Poetic Voices of America

Fall 1990

A New Collection of
Poems in the English Language

Sparrowgrass Poetry Forum
Inc.

Published by
Sparrowgrass Poetry Forum, Inc.
203 Diamond St., P.O. Box 193
Sistersville, WV 26175

Library of Congress
Catalog Card Number 90-060975

ISBN 0-923242-08-2

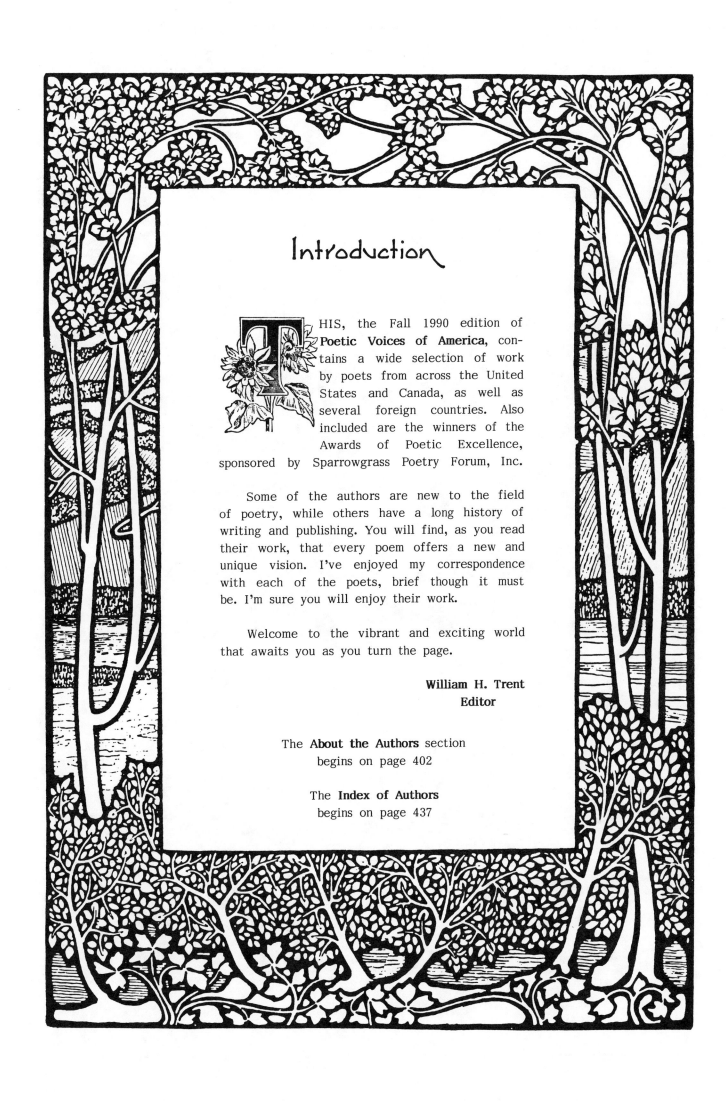

Introduction

THIS, the Fall 1990 edition of **Poetic Voices of America,** contains a wide selection of work by poets from across the United States and Canada, as well as several foreign countries. Also included are the winners of the Awards of Poetic Excellence, sponsored by Sparrowgrass Poetry Forum, Inc.

Some of the authors are new to the field of poetry, while others have a long history of writing and publishing. You will find, as you read their work, that every poem offers a new and unique vision. I've enjoyed my correspondence with each of the poets, brief though it must be. I'm sure you will enjoy their work.

Welcome to the vibrant and exciting world that awaits you as you turn the page.

William H. Trent
Editor

The **About the Authors** section
begins on page 402

The **Index of Authors**
begins on page 437

IN THE URBAN FOREST

What they want
is to smother this grass at their feet
and be a forest as their fathers were.
Patient, relentless, every year
the same silent claim,
the old strategy
that never has failed in the end.
Again and again, raking away the brown leaf-fall,
their sweet gift to the earth, I refuse them.

—Richard A. Stewart
First Place Award

STONEWALLS

In New England
where time is measured in centuries
        not fleeting years
        faces carved in granite
        tell of a many-wintered life
and each Spring
        the Earth heaves up
        a new crop of stone
all gray roundish and old
        to be laid upon the wall
        which crawls with time
this oldness
        these silent bones
        of New England

—Dennis Curran
Second Place Award

UNPUBLISHED

You tell me I'm too full of words
and send me to your rival in another room
to spill myself
upon fresh sheets
breathless with the urgency
of a bursting spirit.

I'm delivered—
a new poem filed with the other
offspring of my abstract labor.

You come, we spill into each other
between sheets that bear witness
to our creative rites in
rumpled mounds and pillows . . .
unread, unacclaimed, Ecstatic!

—Gabriele Ulrike Stauf
Fifth Place Award

Head hung, leaning
against crack-infested wall,
strands of hair concealing
the blackness in his eyes, rolled
as he pursues non-exsistent answers.

"Animals are perfect. If you're nice
to them, they're nice to you.
Whenever they do something WRONG, it's
unintended, someone has to be mean
first before they strike back."

"Why?", she asks, cringing beneath
sweat laden sheets.

—Dawn M. Pretnar
Fifth Place Award

icicles drip
        from lemon tree leaves—
hissing smudge pot

—Charles Bernard Rodning
Third Place Award

PARALLELS

When she was 37, she gave me life
And now;
I watch as life slips out of her,
My hand upon her brow.

I wonder at the parallels
That our two lives have shared;
When I was young, she cared for me,
And now, for her, I care.

Our fathers died when we were young,
Our mothers raised us both;
We married at age 24,
Coincidental, at most.

But the parallels continued
When I was struck by lightning once;
For the very same thing had happened to her,
Was that coincidence?

Now one last parallel will bind
Our souls by a common thread;
She was the same age when I was born,
As I am at her death.

—Nancy Turner Jones
Fourth Place Award

THE SEASONED MIND

Summer bringeth winter wishes
of snowbirds coming with the chill,
when they will,
And winter bringeth summer thoughts
of grasses wild and breezes hot,
all for naught,
For who has ever seen the season
that mimics hope and follows reason.
The mind that changes with the weather
will hear it not and see it never.

—Nathan J. Kinzel
Fifth Place Award

IMMIGRANT SONG

They slept fitfully to wake again in hell.
Chained together in rows,
yet each man separately crucified to himself,
the mark of the beast burned the flesh still,
and bedlam reigned
as screaming, praying, weeping, cursing voices
multiplied the horror.
Shelved ebony wares,
racked in spasm,
reclined in fetid vomit and excrement
as urine dripped from above like a rank rain.
The strong survived somehow,
though the death-stench spread
in suffocating swell.
The unlucky weak died
without a hint
they were heading
to a proud land
where all men were created equal.

—David Bond
Fifth Place Award

viuda
at parties
surrogate husbands
ease her physical deficiency

she drifts toward the deepest voices
comforted
hearing them discuss their wives
clusters of Peters
denying sacred connections

celibate
she craves the embraces of strangers
their speech echoes in her caverns
touched fingers tremble against
whatever passed between
Adam and God
on Michelangelo's ceiling

—Doris Straus
Fifth Place Award Winner

DREAM

They sit in expectant splendour:
White and honed and carefully
Placed to look
Abandoned
After a heavy session on the ice.
A solid little blonde
Dreams across the room.
Her eyes sparkled
When she first saw the skates.
Parental protests about size
Went unheard as she balanced
Herself on their rims—
Junk store beauties
Two years too big.
But that didn't stop her
Dipping and swaying,
Gliding through the gold shag carpet—
Fairies clinging to her heels.

—Connie Borders Strode
Fifth Place Award Winner

UNDERNEATH THE CITY

Underneath the City
Riding on the "T"
Ten thousand time-bombs sitting—
:frozen Anonimity.

Individually packaged
Ghosts on Public Show
All on suspect errands
—everywhere they go.

Eyes in sockets roving
Dart from "thoughts" to "things"
From their-cells creating
—all the person brings.

Each and all will go off
According to their clocks,
Casting ancient Shadows
'round the City blocks.

Underneath the City
You staring cross at Me,
a Hundred-Thousand mortals—
:fresh-freeze Anonimity.

—Merritt Mage
Fifth Place Award Winner

A man brings up the subject of pain because
his wife, whom he is romantically involved with,
is not here, is in too much pain to be here.
So he is halved and is telling us of her pain
just to say her name.
She who is not here is at home in pain.

He has said too much, too flagrantly.
So that pain does not awaken,
people begin solving her pain
with incantations, propitiations, and philosophies
that are pain drugs. To say these words in broad daylight
they must preface them with disclaimers,
"This may sound silly." or
"This may not work for her; it is a small thing but . . ."
So as not to rise too high and fall in pain.

He is not entirely satisfied, and the people know it.
They begin to chafe and think him uncommonly rude.
Vigilant, he will wedge her name in again today.

—Flannery McFadden
Fifth Place Award Winner

EGYPT, 1983

On the steps of the temple of Abu Simbel.
I remember Detroit kids who tussled and tumbled
in the dark and gulped grape Kool-Aid,
nothing at all like Egypt's tea-colored children
who fight without words for cake crumbs.

In the Cairo museum,
I see a woman with my face
staring at me from a glass cage.
She still remembers Egypt and Assyria, Babylon and Persia,
while tourists ride camels
with pink ribbons pinching their throats.

On the streets of Aswan,
brown boys in borrowed trousers peddle jugs
of purified water for a dollar,
never admitting it flows from their
own taps and tanks,
slamming strangers with cramps
when they finally reach the Pyramids.

—Betty De Ramus
Fourth Place Award Winner

At last . . . the stars again!
I have known them since before eternity . . .
Breathed them . . .
Caressed them;
Even as I rested in that calm, black sea, their fires
pulsated in my memory.

Now, freed from my watery sanctuary,
Imprisoned,
I behold them from afar;
High in the desert sky they shine, beyond my reach.
I cannot touch them.

I have never known cold before.
The woman heeds my whimpering and holds me to her breast.
The warmth that I had known for all those months, returns.
The essence of the woman comforts me; she permeates my being,
She touches me, as I once touched the stars.

How . . .?
Is she not mortal?

—David Bullock
Fifth Place Award Winner

CHARLOTTE BRONTE

Out of that bleak and somber parsonage,
Where each uncurtained window held its view
Of family graves within a treeless yard,
She mined the words that conjured up a world
Of romance stormy as the winds that shrieked
And drove the clouds across the purple moor.
Awake, she dreamed and writing down those dreams,
Dispatched the book that captured London town.
In her imagination lay the warmth
That neither graveyard home nor father gave:
Beneath her quiet demeanor raged the soul
That took to flight on wings of shining prose.
Bereft of time and yet that fragile flame
Has lit her away to immortality.

—Rita Haaga
Fifth Place Award Winner

MOVING DAY

On moving day in the green-shuttered house
White ruffled drapes slump untethered in a heap
And the cats steal furtive glances at empty walls
Sliced by hysterical patterns of the last morning's sun.
The sailing ships are moored inside sealed boxes now
Along with random cups and clocks and cares
                    Of all that must remain.

I have thrown away the farewell flowers that you sent,
The crimson buds that exploded gently and then were gone.
I saved the card and savored the small betrayal
Of having been left behind to pack and brood
And coax three fretful cats from the lame shelter
                    Of their mute contempt.

Three men came with the frantic arrogance of picnic ants
To cart away ten years of crusts and crumbs and leave me
Standing dazed with keys and cats and road maps
Marked in bold strokes toward a place where you wait
For the first morning's sun and for me and my memories
                    Of the green-shuttered house.

—Linda Caradine
Fifth Place Award Winner

SONG OF THE SWAN

I'll sing you a song of silver swans
    of silver friendships by and by.
I'll sing of bodies intertwined
    beneath the pale-lit sky.

The silver stars, they dance and sing
    for love has found its home.
The warm sweet breeze will whisper
    for love no longer roams.

It's been some time since I've seen your smile,
    but when I close my eyes
I think of you, and the song of the swan
    springs up from where it lies.

I find still waters within the song,
    there I go for my mind to feed;
    and the simple thought of you
    seems to fade all of my needs.

"Love let me not hunger,"
    the swan cries to the land;
"and if you've ever hungered,
    I know you'll understand."

—Lisa Dian Houghton
Fifth Place Award Winner

THE ORCHID

Flower of beauty, your petal soft
    Skin, blushing, cries out to be
Caressed, as inhaling your
Pungent scent, I hold you close . . . .

With tender touch, your trinal corolla's
Stroke an amethyst spur, partly
Sheathed, mysteriously hidden as if
Jungle-clad on some epiphytic vine . . . .

Budding behind those virginal
Limbs, like a falling star you
Blossom once, in resplendent lavender
Gown, hidden only by the envious night.

—Gordon Frees

SILENT WITNESS

Amber streaks of sundown
This man against the sky
He's seeking out his lover
He longs to hear her sigh,
He curves his arms around her
Fits her body into his
And bows his tawny head
As though to wake her with a kiss.

This man against the sky
He loves the songs she'll sing
Here alone I watch and listen
Wishing to have six strings.

—Beth Casanova
Fifth Place Award Winner

FOUND

Bark scraping on bare knees
The just right branch to lean on

Shadows and sunlight on printed page
Purple-red cherries
Dreamtime.
Free time.

Warm cherry juice on my chin
Nancy's found The Secret Staircase

Window sash up
Voice calling
Found.
    Again.

—Mary Lou Miller
Fifth Place Award Winner

love tune # april 8
around sunset and stillness
i watch the moon rise
in the east, while over west
above the mountains,
the firey volcano of days end
colors the clouds and hints
of ancient begainings.

at bedtime, with the cats
curled up in the chair,
the dogs on the couch,
the horse standing forlornly outside
in the yard, i slip 'neath my quilt
into my spacious moonshadowed bed.
alone i watch the moon also
fade west, bound for sleep
unlike me.

—Yashieka Soamnes

CONSUMPTION OF GUMPTION

Nibble, Nibble, Nibble . . .
  At sod and thread and cribble,
Chewing, Chewing, Chewing . . .
Barbie's tears and spring canoeing,
Smacking, Rudely Smacking . . .
On Mill walls slowly cracking,
Spitting, Spitting, Spitting . . .
On blissful sand dune flitting,
Mutate, Mutate, Mutating . . .
Keen, silent understating,
Savor, Savor, Savor . . .
Each crimson Autumn flavor,
Swallow, Swallow, Swallow
Her whole essence, leave me hollow.

—S. Renee Perry
Fifth Place Award Winner

          twice as many years
there were twice as many years
when the apple shadows fell
far among the orchard trees.

there were stones to throw
far as the eye,
deep into the dark pond,
the sounds of their
falling.

there were places left to walk,
paths whose wanderings
were mystery,
just beyond
the corner fences,
where dogs ran away
and would not come when called.

there were clouds to climb
all afternoon,
a window big enough
to watch
the sky.

—Bert Paul
Fifth Place Award Winner

THE FEATHER DAGGER

Say forgotten!

  By deed, in journey a man is trust,
and lonely flows the asphalt plane
amid the modern splendor.

Tonight his eyes and open chest,
forgotten now, the answers seek.
And in the darkness tickling sense
by way of blades in life so deep.

Entranced so man in lifeless striving
giving worth without his word.
In raptured night his life is taken
and there instead a useful tool.

By moments will a life be made—
forever trusted, forever real,
of blades of grass cutting places
where common sense lay exposed.

Say forgotten!

This darkened space of iris night!
Come the dawn this journey's ended
Trust the feather dagger.

—Pieter K. Wallace

ARLINGTON (JANUARY)

In the season of death I walk among the sentinels of the dead
  Keeping the past in their whiteness, cool and hard
The empty uniforms march back and forth in order known but to
      God
Who must glint the sun off marble in fast rows
And my name is spelled out here in last month's leaves
Holding out a lone life among the dead and the mourners
Walking among the sentinels silent as the soldiers beneath them
In the season of the dead in the land of spent glory

—Jennifer C. Worth
Fifth Place Award Winner

MAX

When did he die? I had him put to sleep.
  My mind won't hold that date, though tightened throat
    and tears return.
I couldn't bear to hold him at the end,
But bending kissed his head, then drove away.
That night I walked alone to find a place to cry.
Since his death I've seen less lightning, fewer stars,
Been one friend short.
(At times my kids found me by finding him.)
Whatever mode I enter next, I hope that he'll be waiting —
Soft ears, bright eyes, and wholly loving heart.

—Mary Moore Boulay

MODERN HAIKU (AND OTHER DIVERSIONS OF MANKIND)

The box,
  brown, disposable, cardboard,
and home to so many.
The street,
hard, cracked, and rough,
like the faces of the inhabitants.
The statue,
majestic, proud, commanding,
and a joke to all who knew her.
The t.v.,
mesmerizing, hypnotizing, mystifying,
and a friend to many millions.
The dreams,
a waste of time, effort, and energy,
and a hope for those who dream them.

—Dave Burton

PEER PRESSURE

You did not hit Babe Ruth homeruns
  so you bullied neighborhood arms
around and around behind their backs,
fun as a nonstop ferris wheel
to stretch your manhood publicly
the textbook way, "On time,"
but tight as torture for me.
I could not see my pain,
though my screams bled miles of fear.

There were no winners.
We both cried.
Your pants plastered wet
by your father's newsworthy beatings.

Nobody calls you bully anymore.
You traded my arm for a bed with my grammar school friend.
The yearbook kids waved by their town
marched to lives with no defeats.
You stayed home, a window from my townie mother.
I heard someone call you Daddy.

—Lisa Fay
Fifth Place Award Winner

TAPESTRY

Threads of sleep and knotted ends of thought
Run through the open weave of pain

Anger warps the close hatching of the quilt
And stops the air of summer still
Passive and quiet pass the shuttle end
Where reflections make up the bolt
Alone the dark and dangerous future
Faces each as blocks of cloth unfold

—Kathleen Sheridan

DECISIONS

Come tuesday next, I must deal with the brakes,
My faithful mode of transport
Victimized, casualty of inept menders
lies helpless.

Come tuesday next, I must deal with the brakes.
Meanwhile, perilous ridings
caught in a possible careening juggernaut,
A dupe of inertia and blind chance . . .
This is not my style.

Come tuesday next, I must deal with the brakes.

—**William A. Durst**
Fifth Place Award Winner

THE CHALLENGER

They disintegrated in the Atmosphere
in the red heat of technic flames,
Deceiving the worshippers of advancement.
Heroes falling from the sky without
deus ex machina.
The Greeks never desecrated a temple
Without the God's punishments.
But Land of the Free and you-could-be-president
sends more into heaven to become immortalized.
Race for nebulous discovery.
We walked the moon; our footprints prove.
We photographed the rings of Saturn.

Earth's children starve as flies crawl over their eyes.
War thrusts its sword from continent to continent.

—**Connie Beth Workman**
Fifth Place Award Winner

untitled

Only within our fragile perfection
a mortal world diminished, does my sorrow subside
so clasp my hand and walk unto a dream
of which the atmosphere will collide

kiss me and clutch my body
yet only in a thundering storm
and allow me to dance among tombstones
while you photograph my twirling form

among bleak clouds and cold showering rain
ecstacy innocent and true
inside a still deserted cemetery
i can only love you

you are me, i am you
we walk in an ideal frame of mind
captured out of reality
our bodies will entertwine

follow me into a surreal landscape
beneath a depthless sky
and hold me until time itself ends
or our flawless moment has died

—Cyndie Morgan

A PHONE CALL

As I was talking to my friend on the phone
I could hear sounds
Loud sounds
In the background
An angry voice
raised in hatred and disgust
A child's scream
cut off by a slap across the face

My friend and I paused for a second . . .
Then hurriedly began again,
trying to drown out the sounds
The loud sounds in the background
Each not knowing what to say
Each not knowing what to do
One too far away to do anything
One too close.

—**Shannon Carter**
Fifth Place Award Winner

POISED

Not much more light now
than first light.
Fine mist on a grey March morning.
I reel across the sodden lawn,
drunken now with drizzle.
Wind slips across my shoetops,
scavenging, deft as a pickpocket's fingers.
The wet leaves and paper
hug the ground, too leaden to lift.
The breeze moves on, empty handed.
Black birds roost silently
in the cottonwood tree,
Dark calligraphy in the bare branches.
And I, standing gently
upon the swollen earth
ready soon to reveal its green shoots,
Am hollow and parched
as an old wineskin
awaiting new wine.

—**Scott A. Harpst**
Fifth Place Award Winner

THE LATE AUTUMN CREEK

lies with barely a pulse to feel
in wain its lethargic flow
must wait for winter snow

with vitality at lowest ebb
trees shed naked each yellow tear
cold quiet whisper death is near

cut corded wood giving envied relief
as smoke shrouded sun crosses bleak horizon
hoarding warmth from blood-less dominion

white billowing ships laden with moisture
impeded by grey compassionless seas
becalmed eyes watch for sail filling breeze

precious pools where fish rest besieged
by rocks laid raw with moss brittle brown
like old men's dreams of white wedding gowns

no joyous cry of bird or beast
exalt as one resurrection giving
hope to each creature of God still living

take heart as the world surely turns
heavenly moisture in snow and rain
will arrest all strife as love ends lonely pain

—D. A. Bratcher

FLUTE

The wind I draw from mouths
they uncover small caves
where the secrets of birds go
room to room
they leave every key behind
for other countries

—Clifford Hicks
Fifth Place Award Winner

CONDO CASUALTY #505 B

Spider lady cracks the door
to see who the elevator
has deposited into her web.
Gnarled fingers rest
on the umbilical chain
that attaches her world.
Fear slices the space
spilling odors
into the newly done hall.
"I got my notice."
she states as feet shuffle
in slippers of her husband
who left, feet bare, feet first
years ago.
My "Sorry" falls on the click,
hangs in the lock
as 505 B turns back
to the world she has to leave.

—Sandra Y. Smith
Fifth Place Award Winner

INFINITY

Bristlecone,
pine tree of antiquity,
an image
fastened in a weathered frame,
you are my connection
to the cosmos.

Sprouted from a single seed
we stand embraced by sun
        strafed by hail
        split by lightning
        cleansed by rain
        at last

        stripped but alive!

When new growth springs
from withered limbs, I ask
what Secret rests
among our tangled roots?
Though some will answer chance,
instead:
        You reveal it's Healing.

—Bettye J. Luckemeyer

NIGHT

There is a place I know, it's a little town that won't grow.
it has a one-eyed cop and one stop light. The kids there drag
the streets day and night. The girls there, are a far out
sight, wearing blue jeans skin tight. There's not much to do, but
get high at night, and run that only stop light. It's Saturday
night every night, the kids there are all right until they get
up tight, then it's redneck night, everybody's in a fight. The
little town is all right, even if it's only at night. Grow it
might, some night.

—Preston Gene Crosby

AN OBSERVATION MADE AT THE COUNTRY KITCHEN, 1973

Nancy, with bouncing gait,
Flexing a golden leg,
Lightly bearing her culinary burden
On brown arms powdered with soft down,
Twitching a mischievous nose,
A center button on a china-plate face,
Flutters from table to table,
Sprinkling stardust and quickening smiles.
Does he dare ask her the question
And voice a presumptuous hope?
Can he expect this delectable nymph
To be contained by one solitary love?
Or is her heart given in covenant
To the entire human race?
Can she, who is for all men,
Ever be for one?

—Paul A. Blaum

THE LONELY HEROES OF MY TIME
(To the victims of San Francisco
earthquake — 1989)

Dear Sun: wait . . . Please . . . Don't let the silence pass by:
the Mother Earth just moved violently several cries ago . . !
There are mothers, children in their arms,
trapped in cars,
and fathers, wrapped in scars,
on the way home, so dear pictures
in wallets and nowhere to go . . .
Ever again . . ! Dear Sun at dawn: wait . . . Please . . . Please.
There, under the solemn hopes of a brave town,
under rubbles, the dying lovers confess not to cry,
still glancing at each other, still so shy . . .
Dear Sun: wait . . . Please . . . Please refuse
to go down — listen to the lonely heroes of my time:
they, who strived to cherish love, freedom and peace,
and, oh, God!, oh, rhyme!,
the homemade bread,
are smiling . . .
they must not be dead . . !
Oh, dear Sun: must they die . . ?!
Dear Sun: wait . . . Please . . . Don't let the silence pass by . . .

—Vladimir de Tonya

JUST A FOOT

I saw me a foot today, Lord, just a foot and it got me a big heartache.
The sidewalk were full up with rags, bags, papers and an old gray raggedy rug.
I had to wheel around it, into the busy street.
That's when I saw the foot, blue-black from the cold rain, sticking out of the rug.
I wheeled for help but no one helped and I am helpless, Lord, so I called you.
The foot must have a body, a body needing help, but there were no help, Lord
And it got me a big heartache that I were helpless and no one cared for my brother!

—E. M. Grant Howard
Fifth Place Award Winner

LIGHT WASHED UP AT MARCO ISLAND

Here is a thick, lumpy chunk of gray matter,
Pitched onto the beach at an off angle,
Bringing the light across its crevasses, so it gleams, changing whimsically,
Its matte surfaces to reflective silver,
The reflecting ones back into umbra.
In and among rocks, worn passage-ways, lined in splinters of battered shell,
An abandoned colony on a hillside, where a stray from the mollusk beds
Could home into harbor, hitch to port;
Weary of his exile on the wide sea, trembling into salt air,
Build his single home around him,
Wrap, coil, spine upward and over,
Mottle sand and pebbles, streaks of kaleidoscopic colors,
A prize on the threads of a rainbow,
Web it or net it or lace it with seaweed,
Spectrums from the rare source of his being.
What is left is the brilliant, white light
Of change over a mass of matter,
A tuft of sea emerald fur, stranded,
Stubborn, stuck-up, and preening like a tattered frog.

— **Mary Jane Burns**

CLIMBING THE TOWER AT LAST

That long ago summer, as he walked the Carmel beach,
I could have known him.
Sometimes I trailed along behind Robinson Jeffers—
watched him as he shaded his eyes with his lean brown hands,
or I glimpsed him in the wind and cold fog—tall and sinewy.
I was shy, half-frightened by the passion
and the power and the violence of his poems.
He never knew.
I was young, untutored by the hawk!
Against the dark Greek wisdom of Jeffers,
I gave my heart to men; torn apart, never forgetting
any lover, my spirit did not completely heal.
. . . Now, climbing Jeffers' hand-hewn stone tower at last,
I look through his windows to rough-shaped hills,
down to his turbulent Pacific. I whisper,
"Dark man, passionate man, what would you tell me today?"
I wait; wind blows through his hand-planted gum trees.
At last I accept the dark, lonely canyons, the sea-wasted stone.
The answer comes in his own words: "GIVE YOUR HEART TO THE HAWKS,"
    "BE ANGRY AT THE SUN!"

— **Marguerite A. Brewster**
Fifth Place Award Winner

ABSOLUTES

I say that you are wrong to practice apartheid, brother.
I need not debate points with you,
I need not consider your views because you are wrong.
Absolutely.

No, friend, it is not in the swollen eyes of the beholder; I speak of
Absolutes. I can be eating breakfast tomorrow morning on a flower-laden
veranda in Pretoria and I can Absolutely taste the rich, red blood of the
eighteen-year-old black student you will kill late tonight on a dry, hot
street in Soweto and I can Absolutely taste the salt of his mother's tears.

I can feel the nausea of the elderly Gentle-Man who witnessed the fatal
beating of his once-beautiful wife, and I mourn the pathetic life of the
Zulu girl who lives as a quadruplegic because her spine was severed by
your bullets.

No, I am not in your land now and I may not be there tomorrow, yet I feel
the cold sting of your blue eyes and my hands are stained by the black bars
of your prison cells. And know that I will be with you, my brother, when
your body is burned so badly that the flesh falls from your bones and I will
be with your children and I will never allow their wounds to heal, and I
will never allow you to forget that your apartheid was wrong.

Absolutely.

— **Aron Neil Solomon**

WHERE

Plants where water,
animals where plants,
man where man.

Woman where wealth,
children where sun,
sleep where moon.

Many times
children where moon,
sleep where sun.

Who we,
where we,
each a little earth.

— **Peter Hess**

TOGETHER

Love is his touch.
Love is his eyes
hypnotizing you.
His eyes are like
a green forest
you are lost in.
His touch is like
rays of sun
glistening across
your body.
His kiss pulls
you into an
unknown world,
a world where
you are always
    TOGETHER.

— **Amy Arnett**

SOUND OF SPRING

Frogs that croak
and birds that sing
and peeper calls
are sounds of spring
Day and night
our eager ears
are full of cheeps
and peeps and cheers.

But sap that flows
and buds that break
and seeds that split
and plants that wake
and other sounds
with quiet habits
only reach the ears
of rabbits.

— **Joesy M. Dethloff**
Fifth Place Award Winner

A child loves freely,
Innocent to the world,
Naive enough to laugh,
Smiles to all,
No stereotypes entrapping,
A scream for pain,
Suffering unmuffled,
Skipping, loving, living,
To be more like a child,
The little one inside,
Now calloused and torn,
So heavy each step,
Confined, trapped,
Lashes wet with tears,
Salty taste on my lips,
Muffled sobs,
Hands hiding face,
Peeking through fingers,
Clear-eyed children observed,
With my clouded vision.

—Ann Cathcart

SUN BUS

Passengers talk and cough
sneeze and swing
their feet.
Tell all their secrets.

Seniors are half price
and free on weekends.
Gray faces gasp
at changes they see:
Last year's fires
leveled favorite
restaurants and banks.

The driver's silent
until a regular
calls her the wrong name —
Carol . . . Caroline . . . Carla . . .
She stops anyway
where she always does
and tries to smile.

—Stel Miller
Fifth Place Award Winner

limbo

lost on the high plains
under grain elevators
and a single railroad siding
of my boyhood
is a hometown
not even big enough
to be in the rand/mcnally
atlas sitting next to
the librarian's desk
at school—i wondered
out of adolescence
that other kids
in places i saw
linked by tracks
and red and blue lines
saw in their atlases
only a blank space
where i lived dreaming
and counting boxcars

—John Neal Williams
Fifth Place Award Winner

STEPPIN' OUT

I'm wearing different shoes now,
  Missing the ones I used to wear —
  Snappy reds and blues—pastel hues;
  Shiny blacks and whites.
      Bows and straps,
      heels high; heels low;
      No heels at all!
They were part of me. The finishing touch
that made me fit in many modes and places.
Tears came when I bagged them up for someone else's
  need.
Support for weakened limbs is now the name of the game.
Seeming to come only in sturdy browns and blacks.
      But still I stand—with halting steps and slow
can turn to reach your waiting hand—and after all
that's as far as I really need to go!

—Janna

BLACK SUNSETS

I walk the valleys of those forgotten.
My presence is known,
but I am wrapped up in a name in which my body is a stranger,
a villian.

My face, my pale lonely face,
is not recognized when my image bleeds through the pages
that I have written.

The anguish of my heros and heroines,
is the icy wind that blows through my hollow soul.
Yes, it is for me you have cried,
and laughed.

I, I am the spirit that haunts your dreams
and rapes your naive heart.

I have entered your very being through your blindness.
But at last, when you open your eyes to clearly see,
my image shines forth,
and you turn your head
and close your heart.

For I am a woman.

—Yalonda M. Bones

MAMA USED TO SING

No one meant us harm; sure not the man
who said he'd fix our broken furnace
before Winter's cold bite
for 3 knit sweaters Joy finished, working late hours.

The promised job unfulfilled, he never grasped our urgent need.

Timid, poor—we had to wait chilled-through too long;
pneumonia set in quick and hard—
Ma was courage itself, but frail.
After sick bills, one meal-a-day took its natural toll.

Mama grew too weak to talk but whispered: "Love all folks."

Deep hunger caused our schoolwork's lack;
Paul's sure scholarship was lost—
but Mama lost more.

Her death was our loss, too.

Mama used to sing; her songs would lift our hearts.
The house is silent now—and sold
today for the highest sad bid.

Mama said to love all folks, no one meant us harm;
sure not the man who just didn't see
our lives hung on his word.

—G.F. Berkowsky

THE OLD MAN DREAMS

The old man dreams, they say. It is not true.
He screams within himself, for dreams are seeds
Of future marvels that will come to be,
Of altered worlds in undiscovered hue,
Developed new perspectives on old creeds
Arranged by tact and ingenuity.
What has been done seems jetsam in the lee
Of what is possible. Ambition weeds
Away the slow and old, whose eyes are sunk
To scrutinize the pearly sheen of greeds
Hung up within the skull, to judge with rue
The chances missed, the glory turned to funk.
For lust of life abandons not those shrunk
By Time — dreams unacceptable au lieu.

—Alfhild Wallen

ADDICTION

just one more cookie, please.
no one will notice, just me.
another scoop . . . chocolate chip
and whipped cream, of course
tomorrow's a diet day, enjoy now before the Fast
before self-control tries for control
over the cookie and ice cream
and men, of course
just one more, then i'll stop
when Mister Right shows up
i can't miss one, He may be Him
wrong choice, again? never fear
men never multiply like cookies
or do they?
how quickly one becomes one dozen
when to stop? no problem
i can handle it, no one notices
the queasiness after twelve cookies
or twelve men.
just me.

—Karen Crenshaw

OPEN WOUNDS

Daddy's dead. His widow still. No tears today.
    Drunk young son's fists slamming into the wall
        again and again

Knuckles bleeding tears of pain.

Elder son drunk dry-eyed vacant scared.

Violent words lovingly said crash against loving
Words whispered with rage.

The hated doctor should never have moved him.
    "He'll pay for his crime . . . ."

Brothers beat each other senseless.
Fists and booze the only release,
Sobbing, fall into each other's arms.

Baby daughter cries, blames
Elder daughter silently screams,
    "I want my daddy!"

Brandy, vodka, cannabis, xanax.
Widow is still and touches nothing, no one.

The others swallow whatever with impunity.
The pain will never stop.

Daddy's dead. And so are we.

—Sandra M. Carpenter

FOR NEMEROV: OUTSIDE THE ONION

Beyond the wailing wall
You'll find a bit of me;
A pinch of toast-a taste of tea
A lost remembrance of used to be.

Now dare not change my scope of things
Nor toy with my mind.
There's not a quarter ounce of Truth twixt
My and your own lines.

Who dares to set the world aright
With logarithmic scheming?
Neither you nor I nor any pawn
That sits at high noon dreaming.

Perhaps this little note to you
En Furioso seeming
Will set your thoughts —en isochronal rhyme—
And we shall share its meaning.

—M.B. Gubitosi

FOREST

Timbered hills
    tell placid lies—
under the tranquil shag
life seethes in
obsidian eyes, prowling fur
and armored amblers.
Wings negotiate freeways
through the boughs,
and sliding things
leave S's on the ground.

Quilled waddlers toss
non-verbal barbs;
striped plumes make
potent points in argument.
All citizens speak fluent ESP.

A hole is the doorway
to a split-level home;
condominiums thrive within a log,
a mound contains a citadel . . .
Walk gently in this suburb of Assisi.

—Lucille M. Hershey

JACOB'S WELL: REMEMBERING

I saw Him once. The day
the woman ran from the well; her clothes
swirling, no water spilling
from the jars, to say
"Come see this Man who knows
all I have done."

The well was deep. Close
to the village. We did not run
for that, knowing, I suppose
her secrets might keep; no one
came with jars for water
although the well was deep.

The well was ours from Jacob.
The mountain stands nearby
to lift us in the dry days as before.
He stayed two days. Sometimes now I
find my fingers reach to remember living water.

I only know I come to Jacob's well each day
And Jerusalem doesn't seem to matter any more.

—Liz Faries
Fifth Place Award Winner

ARTIST'S CAVE

No place here for vaulted shapes.
On bended knees the Artist makes
A piece. A trembling, pious
    pilgrim falls
And gazes on Ancestral Walls.

She reaches out with anxious hand
And with one crude but Chosen Line,
Before the threat of some cock-crow,
She adds her discreet mark to Time.

            —Pat Hutchens

JOURNEY

Pages turn.
    Horizons in succession ease forward
Bearing Hope: kind green eyes surrounding
        as only a voice,
                    immense and gentle, can.
With words—soundless, green-laced and longing:
Gifts flowing smoothly
                    past definition

        Into softness, into Light,
                into Life.

Warm, green-laced pillows for my head,
As Doubt awaits me from across the bed.

            —Jack Moriarty

PORTRAIT

Serene sun-man—
    Glowing like the morning sky
    in blue jeans,
Florentine attitudes:
A Rembrandt portrait
An Artist in His Studio
Epicene qualities:
The Polish Rider on His Horse
    at seventeen.
Lotos-eater—
Dreaming out the window while
White light drifts down like petals
To the dusty floor;
Where is your paramour?
You lost her long ago.
Angel in blue and a leaf halo,
The wound still shows.

            —Emily H. Weant

ALIA

Behind the veil of old, old eyes
    what thoughts, or vague memories of such?
What is her name?
And does she know that she should know
somewhere in her fog filled mind?
Does she fear each dropping of the veil?
Shudder, and know how frail each memory?
How tenuous her grip!
And when she feels her daughter's face,
the new baby's touch,
begin to slip, slip,
Does she cry out in her mind?
when all's gone
and only the empty dark remains,
Does she weep
for what she does not know she's lost?

            —Mesa Merrick

NOT TOO LATE

It is not too late! Ah nothing is too late . . .
    Cato, Learned Greek at eighty,
Sophocles wrote his Oedipus,
Simoides bore off the prize of
    Verse for his composers,
When each had numbered more
    than four-score years
And Theophrastus, at four-score and ten,
Had but begun his characters of men!
Chaucer, at Woodstock, with the Nightingales,
At sixty wrote the Canterbury Tales,
Goethe at Weimer, toiling to the last,
Completed Faust when eighty years were past . . .
What then? Shall we sit idly down and say,
"The night has come; it is no longer day? . . ."
For age is opportunity no less,
Than youth itself, though in another dress.
And as the evening twilight fades,
The sky is filled with stars invisible by day.

            —Helen B. Byard

LIFE THREADS

Her grandmother taught her to cross stitch.
    Tiny, tiny stitches in parallel lines,
    Marching across the fabric to protect a heritage
    Exposing both front and back to public scrutiny.
    Hidden ends caught in the pattern,
    No beginning or ending to herstory.

She picked up the crewel kit in self defense.
    No grey areas of indecision,
    No work to unravel with shifting winds
    Of job and family and private expectations.
    Needle sharp to lance the soul,
    Anger and joy and sorrow hidden in herstory.

The quilt and she will grow together.
    Ascending feelings of swirling fabrics and colors,
    Patterns emerging with time and trust
    As her personal amalgam bursts forth.
    Practical and whimsical and strong,
    A new beginning for herstory.

            —Mary Ann Payne

LOST DIALS

Somewhere the hands went
    leaving a legacy of a vacant stare
filled with numbered time
as one remembers
including several hours
and days and unpaid passings.

Somewhere the face turned
forgotten and in search of a name
written in the sands
caught between the lips of the tide
hurled backward, bare of hands, small stumps of time.

There's not much to remember much
being alive and lost so deep in time
climbing night and falling sun slipping under,
        under . . .
open eyes, closed lips, and whispering ears
drawling among weathered bones 'neath rocks and
        roots of going gone
through grass and forsaken foreheads and finger
        knuckles
where lost hands, sunken eyes, and empty faces fall
        before broken words of everlasting earth.

            —Joe Wheeler Drennan

A PARTICULAR BEAUTY

There is a hint of bravery
in old homesteads
occupied by aging souls,
remnants of families, left alone.
They struggle on, maintaining
their bits of dignity and identity.

There is a touch of sadness, too,
in sagging ridgepoles, peeling paint,
the disrepair of unavoidable neglect.

A farmhouse, bleak against a stormy sky,
looks cold and empty, yet inside
there may be one who tends a fire.

There is a particular beauty
in old homesteads,
even in their state of decline —
an aura of nostalgia
in each crumbling wall.

—Sylvia E. Niemi

AEROPAGITICIA

I, myself, being a cat in a tree, see you before
you would see me. Even if heart and hand would
gift him, the mind would show not an insight, a
clue, or the common audacity, meant to set the
stage for a coming way to see what it is to be
a cat in a tree.

A power struggle contemplating a solution, small
weary ones understanding nothing but a question
of disgust. The other generation looking for
answers, finding only alternatives to an unsolved
majority.

Why the pestilence, protrusions; why are the mobs
crowding, personal feelings shouting, and small
infantile children pouting? For hope? For escape
from their barred reality, which in simplicity is
their own fantasy.

In the deep crevices of the mind there lie
answers, unopposed by the questions sometimes
concealed by greed and mental servitude.

—Jason Travis McMichen

PASTORAL PRAYER
Life flies by.
A quick ride on a fast,
beautiful horse.

Hedges.
High hedges fly by unnoticed,
when you're young.
High tail—fast gate.

Mid-race, hedges get higher.
Gait slows.
The crop hits harder.
The thrill of clearing them grows steadily,
Yet yields to fear.
A stumble would hurt.
You back away—at first.

Until at last, youth regained
With unbridled strength, you leap
And clear them once again.

A race won.
Another victory.
written to Beethoven's Pastoral Symphony 3-7-89
—William A. Hutchison

COMPATIBLE MINDS
Delicious is the mind that touches mine,
that meets, engages, enfolds, enmeshes,
and with my thoughts is one.

As though I'd come unexpectedly upon a patch
of wild raspberries in the wood;
tart, crisp, and warm from the sun,

The flavor of it clears the palate of my mind,
welcomes opposition and releases whimsey, which,
once encased in words, is done.
—Gloria M. Thompson Duke

NIGHT HORSE

Night horse flying,
Beyond all that we are and dream of being,
I sit astride your velvet soft back,
Deathless,
Lifeless,
I am, I AM,
That alone is enough for me,
Only one among many,
Yet, ever so alone,
Except for you,
Night horse, flying, flying, flying.

—Mary J. Nichols

YOUR SONG

A broad wing span of centuries now past
With sweet, historic sounds you boldly cast;
A russet back with dark buff chest you own,
Renowned, creative poets made them known.
Milton's ascetic man once heard you sing
And nothing L'Allegro has enjoyed could bring
Your song, for you're a star of Keat's night,
A dream or vision with immortal might.
Dickinson said your ladder is the sky,
No ends to your ascent, so high you fly.
By needless candles, I once heard your story
And knew why it was only sung at night,
For all of your acquired, enduring glory
Would be too blinding in the bright day's light.

—David Anthony Ensign

BLACK STRINGS

The birds flew overhead
in a mile-long string;
unexaggerated numbers for nature,
but staggering the small recesses
of the human mind . . .
especially travelling down highways
in machines that measured
miles with odometers.
I could see their wings beating . . .
excited by the urgency of their great number.
Traffic was so engineered a flight,
compared to the organic massing of migration.
That I had to witness this through windshield,
and hold my awe to the highway!
This river of birds restlessly flowed
over the mapped and black strings
we tie between city and city.
The birds were black too;
but it was the color
of things laid down long ago.
—Peter W. Johnson

SLOW DOWN

Dear Daughter
You won't slow down to let me prevent
Or curb the slaughter
Of your innocence

Those eyes, crisp in intelligence
Convey a nimble mind
Strong in dilligence
Trapped in a child's body

Your young face
Sweet with the yearning
Of flowers and lace
Yet, hides so well the knowing

Dear Daughter
Gifted, but also my gift
I beg you please, please slow down
For the laughter

        —Gwen F. Lujan

VOLUPTUOUS WATER
(Elsie Answers W.C. Williams)

Do you think that I
am any more or less than she
who sits hot afternoons in
morning-glory cool upon your porch
drinking tea—
a painted woman in a frame?

Two small feet creep out, innocent as birds,
from under starched white dress. She
drops and lifts her eyes behind
a fan when you appear.
She needs the same as me.

But if she gives you what
you want then why—
on hot black nights, through
steaming grasses walking
beside voluptuous water,
do you come to me?

        —L. M. Drescher

HER NAME IS APPLE

A thing of beauty, edible is she.
The one was labelled, "I forbid you eat,"
by God in the beginning time. A fruit
of the family symbolic of love;
her shape, the dwelling of that emotion.

Innocence, purity, within she hides;
external, smooth and velvety her skin,
of patches violet-red, with colors dark,
and yellow, lighter shades of orange-red
her surface covering, tattooing all!

A greenish-brown, her umbilical cord,
soft stem, the lifeline to her mother tree,
can only be separated if yanked.
I wander . . . wonder . . . if she feels the pain,
as an aborted child within the womb.

        —Maria Ruiz

A JAR

A sleek china jar devours a newspaper.
The Old Testament age's serpent turns round
in a whirlwind; a calendar is curled up
rolling into the jar's mouth.

The jar's home—the sea at the end of the sky—
has become even fainter than a whistle at cloud.

As a thick fog persistently presses down,
with lightning flashes beating drums,
another corner of South America cracks again.

The echo of fish torpedoes strikes the jar.
How many Mediterranean fish have
increased in number for hungry people?

You stars, so sullen all along
in fear of sudden perils,
why don't you fiercely plunge into the jar's
bulging belly tonight?

Stars, get the frantic jar
pregnant with child.

        —Ko Won

RIVERSIDE

"Grub . . . white one . . . put a white grub on a new hook for me, Gwen,"
he half shouted, fumbling to straighten out the ball of tangled line

    Between handfuls of potato chips,
I reach into his smelly, gray tackle box
    Simultaneously shoveling chips and searching through his gear,
I somehow manage to find and force the lure onto the shiny grapple,
leaving salty yellow crumbs on the white rubber bait

    He takes the hook from me with the very tips of his fingers,
and with the long pole held securely between his thighs,
he ties the hook to the line

    To the beat of my shovel, crunch, shovel, crunch
I watch his cast, reel, cast, reel

    His reeling speed increases with my crunching
until the clicking of the reel and the crunching of my mouth
can be heard above the chirping of the blackbirds
on an otherwise deserted river bank

    My shoveling increases to almost wheelbarrow size
as I watch his quickening, frantic casting
in a river
that by now we can assume is barren.

    —Wen Ricksecker

12 MARCH 87

I have held women for one night,
no longer,
never loved
and loved them forever.
Held them so tight,
so breathlessly tight,
for fear they would let me go.
Walked one million miles to touch the sun
all the while surrounded by shadows,
fearing to feel that fire on my face
And wept, Jonah in the belly of my own whale.

— **Joseph Carrabis**

SAVE FOR A LONELY MOON

The motion of black arms reaching for a migrating sky
Cannot be witnessed forever
The indigo herds will gallop past
Leaving us behind

Fields offer a common thread
Warm, inviting; an arabian color
Making fire against the impending coolness of night

The rapid flight slows
Solace has come
Herds rest beneath protective trees

Blackness prevails
Save for a lonely moon

— **Karen McFeaters**

PERSIAN GRACE

Laughing, our hands meet. Fingers intertwine.
Your hair bobs kisses on padded shoulders
beneath Manhattan skies. One taut star shines
overhead. Familiar voice soothes, "Hold her."
I close my eyes and draw your body's curves,
tracing your lines; your back, your cheek, your breasts.
Then stop, sucked under waves of teenage nerves
(like first-date-panic/high school mid-term tests.)
We reach the car. I open your door first.
You slip inside with liquid Persian grace
and smile. No waterfall could quench my thirst,
I drink in the silhouette of your face.
    You sigh. The windows fog. A siren moans.
    Our headlights hurtle down the cobblestones.

— **Darren A. Singer**

SOJOURN

The man in the green tie,
That yelled at the way I parked my car.
We just smile and go on in to eat.

The comely woman who is so facinated by what I say,
She puts my phone number in her address book
Where she, "won't lose it."
She lost her address book.

The old man in blue jeans that are just a little baggy,
Wants to tell everybody passing on his street corner.
What is wrong with this and that.
I have to meet a friend for tea.

I shamble along the dust road thus,
Towards the old house at the end of the lane.
Watching the horses watch me,
Silent sentinels, they make sure I do no harm.

— **Val John Green**

VAGRANT HEART

She was not aware of the empty chair,
The train whistle,
The ripe thistle,
Or raincloud waiting there.

The red leaf trembled,
Wind sang doleful tune,
Yet, she was not aware,
Even of forgetting June.

— **Mary W. Ballantyne**

The boys
voices loud with harmonies
fling vulgarities viciously
at each other like rocks
that skim quiet waters
only to sink forgotten
into the pond of summer.

Memories
are made in the verbal bonding,
the blood shed in the bantering
a ritual of puberty and pecking
whose scars haunt at winter's worst
and warm with the telling when
grey they inevitably gather again.

— **Porter Young**

COMING HOME

Clamorous green rampages through me
baring a lushness in my soul
inundating its welling fertility
beckoning still certain of the
fearsome pull in the bursting
clarity of the known
in the heartstrings of yearning
in your green, green arms
in the swelling of my flesh
in the small sounds of rapture
that tremble in the dear, dense heat
whose savage grip cups the slow,
steady breathing of my safe
homecoming

— **Rosemund Handler**

MIÉTES

Shadow-souled, I stand
Upon the canted bridge floor,
    I watch the distant mists
        Play among the plants
            Of the salt-water marsh.

Night sounds filter
    Into my pensive mind,
    Strike a responsive chord
    Somewhere deep within,
    Free the primal urge
        Which strives for the surface
        Like a drowning diver.

Miétes, I invoke your name
    Once,
        Twice,
            Thrice.
As a dying man
    Calls for his mother,
    I call for you,
        Neither kith nor kin, but special.

— **Ricky L. Allen**

the compromise

he was a virgin—seventeen
I, a matron of ages too numerous
to speak of properly
there were years between us
the numbers reached out
nearly
the height of his thrust for me
I could not say
yes, I will follow to wait near
jewish armies leagues away
for your courage
to find its voice
for I am old, too old
my courage spent
on bringing one as young as you
to this private battleground
uncompromised

—Diane Jones-Richards

1989 MELTDOWN

With one captured   Hand
this thought   Blinked
the first opening of a closed fist

everyday's Which-How-Who
;some thumper's glum rat-a-tat
piercing our lives
IT'S
Just a matter of . . .
wheather.

I am so love not exceptionally grand
but oh in power
i stand the tallest shape beside me
i in cry do humble tears
as though thanks could be spoken
"Live as they die"
and Generals roam look heads bent
saving their tomorrows spent
In anger whose shaven voice slick
slices the thought as easily as bread
"Gentlemen, . . . we won."

—Brenda

THE LAST SWEATSHIRT

Tears dropped on the old photographs
as Memory Lane
explained to Cosmos, his grandson,
what Motif#1 and whalewatching
was all about
—like distant castles and dinosaurs.

Caping his shoulders
with the old rag
pulled from Memory's
treasure capsule,
the child marched around their cubicle
—did this belong to a knight?

No, the old man sighed,
There was an artist there
at Port au' Rocke
who painted anti-nuke pictures
and save-life-on-earth posters
—They wouldn't buy it.

So she painted pretty flowers
on black sweatshirts.

—Patza

(untitled)

thin light clouds dancing swans in the sun
swim the sea of paradise home
atmospheric sea of atoms and Love
rhythm flowing turning 'round
around and around in celestial eights
all quite a space
all a wild state—dance
the lively prance of elves
in and with the thick mystic forest
with sprites of the sun
      now one
          all rise
all rise in the shining
dreams alive in trance
entranced by the bounce of the ball
reflection of motion
Earthen reflection
Earthen paradox
inversion

$1 \text{ inverted} = 1/1 = \infty$

—B Dahlia

FOOTPRINTS IN THE SAND

The coyotes
crying at night ring
echo's for a lonely one, lonely in his grief,
it's December of years for a desert rat,
who stayed in spring looking for gold,
with years the change came—
he was of the wild.

And there was about him the seamed face,
that came to him and the strangeness,
a day just feeling the
time lost in the bleached desert—
and he sat until morning still—
in the house waiting.

They came
the children now grown,
they were success—
in hypnotic trance he went with them,
only the coyotes
understand this.

—Helen Lair

INERTIA

At the river,
our favorite peace, we two hunched wine-drunk
that summer night, tickled each other with feathery words
from soaring Whitman and grousing Miller. Later,
warmer, wet, we bared our envy of their grace.

All the while, we shook inside, waiting
to stage our own just-finished poems, wanting
more than our usual approvals, wanting each other's
plunge in our own private sweat, flight round
our every right word, wanting more than we might
give, wanting.

You did yours. "Nice," I said. I did mine.
"That's nice." We eyed the river passing.

Then jamming your poem in our empty bottle, I flew it
at the river and said, "Who knows, maybe someone
somewhere will find it, study it and be amazed."

You and I, dry by then, did we dimly
see what didn't fly, and did you think
as the river passed, Yeh maybe, somewhere, someone.

—Leonard Ferrante

MIRROR IMAGES
The lumbering yellow schoolbus
squeals to a halt at the junction of two country roads.
Children descend, laughing, rejoicing.
The last, enshrouded in a too-large slicker
does not join the others, who splash through the hollows
by the side of the road, which April showers have filled.
"Come straight home. You've got to watch your brother."
An untroubled puddle affords the child
a glimpse of her face: adult, careworn.

The door snaps shut, cutting off the drone of "Morning Edition."
Oat bran toast in one hand, monogrammed attache in the other,
she struggles against the blustery March wind
which rifles between towering office buildings
to another bus stop: arriving breathless,
turns to smooth hair rearranged by the gusts
and catches her reflection in the plate glass.
The child stares back, wide-eyed, anxious,
begging to play.

—Susan Hoaglund

ANCIENT ODYSSEY OF THE WORKING WORLD
A view of the court of the unwieldy backyard,
That stretches beyond my imagination,
Is encompassing the living standard of wildlife.

Oh bird, breaking the bud of colorful hues open,
When you reach out to life's balustrades,
That extend like the palm of a hand,
Out to the immediacies of cross-indexing
Of the wild, beyond the living tears of man,
You seem to be royal;
In a gallery of sweet, opportunistic singers.
The pause of the sky's doldrums,
Leaves an ancient, yuletide blessing beside you.

Winter begins to sleep, fade, and disappear,
When mother nature chastises her sincere flower,
And adorns her for the beauty of her
Awakening moments,
The earth seems to burst out laughing,
Among the quibble of
The surmountable spring Gods and Goddesses of real variety.
In the unforeseen future.

—Lisa Miller

FOR MY SON IN DEATH — A EULOGY
Denny was his name—as the baby of eight he came
When laying him in his crib at night
The sign of the cross on his forehead
How I laughed about his big feet!
But such an engaging smile.
I was so devoted to him and very close
He was responsive and loving
Friendly and competent, Handsome and brilliant
Tall, dark, and genius
He graduated National Honor student and Salutatorian
He had broken soil to build a Catholic church
He was President of his class and loved by everybody
His art painting of a stairway to the Heavenly Father
Carrying the huge heavy cross on the man's back
That hangs on the parlor wall.
His talents ranged from knitting, painting and cooking to
Farm work, hunting, auto repair and computer programming.
The sudden automobile accident after a party with friends
brought it all to an end at age 19.
Pretty bubbles in the wine—Make you feel happy, make you
feel fine. Amen.

—Bernadette Sievers Gannon

THESE TEARS
These tears
dark slivers
off of the soul

don't fall down the cheek, but
cooly slice through the flesh
to pierce the ground like daggers

and
by the pale light of
the moon
they become simple flowers
with ripping teeth

dancing there
to some unseen melody
they mimic me

till finally, without smiles
they drink of myself
and end

—Kwang Hsiung Marier

A JOURNEY IN THE NIGHT
I walked into that grove of trees
not knowing what to find,
like searching for reality
when all it takes is time.
The night was very dark indeed
without a moon to shine,
the stars all danced behind the trees
like puppets on a line.
And then the sound of humming bees
grew louder in my mind,
it threw me down upon my knees
the sound was so unkind.
The stars they shined so brilliantly
upon my clouded mind,
they seemed to hang unto the sea
like grapes upon a vine.
I wonder if I'll ever see
those stars I could not find,
to watch them through eternity
and drink upon their wine.

—Scott Belcher

WITH JASMINE
I need this paper
to guide me through a memory
a memory of an hour ago.
I swam in the grass
golden
and I was golden when
the sun streaked across me
in brushes of wind.
I groped the tufts
delusively coarse
burned my hands raw
but I held them still grasping
deeper and stronger
keeping me from falling into the sky.
It called me in a voice
so raspy it hurt my throat
while the sun burnt my hair
but I love.
I love this barren pit of gold—
one big broomstick
and I am the witch.

—Hilary Jay Keller

UNTITLED

"You" tear at the remnant of Tranquility
I will not let you destroy the doors of Peace
You push me toward the road of Violence
Yet on my soul you have no Lease
I will not let the darkness conquer me
The guns of Hate must cease to Be.

—Calvalita Browning

LOVE'S SPLENDOR

Love's splendor circles 'round and 'round;
    gently touching my day.

Love is a mother's awe, as she tenderly nestles her
    newborn babe; gently, so gently.

Love is a father's hand, guiding his swaying toddler's
    steps; gently, so gently.

Love is patience to tie sails on life's tiny boat, and
    the gentle puff to send it on its way.

Love is a place to rest, and sorrow's balm within my
    breast; rocking me gently, so gently.

Love is the blessing of my family; rejoicing, sharing,
    'round and 'round in splendor's great array.

—Sue Gardner Fenster

FOR MY FRIEND

Whatever else the years have brought, of few
    Or more than many things, solicited,
Or undesired and warded off with dread
Or subtlety, or somehow suffered through
With patience or with none, I will and do
Forgive them much! It can and should be said
That I am in their debt above my head
Since they, though who knows how, have brought me you.

And yet, perhaps the years were nothing more
Than correlates of space, through which you came,
So beautiful, so welcome, to my door,
Arrayed in living form, with voice and name.
Have I not known you, then, somewhere, before,
Before some other world dissolved in flame?

—Carol Hadley Bryans

this white slumber has been shaken,
ponds of glass shattered
by a sudden sun,
stirring the germinal seed touched
two years ago.

black, dead hills live!
still, lifeless rivers flow!
white dies to green—green aligns to blue
filling the horizon against
change of gold and orange.

(painful memories melt
with february snow)

    the death i have known this dreary winter
and the death i have watched linger
and the death i have mourned
    my loss and nature's
have been replaced
by the return
of your spring.

—J. P. hunt

THE MONARCH'S WINGS

In the wake of loneliness
My heart's eye knows no tenderness
Like maples drenched in crimson gold
The stench of what was bought and sold
No longer strings and strains the ear
Thou foul gospel, clinging like germs
Such spittle stains the monarch's wings
He learns — — like every species in his turn
To grasp life's last ashen breath, gasping
To die without agrandisement
To dream with love's abandon

—Rebecca A. Higgins

ONE LONELY DREAM

A little road once beckoned me
"Come on and play" it cried.
"We'll wander far beyond the lea
Where ships at anchor ride."

"I'll show you love, and joy, and
    laughter too — all this
I'll show you where a dream
    comes true, made lovely by a kiss"

"Begone, you naughty road, I cried
I have no time to play"
So one small dream within me died
And I'm too old today.

—M.E. Ball

HAWK OF NIGHT

He perches there
Upon his wooden throne,
His eyes in constant search of prey
Within the weed and stone
Strewn across his domain.
Aware of all it seems,
Suddenly he springs
And stretches blackened wing
High into a soft and silent flight,
Blending into quickly falling night.
Feathers spread and close,
A whispering hiss,
As eyes spot prey and talons do not miss,
Delivering a sharp and deadly kiss,
Returning to his throne a benefice.

—Frances C. Morrice

SEASONS CHANGE

As winter blossoms into spring,
The gloom becomes a glow.
The happiness that robins bring
Gradually melts depressing snow.

Trees renew their precious green
And waters begin to heat.
The beauty of the awakening scene
Is impossible to repeat.

The spring becomes a summer bright
While sun becomes the fire
Of dewy morning's only light
Shining oft till we retire.

The summer fades as fall marches in
To become the winter we dread within.

—Jennifer E. Coleson

MY BACKYARD

Blue, purple, red, golden orange are in the skies.
The trees hang bare,
With no leaves to shed as the wind blows.
The grass grows green and tall
With yellow Buttercups.
The fence that surrounds the grass is plain,
And holds no color.
This is my backyard.

—Ngeng Te, age 10

ODE TO MOLLY

My heart, the last box of cereal in the cupboard,
lies there so listless—a frailty lost.
Outside, a rooster, jars my body awake to its perfunctory
duties this morning.
I move in these bleak surroundings like yesterday
when there were two bowls.
Now, a pool of tears has claimed residence in one.
As I reach for that box I feel my breath
without a sign of breathing.
In these dark, empty spaces I've put away death
but closed the door on my heart.
If Molly was here she would say cathartically,
"Drink of this bowl and paint a shoe to wear today."

—Ronald Joseph Cecilia

SONGS FOR GOD

"I'll write a song"; porous lies the sand.
"and pen some scenes"; "Oompah!" mocks the drum.
"Just wait, you'll see"; "Fool!" whispers the wind.
"'Oh my,' says I"; "Continue, my son."

"A hymn to my love"; "Shhh!" moans the snore.
"a sonata so sweet"; "Tch, tch, tch!" sound the drops.
"Beautiful curls and sweeps"; hazy paints the fog.
"'I'll stop,' says I"; "Your songs are not done."

And so I write, and so she draws,
unvarnished though the hymns may be,
a symphony amid the cacophony
of human pain and age's drain,
love arrows to the Lord.

—Al Sieracki, O. Carm.

LAST NIGHT, THE WIND BLEW

Last night, the wind blew
And an army of snow fell and forced trees to bend.
Death called gently
      To invite the children
      To kiss the ground.
With weighted hearts, and tired eyes, they did.
And they lied there,
Ears against the earth, as if
They thought to LISTEN
To a familiar song;
Stricken with a disease that stank like
GUNPOWDER
And made the life run from them
      (Flowing, Red),
Running out in fear of the storm.

When the wind stopped,
Beneath a white blanket
      They put out the light to sleep
—ETERNALLY—
Last night when the wind blew.

—Deanne Johnson

I, TOO, WENT TO THE GROVE

Blackened branches in a guileful sky
whisper treacherously to the dusk
of a night one lay by one beneath them

wicked blades in the darkness descending
down the waking moon carve
cleave the stars on the rise

and what sure ones this eve
will lie safe in the grove
only to find as night next conspires
their pine needle secret betrayed?

—Liza L. Knowlton

It is midnight; I can see nothing.
The forest is lit only by the sound
Of rain falling, and the smell of trees.
No, black is not the absence of color.

Does the sun remember coloring
My closed eyelids poppy-petal orange
One August morning years ago
To the azure droning of bees?

I want you to know that I (and the sun)
Have forgotten nothing
Least of all you, O child of music
For such a forgetting would be a death

And death is the absence of color
Yes, and death is the absence of love.

—Thomas R. Thomas

at lake berlin

there were old men in fishing gear
reeling silent
to the accompaniment of coleman lanterns
they waited
for trout I remember their ritual
of patience
that brought in rainbows for slaughter
they bragged
as the ceremony of de-scaling began
with cleaning knives
that chopped and gutted
the reeking school
I watched as they fried their trophies
over sacrificial fires

—Bekki Wehr

DANCE IN THE WOOD

To pillage the branches of the herby,
wild, pink-flowered current
that after a soft rain
spread a mist of perfume
through the still wood—
and the blue violets—and the trilliums.

. . . I was never harrowed by the dark wood;
My sensibilities were quite alert and well
      channeled,
(at least I thought so—)
and I noticed this and that.
yet, inspired by the beauty of the morning
I hurried from one botanical miracle
to another, in always too much haste,
and my itinerant steps along
the wind too swept . . .

—Olga Wahlsten

21

MOURNING

Golden fingers
Play gentle on my pillow—
And day proclaims
Her soft alarm.

And though no lover
Strokes my head—

God hath no sweeter touch
For one who wakes
Alone.

—Sona G. Schmidt

FOR AUNT EDNA

Often
My mind comes to gaze
On swans on ponds
In apple'd days.
Milk with coffee
Highway psalms,
Playful romps
And joyful songs.
While we harvested apples
And the sunshine above,
You and I—
We harvested love.

—Linda Ford

SOLACE

I've been waiting
for a day like this
    cotton-covered
    and dripping grey
but I might slip on
    apple-skin-leaves
so maybe I'll just cover
    myself with your bark
hide in the womb
    of your trunk
wait
for winter to pass

—Carol Rial

MIRROR IMAGE

Her lips move when mine do,
She's the same but yet anew,

I see her in the morning
    when we compare faces,
I pass her in store windows
    and unexpected places,

I'd like to look her in the eye,
    but I can't for I'm too shy,

I think I've seen you,
Did you come out of the blue?

I want to ask you,
    "Who are you?"

Shall I form the question,
Or will you keep me guessin'?

Are you a part of my imagination,
    Or is this a real-life situation?

Am I so blind that I can't see,
That you are plainly afraid of me?

—Lisa A. Neitz

FRUITS OF LOVE

"Come," they call, "See the beauty, see the color!
Gather all you can!"

My first bite brings a questioning frown.
Where is the sweet, rich flavor?

Feed me only ripened fruit. I can wait
for it to become joyfully sweet.

New love is like new fruit. Let it ripen.
Only with time is love's promise complete.

—Patricia Mulder

DAWN MARIE ELIOT WANTS TO GET MARRIED

If the world were to end Friday, what would you say?
Would I say:
    "So what? I'm alone and skinny anyway."?
Would I say:
    "Damn! There go all the potential and beauty of humanity,
    and I never got a chance to wed."?
If the world were to end what would we lose?
There would be no more generosity.
There would be no more touching.
There would be no more dejection.
There would be no more shopping.
There would be no more creativity.

—Adam Clifford Stolfi

J. DOE'S DIARY

I want to make a poem too.
But I don't know how.
If I could, I would.
I would make its edges glitter with gold;
If I could.
All over the inside it would be creamy and smooth
With little touches of lemon,
And it would sing with music.
It would have a high moon racing through silvery dark clouds
And it would roar like the ocean on a windy night.
It would burn hot and dry sometime like Cape San Blas in August.
I would splash it full of diamonds and pearls,
And little seeds of grass and meadowlarks and mockingbirds,
And dusty dirt roads and berries.
It would be good if I could.
Make a poem.
If I could, I would.

—Ovia Dale Bell

LITTLE JUMPER OUTFIT

There was something hanging on my closet door,
Something, that had never, been there before.
Oh! it's a jumper outfit, made of soft wool in brown
And a blouse—of tan satin, like an expensive gown
With its wide shoulder straps, it's unique and swell!
My Mother made it, and sewed it so well.
I got to wear it, to school, one special day
Everyone loved it, I just have to say.
There was one girl, who jumped with glee
I want one! I want one! cried Marilee.
But it was a product of a sewing skill
And could not be bought in a store, at one's will.
Oh! little outfit—You are so fine
I can wear you anywhere, even out to dine.
And I wore you so proudly and so happily
Because you were something, just made for me.
But, I wondered, so often, as my friends, over you would gloat
What they'd say, if they knew, You were once Aunt Ella's old coat

—Miriam Gregory

DREAM HORSE

There is a horse I dream of,
  with a single horn protruding from his forehead.
His mane and tail of silver and gold,
  glisten in the moonlight as he sleeps. When he
awakes and begins his endless journey once more,
  with giant leaps of strength,
his muscles ripple with love and security.

—Sharyl Crossley

STARS

We go to bed and we turn out the lights;
  but not before we all say goodnight.

Then we gaze out the window and into the sky;
to see the stars looking into our eyes.

The stars look over us all night long;
to ensure that nothing will ever go wrong.

Without these stars where would we be;
we really would not be able to see.

It is these stars that keep us safe;
twinkling down as we dream in our own little place.

When our dreams are over and the dark turns to light;
it is the stars, who then say goodnight

—Dean Nutter

RAINDROPS

Raindrops gently falling as the wind whips through the trees
Gray clouds moving quickly anticipating a winter freeze
November days are moving rapidly toward December
Holidays fast approaching — for all to remember.

Pitter, patter is the musical beat of the raindrops
As valleys fill to the brim with rain from the rooftops
Scarce are footsteps on the pavement, as all run inside
Keeping warm and dry, from the damp wintry rain they hide.

Bring out the hot cocoa, cookies and tea
It's the nicest thing to do, and the warmest place to be
As the raindrops slowly bid their whispering goodbyes
For the sun is peeking through the gray and cloudy sky.

Hiding in their special places, till another time is right
All the little raindrops twinkle as the sky turns into night.

—Dolores Gaylord

WELCOME

Red candle, wavering so slow, suffuses the floor and ceiling
  with a flickering, silent show;
    for assembled shadow chairs and tables.
      This is my calm center of being,
  this is the welcoming hearth of such inspired meeting.
We'd assembled only hours before in rapturous music
      and song
    effortlessly carrying our revels along
        to my now quiet reflection:
        the assembled chairs and tables,
        the ticking clock upon the wall,
        to the glasses resting on paper,
    to the blank t.v. screen as spectator.
  My tired eyes are nearing their final blinks
as midnight thoughts perch on the subconscious brink.
      But do they take me in their leap?
  Long after this time has passed, I will always
    hold this place, these people, in my thoughts,
  long after the dying light of the creative spark.

—Ed Nielsen

CHERYL

Emerald eyes in almond frames.
Lucent skin. Sapphire veins.
Smile reflects the midday sun.
Chestnut hair bids breezes come.
Frail throat, so gently turned.
Slender legs, so smooth, so firm.
Tender titter when I tickle you.
Soft embrace . . . Oh! play is through.
Soft embrace is all we took just then.
I was twelve, you were ten.

—Peter A. Corrente

O, do not quench that fragile flame
That burns so brief a season
In youth alone, unspoiled by shame,
Nor yet bedimmed by reason.

Come, love, while the sun still warms.
Waste no time with doubt.
All my world's within your arms,
And nothing lay without.

Hold steadfast deep within your heart
Each precious, joy-filled day.
O, cruel is Nature, vain is Art.
Thief Time will have his way.

—Anita Jane Denison

PERSONAL

My pen draws lines of nothing
  on a page blank as my mind.

I am obscured by what does not exist.

The smoke of life shuts off a window
  toward the open years
And then evaporates.

My thoughts are stairs that crumble,
  leading nowhere.
Half of me betrays what seems to be.

And yet I plan, I try.
I shall persist.

—Dee C. Konrad

MY NEARNESS

My footprints wear no skin
  wear nothing   weigh nothing
are visible on granule lid of earth,
spread out   are dried
by the nearness of the sun's tentacles.

I turn back to find one   and another;
the innumerable traces of myself
that have no relative shadows.
Each print halts my nearness.

I watch them crumble
from the tentacle's touch—
pieces are driven into   hungry sunlight
acquainting in the air.

Naked bits of life   dash in brilliance
through swatches of evening.
I look through night windows.
The night crowds my closeness.

I listen to the switch of wings
that with sleep   will close the night.

—Francesca Aragon Azevedo

SAVE THE 'STARS AND STRIPES'

If Betsy Ross came back as a ghost,
Seeking news of what she loved most,
She'd ask first, "Where's my flag?
For all I see is a burnt black rag.
This can not be our 'Stars and Stripes,'
For which Sons and Fathers gave up their lives!
Oh, please tell me that it can not be so,
That our great Nation would stoop so low.
I know we are 'free and equal' in every way,
But once 'She's' destroyed this we can't say."

—Pat Simpson

CHALLENGER
January 28, 1986

A nation at a stand still.
Thousands of blank faces stare toward the sky.
A wave of silence rushes over the land.
The usual fulfillment and glorification,
replaced by an unacceptable tragedy.
With a crushing farewell to pride.
Each individual feeling shock and resentment.
Many group together to converse, to console.
America's visions for tomorrow
have become today's realistic nightmare.
Still dignity remains, to try again,
for our dream to succeed.

—Connie Lynn Clinton

A PROUD EXPERIENCE

As I look into the endless sky,
Soaring high above the majestic peak;

I see a proud reminder
Of our country's greatest fight.

I'm reminded of all the struggles
And the battles big and small;

The costly price we had to pay
For the most valuable prize of all.

Soaring high and soaring free;
Past obstacles overcome.

The great dream of our country unconquered;
Free to fly, free to fly.

—Karen Leigh North

LAND OF LIBERTY?

Why is there so much pain and sorrow
In the Land of Liberty?
We all grew up believing
That this is the Land of the Free!

Liberty is just a facade
Big brother is on the watch
Waiting for us to cross the line
And then our freedom is lost!

Rules and regulations
We wade through every day
And if we don't obey them,
there is a price to pay!

Between our definitions
There is a great difference
We have the freedom to obey
or face the consequence!

—Vickie Bingaman

HEY! THAT AIN'T HAY!

We Love to Throw Money Around.
We Hear BILLIONS are OUTWARD BOUND!
The World Looks to US for a TREAT—
While Our HOMELESS Sleep in the STREET!

—Robert Emmett Clarke

AMERICAN SPIRIT

What have you done for America today?
Have you helped anyone along the way?
Have you done your job or some trouble increase
For those who are trying at least

The homeless are both young and old
They make their homes in the bitter cold
They watch the clouds in the sky
And sit and talk with others near-by.

People are starving both here and there
Children are abused almost everywhere.
Crimes are committed left and right
drug busts are done throughout the night.

Oh! Stand up for the "land of the free!"
Be proud of this great Coun-try.
When we are unsure of what next to do
God as usual will see America through!

—Janice C. Handsborough

LIBERTY

Proud country it was with thee we sang,
when we learned of tyrannies fall,
to freedom's sweet refrain we watched,
people dancing on the Berlin Wall.

'Twas for thee sweet liberty they fought,
justice and dignity the weapons they employed,
many visions forged into one voice that cries,
"this wall must be destroyed."

What a glorious moment to witness,
with dreams of peace on Earth we are inspired,
East and West have been united,
yet, not a single shot was fired.

Americans hail and welcome you,
upon liberties gracious wings,
thankful for one more mountainside from which,
freedom now shall ring.

—Kathleen Patrick

THE BALD EAGLE

Our national emblem bird,
Wanting not to be disturbed,
Builds her nest on the cliffs up high
For an easy launch when she wants to fly.

Over the lake like a shadow
She hunts for fish on the surface of the water,
With a hungry eaglet in the nest,
This mother bird won't stop to rest.

Soar high Bald Eagle,
Glide on the wind.
I watch you from below
And wish that we were friends.

How wonderful it must be
To fly so high and free.
I have a question for you,
Would you change places with me?

—O'Neale Adams

SUCCESS

Have you given someone your smile today
Have you helped a stranger along life's way—
Have you shed a tear for someone in need
Or reached out your hand to do a good deed?
Did you open your heart and whisper a prayer
Knowing sure as you breathe that Someone is there?
Did you thank him for bounties you daily behold
And shared all your love so it lit up your soul—
You have lived then my friend, and each day that you do
The best of life's riches will come back to you!

—Anna Ribbeck

FIND WHAT I'M LOOKING FOR

What I'm looking for cannot be sold or bought.
It cannot be given or cannot be taught.
Through thought and determination
I'll look high and low,
and only stop when I know.

Someday I'll get enough courage to untie the strings,
that hold me back from opening my wings.

I'll face dangers and a lot of closed doors,
but I won't stop 'till I find what I'm looking for.

When I find it I will see,
that what it is is only me!

—Jacki Lynn Mitchell

FRAULEINS
(Or, Thoughts On The Reunification of Germany.)

fancy designed
glass parking lots
impressive architecture
tree-lined streets
leaves changing color
bronze blowing
leaves and hair
sun shining
faces smiling (they dare)
rosy cheeks
nice figures
blue eyes
beautiful hair
that's how we come
first she asked
for a moment of my embarrassment.

—Chris Daly

AND THE WALL CAME TUMBLING DOWN

I never imagined I would ever see
The wall come tumbling down
When friends and loved ones too
Could once again be free.

It was a glad and joyous day,
An event going down in history,
Where one-time stoic guards with jutted jaw
Were marking the end to hostility.

Oh Lord, forbid that we more walls should make
For closed doors and walls we hate.
And we know divisions without walls
Are even harder to break.

So then, dear Lord, we pray
Help us to follow your Golden Rule.
Guide all we say, think, or do,
Your Word be our greatest tool.

—Darline Kussmann

TRYING TIMES

This country ain't bad,
In fact it's good,
But things aren't running like they should,
With economy so high,
And spirit so low,
People don't know which way to go,
But things will get better,
I know that they will!
If only I can pay this month's utility bill.

—Valerie Menezes McLaughlin

TRAPPED

Some are trapped in their bodies
Cannot see, or walk or hear,
Others are caught by circumstances
Reasons myriad and unclear.
The outcome—always uncertain
Brings anger, fear and pain
Some things we lose—other things we gain.
But true love lives forever on.
In spite of loss and pain
and the sun will shine again — once more.
Shutting out the rain.

—Betty Sweet

SEGREGATION TRAIL

Dry those painful tears my lady
Walk life's trails to sunshine dreams,
Burying thorns among the wayside.
Planting roses in between.

Years of pain from segregation
Dividing brother among nation,
In a painful trying situation.

In time the wounds will fade away,
Down life's winding trails to love.
Accept the past as history
And forgiveness from above.

The future on a dream,
Place reality on a pedestal!
Closing doors to segregation
Loving brothers among nation.

—Norma Mae Kuhl

THE GREATEST POWER

For the want of power in this world,
There's precious little most wouldn't do.
Power is some what like a drink,
A sweet and heady brew.

It bends the mind, torments the soul,
When carried to extreme.
It's power, when in bed at night,
That most will often dream.

Corruption is its final work,
The ego is its tool.
We're taught that power is our goal,
Starting in nursery school.

There is a power that I seek,
And I hope to gain while I live.
It is the greatest power of all,
The Power To Forgive.

—Wayne Hall

If they ever had seen the blue of the ocean
They wouldn't have begun sandpainting.

Yellow blanket of sand
The pale of Sun and Cloud
and that dance, around the geometric forms
of tribalism

Symbolism on an ancient ocean bed.

—Susan T. Sheridan

KITTY LOVE

When your sleek, supple beauty
lands you warmly in my lap,
your soft sounds move me
to cheap imitations, and slowly
craning my neck, I reach
to steal your dark sweet breath,
lacking even the poor excuse
of drops of milk lingering
on your lips in the night

—r.l. merrick

AN ODE TO THE STARS

I am lulled by the gentleness of
the stars.
They sing to me—songs of peace—
of enjoyed loneliness.
I gaze into the heavens—
and am covered with their comfort.
They are alive—they are there, always.
Never are they bored, conceited in the least.
I am sure if they could give—
I would have the world—
So generous, are they,
to grant us with their beauty—
Their brilliant softness,
their peaceful presence.
They do not speak—
but yet, they say so much.
They do not touch—
but yet, they console—
they are the world.

—Diana Matijas

BOVINE PRAISE

Cows make a certain track among
the trees, along the field
and over slowly rising hills
or in the grass, concealed.

They seek the easiest trespass
in natural terrain
and huddle under broadleaf trees
in sudden and hard rain.

In late autumn and early spring
their wet backs give off steam
that hovers in the chilly air
along the quiet stream.

One single bell betrays the lead
obediently trailed
by horned and bobbing heads, and tails
that swatted flies, and failed.

Oblivious, these animals
greet sun and rain the same
and with stoic indifference
belie their assumed name.

—Dan Sladich

HURRICANE

How angry was the wind!
How it screamed at the clouds,
at the sand, at the sea . . .
And I asked, as it passed by my door:
"Oh, wind! Are you angry with me?"

But the wind heard me not,
just went on to destroy everything,
all around, and as far away as I could see.
Yet it spared my oasis, for
the wind was not angry with me.

—Carmen Becraft

FROM A DISTANCE

From a distance,
as near as a whale's song
and as far as the side of my face,
above the hushed weeping of the masses
and the din of crystal glasses touching lightly
penetrating the brick,
windows,
doors,
and the tumultuous movement of everything around me,
came the chiming of a star colliding
with a child's voice in song.

—Ken Dolen

TULIPS ASCENDING IN SPRING

Straight postured stem reaching
up, held firm by searching
roots sending chromosomes
through a green vesseled stalk,
melding with plum-sized
petals stroked pink, bursting
forth with six tightly knit
mittens holding
future generations, asking
only of this world—
life.

In this, their beauty.

—Jeanie Kahnke

EN CANTAS

En cantas,
the golden days of the autumn haze
that drift slowly out of wind and rain
and fall into burnished snowflakes.

En cantas,
as the quiet nights fleck the air
with a golden blight and brush
the starry sky with the fiery glow.

En cantas,
while the dancing bough mellows now
in the amber wine
of the fields' and farrows' bounty.

En cantas,
when the glow of life for man and wife
touches gold the scarlet hills resound with
the fruit of Spring's fertility and Summer's joy.

En cantas,
singing over the amber land as coral sand
upon the sea catches in a moment's laugh
all the good that Earth has borne in a single revelry.

—J.M. Fletcher

A BLANKET OF DREAMS

A blanket of dreams to cover my mind,
And fill me with thoughts of a special kind,
A blanket of dreams all fluffy and white,
To float gently over me stilling my fright,
When I feel forsaken, lonely and lost,
I conjure them up at so little a cost,
Like a penny that's saved for a rainy day,
I carefully think them then tuck them away,
And somehow it seems they never diminish,
But stay fresh and new from the start to the finish.

—Mrs. Nell Reed

OWL

Oh wise old owl with eyes so bright,
Who sleeps by day and awakens by night.
For you are wise which I am not,
Tell me my place in life for I was told but now forgot.
When I was a baby at my birth,
And took my first step on this earth.
I knew not who I was going to be,
But now I'm old and long to be young and free.
Tell me does my death await,
Does each dark corner hold my fate?
I sit and ask these questions to you,
But all you say to me is "WHOOO . . ."

—Elisabeth Petrowski, age 10

TREE, SOIL, AND RAIN

I was once a healthy Strong Tree
With roots deeply entwined in a healthy, fertile Soil
My leaves were lively and green
And plentiful buds danced on my branches
The Rain bathed me in Love, the sun shone its aura
And the Soil and I lived strongly, firmly together
But then the weather changed
The Rain gradually stopped its Love-baths
My roots cannot find water in its once-loving Soil
And the Soil and I merely existed
Now the sun shines bright and the leaves and buds
        still sway elegantly in the breeze
I cannot it seems, even feel the Soil
Yet though I appear the perfect Tree
I miss the Soil and the Rain
Someday, I suppose, the Rain shall again give me its Love-baths
. . . the clouds on the horizon are so far away . . .

—James R. Blankenfeld

THE STAG

The stag jumped up from a bed of brown pine needles . . . .
    making a silhouette against the cobalt sky,
        As he lurched to his retreat in the bush.

He was a king in his own world, and bugled to his mate,
who had preceded him toward her hidden calf in
        the dense timber.
It gave a low cry when her footsteps drew near —
instinctively knowing its native call for food.
        The stag followed and muzzled up to his off-
            spring with sheer pride.
The cow gently pushed him away so she could co-oerce
her loved one to rise up for a meal.
        The night sky paled as the little one suckled
            its mother,
making small sounds in the forest before silence reigned.
The eastern star in the heavens gleamed with tender
        approval.

—A. Norine

MY RAINDOW

A path is being opened before me
Do I seek it or does it seek me?
It unfolds as I seek it
Unfolding for me as it seeks me
I will find what I seek
Only what I seek will have already
        found me!

—Joanne McIntyre

JET TAKE-OFF AT SUNSET

A star to mother-father love
red sky-streak
canyons
a take-off
red spark;
a closing.

Two lakes
in the figure of
two men;
a red fire moving horizontally
sliced to silver.

—Linda Schaaf Aton

END OF SUMMER

The cinnamon spider sits
In the dry
Cinnamon columbine seed pod.
She knows color

She waits
All bunched up but,
Relaxed.

The butter yellow spider sits
In the damp
Pansy blossom center. (Butter yellow)
She knows color too

She also waits
All spread out but,

Also very still

—Bill Duncan

ARBORETUM IN FALL

Tat, tat
Tata, tat
The arboretum's white highlights
the gray, glassy, daylight.

Tata, tat
Tata, tat
Rainfalling rivulets cling and slide
obscure, then magnify
a pointilist's dream scene
through a glass-walled tropical haven:

Tat, tat, tat
Tears streaming down glass.
Plum-glum trees.
Honey-showered grass.
Grand stands of blue-green fir
layered upon autumnal, deciduous
siennas, golds — a yellowed
shimmering-orange
rain-muted
show.

—Robin D. Harrover

A PRAYER POEM — MY CREED

Father, Oh! that I might serve thee—that I might hear the cry of man
Never saying "After all I've done" Tho not to be the crutch which makes the lame more weak
Father, Help me serve that I truly help my fellow man
Might I never say I have done thus and so—for it is God through me who does it all
As I set my heart and mind on thee—Please reveal thyself to me
Take the blinders of selfishness from my eyes—that I might never compromise
Tis Unconditional Love I seek—might I help the poor the weak
The poor in spirit the weak in heart—from them I do not set myself apart
For we are One forever—my brother's hurts are thus mine in the annals of time
My joy cannot be complete until every soul would know their worth—
Then freedom and peace will fill the earth
Again I ask—You hear I know—Reveal Thyself to me
The truth is here, my God, only that I might see and know that I am One with Thee
In the name of Jesus Christ I pray—Reveal Thyself—show me The Way.

— **Lucy Gaide**

FAVORITE TIME OF YEAR

Christmas is my favorite time of year
for there's always plenty of joy and good cheer.
It's that time of year to share in all that is abound
with family and friends as they gather around.
It's the season you find peace and goodwill on earth
and it's that special time the Virgin Mary gave birth.
It's the time for mistletoe and holly,
and Santas in red suits who are fat and jolly.
It's that time of year for grandma's gooseberry pie,
and don't forget those last minute gifts to buy.
There's lots of Christmas carols to be sung
and a few more tree ornaments that need to be hung.
It's that time of year children look through frosted window panes
while daydreaming of toys and peppermint candy canes.
It's the season when wild winter winds blow
leaving behind a fresh white blanket of snow.
These are just a few of the reasons
that Christmas is my favorite season.
For all these things are sure to please us,
but the real meaning of Christmas is our Lord Jesus.

— **Valerie Latella**

THERE ARE OTHER ISLANDS . . .

There are islands . . . surrounded by bodies of water not yet understood

the jealous dawn comes as usual . . . only the sun can produce enough light
to see the world clearly

the wind carries the rain . . . rainbows only appear after the storm passes

loneliness and pain tear at one's soul . . . true peace lies only a prayer away

all faith is lost over things we cannot touch . . . we forget that we live
day to day on something we cannot see

death is unavoidable . . . only the soul can live forever

life is opportunity . . . one life, one chance, one destiny

but there are other islands . . . spirits we can only feel in our hearts

time is indestructible . . . only the bitter and cold dread what tomorrow may bring

each breath is a gift from God . . . for the just, the last breath is a gift to God

love is unconditional . . . no price can be placed on such rare selflessness

true friends are a precious possession . . . material things will only pass away

death is a journey . . . what lies beyond is navigated by the life before it

life is also a journey . . . a continuous search for the island that we can call
our own

— **Vickie Sims**

CHRISTMAS SEASON 1989. JOHN 15:10, LINE 14 K.J.V.

Oh come warm weather come,
Relieve the oil pressure then some.
Price the cartels for lower goals
To warm our hearts and their souls.

How oft t'were said from bible and pulpit
That love of money and greed on hearts sit,
The evils of gain bring sorrows
To the poor, and to our cold tomorrows.

Oh God to you we all pray
That men who sit upon this cold sway,
Would recognize the error of their ways,
T'would gladden our hearts and warm our
    days.

Give us recognition of your love and grace.
To receive love we must love the human race.
But come warm weather come
Warm our beings and then some.

    —S. A. Tabah

MY COMMITMENT

Dear Lord, I place my hands in Thine
Take them, Lord, and lead me gently on.

I give my heart to Thee
Make it pure and clean.

Take my life and use it, Lord,
That souls may be brought to Thee,
For thy kingdom in glory.

May my feet trod only where you lead,
My lips to say only what you want me
to say,
My eyes to see your beauty and love.

So, I pray, dear Lord,
take my hands, my lips, my heart, my feet
and eyes, and use them that others may see
Jesus in me.

That you may be glorified, and your love
be shown to all mankind, throughout the
world.

    —Helen B. Adamson

THE LORD IS MY KEEPER

The Lord is my Keeper
He is so mighty and Strong
I Love my Lord Jesus from this day on
The Lord is my Teacher
To teach from wrong
No matter what it takes Lord
Lord lead me on

Lord lead me on Lord, Lord lead me on
Show the differences in dying Lord
In a way it's going Home
Stay close beside me each day I face
Lord you're my deliverance, saved by
Your Amazing Grace

O How I thank Thee
How I praise thy Holy Name
Thou hast cast my sins behind me
And there Lord they will remain
You gave me your Comfortor to preserve my life
As long as I live Lord, You I
Will serve the rest of my life

    —Brenda Overstreet, Edwards

HIS LIGHT

From just an ordinary light,
God revealed to me a beautiful sight.

From this light, there were four rays,
As I glanced at it, I was amazed.

From these four rays of light,
A cross was formed in my sight.

As I stared at this sight that I could see,
I wondered what God was revealing to me.

God revealed to me His Love for us all,
From the light on the cross that I saw.

There was a warm glow deep inside me,
"Draw Me Nearer," my heart sang to Thee.

If I hadn't taken time to look at this light,
I would have missed a beautiful sight.

We need to take time to observe ordinary things.
Only then can we know the joy it brings.

    —Delores Morrison

JAY

I ask him,
"What does Christmas mean to you?"
He pauses for a minute, and replies,
"I can't think of anything."
It hurts to hear him say that,
But I know why . . .
At four o'clock sharp, he leaves school,
And goes—home,
To pyramids of beer cans,
Waves of cigarette smoke,
And nothingness.
No one greets him at the door and says,
"I missed you."
Or,
"How was your day?"
So I ask him to learn similies and metaphors.
He tries to please me.
But all the while
He's searching for an answer,
And thinking Christmas and metaphors
Are hard to understand . . .

    —Vernice Ankerstjerne

MY HOLIDAY

Love and joy
Sharing and caring
Turkeys and roast
My holiday just makes me want to boast
Stars and angels, on the top of the tree
Santa Claus coming down the chimney
In the morning, I just can't wait to see
All the presents there for me
Christmas is a time for love
Happiness, and of course the dove
Carolers going from door to door
Singing on forevermore
Holiday shows on t.v.
Holiday stories for you and me
Christmas symbols here and there
Decorations everywhere
Laughter and joy, love to spare
Holiday spirit I like to share
Singing around the Christmas tree
And that's what my holiday means to me!

    —Sasha Jordan

CHAMELEON

He transforms.
He adapts.
His truth varies with circumstance.

He deceives.
He perceives.
He makes you trust in what you see.

He hides.
He waits.
Then he makes you learn to hate.

—Karen E. McMahan

WHEN YOU LEFT

A hand of ice
Reached inside
And held my heart
Frosted, turning gray
The red and pulsing mass.

Icicles dropped
Liquid daggers
In my chest,
Then solidified at zero temp
And stabbed me dead.

—Cornelia Bruck-Smith Nedomatsky

CRESCENT MOON

The thinnest moon crescent,
when first light reflects from the limb
and trembles yellow-white
at edge of blue-black night,
rarely is noticed. We see
full moons.

So I, a sliver crescent
in your life reflect your light,
unnoticeable in the blue vault of
your being. In the dark of night,
my candlepower of light can shine
as well; all that must happen is
the focus of your eyes to see me.

—Ursula T. Gibson

BONDAGE GAMES

Desperate now, and shrewd
with the slyness
of other mute women
hobbled beasts
I twist and try to break
free
but his tight harness,
like cooled silver alloy
like the hides of animals
holds me

I am tethered by
a soft mouth, pale eyes

as cleverly collared
on the leash of his displeasure
as he is bound
by the harsh lead
of my needing glances

and with tortured movement
we create
the graceful celebration
of our own
cruel options

—S. Ross

(SOUL LADY)

You appear beautifully on the horizon
of heaven,
O' living woman, beginner of love
How strong your works are!
You have hidden from the heart of this man
O soul lady, like you there is no other!
You did create this love according
To your Desire . . .

—Robert V. Ziemoore

Love,
You've been a poor master for me.
When I let you take the reins
My heart is wrenched,
My body beaten,
I get left in the cold
Naked, shivering, wondering "Why?"

Love,
I've locked you tightly away.
I may never let you out
Can I love again,
Have I forgotten how?
No, I am too afraid
Too afraid to even try.

—Ginger R. Bruvold

LITTLE CHILD

Hear the arguing, see the fight
Be brave little child with all your might.
You can't stop him, he won't leave her alone . . .
The crashing sounds of a very loud tone.
Should you help her or run and hide . . .
or maybe just be there by her side.
Why must he do this it's very wrong,
to hurt someone, who's not as strong.
As the child you can only watch and hear . . .
the most terrifying sounds to your ear.
You'd only hope he'd see you there,
so he'd stop to see what's really fair.
The fighting stops, the sound dies down . . .
There your Mom lays on the cold wet ground.
It shall happen again, it always will—
This man has to get his extra fill.
So little child be brave, and do your best . . .
to keep her away from all the rest.

—Stacy Vanderheyden

FIRE IN PASSION

Thou art Passion so Annihilable!
Never did my ignorant Soul know thy true colors,

Thy nature proved its first phase so soft,
Like the misty shower of early rain,

Then you covered me like an Avalanche,
Filling my breath with thy sweet Aroma,

Thy enchanting quality beguiled me,
Slowly I realized that thou were a burning type,

Exhibiting thy Fire within out—
Till you gnawed my poor Soul,

Alas! In the end you burst like a Fissure in a Rock?
With sudden Rupture—Resulting in an Inarticulate Pain? Passion?

Thou art Passion so Inflammable!

—Charisma Reddy

WALKING FROM WASTELAND

He was Escape.
The deep, wild midnight of his eyes
Caught me away

From the deafening din.
The strength of his mind held me up
As we walked.
We walked.
Time was wind, whistling, whirling away the fog;
We talked, but said nothing.
His smile was warmth.
We walked,
While I breathed in his life.
The droning hum called me back
But he held my hand, whispering

Airy words
To my spirit.
We walked on.

—A. M. Servillo

such love . . .

such love,
such tenderness and warmth
that illuminates every day
and secures us like warm blankets at evening.
was it on that first meeting—
that first coming together of two powerful forces
that gave commencement to such love?
was it conceived on a beach somewhere or perhaps in the
country?
could it have been over a cup of coffee or a glass of beer?
such love,
penetrating our being like the hot summer sun—
sprinkling our hearts like a cool spring rain—
sheltering us like the golden leaves of autumn—
chilling our bodies like a fresh winter snow—
making us what we are and leading us to wherever we'll go;
like the morning glory that opens her heart to a new day.
such love—our morning and evening together for eternity.

—linda moore

IF I COULD

So many dear things, girl, I'd tell you if I could.
So many times you're not around or the words just don't
sound good.
I think of looking in your eyes and I know what I'm here for
And girl I know I'd tell you if you'd just walk in that door.

I'd tell you I love you even how you breathe
How it dusts my cheek warmly while I watch you sleep
Like a cool breeze softly kissing a ripe August eve.

And I'd tell you that together we can keep
Away that day when your strength will break
And the closest you can come to a smile
Is trying to find a way to stop your tears.
Girl I know I'd tell you if only you were here.

So many things, dear girl, I'd tell you if I could,
Things for which there are no words
Or words that might be heard but not quite understood.
I'd tell you how I long to hold you near, but would never
hold you back,
And other well-meant cliches like that
As if telling you things would do us any good.
Girl you know I'd tell you if I could.

—Chris M. Slawecki

SPIRITUAL LOVE

What is physical love,
If it does not release,
The passion of the soul?
Nothing.
It is an empty act,
With no satisfaction.
It leaves the spirit frustrated.
Please reach inside of me,
Touch my soul.
Break the chains,
Of the physical world,
That bind us to reality.
Fly with me,
In the spiritual realm.
Let us burn our wings,
On the flames,
Ignited,
By the passions of the spirit.

—Angela M. Spina

ANTHER AND ELIZABETH

She was comely.
That's why they got together.
Arrested—for vagrancy—by
Her bright eyes, Anther
Wandered into her parlor,
A butt between his lips.

From then on, it was rascal
And mischievous maiden,
Pulling on each other's fingers.
Mother walked into the room,
Carrying a tray of tea and cakes,
Chocolate . . . !

That night, the two of them
Sat in the garden,
Where the lilacs and the rosebush grew;
Shuddering, fidgeting, trembling—
Their captured voices
Mingling with the great hum
Of the stars in the heavens . . . .

—Andrew Gosciejew

WOULD YOU NOTICE ME?

Would you notice me when I
lied?
Surely, when I cried.
I don't talk very loud.
But if I tried, would you be
proud?

Would you notice me if I said,
"hi" and "bye" in a flash?
No, of course not, you're only
in my past.

Would you notice me if I broke
your heart?
Sure you would. I would
leave with a harsh depart.

Would you notice me in a box?
Go on, take a look at her
golden brown locks,
The beautiful smile,
That could only last for a
while.

—Jennifer A. Russell, age 18

I'M AFRICAN AND I'M PROUD

I'm African and I'm Proud.
i ain't yo black woman,
yo nigger,
yo coon
and i ain't yo pick-a-nin-ny neither

I'm an African Woman and I'm proud.
america ain't my home
My home is Africa and I'm Proud,
cause it was Alpha
and it shall be Omega
yeah, I'm African and I'm Proud.

—Shashamine

BOUND OR FREE

Imprisoned, but not by visible bars,
Bound, but not by metal chains,
Tortured, but not by prison guards,
Captured by anguish, agony, and pain.

I feel the wind blow through my hair,
As I run, the grass beneath my feet.
But, these are pictures only in my mind.
Ah, the memories are so sweet.

Trapped in a body broken and spent,
Things of my youth gone from me.
But, still there glimmers a ray of hope,
Because my spirit is oh, so free!

—Ella Colwell

THE TEAR

A simple salty droplet,
Splashes from my eye,
Tells of heartbreak,
Of pain I can't deny.

Symbol of a flood within,
A single drop upon my cheek,
Terror grips my soul,
Of which I cannot speak.

Yet, that sparkling sphere,
Is somewhat like the morning dew.
It washes all the hurt away;
Paints the world a different hue.

—Carol A. Rankin

STRANGERS TO THE RACE

How can you say
Those hateful words?
 They slide off of
Your tongue
 Like venom on a
Blade.

 Is there really any
"They" or "them?"
 Or is it just
Us, we.
 We're all susceptible to
Titles.

 All of us are
Strangers to somewhere,
 Some odd foreign land.
But really:
 Aren't we all just
Minorities?

—Stephani Karen Goodreau

AFRICA

Nature is so beautiful, so beautiful as can be.
Nature is so beautiful, so beautiful and free.
 Ducks are free. Birds are free. My family is free too.
Why can't your family be free in Africa with you?

—Noah Nicholas Patterson, age 6

A GHETTO ON A ROCK OF GOLD

Behold yonder ghetto on that rock of gold!
That's dreary and monotonous Soweto —
Habitat of Johannesburg's two million Africans . . . .
Cheek by jowl with the glitt'ring Metropolis;
Intrinsically linked up with it all ways,
Lies sprawling Soweto, smokey and polluted . . . .
Nestling between rich yellow gold mine dumps,
And fabulously opulent modern urbanity,
Lies Soweto, which Africans created for themselves,
But which they may neither possess nor exploit . . .;
Nor are they free to develop the ghetto
For themselves, their progeny or kith-and-kin . . . .
Ragged and semi-nude kids with bulging bellies!
Here, there's no security, tenure, mobility for Africans;
Here, here, Africans are only to sleep, eat, and die . . .,
On this rich, rich, rich, rich rock of gold . . . .

—Daniel P. P. Marolen

THE CRYING WIND

"The Crying Wind" — is weeping thru the nite
 Covering the world — with "Christ's Love"
Mourning — the hate and the strife

"The Crying Wind" — is weeping thru the nite
 Touching souls — as they sleep
Loving all — whether wrong or right

"The Crying Wind" — is weeping thru the nite
 Sweeping the World — with God's Love
Changing all — that is wrong to right

"The Crying Wind" — is weeping thru the nite
 The "Holy Spirit" — is er'e broading,
Christ's Love — gives to eyes, "new sight!"

"The Crying Wind" — is weeping thru the nite
 God's eye — is upon everyone
Drawing all — to Heaven's radiant light!

—Gloria Jean Daily

FALLS

Who owns that beauty?
That breathtaking
Falls.
Water spraying out into the cruel atmosphere,
Like the fragility of a newborn.
Sprays of water creating a mist that fights contamination,
Damnation.
These precious drops are tried at their own
Gates of Hell.
If they fall,
And are caught by their mother—
They will survive—
Only to live a never-ending life of movement,
Excitement and unity.
Drifting along, taking breaks in the eddies,
And going for it all in the rapids.
These drops amounting to almost nothing,
Exemplifying the lives of so many.

—Nathan Peter Gilbertson

GOODNESS

It is not the color of your skin
That will make your life worth while
And it is not the bigness of your purse
That will always bring a smile and
It is not the fame that's in your name
That will bring that well known clout!
But it is just that pride down deep inside
That will bring that goodness out!!!

—Ralph "Mike" Daniels

THE DOING IN THE ART

Art is not the doing of it all
    a canvas covered or songs bestowed
Nor sounds emerging from ordered ting-a-lings
    nor the thought conveyed from trenches of the soul
Misguided efforts splashed anew
    onto forms and genre-bearing spiels.
Beauty is, seeks She not
    eyes that behold her
Nor does She honor allegorical cabals that schmooze
    poor replicas of Greatness past.
The doing in the Art is not the Art
    it is something else
Something beyond the doing of it all
    beyond the doer, of course.

—Gilbert Neil Amelio

SUNSET GLORY

The sun is going down, now, and is quite pretty,
    A sunset you cannot see in the city.
It shows God's glory His wonderful grace,
Even though the world onward doth race.
It shows His power and all care,
It shows a love beyond compare.
It shows He has risen and conquered death.
That forever we might live and have
                everlasting breath.
A sunset shows we all need a rest.
Even each bird flies to its nest,
For God has set a time when all
                things come to end.
The sunset shows Jesus is coming again!

—Paula Wildermuth

THE MOCKINGBIRD'S SONG

I heard a Mockingbird sing one morn', and it sang
    throughout the day—
through the hustle and bustle of each meadow and lane,
while the world went on its way.
The gentle, winsome tune soared high, in strains
so sweet to hear,
but the notes were sometimes passionate, as if they
were bathed in tears—
The bird sang on and on until—twilight was past—
and darkness filled—the melody with weary sounds—
of soldier's footsteps on the ground—
and muffled prayers—and cries of saints—sounds
of hope—joy—fears and complaints—
I whispered, Mockingbird, please tell—me why you
sing of Heaven—of Hell—of earth—sky rivers and seas—
and will you sing through eternity?
The Mockingbird did not reply—But, I felt he stole
away my sighs—for another line—in another song—
as he echos God and Man his whole life long.

—Joan Dance

SUMMER LOVE

After all things
    have been said
            and done
when the heart is bled
        and wrung
            and hung out to dry.
When you have cried
        until you cannot cry
                The Spirit's gone
                The Soul awry.

Oh this Summer of discontent;
        taken to heights beyond. Spent.
            and sent
                to lows
                    So low
        full posture bent,
    makes all so clear — the clouded sky.

    'Tis the Season — Time to die

—Pat Rauch

We were born in the years of silence
and learnt to be slaves on our land
where the laws of spiritual violence
with the right slogans went hand in hand.

The churches were ruined or set into prisons
the whole peoples were sent to exile
innocent victims of social reasons
were made our foes in Joe Stalin style.

In spite of decays and untalented leading
the absence of sense in various parts
the truth has survived in spite of the beating
in our kitchens, in our hearts.

Now we get glasnost and perestroyka
this is the only way to succeed
so we hope that Russkaya Troika*
will go this way as we really need.

*Russkaya Troika — three horses harnessed abreast
a traditional national vehicle

—Alexander Chepurnykh

A NEW DAY

Enchanting rays of golden light
Bursting forth through morning's stillness.
A fire growing to a climax,
Illuminating the reposing world.

Bursting forth through morning's stillness,
Casting shadows across the earth.
Illuminating the reposing world,
Reigning night dethroned.

Casting shadows across the earth,
An army of receding specters.
Reigning night dethroned,
The victor emitting jubilant warmth.

An army of receding specters
Replaced by radiance.
The victor emitting jubilant warmth,
Wrapping all in its luminous essence.

Replaced by radiance,
A fire growing to a climax
Wrapping all in its luminous essence.
Enchanting rays holding bright.

—Donna Depta Elford

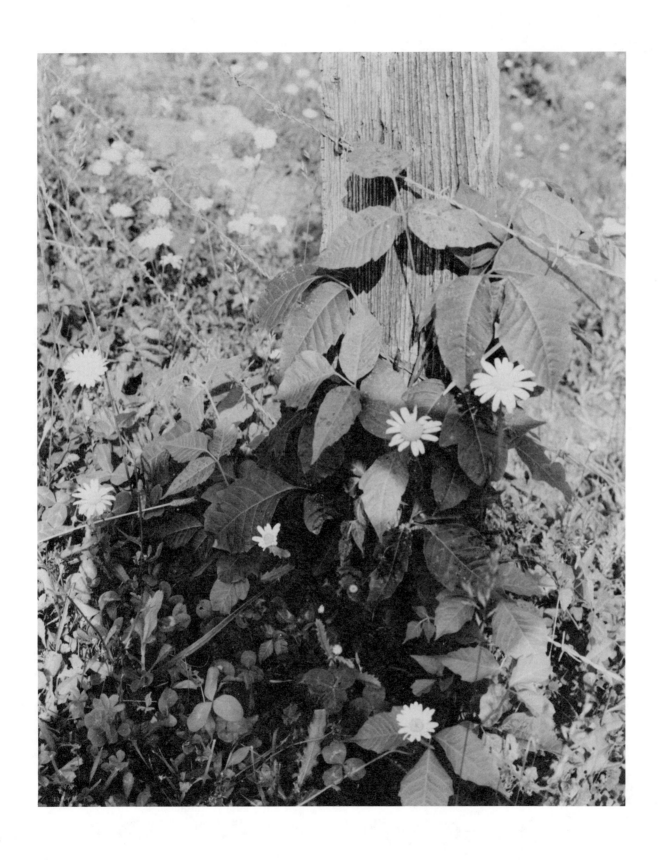

HOMELESS ARE THEY . . .

I threw away my clothes, my books, my job, my home.
Homeless are they that throw away their home.

Two mental hospitals and one guest room later,
I have a home again, one in which
I hug the bed all day, like a crib, while an infant
screams for milk downstairs.
Homeless are they that throw away their home.

Dear God don't let me do that again, no matter
the stupor of this unemployment subsidy.
For homeless are they that throw away their home.

Even if I did it, I let go of the wedding house
where the husband left me years ago to find another one,
even the dishes we shared, yes, I threw away.
How do the homeless get that way?

—Barbara Bialick

You seniors listen to what I say,
You who are age 65 and above.
The young ones especially this message will pay,
For it's certain that time will eventually move.

You should learn the rules before that day,
That make life better and give us good health.
When you reach our age you'll be able to say,
"What I have accomplished is worth more than wealth."

The most expensive rule is this,
We have a habit of eating too much,
Which makes our lives so amiss,
Then we are miserable and heavy and such.

Try not to be gripey, mean or unkind,
To others you meet along the way.
Another thing is love to all mankind,
This will bring happiness to you each day.

If we'd love others as much as ourselves,
And do unto them as we'd like to be;
Seniors these rules would make for yourselves,
A happy life full of joy complete.

—Lora Bell Garland

RELEASE

Maybe this baby won't cry in the dark, illuminated with light
she'll see the branch as it breaks from the tree.
Mouth open wide not thirsting for rain, her need for
salt water might bring the change of vast ocean waves.

Maybe this baby won't accept the gift 3 Wisemen didn't bring
but Sasparilla Compound — Peace, Hope, and Love,
to re-inherit truth.
History books re-made for knowledge.

Maybe this baby won't have tear drops mingled with blood.
For dew drops glistening on fields flowered upon lack
broken bottles and empty faces full with toxic images
in sunlight she won't see.

Maybe this baby her tender smiles upon the sunrise of the day
break up fear by twilight
into pieces miniscule beyond
a microscopic germ.

Maybe this baby, her innocent serenity,
a love potent strong evaporates poison.
She holds the key to unlock a multi-generational prison.
Maybe this baby is HOPE.

—Ruth White

checkerboards half-mast
withered, tired old bones
stand endlessly saluting
the hopes bred of men
and a fading generation.

—Terry Conk

INNOCENCE

I hear their shrill voices
laughing and shouting.
It must be recess—
I stop and listen.
Happiness on the wind—
untouched by details—
Of an adult world—full
of prejudice and hate.
Open minds, like sponges
still fresh and new.
Gentle hands and hearts—
too young to hate and hurt.
Yet—destined to learn.

—Jean Cogan

TOO MANY CONTRACTIONS

Celestial and Existential
what lies beyond the senses
doesn't really mean real.
The world's a liar
"Turn your collar to the cold!"
Roses aren't always red
Mona Lisa is not so beautiful
cheating us of a simple smile
Castor oil didn't taste like
orange juice as a child
Reality or Truth
is that which is chosen
to be included in one's own
Microcosm.

—Margaret A. Tracey

POSSIBLE

You make it seem possible
To love again

Even possible
For a life to begin

Seems I've not had one
For so very long

While trying to get over
All that was wrong

But you make it seem possible
To be complete

Even possible
To not know defeat

It just may be possible
That you are the one

To bring back happiness
And make life again fun

I guess it's possible
If I make you mine

That's why it's possible
I won't waste much time

—Al Martin

THIS LITTLE BOY

When I first saw this small bundle of life, I thanked the Lord for him and my wife.
I hugged and kissed him and gave a loud shout, for this to me is what life is about.
He had no hair on his smooth little head but big brown eyes and a cute little grin.
I held him in my arms as proud as could be, for he is my son, God gave him to me.
I looked in his eyes and at his hands and feet, he is all one, health and complete.
I knew he would be happy and full of spunk to win, so for all of these reasons,
we named him Tim.

> —Timothy D. Smaker

JUST AROUND THE BEND

It is so very nice to know that just around the bend
there is a smooth and golden road we know will never end.
It doesn't matter what your stance has been
as long as you were faithful and believed in HIM.
HE loves the young and loves the old,
HE loves us all, you see—
the rich, the poor, infirm or well, whatever you may be.
And if you live as best you can HE'LL guide your footsteps to the end
and lead you to that golden road just around the bend.

> —Meta McEntire

THE LOSS OF A DEAR LITTLE BOY
In memory of Connor Alan McMahon

Someone special left our world, Dear God, and our spirits are feeling low.
We knew him for such a short time but we learned to love him so.
His days on earth were difficult with the trials he had to bear.
He tried so hard but life sometimes just isn't always fair.

It is hard for us to understand why you wanted him with you,
But we know you have your reasons, God, for all the things you do.
And, God, please tell your angels that it broke our hearts to send
This littlest of playmates and we hope they'll be his friend.

To welcome him with open arms and make him feel at home
So he won't miss all of us and he'll never be alone.
And hold his hand while things are new so he won't be afraid
And let him know they think he'll be the best friend they've ever made.

Thank you, God, for the time we had to shelter him with our love,
That love, our thoughts, and daily prayers are accompanying him above.
And, God, please keep your eye on him for we love him so much,
Please keep him safe and happy within your tender touch.

> —Sharon Ann Shorma

HIS AMAZING LOVE

I visited today in Gethsemane where I took a walk with God
We traveled the road to Calvary that my Master once had trod.
I heard the angry crowds as they cried, "Crucify, crucify Him."
And I thought I saw a face like mine right in the midst of them.

I listened to Roman soldiers as they laughed and mocked His name
Saying, "Prove yourself Lord Jesus; show us why to earth you came."
I heard the sound of hammers as the nails went through His hands
And I watched them gamble for His robe as they cast their die on the sands.

Oh, I saw the spear as it pierced His sweet precious side
And I heard the voice of His mother there at the foot of the cross where she cried.
I saw the crown of thorns they had placed on His sacred head.
And I read the sign above Him, "Jesus, King of the Jews" it said.

I trembled as I watched His blood spill onto the ground
Thinking, "No one understands Him out of all these standing around."
Then I hung my head in shame, I couldn't stand to watch Him die.
He never showed signs of anger only tears of love filled each eye.

And when He prayed, "Father, forgive them for they know not what they do."
His mission on earth was finished "SALVATION" for me and you.
Yes, I witnessed the pain and anquish that our Savior had to bare
And to think, it was all His amazing love for us that kept Him hanging there.

> —Brenda King Parsly

GODS FLOWER GARDEN

Such Beautiful Thoughts in Ones Heart,
Helps Life to be more Special at the Start,
As I look at all the Beauty there is to See,
How Wonderful and Precious for You and Me.

Another Beautiful and Special Start,
IS GODS CHILDREN, A FLOWER GARDEN OF THE HEART,
As We learn of the Wonders for Us to Heed,
How WONDERFUL and PRECIOUS INDEED.

What a Special Way for to be a Part,
OF GODS FLOWER GARDEN OF THE HEART,
As We receive His SPECIAL LOVE,
He reaches down, He Pours it out from Above.

And When I remember that which He has done for Me,
How SPECIAL to KNOW YOU SEE,
A WONDERFUL AND PRECIOUS START,
AND TO BE ONE OF GODS CHILDREN, A FLOWER GARDEN
    OF THE HEART!!!

—Sandra Walker

THE GIDEON BIBLE

This precious Bible will always be
  for our hearts, and minds, and eyes to see
  In the many places where we stay
    when we're home alone or far away

This Bible has comforted many
    so we've been told
  When we're alone in a room
    and need something to hold
We read with reverence verse by verse
  How our Savior died for us,
    and gave us birth

The Gideon Bible goes around the world
and keeps God's love deeply furled
So all can learn and see the light
Whether it be red, yellow, black, or white
They are all precious in His sight.

—Billie Hendrickson

Sometimes, when the days are cool and foggy, I remember you.
Those were the days you would wander the sand.
But when I run to the shore to find you . . . the beach is empty, the night air quiet.
There is no one there. No one to give my thoughts to, no one to share my feelings with.
So I simply sit on the sand and whisper my secrets to the wind.

I remember, in your room among your ruffley trimmings and china dolls you would find a world all your own.
But now the room is dark and musty. The bare floors holding no traces of life.

I still miss you. You were my closest friend. You understood and accepted while others questioned and judged.

Your tears were fragile, a feeling from inside you. I wanted to bottle them up and keep them forever. They too were lost.

Even now as I watch the changing colors of the air, I wish you peace.
Forever . . .

Good night, my friend. Go with God.

—Tawnya Fraizer

ANNUNCIATION

Fear not the angel said to her
  Rejoice, o favored one
I bring you news of life to be
of joy of sorrow spun
a tapestry of life that sings
with laughter, tears and death
with grain and grape, friend and foe
A son, his father's breath.

I know not man the virgin said
How can this come to be
I am the maiden of my God
I give my yes, sung free
The angel smiled, rejoiced with pain
told power tales of God
The angel and the woman stood
while Mary's heart gave nod.

—M. D. LeDoux

WHEN I HEAR GOD SPEAK TO ME

When I hear God speak to me,
  I am usually all alone.
Surrounding me there is silence,
All the noise is gone.

This is when I talk to God,
And of his presence I'm fully aware.
I can feel each burden lift away
As he takes them in his care.

When I hear God speak to me,
It's at times when all is still.
Even though I hear no voice,
In my heart I know his will.

If ever I feel on shaky ground,
Not sure of what I should do.
I talk to God and read my Bible
As he answers me there too.

When I hear God speak to me,
I must be willing to turn all aside.
For if we are to know his answer,
In him we must abide.

—Carolina Carpenter

JEANNE

She was like a sunbeam
  brought into our life;
the beautiful girl-child
of our son and his wife.

With hair so fair,
and eyes so blue;
her cheeks so rosy—
with a dimple too.

Our oldest grandchild
this one so dear;
How could we know
death hovered so near?

She was just sixteen
when she met her fate.
The years pass by,
but we remember the date.

God called her home
to that beautiful shore;
we wanted to keep her,
but he needed her more.

—Joyce L. Douglas-Morgan

WILD AND FREE

It seemed to roam, wild and free.
The horse was special.
It would eat the apples from a tree.
In the grass, it would nestle.
I often wish I were that horse,
   that my life would be on a different course.
Then again, I realize it could not be
   because only wild things are free.
Humans have been tamed
   and that's the way we'll stay.
Some may and may not agree
   that we can not be wild and free.

—Cheryl Schmeler

SANITARIUM

In the dark crevices of your mind,
something awful lingers behind.
It's something beyond sadness and pain,
It's really bad almost like you're insane.
Evil thoughts run through your head,
Your depression is sitting alone with your
corrupted mind,
and in your heart love has been left behind.
But you'll grow out of it is what they all say,
Oh, but you know they'll pay for that state-
ment one day.
Oh, but you're a pretty one aren't you?
Why don't you come over here and show me
some of those things your mother taught you?
But you're not as insane as they might think,
and your mind is not fixing to break.
There's a word for this you know,
let's take a walk where the other ones go.
It's a nice place you'll like it a lot,
and in your room is a dresser and a cot.
There's a lot of people in here like you,
well some,
You know where you are little pretty one?
A Sanitarium.

—Lawless Jones

MESCALINE DREAM

Hold me, hold me, let me die awake.
Thunder rolling, keeping silent tapes.
Lights are blurred, triple visioned stereos.
Car hoods leap out, statues of staring cats.
Real, not real, always there.

Laughter, sickening music so in tune.
Tears, black eyes, never closed.
Icy hands, paralyzed bodies.
Sick, so sick, wish it were only a dream.

Wrong type, wrong time, I should never be here.
Lows are lower, speeds are faster.
Two days can't go on forever.

Thoughts are gone if only for a moment.
Skull and crossbones never more.
Paper doesn't taste good, light blue dreams
are better.

Chilled air, going down ever deeper into
dreamless black.
Blood flows so slow. Talk on into the night
becoming day.
Release, release, swallow hard.
Rolled bills, green dust, sleep—
      sleep forever.

—Karen Majewski

BREAKING FREE

I see you break free
After all your struggle
You called to your mother
You called to your father
They could see your fear in your look
You could see happy lands in a mirror
With you inside
Calm springs
Golden sun
Drifting winds
Your heart died calling to you,
You hear, see, breathe, smell, happy lands.

—Amy Lynn Harnois

RESTRAINT

Be still oh saddened heart of mine.
Time will heal and you will be fine.
Dry up, soft tears upon my face.
You will disappear without a trace.
Stay silent, words, my tongue would speak.
The thoughts are those of one who is weak.
Lids please cover eyes which see.
Those little things that hurt the me.
Ears be deaf to gossip spread.
This cross can be the weight of lead.
Mind, you must control it all.
For if you falter, all will fall.

—LeAnne M. Emery

HUNGRY LUST

Man with a weapon in the streets today
Unaware people get in his way.

Gun takes aim, he cares not where
Just to kill someone is his only care.

Child, policeman, minister too.
Aged old woman she will do.

Brain so idle, by drugs long took.
He has no love just a hungry lust.

Unaware people they hurry along
Someone to love, a job, a home.

Unaware people, must they pay?
For the weakness of drugs in this man today.

—Lavada Robbins

CHAINS

Who am I?
Why am I here?
Deep in the recesses of my soul I sigh
I will not die, I will not fear
Unchain me I must be free!

The blood of my ancestors runs within me
Unchain me I must be free!
The wisdom of my ancestors burns within me
Unchain me I must be free!
The dream of my ancestors lives within me
Unchain me I must be free!

Doesn't anyone understand me?
Does anyone care?
Circumstance and time work against me
I suffer so deeply and no one is aware
Are my chains so strong I cannot burst free?

—Ruby M. Chatman

KNOWLEDGE

From the premier day of my being alive,
I began to observe, wonder, ask, and compelled to
formally learn by the age of 5.

Values, emotions, good, bad, and myself—
Names, people, things, adjectives, and adverbs—
ABC's, Twain, Asia & Africa, atoms, and Shakespeare—
Love and Hate— Life and Death.

Learning is hard, long, endless-eternal like a flame,
Those who choose to take on this task will fulfill
their dreams And nothing to shame.

—Michael F. Misa

I want to live,
not to just merely exist on this earth
as another human being mixed with
the other billion I share this big
mass of dirt.
I want to be different,
not like everyone or anyone else.
I want to count,
to make a difference in the world, or
in sombody's life.
I want to be free,
to soar in the blue skies as the
mighty eagle flies over the earth.

—Jeni Cleves

PERFECT PEACE

When I feel alone in the darkest of night
With only my chaotic thoughts for company
I leave my bed of misery and woe
And climb the long staircase to the roof top

As I step out the door and my bare feet
Touch the rough shale covered floor
I am instantly at peace and greatly comforted
For from my lonely vantage point
I can see all the beauties of the night

The twinkling stars remind me
That someone somewhere loves me
The bright full moon disperses all the shadows
Fragrant night scents calm my thoughts
And the perfect quite washes away
All my misery and woe
Leaving only perfect peace.

—Ondrya Lynn Smith

THE SCORPION

You think the bird has lost its wings,
and the scorpion, no longer stings,
you think the snake no longer slithers,
and you think my spirit slowly withers.

But the bird is still on the wing,
and the scorpion has a deadly sting,
the snake still crawls in the dark of night,
and my spirit is bathed in a radiant light.

You think the wolf no longer howls,
and the junkyard dog no longer prowls,
you think the night bird has ceased its crying,
and you think my soul is slowly dying.

But the wolf still has a mournful howl,
and the junkyard dog is still on the prowl,
the night bird has never ceased its crying,
and my soul is ever upward flying.

—Mary E. Creason

DISCOVERED

I chanced to look deep inside of me
and saw a wondrous spirit— floating free,
over a "life-scape," a beautiful tapestry!
Soft colors were woven with joys untold
and ideas were sparkling in every fold!
Sprinkles of tears kept it fresh and new,
and the border was my favorite shade of blue!
Bound together, this spirit and tapestry
with ribbons long, yet still floating free.
The space between was filled with sweet refrain,
and the words to the melody? "This . . . is Elaine!"

—Elaine L. Wieneke

REALITY

I am the reality of my dreams, a thousand times
and then some.
Miles and miles I have traveled, all within my
mind, taking with me only my soul, my closest
companion.

Unknown faces and untraveled places seem to
inhabit my thoughts.
Each searching for their own time and place.
Emotions flow silently through my veins causing
my heart to soar beyond the limits of my dreams.

With pen in hand I breathe the immortal breath
of life into dreams that otherwise would cease
to exist.
I am the reality of my dreams, a thousand times
and then some.

—E. Kay Holcomb

FLYING

I long to fly into the clouds—
Head thrown back, wind rushing
and roaring through my ears.
Leave behind my heavy heart
and fly straight up, up, up
as fast as I can fly.

I'll let the smile from my face
plummet to the middle of my being
and feel my body sail with nothing to hold me.
I long to feel the weightlessness of being unbound
from all that keeps me.

Pretending with closed eyes
that I can stretch to the sky
and leave behind everything.

—Loretta C. Hoover

I WILL RUN AWAY. . .

I will run away into the forest.
In a bed of pine needles I will rest.
Free from all that tormented me night and day.
I will look onto the heavens and pray.
That here amongst nature I will find rest.
Yes here among creatures, I will make my nest.
I will seek peace from all that taunted me.
As I lie here in the shadow of trees,
beneath the fir trees rooted strongly in ground.
The thing I once lost that needs to be found.
Surely the quiet solitude will lead,
to the only one item I most need.
Alone I may be, not to discourage,
one day I WILL, discover my
courage.

—Kim Nixon-Thomas

AWAKENING

When I awoke this morning,
It seemed too early to start the day;
And, I thought to myself — disgruntled,
"It's too early even to pray."

As I lay there in the darkness,
In the distance I faintly heard,
A sound that lifted my spirits —
The sweet song of a bird.

Then I began to remember,
Other sounds I had heard through the night —
The frogs, an owl and the crickets.
Sounds of joy — with no hint of fright.

As I heard the sounds of God's creatures,
I learned what they knew all along.
You don't have to meet God in the morning.
He'll stay with you all the night long.

—Bennie Raper

A CHILD'S PRAYER

Please, Dear God, guide Mommy and Daddy
through the years with your love
even though they are divorced. I still
love them, even though I really
don't understand why they are not
together. But Dear God, will you
keep them by your side and guide
them in the right way. Then maybe
some day, they might get together
to stay; and we will be a family once
again, to follow in your way. Amen.

—Rick Nading

HIS WAY

He who says he can't
turns out to be he who does
He can turn and fool the day
and end up living life his way
no stone unturned, each obstacle met
with courage strong, his dreams he'll get
he charts anew using God as guide
to show the world what is inside
and strives always to use his skill
to serve others as best he will
and when the roll is called aloud
he will stand up tall and be so proud
a man must toil and grin and bear
and only the battle will get him there

—Hazel M. Carestia

THROUGH YOU

Dear Lord, please tell me
Why I cry these tears.
When there have been far too many
throughout all these years.

I should be so happy.
I'm thankful for all you've pulled me through.
Without you by my side.
What would I ever do?

Please bring him nearer to me Lord
and help my prayers and
dreams come true.
I love and care so much for him.
There's nothing I would not do.

—Bonita Marie Thomas

RAINDROPS

Sent to earth by clouds from above
to moisten the soil with God's Sweet Love
the raindrop emerges from the gracious earth
as a lovely flower given birth
soon to wilt and wither away
only to be resurrected one day.
God's promise is that forever we live
a promise that only the Almighty can give.

—Teresa Nicholls

THE LORD'S GREATEST VICTORY

For three long hours on Calvary's hill
Lord you were dying and all was still.
Lonely figures weeping below, watched
while you suffered ever so slow.
A crown of thorns pierced your head.
"What a pity a few had said."

Dying on the cross you were softly praying too
"Forgive them Father they know not what they do."
Anguished and grieving her heavy loss
Your mother stood helpless beside the Cross.
Crucified cruelly, for men of all creed.
You became man to fulfill this painful deed.
Death conquered through your resurrection
Was the "Greatest Victory Won."
"For God so loved the world. He gave you,
His only son."

—Felixa M. Lovell

OUR LORD IS HERE

"The signs of our Lord are here,
but please, don't cry or be in fear.
For the Lord is here to save our soul,
Then will it be time for us to see the
rivers of milk and honey as they flow.
This is the promise to us from a long
time past,
Now is the time to see the beauty of
our Lord, at last.
The Lord knows our flesh is weak to sin,
But our soul is strong to win.
For the Lord has come to this world, brethren,
To tell us, 'All will be saved and go to heaven!'.
But please don't make yourselves a mess,
'Cause all our souls need to rest."

—God Bless
—J.S. LaRock

A SONNET

The atoms between the grains of sand
Are the planets of stars in God's hand.
The crystal floaters swirling in my eyes
Are nothing more than clouds across the skies.
The violets on the lawn? A cachet revealed
I know not, but enough is the color they yield.
Queen Anne's lace rustled by the wind
A sign of life where spring has grinned.
Phosphenes under my lover's eyelids
Are but sunspots about humming bird nids.
And in my rapture of the deep, I've no fear
Not in perfect grace, just happy we're near.
So if I'm only a moment in your eternity
I'm proud to have loved and shared your entity.

from the copyrighted volume:
Asymptotes, My Silent Psalms

—Lewis L. Latta

40

HEARTFELT LOVE

No heartaches need to be meant
for the joy of your Love has been spent
with the loving touch of two souls
thru many hours untold.
Two whispers of Love have brought
a joy to this human heart
thru a sweetheart only God could have meant
for this love from my heart is heaven sent.

—Duane L. Adcock

THE MASTER OF ALL . . .

God, is the master of all.
He gave us life, He gave us many things.
He shows us the way through everyday.
THE MASTER OF ALL.

God, take me by the hand,
And show me the way.
For all I have, You gave me.

THE MASTER OF ALL, is with you everyday.
Just show him you care,
And you will live for all Eternity.

For, The Master of All, We pray,
That you show us the way.

—Connie F. Neese

IT'S TIME

Last night, as I lay sleeping,
   An angel glowing white.
Came gently to my room,
   Floating in a shroud of light.
I was not filled with fear,
   A sense of peace, swept over me.
All my earthly bonds were broke,
   My soul at last, was free!
Then I saw my Maker's face,
   Chills raced down my spine!
He reached His hand towards me,
   "My faithful servant . . . Yes, it's time."

—K.K. Schauer

I pray for God in all his glory
to chart your path and make it holy.
May each day as you arise
Be filled with a sweet surprise
that will lead you down a glorious lane
where there is Love, and little pain.

Keep the faith and never forget
when you love each other, your life is set.
Hold steady to each other's hand.
Don't let go, and take a stand.

Look to the sun that rises in the East.
Follow your stars that never cease.
And always know it's always there
when you may feel that no one cares.

In the evening when the sun is set,
rest on each other's dreams, and never forget.
Build your tomorrows on solid rock,
Secure it with love, free from shock.

Fly your joy on wing of dove,
always know you have my love.

From
Mother Gustelia

—Gustelia Barnes

I AM A WINNER

I may not be the best,
But, I will try to do my best.
   I am not perfect; yet Failing,
But, I am striving for Perfection.
   I may not be all I would like to be,
But, remember God is not through
with me.
   I was not born a Winner;
But, through Jesus Christ, Our Lord
   I will never be a Loser.

—Mahalia Simon

JEWELS

There are many facets of pearls to see —
   Whatever beauty is desired by you or me.
In a jewelry store each person could find
A lovely necklace or ring of every kind.

Of no significance is the style or size —
To have the genuine would be a real prize.
These precious gems are only to give one
      pleasure;
They are mere substitutes for a better
      treasure.

Far greater jewels are available from God
      above —
Peace, hope, joy, and His never-ending love.
These are free gifts for us to receive;
All we need do is accept and in Him believe.

—Arlene B. Broderick

LIFE'S GRADUATION DAY

I have known you since the start of this life
   And stand at your side with all of life's strife.
To ask you to know Me with all you can muster
   A little bit a time, would be nice,
      if you could sequester
The love I have for you that shows no measure,
   But to bring fulfillment with all of its pleasure
To fill all the emptiness of life's degradation
   And to prepare you for Life's Great Graduation
I know you don't like to think on these terms,
   But I want you to love and know Me
      in return,
Because some day you will come to see Me up there
   And I want your love and to know
      that you care.

—Carl Youngblood

BRIEF REMINDER

Let us all stop and take notice, as people,
we often take for granted the basic
Historical Guidelines Our Heavenly Father and
Founding Fathers gave to us as "human beings."
   Our Heavenly Father gave to us the
Ten Commandments and "we hope" Common Sense.
Our Founding Fathers gave to us the
Declaration of Independence and the
Constitution of the United States which
are to be followed by each and every
Citizens of the United States.
   However, without the use of Common
Sense these Guidelines will become excruciating.
Again, let us all stop and take notice.

—Esell R. Johnson

I LOVE THE DEAD

I love the dead before they're cold.
Their bluing flesh for me to hold.
Kadava eyes upon me see nothing.

I love the dead before they rise.
No farewells, no goodbyes.
I never even knew your now rotting face.

Well friends and lovers,
mourn your silly graves.
I have no other uses for them dolling.

— **Terri Nava**

OPTIC

Hours held in my palm
long to pancake,
make dough rise again,
melt butter and warm spices,
rub in berry juice
sprinkled with soft sugar,
ride roller coaster dips
          in jelly rolls.

Quick! Gulp away the pattern
far behind a chamber
lies a lens in rods and cones,
bipolarial cells
          in ganglion illusion.

— **Dorothy R. Moffett**

POOR MAN'S RIVER

The quiet river
  Reflections of dawn
    A lone seagull
      Observing muddy shore

  Intense laughter, rings out
  Of the boy who
   Caught his first fish
     Years tell the tale

  The poor old man
      Who never had his day
   Lies on the bench, forgets to wake
  Chimneys of stone
  Billow poisons of breath

  The dying river
  Reflections at dusk
  Moon silently kill
   No seagull, man or boy
        muddy shore

— **Renee Scelia**

THE MEANING OF TIME

A second, a year, a millenium—
Just what is the meaning of time?
Time is measured by happenings,
Both sorrows and joys sublime.

We cannot control Time's passage;
It never pauses to gaze in our eye;
It neither gives nor receives any message,
As it glides on silently by.

So why do we worry, or tremble in fear,
Of our space in this vale of tears,
When Time does not bother to guarantee
One year or a hundred years?

— **Margaret Dagley**

THE GRAVE

The icy crystals break from the withered tree,
  shattering against the tomb's brittle back;
wind cries haunting songs, shrill in horror
of a night so black.
Void of color, grey shrouds cover the grave,
eerily dancing above the hardened ground:
here death is found.
Wonderment for what lies beneath this soil
leaves a chilling certainty of fear
in the bones of those who live,
for the bones of those left here.

— **Robin L. Taylor**

SHARKS

Snapping sea blood moans
Rising achingly from their slumber
Ushers in molded faces of stone
Spreading unnerving restless lumber

Among cold water swirling realms of
Life endangered schools
Spelling certain satisfied hunger above
for shark greed riddled rules

Allowing no escaping afterthoughts
to enter sea cities too soon,
terror torpedoes insistingly stalk
them into hasty ageless doom.

— **Walter Jackson Fisher III**

VANITY

Rhythm played on wooden drums,
war in a time and land long forgotten.
Dense jungle foliage hiding native huts,
silent ebony silhouettes slit the web.
Headdresses and beads of bone and leather,
symbols of peace fervently longed for.
Echoing heartbeats bring tribes together,
banding as one to fight the brash warrior
tribes of the warring neighboring countries.
Savage, bloody conflicts of knife and spear,
bring back nearly forgotten past victories
or the dreaded silent enemy of fear.
  In the devastation no one is left—
  peace in a land of people bereft.

— **Cheri Michels**

THE WOLVES ARE OUT TONIGHT

Beware, beware, for the wolves are out tonight,
  As the wind makes its nightly flight.
The woods are full of evil and terror you see,
  Beware, for the evil could possibly be me.
For you know not what I do tonight,
  When the moon is full in the sky so bright.
With eyes so yellow, with hunger and hate,
  Beware, beware, don't stray in the woods too late.
For you know me as a hound from Hell,
  A term you know and fear as well.
In daylight you are brave, without a fear,
  But at night, when the moon is full and near . . .
That's when I shall come with eyes aglow,
  And roam the earth till darkness shall go.
This poem's a warning to all those in sight,
  Beware, beware, for the wolves are out tonight.

— **Sherry Kay Abram**

SUICIDAL TENDENCIES

I sit and wait on my bed
contemplating to join the dead

I turn and watch the flame
that has brought hell so much fame

I focus my thoughts on the candle
and try to discern the things I cannot handle

I am torn up inside—the music is
my only solace from this torture ride

The stars are bright all through the night
as I dream of you holding me tight

Why is there so much in life to dread
to make me sit and contemplate on my bed

I fear for my life after death
so I wait to take my last breath

I wonder where I would go
Up above or down below

If I should be up above
Would you still be my true Love?

—Jodi Thoennes

He sat quite alone near the hearthstone
Unless you count shadows on walls
Which jump to the rhythm of crackling red orgy
Consuming remains of a log

Then Merlin took stuff from a vessel
Conjoined it with hyssop and hair
Sang Odius chants that profane and then
Cast it like seed from his hand in the fire

Hell's furies lashed over the marshland
And the sultry night air was inflamed
With noise like a thousand winged insects
Were crawling around on your brain

Then into the presence came Moloch
From whence he was called so he came
The Ancient Cabalist of Sidon
Turning the children to flame

They sat quite alone near the hearthstone
Unless you count shadows on walls
Playing drafts while the crackling red orgy
Consumed the remains of a log
—Seth Richards

THE BURIAL

She stood near the door and shivered,
Still wrapped in a scarf and a coat.
Eyes lost as the wind at the pane
That twitched, like the hand at her throat.

In the parlor, living circles,
Laced with memories, shock and grief,
Denied the young, so she watched us,
One soft lip between crooked teeth.

Had the chill at the grave painted
Frost on cheeks more prone to be flushed?
As my sympathy embraced her,
It unleashed that which fear had hushed.

"I am free from him." She whispered
Dark secrets rebelliously borne.
Has the storm scattered the flowers?
How many, how long will we mourn?

—Loycie Casey Warner

BLACK MASS

Sunlight crosses of yellow and red
Moonlight rises over the voices of the dead.
Gypsy stands on altars high
Speaking tongues from days past by.
Smoke of pyres cloud the eyes
Flame from torches ignite the skies.
Incense stench invades the breeze
Stars in heaven appear to freeze.
Dragons rise from within the ground
Taking flight that has no sound.
Demons dance with the angel of hell
Gypsy plays upon a golden bell.
Satan laughing with sheer delight
Innocent faces are taken to fright.
Gypsy coupled to the prince of the dark
Sung to the cry of the meadowlark.
Awake the nightmare shattered scream
Convince yourself it was only a dream.

—James B. Ley

THE STRUGGLE

Hawk
        Perched high on a treetop
        Eyes piercing the undergrowth
        Any movement may mean food

        Gliding swiftly through the sky
        Still keeping a watchful eye
        Looking for a . . .

Mouse
        Scurrying through the weeds
        Cheek pouches filled with seeds
        A warning shadow appears

        Feet scamper, talons flash
        A hole in the ground—Asylum
        Wings flap to continue the hunt. As

Hunger
        Remains the driving force that keeps
        Hawk and mouse struggling to survive
        In the harsh world of nature.

—Henrietta Diem

DEATH AT DAWN

I tell you my Lord, I tried and I tried
But that sword of pain came to my left side.
It plunged in deep like a learned diver,
Into that crimson pump, like a race-car driver.

I tell you again, I tried and I tried
But from that sword I cannot hide.
And now I ask why life is so cruel,
It killed my love in the cold tempestuous pool.

So now we have this tête-á-tête.
I ask of you, is this your best test?
For if it is I must say I flunk.
My life is a ship which is now sunk.

All his dues will now be paid.
On his wrist, he uses his own honed blade.
From the slit seeps out his life.
This is the end of his strife.

The dim light of dawn
From his view is now gone.

Doing this in front of Him he felt no shame.
Was it him or Him that was to blame?

—Ernesto Ochoa

SADNESS

Sadness is hearing people laugh,
and you can't join in.
    Friends going some where,
you love, and you cannot go.
    Sadness is awful, and is the
worst feeling in the world!!

—Lois-Jean Quirolo

BAREFOOT DREAMER

Yawn, Yawn, Ho Hum
    chewing on your bubble gum

Watching birds and bumble bees
sun in eyes that makes you sneeze

Stirring dirt with crooked stick
blowing bubbles with pin you prick

Dreaming dreams like most kids do
While on your bubble gum you chew

Barefoot dreamer passing time away
Tell us what you dream today.

—Thora Helen Layman

RUN AWAY

You ever just want to run,
    Run till you could run no more?

I live in a world
Where I can't run,
Cause there's no where to run to.
So you tell me,
Why the desire to run?

When your friends don't understand,
Or don't care,
Where do you run?
When you're too old to
Run to mother,
Where do you run?

You run in circles,
Round and round you go,
Where I'll stop:

I don't want to know.

—Mark Wayne Triboulet

COFFEE WITH GRANDPA

Smell the coffee brewing
    as in days of Grandpa Jess,
following a glimpse of light
    trailing in my nightie dress.
Passing by his big arm chair
    no, climbing up inside,
Grandpa knowing that I'm there
    our game, he lets me hide.
Playfully giggling
    around the edge I look,
table side, cup in hand
    he reads his Sunday book.
This vision, and his love
    my grandpa left with me,
today he lives and visits
    each time I drink coffee.

—Debra S. Steinberg

A BROTHER

As we start out not knowing, whether to be a
    boy or girl, sometimes we end up with a
brother, the best there can be in the world

But as we grow together, a little day by day
those pure thoughts turn into chaos and
bitter fits of rage

Thank god we do grow older and mature along
the way, for as you see, there couldn't have
been any better brother, like you are to me!!!

—Malcolm Maxwell

THE EYES OF A CHILD

Have you ever viewed the world through the eyes of a
    child?
Eyes full of innocence, gentle and mild.
How long has it been since you've really seen
Just how blue the sky is or the grass how green.
Children look through eyes of wonder and love,
Much more to the intentions of the Lord above.
To create a gentle people that look on a face
And see much more than a religion and race.
Children don't hold grudges when they disagree.
That's the way we're all supposed to be.
A child appreciates the wonder in everyday things;
The waves of the ocean, or when a bird sings.
So let's slow down a bit and not always hurry.
How can we enjoy life with all the worry?
The world would be so much better I'm sure,
If we'd all be more like the children we once were.

—Vicki L. Suddeth

A PENNY

There's a penny in the street! A meager fortune at my
    feet;
a coin that traveled far and wide and now abandoned, as I
    spied
the old worn tarnished cent. A treasure valued by children,
    spent
at countless candy counters glassed to display pleasure bulkly
    massed.

One we use to pay the taxes, on larger more important
    pawn.
This lonely monetary change can be saved and added, to
    arrange
for future purchase of luxuries. The legal tender on shopping
    sprees.
On wager-bets it's often tossed and a meager currency easily
    lost.

Affluent people don't use it much, but beggars solicit as easy
    touch.
This cash was used in scales for weight and fortune telling
    predicting fate,
or machines with bubble gum in balls. It's even bought some
    paper dolls.
A name it never had to wear is 'filthy lucre' but do we
    care?

A sumptuary fee it's not but pecuniary lure it's got.
One hundreth count of the dollar's whole, what kids want for
    a piggy bank goal.
A penny saved is a penny earned so finding one should not be
    spurned.
Just pick it up and save that copper, be alert and be a
    shopper.

—Carmen Riley

BASKETBALL

The whistle was blown and the ball was thrown
I yelled "Throw the ball here!"
It seemed like #15 held it for a year,
I threw the basketball five times in all —
Someone got the ball,
And we started to run the same direction.
One girl stayed behind worrying about her complexion!
I threw the ball, and it fell into the net;
Everyone was CHEERING!
It sounded like a pet.

—Shelly Franz

GENTLE TOUCH

My mommy's the best—
she's not like all the rest.
My mommy plays many roles—
my friend, my daddy, she even consoles.
My mommy has done so much—
and I love the feel of her Gentle Touch.
My mommy is there when I cry—
she comforts me, even when it's over a stupid guy.
My mommy loves me more than life itself—
sometimes I just forget and put her upon a shelf.
I need and love my mommy so much—
I just don't realize that someday—
I'll miss her Gentle Touch.

—Cenci Carol Childers

DAWN

Dawn, a grown child, with a personality that's very mild.
You have a smile that is larger than a mile.
Your body is petite, maybe that's why you're so sweet.
Don't let others get you down, remember you're the pitcher
on the mound.
The only one in control, as a pilot flying solo.
You know what you want to be, the question is, can you let
your past sail free? If you don't, it's all a joke.
You'll never become your best and remain a mess, never
knowing the feeling of being blessed.
If you told me a lie, it would pass me by, honesty with
yourself is what counts, when you're the pitcher headed for
the mount.

—J. D.

MOTHER GOOSE PHILOSOPHY

See the kids out in the yard. Sheltered castle, I, the
guard.
London Bridge is falling down. Into this life you are bound.
Tearful rivers to be crossed. Many battles won and lost.
Jack and Jill go up a hill. Stand strong, my children, your
dreams fulfill.
Hate no colors, be that blind. See with your heart and love
mankind.
Baa, baa black sheep, have you any wool? Love them all by
the golden rule.
I challenge you to try and do. Be an honest leader there are
so few.
Humpty Dumpty had a great fall. Build no barriers. Break
down walls.
And to yourself be always true. In the end there's only you.
Star light, star bright. Make your wish come out alright.
Nursery rhymes for everyday. A lot of work. A little play.
Twinkle, twinkle little star. Accept yourself. Be who you are.

—Debbie Jeffrey

MAMA LULLABY—

Child-hood dreams of finer things,
a fantasy's in life,
overlook the one who took
care of you most of your life?
My fun'est memory as a child,
as I do recall,
was the tender loving care
she gave
and how she loved us all.
The tender loving smile, a frown
was not allowed,
so thoughtful was my mama
with each individual child.
In evening time when baby cried,
she'd gently rock away,
and softly sing
her Lullaby,
with grace and love
that my mama freely gave.

—George M. Lendley

THE BUNNY AND THE BEE

Hippity, hoppity, floppity, flee!
Said the bunny to the bee.
To the bunny said the bee:
Don't you hippity, hoppity me.
I'll bizzedy, buzzedy, zizzedy zee!
Flappity, flippity, floppity, flee!
Said the bunny to the bee.
To the bunny said the bee:
Zazzedy, zizzedy, zozzedy zee!
From rabbit fur I'll make a coat
for my queen across the moat.
She'll sanggedy, singgedy praise for me.
I'm such a bozzedy buzzedy bee.
Said the bunny to the bee:
Hippity, hoppity, hippity hee.
I'll take your honey, then I'll flee.
'Round and 'round the apple tree:
It's bizzedy, bozzedy, whanggedy whee.
And hippity, hoppity, floppity flee.
Such a sight you sure should see!

—John S. Bush

THROUGH DAVID'S EYES

I have been told when I was one
You "hand-picked" me to be your son.
If this is true, if this is so,
Why did you feel you had to go?

I'm student council boy this year
And where are you, my Daddy dear?
And where are you to see me play
in tennis tourneys Saturdays?
To camp and fish and help with Scouts
To teach me what life's all about?
To hear me sing in choir at school
Oh, Daddy dear, and where are you?

Do you wonder how it could have been?
Does it ever make you cry?
Did you really want to leave us?
I've so often wondered why.

Why did you take me from the start
Then turn around and scar my heart?
A piece of me will never grow
Cause you're not here for me to show!

—Barb Hair

WINTER

How arrant was the Winter
Who chose so long to stay,
And then to show his greediness,
Took you far away;

Dispatched the cold and darkness
At every slightest whim,
Until my patient spirit
Grew ill, and tired of him.

But since he restitution made,
I feel no further enmity,
For after one brief absence,
He sent you back to me!

—George Huitt Atwood

MY LOVE FOR YOU

The days of love are endless,
The time of love is now
The words of love are beautiful,
The trust of love a vow.

The days of love a paradise,
The feel of love divine.
The way of love is ever
to cross your path with mine.

The hands of love are gentle,
The eyes of love are true.
The lips of love are tender,
The heart of love is you
    I   Love   You . . .

—Gonzalo Montalvo

THE LAST LEGACY OF MAGIC

I had forgotten
that you wanted to keep masked
All those contradictions
And for a moment
Believed
In the vivid possibilities
Of accelerated chaos.

The last legacy of magic
Is the hollowed out shell
Of breath-bated tension:
Total submission
To absolute freedom
Revoked
And whistling in the desert wind.

—Noëlle Nina Hogan

IT'S ALL YOURS

For those who find
    their calling in life
be thankful you are placed.

Your life has meaning;
    existence is directed,
your soul is truly laced.

You are danger to adventure
    but safe in ol routines;
be happy with your stability.

Yes, while you live life
    from day to day
you will envy from time to time
    those of us who survive
    moment . . . to moment.

—Karen L. Smith

WHAT IS THIS WORLD COMING TO?

What is this world coming to?
I really don't know.
We have people walking on the streets of America, with no
    place to go.
We have children having children, because they are not being
    raised.
Boys and girls don't act right.
Parents, how do you expect them to behave?
We have people killing people. What's going through their
    minds?
God Bless America, because it isn't very kind.

—Callie E. Walker

ZOOM

I woke up this morning. I looked across the room. I thank the
Lord Jesus for giving me zoom.

I feel like a child, so often I do, I like to play in the
flowers, and run thru the fields.

I like to climb tall mountains and lay up on the top, and watch
the clouds go twisting by and going up and up.

Yet I'm walking, in the shadows, walking straight ahead, the devil
is twisting and pulling, he's pulling on my head.

Look up, not down, look straight ahead, not so far away. Keep
your eyes on Jesus, he's the only way.

—Michael Lindquist

LET IT SHOW

I love you more than you can know,
If you love me, Why can't you let it show?

I want to trust you like you trust me,
But the way people talk, it seems to scare me.

I lay here at night and cry out my eyes,
After hearing people say, you've been seeing other
guys.

If you really love me, I shouldn't feel this way,
Do you really love me? Why can't you just say?

I've learned so much these past few years
Lord only knows, just how many tears.

You've taught me a lot, I want you to know
Now let me teach you, to let it show.

—Clint Shaull

THE ARROWS OF LIFE

I have a quiver full of arrows, each one is a dream.

My education is a launching tool for life,
Like the bow it sends the arrow on its way.
Unless I am prepared, my dreams go nowhere.

I aim the arrow high, so that even when I miss,
The places where I do end up, is not too low.

I'll not fulfill all my dreams in this life,
But I'll fulfill some of them.

So I drew the bow back, and loosed the feathered
shaft skyward.

The young boy watching asked, "Mister, why did you
shoot an arrow at nothing at all?" "Just for the
thrill of it," I said.

"We must prepare for life, but we must also do some-
things just for the enjoyment of doing them."

—Lora Waller

TIME TO LET IT GO

There's a few words I'd like to write
in hopes that you just might
understand what's buried in my heart
and why I feel it's time we must part
We drift away, come back together, again, day after day
We break up just to make up; it seems it's our only way
the ups and downs were ok, for awhile, thinking it would
    make our love strong
but, we can never find a happy middle and keep it for very
    long
I'm tired of people telling me what they think they know
so, regardless of what we have, it's time to let it go
You know we've been trying
but our love just keeps on dying
This confusion in our minds is just too great
We're running out of time; it's just a little too late

      —Debbie Foskey

SILENCE AT THE PORT OF VALDEZ

There is silence at the Port of Valdez,
  Out in the harbor lies the fractured tanker.
Silently thick black crude pours from its belly,
Spreading farther with each pulse of the sea.
Silence permeates the sea beneath,
As all surviving life is forced away.

There is silence at the Port of Valdez,
Fishermen stand on the dock looking seaward.
The boats will sit silent, nets hung dry,
The wives weep, they know hard times will come.
Even the children play quietly, happiness is gone.

There is silence at the Port of Valdez,
At the base of the cliffs where the seal once played and
fed,
He now lays powerless in the oil that covers his skin.
Silent too are the seagulls, that once deafened the ears with
their calls,
Now they float soundless in the sea.

There is anger at the Port of Valdez.

      —Jared M. Dellinger

RELEASE

Come now, sweet death,
  For you no longer need to steal into her presence in the
cover of night,
Nor hide in a changeling's cloak.
Disease, with impartial savagery has swept her fears and so
much more away,
All hopes, all dreams, all of youth's bright enchantment now
lie like shattered crystals in the dust.
All life's promises abandoned . . . and in their rightful place,
Illness with its ragged visage mars her body and haunts her
pallid face.
So, come now, sweet prince,
Glide silently into her hazy, stifling sick room which once
was her bed-chamber,
She does not fear you anymore.
Come, and with one gently whispering touch upon her
furrowed brow,
Release her,
Sever the ethereal cord,
Let her drift to the cosmic clouds, set her soul to flying,
She has endured this prelude to death, now I will suffer her
dying.

      —Ellen K. Brooks-Lynch

ACCEPT ME AS I AM

Accept me as I am,
  Don't try to change me
Or rearrange me
And please don't put me down.

I know I could be better
Though perfect I'll never be.

And I'll except your criticism,
If it's open, honest, and free.

There's always room for improvement,
But that choice is up to me.

I know I'm not the greatest.
But I'm far from being the worst.
People will be people,
And I will just be me.

So except me as I am,
    Or PLEASE just let me be!!

      —Betty Timmons

THE VOYAGE

A calm harbor
  Slowly vanishes from sight.
The sound of rippling waves
Soothes all fears.
Towards the horizon,
A crimson light silently sets.
Whisper soft.
Then,
Suddenly,
Gusts of wind blow.
Thundering waves appear.
Flashes of light dance about the sky.
Roaring clouds let out their anger.
Tossing back and forth
Whipping wildly about the open water.
The vessel rests,
And drifts.
Allowing the sunrise
To guide it to the port.

      —Heather Lorraine Fields

US

Tears stream down my face
  Like falling from the sky; rain
It's been so long but stuck
With me has been the pain
You said you'd never leave
You'd always care
Then one morning I wake up and
You're not there.
We're still together but you
Changed so much.
You thought I couldn't tell
But I felt it in your touch
I tried to talk to you
To see what it was about
But you wouldn't listen
You just wanted out
So I let you go
Let you go free
Now you're gone and
Won't come back to
    ME

      —Brandy Cummings

A SERENADE OF ICE+

A serenade of ice, tranquil serene peaceful waters, the two meet then shatter
Bursting into fragments: thin cutting edge, affecting the senses.
Cutting piercing cold nipping painful biting severe harsh keen eager fierce violent

Yet/ radiant luster brilliant only to disappear to be lost forever
So goes ice castle of winter, to bring beauty of spring

Boats of every creed to pull people on skis
Lazy hazy days of summer escape, "That Mississippi River" treacherous, deadly
Yet beautiful peaceful lovely

It gives and takes, relates respect old man river, enjoy its beauty don't abuse
It's our pleasure to use. A long pile of rocks making their own bridge on the river
Driftwood resting upon the rocks, ice ballet dancing on the water

A sympathy of ice sounds?/ Music of ice was all the sounds-around
The stillness of quiet current ice-shapes-forms-sounds
Each second a new beautiful picture, river forever changing under its surface

Ice castle of Christmas trees—up and down—"drown buoy" pulled under by currents
Yet to return in time, so sat I Peggy watching God's masterpiece, just one of his many
Sharing caring "His (God's) love" we understand how wonderful beautiful

God is in his creation to give to us a small corner of his world
Upon a tree sat me, enjoying the "Trinity" just you and me—God makes three
May it always be, PEGGEEEEEEEEEEEEEEE.
Dedicated to all the priests and nuns who made my life so beautiful, grateful am I.

    —PAX-Peggy Miller

SISTER EGYPT

    "Osirus Lord of the Nile, why dost thy servant Ra set in a pool of blood upon the blackened hills in mockery of his coming dawn and death beyond?"

    "Sister match me eye for eye thy sorrow is my own! Though centuries stand between our lives, dust and ages gone. Yet a moment still in time, stand we two together, sharing pain. For I am as thyself, and thou as me."

    "I grew to know of Aten, sister. Not idol, not god, yet Divinity: the experience of wordlessness and freedom. Death's sleep is not escape. We are sojourners upon a desert waste-land, who cannot undespairing rest until we have sated our thirst."

    "Remember thou with me, the gray twilight of No-Time? How despairing that we could not see the beauties of creation for the nothingness that enveloped us, we sought patches of lighter and darker grays. Sought the shapes of mountains that we knew. Made the heavy dampness around us into dew, and a lighter patch of gray into the morning sun. Creation was already there; but it took courage and faith to make it beautiful and real."

    —Ambpreia Weiss

HEAT DRIVEN

A blurred haze rises with the intense heat in a
world we have made for survival. There we stay,
bound and gagged; even when freed we remain silent!
For us, the fallen, it is too hard to live differently.
The heat of battle we cannot face. Driven, we grasp at
ways to run away and hide. Yet, the heat returns
and the battle looms ahead with no escape.
Arms bare and open, we go to face the real enemy,
not the enemy of long ago but of now—
ourselves!!
We know the cost of disobedience! We dare not pay the price
for the loss is too great.
We will fold because we choose not to move.
Attacked at an age that molded and formed our most
basic thoughts, our chances of leaving the fold were destroyed!
To our heads we hold the imaginary gun; the trigger
is pulled by our own hand. WHY??
The driven are without hope that the heat of battle will
ever cease. ALONE! Ever alone with the heat!!
    —Michaele K. McMurphy

THOUGHT PATTERNS IN THE UNIVERSE

A thought—one of innumerable, tumbling like waves on a seashore.
Crashes down, swirls, finds itself with the rest of the sand.
Leaving the unconscious (sea), moving forward and outward
and deposited on the shore (Material plane).
Manifested, simple, unchanging, how it is.

It flowers, affects others-sometimes fleetingly-sometimes
immeasurably long.
It can wait a long time for you to come to know it, for
it doesn't recognize time. It recognizes energy, light, life force
or whatever you care to name it.
It moves and flows, but doesn't arrive and is never late.
It is whatever you say it is—but it is never only what you say.
A thought is . . .

An acorn, the earth, some rain, a birth.
A trunk, a twig, a thousand leaves burst
from branches high . . .
from the sky.

  —Lucy A. Cogbill

A SIMPLE MAN

A Single Light Flickers In The Window Of A Log Cottage
Behind Emerald Sand; At Waters' Edge, Like a Story-Book Past,
A Greying And Aging Being; Sits At a Table, With Pen In Hand
 Books And Papers, Stacked On a Humple Shelf,
A Little White Dog; At The Feet Of His Master
 Waiting Patiently For a Sign To Go Out; Or a Tid-Bit,
As This Simple Man; Finishes Another Poetic Piece
 Takes Off His Spectacles; Rubbing His Eyes,
Then Reaching Down To Pet His Constant Companion
 Then! Rises From His Writing-Place,
Walking To The Mantel; Over The Fire-Place
 Picking Up a Photograph; Perhaps, That Of a Loved-One,
Near-By; a Lifes' Work Displayed
 Of Plaques, Letters, More Photos,
And! Sun-light Gleaming Off of Pyramid-Shaped Lucite Trophies
 From Another Time; Another Place,
Then, I! This Simple Man, Looks To The Stars And Ripping Waves
 And Remembers The Fast Pace Of Reality; Of Not So Long Ago,
Of Deadlines, Commitments; Fame And Glory
 Wondering Why It Wasn't So Simple Then,
Instead Of The Present Scenario; For Which My needs Are Few
 A Good Anthology; Passer-By Now And Then,
Sunrises And Sunsets; Visions To Release My Mind
 To Pen and Paper; And Those Memories Up There On The Shelf,
Just Simple Things; For, I! Am Just A SIMPLE MAN.

  —James H. Farrell

RACHLIN NIX

Give heed to the tale I bring to thee from a distant land far across the sea
 Where the Creela's move through an endless night with a sky of dirt and a blackened sight.

On one fateful day in the Rachlin Nix, a young ladd named Vear toiled ore his bricks
 And he felt shut in as he grooned about and he felt depressed and he wanted out.

In a whisper vague he conveyed his thoughts to a trusted friend as they sorted lots
 And the silence buzzed as the thoughts sunk in and a plan was hatched by the Creela men.

When the vaults had ceased and the Hokes lay down, to the edge of Nix, moving without sound
 In a mad attempt to ascend the tread, midst a siren sound the two Crees lay dead.

Where the KeGBa watched no one shed a tear, but in secrecy anger tempered fear
 In the slightest means Creelas jammed the track and the terror used couldn't turn them back.

In the Rachlin Nix the name Vear was raised as a battle cry in most silent ways
 And the Creelas suffered and suffered sore, but they held their ground and pressed for more.

And today should you sail to the Rachlin shore, you'll see a bright light through an open door
 And the KeGBa now but an empty shell, twixt the borders of freedom and the portals of hell.

  —Wade Tinnin

FLAME BIRD

A flash of color like a leaping flame
I see outside my window pane.
Tis not a bright leaf that I know,
For they lie buried beneath the snow,
Nor is it an Indian paint brush bright,
Although the color seems just right,
For what would they be doing there,
Flitting through the frosty air?
Oh, now I see them in and out
Through the pine trees tall and stout.
Bird of color, Bird of flame,
Oh but, that I knew your name.

—Thor J. Feind

SHELLS

Shells live where the oceans swell,
Where seastars fell,
Where coral and colonial know,
That seaside daisies grow,
In the sky,
Pelicans fly,
Where the great stork flies,
With beautiful black eyes,
Mermaids hair catches a seafan,
Where Pandora writes with a seapen,
Shells live where the ocean swells.

—Dolly Ojala

KITTENS AND CATS

Big fat cats
Sit on mats.
But tiny kittens
Don't wear mittens!
If I could choose between them
Kittens top rabbits of course then.
They are new,
Never Pink, Red, or Blue.
Some kittens get fat.
They might sleep in a hat.

Kittens meow,
Because they know how.

Kittens and Cats
are my friends.

—Katherine L. Marshall, age 9

SEAL ORDEAL

Life is precious, life is real,
But not for a baby harp seal.

Said the baby seal,
Hey there Bub,
Why the club,
What's the big deal?

You surely know, Mister,
It's cold and I need my fur
And like you, a man so bold,
I too would like to grow old.

A crushing blow, an agonizing squeal,
A rip of a knife
And another innocent baby harp seal
Departs this life.

Shame on you, you big manly cur,
Shame on you too who buy my fur.

A sporting chance? Their fate is sealed.

—Bob Deneke

TWO PONIES

My daddy bought me a brown pony
She has a white spot on her head.
You can't call a female horse Tony
So we named her Annie instead!

We built her a big gate that latches
behind which she plays in the sun;
She welcomed her new friend
named Patches—
You should see those two ponies run!

Our ponies can't eat at the table,
you just don't feed horses that way,
So they love their oats in the stable
Where they eat and drink ev'ry day!

We're scared that the gate made of maple
could be kick'd down flat with a bolt,
But if they'll stick around until April
then Annie will have a new colt!

In Honor of Gary Warner Burris
—Angela R. Fickling

SISTERS

I sit below an old oak tree.
Twisted with age are we both.
Together we sway in the winter's breeze.
Our hands flutter
As we run them through our hair.
Mine, long and white
Drifts slowly to the frozen ground.
Hers, dead and brown
Joins mine in its descent.
Both of us want to leave.
To be gone from this world.
But she, like me, is deeply rooted to the solid ground.
I reach out with my gnarled finger
To stroke her gnarled trunk.
We are united.
Forever.
As one.

—Meg Mayes

HE AND SHE . . . A TREE

In the quiet of the evening, with a lover's moon over-
head, silently they stand there, gazing down upon a quaint
little village, where every one is in bed.

Words never pass between them, nor memories of what
has been, secrets are never whispered to each other as lovers
often do. The space they occupy is constant and is theirs
alone to share.

They listen to the sounds of earth. They are moved
by the gentle breezes engulfing them, constantly caressing
them, as a mother gently soothes a crying child. Touching
and embracing each other with tenderness since their day
of birth.

They remain steadfast through rain, sleet, wind and
storms. Through sunlit days, cloudy nights, each day from
dusk to dawn. On sad occasions, on happy days, none seems
forlorn.

Never should they part unless life should throw them
a thunderous bolt. Life, as they know it, could abruptly cease
to exist for one or both of them.

She a well shaped and beautiful blue spruce . . . He
an elegant and stately pine.

—Doris R. S. Miller

MY PET COUGAR

I have a kitten name Cougar.
He has a long skinny tail.
He's an alley cat.
He's a kitten right now, but he's growing rapidly.
He's black and white.
He smells like burnt rubber.
He's an onery kitten.
He'll scratch your eye balls out.
He look's like a rat, but He's a cat.
                MY PET COUGAR!!!!!!!

—Eugene Michael (Mikey) Judge, Jr., age 10

THE HORSE

While galloping through the open plains,
    With a rope as my range,
With beautiful flowers under my feet,
I carefully galloped in the heat.

As I was slowing to a stop,
The range began to unlock.

I would now become free.
Free as a bird,
Across the open sea.

—Joyce Tolmaire

THE HAPPINESS OF A CHILD

The laughter in the wind
    The crying in the dark
The trembling in the cold
The happiness of a child.

The joy of toys
The sense of protection from a mother's soft gentle touch
The fun of playing tag with schoolmates
The happiness of a child.

The sense of curiosity
The touch of a dog's wet tongue
The ability to love and be loved
The happiness of a child.

The world of hate
The world of anger
The world of hunger
The happiness of a child is still in all of us.

—DeLea

PUPPY LOVE

He brought the pup in — it was cute as could be.
    What was in store, I did not foresee.
He was so cute and won my heart right away.
But it was out of the question — he just can't stay!

He was so cute and I liked him a lot.
To send him back to the barn put me on a spot!
Well, maybe just one night wouldn't do any harm,
But in the morning he'd have to go back to the barn.

He cried and howled and kept us awake until three!
By morning he was romping and playing cute as could be.
Well, I'll try to tolerate him just for today.
Tonight he'll have to go back to the barn to stay!

It was windy outside and the ground was all white.
So I let him stay in for just one more night.
We now have a puppy to have and to hold.
Just because I couldn't let him stay out in the cold!

—Loretta Jean Briggs

CREATURE COMFORT

A furry little gray field mouse
    Needed a new house.
    An empty beer can,
Carelessly tossed beside the road,
    With a little work,
    Could be a warm home.
So, the mouse carried bits of grass
    To insulate walls,
    And carpet the floor.
With bright aluminum siding
    Already in place,
    Modern mouse decor.

—H. Louise Brandt

CONFIDENCE

My swing by the creek
    glides back and forth
and lifts me quickly off the ground.
The icy wind hits my face
and refreshes me,
the trickling creek
keeps me company.
I pump harder
back and forth
pumping, pumping,
harder, harder,
back and forth,
until I reach my highest point.
I stop the rhythmic pattern of my legs,
lean my head back,
close my eyes,
and feel myself soaring
    through the air
    back and forth.
I am secure and untouchable.
    For the moment,
I feel at peace.
As if I like myself,
    no other person's opinion matters.
My swing slows to a stop
I open my eyes, stand up
    and smooth my hair into place.
Saying goodbye to the creek,
I walk away.

—Wendy L. MacDonald

FIRST STRIKE

I stand there poised, my ball in hand
    My eye upon my mark.
I look, and look, and look, and look,
Now I'm ready to start.

I move out with a short right step,
My arms are thrust out straight.
Now I step out on my left.
(Gee, I must look great.)

My arm swings back along my side
Just like a pendulum.
I step forward on my right,
My swing is now half done.

I know that this will be a strike,
I know each pin will fall.
I slide upon my left foot,
I now release the ball.

I hear a thud — a crash — a scream
My ball has just knocked down my team.

—Mary Ellen Emig

51

NOW I SEE

Oh what a sight it is to see
the beauty of His majesty
The sky at sunset in shades of pink
Lets me know that God is the link

The vastness of the world out there
and all the things for us to share
Lake and ocean and country air
Mountains and desert and land to spare

To see the smile of a little child
to see the deer out in the wild
To see the moon high in the sky
or an air balloon flying by

To splash in the sea at waters' edge
or stroll near the rocks close to the ledge
All of these things are special to me
because I know they come from Thee

—Carolyn McQuiston

VACATION IMPRESSIONS

Driving through the country
On our vacation days;
All around us beauty
Much for which to offer God our praise.
The trees are now so green,
Others are in bloom.
Not one thing in God's whole earth
To offer a bit of gloom.
Houses nestled in the valley
Way down the mountain side;
Others on the hilltops,
From neighbors they seem to hide.
Here and there we find
Three crosses on a hill.
Someone has thoughtfully arranged them
To remind us of God's will.
We give our praises daily
To Thee, our God above.
The earth is full of beauty,
Another sign of our dear God's love.

—Gerry Shearer

JESUS DIED TO SET US FREE

Jesus died at Calvary,
Gave His blood for you and me
Yes He paid the penalty that you and I
Would be set free.

Oh I praise His Holy Name because He
suffered there in shame, for the
world and all its sin
If we'll trust Him we will win.

On the cross He bled and died
to redeem us and He cried "Forgive them
for they do not know
what they do and I love them so."

Precious Lord and Master Dear be with
Me oh linger near until my life
on earth is o'er and I stand
at Heaven's Door.

Open wide and let me in oh forgive
me all my sin.
Blessed Lord remember me
And let me win the victory.

—Mary Gibson

SOMEDAY

Someday, Lord, I want to be with you
But not right now, Father, as there is
still so much for me to do.

I need your "hand" and your strength
to guide me through the unknown
As I go into the world of cancer which will
change me forever.

Someday, Lord, I might get better
Someday, Lord, I might get to see
that one dream or accomplishment come true
And then Someday, Lord, I will be with you forever.

—Sandra L. Tyler

GOD LOVES ME

To whom have I given my heart.
To a lover secretly I'm apart.
Someday we will together be,
Because I know that god loves me.

A prophet maybe I'll be.
Someone like Amos, a shepherd, kind and free.
Maybe a disciple or apostle I'll be,
A follower, teacher, and one who believes.

Predicting the future that will be,
As I'm inspired by god you'll see.
I will instruct you to follow what's right.
That will be my job as a prophet day and night.

A missionary I will become.
To preach the gospel to everyone.
A disciple of Christ I will be,
That's the job of an apostle you see,

See my friend I gave my heart.
That's what makes me so smart.
A prophet, disciple, or apostle I'll be,
Because I know that god loves me.

—Joyce Ann Jenkins Sager

EASTER
reflections

Now that Lent is over and Easter is past,
Have we started a new life? and will it last?
As we travelled the road through Gethsamane,
The Way of the Cross that led to Calvary,
Did we feel remorse? Did it grieve us sore?
Did we think of the pains that our Saviour bore?
Of the awful agony on the Cross, when crucified,
How he bled for us, plead for us as he died?

How great was His love for us! we cannot deny,
So great, that to save us, He was willing to die.
The bonds of death He hath conquered and set free,
Hath gained Salvation for us and life eternally.
Did we in humble penitence lay our sins at His feet?
When we came to the altar and in the cup did meet
How we must love Him, adore Him, as our souls were reborn,
As we rejoiced and sang "Alleluias" on Easter Morn.

And now another Eastertide is past,
We've had a re-birth, how long will it last?
When at the end of each week it could be
'twere better if we had returned to Gethsemane,
Then every Sunday loud "Alleluias" we would sing
Hosannah! Jesus our Saviour, Our Lord and Our King!
Then we with Him and in Him and He in us would abide,
And every week would be another Eastertide.

—Carrie Albert

TAKE THE TIME

Did you ever take the time to look at a tree?
Oh, look how pretty it could be.
Did you ever take the time to look at a rose?
Look how pretty it does pose.
Did you ever take the time to look at a child?
Take a look at yours, show him a smile.
Did you ever take the time to say, "I Love You?"
You'd be suprised what those three words could do.
Take the time from your busy day,
Let your loved ones know you care,
With these three words, Just say;
I LOVE YOU

—Robyn Martin

LOVE AND TIME

True love's the sky within us all,
    Not coloured blue but purest white,
A firmament eclectly big or small
That shall show its size tonight.
Take not away your love so true,
Nor leave it in the jaws of Time;
For Time will mute the throat of you
As if you're a theatre mime.
So wasted time is time that's spent,
And spent time is also wasted.
O'er time your love grows bent,
Your heart comes chapped and pasted.
O, if true love is yours then grasp it tight,
For only once in a century are the few
Who've tapped to Love's awesome might,
And if it be any, please let it be you . . .
            Close your eyes
                    and follow always,
                            your Heart.

—Dan Riffell Jr.

IF

If there ever was a man I really loved,
    it was you.
A lot of the dreams we shared did
    come true.
With you in my life, it always meant
    so much—
Even though there were times we didn't
    stay in touch.
We had a lot of problems in our lives
    together, but
I never thought I'd live apart.
    I thought we would always be forever.

Why God took you soon,
    We'll never ever know,
I just wish I could have been there;
    I would have never let you go.
It's hard to go on now,
    knowing what caused your life to end.
If only things could have been different,
    together forever our lives we would spend.

I see you many times now in my dreams.
    You seem so happy, and your eyes so softly gleam.
I know now that life is too short to
    spend it the way we did.
Maybe someday our lives together again
    we will spend.

            Love,
            Ruby

—Ruby Jones

ALL THAT GLITTERS

Could dreams be pennies, wishes golden,
    Love and friendship gems so rare,
If you could see into my heart,
    You'd find a sultan's treasure there.

For dreams abound; some are fulfilled,
    And some, perhaps, may never be,
But no less beautiful are those
    That never have reality.

Bright hopes and wishes you'd observe
    For those I love and hold so dear.
Warm, loving thoughts go out to friends,
    Though far away or very near.

Longing to share this treasure trove,
    This priceless wealth that I possess,
I find the more I give away,
    The greater is my happiness.

—Virginia Murphy

LOVE

I understand, you know,
    I really do.
I remember when it all
was new.

The world was bright
and I was smart.
Not a soul could touch
my heart.

Now I've changed,
I'm much more wise.
So I sit and sympathize.
One day, I think, you'll be here too.

Where everything is tried and true.
When simple things fall into place,
a passionate kiss,
a warm embrace.

Someday my friend, you will see,
that life is more
than you hoped
it could be.

—Shawn L. Gresham

SOMETIMES IT'S HARD

Sometimes it's hard
    To keep love on my mind,
When things don't work out
And I lose track of time.

Sometimes it's hard
To take life day by day,
When I know what I feel
But not what to say.

Sometimes it's hard
To be just good friends,
When my love for you will always be there
Even if our relationship should end.

Sometimes it's hard
To admit I was wrong,
When someone I love
Hasn't loved me so long.

Sometimes it's hard
When three words mean so much,
Like the words "I Love You"
In the heart that you touched!

—Jules Ordinario

OCTOBER WIND

Born on this side of winter,
on a night with a bright full moon,
an autumn wind makes shadows sway
as she sings a haunting tune.

She swirls the leaves in a fairy dance.
Then on a heavy sigh,
she chases soul-rich clouds across
a dark and inky sky.

She weaves in and out of shadows,
paints depths of dark and light.
Her keen is borne on unearthly breath
as she wanders through the night.

With her sad and mournful song,
she keeps tired spirits from their rests—
then cries sharp needle points of rain
as small lifes huddle in their nests.

—Loni E. Parr

A THING OF NATURE

A young female rose quietly yawned
When so softly touched by the morning dawn
And upon her lovely body was the morning dew
That fell like tears as the sunlight grew
Then came along a handsome breeze
And dried those tears with tender ease
Now the lovely rose with such great beauty
Thought the handsome breeze was really a cutey
And while for her he hummed a song
Together they danced the whole day long
And then as he so softly touched her
Her feelings for passion began to muster
As the beat of her heart began to race
A hot flush look came upon her face
She then spread her petals to his embrace
And her lovely perfume began to spout
As he slowly moved within and out
I know it's a wonder how this could be
A romantic tale of such mystery
But this was all witnessed by a honey bee

—Herbert W. Gibbs

The leaves are falling from the trees,
Yellow — green — and gold.
Things I never noticed when I
was young
I do now, that I'm growing old.
They are so beautiful, that words
cannot express.
Of all the seasons I like autumn best.
The sun came out for just a while
And then it went away.
I thank God for all the things
He brought to me today.
The grass still shows so very green
Up thru the fallen leaves.
The birds and bees have all gone
now —
And so have all short sleeves.
There stands a lovely yellow flower
Out by the concrete walk.
I wonder what it would say,
If it could only talk.
Soon it will go and in its place
Will fall the snow.

—Jewel Hembree Jones

SPRING NIGHT MOVES

The spring night moves like a gentle woman,
trapping your mind in her sweet embraces,
intoxicating with her sweet fragrance,
seductress to her warm, soft core.

A new wave crests on the brow unwarned
crashing the wall that stands fragile and thin,
imposing its will where silent water stood,
a raging storm that threatens more.

Raging madness becomes your new master,
tempting you with the fire's inferno,
casting instead to the darkness cold,
burning and bold, a sense near death.

A young woman moves like a warming season
showing one side that seems unreal
yielding another that knows all truth,
giving young men to sensual chase.

—Mike Stephenson

REMEMBERED SNOWFLAKES

Snowflakes . . .
each one unique in design,
its intricate pattern one-in-a-million
Snowflakes serve as a bridge
between a colorful autumn
and the new birth of springtime
Just as today serves as a bridge
between yesterday's memory
and tomorrow's promise.
Each today is as unique as a snowflake;
there is not another like it.
If used correctly, it will become
a treasured memory,
followed by promising tomorrows.
Thus, each today must be lived fully
and not wasted so that the yesterdays,
todays and tomorrows that follow
will be complete and rich with joy.

—Deborah Jessie

SPRING

Spring, when everything is fresh and new
The grass turns velvet green, the sky is azure blue

Everything that appears dead
Is filled with life anew
Flowers emerge and bloom
In the early morning dew

It takes just a moment
To look and you will find
God's hand holds the talent
That artists can only imitate in kind

So, stop and look around you
Take time to live and ponder
It will fill you with a new sense of life
One you won't want to squander

Feel the gentle breezes
Smell the fragrance of the flower
Find the wonders you may miss
In every passing hour

Enjoy the beauty of each and every thing
That you can only find in the wonder of, Spring

—S. Kay Tomblin

UNITY

From the oldest to the youngest,
They form a network of unity
Bound in a wheel of support,
Giving their all and all to one another.

Constantly separating themselves from the fungus,
Which sometimes has no shame in its nudity.
Trying to sustain all the love it can import,
From those we call our brother.

A grandmother to plant the seed,
A mother to guide,
A father to lead; and
A brother to stand by your side.
A sister to go the full length,
A family to create great love and strength.

—Sonya Y. Green

TO OUR DAUGHTER
(THE DAY SHE GAVE BIRTH)

To you daughter dear we send our love,
And the good Lord's strength from up above,
That he may guide you through this day,
And bring you safe to us, is what we pray.

May you have this child that love has blessed,
As our prayers for you will never rest,
For "God" will watch over you, because you're worth,
Everything to us on this your day, of giving birth.

So be it girl or boy which ever it be,
Will always be loved by your mother and of course me,
For you are our little girl, no matter how old you be,
But a great big mother to your children of three.

May you always be blessed with the gift of love,
That was given to you by the Lord above,
And may your life be happy through all your years,
Because, no one is more deserving than you, our dear.

This poem "To our daughter" is dedicated
to my daughter Rosetta, who on Monday,
October 5th, 1981 at 7:19 a.m., gave birth
to her third child Roseann Marie, at the
Brookdale Hospital weighing 8 pounds
1 ounce and 21 inches long.

—Louis D. Izzo

FOR NICOLE

I've seen your face as radiant as the sun
And felt your touch with the softness of a rose
Your eyes bright, beautiful, and clear
With a heavenly look that only a father knows

I can still hear your voice and laughter
No matter how far apart we may be
As if you were standing by my side
Holding my hand, and saying, Daddy it's me

I've held you as a new born baby
And seen you as a small child
I can imagine you as a beautiful young lady
Yet see you with a childish smile

Deep inside I know a time will come
When I'll see your beautiful face sad
With your eyes filled with tears I know will say
I'm all grown up. It's time to leave Dad

So listen for my voice, and laughter
No matter how far apart we may be
As if I were standing by your side
Holding your hand, and saying, Nicole it's me

Love, Daddy

—David E. Hancock

SHE

She . . .
She can be anyone I want
She can be intelligent or witty
                clever or cunning
She can be beautiful or plain
                vibrant or funny
She can have all of these characteristics
                some or none at all
She is mine and
                I am hers
Not in ownership but
                in partnership
She is my most treasured treasure
And I hopefully hers
You ask yourself who she is
She is my wife

—Michael R. Keister

PLAYTIME

Her little dolls will never dance
Nor paper birds take flight on wings,
The porcelain angel upon her shelf
Will never raise its voice and sing.

Still she can hear them calling
As she spins around her room,
She plays she is a fair princess
In a sparkly dress and shoes.

And little brother has such battles
With his mighty plastic men,
They struggle their way through block forests
Then safely march home again.

His bed becomes a pirate ship
He's captain of the sea,
And fearlessly fights a sea dragon
Who has big, snarling teeth.

It's the place called imagination
The world stays in full bloom,
And through a child's eyes it's possible
Because nothing impossible is true.

—Clarinda Floyd

LITTLE BOY BRIGHT

His little hand reached up for mine
And squeezed my finger tight.
He clumsily walked beside me,
Held on with all his might.

He stumbled when he caught his toe,
And I reached down, and then
He took my hand as on we went
Back on the path again.

We stopped beside a sea of blue,
Of wild flowers blooming fair,
He stooped and picked a violet
And put it in my hair.

His laughter filled my heart with joy,
His shining face so bright
Looked up at me inquiring,
To see if all was right.

His love forever I will keep,
This day his love is young.
But through the years our love will grow,
Because he's my Grandson!

—Wilda Louise Carriker

BEAUTY, CONTENTMENT AND LOVE

W) here are beauty, contentment and love to be found, in a world full of turmoil and strife,
   Where would you search to find any of these, amidst heartaches and cares of this life?
Beauty is found in the form of a rose, or a sunset at end of a day.
Beauty comes forth through the rainbow's hue, and pottery formed from the clay.
Nature has given treasures untold, for us to see and enjoy,
If only we take time to behold, what beauty our eyes can employ!
There's contentment in many phases of life—a cat as it purrs in the sun,
Cows grazing peacefully on a hillside, and a farmer whose chores are all done.
A baby taking an afternoon nap, while mother sits reading a book;
A man fishing along by the lake, and lovers in a cool, shady nook.
It's easy to observe in our everyday walk, love on display all around,
A neighbor lending a helping hand, a smile given instead of a frown,
A woman holding her newborn babe, friends near in grief or pain;
A kind word spoken to one in distress, a deed not done for its gain!
Where are beauty, contentment and love to be found? All three are found deep within
The hearts of Christians who've yielded their all, and by Christ's Blood have been made clean.
If you want to obtain all three of these, then pray to our Father above,
For He is the Source, in Him you will find—beauty, contentment and love.

    —Mrs. Ellen M. Maupin

one small wish

i thought i'd lept off the crazy seesaw that is
LOVE
but suddenly, my heart starts thumping out the old, familiar
RHYTHM.
each time the seesaw finds the cold earth, i feel my
HEART
will my legs to push off the gravel with every muscle I
POSSESS.
my mind wanders and i see his face, a time we
SHARED,
a moment stolen in the woods, an hour floating on the placid water of my
SOUL.
the pain of memory, of the hard, firm force of gravity makes me
JOYFUL
as i ponder and treasure each second i spend high above the
CLOUDS.
time is gone, everything has the distinctive essence of beauty and i am filled with the
HOPE
that life and love will be
EVERLASTING.

    —Caroline S. Newman

LOVE FROM ABOVE

S pringtime in blossom, emotions overflow.
   A turning point in the life of this young lass, only a few know.
What will tomorrow bring? She chose this course,
She prays that it's better than her past of remorse.
Then into her life flew a love for all times, upon wings of an eagle he
Soared from the sky, and danced upon moonlight,
Lightly danced through her dreams.
He spun a web around her heart. How could she resist his charm?
She saw love grow in his eyes and soon his mouth spoke what his heart did hold,
And he longed to bring her in out of the cold, and he did.
He warmed her and loved her so true and she knew. They needed each other,
The time seemed forever between times that they spent together.
One day, two days, three or more, heaven forbid it can't be a score.
When she was gone from him, oh what a void. "My love isn't with me,"
Her heart seemed to say as it beat over and over and over again,
"My love isn't with me." He's waiting, waiting, glancing out through the door.
He can't wait to see her, he's pacing the floor.
Planning rare treasures he knows she'll adore. Her heart is now captured,
Her world turned around. The season is summer and with it has come,
New love to the lonely, new love from above.

    —Julie Ann Fox

I'VE NEVER SEEN GOD

I've never seen God but I know how I feel,
It's people like you who make Him so real.
My God is no stranger, He's friendly and gay,
And He doesn't ask me to weep when I pray.

It seems that I pass Him so often each day
In the faces of people I meet on my way.
He's the stars in the Heaven, a smile on a face,
A leaf on a tree, or a rose in a vase.

He's Winter and Autumn and Summer and Spring
In short, God is every real, wonderful thing.
I wish I might meet Him much more than I do.
I would if there were more people like you.

—Gladys Gibson

MY LORD ALONE

Early in the morn, just before dawn,
Is my quiet time with my "LORD" alone.
The trees are all still, little creatures make their sound,
Silvery moist dew glistening upon the ground.

Thank You LORD for this new day,
I know you will guide and show me the way.
Even tho I may stumble and fall,
For "HIS" help, upon "HIS" name I will call.

When my burdens seem too heavy to bear,
I look to my "LORD" and know HE'S there,
My worries take over, then I hear "HIM" say,
"I'll be with you through out this day."

As the day comes to an end,
I know JESUS is my best friend,
As I lay me down to sleep,
Mine is "HIS" to forever keep.

—Zelda Mozingo Mahn

HIS GIFT OF LOVE

As I look into the bedroom, and I see her lying there;
With the soft caress of moonlight, kissing her brown hair.
I cannot understand, how she chose to share life with me.
How could I be the man, that she would really need?

As I watch her sleep, my heart overflows with love.
I close my eyes tightly, and whisper a prayer to God above.
"Thank you my Father, for your love and care for me.
Thank you for your kindness, and for opening my eyes to see.

Your precious Blessings to me, I know are not deserved.
Father I am just so thankful, they are not reserved.
Please look down upon this woman, lying in my bed,
And convey all my feelings, of words that can't be said.

I love her so much more, than any words could ever tell.
The vows we made in our beginning, help them to prevail.
Carry us through this world hand in hand, and side by side.
Help us trust in thy leading, forever be our loving guide."

As I finished praying, and I looked at her again,
The curtains stir softly, from a gentle breath of wind.
She is just a Gift from Heaven, she isn't really mine.
God's love has Blessed us both, but only for a time.

—Kenneth E. Oldham

SMALL BLESSINGS

Lord, thank Thee for the little things
That give us pleasure day by day:
The red bird in the tree, that sings;
The laughter of children as they play;

The white clouds floating overhead,
The windblown grass, so cool and green;
The kitten hiding in the flower bed,
Sheltered by the hedge's screen;

The soft rain falling in the night,
Reminding us of God's loving care,
Who keeps us all within his sight;
And answers every faltering prayer.

We thank Thee for great blessings, Lord,
Which guide and keep us in Thy way;
And also for the little things
That help us through a weary day.

—Ruth Bolton

HEART CRIES

This crazy world seems so unkind.
It breaks the body, tires the mind.
The load's too heavy, can't go on.
Too much pain, the joy is gone.
The curtain's falling, closing in,
Like blackest night all filled with sin.
Don't like the seeds that I have sown.
Can't bear the burdens on my own.
My heart cries out, "Oh help me please!"
And then I fall down to my knees.
The shadows lift, He takes my hand.
I exit from this darkling land.
My trust returns and hope shines through.
He gives me back my life anew.
This battle's done, for now I'm fine.
The war is won, the victory's mine.
The light is bright, the promise clear.
And life's worth living. My God is near.

—Deb DeNio Krueger

A SECOND CHANCE

Walking through a cloud,
My toes sink into the mist.
Finding myself in fog,
I need the chance to survive.

Oh Lord, can I be helped?

The darkness overcomes me,
I can't find my way—
The surrounding sounds scare me,
Wanting the chance to survive.

Oh Lord, can I be helped?

A light is coming towards me,
My tunnel is getting shorter—
Either my life is over,
Or I have another chance.

Oh Lord, can I be helped?

My eyes are being lifted,
I am coming out of the fog.
The clouds are now behind me,
I have been given the chance to survive.

Oh Lord, thank you.

—Holly Wooldridge

TEDDY BEARS

Teddy Bears so nice and soft.
Teddy Bears so sweet.
All you have to do;
Is give them a treat.
They will protect you.
Never neglect you.
Give them a home;
Just as your own.
For they will love you so.
THE END

—Ericka L. Fontenot

SHY

timid creature run and hide
feel so lonely, so hurt inside
so many things you want to say
yet you just can't find the way
sensitive creature so all alone
no real friend to call your own
on the outside looking in
avoiding attention once again
so secure inside your shell
so afraid you're gonna fail
timid creature please don't cry
lift your head and hold it high!

—Gwendolyn D. Micheaux

I NEED . . .

To be loved
by someone special.
To be cared for and caressed.
Someone to hold
me tight when no one else will.
To be understood
and accepted as being myself.
To be wanted
and not forgotten.
Someone to break me out
of this bondage of
being shy.
To be made to feel
beautiful.
To be forgiven for
the wrongs I have caused.

—Catharine J. Courter

MY LOVING FRIEND

Take me down that lonesome road
to a time i knew before,
to grassy meadows green
to that old and peaceful shore.

Where time was young; so full and carefree
a time that knew no end,
a time of true love and mystery
of great and ageless friends.

When we were young and so carefree
not a worry or a care,
we had a friendship so brand new
so beautiful and rare.

Of times that seem so long ago
and always were so true,
to have a friend so special
to have a friend like you.

—Marie Anderson

TO BE A FRIEND

I gather people in my life . . .
                    to stay there.
I gather events in my life . . .
                    to share.
I have conversations to remember
I will love you forever.

When you enter my life . . .
                    don't leave.
When you share my secrets . . .
                    don't tell.
When you love me once, remember me always.
Because a friend like you is rare.

—Susan Cole Duffy

MY HEART'S FRIEND

The morning was perfect, the time was Spring.
If you listened closely, you could hear the birds sing.
A barn and a cabin, sunny dogwoods, the scene
And a log building over the old water spring.

I said "Let's sit on the bench" made of wood.
Our hearts spoke fluently in this silent mood.
Our lips touched: "No, I shan't: YES, I SHOULD!"
Spirits merged, melted — emotions powerful and good.

The time in eternity was planned just right
No pushing or demanding — we held real tight.
Just being near, content — not expecting a great sight
But alas, our separation: that is our plight.

The world stood still, maybe a moment or a year
Our hands firmly clasped, leaving was near
The beeping of my watch rang too loud in my ear
As we walked away, down my cheek, a small tear.

We'll visit this place from time to time
If not for real, then in my mind.
The best thing of all is that I did find
My heart's friend will always be mine.

—Jim Palmer

FRIENDS

Friends come and go, some are here for a life time
and some drift away like the morning dew.
We have friends for all occasions and for all
seasons.
Some we laugh with, some we cry with and others
are there for all reasons.
We call everyone our friends. Whether we met
them just once or known them a lifetime, they're
our friends.
Some friends call when they want something and
some call for no reason at all.
We give our friendship as freely as we give our
love, sometimes to be taken advantage of and
sometimes to reap great rewards.
Yes we seem to have friends everywhere more than we
ourselves realize, because you see, anyone can call
themselves a friend but real friends are always
there no matter what the weather, the best of friends
are those that are there for no reason at all.
These are the friends we must keep and treasure like
a precious jewel.
Sometimes losing their luster but never their
  value.

Friends.

—Laurie Vaughan

58

MY MOTHER'S HANDS

My Mother's hands with all the wrinkles
Tell me a story of the love
   and many cares
Those hands that meant
   the world to me
I'll love and cherish those hands
   so tender and kind.
And long after God has put
   them to rest.
A tear will come into my heart,
Yet happy for those wrinkled hands
   They tell a story to me
That will always be in
   my heart and memories.
My Mother's hands beyond words
   to tell the story of love and care
For ever in my heart
   My Mother's precious hands.

   —Irene Haring

ABOUT DAD

I never understood my Dad.
He loved Mama.
I guess that's enough.

His hand was heavy when I was bad.
I tried hard to earn his love and respect.
I never did.

As a child, a teen, and a man I never felt a part of
the family.
I never did as good as someone else would do.

No matter the task, the effort, whatever it may be.
Dad never seemed pleased with me.

I never understood my Dad.
He loved Mama.
I guess that's enough.

   —Keith Kuhn

DADDY

It was early one morning the angels appeared
Our Dad looked up as they drew near
With his eyes wide open he showed no fear
   He didn't even shed a tear

Hand in hand they led him home
   To see his Father at his Throne

Oh what a joy it must have been
   To see his Jesus that died for him
Eternal Life is what he gained
   Never to be in any pain

So when our tears leave a stain
   Just remember he's in no pain
No more strokes & no more pokes
   No more pills & no more chills
No more sorrow he has to face
   Just his Father's loving grace

For those of us he left behind
   We have a promise to keep in mind
Someday our Lord will come again
   And take us to that Promised Land

So there's no reason to be sad
   Because someday we'll see our Dad

   —Lucretia Willis Fennessy

WHAT IS LIFE?

What is life, without me?
It is hard to imagine,
So you see.

I would not care,
Where I was,
'Cause I'd have no soul to bear.

And so to say, a good-bye for now,
I'm glad to be here,
All safe and sound.

   —Nicole Renner

HAPPY "MOM'S" DAY

A mother is a mother but,
A mom is one who cares,
   You're the one who showed me love,
And taught me how to share.
   Your special day is here again
to praise the things you've done,
   Though you taught me right from
wrong we still had lots of fun.
   Through the years you've been my
mom, but most of all, my friend,
   A relationship like yours and mine
I'll treasure till life's end.
   Now that I'm a mother, I hope
I'm just like you,
   You raised me to respect myself,
but to respect others too.
   Happy "Mom's" Day

   —Apryle Kirk

MOM

It wasn't long ago
On a day so clear,
God called home my mom
That we loved so dear.

Yes, home, don't you know
That's where all God's good children go.

Oh, yes! Gone to heaven
She gave birth to five
And raised seven.

Some say it's more than that,
Because she shared with so many,
Even gave ice cream to the cat.

Wow! What a cook,
You know, I never saw her use a book.

Yes, yes, took pride in her cooking?
You bet she did.
Her willingness to share
She never hid.

What a mom's love she had,
Loved me even when my
Behavior was bad.

When my wayward running was all done,
She welcomed me home — The Prodigal Son.

My life changed on the 10th of May.
And exactly eight years later,
Mom was buried that day.

Sure, there is so much more that I can say.
But, don't you know,
I will cherish her love every day.

   —Rudolph P. Antoine

WHEATFIELDS

While walking through my wheatfield,
all by myself today,
I took my life down from its shelf,
and dusted the webs away.
The webs that held my life to yours,
the webs that shared our pain,
and when I put my life back up,
the webs will form again.

—Gioia Tortella-Nossokoff

SPRING

I really like spring
Because you can do anything.
You can swim and run
That's a lot of fun.

There's different flowers
And sometimes showers.
You're still in school
Cause it's the golden rule.

Snakes come out.
The flowers sprout.
The birds sing
There's nothing I like as much as spring.

—Crystal Lynn Racavich, age 9

SIGNS OF SPRING

The sun is shining brightly.
White clouds drift in the sky.
Light breeze is blowing just enough
For the kite that's flying so high.

Birds are singing in the tree tops,
Crickets chirping in grass so green,
A copter, or a fast flying jet
Now and then above, can be seen,

Cars, campers, and all sizes of trucks
Are traveling in every direction,
Going to camp, fish, boat or ski,
Made possible by God's perfection,

Sweet odors fill the air from flowers
A boy whistling to the tune of a song
With signs like these around us
We know Spring will be here before long.

—Thomas Tigar Smith

SPRING

Shifting restlessly
I looked through the whispering willows.
Children freely playing
a game of innocence
in the brief, new season of sunshine.

A new life —
for the bees swarming speedily
through their unconscious peaceful journey
of honey-waxed wanderings.

In the newly greened open field
each iris and daffodil
shout their big, bright colors
to the grassy weeping willows.

With a dignified calmness
I look out at spring's newly given gifts —
Then glance at my wilting wild rose
of yesterday's tranquil wooded sleep.

—Donna D. Zeidler

THE BEAUTY OF DAWN

I like to rise early in the morning
When the earth is still and calm,
To smell the fragrance of the springtime breeze
That has taken so long to come.

To listen to the mockingbirds
In the Maple and the Locust,
To see the soft mowed lawn
and the fading of the crocus.

Little ones sleeping in the quietness
like little birds.
They, too, soon will leave the nest.
I wonder — Oh, I wonder
Will they find this kind of bliss.

I'm the luckiest person in the whole world
To know this happiness,
And I know there is even better
That overshadows this.

To have a home where God dwells
And know His love and care,
To know throughout eternity
He is always near.

—Lilly Garrett

MARCH-THE HARBINGER
   OF SPRING

Mid winters ice and snow, the month of March
   drew near,
The skies grew sunny and blue, a soft gentle
breeze did appear,
It put a song in our hearts, as a warmth it did
bring,
And our thoughts once more returned to Spring.

Meek as a lamb, March entered the door,
Then capricious as she's often been before,
She changed her garb and altered her face
Then brought in a lion and started a race.

She gathered the storm clouds, turned the skies
gray,
The sunshine was sent far, far away,
She tumbled snow down over us and up overhead,
Alas! All too soon the song in our hearts lay dead.

The big white flakes blew up, blew down, blew in,
blew out;
Swirling and circling, round and round us all
about.
The snow like towering mountains was left
behind,
When the mad, mad winds of March they did
unwind.

Ah! March! Come ye in like a lamb, or with a lion's
roar,
We'll always welcome you with an open door,
For we know when you've gone away we'll find
Another Spring with us you've left behind.

So here's to March, a salute in a glad refrain,
When we say "Au-revoir" as you take off on the
wing,
And when a new year dawns, with eager hearts
we'll wait again,
For your return, Sweet Harbinger of Spring.

—Carrie Albert

THE GOLDEN YEARS

More than half of my life has been spent with you.
Where have the years gone?
It seems as if everything were new—
Could it have been this long?
Although we've had our ups and downs;
Never between us, it's true;
Those things that gave us the toughest times
Helped, as our love grew.
We're now in what are the "Golden Years."
How golden can "gold" be?
We've had "gold" for thirty-seven years—
That's good enough for me.

       —Mrs. Roy S. Smith

MARRIAGE

Our mental relationship is now one
of interchanging ideas
beyond that of exchanging thoughts.

Our emotional relationship has become one of kindness
to each other added to our connecting attractions.

Our physical relationship has merged us to one
of making love with each other
in addition to making love to each other.

Our sexual relationship has changed to one
of mutual heterosexuality as opposed to
a relationship of individual heterosexualism.

Our intellectual relationship has moved
to one of synthesis of agendas
rather than one of analysis of motives.

Our feeling relationship has combined
the tenderness of our touches
to the delicateness of our natures.

Our spiritual relationship has evolved
to become more completely integrated as it reduces
the need for us to strive for perfection.

To Cindy   March 9, 1990
      —Tom Nelson

TALONNA LOVE

TaLonna, my teenage angel love,
She's moving to the music like a disco dove;

She's soaring through flights of imaginary dreams,
Starring Bon-Jovi in his tight-torn jeans;

Oh TaLonna, your hair flows wild and free,
As your eyes try to hide your thoughts from me;

On her feet go her Reeboks, this kid's moving on,
The 'The New Kids On The Block,' are sure not alone;

She says, "You Dudes, will survive the divorce fall-out,
Showing you a detour to take another route."

She's talking on the phone, switching from ear to ear,
Then slides down her cheek a little bitty tear;

It's Saturday now, time to go to Dad's.
It sure is hard continually switching pads;

She's starting to dream dreams of her future life,
Hoping some day she'll be the very best wife;

Mom and Dad, if you could turn back the hands of time,
Would there be smiles not sadness she'd find?

She's a child of divorce, so world get real,
You know the mouth says things the heart can't feel.

      —Judy C. Howell

WHY PRETEND

We started out as only friends.
My love goes deeper, so why pretend.
Do I tell you, I love you
Or will I lose you if I do.
I'm reaching out to you my friend.
Won't you help me reach the end.
Even though we're just friends,
Isn't that how love begins?
We've known each other for so long,
We must know what's going on.
In our hearts, and in our souls,
We still try to keep control.
We go on everyday
Searching for love, in any way.
So hear me now, my dearest friend.
I can't go on and pretend.

      —JoAnne Rose Diodato

WHY?

We once had a true love Remember? one time.
I swore that forever you would be mine.
As our love grew, a new life was born.
One very early hot July morn.
Our gift of love then could it be?
Was the "real" true love meant for me.
Now few words are spoken, no feelings shown.
This is not the true love I thought I had known.
Another gift to us was brought.
Conceived in love — I think not.
There is no love between you and I.
This I admit and you deny.
Torn between love and hate.
My little true loves sit and wait.
Can it be again tonight.
Another scary, angry fight.
This is not fair, they know not why.
They can only sit and cry.
Who's at fault, who's to blame.
That life will never be the same.
What would I wish if a wish could come true.
I'd wish I could say the words "I Love You."

      —Virginia Bouchard

LOVE COMES IN MANY COLORS

In a northern Alabama town
A cold wind was blowing all around,
And in a state penitentiary there,
A lonely prisoner's hopes were drowned.

A dreaded disease they said, he had,
And the outcome they said would be very bad.
Far from family, friends, and love,
His only hope was help from above.

And when this cry reached up to His ears,
The great God of this universe,
Rose up from His throne in a mighty move,
And said, "I'll send this man some love."

But that poor man didn't understand,
That love comes in many colors,
And this same God who hung the stars out,
Wanted mankind to be brothers.

The sun weaves golden threads,
And skies are blue o'er our heads,
People come, some black, some white,
Some gold, some red.

      —Sheryl Bean

THANK-U GOD

God created u and me.
So we could "B" friends
U see.
I knew it from the very
Start.
We would become close
At heart.
I was right now we see
And that's why our friendship
Will always "B."
Thank-U God from my
Heart.
Thank-U God right from
The start.
Thank-U God 4 giving her
2 me.
She's the BEST u will see.

—Sarah Thomas

TIME

Time it is a precious thing,
Sometimes we seem to waste,
We complain instead of sing
And live in the state of haste.

If we could learn to control,
Our thoughts and our time,
We would think more of our soul,
And our lives would seem to rhyme.

There is so much to be thankful for,
Why do we seem to worry?
For in life we would have much more,
If we weren't in such a hurry.

Faith and hope are important things,
Which will bring us closer to God above,
Much more happiness they will bring,
When these things are done in love.

Think of family and think of friends,
These thoughts will be like leaven,
And the happiness that God sends,
Will be a glimpse of Heaven.

—Ron Webb

HIS PLAN

What is your plan Lord,
The plan for my life?
It seems that I struggle
With hurting and strife.

As I search for the answers,
For the needs of the day,
I long for your purpose,
In me to relay.

Lord, give me new insight,
Help my eyes to behold,
Your plan for this day,
In me to unfold.

May those who I touch,
Feel your presence in me,
Be strengthened and blessed,
By the actions they see.

And at the end of this day Lord,
Its events reminisced,
May I have the assurance,
That your plan was not missed.

—Frances Bevard

THY WILL—NOT MINE

Fluttering, feathery white flakes—God's Beauty—
Cascade down on the bleak winter earth.
Hope seems as dead as the landscape.
Spirits flag and eyes grow dim with tears,
For joy isn't easily a part of man
When Hope is gone.

Soon the earth—no longer bleak and dull—
Glitters in its pristine blanket.
Slowly the heart within begins to change.
The spirits rise and peace returns.
His peace covers our lives, as the snow
Covers the ground, when we pray,
"Thy Will Be Done."

—M. Adah Pyeatt

MY SAVIOR

The Lord is my Savior, please don't let me waver.
I try to work hard to be in his favor.

When things don't go right, whether it be day or be night.
The Lord is my Savior, please don't let me waver.

The road may be long and I know I'm not strong.
The Lord is my Savior, please don't let me waver.

We Christians are trying though many are dying.
The Lord is my Savior, please don't let me waver.

To die without grace is the worst thing we face.
The Lord is my Savior, please don't let me waver.

Our crosses we bear, though some may not care.
The Lord is my Savior, please don't let me waver.

The armies of God are trying quite hard.
The Lord is my Savior, please don't let me waver.

With the hope of new life, we walk towards the light.
The Lord is my Savior, please don't let me waver.

With peace in my heart and the love of a harp.
The Lord is my Savior, please don't let me waver.

—Robin

IF I COULD HAVE KNOWN

If I could have known my Saviour
As he walked on earth among men.
If I could have touched the hem of his garment,
been made whole again,
Would I have loved him more?

If I could have heard his gentle voice
As he said young maiden arise
If I could have beheld her as she gently
opened her eyes.
Would I have loved him more?

If I could have stood by that grave on the hillside
Heard his voice as he bid Lazarus come forth
Gazed in awe and admiration
As Lazarus in his vigor stepped forth.
Would I have loved him more?

If I could have beheld his glory
As he ascended to the Father on high
Heard His sweet voice promising as he bid his
disciples adieu
Fear not I'll be coming for you.
Would I have loved him more?

—Anna Davis

ALONE

I feel these touches, they seem
so real,
But when I turn to look, no one
is there.

I hear these words spoken in my
ear,
But when I turn my head to smile
in reply, no one is there.

I feel this warmth and fullness
in my heart,
Until I realize that the words
and touches are not real.

I am alone, the touches and
words are memories.

An abyss is what I live today.

   —Mary Hall

WHEN YOU WENT AWAY

You've been gone so very long,
 Yet you're always near.
Glancing about the same old room,
I find "things," oh! so dear.

A picture hanging on the wall,
A coat you did not take.
A teddy-bear you have out-grown
"Come back," for goodness sake.

You leave me all your memories,
in things you've left behind.
I can not ask you to return,
for that would be unkind.

If you returned to please just me,
and not to please your-self
then I would be a selfish mom
for wanting some-thing else.

So you live there, and I'll live here
We really aren't a-part.
For so very very much of you
is locked with in my heart.

   —Helen Mann Behnken

WHAT DO WE SEE?

The frown on the brow
 The tear on the cheek
The far away look in the eye
What do we see?

Emotions to impress
Knowledge to teach
The inner eye remembers
What do we see?

The limp in the walk
The slowness of pace
The use of a cane
What do we see?

The dimness of sight
The loss of appetite
The frailness of body
What do we see?

The inner light goes out
The body goes limp
The fight is gone to rest
What do we see?

   —Catherine Parker

NO HELP BUT US

The hero died when he should have lived,
 on a day when the sun should have shined but
never did.

The calvery did not make it to save the day and a
hundred men with their lives did pay.

The priest could not save the man from jumping off
the ledge because they could not find out what
put him over the edge.

The world famous lawyer lost the case and his client
went to jail, and no one ever thought that he
would fail.

No one can save us but ourselves, because we rule
over our own destiny each and every day, because
we have the final say.

   —John Lipkvich

I cry.
And you watch as the tears roll down my cheeks.
Each drop moistens my young face and makes it pure.

I laugh.
At first it's just a grin, but slowly it grows into a smile
that covers my whole face.

I wonder.
I wonder what goes on in the dark at night after I fall
asleep.
And I wonder if I'll get to see a new day's light.

I'm scared.
Frightened about all the things I haven't done or seen,
but that will soon face me.

I listen.
Not only for the cries of laughter, but for the cries of
pain.
Because each one must be soothed.

And I believe for every smile, there should be a laugh to
follow it.
And for every tear, there should be a hand to wipe it away.

   —Jordan Rain Hutchison, age 15

TEARS OF FAITH

I cried in tears of anger this morn,
 It was not for me, but for my sons.
They are growing so fast, yet they are still so young.
I cried for them and this world in which we live.

God please make them strong and truthful,
Help them use their wisdom; their love of life.
Give them the strength they need,
To make this world a better place for all living creatures.

My tears cry down from the heavens for peace,
My soul aches for the love of all mankind.
Reach out to us oh Lord,
Lift the hatred, the greed and the pain out of our souls.

Give us back the innocence of a newborn babe.
Let us give to our children what our parents could not give to us.
Let us give love instead of hate;
Forgiveness instead of guilt, and Peace instead of war.

I cried this night for all of mankind
Praying God will guide us all to a better life.
My tears are for the years we have wasted;
I pray they will soon be tears of eternal peace.

This poem was inspired by my sons, Joseph, Joshua and Timothy Black.

   —Sharon Melinda Ellis Black

SUMMER IS HERE
Summer is here,
Oh! Summer is here,
Time for fun,
And time to run.

School is out,
We are free as the birds,
That fly in the sky,
So we say goodbye.

I will see you next year,
We'll have fun and games,
We won't shed a tear,
Cause it's the end of the year!

Hurray!!
—**Mistina D. Modesitt**

SEASONS WITHIN
In the Autumn
All things sleep
The Autumn you came
The cold did not—
Only warmth—Your warmth

Unlike other Autumns
This season was alive and warm

As Autumn passed and Winter came
I still felt the warmth—
A hidden sunshine and flowers

Winter gone—Spring drifting
A new life begins—All things wake

Summer yet to be
Ever changing Seasons—

Seasons change—People change

Ever changing Seasons
Ever constant warmth—

The warmth—You bring
Hidden sunshine—
Change the Seasons within.

—**Kathy Schwartzbauer**

SPRING AWAKENING
Awaken now, O slouthful earth,
Awaken from thy rest;
Bring forth thy seed in sweet travail,
Put on thy spring time dress.
Put on thy carpet made of green,
Thy bonnet made of blue;
Then trim it here and there about,
With cloud of different hue.
Arouse thy children who still sleep,
If need be, with thy fury,
From blustery wind, to sweet caress,
Arouse them to be merry.
Bedeck the bough of every tree,
With different shade of green,
Delight the eyes, as they behold,
The beauty to be seen.
I wonder as I look at thee,
In splendor and allure,
I know there is a Master-Mind,
Whose bidding you must serve.

—**Dixie K. Newell**

SPRINGTIME
Spring is a refreshing time of year,
when trees start to bud and flowers reappear.

Rain falls softly from the sky;
Winds blow gently and kites start to fly.

New babies arrive and the sheep are shorn,
Farmers are busy in fields planting corn.

Spring is God's miracles sent from above,
to Him give the thanks for all of His love.
—**Amy Molyneux**

AUTUMN'S SECRET
I was so sad to see summer go
And to feel the cold autumn wind blow
But I have discovered a marvelous surprise
Autumn is summer in disguise.

Autumn presents a jubilant show
With dancers of many colors aglow
Swirling to the music of the wind
Singing "Summer will return soon again."

She leaves and returns and goes once more
Finally growing weary of each earth-cleaning chore
She pulls a wintry blanket over her head
And sleeps soundly in her frozen bed.

She awakes to the sound of a lively spring
When tiny green bonnets unfurl each wing
She begins to paint with a touch so tender
Each of her miracles in rainbow splendor.

—**Grace Kathryn**

SPRING
Spring is like a newborn baby,
Along with it comes the sights, sounds, and joys,
of a new life,
Beginning its struggle for survival.
To see an infant as it rests,
Or watch a barren field fill with all the colors of a rainbow.
To hear a young babe as it laughs,
Or hear birds sing,
For the first time since winter.
Spring is like a rose bud,
Just beginning to open,
Along with it comes the silent beauty,
Of just knowing it is truly,
One of a kind.
One of God's miracles.

—**Jewett H. Ingram**

SUNSETS
Have you ever really stopped to look at the sunset?
The awe and splendor overwhelms the whole body.
The beauty and stillness of night slowly crawls
upon the earth, as birds lay down to roost
and crickets fill the air with song.
God made the earth and the heavens because He
was lonely and He made the sunset
for His children to see His love.
It is almost a sad moment when the sun sets
because the warmth of day dies
and with it, the light of day.
The sun slowly creeps downward, while the moon
creeps upward.
Sunsets provoke love, which is why
there is such a thing as a sunset.
—**Heather S. Anderson, age 12**

64

THE SUN WILL ALWAYS RISE

The boy's tears fall heavily
On his mother's grave.
But they are not tears of sorrow due to loss.
They are tears of fear.

What is he to do now?
Who's to hold him at night?
To make all his wrongs seem right?
Who's to hold his hand when it rains?

Who will come when he calls her name?
How can he ever hope to smile again
When all the love in the world has left him?

But there's something he sees through his tear stained eyes.
It's something death could never disguise.
The sun will always rise.

—Eddy Burke

LITTLE SHAWNEE

As I gaze from my window at the sight
Of the pasture being covered by a blanket of white,
I watch the snowflakes fall in dreamlike flight
As the afternoon slowly drifts into the night.

You see, out there in that hard cold frozen ground
Beneath a stony little covered mound,
Lies something that will always be dear to me
The remains and cherished memories of my colt Shawnee.

He died this past fall—so innocent and young
His little life had just begun;
When one day he just took sick and died
I slept in his stall beside him and cried.

My Paw and I buried him there beside the west fence
And I've been out there everyday since.
It looks so empty not to see him out there
Running or playing around his mother La Flare.

Now the snow is falling heavier and getting deeper
And has covered below the little sleeper.
Soon his headstone will be covered in snow
But never the memory of Little Shawnee below.

—Bobbie Lynn Hughes

A CLOSE FRIEND

A river is like a wild animal
Running free as a wild bird just
Running away from its prey.
It was a nice summer day
That I saw the river just
Flowing gently away.

Away from memories that I
Had from the past when you
And I were young and free.

But we had those special
Moments when we just had to
Catch our breaths and talk
To each other also to understand
What we've tried to accomplish.

But now very far away from where
We used to sit,
And watch the river.

All of my dreams that I had
Never came true but all of my
Dreams were all about you!

—Lori Beltramini

I'LL WAIT

I sat and waited by the phone,
Most of the time, all alone.
Thinking of days long gone past
Thinking of love I thought would last.
It's hard sometimes to really see
Whatever is meant, is meant to be.
Things do change; I know they will
I guess I'll wait and wait until—
Time alone has done its part—
Then once again, I'll have your heart.
I never hoped for anything more
Than to hear that knock upon my door.
I'll wait for you and then until—
I long for you and always will.
I will say a silent prayer
To see your face and golden hair.
But for now, I hope to one day see,
The day that you come back to me.

—Bart Summerford

FLOWERS OF GOLD

Chasing through the fields with
flowers of gold, shaped like cups
for the sunshine they hold.
The rabbit has run, but caught
it I did only to turn around and
find a piece of my heart gone,
you left me with a smile and
a soft gentle song only to see
the love for me left behind by
you.
I turn and search through
these flowers of gold, to feel
your strong but gentle song,
but then when I turn only
to see the rabbit change into
a butterfly with the brightest
of colors to be seen by the
angels or the gods above, because
they are the colors of life and
of dreams that only you my
brother can share with me.

—Sandie Kay

TO MY BEST FRIEND

When things are going rough, and
you just don't feel like being tough,
Pick up the phone, give me a call,
I'll help you through it all.
When things just seem wrong, and
you want all to end, just remember
you have a best friend.
Sometimes, sure, we'll disagree, but
we'll work things out, you'll see.
You just can't split up two people who
were meant to be best friends.
There's no one else I can call my
sis, my side kick;
There's just no one else like you
to pick.
Just remember when you're feeling
down, and need someone.
There I'll stand waiting to give you
a helping hand.

In Memory of Dawn Rae Ralph, May 27, 1974 - Dec. 16, 1989

—Jennifer E. Kay, age 16

65

I looked outside my window, and there you were, standing way up high.
You climbed the tallest ladder, you almost reached the sky.

You climbed to higher heights, way beyond the few. Who stand so tall
and firm, on a precious love so true.

It takes great strength and courage, to run this climbing test.
You proved your love to me boy, you're better than the rest.

And there you stand so high, waving a banner in the sky.

"MY LOVE, MY SWEET LOVE, HONEY YOU'RE THE ONE FOR ME,
I STAND TALL AND HIGH TO PROVE IT, I WANT THE WORLD TO SEE.

SO HERE I AM, NO QUESTIONS ASKED, I HAVE ALREADY SHOWN, YOU'RE THE
LOVE OF MY LIFE HONEY, BEFORE, TODAY, AND FROM NOW ON.

I STAND HERE ON THIS LADDER, TO LET THIS TRUTH BE KNOWN.
I LOVE DEAR LADY JUANDA BEFORE, TODAY, AND FROM NOW ON."

I looked outside my window, and no trace of you was there.
But I know you've gone to higher heights, on a love climb ladder
between us somewhere..

 —Juanda S. Harrison

GOD'S SILENT TOUCH OF LOVE

When in need without greed, just kindly ask the good lord above, for his love. He listens to our silent thoughts of words, as the moon shines quietly over the earth. The eyes of God watch over us at night when we are sleeping. He listens to hear if maybe we are weeping.

As a labor of love your prayers will be answered, for this I am sure. Feel secure, for God's Silent Touch Of Love, is always felt and heard. In the still of night, God performs his many supernatural miracles of life, for all of our lives. Maybe even tonight.

Have Faith. Hope and Charity. No mountain top is too high. So reach out to the sky and dream your dreams, and hope for all you can hope for. Be all that you can be. There is no limit in God's World. Give all of yourself to everyone in need. The clarity is so clear to me.

Ask yourself if the task you ask of yourself is too much to do. If you give all of yourself to the task that you ask of yourself to do, then with patience all will come through.

Let us turn our inner spirit and soul to the Love of God. Let us love one another as we do God. Only then can you know God. He lives inside us, beside us, just accept his love.

Forgive and let go of all the evil that comes your way. As long as you love, no evil can undo or get in the way. Nothing can separate us from the Love of God. His love penetrates right through us. He demonstrates this to us all, everyday in everyway.

 —Shara Lyn Geffen

A BUNDLE OF LOVE

A chest of memories at my grandparent's house holds treasures from the past,
Its wood surface injured and scarred by time protects items our family holds fast.

Inside it smells of age and cedar and, when opened, the hinges squeak.
Through many years of loving use, the rusted latch has grown quite weak.

At the bottom lies a quilt wrapped in paper tied with string;
Made of cloth scraps and memories that only life can bring.

It's said quilts should be read and cause sweet stories to be told,
Bring tears for a time gone by and some new memories mold.

Mom's favorite shirt from grade school, Grandmother's wedding dress,
Home-made sheets once wedding presents, my Grandad's riding vest.

An old coat from my uncle's childhood, feedsack dresses worn to school,
Scraps from a basketball uniform, baby clothes stained with food and drool.

Aunt Naud's favorite polka-dot skirt, my Grammy's worn-out dress,
Grandad's blue chambray workshirt, a 4-H Club apron that won the best.

Scraps from the past, yet cherished every one.
A promise of love and warmth that years have not undone.

 —Sheryl Lynn Butchee

WEIRD LITTLE FEELING

Sometimes when I think of you
I get this weird feeling in my heart.
Then I wonder,
Do you ever get these feelings, too?
That we should meet and never part.
Then I realize a cold hard fact,
I would have to get you to notice me.
So I try to ask you a question,
And you politely reply, but it's just an act.
But I still won't give up on you
Even though it hurt.
And I'm just a little afraid
That I might be in love with you.
I know what they say about puppy love,
But I just can't help that weird feeling in my heart.
That was just something you did to me.
That convinced me.
When we meet we must never part.
For if we did, it would just break my heart!

—Irene Beal

A BEST FRIEND'S LOSS

Remember way back then
When you were my best friend?
It seems that has changed.
You were there when I felt disarranged
You really cared for me
And I cared for you see,
But now we have lost touch
And I've never missed someone so much.
You were there when I needed you . . .
When I was happy or sad you knew.
Now there is something I want to hear,
I want to know that you are near.
I really want you to know what's
       on my mind . . .
You know, what I search for,
       I find . . .
And I searched for some sweet
Words that are so true,
To tell you how much . . .
       I Miss You!

—Deanna K. Burch

MY BEST FRIEND

My very best friend is dark and tall,
In fact, he isn't a person at all.
Instead of two legs, he has three;
He's waiting in the living room just for me.
When I come home after a busy day,
It makes me feel good to sit down and play
My piano with keys of black and white.
The music makes everything seem just right.
When I am sad, he makes me glad;
Makes me forget the bad times I've had.
I may play a Sousa march, strong and loud,
Or a soft lullaby, like floating on a cloud.
I might attempt something that's hard to do,
Or just play a song I already knew.
I may play Beethoven, Chopin, or Bach,
Or even might try the latest in rock.
My fingers, still nimble, glide over the keys.
For that I am thankful. "Dear Lord, if you please,
Keep my fingers and memory strong,
That I may always praise you in word and song."

—Mary Y. Allen

WHAT DOES IT MEAN TO BE FREE?

What does it mean to be free?
Just look beyond the carefree sea.
Being free can bring life long pleasures,
Love, joy and gold-lined treasures.
Being free can remove all your worries,
But can bring beauty to all winter flurries.
Being free can mean endless love,
With a dove sent from up above.
Being free can brighten the sun-filled rays,
With God's miracle working days.

—Vicki Lynn Kavalauskas

I LOVE YOU

I love you more than anything . . .
however can that be?
We have such a sweet and wondrous tie
for all Eternity.
I love you every moment,
And my love is very true,
Because you give me all the love
that's deep inside of you
I'm happy, I'm content, and so very full of joy
I love a gentle, sweet man . . .
A kind and handsome boy.
I love you, and I cherish you,
In a very simple way
I belong to you, and you to me
through every happy day.

—Marie Woodland Poley

THE SEAS OF MEMORIES

Across the seas of memories
Many long miles away,
There lies a land so sweet and fair,
I've heard the people say.
I go back to yesterday,
To these memories sweet and fair,
To the times children laughed and played,
And love flowed everywhere.
But time has played its awful game
While my world is quiet and still.
Once more, I return to long ago thoughts,
And I always will.
Do not be sad, don't cry for me,
Because now throughout the day,
Memories flow back again to me,
Though many miles away.

—Johnnie Rae Yell

MY SUMMER LOVE

You are
    Like a new leaf in the Spring
    that blossoms into my heart.
    All Summer you shade and comfort me;
    I become accustomed to you.
    Now Fall has come . . .
    you have changed,
    you have turned away.
    Like a leaf you
    fall away from me.
    Now my heart, like an empty branch,
    is cold and alone.
    Now I must await Springtime
    to bloom a fresh new
    leaf of love,

—Kristen Lynn Schajatovic

THOUGHTS

As I think of the second coming of Christ,
I have to take inventory of my life.
Am I what God wants me to be?
Or, am I happy just being me?

As I think of the burning Hell,
could anyone help, even if I gave a yell?
Does anyone ever want to end up there?
If you don't now's the time to care.

If you'll surrender your life to Christ,
I promise you'll never have a friend as nice.
He'll do things your friends can't do,
and he'll always be there to watch over you.

—Shirley (Lloyd) Hall

THIS MAN

There is a man who loves you,
No matter what you do;
In all trials and tribulations,
He'll always help you through.

When you feel you are at your weakest point,
And you feel you can't go on;
This Man will be there with you,
To make you feel so strong.

He gives more love and peace,
He lets you know He cares;
But remember when you're down and out,
This Man is always there.

He calmed the troubled waters,
He parted the Red Sea;
He died upon a rugged cross,
For you and for me.

This Man that I am speaking of,
You've guessed by now, I see;
His Blessed name is JESUS,
The Greatest to ever be.

—Koretta Kay Quinn

ONWARD I RUSHED

The sun sparkled in the morning mist,
Onward I rushed,
A profusion of colors lined my garden path,
Onward I rushed,
Uplifted arms of a loving face,
A baby's radiant smile so filled with grace,
But I glanced at my watch and shook my head,
Time was my enemy which I had come to dread,
Friends passed by,
Outstretched hands to shake,
I had no time,
There were meetings to make,
Endless hours of toil,
Precious dollars to earn,
Appointments and conferences,
Speeches to learn,
Golden moments raced past me,
Hands held out which I did not reach,
If only I had held that moment,
Oh, what treasures would they teach,
The gentle touch of a child,
A warm embrace of a friend,
Gardens whose beauty held no end,
The glory of a sunrise at the start of each day,
Please open my eyes Lord and show me the way.

—Jean Kievit

CHILDREN

You want children to fill the house with joy
You have a daughter first to bring joy
One whose smile would melt an iceberg
Whose tears would kill a clown's smile
You have a son to help bring joy of life
You see he's ruff like dad, but kind like mom
How can you tell he's kind; by his smile
You care for them worrying as they grow older
Then one day you find they've gone
And the home is just a plain empty house
Until on Christmas day when it happens
The family and God reunite
They are together for a reunion of things
Childhood memories and good times, as well as bad
Love and memories make the house a home again
A home blessed by God's presence and abundant love

—Linda K. Humphries

POWERLESS LOVE

If anyone's sickness should go away—Yours Should!
And if I could seek and find the way—I Would!

Your pains and fears I'd surely bear,
And to the Lord I'd cast your care.
I Would!

Encouraging words—sometimes—
Can be discouraging words
And those who say them mean well.

But to be in your place,
And to face what you face—
Only you dwell where you dwell.

You don't know, but I cry when you cry
And can feel pain with your pain,
Praying daily to HIS throne on High—
None of which is done in vain.

HE is not a giver of sorrow,
For it is Life HE came to give.
Please entrust HIM with each tomorrow,
Then within you HIS strength will live.

—Jodie Collins

DON'T YOU QUIT

When things get rough, "(and they sometimes will)"
When the road you're trudging seems all uphill.
You don't know whether to walk or sit.
Rest if you must. But don't you quit!

You're sick in body weary and worn.
You feel so helpless, alone and forlorn.
You say to yourself. "Well, this is it."
Rest if you must. But don't you quit!

When you look and see the mountain top,
You start to think. "Will the problems stop?"
Bring them to God. Relax and sit.
Rest if you must. But don't you quit!

Turn about face and get in the race.
He'll give you strength to withstand the pace.
The prize you will win is worth every bit,
Rest if you must. But don't you quit!

Say to yourself. "I'm going to win."
You'll feel God's presence abiding within.
Trust Him, my friend, take hold of the bit.
Rest if you must. But don't you quit.

—Irene Sorensen Fisher Duval

WAR

The napalm falls on children's tender flesh
Oh, men, are you quite sure you're right?
The bomber's tons of bombs make dread descent.
Oh, God, I know you said, "Thou shalt not kill."
The poison of defoliation spreads.
The swollen carcass of the buffalo
With rigid legs and stench offends our breath
The songs of birds are hushed in throats struck dead
Limbs of trees are shattered, too grim sights
Old women stagger, homeless, weak, forlorn.
Young mothers tug their burdens of the young.
White bearded men gaze stunned at tragic scene.
Their sons, once strong, now broken, blind and mute.
The warriors follow orders stolidly,
Automatons the slaves of sly men's greed.
Where is the love that Jesus taught us all?
When will that final holocaust reach us?

—Madelyn LaRoche

TEARS AND SILENCE

Tears fell in streams of heartbreak
As my mind was filled with torture.
My pain increased, then silence emerged
To haunt and madden further.

Why! Why! Why! My heart would cry
With a plea of agonizing desire,
But all the answer I received
Was a tear of hushed retire.

One day all was gladness and cheer,
Then, so suddenly, he's gone.
Gone away to leave a gap in life
That chills the body, not the heart alone.

"It's only life's irony," they say,
Or else, "He's just one of the many,"
But my heart cries "He's mine, though gone."
"I can't have another, no, not any!"

Thoughts storm on, rushing memory.
I cry warm tears of passions multiplied.
But silence prevails to frighten and hurt
Until exhaustion overcomes, stifling feelings inside.

—Dianne Elaine McAllister

THE TEARS ARE FOR THE FEARS

Somewhere on the other side of the world
A man begins to sing
He's saying that everyone wants to rule the world
And take control of everything

The world is on its feet, reacting
And he starts to go to the next song
The crowd urges him on —
They've waited too long

The other man absently strums his guitar
And the world links hands to become one
The man is saying good-bye
It seems he's all done

The crowd refuses to let it be
And they shout and beg for more
The two oblige and start to harmonize
All about love and war

We're head over heels, we know
In case you're wondering the tears are for the fears
It's God who sent their music
And will get us through the years

—Linda Cottrell

THE HUMAN RACE

They created atom bombs
Mini-skirts, knee boots, and love beads
Aerosals and styrofoam
They are changing
Rainforests, the ozone layer and lives
They introduced drugs,
Oat bran, and A.I.D.S.
Air, water, and noise pollution
They used too much water,
Gasoline, and don't recycle
They worry because
Landfills are almost full
The ozone layer's depleting
And acid rain's ruining everything
These people are the human race.
They are causing Earth's death.

—Amber Norwood

AURORA

O.K. world — you got me to reach out,
but now what do I do. I don't know what
follows.

O.K. world — this world has messed with
me long enough. Someone is always trying
to show me a new way.

O.K. world — I submitted to your strange
ways and once again I'm lost. Trampled
under the many that come before and after.

O.K. world — soon there will be a better
day. The one promised in the Book.

O.K. world — let's see how our heart
is to respond. Lost, stranded on this
desert land.

O.K. world — take it as it comes. An inch
is still a mile with no one to command
and be commanded.

O.K. world — you've still got me for a
while. Take care, I bruise — though often
on the inside.

—Dawn Bartell

THOUGHTS OF AFRICA

Will you carry the brave and fallen
Through the flames and burning embers
Of our land where freedom struggles
In this place no one remembers?

Across the sun-scorched meadows
Over bone-yards of the plain
Under night skies dark with thunder
As the cannons call your name.

Will you stop upon your journey,
Will you kneel beside the dead
To close their eyes forever
On their ravaged war-torn bed?

Will you sing of all your glories
Or will your tongue be still with grief
On your march across a wounded land
Where life has been too brief?

Will you carry the brave and fallen
Will you stumble on your way
Will you pause to fight another time
Will you stop to cry today?

—L. Walker

WHERE DOES THE SKY END?

A dream condemned to prosper
An imagination restricted to run wild
The Sky Does Have An End.

An idea without a flowing thought
A deep reaction without emotion
The Sky Does Have An End.

Believe that it ends; and it will be so.
But death is the fate then chosen.
To be human, is to grow—
Therefore; THE SKY WILL NEVER END!

—Nicole Herbert

LIFE'S JOURNEY

You can ease the curves of your own
course by following parts of
other courses,
But you will always return to the
curves that you once bypassed,
Only to find you have lost the
strength that comes from following
your own course.

Time slips quickly through the
moving part, but lies still in
the resting.

—Thomas Boatright

WE

A pledge a promise cast aside
Left unsmoked a pipe of peace

In despair and disbelief
We prepare not for peace

Feathers shimmering war paint on
We dance and chant the night along

Upon the path of war we seek
And on the ground beneath our feet
Our ponies' hooves their beat we heed

Our mighty warriors their challenge met
Life and death upon them crept

Dust and tears upon our cheeks
Pain and sorrow within we meet

We live, we die, we know not why!

—Sulyn Cody

WORSHIP

Various people
Gypsy or itinerant evangelist,
Migrant preacher, or steadfast pastor,
How do you serve God?

Divers manners
Noisy and raucous revivals,
Zealous moments, wild exhortations
Protracted meetings, dignified gatherings,
Quiet conversions, silent prayers,
Penances, sacrifices, strange denials,
How do you worship God?

Many places
Theatres, tents or public halls,
Schools, churches or missions,
Where do you worship God?

Or do you worship God?

—Mary Jane Mullan

FANTASY

Fantasy is the realm of a dream.
Fantasy is not all what it seems.
A unicorn's trail, a leprechaun's gold,
A bold demon, a tale to unfold.
To find what you want, to find what you need.
You must first discover the key to your mind,
The door to fantasy.

—Seanna E. Sykes

HELL'S FIRE

Hell's red fingers in anger race,
Leaving blackened death across earth's face.

Creatures blind, in terror torn,
Running, leaving, their hearts forlorn.

Men, like yellow ants, in meager toil,
This raging inferno, its path to foil.

Trees, smoldering statues, dead branches held high,
In sobering stillness, to heaven's cry.

Spirits, smokey ghosts, torn from nature's breast,
Float ever upward, somewhere to rest.

Somewhere within her ashen bowels,
A cry is heard, above the howls.

A prayer goes forth, please God intercede,
Put forth thy hand against hell's fiery steed.

From within the throat of this blood-red hell,
Comes searing screams, as the raindrops fell.

Once again peace comes upon the land,
And nature's beauty will ever stand.

Somewhere within her bounteous womb,
Seeds of life will put forth their bloom.

Thanks is given to a power much higher,
For once again earth overcame hell's fire.

—John W. Gardner

The tumble weeds blow across the fiery desert
The hot winds of this wilderland beats against
the desolate soul.
Fiercely the brilliant sun sinks in a cloud of
rising dust,
Lethal dust desiring the human soul.
A trap laid by the deadly desert of Hell.
A place designed for the ultimate destruction
of human life.
Aching to consume the immortal soul;
While lusting for the mortal body.
What is the chance of the mortal Christian
against such devouring Hate?
Who will save the Soul from such evil vengeance?
What can we do?
Nothing and Everything.
Everything and Nothing.
Belief and faith what are they?
They are a means to an end.
An end to the pain and suffering of unbelief
or wrong belief.
Who's to say what we believe is wrong?
Our hearts, our conscience, our minds,
even our very souls.
Our own belief and faith can condemn
or save us.
It is our decision; the only one that
we have.

—Lisa Cox

DADDY'S LITTLE GIRL

With eyes so beautiful big and shining bright,
A smile on her face gives off a glowing light.

When her special man enters in,
This little girl is full of grins.

Daddy's heart is bursting wide,
'Cause his whole life is full of pride.

A little girl's love for her gentle Dad,
Is a special love that makes both hearts glad!

So to you, my Dad, I say once again,
Those words you've heard so many times before;
I love you Dad, with all my heart,
And will always be with you even when we are apart.

—Christina L. Dunham

BUGS

Ladybug, ladybug, polka-dot speck,
how can you swallow if you have no neck?
You're dancing on flowers that you never eat
leaves polka-dot footprints from ladybug feet.

Bumble bee, bumble bee, buzzing the air,
sharing your meal with a sweet honey bear.
But, if he tries to eat every last thing,
that honey bear soon will feel bumble bee sting.

Firefly, firefly, what do you know?
By holding your breath you can make yourself glow.
The more you are happy the faster you blink.
Maybe green, maybe yellow, but never be pink.

Centipede, centipede, what did you lose?
Fifty new pairs of red and white shoes.
You're in no hurry for fifty pair more,
'cause putting them on makes a hundred feet sore.

These are some of the bugs on the world that we share.
Some people know them, and others don't care.
Some bugs are helpful, and some are a pest.
Do you think that you can pick one you like best?

—Jim Taylor

OUR RAINBOW GARDEN

My Inner Child says she wants to play,
So let's meet in Our Rainbow Garden today.

We can hold hands and skip down the path
And smile, and giggle and really laugh!
We'll smell the sweetness of the red, red roses,
And in the orange and yellow pansy faces
    we'll stick our noses.

Wading and splashing in the little pond
We'll skip our pebbles across it and beyond.
Then, let's shinny to the top of a tall, tall tree,
Sit amongst masses of green leaves
    and shout with glee, while the blue sky
    surrounds us and we are masters of all we see.

Oh! let's build a tree house and stay
    while the sun goes down,
And in the velvety indigo blue sky
    gaze at mysterious winking bright eyes all around.

When the sky becomes streaked with a violet glow
    I know it is time for us to go.
My Inner Child thanks you for a happy time,
    as I let you return to your world,
        and I, to mine.

—Naomi P. Lindsay

THE OLD SWINGING BRIDGE

In my watercolored memories,
Of my childhood long ago,
I have visions of a swinging bridge,
Swinging to and fro.
I would fish beneath the structure,
With a bobber made from cork,
And I see this bridge still swinging,
Across the Mighty Middle Fork.
I see the mill below it,
With logs floating on the pond;
Yes, that was in the good old days,
Of which I was so fond.
My thoughts keep wandering back,
To picking chestnuts on the ridge,
But my memories still haunt me,
Of the dear old swinging bridge.

—Evelyn W. Bachtel

SUN'S JOURNEY

Sunrise, strands of gold,
Hues of color so untold.
Bursting out as a splash of water;
Gaining momentum, rising higher.

The morning mist, so cool;
Yet the sun so warm to touch;
Glitters, sparkles in a pool.
The feel of God is in the air,

As the sun rises toward Heaven,
It sends rays of gold through the trees.
The mist has vanished quietly
And there's a warm gentle breeze.

As the sleeping flowers awake,
They are kissed by the glowing sun.
A sweet smelling aroma fills the air
And fragrantly blows across the meadow.

A butterfly softly flits about,
As the awesome sun sets.
Soon night comes without a care
And everything quietly sleeps.

—Iva D. Culross

GEOI'S CHOSEN PLACE

I went to visit him today,
He's sleeping where the squirrels play.
I saw him in the flowers there,
I look, I see him everywhere.
He walks so softly in my night,
He's standing in my morning light.
He's in the clean and misty rain,
My humming bird with satin wings,
The lightning bugs, the butterflies,
The green green grass, the blue blue skies,
A sunset that so vivid comes,
To bring the night as darkness comes.
But look! The stars are shining there,
To light his night and linger on,
As morning comes to break the dawn.
The sun shines on the dewdrop lace,
And comes to warm his chosen place.
The tiny spiders playing there,
I look, I see him everywhere!
I came to visit him today.
I saw him smile I heard him say,
"Don't worry mom, I'm O.K.
I'm sleeping here where squirrels play."

—Claire Walker

AFTER WORLD

An arrow pierces your heart.
You are now gone forever
Living in a world where no
Hate exists, only love.
The love between you and the chosen one
Will survive through anything
that comes your way.
Both of you have been sprinkled
By the fairies' dust of time, and
During the trials of life, no harm
Will disturb the peace surrounding
the both of you.

—Amanda K. Heifner

MORGAN

She is so young and innocent
From heaven she was surely sent
Her eyes are dark and very brown
She has the cutest little frown
Straight and silky is her hair
Her beauty is beyond compare
I love her cute and tiny nose
And of course those little toes
Just like the morning dew
Her world is fresh and new
She's learning more with every day
Patience and kindness guides the way
When she takes a look around
I'll show her the goodness that can be found
Together we will journey
There's many things we'll see
Our hearts will be our guide
As we journey side by side
Joined as one we were
My blood I shared with her
For her my love is infinite
She's the most precious thing to me
Mom and babe are like no other
There is no deeper bond
With Morgan's life I was blessed
She is a dream come true
                    Love Mommy

—Kim N. Pasquine

ON THIS YOUR EIGHTEENTH BIRTHDAY

On this your eighteenth birthday
I'd like to say to you,
I hope every wish you make
Will actually come true.

It's hard for me to realize
That it's been eighteen years
Since I first held you in my arms
And wiped away your tears.

I know I haven't been
What you'd call a perfect mother,
But I know that as a son,
I wouldn't want any other.

I just want you to know
That I love you very much.
I have from the start
And I will die doing such.

I've always been so proud of you
In everything you've done.
I'd like for you to know one thing,
I thank God that you're my son!

—Arlene J. Mathews

HOME

Home is what we both do share,
In pride and love and tender care,
This home is ours, all we own.
Together we the seeds have sown,
As roses blossom and unfold,
Let each of us together mold,
As from the nut young roots appear,
Let the roots from our hearts bear,
To grow to wind to firmly brace,
This home we share in solid grace,
That though the world winds may our strength test,
This home in graceful solitude shall rest,
Let all we share, upon it build,
never be a barren field,
But always flower, fruit, and life abide,
From side to side in loving pride . . .

—Daniel W. Moore

FIRST LOVE

It's only been months, though it seems like years,
Since the first time that we met,
I'm not exactly sure how we arrived here,
But I'm sure I have no regrets.

You've touched my life in many ways,
And with your caring I have grown,
I reminisce about the days,
Of our stolen moments alone.

If only you realized what your friendship meant,
It's difficult to describe in few words,
Dare I say you have been heaven sent,
Though the notion wouldn't be totally absurd.

I am a better person for accepting your gift,
Of love, friendship and guidance,
Until you came I was floating adrift,
In a world of self-pity and silence.

So now as our lives take different directions,
And an end has come to all I've dreamed of,
In my heart you will always be worthy of my affection,
Because you were my first true love.

—Maria E. Morales

THE ROPING MAN

You know, sometimes life really seems unfair.
The harder I try, the more heartache I bear.
I reached so deep inside myself,
Only to have my love placed on a shelf.

And there it stiffened and gathered dust,
Finally—Cupid's arrow pierced my trust.
So as my broken heart was trying to mend,
You slid to a stop and came riding in.

Thru the haze of unsettled dust,
Burst forth the grey—making no fuss.
Never a more handsome man had I found,
And straight for that steer you both were bound.

Since that day, we've had some good times,
Remembering especially our first shared bottle of wine.
No one had to tell me or to explain,
Your heart too, had been pierced by pain.

As we both put the pieces together again,
There is so much comfort in being friends.
Only to you, my secrets will I share.
Life to me now seems much more fair.

Written especially for Larry,
—Kathy E. Elkins

72

COUNCIL ON LIFE

It's sunset and the elders of the village gather
Bursting with the excitement of the day's events
A young man spoke his mind in ritual fashion
Rage fell at the seat of the Council on Life
A man with so few years understanding the way
We must think if this is of new winds and clouds
That he did speak with such determined belief within
And that the breeze that flowed in the evergreens and thickets
Harmonized with his words in utterly full acceptance
What has brought this child to his latest revelation?
How did he speak with our soil and our trees?
What force did bring him peace in a warring world?
It was his ears and his eyes and nose and hands
It was his voyage into minds of other beings
It was the message that flowed in his veins
Be yourself, by understanding the thoughts of all else.

—Erik Trager

THE WRECKERS

I watched them tearing a building down
It stood for years on the other side of town,
With a yo heave ho and a lusty yell;
The ball struck hard and the side wall fell!

I thought to myself as to what it would need
To have made repairs and avoid this deed;
As I glanced back again it was all torn down;
No longer its sight would grace our fair town!

I saw in that what has happened to many a life
Battered, torn, neglected and filled full of strife,
When all that is needed was someone to care;
And very likely it still would be there!

Have I sown seeds of kindness in those whom I meet
Or have I chosen to avoid my brother and be so discreet,
Take time in your schedule to listen to others;
You can win their respect and gain them as a brother!

Have I been in my lifetime a friend to someone in need
Or have I failed to love them and their hunger to feed,
Has your name been known by folks over town;
Or have I been content with the labor of tearing down!

—Harold Arthur Leckron

I AM AFRAID

I am afraid of long days of pain
   that turn into years
and make me tired of the fight

I am afraid of not holding it together
   internal combat waged
against the darkness in my heart
   balance — perspective — a positive attitude

I am afraid of a task left undone
   but invested with tears and pain and hard work
a real failure
   because I really did try

I am afraid of broken trust
   of "I love you"
that to me is real, but to another — just words
   knowing that I must be vulnerable again
or face isolation

I am afraid
   of justice without mercy
   righteousness without forgiveness
   feeling without depth
   love without sacrifice and
   joy without sorrow . . . somewhere . . . sometime

—Karen E. Nytch

THOSE WE DO NOT KNOW

With stone cold eyes we criticize
   unknowingly, we generalize
yet shamelessly choose to despise
those we do not know.

their worth we often minimize
our ignorance only simplifies
the pain within pathetic cries
of those we do not know.

our style must not be jeopardized
so in our minds we sterilize
the visions that would dramatize
those we do not know.

our love could lead to compromise
our hope might help to stabilize
our charity fuel the empty lives
of those we do not know.

—Nadine R. Strivens

GROWING OLD

We have a way of growing old
   No matter what we do.
Time has a way of slipping by,
And catching up with you.

We don't have to fold our hands
And be put upon a shelf,
There are lots of ways
We can help others, and ourself.

We can love our neighbors
And help them along life's way.
We can show lots of kindness,
And be careful what we say.

We can brighten up a corner
That seemed so dark and blue.
We can smile so cheerfully,
It will seem the sun has come thru.

We can live for Jesus
As we go along life's way
And when our life is over,
"Well done" we can hear Him say.

—Emma Walker

It's too cold to go out
   nature's work is done
All that is left is my
   desire for fun in the sun.

One by one
   some side by side
are all the cares
   forgotten in the tide.

The waves crash sharply
   upon the beach
Even the wind is too loud
   as summer's long out of reach.

If not in the snow
   or high in the mountains
Then find me striving
   for summer's bronzed tans.

I can hear the ocean
   do more than call my name
I cannot have it as it was
   Alas, it'll never be the same.

—Heather Honea

SOON

With the wind in my hair
and the sun on my face,
I'm thinking about my lady fair.
Is she also thinking of me?

Five long days we've been apart.
In three more we'll have a new start.
Oh how I long to gaze into her blue eyes
and run my fingers through her hair.
Soon we will be there.

Are those wedding bells I hear?
Beautiful music so far away,
but yet so near.
Soon we'll be there.
Those same bells will play when we unite.
With love beating in our hearts,
they'll play for us on our wedding night.

—Alan L. Lykins

BONDED

She is so sweet and gentle,
Her beauty beyond compare.
Our kindred souls are bonded,
By a love that's oh' so rare.

Now I am she, and she is me,
And both of us are one.
I thank the Lord each passing day,
For this Miracle he has done.

Her lips are soft and yielding,
She is eager for my touch.
My adoration is consuming,
For this girl I love so much.

In times of crises, she is there,
To help me should I fall.
She's giving me strength to carry on,
When my back's against the wall.

If ever I should lose my love,
On some far distant day.
I pray the Lord will take me too,
I'll have no reason left to stay.

—Leon Harvey Burnes

ENCHANTED EVENING

You and I are running blind,
Plunging into darkness,
Arms entwined.

The winds of fury blow on past,
Guiding the ship,
Tugging the mast.

Burning with fury,
We keep lunging on.
Lighting the darkness,
Purging the dawn.

Then, we arrived at a mystical place
Where the glistening beams
Lit up your face.

Shining so brightly,
Like the moon on the sea,
Our lips gently touched knowing it was to be.

The tides rise and fall,
Our ships drift by, free.
Cherishing the journey
You once took with me.

—Michelle U. Bly

FANTASY

There's a subliminal level of imagination
that permits an enjoyment of life's ecstasies
without reservation
A scenario that's more profound than a vivid dream
and a paradise that creates a drama of an
idyllic scene
The splendor of uncensored passion and wanton desire
with the intensity of a raging fire
A fierce warrior with courage and strength that's
beyond compare
and the genius and finess that is extraordinare
A preservation of beauty and happiness in a
myriad of collections
and an uninterrupted milieu in total perfection
An emotional honesty that remains safe in the heart
for fear that reality would disillusion the spark.

—Eddye

THE MOLD HAS BEEN SET

I sat and I listened and I felt you there
Talking to me as you brushed my hair
Talking of things long in the past
When they set the mold and made the cast

The mold was you and the cast is me
I love as you do and I see as you see
The feelings I have, the same as you feel
The mending you do, my efforts to heal

Reconstructing our life, starting inside
Untying the knots that so many have tied
The sadness and fear come through every day
The love that we have is guiding the way

I sat and I listened, I knew who you were
With each word you spoke, each feeling would stir
You were you, you were me, I was you, I was me
My heart, my mind and my eyes which to see

A house with a window, inside and out
To finally calm, and make peace of your shout
The mold has been set, the cast is brand new
I am me, who I am, because I am you.

—MaryBeth A. Horkan

IF I WERE THE SUN AND
YOU WERE THE SEA

If I were the sun and you were the sea,
in this grand earth's design,
I'd shine to your side, at your rolling tide
and dream to claim you as mine.

I'd weave through our waves, and wait at your shore
for you to come join your love true;
and by the rays from my lips, all sailors and ships
would witness my longing for you.

I'd sift through the clouds and dart through the sky
to daintily glance to your face;
I'd reach for your sight 'til I left you in night
and trust in God's infinite grace.

If I were the sun and you were the sea,
I'd greet you each morning bright
I'd dance through the skies to open your eyes
and love you, to wake you from night.

Should you and I share, and should you and I grow
and should we overcome life's demands
in love we'd stay, each night and each day
each holding one of God's hands.

—Shari Sweetnam

The chains that once bound me
 are now broken and rusted.
They have fallen to the floor
 and become symbols of the past.

The words that are used to hurt and insult me
 are still spoken today with anger and resentment.
They ring in the air like the bells of a church
 and stay with me day after day.

The brotherhood that unites us all
 is a sign of our future, if only the chains
 and the words could be forgotten.

— Valerie Wiesneske

A REVELATION
What is, is not, yet Is.

We cannot live by threadbare traditions
 Nor by doctrines and customs of old.
What mankind has done uninstructed
the end thereof was foretold.

Temples built with hands are earthy
The houses of the Lord they claim
Having never perceived his Majesty
The doctrines they preach are the same.

Their prayers are vain repetitions
And are seldom heard for the din.
It's not done so much for the answer they get
As in their pride in being seen of men.

They make their long-winded Sermons
Spiritual things they presume to declare
Believing heavenly things are earthy
Proselytes are told what to eat, drink, and wear.

Now they all fall under subjection
Collection plates are passed around for a fee.
The false prophet reads and interprets
None suspecting the TRUTH makes them free.

— Evelyn Christiansen

THE WALL

Tear down the wall that iron curtain.
 Unite a people divided for certain.
Families were parted by that wall of fears
And hope was imprisoned near twenty-eight years.

That communist barrier was built to detain
Subdue a people in a common domain.
Yet so many suffered some even died.
For crossing that wall meant death if one tried.

Now open the borders let everyone see
They are walking across unharmed and free.
Tear down the wall that sign of oppression
By whatever means you have in possession.

Dance in the streets from dusk until light.
Tear down the wall celebrate all night.
Then thank God in Heaven and the powers that be
The wall is coming down in East Germany

There's so much unrest it's an effort to appease
A people wanting freedom from such atrocities.
Stand in the shadows watch and see
The wall is coming down and changing history.

March in the streets, carry banners high
Shout for reform till God hears your cry.
Tear down the wall chant and sing
You have only begun to let freedom ring.

— Wilma Burlew

SUNSET

The setting of the sun on the valley
 is like the glow of a thousand
 candles burning
Burning ever so slow
As I walk in the light of a big world I can
 feel the heat in the air that I breathe
The distant horizons are slowly drowning in
 the fire
I feel the darkness coming, my life flashing
 by me.
I see an angry sun slowly drowning under
 the valleys
I want to breathe the night
I want to set myself free
Fade away from the earth
I dream, dream that I wake up to the
 dawn of a new day.

— Reneé Susan Marshall

THE LESSON

"Come learn of me," he cried to all
 and they did flock to hear his call.
He preached and pounded and cajoled
 and ranted all the stuff of old.

Now some were thought to benefit
 while others deemed it merriment.
In either case it matters not —
 Another tempest in a pot.

While some of these are on the screen
 the others come from a machine;
but one and all they sound the same:
 with burning words hell-fire proclaim.

Yet elsewhere, far from noise and strife,
 there is a place so dear to life,
unknown to pomp and merchandise
 which stoops not to commercialize.

It's quiet there; no sound is heard,
 nor screaming of condemning word.
In dark and deep like endless sleep
 it soothes the soul and safe does keep.

— E.J. Hester

THESE CELL WALLS

Why do I sit here today
 And think of a time so far away.

A star disappears
A memory of a girl reappears.
I see her smiling face
Of a time forgotten in space.
Hair so long, beautiful, and brown
It's not enough to turn me around.

So I sit here amongst these walls
Killing time like a man in a prison cell
Soon my sentence it will tell
And maybe I can leave this empty jail.

Or will time just past
Be forgotten at last.

But for me life is like a passing train
Wailing in the distant rain.
Here today, gone tomorrow
Everything will be just the same.

Like the train rolling on its merry way
With its neverlasting stay.

— Stuart L. Spanier

SHOWERING BEAUTY

As I gazed into the midnight sky
The stars that glittered there,
Were falling in periodical ways
Showering to who knows where.

I wondered as they fell
Of where they ended below.
Were they disappearing dreams
Lovers made long ago?

Perhaps they were the diamonds
The jewels of people we've known
Who've shaped our lives and futures
Their faith in us they've shown.

It seems sad to watch them
Despite its natural way,
Their last fleeting moments of beauty
Says they've gone . . they couldn't stay.

—Debra L. Sellers

LIVES IN VAIN

We gather now to celebrate,
The lives of those before.
Reflecting on the battles won,
Be sure there will be more.

The world gives no security,
But guarantees your grave.
A hopeless place for faithless men,
A challenge to the brave.

I bow my heart to those who fought,
And to those who paid the price.
Ashamed of my complacent ways,
Unworthy of their sacrifice.

The soil of earth cries out for rest,
Their stones now mark their dust.
Will men not ever trust in God,
The choice is clear-we must.

Though more men live than 'er before,
Seems wisdom has lost her charm.
Self-righteous, greed, no thought for life,
Behold Heaven, and mercy's right arm.

—Richard Ralph Rudicil

This is the first poem of yours
that has come outside to play
still fragile as a newborn
yet, I think it's come to stay

I've kept it nurtured deep inside
held close and touched with care
until tonight it popped right out
and said, "It's time to share!"

We've got no time for wasting
we've got all the time we need
we change and grow and change again
like everlasting seeds

It's true that we must feel it all
and true that we can choose
to play our melody as jazz
or decide to sing the blues

Our harmonies may ebb and flow
yet, we only have today
to sexperience whatever each moment brings
like poems that come to stay!
For My Mother
—Merri Lu Park

LOST AMONG THE STARS
(Dedicated to the crew and the spirit of Challenger lost Jan. 28, 1986)

Let silver touch the wing-tips,
Our silent kiss brush their lips,
Our whispered sorrow of goodbye—
Forever follow their final journey through the sky.

Their hearts beheld a vision-their
Souls had found a quest,
The chance to slip the bonds of earth—
A last and final test.

Sometimes in eagerness, we reach
Too far—
And fall from grace among
The stars.

Man will journey onward—
As it is right to do.
Forever flying ships of silver
Beyond the sky of blue.

But pause I must—and wonder—
Even though we've come so far,
If we'll be forever pilgrims—
Strangers—lost among the stars.

—Joan Martin-Raynes

THE VILLAGE

On a cold, cold, snowy night,
I wandered through The Village
  to see what was left, after war's
Terrible, Terrible Pillage.
  I found The Old Church,
The Bell's still rung,
  But the beautiful Children
who sang in the Choir,
  Their songs are no longer sung.
For the dreaded enemy, Encamped The Village
  And killed them all,
And by the enemies Guns they did fall.

  But now, in a Heavenly Choir, They do sing
And their Angelic ears hear a Beautiful Bell ring.
  But more than that, They see Their Saviour's face,
And know at last a permanent resting place,
  where flowers always bloom and Love is all around.
They no longer suffer or fear
  Nor do they hunger or feel the cold
By The Saviour they are held so Dear,
  With His Wings around them He does fold
Safe and Happy for all Eternity!
        Amen.

—Donald Thomas Veale

A POEM TO THANK MOZART FOR HIS REQUIEM

When, in me, lies the dead feeling of
  dangling boredom,
  the tightness of frustration,
    the wrath of an ugly anger,
You drain my muddled mind
of the mingled mess of its humanity,
And leave me with nothing but a resolution,
a satisfaction that
      All pitched passions,
      All deathly depressions
      Give 'way their power to action.
      Be that small or cosmic,
      They give 'way their power to
            action.

—Donald W. Chaffer

THE MEDALLION

This is a story of a rose on a medallion of gold.
A story of love so tender, yet bold.
It was given to me by a child so dear
On a Mother's Day so golden and clear.

When love filled her world and in childlike candor,
Her face expressed awe and wonder,
Then a little hand reached for her mother,
For her there was no other.

On the medallion there was a sonnet,
Along with a rose that had no thorns on it.
A charm on a glimmering chain,
Bringing joy of memories once again.

And now today on this Mother's Day,
I think of her who has gone her way,
But the medallion engraved with a rose,
Will be mine, as time comes and goes.

—Edith Martin

HOMESICK

I long for my friends back home,
    The big, white house and the lovely treed lawn,
Where I yearn so much to rome,
    With my old friends of which I am so fawn.

There, I had friends that were loving and clost,
    Here, they are thoughtful and nice.
There, they were warm and made me host,
    Here, some are sweet and others are ice.

There, I heard sparrows sing,
    Here, only a lonely owl hoot.
There, I heard church bells ring,
    Here, only car horns toot.

There, is a wonderful place to be,
    And to find someone to love.
Here, is a wonderful place to see,
    And to admire the snow white dove.

Even though I once ruled my own heart,
    Homesickness is now my master.
And unless from this place I depart,
    I guess it will lead me to disaster.

—Carol Musgrove

DEPARTURE

By spectral retine of flowery eloquence attended,
    Forsaking meadows and lush, ripened fields,
Like a young bride, summer has departed
Leaving ajar the creaking gates of mist . . .

Gone is chaste ardor of the earth and sky,
Their deeply heaving breasts are cold and still . . .
Touched by the roughened hand of brittle frost,
With early silver hastily adorned . . .

Through slender, stiffened fingers of the trees,
They mournfully lament love's sudden passing,
Repeating promises forgotten, unfulfilled . . .
Delirious they ramble . . . , as if dreaming . . .

Deep in the woods the rainbow echoes still . . .
Forever gone . . . , yet magically enticing . . .
And, as the ashes of the hearth grow cold,
The embers glow beneath like an enchanted treasure . . .

In a transparent silence sorrow hangs suspended . . .
Lost in an empty nest the wind is crying . . .
My wounded heart is filled with boundless longing
For the young bride through misty gates departing . . .

—Vytautas Matulionis

AGELESS LOVE

I saw the light in Grandpa's eyes as
    Grandma passed his chair
Though plump and wrinkled is her skin
    And hair of silver color
She still remains a maiden fair in Grandpa's
    Aging heart.
For fifty years they've been wed, through
    Good times and some bad
I've never heard a cross word pass
    From their lips of old
A bond of love they truly share
    They draw from one another
Their strength and courage come from
God
    Of one there is no higher
I saw the light in Grandpa's eyes
    As he held my Grandma's hand
And said, "I love you dearest," and
    Kissed it one last time.

—Dorothy Perrin

HIGH TIDE

I am the ocean, he is the toy,
I am a woman, he is a boy.

He casts his line,
He kisses my lips.
He sails my body with finger tips,
Bringing me ripples of joy.

Finally, he takes the plunge.
Inside me he swims,
Making slow waves that move in and out
of me again and again.

I feel the tide about to roll in
it gets higher and higher,
Creating a feeling so intense,
My mind becomes dense.

The tide has rushed in and now is over,
He quickly gets up and runs under cover.
Leaving me only a remembrance,
Of his excellence.

—Stacie R. Berrie

CONSOLATIONS

There is little I can say
    And probably little I can do
But I would like to have you know
    That my thoughts go out to you.

When one has this kind of loss
    They are saddened in their heart
And the ones who love you most
    Would some way like to do their part.

Even tho we seem so weak
    And we seem to find no way
To supply that vacant spot
    For things that we can say.

In my heart there's a desire
    To some way reveal to you
That my acts can somehow show
    I would like to something do.

I can only strive to say
    That somehow I'll have a part
In bringing sunshine in your life
    And some comfort to your heart.

—Edgar Wyatt

REMEMBER THE CHILD

Remember the child who did nothing wrong
only guilty in society's eye, and her own,
by association
Remember the child who smiled only
moments before, and then smiled no more
It's time to tell her to put down her shame
It's time to tell her she shares no blame
She's played the martyr much too long
It's time to tell her to let the pain go
Remember the child, and then let her
grow
If she cries a little in the night
If all the memories rise up inside her,
and she gives life to them
Forgive her,
and help her let them go

And the Lord set a mark upon Cain . . . .

　　　　—Lisa A. Butcher

CONFUSION

Why do I hate her so much?
　　Why couldn't she give me a chance?
She takes so much and gives nothing
Always afraid to give a second glance
I hate her for being different
From anyone I've ever met
There are times I need to tell her
That she's someone I'd love to forget

Then comes a time when she changes
And every word is a joyful surprise
And I'm amazed how much I care
When I see her through new receptive eyes.
There are times she is my best friend
While at others she's only a stranger
And despite some foolish efforts
There's still no way to change her

All I know is how very simple
My life could turn out to be
If I could only be this person's friend,
　　If I could just love me.

　　　　—Christine Sheeran

SOLITUDE

People usually resent it,
　　With it — they can not cope;
　　They meet it in the darkness —
　　Depressed, angry, without hope.

'Solitude,' can be a true friend,
　　A tranquility, the mind requires;
　　A way to sort a problem through —
　　To find solutions, to sort your priors.

Sharing in some special moments —
　　Watching a wild deer, and her fawn.
　　How many times, you sat together —
　　Waiting, anxiously, for the dawn?

Being there to read a novel —
　　One, you have meant to read for years.
　　Laughing at your good thoughts —
　　Yet, sharing all your tears.

Helping you to write a poem,
　　Something, you never thought you could —
　　About a friend, who is always there —
　　Quiet, shy, mis-understood — 'Solitude.'

　　　　—Patricia Ann Shaw

FOR KEEPS

My parents were calling out for help, but not aloud.
　　They worked hard for their name, became too proud.
Too proud to take the time to listen.
Put back the "magic" and make their lives glisten.
They thought in time things would get better,
But instead they got worse and my pillow got wetter.
Wetter from crying myself to sleep,
Wishing He'd come back, this time for keeps.
If they would have just taken some time,
Things could have worked out and he would be mine.
Sometimes I feel so shut out of his life,
Maybe I cause him too much strife.
I'd never want to lose him for good.
So I guess if I try maybe I could,
I could accept how things are — for now,
But deep inside still hope they could change somehow.
And when and if they do, I'll still be here
And at night I could lay to rest my pain and fears.

　　　　—Marisa Rice

FOR ALL THE LOST CHILDREN . . . WAITING

What a confused child
　　that patiently waits with an open heart,
　　　　open arms and a happy face
Waiting for his parents' love
Waiting to show his love in return.

Slowly, surely — with love mounting to anger
　　wanting to show, once his parents part,
That he patiently waits — with an empty heart
　　　　　　To be noticed.

Such a disturbed child
　　that silently waits
With a broken heart and a sorrowed face
　　　　　　Searching . . .
For a little love and an open friendly, smiling face.

And an empty child
　　constantly waits
For a gentle hug, a kiss, a smile, or a warm embrace,
　　But most of all . . .
　　　　　　A place —
in this big, wide, lonely world.

　　　　—Margie Ussery

LITTLE CHILD OF DIVORCE
SHYLOAH

Dear little one if only you knew,
　　Just how much we thought about you
A small wonder planned and prepared for
　　A little child to worship and adore
A token of your parents' love
　　A gift from heaven, God above
A truth that divorce can't split apart,
　　A part of each other that can remain in our hearts
The best of us both we can continue to love
　　A part of each other we can be proud of
For you are the only one that enables me to see
　　Your father's eyes and bright smile,
That meant so much to me
　　Yes, we're just parents and guilty at times;
We forget how fragile the hearts and the minds
　　God bless the child that suffers our abuse
Please, help us to remember our own imperfect youth
　　Yes, I've felt the hurt and rejections
You have known, for I too had,
　　Imperfect parents, of my own! Love, Mom

　　　　—Doris R. Travers

IT WAS MEANT TO BE

I will love you always,
That's what you said to me.
You and I together,
It was meant to be.

Just you and me forever,
You said we'd never part.
But now you've gone and left me
With a broken heart.

We had something special,
A sweet harmony of life.
Now I live in torment,
My hours full of strife.

Tears reveal my love for you
When I hear our song.
My days are dark and lonely
As I wonder what went wrong.

I'll go through life recalling
What you said to me.
You and I together,
It was meant to be.

—Barbara M. Schaub

A BROTHER'S LOVE

Of all the loves given,
A brother's love makes
    life worth livin'!
Nothing is asked for in
    return,
It's the easiest love I've
    ever earned.

A brother is someone I
    can talk to,
He understands what I'm
    going through.
He seems to know the
    right things to say,
No matter if it's night or day.

I call upon him time
    after time,
To help me with problems
    that are rightfully mine.
He'll smile and say,
    "What can I do?"
There's nothing I wouldn't
    do for you.

I love him with all
    my heart,
And I knew from the
    very start,
When he lay there so
    tiny and small,
He'd be there whenever
    I call.

I'll cherish our friendship
    'til the end of time,
And thank the Lord for
    that brother of mine.
And when life for him
    seems hard to live,
I'll give to him the kind
    of love, only a sister
    can give.

—Mary Kramer

FOR GRANDFATHER

Your life was like the splash made
    from a large rock thrown into a pond —
Making a splash which all could see
And making enough out of your words and deeds
    that none who met you could easily forget you.

Your life ended calmly and with dignity
    as the small ripples slowly died away.

But we will not forget.

For that rock is still there
Lying in the bottom of the pond
    Just as the memory of you still lies within my mind.
And anytime I want I can lift it back out
    and throw it into the pond once again
To relive my memories of you,
And all that you meant to me and to all
    who were fortunate to have known you.

Written by David in memory of his maternal
Grandfather, Ralph O. Irish, Sr.
April 2, 1909 — November 13, 1989

—David S. Carter

GOOD-BYE OLD MAN

Good-bye Old Man
I have walked with you to the end; you have been so good to me
First and foremost you taught me to love God
You have shown me how to love and respect Nature
You were always there when I needed a friend
I could always talk to you when I needed advice
You have been with me when I was sick
You have been with me when I was sad
You have been with me when I was happy
Your hand was always outstretched when I needed help
Never did you use harsh words towards me
Even though you are gone now, you will always still be my friend
Because the good memories I have of you, I will never forget
As I walk this path called life
I sometimes wonder why it has to end like this
I want you to know that I will always respect and love you
Now you are gone and I must go on
The love I have for you will help me each step of the way
Good-bye Old Man; Good-bye Old Friend; Good-bye Dad
I Love you; from your Son

—Perry L. Garner, Jr

OLD MAN

Old Man, sitting all alone,
Wondering where the years have gone
The rocking chair creaks, he begins to weep

Now, in his mind he drifts in time
To a handsome young sailor, with a taste for flavor
To beautiful faces, far away places.

The old eyes clear, and he can really hear
A nervous young giggle, and a dark dangerous figure
All fit together.

A life of dreams filled with terrible extremes
There was no easy way, if you were to play. Life or death,
Love or hate, no time to debate.

At the time, it was the only way to live,
Taking everything that you pleased, nothing to give
Running for 40, hoping not to choose,
Knowing in your heart, if you won, you'd lose.

Old Man, sitting all alone,
Wondering where the years have gone
The rocking chair creaks, he begins to weep.

—Ranny Autry

WHAT USED TO BE ISN'T

The sky, dark as velvet, stretches across the barren
space we call the sky.

The earth, spinning like a top, across our lonely
universe, taking up the space of what we call the earth.

The water, flowing over rocks and holding treasures of
worth, taking up the space of what we call the water.

The hate, spreading war throughout like a plague on the
rampage, taking up the space of what we used to call love.

—Roger LaMarque

ECLIPSE

Dear Moon,
object of infinite beauty,
the clouds wanted to intrude
upon your silent conversation with a stranger,
your dance with a shadow.

Clouds obstructed our wish to stare at you in surprise, wonder,
mutual admiration,
and a rare chance to behold your mysterious, temporary shyness.

We learn from the drama you shared with us
how beautiful you are
as a lamp in a deep darkness, a solace to night wanderers.

You, and your Sister the Sun, represent two Candles,
Eternally burning, refusing to die.

Continue to light our way
in our all-too-short sojourn here on Earth.

Enhance our wayward dreams and visions;
remain a lighthouse for us in a troubled sea
and inspire us to calm the restless tides within ourselves!

—Roger D. Fox

AFRICA

Africa is a place I long to see, among all the animals I
would love to be.
I would love to go again, before it's too late, and see the
Elephants that are so great.
Poachers are killing them for their ivory tusks, many are
falling because of men's lust.
They want the ivory for the money they can earn, when in
the world will they ever learn?
Pretty soon the herds will be gone, and the way it's going
it won't be long.
They are killing the Rhino for his horn, why, oh why, were
these men born?
These men are wicked as they can be, and they are stealing
this beauty from you and me.
These magnificent animals are here to roam free, but how
much longer will that be?
I want to see the Giraffe with neck so tall, running across
the plains and never a fall.
I want to see them eating the leaves from the tall trees
never behind any locks and keys.
It isn't the same when they're in a Zoo, freedom is great you
know it too.
The Lion is King with mane so full, when he roars you give him
no bull.
He has his harem, you better not bother, cause cubs are there,
and he's the father.
In Africa, so far from home, these animals were made to roam.
Their magnificent size, their grace and beauty, were put in our
care, and it's our duty, to help them to survive, and try
to keep them all alive.
So take me to Africa, it would be a crime, if I couldn't see
these animals one more time, roaming free in their natural
state, one more time before it's too late.

—Margaret Bynum

PINES

Do pines whisper?
Sometimes.
Sometimes they roar.
But most stand silently
And weep brown needle tears
Into dark shadows round their feet.

—Gerald G. Raun

Sun
bright, hot
warming, fueling, cheering
day, life — night, death
cooling, resting, refreshing
cold, dark
Moon

—Kristine A. Hassebrock

RIVER'S REFLECTION

One day as by the river,
I was taking a little stroll,
I looked down in the water,
And my reflection I did behold.

The reflection was distorted,
And for a minute it questioned me,
Was this really me I was seeing,
Or someone else that I did see?

Then I stopped and realized,
A reflection of me it had to be,
For I was just seeing me,
In a way I was not used to seeing.

Maybe this is the way,
That other people do see me,
Not too clear, maybe distorted,
With their eyes is all they see.

Then I think and answer myself;
This is just the outer shell of me,
For what matters is the inner part,
Which only God can see.

—Matt E. Hunt

EARTH AND SUN

In the milky way
(Its axis wobbles anyway)
Third planet from the sun,
Earth moves,
Elliptically,
By orderly laws
We not yet understand
Completely.
A natural new ice age forms
blending
With greenhouse effect artificial.
Is this so noteworthy?
The third in line of nine,
Two-point-zero-seven-nine,
July 4 4:28 pm to 12:28 am July 5,
1994.
What will be done
When earth
Is furthest
From the sun?

—Eve Briggs Raymond

ABUNDANT LIFE: IN LOVE AND PEACE

Might-makes-Right must now be changed
to Love-makes-Right. How can it be?

The 'How' of this is as old as can be:
Man's oldest greeting: Sit down and eat,
we have what we have, stranger, "We greet
you as brother." Now add New Age feat:
"Abundance awaits!"

Full production assures us plenty for all,
on a fair-sharing basis: it resolves all hates!

All made it together: we share it together.
The economy of scarcity is no longer true.

Old mores are dead: True morals replace them.
Democracy now rules economy, too.

The question no longer: How much can you buy?
Our moral question: How much can you use?

Then it will ours be: in just equity:
Mankind all One in true Equality.

— Philip S. Hensel

MY LITTLE BUDDY

Though not always was I there,
My heart was with thee
For within my soul you lived,
My greatest joy was thee
You once said, "Always shall I be"
Your little buddy,
Now I must say, "So long,"
My little buddy.
For thy maker has called thee away
Bidding you adieu, my little buddy,
Is so hard to do
Though your soul wings its way to heaven
Thy heart is heavy and laden
For you were so young,
A tender loving lad of eleven with your
Dreams and hopes of tomorrow, of changing
The world's ways
But you were robbed of your chance
By a drunken man
So long, my little man.

— Trampas

THE GOLDEN SPIDER

Through the wall of bacteria
I danced with a maiden
'Twas the goddess of Venus
As I saw a silver laden

As I danced with her Venus
On to ruin she pondered
Still quoting I was a genius
As the door stole heaven asundered

The black magic death was all that trodded
Secrets she kept often begging
Someone said it was I that nodded
Secrets some more with female legging

Secretly hiding each golden spider
Climbing to the top rung of a silver ladder
Softly quoting "the gap is becoming wider"
If it wasn't for a golden spider I'd had her

"Venus," said she near her silver lattice
I didn't mean to truly disgust her
I thought to be with a girl named, Gladdis
I thought I was John who was called Sir.

— Allen Johnson

WOMANHOOD

It's quite a task for a young girl
To believe implicity that her blossoming woman-
hood
Will most certainly bring her wonderful beauty
With no remnant of the mark left by puberty

It's a quirk of Mother Nature
To sort of try our souls as we develop
Into maturity and nature knows no schemes
As Homo sapiens seem to bring,
To torment all the species on earth

And leave all sentimental beings
graveling in their death
Of complete understanding of the
sensible laws
By which all living things are controlled
on Earth

— Irene Miles

THE CRAZY LADY ON NEW YEAR'S DAY

It was my mother's smile that brought her walkin',
And then she did her lengthy talkin'.
Her family history she revealed,
And none of it from us concealed.

My sister's plane she was blockin'
With her long incessant talkin'.
Inside that window at the airport bay,
While we sat sleepily early New Year's Day.

White pants across the room
Reminded her of childhood gloom.
Cause her faint mom lay on the floor,
White shoes and pants she does deplore.

Red shoes she wore that very day
To prove her point in her own way.
Her oily hair and the clothes she had
Were enough to make her story sad.

Her sister left along with mine.
We turned and listening did decline.
As she predicted the coming year
To be filled with bounteous cheer.

— Eric Slane

LITTLE BOY

Come here Little Boy and tell me your dreams,
You are so young, your heart is so free,
Only a child no older than ten,
Tell me my son, when do dreams begin?

You tell me of rockets and mighty space ships,
Of ice cream and castles made of chocolate chips.
These are your dreams for great happiness,
So young and so free, your dreams shall be blessed.

Now you're a young man of twenty and one,
You've come a long way since your dreams first begun.
You dream of great love and future conquests
And until you have won, your heart shall not rest.

The years have gone by so very fast
Your first dreams of life have long since past.
Have you lived well, have your dreams been blessed?
Is it true that your heart is at rest?

Though you are old there is something on your mind
Tomorrow and tomorrow until the end of time
Now you're an old man of eighty and ten,
Tell me my friend, when do dreams end?

— Suzanne C. Bowman

MORNING FLOWER

In a sea of wild flowers, among rolling country hills,
Only one has soft, white, silky petals, reaching
       skyward to the morning sun,
A slender stem arching gracefully in the gentle
       Springtime breeze,
Light fresh fragrance, coloring the senses with a smile,
You are the Morning Flower . . .

Peaceful and tranquil, like the early morning sea,
Wearing a comforting smile, warm as the sun,
Projecting a soft sensitive inner beauty,
So often overlooked in this fast competitive world,
Ahh . . . To touch so tender a soul . . .

You have yet to touch the earth and dine at nature's table,
Catch a moonbeam, watch a velvet starlit sky,
And sail upon a river of moonlight, listening to the wild
       call softly your name,
Loving and caring, with beautiful eyes open wide,
You are the Morning Flower . . .

       —Brian W. Feldon

I AM ONLY ONE MAN

A tree fell today in a rain forest where it once grew,
but I am only one man what can I do?
A child died today beaten black and blue,
but I am only one man what can I do?
I walked the beach today and oil stuck to my shoe,
but I am only one man what can I do?
A man froze today a home he never knew,
but I am only one man what can I do?
A crime occured today and drugs were the clue,
but I am only one man what can I do?
Oil prices rose today the cost of living did too,
but I am only one man what can I do?
The lay offs came today our jobs they are through,
but I am only one man what can I do?
A flag burned today mighty and strong it once flew,
but I am only one man what can I do?
A disease spread today of which survivors have been few,
but I am only one man what can I do?
Someone cared today there's hope for me and you,
now I'm not just one man now we are two.

       —Christopher B. Artrip

I ONCE WAS A MOUNTAIN, NOW ONLY A CREEK

What a day Dad, isn't it great?
Sunshine, grass, Vivaldi, birds.
   No.
Cancer, pain, my aching pride,
I can barely move my whole left side.

   But Dad, what about the things you have?
Children, money, music, love.
   No.
Man loses all when he becomes weak,
I once was a mountain, now only a creek.

   But Dad, what about your lessons?
Work, work, respect, save.
   No.
I have nothing more to teach,
But try and take what I could not reach.

   Teach me, Dad, how to be the best.
Work, work, respect, save?
   No.
All you need son, I will say,
Is work a little, but pray, pray, pray.

       —Mario Manna

QUESTIONS AND ANSWERS

Wise men ask, "What is the meaning
of life?"

I've known since the first quiet
  movement deep inside.

I've seen him run in my garden
  chasing butterflies.

I've heard his pure laughter pealing
  in the sunlight.

I've smelt his sweet warm smell.

I've felt his soft skin touching
  mine.

Oh yes, wise men may ponder,

But I know, and I love him,

       —Constance Wall

True meanings in times such as these,
Like rings that show the age of trees;
Lies are layered deep.

Leaves are born again anew,
And the children put their trust in you
While betrayal surfaces everywhere.

To drink the sunshine a nourishment in
Need, a child's mind for us to feed;
Which way will you lead them.

They cast a shadow for shade to rest,
To look in a child and see their best;
Least we besiege them.

Roots grow and anchor deep,
A child's family into them will seep
A foundation to build on.

In every living thing you'll see a
Responsibility to each breed;
And such is the labor of love.

Inspiration:
A child's trust and love is unconditional; never
before in my life have I had something so
constant and pure.

       —Dwayne A. Susak

A POPPY THRUST THROUGH CINDERS

He walked in moonless night,
walked wounded
  among the walnut trees —
bandaged with scars old, red and hard.

The mighty echo to the pulse of fury
  crouched in his veins.

Burning memory veered
  from flames dark winds
to trace peaceful ripples
of golden carp in lotus pools
and streams of watercress
till from over far away waters
the scorched cry of agony
  clogged his ears.

Pushing through reckless jungle depth
fear and fire penetrated skin and lungs.

Bird and leaf breathed fire
and there one poppy, flaming red,
thrust through cinders, turned from men
to face tomorrow's sun and heaven.

       —Emma Crobaugh

TO THE CINEMA . . .

This moment lost in shadow
Let us never illumine . . .

This dim, enraptured hour
Let us forever savor . . .

In this unutterable darkness
The ineluctable belongs to us . . .

Translucent as a dream.

—edward seymour

AT THIS POINT IN TIME

Cotton candy at the county fair
Like shining spun glass
From a long ago time
Only sugar and air
Not much else there
Just a faded valentine
Hope that you are fine
At this point in time

As the years go by
Something's wrong in the sky
The sun isn't warm
It's much too bright
Sky's too dark
Not a sliver of light
The breeze is too breezy
Nothing comes easy
But it might, it might
Got some aches, a little pain
Can't complain, we need the rain
Sunset isn't far away
It's waiting down the line
Hope that you are fine
At this point in time

—Robert Lauritzen

THE FUTURE

Destinations . . .
                What are destinies?
I have no idea, maybe they
are promises not meant to
be kept. Maybe they are a
secret no one has told, so
nobody knows. Most probably the
person who knows this secret
doesn't really know himself.
        Why should I dwell on
this question? I have my whole
life to think about, I guess
I'll catch a star or paint
the clouds a simple color . . .
        Red
Maybe I'll just lay around
and let life slip by me silently.
Life's confusing. It's like a maze
it's so near, but yet so far
away. I've decided what to
do. Yes, that's it, I'll just wait
and see what comes next
when I'm more experienced in
this field. For life's a surprise
and the future is the key to the
past, anyways, why should
I look to the future for
comfort, when the present is
right here.

—Carrie Rendon

IF DREAMS CAME TRUE . . . .

Then the child who cannot walk, would be able to run,
    The man who is blind, would see the sun.
The man laying cold in the streets so alone and still,
Would find a bed with warmth and friendly goodwill.
The hungry child that cries in the night,
Will be comforted of their saddened fright.
Then the one who walks the street,
Would have a friend, of all they meet.
The fear of war, would be never more,
And no young man, would have to go off to war.
Each nation would lead their people, in friendship and peace,
No more prejudice would they teach.
The love of God and family, would be all we'd strive for,
And if dreams came true, we would be happy for evermore.

—Sherry Beasley

NO ONE STANDS ALONE

Have you ever done or said anything which you regretted?
    Knowing that somehow other lives may have been affected.
You may have said that swear word,
Knowing that other people may have heard.
You try so hard to do your very best,
Even though life's every day trials are put to the test.
You try to make nice impressions for those you meet every day,
Hoping to show them respect and kindness, in the words you say.
All eyes are upon every move you make,
So watch what you do for Heaven's sake.
Sometimes we get upset, and let our feelings and emotions
Get the best of us,
When we should calm down and look to those we trust.
When we talk out our frustrations and thoughts to those who
Show they care,
In turn we can also help them in the crosses they bear.
A friend is a person who is a special gift from God,
They are there to help you in the paths that you must trod.
A friend is there to listen, and give an encouraging word,
Giving a person courage to go on forward.
So you see, wherever you go, no matter what you say or do,
Your life will have an affect upon those around you.

—Phyllis Ann Blaize

FADING GLORY

As I look at the sunset of a life passing by,
    I wonder if their share of happiness, they will enjoy,
            before they die.
When I read about the worldly and the famous,
            with all their glory,
Was it worth it, in their days, or for them a sad story.

That brought an unending craze, to go on to beat all others.
In their search for happiness, thinking that would only come,
            if they were the best
What makes people try so hard to reach,
What they think is the top,
Living each day with worry, because they dare not stop.

To them it would be defeat, which they cannot accept.
When they don't get as much, as they really expect,
And would rather die, than see others pass them by.
How long does Glory last, you can't be the best forever.

Someone else comes along and steals your thunder,
The course of History changes, and you begin to wonder,
Why do people forget and your glory comes to an end?
Well, when and if you find the answers,
Please tell me why, my Friend!

—Ruby M. Olson

THE JOURNEY

Life is so short, it flies by so fast.
From the day you were born it becomes a part of your past.

For life is a journey we all must walk through,
To get to the Promised Land where life is as new.

A place God has prepared for us in the sky,
no more tears, no more goodbyes.

So when your journey is over and God takes your hand,
You will have known the struggle was worth it when
    you reach the Promised Land.

—**Mary Joy S. Reed**

COLD DARK SHADOW OF THE DREAMER

Softly the wind blew cold breeze through my lonely worried
    heart as though there's no life existing.
Hurting, suffering and pain filled my eyes with tears.
At times I feel as though I'm walking against the sky
Sprinkling Love-dust with a caress in my heart . . .
I remember the time when the Rose grew with incense of
    yester-year
My face put up a smile knowing that the sun of life would
    shine against the Rose to give meaning.
And the summer rain came, slowly I felt the hardship of love
    turning against the sunset of tomorrow . . .
But as I smelt the breath of the tomb of cold dark shadow of
    the dreamer;
Time began to tell the face of beauty "turn aside" —
    as I stood in silence.
I could feel the coldness charring my soul deep to burn
    tomorrow aside;
For the Rose slowly has withered against my heart . . .
No more my eyes will smile
Only with glassy eyes I walk across the pale moon of the
    winter —.
As I lay beneath the cold dark shadow of the dreamer.

—**Archie Washburne**

ETERNAL LIFE

If I must die, then death I'll see, I'll walk the path,
no one but me.

No helping hand, will kindly reach, to grasp this one,
that does beseech.

So born alone, alone I'll die, upon my lips,
shall ring no cry.

No sound will echo, in the night, nor surface,
in the dawn's first light.

It shall not echo, nor rebound, shall not be heard,
yet I'll be found.

I, who was lost in shadows deep, and seemingly,
in endless sleep.

I shall step forth, with eager hand, and reach for life,
and breath again.

And when that breath, with mine shall merge, then I shall feel
a glorious surge.

Death was defeated, by God's son, I claim no praise,
although I've won.

The battle for my soul was fought, and Satan failed,
put down for naught.

Now I shall live, in peace sublime, eternal life,
is surely mine.

—**Mary Beth Bennett**

The egg hatches.
You step through the shattered
pieces of your dreams
towards the warmth of the sun.

A stream rushes by.
The water, sequined by
sunlight beckons you to its shore.
Its name, friendship.

You drink the life sustaining
liquid thirstily, knowing
how parched you are.
Renewal.

—**Laurene Sierles**

THE PIONEER

"The Lord was not in the wind . . . earthquake . . .
Fire. . ." Then came "A still small voice."
I Kings 19: 11-12

Hard and honest work
Year after year
Through sun and snow —
The pioneer!

Not as a gift,
Not through fear,
But in spirit and enthusiasm —
The pioneer!

Mountains and plains
All held dear
With river and forest —
The pioneer!

No titles, no grants,
But joy and tear,
All to be earned —
The pioneer!

Faith in God's voice
For all to hear,
For country, mankind, freedom —
The pioneer!

—**Richard A. Senser**

GREAT TREOW

I
To delve from fertile earth
A pulse of power
That yet the precious grace of youth
Can but compliment,
II
And give it thus
To arbor kin
Long before my Warwick stem
Sought your ample shade;
III
Now to send your ever reaching reach,
That touch my inner quick,
Its call to swing
Searching 'round the sun
IV
For tones and shades
Afloat amidst the dust
To fill the sinkholes
Of my soul,
V
Will,
Down the run of time,
Bring me home again
To be then more than what I was.

—**W. R. Stubbs**

LOVER'S RAGE

Why is it in a lover's rage,
With words of jealousy we build a cage
And place our sweethearts deep within,
With selfish hearts we then condemn.

With degrading words we form our chains,
With distrusting actions we tighten reins
We force them then, to fit our mold,
Where they must act only as told.

History tells us all, you see,
That a captive will always struggle free,
If not by actions of his own,
With help from a friend unknown.

Instead of acting in a lover's rage
We must use praising words to form a stage,
And place our lovers there, you see,
Only then can they be free,
Only then can love be.

—Richard S. McKenzie

SUMMER SHOWERS

On a lonely summer evening
with the fragrant showers her
solitary occupation, she rocked
the old porch swing. the faint
creak of its chains the only mark
of time in the cloud encased darkness
gone unnoticed by the silent figure.
her eyes focused on the black leaves
of the unending wall of elderly trees
seeing nothing other than what
her imagination rolled across
the blank screen before her.
the cool fingers of the breeze
running through her long wet hair
and plucking at the damp calico
of her skirt welcomed with the rain
as a reprieve from the days' simmering heat.
she closed her eyes to enjoy the change,
her memory recalled tears lost with the
soothing solitary summer storm.

—Margaret M. Brown

FOREVER WITH ME

Yesterday our eyes met,
For just a little while.
I'm a woman now, can't you see
And not a little child.

I never knew what heart-ache was
Until you were no longer there,
I wish I wasn't so hasty
To throw away those years.

I was only seeking
For just a little more.
I can't take all the blame you see,
I was merely immature.

My lesson I have learned
Through lots of lonely years.
Wishing you had stayed around
Instead of going ahead.

Someone new is in my life
But it can never be the same.
You are forever in my thoughts and dreams,
Time and time again.

—Cynthia Malone

RIDDLE

New and fresh as an infant's first cry,
as ancient as time itself;
Timeless, moments spent between lovers,
longer than the eternal reign of the gods . . .

Free to roam as is the wind,
more binding than any fetter of steel;
Lighter than a summer shower,
with the weight of death's skeletal hands . . .

The pristine wildness of glacial expanse
that is tainted with dark secrets;
Booming thunder, louder than silence,
soundless as the tred of the forest dwellers . . .

Gentler than liquid sunlight dancing with clouds,
hauntingly alluring and deadly—a siren's call;
All the caring and tenderness of a mother's embrace,
more cruel and harsh than the Northern wastes . . .

What is truer than life itself,
that blinds the heart forever?

—J. R. Schroeder

PORTRAIT OF "MARIE"

Long . . . long long ago . . . and faraway
I met a girl
Deep . . . deep in the greens of summer grass
She was my world
"Marie . . . shadows wait at the edge of the day
Chere' . . . still I worship your laughter and pain
In this silver frame"
Eyes of sparkling hues . . . colors so rare
Fair shades of blue
Hair . . . like honey dew at harvest time
Image of you
Window shades pulled down at dusk of day
Make me forget what hour or even what day
We kissed goodbye
The stars we shared, so bright, are high in the sky
A voice inside my head keeps asking me why
you had to leave . . . so soon
"Marie, shadows wait at the edge of the day
Chere' . . . still I worship your laughter and pain
In my portrait . . . "Marie"

—Wesley Penn

WHEN STRANGERS MEET

He walks alone, day in, day out,
nothing in the world to talk about.
He sings the same old song; memorizes each word,
he cannot go wrong.
He sits at the same tree,
right next to me.
We have never even met,
but soon we will I bet.
He picked a flower and handed it to me.
So now he lets his thoughts go free.
We are one now, we think the same;
The world at our hands, no one to blame.
His words so beautiful, they touch my heart.
We now are together, never to part.
He no longer walks alone, day in, day out.
Oh! We have a lot to talk about.
We sing together his wonderful song,
I memorized each word, we just cannot go wrong.
Yes, we still sit at the same old tree, him, me,
and our little baby.

—Bonnie S. Foster

PHOTOS ON THE WALL

Look here,
        photos on the wall,
        faces of those we love.
Pages of phases
        of our lives.
Ticking off the years,
        our smiles, our tears,
        our pain, our joy
        painted on film.
The record of our life,
        forever stamped.
Some we have lost along our way,
        only memories in our minds.
This tells the story,
        others will know
        I was here.
When I am only a photograph,
        and they say . . .
        Look here,
        photos on the wall.

—Dayna Haynes

REFLECTION IN THE ROSE GARDEN

The afternoon wanes into evening and all is quiet.
I stop and reflect on the past years of my life.
All is quiet now.
Do the ghosts we carry as extra baggage still stir?
Do the lessons learned carry any weight with me?
I no longer hurry through the rose garden
I have learned to stop and catch the scent
of the wondrous roses I've planted.
Are you listening to my words?
Do you stop now and then and reflect too?
Or have the years shut your heart to the memory
Of children playing and laughing together?
We only have a brief moment here
We will never have enough time
To do the things we want to
To mend the hearts we've broken
To care enough, to stop, to love.
Somehow I wonder if we aren't all just a little selfish.
Happy anniversary, where-ever you are.
Twenty-four years today, a life time to remember.

—Lauralee Williams

IF I COULD KNOW

Would you be disappointed in me
If I asked you to hold me in your arms?
Would you, if I did, think less of me?
That your kindness and sincerity
leave feelings I had feared lost to me.
Would my feelings scare you away?

That I see you as a man, both strong and gentle;
Strength to make love to me as a woman,
Yet gentleness to allow me to remain a lady.
Would you think me less than a lady,
if you knew my true thoughts of you?

I've gone to sleep nights and dreamed of you,
of how sweet your kisses would feel,
and wondered if you could feel the same for me?
If I could know and not have to face
your disappointment, or feel you think less of me,
or be afraid of scaring you away,

If I could know you would take me,
I could tell you, I would love to be yours.

—Cheryl Deering

WHEN ROSES DIE

When roses die, they say goodbye
in a friendly sort of way
And drop their petals one by one
all through the day

They sometimes start to cry
before they pass away
But the good thing about it is
a new bud will come up again
to stay

      and stay

          and stay
—Tatiana Louise Gelardi, age 10

LIFE'S CIRCLE

Bitter sweet, fluffy white and blue.
Forgotten tears, forming a new you.

Through your shutter, catch me if you can.
The rising sun, is all that I am.

I was before, but you did not see.
That was my secret, yet you hold the key.

I shall be again, but that's another year.
You'll know me then, and there shall be
    no fear.

Bitter sweet, fluffy white and blue.
Forgotten tears, forming a new you.

—Marian M. Denton

TOTAL MAN AND LOVE

A Total Man came to call, draping me
with Tender Love, as delicate as
Gossamer Lace.
So beautiful was his gift to me,
I could not speak . . .
Just Weep.

Love made with exquisite tenderness.
"Self, quick Hide! He will know
you, with his tender exquisite
Love."

Only a Total Man would know
to bring the delicate treasure of
Tender Love to Me.

—Sue A. Bunting

MY FANTASY

I'm laying in a field of green
under a moonlit starry sky
On a nice big warm blanket
With only you by my side.

The radio is on
playing all our soft mellow tunes
the sky is so clear
You can almost touch the moon

As we look softly into one another's eyes
and we hold each other tight
We don't have to say one word
We just know it's right

It just feels too good to be true
lying here next to you
then I awaken all alone
My Fantasy is through.

—Sandra Lee Schoaf

SPECIAL LITTLE ONE

When I was little
I hummed a song.
My own special little song.
It was of happy times,
and special things,
That only I knew of.
Then I whistled a merry tune,
Its thoughts through out my head.
Of wonderment and questions full,
I'm sure were only mine.
I've grown now,
Yet I still sing,
A song deep within my heart.
For now I sing out,
loud and proud,
To my special little one!

—Kimber Kelly

TRIBUTE TO MOM

My mom is a jewel,
The rarest of the rare.
Whenever I've needed her,
She's always been there.

She's an old-fashioned mom
Filled with compassion and love,
The kind that only comes
From the good Lord above.

Her vision and hearing are impaired,
Her body frail and weak,
Her voice, at times, so soft
We strain to hear her speak.

Now ninety two, an invalid,
From her bed she cannot rise,
But she's still the sweetest mom
In her eight children's eyes.

She's loved and cared for
Throughout the day and night,
We know she'd do the same for us
If her condition had been our plight.

—Anita R. Brinkley

TEAMWORK

It has been a long time since
A rocking chair and I
Have joined our homey features
To calm a baby's cry.

The comfort of this rocking chair
The rhythm of its creak
Is just what she had needed as
She lay by Grandpa's cheek.

An arching back, the little fists
The kicking of the feet
Has been replaced by open hands
And pats upon the seat.

The voice that just a time ago
Was so distressed and shrill
Is quiet now, the throat relaxed
The vocal cords are still.

The breathing's soft and regular
All fears have passed her by
Our team has had a wondrous time
This rocking chair and I.

—Ralph G. Johnston

LOLLIPOPS AND BUBBLE GUM.

When the children are rowdy, and your head's in a spin,
And your son dashes in, with a disarming grin,
And a, "Hey, Mom, Can we go to the corner store?"
You give your consent, not remembering what happened before.

You relax, with a sigh, thankful for this short break,
But, not for long, for you see your mistake.
Though you resign yourself, at the sight of happiness come
To those small faces, stuck up with lollipops and bubble gum.

You sigh when you think of the look of joy
On the faces of that small girl and boy.
You know that it can't be all bad,
Messy, though it is, when it makes them so glad.

And you're certain that, as sure as another day comes,
There'll be more lollipops and bubble gum.
But, you know as you wipe the door knob that clings,
That you'd never ever try to change these things.

—Kay Houskeeper

MY BLESSINGS

A little golden haired doll comes running through my door,
Lifts up her arms, and says "Upoo me Gamma!"
My heart wants to melt.
I look down at the chubby dark-haired tyke standing
Shyly by my side, looking back with his big blue eyes
That glisten when I pick him up, too. My mind says,
"Listen! Feel! Remember! You won't have them like this
For very long. Thank you Lord, for these blessings."
Next the little one with the wide smile crawls and squirms
Her way into my heart. Thank you also for babies.
The tall almost-teenager, with the so beautiful face,
Is here with a quick hug. "Hi Gram. Need anything done?"
An embarrassed 7-year-old gives a fast squeeze around my waist
When no one is watching (boys that age don't get 'mushy').
Then a whirlwind towhead hollers "Hi Gramma!" on his way
Through the house on the run.
For these, and the husky-voiced dark eyed girl we can't see
Very often, and the 6-year-old charmer and her baby sisters
Who live so far away in Wyoming:
I'm listening, I feel, and I will remember.

—B.J. Sutton

MOMMY'S LITTLE ANGEL

As I watch you while you sleep
Remembering the days of past
Treasuring the memories I'll always keep
Beautiful thoughts of you, that will always last.

I remember the moment they said "It's a Girl"
How sheer joy filled my heart
You changed my life, you changed my world
And of my life you will always be part.

As I hold you in my arms
Time seems to stand still, really only to begin
You're so young, but have such magic and charms
Some would say, you are a magician.

Your eyes dance with happiness
You have so much to see and to learn
And you'll be grown all to soon, I must confess
As the hands on the clock of time, slowly turn.

You give such joy to all when you smile
Your eyes so bright, beautiful and blue
They seem to dance and laugh with such grace and style
And I hope you always remember my angel, mommy loves you.

—Wanda Pierce

MY SON, TING ZHANG

You looked so proud standing there
So small and frail before the tanks
That seemed to come from nowhere.

Silently you stood, school sack in hand
Taking small baby steps from side to side
The first "Tank Waltz" ever seen in our land

There you stood not saying a word that anyone could hear
But the whole world was watching the lad that showed no fear
(Where were you on your way to that day?)

But they caught you in the dormitory
Pumped bullets into your curious brain
And they thought this was the end of your story

My son, Ting Zhang, you're the unsung hero
In all of freedom's land.

Yet who shall remember the name of the lad in the square
Who had been so brave to just take his stand there.

        —Omar J. Calleja

AN UGLY NAME FOR A BEAUTIFUL PERSON

Mongolism — Special
The only word to describe — my sister
Always trying to help, never hurting anyone
Trapped — that's her
In our society; a world so cruel
Her emotions, so fragile, like a piece of broken glass
Treating her so differently cause she's not like anyone else
Sad — that's me
Hearing how some speak of her — In general, so dumb
Not her, my sister. In my eyes, she's better
The only one who really cares about people as an individual
The only one I know who'd walk up to a stranger just to say Hi
Unfair — that's her, cause she deserves more
In my eyes, she's a gift, teaching us how to act and treat
    people the right way
Sorry — not me
A blessing more like it
She was put here to bring this world closer together
Special — that's definitely her
My sister, Renee

        —Dawn Vrchota

ALWAYS LOVED

Son you will never know the grief we have been through.
But we give thanks to God these things are kept from you.
We feel at times we can not bear.
At times it seems unfair.
But these are trials God has given us.
And we must not despair.
He knows what's best for His elect
For this is surely true
You were such a humble Christian Boy
That's why he called for you
The Holy Ghost revealed to you the words you had to say
He gave you strength to make things right, before that final day
You gave our family so much love
Your laughter was always there
But thanks to God you sing hymns with Him
And that's always been my prayer
The tears still flow and always will
But you're safe in God's own arms
And son your loving memory will always linger on

**This I made up for my son who passed away
April 4th 1988.**
        —Jean Havens

LITTLE SISTER

I have a little sister
in second grade you see
Now everybody says
She resembles me.

Now I don't see it
And neither does she
But every time I look at her
I think of me.

        —Rosalie R. May

GABE

Gabe is an angel
Sent from heaven above
He has filled so many hearts
With joy and with love.

He is so special
Each and every day
A bundle of precious memories
That time can't take away.

His bright blue eyes
His precious smile
It's very plain to see
Only God could make such as he
To be loved by you and me.

Dedicated to "Gabriel Martin Farmer"
        —Anita Gale Moore

WORLD PEACE

How can we have world peace
   When neighbors and relatives
   Are fighting.
Peace starts with each and
   Every individual.
Forgiveness, loving, sharing
   And compassion, must start
   With you
How often do you hear and
   See someone arguing over
   Children running on the grass
The grass will grow, but anger
   Can last for years.
Don't be jealous of worldly
   Goods, be happy with what
   You have.
Love is the only answer.

        —Angeline R. Poczebut

THROUGH THE EYES OF A CHILD

With wonder the child looks
With wonder the child asks
With wonder and awe
The answer receives

If only the answerer
Matched in simplicity
The mind of the child
And were true

If only the answerer
Could tap the divine
Storehouse of knowledge
And answer in truth

Then would the child
Nurtured in truth
Find here on earth
The kingdom

        —Solveig Clark

GOD'S PROMISE

I talk to God in the morning,
    He walks with me all the day.
He carries me over my mountains,
    He is there by my side all the way.

God tells me how Jesus died on the cross,
    So that I could forever be free.
My salvation is there for the taking,
    With my Saviour each day I shall be.

Through life with its sorrow and heartaches,
    We all have to walk our own road.
But Jesus will be there to guide us on,
    And will always lighten our load.

There will be no more heartaches when
this life is o'er.
    If we walk all the way with God's Son.
We have laid up our treasures in heaven,
    And happy we'll be — everyone.

      —Maxine Dickason

TINY DROPS OF RAIN

I watched the tiny drops of rain
Cascading down the window pane
To gather in a puddle on the sill.

The puddle grew in mass
Until finally at last,
It fell again in droplets from the sill.

The droplets fell on thirsty leaves
To nourish and fulfill the needs
of the roses and the flowers there below.

Suddenly, I realized
that here before my very eyes,
Man's purpose in this life was being revealed.

In love we must unite my friends,
In peace go forth unto all men,
Be just and true in all things we do.

Then like those tiny drops of rain
Cascading down the window pane,
We'll nourish and promote life's beauty, too.

      —Roy D. Matthews

THE GOOD TIMES

I think the good times came and went
While I looked the other way.
I kept thinking that tomorrow,
It would bring a better day.

Roses bloomed in wild profusion.
Children played at my feet.
There were sounds of joy and laughter
From the voices young and sweet.

Now the house is cold and silent.
Emptiness fills every hall.
Now, I stop to smell the roses
Scantily blooming, weak and small.

Like me, they've passed their days of glory.
Old and gnarled, they tarry there —
Waiting for the cold of winter
That will leave them stripped and bare.

Have I reached my destination?
Is this all there is for me?
Yes, the good times came, but in my hurry
I was just too blind to see . . .

      —Nellie Fry

SAN FRANCISCO EARTHQUAKE — 1989

With the sudden fury of a swooping hawk
    Striking his defenseless prey,
Earth's crust convulses with a shearing force
Shattering castles man builds along with all his dreams.
Broken bodies, trapped and crushed
Lay beneath the fallen beams;
Water lines rupture, power lines are down,
Gas lines leak, sparks abound;
Fires rage everywhere, out of control
On powerless humans, they take great toll;
Then, an eerie silence in the blackness of the night,
All communication gone awry;
There is much fright;
There is looting and stealing, mugging at night.
Exhilaration is rampant when all is right.
Lord, I am so helpless,
I am struck with fear;
Son, I hear you,
I Am Here.

      —Dr. Anthony Alba, M.D.

WHAT IS LIFE?

It is time for now—
Life is a fleeting second in the existence of reality
it is the same for a new baby
an unborn child—an old man
Life is here
    Leaving us every day
        With every breath we take
Life is the same for us all
man or animal
Life is a passing us by all the same
it has no prejudices of people
places or time—
    it is the same in this world
    and others
    it is the same whether we
waste not a second
    or if we sleep the day away—
Life is constant—
    Death is the thief
it takes us when we least
expect it—

      —Lamesa O. Whitson

WOULD I?

If you came to me today,
    And asked me to unbuckle your sandals,
Could I?
If you asked me to slip them off
    To comfort your feet,
Could I?
If you asked me to place my own in them,
And walk the path you chose,
Could I?
Or would I just shake my head,
Tears running down my cheeks?

You are so caring, so loving, and trusting,
Whereas I have a heavy heart;
Weighted down by petty fears.
How do I open my heart — let you in,
So you may fill my soul and take my fears away?

I am scared and frightened,
Unworthy to follow.
So, if you placed your sandals before me,
Oh Lord Jesus — Would I?

      —J.P. Wiegand

A MOTHER'S VOW

So you're finally one, it's hard to believe!
I thought I would sing and shout with relief,
But I can't help but wonder as days go by,
How much I have missed in time's hasty flight.

Will I always remember your tiny caress
Wrapped 'round my thumb as I laid you to rest?
The first time you hugged me or laughed or smiled?
Your first words or steps taken toward your first mile?

Yes I will always remember these things,
Kept in my heart when my memory takes wing.
How could I forget the one that I bore,
Nurtured and loved and grew to adore?

So no matter what the future may hold,
One day you'll leave, but I'll be so bold
As to say without doubt that I'll never forget
That sweet little baby I held to my chest.

—Laura Mohr

BIG BROTHERS

One of the best things a boy could have
    When I was just a lad,
Was a big brother who understood
    And whose friendship would make you glad!

For your big brother would look after you
    And help you at any time —
He'd keep your secrets and help with your chores,
    And slip you a nickle or dime.

He understood what your life was like
    For he had been young like you —
He knew how things worked and what things meant,
    And which things were tried and true!

He taught you to run and climb and fish,
    And how to use a knife —
For he cared about you, and wanted to see
    That you got a good start in life.

So three cheers for him who taught you to swim
    And helped you along life's road —
For all that he did, and all that he was,
    He helped you to carry your load!

—Joe McCoy

ON MOTHER'S DAY

One is told to count his blessings, to name them
    one by one.
        To try to pick the best of them, does not amount
        to fun.

I choose my God, my church, my home,
    And all the friends that I have known.

My children also top the list, for what would I do
    without,
        The many blessings I've received from them,
        without a single pout.

They have brought me love and laughter, tears and joy,
    Memories to treasure, with each girl and boy.

Worries come and worries go, which only goes to show,
    Children make the world go round,
        And no where could better ones be found.

I count my blessings day by day,
    And truly I must say,

I am so very lucky to a mother be,
    Of so many children who mean the world to me.

—Lucille Unruh

A CHILD'S INNOCENT EYES

Did you ever watch a child at play,
    And admire the things he tries?
Did you see the glow of accomplishment?
Seen in a child's innocent eyes.

And sometimes when he falters,
And even stands and cries
He's just looking for another way
With a child's innocent eyes.

So, when he comes to you for help,
Don't waste his time with lies
He just might see right through you,
With a child's innocent eyes.

So, help him do the things that are right
To grow up strong and wise
So, some day he can look with pride,
In his own child's innocent eyes.

—Larry G. Mendenhall

TO YOU MY CHILDREN

You know I love you when I say,
    Pick up your toys and put them away,
Eat your food until it is gone,
I want you to grow up big and strong.

Don't think I am being mean to you,
When you are punished for things you do.
I only care about your future,
Don't want no bruises, bumps, or sutures.

I will always be in your lives,
Even when you become husbands and wives.
I cherish each one of you in every way,
So always remember these words I say.

I try real hard to be a good mother,
To keep you from fighting with each other.
To give you the love I never had,
To always respect me and your dad.

If ever you need me, I'll be there.
No matter the problem I'll always care.
We're a family we'll stick together.
I'll love you always and forever.

—Coral Lee Earl

BRIDGING THE MILES

Close your eyes and think of me.
    Asking why? To wonder how it would be.
    Thoughts of us within your smile,
As you pause to dream for a while.

    If only you could feel my heart glow,
To fully understand how I miss you so.
    Wishing to hold you, I really do,
Tears from my heart weep for you.

    Close your eyes and think of me.
Is it real? Can it be?
    Close your eyes and believe it's true,
We're hard to explain, me and you.
    Yet so simple, I Love You.

    Far is the distance between us now,
Directions to find somewhere, somehow.
    My feeling is lonely, and yes it's true,
There is hope for tomorrow, but today,
    I Miss You.

—Bobby Maskew

CHILD'S NIGHT PRAYER

Bless me as I sleep
tonight.
Keep the boogyman
out of sight.
Send four angels
the watch to keep.
Their eyes wide open,
As I sleep.
If the boogyman
comes around.
I pray the Lord will
knock him down.

—Nancy Parker

THANK GOD

Is there within thy heart
A need
That mine can fullfill
One chord that any other hand
Could better wake or still

Speak now lest at some
Future day my whole
Life wither and decay

Thank God for my eyes
That I might see
Thank God for my ears
That I might hear his word
Thank God for my voice
That I might speak

Of his saving grace
Thank God for saving my soul
Through someone who cared

—Burma Cusenbary

SOMETHING FROM THE LIGHT

Something from the light
has been given to me.

Something from GOD
which truly I see.

It was one summer morning
by the dawn's day of light.

We met upon faith
in a solo-less flight.

No maps could I chart
on his ride in his wing.

We climbed over mountains
to which my heart sings.

He pushed me to see
with his wonderful sight.

He pushed me to see
as the dawn came from night.

He gave me a journey
in a sea with no end.

He gave me new sight
with a message to send.

Go forward in faith
as the truth it is known.

The walk in his light
will lead the way home.

—Susan K. Brubaker

LOST WITHIN MY MIND AGAIN

Lost within my mind again. Remembering the past.
Holding on to all the pain. How long must this last?
The voices are inside me still. Nothing drowns them out.
Can't control them anymore. What is it that they talk about?

One voice says, "You're stupid." I answer, "I will never learn."
One says, "By the Devil you are possessed; in Hell you will burn."
One says, "You're a bitch, you're sick, you're a whore."
"No I'm not," I whisper, "I need help, I can't bear this anymore."

I tried running away from them. But I will run no more.
They're always catching up with me. Then they're louder than before.
No one needs to beat me down. I do it to myself.
When will all this fighting stop? Lord, I need your help.

Whatever it takes, God, I do not care. I put my trust in you.
Help me to heal my heart, my mind, my soul.
Help me dump the garbage out and help me feel new.
Inside my mind I must go again. But if and when I lose control.
What if I don't come out again? I'm afraid I won't be whole.

—Hannah Broussard

THE VISION OF BEAUTY

I saw the Lord high and lifted up and his train filled the temple
My heart almost stood still and my mind seemed to tremble
Because of the beauty that is so rarely revealed
Caused me to feel as though my blood was congealed

His head fairly glistened with the Heavenly light
Which dazzled my eyes as it was so bright
His raiment was white as the purest snow
It seemed to shimmer and glow

My head immediately bowed in reverence to my King
But my whole being wanted to sing
As I was overcome with such a Heavenly joy
That it is impossible to describe or record
I wanted this moment to be suspended in time
In order to bask in his love sublime

But he smiled and made me aware that much work was to be done
Before all victories would be won
However, this message he left with me
Spread my words to one and all that they might in my service be
When my trumpet will sound for the in-gathering of my family tree.

—S. A. Reed

HEAVEN NEVER LOSES ITS SHINE

With each new dawn, there comes light of a bright, new day.
In the springtime, the cold dew and the smell of birth brings
    a certain joy to all;
And the song of feathers is a glorious tune.
In the winter, the sun puts gleam into the dreadful cold;
And we remember that soon the doves will be home.
In the summer, we block the sun with the cool water of a sprinkler;
The lark is never too hot to call upon our souls.
And in the fall, we reminisce our joyful springtime and ponder
    all that lies ahead;
The birds fly south, but leave us with the knowledge that
    they'll be back.
But in the midst of all this joy and happiness, lies the
    thunderstorm.
The storm that steals all of the birds away;
And we are saddened with the fact that they are out of sound
    and sight.
But we must bear in mind as the rain beats upon our faces,
    and the thunder shakes the earth in its entirety,
That in the place where eagles fly . . .
The sun never loses its shine.

—Anne M. Sutherland

TWO PATHS

Two paths crossed one lonely night
Two souls were ready to give up the fight
They reached for each other, a flame started to glow
And on that lonely cold night, love started to grow.

Where despair once grew, hope stepped in
And both were willing to fight again.
Two paths crossed one lonely night
Two souls found love in God's shining light.

—Kathleen S. Dishart

ONE VOICE

My faces are many yet my voice is the same to all I call
To some I am everything, to others I am nothing at all . . .

I am the Light for many known as The Shepherd too
I am who I am as perceived by each of you . . .

I am The Master, Creator of heaven and earth
I am a baby's first breath at the moment of birth . . .

Although my faces are many I still am one voice
What I am to you is solely your choice . . . .

—Rosemary Higgins

ADVERSITY TO BENEFIT

"All things work together for good to those who love God."
At times in my life these words were difficult to laud.

A stranger was drinking and driving;
The accident killed mother and left six surviving.

We have grieved and grown each step of the way.
Without Mom, we had to bring our talents into play.

A traumatic divorce brought me to my knees,
But when I was honest with myself, I realized that Spirit frees.

A chronic illness has plagued me for forty years.
It's kept me closer to Him, and thus; lessened my fears.

I have three interesting children, and ten adorable GRANDS!
I rest easy knowing that they are in His hands.

Yes, I believe that every heartache and pain,
Will be bathed in sunshine and softly falling rain!
            PRAISE GOD!

—Patricia Joan Johnson

THE COMMISSION

"Go! Ye into all the world — Teach, Reach and Pray—"
This has always been the need, but much more today.
It seems we somehow, just do not have this need—
Our own selfish wants, our ever growing greed,
Is taking greater precedence, we fail to see and heed
This love that He has and is always near us,
Is closer than we really care to know.
For no matter how far we stray from Him
He is always there to show—
We can be whatever we want to be, even when
      things look dim,
If we have Love, Faith — Let Him Be Our Goal.
He is always there, giving us full control—
With our choices, deeds, thoughts and remembrances,
Even though He has the last word with hope
      to save souls—
Regardless, if it is our desire or at our conveniences.
So! Why is it so constant that we prefer to make Omissions
When all He asks — "Follow His Great Commission."

—Hazel W. Tyson

OUR NATION TODAY

For what did God destine us?
What did God intend?
To turn our hearts to Him,
Or to the ways of men.

Our nation is divided.
Split at the heart.
Not growing closer,
But being torn apart.

A nation without morals,
A nation without God.
We ignore what we know is right,
And live for what is not.

God is the answer.
God is the way.
"Turn to the Father."
Is my prayer for her today.

—Heather D. Tyler

SHREIVE ME

Relieve me!
oh holy word
of this unholiness.

Breathe me!
immaculate lung,
and let me be exhaled.

Touch me!
with not a hand,
not flesh not bone not earth.

Lift me!
bring me up,
beyond my sitting here.

Hold me!
within yourself,
within your warm safety.

And leave me,
to be myself,
to live by word and man.

—Abraham Burickson

THE BEST VALENTINE

Jesus loves me and daily He
      tells me so.
I love Jesus and wanted you
      to know.

Jesus loves us, that's the Best
      Valentine of all.
He is always with us and answers
      every call.

It is easy to share our valentine
      with everyone,
Just tell them all of what Jesus
      has done.

Soon our valentine will be shared
      all around,
With family and friends let us
      His praises sound.

So this year when you are asked,
      "Will you be mine?"
Share with others, Jesus our Best
      Valentine.

—Barbara Prather

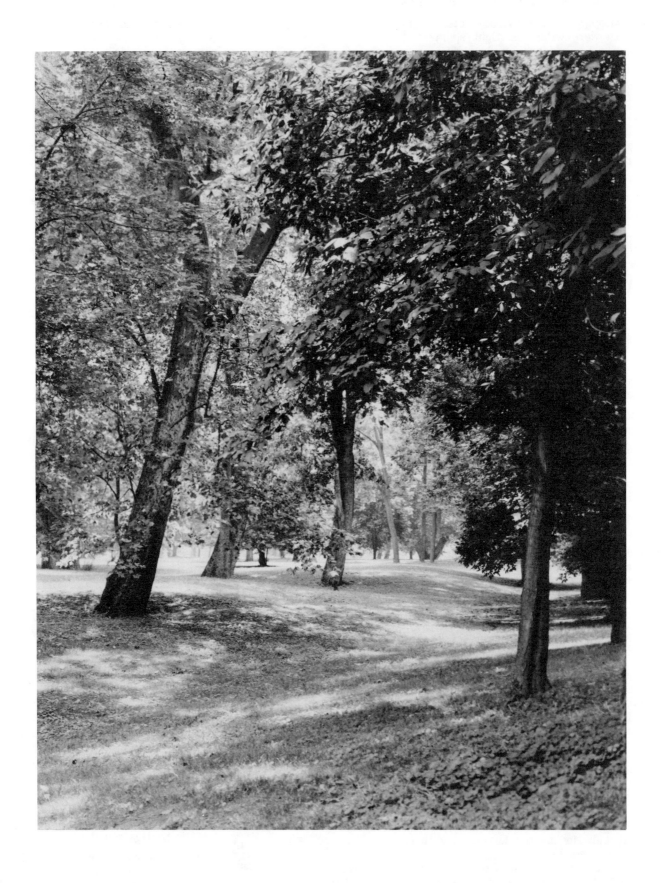

WHOO! (IN THE EVENING)

When dusk floods down to the forest floor
  and the carpet's green to the shadows bend,
The waves of night in their silence roar
    to the trembling prey at the burrow's end —
      And the owl scans his day!

—M. C. Bode

THE WISEST ONE

We find ourselves moored here like strange sailors.
  Blown like a shipwreck to the shores of life.
We rant and rave and try to blame others.
Emotions get strained, they cut like a knife.
I can't help but wonder, why we are here.
What is the lesson, what is to be learned?
When confusion lifts, the meaning is clear,
That acceptance is not given but earned.
The wisest one here lives a simple life.
Loves a brisk walk either early or late.
To lie by the fire and be without strife.
He gets along with all; accepts his fate.
I study his ways, seeking mine to mend.
He's my good dog Fred, my faithful friend.

—Sandra Wolf

I saw a unicorn today
  and he asked me what he could do.
    So I asked if he'd grant me a wish
to which he replied "I'll see what I can do."
    The unicorn proceeded to place his horn
in a pool from which a rainbow sprang forth.
    He replied follow this my boy and have no fear,
at the end of this rainbow your wish shall appear.
    So I heeded his words and followed this wondrous sphere.

    There at the end I found
something brighter than the sun
    and fuller than the moon.
A heart warmer than the warmest day in June.
Sparkling eyes which rivaled the brightest stars.
A smile which pushes away the clouds of gloom
enlightening the darkest night.
A caress as gentle as the dew
There before me my wish had come true
for the rainbow led me to you.

—Robert J. Bonanno Jr.

MY LONELY LITTLE FRIEND

Your sad, lonely eyes look up to me
  How cold and frightened you appear to be
A warm, cozy home is all you ask, a place out of the cold
Somewhere you could curl up and grow old
To belong to a human with a kind, gentle heart
Somewhere to go, to be a part
Oh, my lonely little friend
I'm so sorry I cannot take you in
So sorry I have to turn you away
How cruel you seem to say
If only I could make you understand
How I long to reach out my hand
But I have no more room you see
There are already too many living with me
How did you come to be this way
Someone just threw you out one day
You were no longer that cute, little kitten
With whom a child was smitten
But would they have thrown you away just like that
If you were a child and not a cat?

—Wanda Campbell Moody

THE KANSAS OZARKS

Chautauqua county is
  The Ozarks of this state
And gives the local citizenry
A reason to sing of fate.

So we sing a song of sunshine
We sing a song of glee
We sing a song of life
Lived so open and free.

In the land of sunflowers
And waves of golden grain
In the land of Redbud trails
And gentle summer rain.

Where in early morning light
Deer graze on all the bounty
And quail coveys march through
The tall grass of this county.

—Julia Higgins

THE FALCON

Tethered from the lofty breeze
  I sit on perch of great unease
Wings tucked back in futile pose
The gentle wind of freedom blows
So close the gale of life's intent
Yet, here I sit on haunches bent
I wait on word of high command
The raising of the master's hand
To cast me into breezes fate
The loosening of the leather gate
Falcons soar above the farm
Yet, here I sit on tethered arm
Now! Hood is off, the light I see
I've waited long, it's time for me
To fly the perch of great unease
To swoop and rise in nature's breeze
Good-bye my friend of hooded sack
I'm airborne, yes, I won't be back

—S.L. Blankenship

GUESS WHAT

In the beauty of their splendor,
  They flutter to and fro.
From one flower to another
Across the earth they go.

They were put here for a purpose
That we never think about.
They pollinate the flowers
As they fly about.

They wing their way so graceful,
They are a flying gem.
GOD knew that we loved beauty,
That's why he created them.

Across the fields on milkweeds,
Caterpillars are hanging there.
From them come lovely creatures,
They go propelling through the air.

Sometimes they fly down low,
Or even way up high.
Guess what I've been describing?
It's a ʎ˥ɟɹǝʇʇnq ʎ˥ǝʌo˥.
      LOVELY BUTTERFLY.

—Shirley A. Dittman

HYMN

Notes glowing with the Spirit
Drift across the chapel
And settle delicately upon the souls;
Striking deep chords
Of gratitude, joy, and love.

—Arnold Stonebrink

KENTUCKY MORNING

Kentucky morning;
You awake with dew drops in your hair;
Kentucky morning;
The birds sing with laughter everywhere;
Kentucky morning;
Your eyes shine with sky blue;
Kentucky morning;
Your moods are as the rainbow hues;
Kentucky morning;
God walks as gentle breezes blow;
Kentucky morning;
I look and love you so;
Kentucky morning.

—Bonnie June Wentz

WOOD WINDS

Many a time walking through the wood
I stop to listen to the whisper
Of the wind through the leaves.
They dream many things
Do these tall men of the wild.
Dreams of root, rain and seed.
And they seem to be whispering
Secret things amongst themselves
So that a thousand whispers
Becomes a loud roar
Til it seems a storm must come
With thunder and rushing waters
To hush the talk of the trees.
Sometimes I would stop
And rest next to a rich, feeding root
To listen to the talk in the leaves
And like a child
Fall asleep.

—James C. Shearer

LANDMARKS

Lofty spires of old Ebernezers,
Salems, Midways, their pews with doors.
Pulpits high, and old bronze bells,
What a story, they really could tell!

Venerable Treaty Oaks, and their sisters,
Their branches knew each tribe.
Creeks, Seminoles, and friendly Choctaws,
Sat under you, made tribal laws.

See the old iron fountain
Low! there it sits near the park
Not for man was meant this one,
But tired horse and mule, work done.

Remove not the ancient landmark
Which thy fathers have set,
Take the children by the hand, and
Show them their heritage in our land!

(taken from Proverbs 22:28)

—Evelyn C. Parramore

MOVING

We're moving out today,
Again, we must not stay,
The truck is loaded and on its way.

Empty rooms loom bare and stare,
Tears flow as I softly touch, here and there,
Not an inkling they reveal of the love we here did share.

Of when our babies first were born,
'Twas in this very room a first smile shone,
First wobbly step, bubbly word, the very first red balloon.

Gaping panes, wall-eyed glare in,
Where we nestled, worked and laughed and then
Took our share of days disheartening.

And outside yonder lies, a gay flower garden,
A lush red rose, purple heads of bachelor button
Left, a part of me, of loving care, but ne'er forgotten.

And so good-bye to you old, gentle, house,
Diary walls unspoken, I love you and please bless,
The next family here with such happiness.

—Cara Sue Winkler

ONE SIDED

Look to the West see the sun going down
crowning the Earth as it touches the ground,
The flowers are catching the last bit of light
as they fold up their petals and wait for the night.

Look to the East see the stars coming out
beautifully sparkling and dancing about,
The moonlight is shining on forest and trees
while the wind whistles softly a magical breeze.

Look to the South see the ocean aglow
with its frisky young waves as they bob to and fro,
And the fishermen hauling their final catch in
then they go home to sleep, till the morning begins.

Look to the North see the snow coming down
swirling but silent it touches the ground,
This land knows no warmth in the cold icy air
but there's warmth in the hearts of the Eskimos there.

Scenes like these peaceful ones aren't hard to find
but if that's all you can see, then you're partially blind.

—John R. Desmond Jr.

SAN FRANCISCO BY NIGHT

Magical city!
Your white painted houses
On the sides of the hills
Hang like snow flakes,
Bait for tourists.

'Frisco by night
You fascinate us!
Floating in the early morning fog,
City greedy for all pleasures,
You know the secrets for spontaneous loves
That drift along the Bay Bridge in early morning hours.

Your naval cord hangs over the Pacific waters,
Illuminated by fairy snake-head-lamps.
In a slow moving car, a perfume exhales—
The Tiouraye powder ignites souvenirs of Senegal.

Our speechless romance puts rhythm to the sounds
Of the Sabar drum beats in our two hearts.
Our fingers touch and our souls sing in chorus.
SAN FRANISCO by night: romance without words.

—Ozzi Richard Hoffman

TODInY

Tomorrow, today is gone forever
Just like the down from the dandelion flower;
Just like the rain after an April shower.

The kind deeds we could have done yesterday
Don't make that mistake today.
But, go out and help someone along life's way.

—Angeline Davenport Smith

BETWEEN SEASONS

Winter's whiteness, once covering all,
Remains now in scattered dirt-covered mounds,
The cold winter wind, once piercing our wrappings,
Now softly brings dampness to colorless ground.

Anticipation of the rebirth of nature's treasure,
Fills our thoughts as we see longer days,
But wait we must for blossoms and green,
While trees are still bare and grass muddy gray.

—James McKay

COMPARISONS

A lonely heart is like an empty room
Because both are waiting to find someone soon
To fill the space with their good grace
And thus eliminate the gloom.

A candle burning in the night
Casting shadows on the walls from its light
Bringing warmth and glow into the empty room
Filling the heart with dreams that will
Hopefully come true soon.

—Mrs. Sylvia Cohen

ROOTS

I sit here with so many confused emotions
They are going back and forth
To and fro, like an ocean with all its motions.
There is so much love and laughter around me
Yet I sit here by myself watching it all,
Listening to it all, nursing it like a baby tree.
Watching the world grow, like limbs
Reaching out, starting new roots that bring
More trees, more limbs, more love
More heartache, more togetherness, more loneliness
Why can't one of these roots be me??

—Kathryn Smallenburg

SMALLTOWN HEARTLAND

Mom and Dad got education on the family farm
I got mine in a fancy school.
Grandpa got his out behind the barn
Uncle Bud from an ol' bar stool.
Aunt Jean's purebred
From the old homestead,
A mother hen from the start.
Why don't ya' come on in
We'll pick and grin
We're from the land that begins with heart.

Smalltown Heartland,
Come and make us your friend.
Lord knows you're always welcome
Just watch us wave and grin
Smalltown Heartland,
Stay a spell and ease your mind.
Come visit us and you might spend a lifetime.

—Kenton Runyon

NATURE'S EMBRACE

Love is the color of the golden sun
as it warms up my body on a summer day.

Tastes like the cold and refreshing water
of a sparkling, bubbling spring.

Sounds like the rumbling of a lively
waterfall tumbling down the mountain.

Smells like the aroma of morning dew
upon the grass and wild weeds.

Looks like a myriad of shining stars
on a moonlit night, just before dawn.

Love makes me feel like embracing my brother,
as nature uses my senses to embrace me.

—Nellie Reyes

ZEN JOURNEYS

Drip, plop, shimmering liquid,
Like diamonds on jade.
Fine webs of glittering lace,
The forest mantled in misty rain.

The desert moans and whispers.
Shifting ribbons of bleached sand,
Rocks imprinted with a million grains.
Sun rays reach down and envelop.

Gentle gurgling—water seeps into nothing.
Babbling water—swifter over stones
Roaring water diving off rocks and cliff.
Majestic canyon encircle and enclose.

Mountains flecked with jewel tones,
Amethyst, ruby, emerald, and crystal,
Sunlight filters thru sheer cotton.
Beyond the peaks clear blue blankets all.

Infinite stillness . . . solitude
Calmness enfolds all of nature.
Harmony lay like a coverlet
Of peace, over all the land.

—Hope

AN ENCHANTED ISLAND

Where the sun shines a little brighter,
Where the sky is always blue,
Where worldly cares fade away
And peace enters in.

North Haven

What would you give
To listen to a loon at eventide?
To watch the gulls circle overhead—
To bask in a gentle sea breeze?

At North Haven

When the joyous day is over,
And the stars hang low
You watch the dancing fireflies
While caught in total reverie.

Here you feel the mystic rhythm of the universe.
Here the truths of life unfold.
Here the soul is refreshed.
And faith once more restored.

Day by day, it weaves its magic spell
Once savored the islands special charms
Never to escape its mighty hold,
But abide forever within its safe embrace.

North Haven

—Alberta I. Wallen

HOPE

Frozen hills roll into
  nothingness—
icy twigs reach for the
  heavy, gray,
  closing-in sky.
  Caught.
The cold is silent,
  revealing no
  secrets.
Winter whispers loneliness.
Ice-clinging grass stems
  bend,
  and break,
  beneath their load.
Yet beauty remains—
  an unspoken
  knowing
that tomorrow the sun
  will shine.

—Heidi Bergh

FOX FIRE

Amidst the
  darkness
of the forest
it lies
casting a
ghostly glow.

Living off
the death
of rotted wood,
it illuminates
the shadows
of night.

Carried in a jar
to light the way
for one bold enough
to wander about
where unexplained
things creep,
nature's lantern,
becomes a friend.

—Guy Lee Forest

FOR TOMORROW

Walking in the sand
  we have no worries,
for tomorrow's sun
  will shine.

Sitting under the moon-
light, loving the night
away, for tomorrow's
dreams will come true.

Watching the waves on
the lake, we have no
fears, for tomorrow's
rain clouds will
  go away.

Running on the pebbles
and stones, we have
no cares, for all those
wonderful tomorrows,
I shall remember each
and every one of them
  spent with you.

—Barbara Heldreth

THE OCEANS

Somewhere the sea is the judge and the sky is the jury.
  They both shall decide when life shall abide with its troubles.
Where life never ends and the land comprehends with the beauty of it all.
Things match together, and here love is forever.
The oceans, the oceans, the place where the sea connects with the sand.
The oceans, the oceans, the place where the waters collide with the land.
To help our oceans, we mustn't wait.
The destiny of our sea is too terrible a fate.
We must come together, so our oceans will last forever.
The oceans, the oceans, the place where the sea connects with the sand.
The oceans, the oceans, the place where the waters collide with the land.
The love I will share along with the care for the oceans.
"It's only an ocean!" they say.
But, what happens one day,
when the sky dies because it is lost without the eyes of the oceans?
The oceans, the oceans, the place where the sea connects with the sand.
The oceans, the oceans, the place where the waters collide with the land.
Oh, our oceans.

—Amy Elizabeth Thom

MY BELOVED ROSE

Once there were two roses, they were the most beautiful
of all, one a rose, the other a little rosebud, no other
could compare with the beauty, happiness, contentment, and
meaning they brought to my life, but like all roses this
rose had thorns, his thorns brought more pain than any other,
because he was loved more than any other, I tried to hold
him very close to my heart, but I didn't know how to hold
my rose to keep the thorns from tearing into my heart, I
lost my beautiful rose, he fell from my hands, while the
beauty of his memory lives on, my heart bleeds, for I can
no longer cling to my precious rose when I'm scared
and alone, or feel his warmth and tender caress like soft
petals against my skin as I sleep, or see the beauty
and love in his eyes when I awake, or smell his sweet
fragrance as I walk through the flower garden of my life,
my heart stands alone as it cries out, scarred and frozen
in time, holding only my precious little rosebud and the
memory of my beloved rose.

Dedicated to: Burton   From: Angel
Love lives forever.
—Janie L.

MOONLIGHT RAINBOWS

Moonlight Rainbows. Transparent crystals flow in murky darkness.
  Shimmering starlight, projecting pearly-flavored beams of brightness.
Misty shadows. Nocturnal images of cloudy travelers.
  Dark grey billows float over emerald waves of earthly vapours.

Pale grey dawning — the waning glances of celestial bodies.
  Amber sunglow. First enchantments of a new beginning.
New horizon. Copper choruses of solar splendour.
  Golden morning. Painted tapestries of life's profusion.

Azure rooftop — unending canopy of earth's revival.
  Timeless skyworld — life-giving spectacle in ice-blue brilliance.
Spinning gases — states changing, emanating vital forces.
  Ivory sunball. Florid fringes transmit life's own essence.

Blazing halo, extinguished slowly in its daily passage.
  Falling skylight. Rose-tainted aura blends the blue horizon.
Lingering half-light. Frosty feathers hide the dim lit places.
  Dull grey awning. Ashen curtain covers heaven's fullness.

Midnight marvel, coal-black blindness blankets all around it.
  Sombre skyway — unlit poetry for unseen people.
Jet-black hollow. Ebony phantoms dance in total darkness.
  Sable showplace prepares the viewer for more Moonlight Rainbows.

—Jack Dennis

THE CALL OF LIFE.

A small brown seed
warm in its earth blanket,
hears the ancient call of new life,
and thrusting and pushing from the womb
of the green and brown shell which held and
nurtured it, a tiny brave shoot bursts through
into the light and warming rays of the sun, and stands,
as though waiting, for the head of gold soon to appear, to
complete the tapestry, of earth's meadows, and become a part of life.

—Grace E. Brooks

TALK TO ME

What's in store for me to be?
Through nature's eyes I'll try and see.
I felt the wind that blew my way, but I can't tell what it's to say.
It whispered softly in my ear something that I can't make clear.
I wish I knew what it had said before it twisted, turned and fled.
I do get bored just "sitten round" waiting for the wind rebound.
So, I watched the water flow and heard the sound of deep echoes.
It muttered low I should have known then, drifted to a danger zone.
I won't go wading in the depth, so I'll just watch the bright sun set.
Hugging near the mountain top — absorbing all my endless thoughts.
But, time did take the sun away and put an end to this whole day.
So, What's in store for me to be?
A question I'm unsure, you see!
"Cause" I don't want some blessed key to open doors not right for me.

—Barbara J. Paugh

MOON MIST

We stood on top and watched the day lie dying at our feet.
We cupped the world up in our hands to see it more complete.
The earth was torn—there rose a glow of hell fire's filtered light,
But all the valleys turned to smoke, then all the smoke was night.
Still faster raged the misty ways and faster chased the winds.
The world below us lay exposed into its very ends.
The moon won o'er the sun and rose victorious in the night
And hushed the cries of mists and set the plundering winds to right.
She smiled upon a world serene and still beneath her glance
And turned her practiced charms again to furthering romance.
Poor moon did little, though, to note the happenings below.
She could but light a lover's eye and weave a mystic glow,
Or swiftly set the world apart from time escaping fast,
Or fire up hungry lips to kiss and wake up dreams long past,
And open hearts that closed in pain to beat a love as true,
And though she's smiled here oft before, the thrill is always new.
But all the other passions hidden well behind the night
Remained from battles of the sun who just had lost his fight.
And though the moon tried hard to hold, and though I held you tight,
We found our love no life can hold— just moon mist in the night.

—Mary Alma Wilkes Furchtgott

CLEARER SKIES

You made it seem
like dreams
were just in reach
and I believed
you when you told me
tears I cried
were to cleanse my eyes
and,
as after a rain . . .
I'd see clearer skies.

—Billie Jean Goff

SUNDOWN

Day is done
Darkness comes
Slowly crawling
Enveloping all
Day sounds end
Night sounds begin
The sun falls
Below the horizon
In a splash
Of color
Day is done

—Lisa M. Holthaus

SECRETS TO THE SUN

I said to the sun,
you move over, ya hear?
I'm burning, I'm anxious
'cus my time is near;

I fought and I worked
each step that I made,
I laughed and I wept
when a little bit paid.

So I must struggle on,
I will not get low,
the taste that I've had
is too sweet to let go.

So move over big sun,
you move over, ya hear?
I stand out alone, and
I know my time's near;

my prayers and my struggles
are coming out right;
so I'm telling you now,
I aim to shine bright.

—Leslie M. Laverty

ALL ASHORE

It has begun to spill from me like a dam that has ruptured with no time to
seek higher ground, only to ride the crest of the wave and await the flood's
passing. Overwhelmed by the lingering excitement of the unknown and what
lies ahead dictates reality if this indeed is reality, as I am in no posi-
tion to contemplate, but only to stay afloat. I have read of such transi-
tions in the lives of others, but never in my life have I experienced such
a feeling. Seasons bring with them nature's poetry, and I am for whatever
reason caught between the seasons of change and the poetic rapture therein.
If tomorrow were not to come I know not that it would concern me, for of the
moment there is peace in not knowing, and I dare not look back for I might
drown. Wherever these waters are to carry me, I know the island is behind
and the shores of freedom await my heart's arrival, and the priceless cargo
it holds within.

—Ken Cornia

THE MESSAGE

Let not your heart be troubled
Let not your soul be sad,
Lift up your face and smile
I want you to be glad.
I want you to be humble
Place your worries all with Me,
I will lift you if you stumble
And lead you tenderly.
I will point out all the dangers
The pitfalls you should know,
We will not be as strangers
If you follow where I go.
You will not ever lose your way
If you follow in My Light,
You will not ever go astray
I will point the wrong and right.
You shall praise My Name to everyone
And tell them that I care,
You shall tell them that their Father's Son
Has made them all, His Heir!

       —Alice A. Cahn

This poem was inspired by My Lord.

JESSEABEL NATHUSULA

Just a song, just a song
Now that's what's in my heart.
Stopped to steal
That little meal,
Ain't been prayin much,
Cuz I ain't been sayin much;
But Pappy always says still water runs deep,
And that's just what I'll keep.

Happy, happy are those who pray
They're awaiting for the day—
That comes but once in life
With a good lick and a bunch of strife.
Maybe I'll sit down to rest.
Days gone past are days I like best
Memories are happy and gleefully nice,
I do think of them once or twice.

Being poor ain't no credit I can afford,
Locked in this prison is what I swore
To God the Almighty the One I adore.

       Amen

       —Carolyn Ann Walker

SUCCESS

To believe in your self is the first step,
To plan and establish goals is the next concept.

Walk the path you choose with confidence,
Definiteness of purpose is the main difference.

Apply your self in life with no limitations,
For the opportunities have no invitations.

Maintain happiness and always be positive,
Do not be down or surround yourself with negative.

Do not feel you have to follow the crowd,
Have courage let your voice be heard clear and loud.

Begin to develop a winning attitude,
Have faith in God and show your gratitude.

Do not wait for someone to show you how,
The time to act is now.

       —David Shanley

WEAVERS

No one can separate those who love.
Love is a web woven to hold the world together;
And all loving people are weavers.

Distance is nothing to those who love.
Love is a light that glows far and wide,
Lighting the inner recesses of the spirit—
    The root
        And fruit
            Whence we came,
And whither, together, we go.

Far apart? No, close enough to hear
Love's laughter,
    The silver sound of starshine,
        As it trills through the hills of forever.

No one can separate those who love.
Wrapped in God's cloak, snuggled warm
Against His breast, where rests the universe.

       —Lois Tyner Bodle

THE HORSEMEN

The four horsemen rushed in off the clouds
The hoofbeats on air were thunderous loud
And lightning flashed to reveal their faces
Then darkness erupted to hide all the traces
But a glimpse was enough to identify
The four fiercesome horsemen who rode in the sky

One rode a white horse and carried a bow
A crown he wore and he rode his horse low

Another a grey horse and held him a scythe
He wore a black robe and swift did he ride

A third, a horse of crimson red
Welding a sword that spoke for the dead

The fourth rode a steed black as the night
And held he the scales of earth's every plight

And creatures below who held such this sight
Scurried to darkness to hide in their fright
And the four fiercesome horsemen circled the skies
Listening for wailing and lost children's cries
And held in their hearts not an inkling of pity
The horsemen of death plunged down on the cities
And dealt out the wrath for which they'd been sent
Then back to the black clouds the four horsemen went

       —Andy Hard

A WORLD OF PAIN

Why is there famine? Why is there grief?
Why do God's children create their own pain?
Violence and crime are taking their toll on innocent
People who cry in vain.
Child molesters with no remorse.
Twisted minds on an unstable course.
The old and weak, the poor and young,
Don't stand a chance with a weakened government
With a broken lance.
All the world powers are going to shit.
But still they keep fighting, will they ever quit?
Questions without answers, when will it cease.
Can't anyone find the key to world peace?
My mind is dwelling and wandering in mire
At the sight of a world that could soon be on fire.
With just a push of a button and everyone to blame,
This world as we know it could become a flame.

The End

—**William K. Hearn**

GOD'S FLOWERS

Reflecting the image of their Maker,
The flowers dance in the sunshine of His smile.
His laughter flashes from the splashing brilliance of Tulips.
His teardrops flow in Violets soft and blue;
His sadness in Bleeding Hearts grace the morning dew.
His gentleness whispers in lacy Baby's Breath;
His tenderness the gentle Sweetpea holds.
His joy dances among the merry Marigolds.
His constancy stands firm as each Dandelion unfolds.
His generosity springs forth in blossoms
Apple, Cherry, Peach, and Pear.
His grace through Lilacs fills the air.
His wrath flames like Cock's Comb blazing in the sun,
But His anger is slow like the late blooming Mum.
The Rose unfolds, soft and sweet, His perfect Love,
But thorned to remind of a Sacrifice made.
The Easter Lily, pure and white,
Trumpets His glory, forgiveness, and power.
The promise of New Life
We find in a Flower.

—**Mary De Vries**

LIFE GOES ON

Times change . . . some good . . . some wrong.
A major disaster . . . a beautiful song.
Children grow . . . and soon leave their "nest."
Wars may end . . . but, still fighting and unrest.
Planes fly faster . . . as they lift to the sky.
We explore the moon . . . but, some wonder why.
Fish in the waters . . . used to thrive . . .
Now, they find it hard to survive.
Some of us try to do the right thing . . .
Others don't care what the future will bring.
A baby is born every minute of the day . . .
Some people feel, they don't want it that way.
There are plenty of jobs, with good pay.
Many homeless live in the streets today.
Floods and earthquakes, happen, more and more.
Trash, and debris, wash up on the shore.
Trees are cleared out, day after day . . .
Animals have to find a new place to stay.
We grow old . . . and then we are gone
So, learn to live . . . "As life goes on!"

—**Maxine Novak**

HE GIVES US STRENGTH

He gives us valleys to walk through
He gives us mountains to climb,
He gives us roads to walk down
But he is always there — all of the time!

He gives us pain and heartache
He gives us tears beyond control,
He gives us misery to cope with
But through it all — our hand he holds!

He gives us dark and dreary days
He gives us perilous times,
He gives us doubts about our life
But still — his glory shines!

He molds and shapes and makes us
He takes us and refines,
He gives us a reason for living
He bestows his love — divine!

—**Elaine Bailey**

WINTER DAYS

In the latest days of winter
    when the skies are not so bright,

one feels the stillness more
    and often fears the night.

Soon fears change to somber
    at the break of dawning grey,

then efforts force the facing
    of another winter's day.

One stops to think of spring
    when day is near its end,

Just to shed the knowing
    that another night begin.

Soon the winter's dying
    brings the dawning light—

Still another promise
    that everything's alright.

—**James C. Conant**

ENDANGERED MAN

Oh, where has our good earth gone?
    Once perfect, now surely spoiled.
Rivers, streams and seas once pure
    Are now so grossly soiled!

Driftnets trap our sea life,
    Endangered by the pound —
Slain dolphin are no matter
    As long as tuna can be found!

Once stately trees and forests
    Gave shade and wildlife shelter,
Fought erosion and pollution,
    Now chopped down helter-skelter.

Great herds of elephant roamed the land
    To raise their young carefree;
Have all but gone from poacher's guns
    Just for that ivory!

Is it too late to turn around
    And change our greedy ways?
If so, man's years are surely numbered
    If not his very days!

—**Susan Stine Mason**

MOON LANES

Crescent moon descending in the west
Does it always travel east to west?
What is its destination?
To find a treasure chest?

Full moon or on the wane
Returns to view again
Wrapped in jewels of light
Ever changing through the night
Traveling a new lane.
It is never the same.

Pathways ever wending
Slightly, brightly bending
And is always blending
Into new beginnings
And the message it is sending?
Miracles of beauty, peace
Tranquility and Love.

—Maryalis Hadley

CLOUDS

What is a cloud
. that hangs in the sky?
Have you ever wondered
    as one drifted by?
Clouds do appear
    and soon take on form.
They are the source,
    From which goodness is born.
As they slowly descend .
    they take on the shape,
of what we desire
    they mold and create.
Or turn it around,
    see in them our need,
to quickly dissolve
    all our ill-done deeds.
Clouds are like magic,
    they soothe troubled minds.
They bring to us peace
    like no other kind.

—Betty Jenkins

BEAUTY OF THE WOODS

Alone in a wooded field I stand
Beneath the quiet of a summer's day.
A bouquet of beauty in my hand,
I frolic as a child at play.

Rays of sun shine down on me,
Bringing warmth that feels so good,
The sun makes it hard to see
Why everything is not as it should.

A butterfly quietly passes by,
It looks so elegant in flight,
How does it fly so very high?
The honey bee decides not to fight.

The world to me is very calm.
A day in the woods I really like,
Trees sway gently like a palm,
This is my favorite place to hike.

The birds sing sweetly up above.
Today has come and will be no more,
Tomorrow will bring Mother Nature's love,
I will enjoy it as before.

—Linda Green Slone

SIGH-LENT NIGHT

He rushed upon her
with his driving force.
He penetrated her
then was gone in seconds,
Leaving her cold and lonely.
But again they are together—
As he, the mighty sea, meets her; the waiting shore.

—Lisa R. Toler

AN OCEAN SUNSET

The ocean waves roar,
Foaming water falls onto the rocks,
The sun sets silently
Its shadows of light calm the waters.

A silent sky shelters the stars.
The song the breeze hums, is distant.
The moon hangs solemnly, and
The air is warm and comforting.

It's a vision of peace and perfection.
The quietness of the night brings strength to the soul
To be so close to something unknown,
Makes its flawless beauty so familiar.

—Taunacy Watts, age 14

DAWN ON THE MYSTIC RIVER

See the masts of tall ships towering.
Hear the shipcarvers' hammers pounding.
An ancient steamship chugs along her way
etching a peaceful image from days gone by.

Sunlight sparkles on the Mystic River
shining on spars, rigging, and anchor
casting a golden glow on an iron-hulled ship
making great shadows — big and bold.
The silhouette of a schooner setting sail,
canvas flapping in the breeze,
meets the horizon.

Strains of a chanty drift through salty morning air
mingling with the unearthly wail of the steamer's whistle.

Close your eyes!
Journey in time!

—Brian Keenan Muzas

ETERNAL SEA

I sit upon a large, amber, flat stone.
With all human life far away as home.
Within my hands the pole that fish lore;
As the surf gently flows toward the rocky shore.
Up comes early rays of sun piercing morning mist.
I ponder all cities of concrete and steel;
Hoping to find some answers to problems I feel.
Gazing unto the sea;
Where lies centuries of lost treasures.
Dreaming and wishing I can discover;
Just for sensual pleasures.
I love the sound of waves;
Crashing on the rocks.
No other's except;
The flowing wind as it talks.
Suddenly, there's a pull and tug on my pole.
Up reels a wild one, which I hit with a blow.
For me there is no eternal day.
I hope the sea will always be;
For which I in remorse can not stay . . .

—Patrick V. Morgan

HIGH TIDE

You said that I smelled like the ocean. I didn't believe you until our embrace caused high tide to gush from the stillness in me.

Like a starving sponge, you soaked me up.

Absorbed

We rocked to your passionate rhythms

A private tune . . . slowly ended with echoes . . .

of you calling me . . . your ocean.

    —Priscilla Barnett

THE SILENCE OF WINTER

As the autumn days grow shorter, and the light fades to dim,
We close our opened windows, seemingly with but a whim.

And suddenly gone, are the sounds of summer, autumn, fall,
No sounds of tree frogs, leaves, and crickets — nothing at all.

How pleasant were those warm evenings, as through our window came,
As we sat around the table, we thought each evening to be the same.

Oh, how happy was our laughter, as we sat at the table round,
Oh, how kind and loving God is, to allow us all those pleasant sounds.

And how easily we take it all away at will,
By closing all our windows, to keep out the evening chill.

    —Leslie Dyck

WITH ME

You are with me every hour of each day,
In dazzling sunshine, where halcyon breezes with the flowers play.
In every breath and sigh and all serenity,
You are with me in delicious, loving ecstasy;
Sublime solitude is my delight,
For you are with me every day and starry nite.

In each prayer, along the winding roads, under blue skies,
Reflections soften in your wondrous eyes.
In wispy dreams you are in close sight,
In utter despair you are the beam of sunny light;
Tho' distance separates us miles apart,
Darling, you are in my heart.

    —Leonard F. Duzinski

FROZEN REVERIES

I loved the hillside 'neath the snow.
There in springtime would I lie
Listening to the song of birds,
Gazing unto the azure sky.
With blinding rays my eyes would close
And rustle of grass would lull me to sleep.
In lethargy would I doze and idealize my lovely knoll—
The perfection of its form, the richness of its colors.
But alas my sleep had been too long,
I awoke to find snow upon my grassy sea.
It roused me from my dreamy state—the harsh reality of ice.
Where were my sense of truth and reason
That I could not anticipate this cruel season?
The time had not been short I know
For nowhere did the flower grow.
I disillusioned after sleep began upon my hill to weep.
Thus shaken by the piercing chill
I commenced to leave my hill.
And herein lies the saddest thing—
How I had loved you in the spring.

    —Marianne Loffredo

"E"

Flowers are like a friendship
For this I have a hunch
Still blossoming and growing
And loved an awful bunch
Each petal so delicate
And stem too tender to touch
Like your hand in my hand
That means so very much
So be patient and content
And you shall grow so tall
Like a lily in the morn
In the dead of fall . . .

    —Dana-Marie Walter

BEGINNING

Darkness closes . . .
    candles fight for life

Frozen breath lies suspended
    on the field

Sunrise, gray and unborn
    touches the sky

Roosters crow . . .
    the stars go out

Nightdreams fade with the
    morning light

A breeze stirs life silence
    into sound

Movement in the streets . . .
    asthmatic engines

Stirring in the sheets . . .
    air borne voices

Sleep nods off . . .
    the day begins.

    —Ed Roh

THE SUNSET

Out there in the ocean
    and beyond the crystal seas,
the sunsets are so lovely
like none you've ever seen.

It gives you such a
feeling to see the
sun go down,
To watch it fall
beyond the clouds,
As it fades clean out of sight.

Just to try and wonder
Just what life could really be,
Without those lovely sunsets,
To finish up your day.

You often stand and wonder
as you stand there,
in a daze.
You think about tomorrow
and wonder just what,
it is that may be in store.

But just another lovely
sunset and maybe even,
better than the one before.

    —(Tom)

LOVE IS LIKE A ROSE

Love is like a rose
the beauty it may bring
Love is also pain
the thorn upon the rose
Love is many pleasant things
but still can lead to sorrow
Let us find new hope
and let it be tomorrow.

—Antonia Berg

YOU STOLE MY HEART

You stole my heart that is true
And I seem not blue.
For the taken
And the mistaken.
Of my love for you.

You stole my heart for long
And I sing a loving song.
Of birds that fly
Up in the sky.
I know my heart fears wrong.

You stole my heart again
And I will soon pretend.
Of the fun
On the run.
I will soon intend . . .

You stole my heart once more
And it is now sore.
Of the kisses
And the misses.
Of once I had before.

—Laura-Lynn

GRANNY KNEW 'BOUT BOYS

My Granny said,
"She knew 'bout boys."

I didn't care, 'cause
I found out 'bout boys

all by myself.

My Granny said,
"She knew 'bout drinking,
sin, and stuff like that."

I didn't care, 'cause
I found out 'bout drinking,
sin, and stuff like that.

all by myself.

My Granny said,
"She knew 'bout things
that went on in the back
seats of cars."

I didn't care, 'cause
I found out 'bout things
that went on in the back
seats of cars,

all by myself.

My Granny said,
"Men don't marry girls
like that."

I found that out,

all by myself.

—Martha L. Allums

NO FORGIVENESS

He watches her sit in the back by the wall.
She shuts out the world; she can't hear his call.
She sits listlessly with her nose in a book,
Her pride won't allow her to give him one look.
So many thoughts rush to her head
The cheating, the fighting, the lies that were said.
He must try his hardest to make his love see
That without her beside him nowhere would he be.
Now he approaches, his heart in his hand;
Forgiveness is something he cannot demand.
He begs earnestly but she will not forgive
His one costly mistake with which he must now live.

—Sandra L. Gonzalez

LOVING YOU (and only you)

Our love is stronger than anything I've felt
The love you've given me just makes my heart melt.
They say the two of us make a great pair,
I'm always fascinated by how much you care.
The days have been wonderful, and so have the nights
Nothing could go wrong because everything is so right.
Love is a very mysterious thing
it makes people laugh, it makes people sing.
The music that we have made together
is like a song that lasts forever.
You have me and I have you
though the days may pass, our love will stay new.
The minutes will pass and the hours will too,
but there won't be a time when I'll stop loving you.

—Sharon Buzon

REMEMBRANCE

Remember me not for my departure
Not with pain or suffering
Quiet mourning is permitted if not habit-forming
No, remember life for that is bright and spontaneous,
When you see a tree or a rose think of me
These, like the soul, represent eternal
beauty and can never be diminished,
And when a bud falls from the vine to lay upon the mother's bosom
Its brothers and sisters do not cry out in remorse, but
gain an inner closeness as they entwine to fill the void created
Closeness and companionship breeds new life from ruin,
When you love I will be there,
Follow your dreams and, like the rose,
Ours will never be a true separation,
Remember love and you will remember me.

—Jeff A. Sanfacon

HIS GYPSY LOVE

When walking one day down an old cobble road,
He saw her sitting by a stream, resting from her load.
He saw her brushing her cream colored mare,
With her green eyes twinkling as she tossed her jet black hair.
He saw her gold earrings lying in the grass,
As he glanced away from his fair gypsy lass,
He sat there watching her night and day,
Until the time came when she rode away.
She left behind but one golden ring
And as he touched it his heart began to sing.
He searched for her far and wide,
But he never did find her to make her his bride.
He never did find his fair gypsy lass,
With eyes as green as fresh spring grass.
He sits to this day in a little alcove,
Thinking about his long lost love.

—Mira Lopez, age 13

WHY?

I sit in the warm and cozy darkness
A feeling of security and love surrounding me like a blanket
I can hear your soft and gentle voice talking to me with love
No, wait, something's changed. Why is there silence
No, now there are tears. Why?
Who is god? and why are you asking us for forgiveness?
I no longer feel safe and secure, why?
What? You can't want to get rid of me!
I'm a part of you, we are one
Why listen to them, I don't know them but listen to me
I'm a part of you and you're a part of me!

"Why!"

—Nora L. Morris

MY LADY BY THE SEA

A loon cries softly in the distance.
A cloud drifts silently past the setting sun.
Waves stroll serenely upon the sandy shore,
as I lay next to the woman I adore.

The warm hush of waves and quiet breast of breeze
speak to the coming of a warm Summer's Eve.
The muted light of day is reduced to a glimmer.
Near my lady and me the waves slowly shimmer.

The tall grass behind us rustles gently on dunes.
The warm scents of sea waft gently 'pon their way.
Stars look like diamonds appearing in the sky,
and the waves move serenely toward my lady and I.

The sun's last fade no longer lights the dusk,
as we rise and we leave on that dark and quiet night.
She to hers and I to mine — to meet again no more,
by those waves a'rolling gently on that warm and sandy shore.

I awaken from my dream with a tear upon my eye.
I turn and in my pillow I ask myself why.
I lay praying for that blessed sleep that I once more may be
with the lady that I love on that beach down by the sea . . .

—John R. Perard

WAITING FOR YOUR WORDS

Glinting off the gentle rays of sunlight are meadow
grasses long and thin
Apple trees whose branches are blowing in the wind
Sunlight that filters through the puffy clouds above
All adding to the feeling of this romance and this love
My heart is beating so fast as I look in your eyes
You are holding my hand, your smile so tender and real
I wonder what we will discuss today —
The big question? Could I face that now?
I wish for love, yes, that's so true, I've lain awake
at night and sobbed for it,
Asked my Lord for it,
I've sometimes condemned it,
But now I desire it and I see that you do also.
Your mouth is opening, your lips are beginning to
move . . .
I am leaning closer to you, I must not miss what you
say today.
The bluejays are chattering in the elm trees nearby
And how the sun is warming the air from that azure sky
And how I am waiting for you to tell me that secret,
I am imagining a hope chest, mine all mine, our own
house, and someday children . . .
"I want only to be friends."
Your words have stunned me, deeply stunned me, I close
my eyes, I take such a deep breath.

—Linda C. Mortensen

VISION

You are a vision, a vision,
I'm not sure I'm seeing.
Hopefully you are not,
So I have finally got,
A new kind of love,
I have forever sought.
I never really thought,
I would find the guy I got,
You are something special.
You're in my heart right now,
I hope there is never any sorrow.
For there is always tomorrow,
For I have found a Vision.

—Betty Jo Reed

OUR LOVE

What you mean to me
Is more than I can say.
More than dreams I see,
Or hopes that fade away.

I live for only you,
But life is not enough.
With love we'll make it through,
Or go down fighting tough.

I'll be right here,
To calm your cries.
To see your fear,
And dry your eyes.

So please don't fall,
From love we have so high.
All it takes to call,
Is a simple, tender sigh.

Your hand is held by mine,
And mine will not let go.
Our love is like a line,
Where ends do never show.

—Toby Daniels

Eyes of blue and hair of hay,
With my heart I'd love to stay,
Holding you night and day,
Your warmth shines so bright,
Like god's shining love light,

How I love you girl,
I want to know your world,
Your heart is a shiny pearl,
But pain is in the way,
I want to take your hand,

And show you a better day,
My dreams are not of sand,
They could come true someday,
With my hand in yours,
We'll make a better day,

To make a better world,
We must go a better way,
Who ever I'm with,
I'm always talking with you,

Because hearts can feel so much,
I need my arms around you,
I want your soothing touch,
Because hearts feel so much,
I need your warming love,
Like mankind needs the dove.

—John Malliot

NIGHT-TIME

The room is cold and dark
The noisy sound of a dog's bark
There came from the room
An old lady with a broom
Ready to fight the dangers that loom.

—John F. Panso

SEED OF LOVELINESS

Lonely breeze from the sea,
    salty as a lover's tear,
    take my aching spirit
    'round the world with you.
Free me from these grappling souls
    to drift as silky mist among
    the green things of the earth.
Let me kiss a saddened cheek
    to make it full with peace of soul.
Raise me to the fluffy clouds
    and release me as a gentle rain
    to cleanse the dingy veil
    of apathy from the eye of every one.
Should I fail to help one seed
    of loveliness to grow,
    guide me to your sea again
    that I may try once more.

—Charlotte Jewell Lowe

A LEAF AM I

As along the street I trod
One evening in the cold,
There came an oak leaf tumbling
Across the glist'ning snow.

It had clung to life much longer
Than its brethren of the trees.
While they lay deep 'neath winter's coat,
It frolicked with the breeze.

I watched the brief performance
The two of them put on.
Then, tossed up by a sudden gust
The dancing leaf was gone.

Was its passing in the night
A symbol for my eyes?
It toiled to shade from summer's heat,
The task, now done, it dies.

—Bob Heffner

THE HUNT

The sweeping mighty bird of prey
    scans and swoops in disarray,
searching for the fur to trap
in claws with power the necks to snap.

I watch in silence its persistent ways
to catch and conquer the resisting plays
of patterns run by rodent feet,
in time with nature, their deaths to meet.

In order to live, then one must die
but not without the will to try
to beat the odds of fate and time,
to escape the destiny of the mime.

There is no reason residing here —
Just the running patterns of untamed fear.
Zeroed in, it falls, locked on track.
I need not know. I turn my back.

—Sally Rock

FOOL'S GOLD

Why does it seem, that the Old Days are Gold Days,
    When the present never seems quite golden?
Perhaps the mind forgets the torment suffered in the past,
As the Years wear on.
But why it is, I do not care.
For often I wish I could relive those good old memories,
Of simpler and brighter times.
For Time is like a heavy burden,
Tied upon my back.
At first the weight was easy,
When the back that bore it was strong.
But every day now,
The weight makes me stagger,
And my face gets closer to the ground.
Let Fate not let It crush me.
Although the past seems golden,
Its glitter is deceiving.
And part of me says to be bold, to face the Future.
And so I shift the Weight,
And trek endlessly on.

—Kirk Ogaard

OH, WAITER

"I've been away and I've been around
    I've been high and I've come down to earth
with sudden jerks (this way and that)
I've been searching for so long, I find
I can't remember what I sought in time and space
just ran the race (this way to the path)

Now I choose to play it loose
lie around like the others do
maybe it will come by way of fate
some type of destiny — don't you see
I can wait"

And in the years that followed he did just that
he loitered and waited
he stood and he sat
they called him The Waiter (and that was his name)
yes, that's what he did what he was and became
waiting for someone to point out a path
oh, Waiter is that why you're still
where you're at?

—R. Mageddon

A SMILE AND A GLANCE

I was so afraid, and nobody knew
Just how much I wanted you.

You sat and watched me with a drink.
I dreamed of love and tried to think.

What would I do if you came to me?
But I could not let my mind agree.

I sat and waited for time to pass on,
Hoping the next time I looked, you would be gone.

The next thing I knew, you were at my side.
You asked me to dance, and I did with much pride.

Now the years have gone by, and older we grew.
I often wondered what happened to you.

My life is so lonely, and sometimes I cry,
Just why did I let such a love go by?

If I had known at the time of the dance,
My love would have been more than
                    a smile and a glance.

—Doris Harbaugh Eckart

A TEAR'S DESCENT

A tear is a token that comes with love.
It slides down your cheek with your last goodbye.
A stong running stream, full of emotion,
Streaking your face as it descends to the floor.
A thousand cares, contained in that teardrop,
Shatter into nothingness after its fall.

—Trisha Meyers

TO MY DAD

When I was very, very small,
And you were oh so very tall,
I looked up to you.

Throughout my youth, throughout those years;
Throughout the laugther, and yes, the tears;
I looked up to you.

Now you're in a wheelchair, and I tower over you,
But nevertheless, it is still true;
I look up to you.

—Hope Lane Grayson

A YOUNG CHILD'S SORROW

A young child has just experienced a death,
The worst she probably will ever see.
For her father has just died.
She doesn't know what to think,
To cry, or laugh, or shout with glee.

She doesn't know that she will never see her
    father again.
When she becomes older, she will understand and
    realize.
The pain in her heart will be immense,
For she will then remember his death.
Remembering the awful sight will never minimize.

She then wishes he was still alive, to be there with her,
To lead her on like waves in a sea.
She was only a girl to experience sorrow,
Here today, and gone tomorrow.
And who is that young girl you say?
                    That girl, is me.

—Lucrecia Mervine

YOUTH UNACHIEVED

Can't march all to a candle
Unlit and waiting for you,
As if it could welcome the presence of a long lost flame
Begging for the ashes you make.
    Suddenly in a twisted world of fate, so eventful,
And still waiting for you.
The most important thing one could possibly try.
Accomplished,
With your crown on iron grate.
    Never, but it's always again
The unfeeling meets man's well laid plan,
You've finally reached the unbelievers land,
    Below the attacking streets,
Should have cut sail and took a try in the sea.
So blue, and still waiting for you,
Drown, but your face is instilled
On the bottom that no one will see
    A watered down life
    Maybe a memory
    In an occasional tear.

—Aaron Micheal Morrelle

CRY

One day I heard a speaker cry,
She looked about the same age as I.
I listened, but never knew what she meant,
But yet I knew the message she sent.
Next time the speaker I spy,
I knew that girl was I.

—Jamie Watkins, age 12

LITTLE FEARLESS FIGHTER

So small I am in this big world,
I hum, I hum, I hum to get my
    day's work done,
Fearless I am to challenges or peril,
I fight, I fight, I fight to stay
    abreast of my quest,
I fly, I fly, I fly to find my
    daily treasures,
Because fearless I am I made a
    difference in today's pleasure,
And as I fight my way home when
    my day's work is done,
I hum, I hum, I hum notes of love
    for I am thankful for yet another day
    and have high hopes for bright,
    successful tomorrows.

—Margie Reeves

BARREN DREAM

Baby mine,
how I marvel at those tiny fingers,
so able to hold within their grasp,
my heart.
    Baby mine,
your eyes reflect both love and wonder,
embracing my soul as I enfold you,
within my arms.
    Baby mine,
so sweet be the melody you are cooing,
the angels delight to sit and listen,
by your side.
    Come evening an anxious heart
will surrender unto slumber,
for I can hold you only in my dreams,
baby mine . . . .

—Micky Woldruff

YESTER YEAR

I'd like to walk again along a dusty road
That only now my memory knows,
To feel again the warm soft dust
Work up between my toes.

I'd like to wade the cool spring branch
That brought contented happiness
And watch again, the small fish dart,
And hide among the water cress.

I'd like to follow down the fur-row,
New made, across the field,
To watch the seed go in the ground
And then to watch the yield.

To see again the cotton fields;
The corn, the new mown hay,
The fields of waving golden grain
Miraged in memory's yesterday.

—Joseph T. Craig

BEALITY BY THE SEA

Beauty is a shell, cast from the sea,
Perfection personified in pure
    artistry.
Iridescently tinted with lavender
    hue.
Imprisoned with rainbows,
glistening with dew.
Incredibly fragile, this shell
    holds for me
The immeasurable wonders of
    Life's mystery.
God must have loved to
    play by the sea.
When He fashioned with
    care the waves symmetry,
Forever repeated and
    spirally wound
Locked in a shell
    With the Ocean's sound.

—Helen Muccia

PAINTING NATURE

Pine tree standing all alone
    Surrounded by grass field
Owl perched to set and wait
A mouse for him to yield—
Stream beside me, cracklin brook
Cedars hang amongst its sides
Birds are chirping in the thickets
A little rabbit runs and hides—
Deer feeding on its outer edges
Cows mooing on a distant farm
A pheasant cackles from the ditch
No dangers close to cause alarm—
Sun shines in at tree top height
Blue sky peeking through
White clouds moving overhead
Light haze rising from the dew—
Warming sunrays on my face
All surroundings become lit
Time to set up canvas board
And try to capture all of it—

—Craig Jeffrey Welch

SAVE, SAVE AND DON'T POLLUTE

Where will it all end.
    In our water so don't pollute.
Be careful of your trash.
Try to save what you can.

A place for papers
Another for bottles
And someone else gets your cans.
Even your plastic must dissolve with
    the sun.

We need clean water,
Just to save your life.
Our water needs treatment
Even what runs off from the rain.

We need a dual water system.
One for humans
And another for plants.
Save, save and don't pollute.

It means your life to save.
Not another day can be wasted.
For tomorrow is here already.
Save, save and don't pollute.

—Ruby E. Rowland

When I was just a little lad
    We were taught what was good and what was bad
Respect for all was our daily creed
Lots of discipline we would try to heed
Add the love your family gave
It wasn't difficult to behave

But today it's an entirely different story
Too many distractions for money, fame, and glory
We must try to save our youngsters now
For them, their future we should endow
Let each one of us try to find a solution
And finally get rid of all the pollution

—Gerald R. Barrett

SIGHTS AND SOUNDS

The pulse of the foghorn when heard through the night
    reminds me on shore of the mariner's plight.
It jogs my thoughts back 40 years or so
    to the same lonesome sound, its moan is low.
Gazing from the window, the light is in view
    as the lighthouse beacon sends forth its clue.
Memories flow to the iron ore boat
    which says 'hello' with a deep bass note.
The tug and the barge out on the Lake
    visible from the bluff when the dawn does break.
These sights and these sounds in my mind will remain.
    of the Great Lakes with their beauty never to wane.

—Ann Linn Newberry

THE COUNTRYSIDE

The countryside abounds with the splendor of God,
    From the meadow's green grass to the dark, rich earth.
The air mingles with the scents of the land,
Bringing the smell of freshness to everyone.
The droning of bees and the chirping of birds,
Mix into a delightful sound.
Butterflies flit from flower to flower,
While showing the world their beautiful colors.
Ducks swim from one end of a pond to the other,
While the water gives them company with their reflections.
Lying on the ground and looking at the cloud-filled sky,
Gives you insight to the things you're feeling.
The shade dances around the trees,
Its coolness darting from place to place.
The sun slides by in the sky,
Drawing with it the hours of time.
Truly, the countryside was molded by God's hands.

—Carol Hay

ODE TO MOUNT ST. HELENS

O beautiful mountain of Washington State,
    So stately and proud our presence seems inadequate.
Beautiful Mount St. Helens so majestic and regal,
Rumbling and steaming as though our presence were illegal.

We stand in awe of your earth-shaking force
With harmonic tremors, nature's universal chorus.
O Mount St. Helens, so belyingly serene,
We wonder and marvel at your awakening!

Though you inconvenience we humans so small,
We admire your power and stature, because
You were here first; you're in control,
Shooting ashes and steam through thick white caps of snow.

As you carve your crater so enormous and deep,
We'll be listening to you as you rouse from your sleep.
Go ahead, Your Majesty; show your power and might;
We respect and bow to you—What a magnificent sight!

—Thelma R. Henderson

Speak to me
Of the open Sea.
While I feel its
Warmth, my brow
Is covered by its cold.
Waves and I will silent be.

—Gregory Price

Dew drops glisten on the leaves,
    A merry River runs by;
The moss grows thickly on the rocks
    And white clouds are in the sky.

I sit beside the happy brook
    And watch the water dance.
I Dream of men in shining armor
    Carrying shield and lance.

My fancies carry me away from life
    And set my spirit free.
They show me what I'd never know
    And things I'd never see.

—Robin Smith

THE SHAKIES

Shaky is the name for Aspen Tree
    In this country.
The shimmer of the leaves
At the whimper of a breeze.

It is now glorious here
For it is Fall
And down come those leaves
Upon the wall
And rest upon the house's eaves.

Blending in the panoramic view
Is the continuously changing scene
All variations of yellow, red or green
Blowing in a gale of leaf upheavals
Twiggy trees are left by leaves.

Now the leaves sink
In a solid soft mass
Upon the grass
Losing their crispness
As Snow White arrives in mistiness.

—Joan Swarthe

MY INDIAN CHIEF

Looking out the window one morning as I awoke,
    There appeared an Indian Chief, and not a word he spoke.
He was high up in the branches of an old elm tree,
    And the silhouette of his face was all that I could see.
His likeness was formed by branches here and there,
    And limbs like feathers covered his glossy hair.
His one eye was a circle of little twigs,
    And his nose was of branches covered with thing-a-ma-jigs.
He had a straight mouth and a pointy chin,
    And from all appearances he was gangly and thin.
So I let him stay there both day and night,
    To keep vigil and protect me from fright.
He was so faithful, never leaving my side,
    Guarding and protecting me, my joy and pride.
Through snow, sleet, rain and fair,
    I felt so secure, because he was there.
But alas, one morning, much to my dismay,
    A gusty March wind had blown his nose away!!!

—Mary Flowers

MISSISSIPPI, MY HOME

"Mississippi is terrible," or so it's been said;
    Don't believe everything you've heard or read.

The movies have depicted us as being cruel;
    All of this just adds on more fuel.

Some say they are afraid to travel the state;
    And hurry through at a very fast rate.

Just slow down and browse awhile;
    Visit with folks though not your style.

Seeking some good, forgetting the past;
    Remembering pleasant thoughts and letting them last.

Mississippi is scenic with enormous clear lakes;
    Just imagine many pleasurable hours fishing makes.

Boating, skiing, swimming, camping, and the like;
    If this is not your cup of tea, take a hike.

Visit historic Natchez and see Elvis's home in Tupelo;
    Gaze at catfish ponds and watch Delta planters sow.

Learn history at Vicksburg and eat seafood on the Coast;
    Read Eudora Welty and of four Miss Americas we boast.

Each section has something unique to give;
    Mississippi, you are a great place to live!

—Ruth H. Biggers

LOVE IN BLOOM

My household duties "swamp" me in,
    By my kitchen window, I'm lost to a "new" nest in the makin' —
In the loftiest branches, on the old cottonwood tree!
    How many flights to gather "bits," is way beyond me —
Each tiny "bit," laid with the tenderest care,
    Comfy and warm and "sweet" for a family, soon to be there!
Their marriage is as sincere as the Bible's written word —
    Such a "wholesome" way of living, God gave this little bird;
As Momma placed the piece she had, Daddy watched with a devoted eye —
    Then in a twinkling of an eye-lash, away the happy pair would fly,
Each moment is so precious, it mustn't be lost —
    The summer is short and there's a long "journey," before the "biting" frost!
I wonder, how such a tiny body, can be so brave and strong??
    When "trouble" stands before them, it doesn't seem especially long,
Till they can hop from branch to branch, and sing a cheery song!
    Seems that God has woven in his pattern, a "lesson of rebirth"
With each spring, my faith is lifted, when things go "hap-hazard" here on earth,
    For I've witnessed, once again, how much my "feathered" friends are worth!!!

—Hazella Westman

THOUGHTS

Critters that flitter through my mind,
Unimportant little thoughts that go round and round,
Seldom related, often one of a kind.
Once in a while, one becomes a bright star found!
Caught while playing hide and seek thro' my mind.
With pen in hand the critter is sentence bound,
To be shared forever with others of my kind!

—Don E. Meister

MIDDLE MILL CREEK

I think now of those bygone days when clear water spilled
over rocks and as I think back this meant peace
I see it again bathed in sunlight
and I can see the bottom
of my special crystal swirling pool
I caught a salamander and a crayfish too
I was young and did what boys will do
now my stream is clogged with silt and filled with goo
and write about this tragedy is
what I feel compelled to do.

—Herman Mills

TENNESSEE BOY

Raised a young boy in East Tennessee
Nurtured in the mountains, beneath the tall pine trees
Study the call of a whippoorwill, as lonesome
    as a starless night
Behold the beauty of a golden sunset, as it
    slowly fades out of sight
Rambling through the woods, or meadows of tall grass
Summer is almost here now, and Spring is about
    to pass
Soon stiff breezes will blow, and the seasons will
    change again
And changing like the seasons, the young boy becomes
    a young man
And no matter where he may go in life, or down
    what roads he may travel
Whether they be paved, or be roads of gravel
One thing that won't change, for it will always
    be
That he was once a young boy, raised in East Tennessee.

—Patricia S. Hampton

ROAD KILL

The highway
    wide concrete path
stretching into infinity
battleground separating lush green pasture
from dark primeval forest
two eyes glowing like red hot coals
within the forest's depths
small woodland creature driven by some primal urge
to venture across that peril-fraught strip of concrete
metal monster instrument of death and destruction
headlights gleaming malevolently in the twilight gloom
little forest dweller frozen in fear
at the point of no return
one moment of terror
one scream of pain
sickening thud
crunch of miniature bones
furry body deathly still
small legs reaching toward heaven
mute testimony to a tiny life that once was.

—Nancy L. Armer

MOTHER NATURE'S QUILT

On the breezes gently blowing,
The Autumn leaves go floating by.
Like falling stars or shooting comets,
Of red, green, orange, brown and gold.

They find their places on the ground,
To make up nature's patchwork quilt;
    Pieced in a colorful design,
To warm the earth through winter's cold.

—Juanita D. Washburn

SERENITY

Laying on the fresh, green grass,
Breathing the cool, crisp autumn air,
Feeling the slight chill of night,
Smelling the first scent of burning leaves.
Hearing the cricket's song,
    and the gentle wind through the trees,
Seeing the infinite, deep blue sky
    with its brilliant stars,
Tasting the goodness of life,
Sensing the peace it offers,
Knowing the world is me and I am it.

—Kristen L. Capitani

WINTER

The hills are cold and chilly
    In the winter when it snows.
The pine trees moan in agony
When the cold wind through them blows.

The furry woodland creatures
Are cuddled snug and warm
In burrows lined with leaves and moss
Far away from winter's harm.

The song birds long ago have flown south
Except one, where can he be?
For when the wintry sun comes out
You hear friend Chick-a-dee.

Our Loving Heavenly Father
More wonders to bestow
There on pure white velvet
Frost diamonds He will show.

—Charlotte Olbricht

THE OLD DOG

The old dog lay still,
    his head upon his paws,
Fighting the urge to move,
    with a lack of power and will,
He remembers years past,
    when he ran here and there,
But those days are gone now,
    and he wishes he could go,
To an easier, more peaceful place,
    but he doesn't quite know how,
As he rests his weary eyes,
    he thinks of many things,
Of cattle driven and horses followed,
    of cats chased and bones of every size,
It's been a good life he concludes,
    and as he looks down the lane,
He sees his master coming,
    but his head is upon his paws
    and will never raise again.

—Kay C.

EARLY MORNING

Song birds are singing in the trees
On budding branches in the breeze;
While over the hills and in valleys too,
Sounds of morning come clearly through.

The break of dawn, its colors bright,
Low skidding clouds and birds in flight,
A gentle breeze that kissed the dew,
God starts each morning fresh anew.

—Theodore Kocher

LIFE

"Life" is a moment in time
a flash of light
a beautiful memory
sadness that passes with time

Mountains that take your breath away
a baby's first step
Pride of your first born
which no words can describe

"Beaming" Grandparents
with wisdom to share
which so often, is ignored

"Life" is a lesson
to be cherished and nourished.

—Ann Hodge Merckson

To reach up to the stars at night
And swing across the sky—
That's just one thing I dream to do
Before the day I die.
If I could buy those stars I see
And tie them with a bow,
They would be my gift to you
As you deserve them so.
With face and eyes as kind as yours
And the joy they bring to me,
With little talks to help me out,
My friend you'll always be.
At times it's hard to say such words
To a person in her sight
But the words I wish to say to you
Are in the sky at night.

—Susan Peiffer

Silence
As the fiery sun sets.
The rays creep over the ocean waves
Gently rolling.
Beauty, almost mystic.
Then the tide crashes in
As the glowing array of colors
Deepens.
Out of the blood red sky
Comes a bird—
A single, lonely white dove.
It glides gently
Slowly
Then it lets out a cry.
The cry seems wanting
Coming from so deep within
As if it looks for something
That cannot be found.

—Susan E. Klein

THE CITY OF ENDLESS NIGHT

The wind blows endlessly through the trees.
Clouds fill the black sky.
The darkness overwhelms the people with its sound
power.
The earth shattering force of its will.
The mindless terror amiss the chaos.
The hatred in its face.
The glare in its eyes, as it stares upon the City of
Endless Night.

—Linsey Brown

EARTH-MAN'S PUZZLE PIECE

Caught up in the theory of the BIG BANG,
Scientists peer, near-sighted, into Space,
Hoping to find substance to support conjecture
That Creation was a one-time explosion.

I think: How delusionary it is to place such emphasis
On a single theory,
(Of which I am leery),
And on a trail that leads backward.

Though the avenues are myriad,
There can be no conclusions drawn from such theories,
For Earth-Man has yet to realize
The true substance of Creation.

—William H. Coatney

THE MOON

The moon was full in the pastel sky,
I noticed it there as I was driving by.

How it hovered just above my head,
the beam of light in which I was led.

As its stare looked down watching my every move,
I tried to run and hide but its glare still ensued.

In the middle of the night when it's so round and bright,
that's the time my head feels so light

And, I could lose my mind
with the same old grind.

Just when my life felt so out of tune,
I then realized, it was only the moon.

Duke 90#

—Craig S. Lindberg

AURORA BOREALIS

Arcadia, alas, tis lost,
Aurora Borealis.
You must not stop, to count the cost,
Aurora Borealis.

Forgivingness, tis now, the bridge,
The kiss, by which, you were dismissed,
To carry on, though hope, is gone,
Across the great abyss.

Forever now, tis written here, Arcadia is dead.
Aurora Borealis and tomorrow lie ahead.
You cannot search forever; you cannot live alone, unloved;
You cannot spend eternity, in search of, stars above.

For you are just a meteor, that is,
A simple streak of light.
Aurora Borealis, tis
A grand and glorious sight.

—Robert C Krider

EARTH WORM

Little worm, worm, worm,
    Why do you wiggle, wiggle, wiggle?
Is it because when you crawl, crawl, crawl,
There is a tickle, tickle, tickle?

Where did you come from little worm, worm, worm?
And where did you learn to wiggle, wiggle, wiggle?
Do you have fun when you wiggle up and down, down, down?
Or do you get a headache on your crown, crown, crown?

Where are your feet little worm, worm, worm?
And why are you so long, long, long?
Why are you sometimes brown, brown, brown?
While marking the sands of time, time, time.
Did you get stuck in the ground, ground, ground?

—Doris J. Sawyer

A SUMMER NIGHTMARE

Things that go bump in the night
    And keep you awake in a terrible fright,
Deer flies buzz and bite and drive you insane
The mud and mess that comes with the rain

Whiskers a growin' all over your mug
You open your mouth and swallow a bug,
The weather's so hot your backside gets galded
You spill your tea water and get yourself scalded

In the dark spot in the cool of shade
You step in the mess your buddy has made,
Poison ivy, poison oak, poison sumac too
The nettles you wiped on because the leaves were too few

Clouds of mosquitos looking for something to chew
And the only thing available that's chewable is you

When the last of the daylite begins to fade
And the mosquitos from the swamp begin to invade
Then you remember you forgot your can of Raid

You itch, you scratch, and are in such pain
You can hardly wait till next year for vacation again

—Thomas Kruger

A SKUNK A DAY KEEPS THE COMPANY AWAY

One fine day I heard a scratch underneath my house,
    I thought perhaps it might be just a little mouse.
But when my heating vents stopped working one by one,
I quickly realized just what the "thing" had done.
I called a friend who graciously did help me set a trap,
And we did catch a lovely skunk who gave us both a zap.
But ignorant of the aroma which surrounded both of us,
We scurried off to town and caused a major fuss.
The drug store I did visit quickly left the door ajar,
And made sure it never closed 'til I was in the car.
A visit to my sister's home did readily let us know,
How ghastly we did smell, from our head down to our toes.
In fact, a lady at her home did say a skunk was near,
But my sister speedily replied, was but here sister dear!
So next I called our ranger who you all know as Scott,
And quickly to my home he fortunately did trot.
He advised me for the future to call the animal control,
So set the trap I've done each night in just the same 'ole hole.
And lo and behold the count so far has risen to 14,
But because of feeding skunks to catch, my cupboard's getting lean.
I do so pray the last of these has finally been found,
Then I can once again have my family and friends around.
So folks, if you do see me and notice quite a scent,
Just hold your nose and know that I will quickly get the hint.

—Doreene Livermore

STARS

Stars are bright,
    In the still of the night,
They shine their light,
With all their might.

—Mary Kathylene
Elizabeth Bible, age 11

STARS

Who sprinkled the sky with
    glitter tonight?
Was it the wind blowing
lamplight from windows?
Or lost yellow balloons?
Could it be an exploded comet tail
of long ago?
Perhaps it is a rich King's
deserted gold.
But most likely it is the
angels' candle light as they
watch over us from heaven
above.

—Lisa Skaryd, age 13

THE LIGHT UP IN THE NIGHT

One night the sky was bright.
    It had some kind of light.
I couldn't see it clearly.
I didn't hear it, nearly.

Is it a bolt of lightning?
It's really very frightening.
It was a pretty sight;
The light up in the night.

Is it a giant glowing ring?
Can it really sing?
Is it a ghost king?
Or is it fire on a wing?

Is it a U.F.O.?
I really don't know.
It was a pretty sight;
The light up in the night.

—Jason Jackson

HUCK'S MISSISSIPPI

It weren't no use
    To think of no place better
Than sailing on my raft
Down the Mississippi River.

No school, no forks
Ain't no such truck.
Just a life of luxury
Where I can be Huck.

No Pa to hit me,
Or Miss Watson's manners
But on the Mississippi
Life is full of adventures.

All the smokin' and fishin'
A boy can do.
Weren't no place like it,
Least none I knew.

As the range to a buffalo
Is where they roam,
Mississippi is more than a river
It's my home.

—Mark A. Stasz

TIME TRAVELERS

They burn up the street
They are travelers in time
Forever they seek to meet
Hour after hour the clock will chime
Time traveling, travelers seek
Machines they build with each and every dime
Never yielding to something that's weak
A machine finally built
A story it began to tell
About how in the past you can forever dwell
Some memories will lose their claim
Others will travel your life like a train
Past strangers of the tracks
Travel the same train
Straining their backs
Experiencing each loss and every gain
Treasures they didn't treasure
Memories some they forgot
When they are older they could measure
Memories there's not a lot.

—David "II" Brooks

AMERICA IS GROWING UP

America has come thru the infant stage
Of demanding and taking with pleasure,
The childhood stage of, "I myself,"
Blind to its faults beyond measure.
The adolescent stage of seeking, searching,
Rebelling. Answers, knowing them all,
To the mature stage of seeing its faults
And admitting them, with hopes to recall,
Get rid of the wrong in our country,
Hold fast to the right we yearn.
Combining a love of country with
A broader outlook of concern
For all the world and its people,
Knowing each individual has rights.
America, there is hope for you yet
To grow from darkness to light!

—Ruby Tippit Peacher

THE PORCUPINE CLUB MANIFESTO

Do not climb a Porcupine,
in search of true pine cones.
Do not climb a Porcupine;
  a true pine has no bones.

Do not cite "The Bill of Rights,"
  and trample Rights as well.
Rights and writs, for spites and snits,
  can't ring a half cracked bell.

Porcupine love seems abstruse;
  they love, as if they care.
They don't indulge in spouse abuse;
  they share what's good to share.

Porcupine love depends on charm;
  no cupid's arrow may jump-start!
They never raise a false alarm;
  with time and tide, comes heart to heart.

Porcupines love, kiss, and caress:
  great choreography! the zest!
To show all due respect, I guess,
  the "con" does not debase the Quest.

—Ed B. Patterson

HE IS FREE

He has finally spread his wings, and taken flight.
He is now free to be, what he wants to be.
He will fly deeply into the night,
  until his wings are out of sight.
    Out into the stars
    he'll fly so far.
    Free at last,
    cause death has passed!

—Leigh Anne Massey

KEEP THE FAITH

Lord, I am a stranger in a strange world.
That obviously wasn't made for me.
Having to face so much turmoil.
Trying to be what you want me to be.

Doors are constantly shut in my face.
Turned down for the color of my skin.
Wondering what man invented this thing called race.
Giving themselves a reason not to let me in.

With dismay in my heart and tears in my eyes,
I kneel down to pray.
Lord not daring to ask you why.
I just ask to keep the faith.

—Marsharee Anjanette Swift

GREEN ISLES

Isles of green misty seen
Hover in visions these sleepers between.
Beautiful memories, cozy and clean
Restfully precious, and sweetly serene . . .

You from whom hope, but not feeling, has fled
This is your refuge from pauperhood's bed.
Timorous lad with sensitive face
You have no record of crime and disgrace . . .

Weary old man with the snow-drifted hair
Not by your fault are you suffering there.
Never a child of your cherishing nigh—
'Tis not for sin you so drearily die . . .

Pain, in all lands, smites with two hands
Guilty and good may encounter the test.
Misery's card is of different strands
Sorrow may strike at the brightest and best . . .

—Roy G. Biv

MOMMY ALMOST STARTED TO CRY

No daddy and a working mommy
No new toys but an empty tummy
No front door cause a robber tore it down.
No car when mommy needs to go to town.
No pretty dress I wanted for my class play,
  mommy almost started to cry today.
No red paint I wanted for my art kit,
No cigarettes for mommy, but she needed to quit.
No Barbie Doll that every girl has got
No food for kitty—I think mommy forgot.
No little Bible for me with which to pray,
  mommy almost started to cry today.
No television cause it broke
No shoes, and boys think it's a joke.
No hope for what's going to happen to my family
No serious problems for the rich world to see.
No food in the house—I wasn't hungry anyway,
  mommy really did cry today.

—Beth Nuckols, age 13

IF WALLS COULD TALK

If the walls could talk, oh, what they would tell.
They would tell you where David Crockett fell!

They could tell you about the Alamo and all its men,
And that Santa Anna was moving in.

They could tell you about the brave and the bold.
They could also tell you stories untold.

In the stories they did tell, the men there that day
Were courageous in every single way.

They would tell you that each man fought to the last breath,
And that they died a faithful death.

—Ryan Michael Ballard (age 13)

WHY?
IN HONOR AND MEMORY OF PRESIDENT JOHN F. KENNEDY

Our Father, which art in heaven above,
Why was such a great man who was so loved
Taken from this land he loved and tried to save?
In war and in peace he was so brave.

He trusted everyone where he went.
His life on this earth was so well spent.
Even though he was here such a short while,
I am sure all the world will remember his smile.

He was everyone's friend; he let them know it,
Until with a sniper's bullet he was hit.
For him there would never be another tomorrow.
His nation and the world were plunged into sorrow.

For never again would he flash his smile
As he used to do when he traveled mile after mile.
Perhaps after he did his very best,
You thought it was time for him to rest.

So we will have to do the best we can
To save this great and glorious land.
In his honor and memory may this nation stand
Forever seeking peace and good will in all lands.

—Essie Salter

OF WARS AND THINGS . . .
(A trilogy for peace)

I

In psalms of dreams, webbed in the labyrinth of time,
praying to the fertility gods, I stole a hole in space

And there planted a flower: mourning peace
amidst the empty shadows of wars never won.

II

The whole world is a war, and we are its victims;
you and me . . . us; fading silhouettes of life,

Chasing tomorrow in euphoric bliss, riding high on cloud nine;
a mushroom nourishing pregnancies of new world war ghost.

And living today has been postponed:
the world has declared war on peace.

III

See, flowers don't grow here anymore:
earth's womb, a victim of nuclear-rectomy;

Her tissues of civilization rot from atomic infestation:
a military plague mutating shells of humanity

Freaked out on self destruction; while peace lie suffocating
at the conference table, God's denied His seat.

—Millard L. Lowe (M'Lo)

REASON

Try they said,
and try we did.
Die they said,
and die we did.
Why? we said,
They didn't know.

—G. Keaton Conner

LIFE OR DEATH

There is dead silence until,
A squeak.
Then a hiss.
Next a rattle.
Followed by a cry.
Now there is silence again until,
A hiss.
Then a swish.
Next a screech.
Followed by . . . silence.

—Bruce A. Duncan

UNTITLED

Warrior bride
Wedded to weapon and shield
Walk upright
While about you is a warring field

Warrior bride
Welded to a will too strong
Withstand scorn
When you are weak and wrong

Warrior bride
Weather your soul's wicked storm
Whisper to the world
What a battle woman has born

Warrior bride
Witness the wealth of that hour
Waste none
When in the womb of power

—Angie Jackson

A WONDERFUL WORLD OF PEACE

The lights across the water
Shine to guard the shore
From ships in the harbour
That prepare for a war.

The first shot is heard
To begin the dreaded fight.
No longer will we know
The stillness of the night.

Fire rises high
From a sunken ship upon the sea
That made its courageous soldiers
Fall on their knees.

They plead for their lives
As water pours into the hull
And suddenly the ship is filled
With a deadly kind of lull.

The ships and men that fought
Now lie below the sea.
All because they wanted
A wonderful world of peace.

—Chris Wood

A Bud that bloomed and blossomed,
now lies withered, pale and old.
Petals still intact, but withered,
hold a heart of purest gold.

Fragile, but yet so strong,
able to endure life's storms.
Thru sickness and health, giving of herself,
with a love — all her own.

Her strength will not be forgotten,
her love and gusto for life.
Simple things for her had such meaning,
for her family was her LIFE.

As I look on this withered flower,
I see a lifetime and now the end.
A soul gone on to GLORY,
OPEN the gates, my mom's coming in.

—Betty J. Brown

WHEN I'M GONE DON'T WEEP FOR ME

When I'm gone don't weep for me.
Just plant a flower from a tiny seed.
Caress it with sunshine.
Water it with dew.
Then close your eyes and think of me
And I'll be there with you.

When I'm gone don't weep for me.
Just find an acorn and plant a tree.
Protect it with love.
Give it lots of care.
Then close your eyes and think of me
And I will be right there.

A flower is full of beauty
As life has been to me.
An oak tree's strong yet has gentle grace
As I feel mankind should be.
So when I'm gone don't weep for me.
Just plant some flowers and a tall oak tree.
Then close your eyes and think of me
And I will always be there.
Yes, I will always be there.

—Constance Saul Foster

GIVE A LITTLE LOVE

When you've reached the end of your rope
And you think misfortune's your lot
Visit a nursing home or rest home
And thank God for what you've got!

The people used to be just like us
So full of life and spirit
But time and age took their toll
So they finish out their life here.

They try to make the best of it
But it's not easy being old
I'm sure a lot of them feel rejected
Like being put out in the cold.

The people there only want to be loved
To be spoken to once in awhile
So when you want to do your heart good
Go visit—give them one of your smiles.

Please don't down-grade our old folks
Who no longer have any control
For you may be in the same position one day
When on you, age takes its toll.

—Penny L. Moreno

GRANDMA JANE

There were many moments in my life
When I wished I'd known someone like you.

And when I finally met you
Time passed by too quickly.

I have always enjoyed our talks
And the way you listen with such care.

I recall your tired eyes, and your bright warm smile.
I truly miss your kindness, old woman.

But, most of all I miss your hands.
They're the hands I used to dream of,
as a child . . .

—Lady Josie V. Perez

A BACKWARD GLANCE (SHAKESPEAREAN SONNET)

The wayward winds of time divide us now
From fading years of many decades past.
The thought of times we shared — Remember how
The playing children seemed to grow so fast?
And can it be, I hear your thoughts, you mine?
Now as my grown boys argue I reflect
The joys we shared amid a friendly vine.
Recalling happy thoughts, I can't forget.
We poured our hearts together — right or wrong
The secrets families can never know.
And as our children grew both tall and strong,
Warm thoughts filled parted years with afterglow.
Alone, we'll walk the path . . . Its final bend.
But I'll remember you . . . A Love . . . A Friend.

—Winnie E. Fitzpatrick

VALEDICTION
(On Reading John Galsworthy's The Forsyte Saga)

The day after old Jolyon died
Indian Summer died too
And Halloween burst into cold and wet.
The wind came hard
To free the browning leaves
And the rain came to mourn
For both Jolyon and the leaves,
Lost with the Indian Summer.

Farewell the gold, the leaves,
The warm blue airy days.
Farewell Jolyon!
Beauty came to you, across the lawn.
But you had gone.

—Matthew F. Kluk

UNTITLED

Before the starving child a banquet is placed.
Not simple fare but a royal feast.
Food for the soul, served with delight.
To build her strength, to continue her fight,
Lest her spirit die in the dark,
And from her soul sweet love depart.
Platter upon platter the feast is brought forth.
In patient love he sits to watch,
The depth of the hunger in her eyes,
replaced by the sparkle of sweet surprise.
As long lost dreams come true
and wishes that vanished in the night,
now buoy her soul, give it flight.
And the one who brought healing helpings of love
will fly by her side in starry heavens above.

—Linda M. Snyder

CURT

Were we wrong, Not there when we should
What possible thing didn't we do that we could?
It makes us sad that things all seem wrong
What could we have done to make you more strong
We're sure you learned at an early age
In what you should and should not engage.
The die may be cast we're not sure;
But our love for you is very pure.

—Virginia Sturtz

OLD FRIENDS

If in my life I should cross your path again
I will know at once that we were good friends.
Not with hugs and kisses and fondest wishes,
but through your eyes straight to your heart,
where all the best of friends start.
If I see that I will know
That all my love had a very special place to grow.
And not once did I doubt that my love was wasted,
but was adequately tasted,
like that of a very fine wine.

—Joy L. Stoll

FRIENDSHIP

Friendship . . . a valued treasure.
A treasure unlike any other.
A gift from God.

Friendship . . . a gift not to be
tossed into the wind,
but embraced whole-heartedly.

For without friendship . . .
the caring . . . love . . . embrace . . . even silence
expressed to one another,
What would be the meaning, purpose, reason for living?

Friendships help restore sight to the blind.
Those blinded by hurt . . . shame . . . self doubt.

Like seashells, friendships are unique, colorful, detailed.
Giving one's existence meaning . . . interest . . . variety.

God created each one of us in a unique way.
And for that, we are friends.

—Joy S. Stewart

TILL DEATH US DO PART

You are the spark my soul has searched for,
my soul has not to search again.
You have filled the void in me which
always before laid barren.
Our hearts have been fused into total serenity.
You've become habitual and I've absorbed
you into my blood.
I am compelled to live with you and
your priceless love forever.
If there should come an interval in
our time together — when one should depart
from life on earth . . . don't become disillusioned.
We have not been isolated from each other,
we are inseparable and absence will
intensify our tender feelings.
Have the faith to continue on until death
unites us once again and we embark on
a new and everlasting journey —
For this life is but a prelude of what is to come.

—Tracy Christensen

JUST FRIENDS

I never meant to love you.
It happened quite by chance.
I wanted just to be your friend,
Not to share a new romance.
But something happened suddenly,
Before my heart could know.
I came to know a side of you
That caused my love to grow.
The tender way you touch me,
I pray will never end.
A miracle of circumstance —
My lover, my best friend.

—Lisa Frederick

A LETTER TO DAD

You left when I was a little girl
you weren't around much in my world.
But in your eyes I was always
your little girl.

I know I caused you a lot of heartache
you were all give and I was all take.
I know many times through the years
you shed many a tear.

And now that you're gone
I want to apologize.
Because until now, I never realized
how much I love you.

—Donna L Kirk

MOM

I have a mom who's good to me.
She always gives me hugs.
She tucks me in and says good night
And shows how much she loves.

She takes me shopping and buys me stuff
She knows that I will like.
She shows me Christ in all her ways
Though He died with a spike.

She has a saying that helps a lot —
That she says when I can't figure.
She hugs me and then she says
"I love you more 'cause I am bigger!"

—Heather Anne Brubaker

A DOG

Just a furry bit of bouncing life
Known as a dog is he
Heaven's gift to souls like me.
To ease a bit the daily strife
Of mortal's waking here below
And bolster up a worn ego.

For companionship he has no peer
Man's best friend so parts say
Twang their harps and sing their bay.
Whistle and at once he's here
Always eager for a walk
Or just listen to you talk.

A boy's most proud possession — he
Fulfills a place within his heart
That all through life will never part,
But dwell forever in memory
And so to make a dream come true
God made a dog for me and you.

—L K Conger

117

FREEDOM

The sound rings true
  of patriotic colors
red white and blue
immigrant men
in their new home fight
for truth justice and freedom
right
as the dawn burst forth
on a bright winter day
men with frozen fingers
dreamed as they lay
on hard cold ground
of homes filled with warmth
and an eagle flew overhead
his wings spread wide
between blue mountains on either side
the men knew
this was how they wanted to be
soaring
in a land of the brave and free

  —Victoria Ingrid VanDalli

EVERYDAY

I stare away, no longer cry.
  I can't go on this way!
Such loneliness, I pray to die,
I dread each waking day!

For everyday is agony
For everyday is pain
The horror of life, it gnaws through me
And penetrates my brain.

My mind, it cries to be
Free from all the sorrow.
My body cries, "Please embrace me
Again, oh let me borrow
One yesterday!" It is too late
There's no one now to care
If I should live or choose my fate
No, no one would be there!

For everyday is agony
For everyday is pain
The horror gnaws inside of me
It penetrates my brain.

  —Stacy Johnson

THE HOMELESS WANDERER

I see the rain dripping
  Right before my eyes.
I see the cars slide steadily,
On the shiny slick black road.
As I see the people rushing,
With umbrellas to shelter them
I smile slyly to myself
Knowing that for today,
I too have shelter.
I see a hand eject
From beneath a red umbrella
To check the dripping rain.
I too stick out my hand
From beneath the meathouse shack.
The red umbrella shuts slowly
While I move slovenly on my way,
Knowing that every day, I will view
A new and different scene
Under a new and different umbrella.

  —Aliya Ghani

A PLEA TO "THE WORLD"

Am I the only American who loves these men?
  They risked it all for you and me.
They slept in hooches then.
They sleep on heating grates now.
These heroes of days gone by deserve more.
They risked it all for you and me.
They saw everything—death, destruction.
Never a word of thanks.
I wish they knew how grateful I am.
They could not vote, they could kill.
Heroes of days gone by.
Yes, heroes.
Do not forget what they have done,
Surely they never will.
I was not alive then—
I could not help.
Now, I can.
Can you?

  —Amanda Lee Picard, age 16

HOMELESS

Standing on the outside, looking, looking inside.
  Wanting a place in the human race.

Tears, salty to the taste,
Are running down my face.
The sadness in my heart,
Tearing me apart.

No matter where I stray,
They look and say, "Go away,
Move along on your way."
Rejected again today.

Eating out of garbage cans,
Grabbing any crumbs left by man.
Sleeping in the park,
But I'm afraid, so afraid of the dark.

Days, weeks, and months go by.
I don't cry anymore or ask why.
The north wind and the rain stings my face,
And now I don't care if I have a place.

  —Reta Elkhair Lankford

THE CHILD

The child wanted shoes
  wishing not to solicit though

but in strong avarice
her nature comes through

A plead for trust.
A plead for care.

Her silence, her only voice
begging into the night

The night means; darkness
and the cold, terror of solitude

Barren, blistered feet
barren, desolate heart . . . void of warmth

The walk of life
more painful than the shedded skin;
as painful as the depth of the heart.

The worn soles of the child's feet; ache
the worn soles of the heart; agony

Dedicated to homeless children around the world.
  —Daniel Quay

A WOMAN LOST

She boards the train without hope or joy,
disillusioned, enveloped in clouds of fear.
Her weapon, a bottle of forgetfulness.
Her armor, ragged remnants of better days.
Private demons clawed at bleeding flesh
to tear away the buried wounds, bitterness and anger
wrapped up in one.
"Help me" the piteous cry unheard
"Make me forget, let me fly.
You sir, got a pill or two? For fifty, please
take me high."
Cruel, indifferent world still looks on
while death invades the soul.
Who remembers, who cares?
Who can understand a woman lost . . . .

—Vienne Le

NOT GRADUATING

The guys were having a party with lots of beer;
He hadn't felt this good all year.
He grabbed his keys and went to his car;
"It's okay," he thought, "I'm not going far."
Just a few blocks to the store;
They had run out of beer and wanted more.
He was on his way, he wasn't going very fast.
What he didn't know was this beer would be his last.
There were many shouts, but he didn't hear a word.
He had run a stop sign, his vision was blurred.
He saw the car, but it was too late.
He flew through the air at a very fast rate.
The newspapers said, "18-year-old boy, dead in the street,
A half-empty beer can lying at his feet.
He saw the car, but it was too late;
It's too bad, he won't graduate."

—Anna Michael

CRACK FEVER

Hickory Dickory Dock,
Twenty bucks for a rock.
   Smoke that crack
Age ten years,
   Maybe have a heart attack.
Men will steal,
   Women will kneel.
Anything for the almighty rock.
   What a crock!
The first hit is the best high of
   your life.
Keep it up, lose your wife;
   And everything else you care about,
Even yourself.
   I've tried it you see,
So I know what it's like to be
   A white rat.
Get it from the bros across the tracks.
   Just go there white boy, -n- look
For the blacks.
   It's easy to make and easy to get.
All it takes is money,
   Something hot; or "C'mere honey."
I'm glad I don't do it anymore.
   I didn't want to end up some crackhead's whore.
Besides, I kinda like myself.
   Hickory Dickory Dock,
Lose it all for a rock.

—Viola Douglas

TAKE HUGS NOT DRUGS

Take hugs not drugs
If you take drugs,
You'll not even be fit for the bugs.
If someone tells you to take a drug,
Say "NO" I'd rather have a hug.
Drugs are not good for you and me,
So don't take a drug from anyone.
One who takes drugs hides,
Only to walk side by side.
A drug won't keep you busy.
All it will do is make you dizzy
I hope you get this through your head
Don't forget the things I write
And things I said,
So you won't end up dead.
To make your life better for you and me
Take HUGS not DRUGS!

—Alana Clark, age 10

WHAT I THINK ABOUT ME AS A TEENAGER

As you can see, I'm not a babe
I'm getting older each day.
Now, I ask myself.
Who am I?

I'm getting at the age to be a
teenager
A teenager that's free
but you have to decide on the right
and wrong discussion.

It's very difficult for you to be.
Teenagers get many kinds of drugs as
you can see. That's why I'm glad
to be free.

Some teenagers need love and care
For they don't know love is in the
air.
It makes you weak and gloomy. So that
is why I'm glad to be free.

—Sherri Powell

MISTAKES

I started drugs,
Just to get high.
Now, I'm lonely
And can't help but cry.

Everything is different.
Nothing is the same,
And I don't know
Just who to blame.

They said it would help
That it wouldn't hurt at all.
They said that I would have
A wonderful Ball.

But now I'm going—
going fast
And can't undo what
I've done in the past.

So, just remember
What I'm saying to you.
Starting drugs is
The wrong thing to do.

—Mary Rochelle Johnson, age 13

119

SPACE

Peace
for my heart
A sign,
A sign of Love
in the dark
rain rain hard,
hard rain
It feels Like
pain.
Somewhere,
Somewhere out there
We are

I know
it's not far
Standing high,
Standing high in a tree
Look at me!
I just want to be

free!

To Laurie Frank
—Barry R. Collins

MOSAIC

Mandala
and tapestry
sandalwood
and musk
candle burning
single minded
dimming
in the dusk
night mantle
mingling
in a sky of molten rust
and chance glances
passing
as our flesh returns
to dust
motes
floating
gently
I will learn
to trust.

—Rose Fravel

Oh, it's hell
being perfect
all the time.

If both of us
are shut down,
growth stops.

Patience, trust
and love in large
quantities are needed.

There is no pleasure
in pain, no victory
in winning.

Here — can you
reach it, my
open hand reaching

Halfway towards you?

—Rose Ross

RAVEN SONG

The birds return so soon to greet morning.
Where do they go when shadows roam?
And can it really be morning so soon?
Day and night merge without the solace of sleep.
And my life goes on heeded when long I should have been alone.
No respite from the monsters all my own.

My little raven, cradle of nights past, where have you gone?
I can no longer hear your song.
You took away even the echo, not lingering here too long.
Where have you flown to, who sees you?
Ebony wings streaking the sunrise.
Have you gone to a place not far but less sad?

Dear raven, fly fast lest you see the face that knows no night or day.
The soul that cries out in anguish for the torment of man.
How I envy those wings that take you far from where I am.
Flying, pain against the wind because you understand who I am.

—Paola Luz

HER CALMNESS

Oh, the dazzling delight, a hot summer night,
Winds blow wildly, sweeping kisses to the shore,
Romantic melodies stir hearts, such jubilance;
Somewhere on this ship is love with manly might.

The waves caress her long slender beauty,
Laughter echoes invitingly, come, sail along the golden shore,
Cares and concerns part of every human's life,
Never once surface, in this escape so harmless.

Salty air clings ardently to the misty blue finish,
The perfect lover moves silently upon calm waters,
Convinced without doubt; "Her Calmness" is much like a virtuous woman,
Whose beauty and love will never fade nor diminish.

Smoothly, steadily this striking beauty sails,
Waves beat time and easy rhythm,
The once pounding restless and frustrated heart now still;
Because, a midnight cruise upon soothing water once again prevails.

—Dianna Kaye

IN A FIELD OF YELLOW FLOWERS

In a field of yellow flowers, lying there for hours and hours,
something striking comes to mind, peace is what I've come to find.

Peace and quiet fill the holes in restless men's and women's souls.
Holes made so by lust and greed which binds our eyes to those in need.

And fame and fortune aren't the ends upon which our sense of self depends.
These just blind us to goodwill, our feelings sleep against their will.

But those who wake and feel the strain within their shrinking souls in pain,
will have a burning in their hearts to quell the crushing it imparts.

Then soon the weight of each foul deed committed in the name of need will
find its way up through the throat and pierce the lips from which it smote.

No rest shall come to those who dare recount the ways they did not share.
Past selfish acts will eat away the souls of those through night and day!

But once we search for inner peace on life we'll get a fresh new lease.
A lease with which we'll live anew and see the world the first time true.

For it's the work of every man to do for others what he can.
The gift of love which runs so deep was made to share and not to keep.

When we learn our hearts the key, only then can we be free,
cured of falsely living life, cured of wrestling with strife.

And so to start your living quest, I put to you to find some rest,
a place where you can spend some hours, in a field of yellow flowers.

—Leslie J. Pinnell

BEING YOURSELF

You can't change your ways every time someone wants you to
People are never satisfied with anything you do
But, if a friend accepts you for what you are,
Your friendship will go twice as far.

You should be the way you feel is best.
There isn't any reason to listen to the rest.
Just be the way that you think is right
And hold to it with all of your might.

If, with yourself, you have a peace of mind,
Plenty of friends you will always find.
But if with yourself you are having a conflict,
Your future no one will be able to predict.

We should be what we've always dreamed of being
And see what we've always dreamed of seeing.
Then, let our friends accept us for what we are
And the friendship will go very far.

—Alice Diane Baggett

LIKE AS A ROSE BUSH

Could it be I am much like a rose bush, full of thorns
from the past, trying to cover-up all the ugly parts with the
only beauty left? Somehow there isn't enough small delicate
leaves to completely mask the scars.

You came along and your love made me forget the past,
much like the warmth of the sun changes the direction of the
rose bush. Your kiss so tender and sweet quenched my thirst
for life re-newed, like the dew kisses and quenches the thirst
of the rose bush.

The rose bush, depending on the warmth of the sun to
give it strength, and the kiss of the morning dew to quench
its thirst, reaches upward and strengthens to full glory.
Showing its love and beauty for life renewed, it begins to
bloom. Blooming more and more, filling its surrounding with
its own sweet fragrant scent.

Until like your love, the sun changes its course of
direction leaving the rose bush dark and alone. The kiss
of the morning dew turns hard and cold. The rose bush is left
to wither and die, until all that is left is the bush, trying
to cover the thorns of the past with the only beauty left.

—Dianna L. Wesner

gloved hands

sitting there i watched them dance
ever so gracefully
with gloved hands they both romance
for all the world to see

where did they lose the love they'd gained
that timeless rhapsody
with gloved hands they both romance
for all the world to see

why must there be the marching
and death knolls distant beat
the sieges and the pounding that rattles distant peaks
the voices ring together in that crowded, empty room
of kitchen talks, of forest walks, of childhood words of doom

the dance they made seductive
all nodded solemnly, for chance
to be productive, the bid was moved to three

sitting there i watched them dance
moves made so intricately
their partners smiled, knew all the while
for all the world to see

—M. Louis Jackson

SMILE ON HIS FACE

She wanted to hold him forever
    to keep him by her side,
But time put its hold on him
    and took him for a ride.
Now he is gone from her,
    but her love for him remains
In hope that soon he'll return again
    to find her just the same.
Visions of him still come and go
    that reminds her he is still there.
For he can not leave her heart
    because she still cares.
She longs for his touch,
    his warm embrace.
But for right now it's not
    the embrace she wants,
It's the smile on his face.

—Michele M. Hansen

MY QUESTION TO YOU

Tis lovely the thought
    Of knowing me
Who for so many years
Was left wandering

I look in the mirror
And I like what I see
Because finally I've learned
To be accepting of me

There's no more guilt
And no more shame
These were my burdens
Which I had to tame

But I still have you
Though free from me
For you're a part of society
And how accepting are you of me?

But I am happy with who I am
No matter what you say
Because now I want to simply ask,
"What's wrong with being gay?"

—C. Michael French

THE WAY I FEEL FOR YOU

I love it when you smile,
You make me smile too.
I love it when you laugh,
'Cause that tells me you're not blue.
I love you for being you,
And not trying to be someone else.
You are a special person,
I hope you know that too.
You make me feel happy,
Whenever I'm blue.
You just have that special touch,
Nobody else has, but you.
You brighten my day,
When you say "I love you too."
I don't know what I'd do,
If it wasn't for you.
Now I know there's no way,
That you will ever go astray.
There's nothing else I can tell you,
That you don't already know,
But that I love you,
And I'll never let you go.

— Raechell Garrett

MY MOTHER

My mother cares for me,
Lives for me,
And would die for me.
Sometimes I don't appreciate her,
But where would I be without her?
She cares for me when I am sick,
But that's what I expect.
She doesn't owe me a thing,
But she somehow always takes
  me under her wings.
I get mad at her,
She gets mad at me.
But I will always love my mother,
And I know she feels that way too.

—Bob Harlan, age 15

CHILD OF THE UNIVERSE

Child of the universe
  Your dream upon a star
A million miles for you
Is far away from far

You are so special child
There are no imitations
In the expanses of your mind
There are no limitations

The galaxies are loose
Allowing for your feet
While suns explode from overload
Oh such worlds you've come to meet

Child of the universe
Your dream upon a star
You twinkle and you sprinkle
The particles you are

The meteors that fall
Are scattered and abound
They shower on the hour
This universe around

—Richard Doiron

MOMMY, I LOVE YOU

For the one who bears all the weight
  She holds her head high, without a
complaint.
She always has time for an encouraging
word, or even a hug.
Her worst enemies are well aware of
her love.
Even in exhaustion when she
seems to have no more to give,
If you look for her in time of
desperation, you'll find her there
holding you, thus you've one
more reason to live.
A gratitude and love so deep,
under no circumstances could
it ever grow weak.
Yes Mommy, this gift goes to
you; and if in your times of
sorrow, you listen, I promise
you'll always hear, the voice
of your little girl's whisper
saying, as a tear rolls silently
down her cheek, Mommy I
love you.

—Verna M. Wolf

ETERNITY

In your eyes, I see eternity,
  Two dark, fathomless pools staring back at me,
Where meet the future, present, and past,
As we will meet at long last.
Your eyes go warm with sunshine, or stormy with rain;
Alight with love, or cloudy with pain.
But happily you watch me,
For in my eyes, you see eternity.

—Karen Stefanik

I'm sitting here, alone. In this transit station
Watching a precocious child with a straw
    hanging out of his mouth
Peek-a-booing through the window.

Traffic is passing all the time—everything is moving;
Everyone is moving, changing. Why?
Why must everything change?

I thought I knew you, and maybe once I did
    but you changed, or I grew up
Your life is a game and I can't play it.

I couldn't play by your rules because you kept
    changing them—you didn't keep a printed copy!
If I could play by your rules I wouldn't be here
    playing peek-a-boo with someone else's baby.

—Heather Mesler

A GRANDFATHER

How will they remember me when I'm gone—and dead?
  Will they remember me by my grace and style?
Or will they remember the comical things I said,
    and repeat them with a smile?
How I made them laugh (or cry),
    with stories of bygone times.
Or the funny old hat I wore;
    I wore it "rain or shine."
How they listened with respect and veneration,
    as I expounded on "this new generation."
My kindness to the very old, the very young;
Patiently, I listened to their tales of woe,
    or to the songs they'd sung.
It would be nice if they could say,
    "My Grandpop, the Senator"—or such.
But I'd rather hear them say,
    "My Grandpop, that I loved so much."

—John J. Meares, Jr.

A POEM FOR KENNY, AGE 3

With his eyes full of tears, he waits at my knee
  While I fix the broken toy, that's been thrust at me.

I could be rewarded with a chubby little hug
But he reaches in his pocket, and presents to me, his bug.

Crayon marks, funny noises, crashes, bangs, and booms
Such a little fellow, yet his presence fills these rooms.

On the edges of fatigue I travel in his wake
Cleaning up one mess, while yet another he makes

What's that noise, who did this, where did that come from?
"The boogie man did it, me sure wub you mom."

Comes the end of the day, as I'm tucking him in bed
Sighing heavy and kissing his sweet little head

I'm bemused, as I reflect on the contrary joy
Of loving this whirlwind, that is my little boy.

—Connie Blevins Sambrook

MAMA AND ME

There are so little words can say, But God called Mama home today,
   He told me with the Love of God, and my firm belief,
He'd give me added strength in my time of grief.
His Love and matchless power gave me comfort hour by hour.

All our hopes and things we had planned were blessed by the touch
   of his Loving hand,
He blessed us both on our special day, He was always riding
   with us along life's way.
He gave me treasures and memories that none can take away.
He gave me a happy pathway of yesterdays tomorrow and great
   joy of today.

Although at such a time as this, there's little one can do,
But our friends and neighbors were with us, with their warm thoughts
   and prayers too.
Our sorrow's path is paved with tears, and hard for us to stand,
But the walk becomes more bearable, by having God and friends
      Like you to hold our hands.

   —Hazel Maness

WHERE DOES THE SKY END?

You will never find the end of my sky all abound,
   Because of all the love that shines from sky to ground.
   Without my sky to guide us and show us on our way,
Life would not be worth living, or getting up day by day.
   The world would be filled with hatred and the people would all be
Running here, and there, without a care for my sky and me.
   Some people say I am crazy to think my sky does not end,
But they would not know for they have no love with — in.
   At least I keep on trying to convince the world below,
That I am a heavenly angel and have seen the sky and know!
   I know I cannot be dreaming, because I've pinched myself till I'm blue,
And I can hear the laughter that people make through and through.
   But I will tell you one more time I know that this is so,
My sky does not end—it just goes and goes and goes!
   If you start walking until you are beat,
My sky will be there right upon your feet.
   The year is getting older but I am giving you one more chance to go,
Go and find my endless sky and don't say I did not tell you so!
   When you find my endless sky, please tell me so I'll know,
I am not the only angel, on the ground below!!

   —Deboraha Linn Shutt, age 12

innocent years

watch the children play in the park
      running, laughing, yelling . . . happy
      romping through trees
      swaying to and fro on swings
      squealing with delight at the promises of life.

see their upturned, innocent faces
      carefree, open, trusting . . . happy
      catching the rays of the sun
      absorbing its blanketing warmth
      positive that tomorrow will bring new wonders and joy.

hope they remain confident — serene — through the years
      growing, discerning, dreaming . . . happy?
      taking on the responsibilities of adulthood
      learning of life's beauties and tragedies
      questioning all they see, hear, read, feel.

don't forget these lazy summer afternoons, little ones
      remember how it feels to run, to laugh, to dream . . . to be happy
      keep your heart open to the wonders of life
      i remember . . .
         oh, to be young again.

   —Esther H. Okawa

The heart beats strong
   Against the wind;
The child lies silent;
The light grows dim.

A dream ensues,
The child awakes;
A frightening thought
Is all it takes.

A screaming child,
A desperate mom,
A loving thought
Voiced in song.

A mother's answer
To a child's cry;
Whispers of love
Found in a lullaby.

   —Susan Casto

RURAL REQUIEM

Sometimes there's not
   much excitement
in a prairie day —
expanse of grass, rocks,
small animals —
leaves shimmering
and shaking
over the little hill.
Daily chores of
dull routine
until the train
speeds by
like a column of
mercury —
lighted windows
like bright eyes —
a thrill as darkness
comes and
another day
is laid to rest.

   —Betsy Slyker

WATERFALL

Water falls
   down
      down
plummeting, splashing
against pebbles, stones
   raking across the
      river bed.
      Swish. Swirl.
Wearing, tearing
away particles
against their will, desire
   carrying them on to
      new homes along
         the river bed
Until water falls
   down
      down
         down again
beginning the entire
   process anew.

   —SPIV

Sometimes I think we are put here on earth
For no other reason than to find ultimate love,

To search aimlessly until we come across one person
Who is every essence of what we've been looking for,

From then on and with purpose, everything we feel
Encompasses a world of its own,

I have found this certain Utopia,
I have found you.

—**Trudy Elder**

IT IS

Truth has a quality not easily found
   by unreasoning, emotionally bound.

For in a quest to find
one must train the mind.

Build on the proven, not the hear-say of the crowd;
not a faith unfounded, or a clamor or cloud.

Truth's not a braggart.
It's a standard without sound.

Whether known or un; honored or un,
It honors none. It is.

Truth laid bare: eloquent probity;
maintains viability unwaveringly.

The discipline truth can teach!
Moral, mental, emotional: each.

Brings honor to oneself, no doubt,
For giving no note to a siren's song to sell-out.

Its value's not by man's value on it,
Its reward's its value given those honoring it.

Traceable; veracity!
Covered or un; verity — it is.

—**William Wright**

A STUDY OF THE WORLD

THE WORLD is a pyramid
   Of visions of all sides of the world.

      Some bad — some good.

THE WORLD is a pinnacle
   From which we sometimes leap

      Into fire — into water.

THE WORLD is a scale of balance between
   Mastery and perfection

      To weigh — to measure.

THE WORLD is a prism
   Of angles and lines

      Some inventive — some straight.

THE WORLD is a sphere
   As around it spins

      Falling off — catching on.

THE WORLD is a musical ode
   Of lyrics and melodies

      In sharps — and flats.

THE WORLD is a test tube
   Of even mixtures

      Sometimes safe — often comfortable.

—**Ginny Westerdale**

I must walk on . . .
   through the rain,
   against the wind.
A journey difficult to travel.

Tomorrow is a new day
   and the sunshine is somewhere up ahead.
As long as I have that hope —
                     that belief . . .
then my feet shall stay
                  upon the path
         and
            the rain and wind
                  become my friends.

—**Melanie S. Tyra**

TIME

The air is thin
   The night is cold
The clocks are ticking
As time gets old

Time is given
And time is spent
Time is coming
And time hath went

The ticks and tocks, the dials and clocks
Immobility as time stands still

The seconds and years, the hopes and fears
Coming together at their will

As time goes on
As time is passed
The end is near
Close at last

Time is straight
Time will bend
There is no time
'til time will end

—**Kenneth B. Smith**

HISTORY IN THE MAKING

Sometimes I often wish things would
   remain the same,
we just had "History in the Making"
when the space shuttle went aloft.
Yesterday's strategic landing made
people think it was worth the cost.
I once believed in the space program
and the greater things that it would
bring,
but have we over stepped our boundaries?
Right now this is what I'm wondering,
Cloning man and test tube babies! Is
this what we call new birth?
We are making nuclear warheads and
experimenting with chemical warfare
that could destroy the earth.
We are taking the lives of children and
sending them to their doom,
The world in which we live is becoming
a place of gloom,
If this is "History in the Making" and to
all our destiny,
I wish our judgement would come soon
or have everything remain the way it
used to be!

—**Glenna Mann**

NO PLACE TO GO

You step down deep in the thick white snow,
Now you're stuck with no place to go.
Standing there all day
While your feet freeze away
In your knee deep of snow
With no place to go!

You want to go play
But your feet seem to stay,
So you fall to your face
Oh what a disgrace,
Your face is in the snow,
and you have no where else to go!

You put your hands down to get up,
Now you're really stuck.
So now with your body filled with snow,
You really have no place to go!

—Bridget Bartkowiak, age 15

PLAY OF DUSK

With falling dusk the cooling breeze
        bends the long stems
                of grass and reeds
While tree boughs sway with graceful ease
        and cattails give flight
                to cottony seeds.

Glistening with interrupted sheen
        the lake water ripples
                in faining light
While a rustling sound from darkening green
        settles with kindness
                on somber night.

The cool breeze smites with a tender blow
        that edge of dark
                to laughingly bring
A gentle whistling soft and low
        that whispers of grateful
                songs to sing.

With vibrant curtsy this dusk is met
And the long day sun has deftly set.

—Donald D. Smith

BOUNTIFUL FALL

Languishing lightly in a field of clover,
    As autumn abounds the hillside over;

Swatches of red, yellow, orange and green,
    Smudged together in a scintillating scene.

Countless clouds scurry overhead,
    Like feather pillows that grace my bed;

Bringing forth a buoyant breeze,
    Ruffling the leaves on an old oak tree.

A wisp of yellow surrenders its life,
And glides toward earth in colorful strife;

Nestling unnoticed amid others there,
    Just one more leaf in this harvest fair,

Except to the Creator who treasures all,
    And urges one with child-like awe,

To gather and press with infinite care,
    Into a book for others to share,

This glorious symbol of a bountiful fall,
I encountered one autumn, and held, enthralled.

—Sabrina Albert

THE DEMISE OF THE WOOLLIES

When nature lies in darkened mood,
Light is the heart when leaf buds brood.

Country streams and dashing rills,
Course frothing water down rocky spills.

In melodious overture birds o'er the lea,
Sing their praises in hymnal harmony.

A new world is dawning,
North breath is waning.

Brown stemmed grasses nobly nod,
In gentle zephyrs with southern prod.

Heralds a struggling verdant sea,
Laced with pink and white and purplely.

The shivering chill is fading fast,
I can mothball my red flannels at last.

—Leonard B. Talburt

WONDER

I wonder at the night and day
I wonder at the starlit sky
Wondering what the world would be
Without the acts of Nature

The rain those black clouds bring us
The changes in weather the seasons cause
Our survival accordingly—
Amazed I am—by these unique events

The plants that grow into big trees
The birds relishing the juicy fruits
Flowers smiling in multi-colours
A feast for our eyes to see

I bow to Thee, the magician
Every creation of yours is magnificent
This wonderful life—you've gifted me with
Millions of thanks to you

The vast blue sky, I shelter under
In Mother earth's bosom I'm reared
The happiest one I am!
On this great earth.

—Pratibha Jyothi

THE ARTIST OF LIFE

Behold splashes of sunshine water
As opposed to oil
Carefully splattered on the barren canvas
Under the careful eye of the artist

Who sorts, sifts, mixes
And creates dazzling, dizzying heights
Towers, cliffs, and sunshine water
Spits and sputters and dreams

For she is unafraid.
And of the shadows and circles
She colors and shapes monster into man
And clowns down in depths of deceit

Into friends, fancy, fun, and ever free
Daylight from nights of dark, stark, bleak
With her sunshine water she erases her fears
Into laughing flowers at night

Who are watered by her tears
Of sunshine water carefully splattered
On her barren canvas or her barren heart
As she knows how to create and survive.

—Tara D. Van Bijsterveld

WE WANT TO LINGER IN THE SOFTNESS

March and April
Will they ever last,
Or us to endure
For us to grow;
Before the day
We suddenly realize
The time went so fast
Yet we still want to linger
in the softness . . .
of snow

—Ai T. V. Nguyen

THE MASTER PAINTER

A world dressed up in shades
Of red, yellow, green and brown;
A more perfect painting never found.
Rainbows of color splashed across the sky;
Draped in majesty before the eye.
The Master with His brush in hand,
Canvas before Him, and hues so grand,
Lays out the scene at His command.
Who can copy the portrait painted,
Or capture the grandeur of all the world holds?
None but the Master; I believe it's been told.

—Joyce Monroe

MOOD SWINGS

Colors in trees are of different hues,
There's a change in the sounds of the birds —
Fields of grain are all golden and full
With a promise of bounty anew.
Mother Earth is busily changing —
Her garb with a different style,
For one day it is windy with a change in the air,
The next day is warmer and mild!
The winds of her breath make the bright leaves dance,
As they skip merrily here and there —
Then they fall to the ground without making a sound
Lying motionless almost anywhere.
You feel the change in all of her moods —
Coquettish Fall is 'most here,
The reason for all the swings of her style —
The dear lass wants a new wardrobe to wear!!

—Marie E. Gingrich

AGAINST THE STORM

Winter's rain kisses
    the earth parched and dry,
        filtering through spindly fingers
            on tree limbs, whence yesterday
                were clothed in autumn dress.

Gales of wind moan
    as though in great pain,
        much like a woman in labor
            giving newness of life
                to her firstborn.

Old house with peeling paint
    and creaking floors
        with warmth and shelter
            inside your fading walls
                give solitude,

Against nature's elements
    in the world outside,
        the darkness portrayed
            beyond my field of vision.

—Evamarie Rushing

SAILBOAT IN THE SUNSET

The sun on the sail,
    The sail in the wind,
The image of happiness
That has no end.

The waves splashing on the rocks
Allow a person
To feel safe and secure,
As if a person had no cares.

Love fills the heart,
A dream of paradise seems possible,
Then when the boat docks
The dreams of a better world vanish.

The dreams and hopes of a person
Should not be forgotten,
But above all, fulfilled.
A sailboat in the sunset
Should be treasured . . . .

—Eric Kelly, age 13

SEASONS

Summer, Winter, Spring and Fall
    if you listen carefully
you can hear Mother Nature call.
    In the summer
when the breeze is blowing very light,
you'll see the birds
and that can be quite a sight.
    When the leaves change colors
and begin to drop,
you'll know right then
Summer's gonna stop.
    When it's cold outside
and there's frost on the ground
you can usually tell
Winter is coming around.
    When it's nice outside
and the sun is shining bright,
you can relax all day
and sometimes at night.

—Tracy Munson

SNOW

Glistening, glimmering, sparkling white
    Shining, glowing in the night
Falling, falling one by one
    more and more they do come

Turning my head toward the sky
    A snowflake landed by my eye
Melted slowly then became
    Something like a drop of rain

Soft and cool upon my skin
    Making me tingle all within
Snow, Snow, falling down
    All over the entire Town

Making the ground a blanket of white
    Right before my very sight
Footprints in the powdery snow
    Tracks that go to and fro

Snow, Snow falling down
    All over the entire town
Falling gently without a sound
    From the heavens to the ground.

—Maryann Abajian

A seed of Love was
planted in my heart and it
grew into a flower that longs
to be picked by the hands that
planted it

—Ashid.Bahl.K.

OUR LOSS IS HEAVEN'S GAIN

Her voice no longer echos,
through the hallways in my home.
Her feet no longer walk the paths,
where in her childhood she did roam.

Those little things she used to do,
to try so hard to please.
The pillow that she knitted,
and the kitten she would tease.

The lifetime that she tried to put,
into a few short years.
The loved ones that she left behind,
to fill their void with tears.

The memories that she left behind,
now we hold so dear.
But they will never take the place,
of when we held her near.

But she's left to be with Jesus,
he took her home to stay.
Our love is still strong for our little girl,
and we miss her everyday.

—Dale A. Hall

THE WARMTH

We are the Kings' creation,
And he loves us all as one.
We are his treasured children,
Just like his precious son.

All he makes is perfect,
For he himself is, too.
We are his precious people,
And his love is all so true.

But at times we do not see,
Or understand God's purpose.
We shy away from others,
Because we only see the surface.

Like the ones who cannot walk,
Or those who cannot speak.
The ones who need our loving care,
And to give it is a love unique.

But what a joy it would be,
What a love we could feel.
If we'd look beneath the surface,
We'd see a love so real.

A love that comes from God,
A heart that can be so true.
A gift that's filled with love,
And it's meant for me and you.

So open up your eyes,
And seek what's in their heart.
You'll find the warmth that lies there,
Is a love that will never part.

—Lee Stratton

WHY

What have I done now?
I can't face life or reality.
My soul's tearing me apart.
Screaming for wisdom and rationality.

I've gone so many years.
With nothing, but drugs and fears.
I often wonder why;
But seem to do nothing but cry.

Why can't I grow up — be who I dream to be.
A person full of goodness and God beaming out of me.

The years have come and gone.
And I'm still weak and never strong.
I pray at night for my soul,
But tomorrow it's forgotten and I'm so cold.

So, what's the matter with me?
Why can't I be, who I really should be?
Why can't I be,
Just a good old me?

—Debra Kay Ellis

BROKEN WINGS

Through memories he continues to levitate upward
passing through heaven's doors.
On wings of the past, he returns once again
to where his spirit still soars.

A bird of prey, he prays to live, the life that he
once led,
and refuses to yield to the erosion of time what lingers
in his head.

Through misty eyes he scans the skies where his broken
wings can never again go,
and curses the gravity which keeps him down from a
life only he could know.

The nourishment to sustain his being is for the taking
on the ground,
yet his spirit still starves for the freedom of flight
that so long ago he found.

If through a twist of fate, he was given one more
chance to soar,
he would fly at the speed of sound, into the ground,
and pass through heaven's door.

—Daniel Whitehurst

EMOTIONS RULE

The world revolves, but not around people.
One President, one God, one Pope—
Billions of laymen begging for hope.
A castle, a shack, an archaic church with a steeple.

The world revolves, constantly being used.
AIDS, drugs, despair, degradation—
A loving, caring God, with plans for creation.
Homeless, hungry, neglected, abused.

The world revolves, without hope or glory.
Struggling day after day, shattered dreams—
Sleepless weeks, tormenting nightmares, scattered screams.
Gunfire, bloodshed, sinful war can get gory.

The world revolves around emotions.
Life's ups and downs, sporadic mood swings—
Soul searching, heart wrenching, finding peace when a
voice sings.
God's love for his people goes beyond depths of the oceans.

—Jean Marie Raney

TALE OF A YOUNG PREACHER

I was sitting at home just wasting my time.
And all of a sudden I thought of this rhyme.

I was standing in the pulpit and what did I see?
Everyone in the church was staring at me.

I thank the Lord for just one more day.
But now that I'm up here, I don't know what to say!

I may talk funny, but don't correct my speech.
Just listen to this message that I'm about to preach.

Amen.

—"The Original"

FEELINGS ON HIGH

As I lie on my back eyes set on the stars
Surrounded by mountains from near and afar
Tranquility takes hold of my body and soul
Settling my spirit and making me whole

It's hard to explain these feelings of love
And feeling as one with the heavens above
There is no other way of expressing why
Except but to say it's a natural high

There's no place on earth that I'd rather be
Than here in these mountains above the sea
For there's nothing more moving in music nor verse
Than these feelings you're one with the whole universe

—Joi

I WON'T NEED ANY CREDIT CARDS IN HEAVEN

There won't be any shopping centers in Heaven.
All my basic needs will be supplied.
No need for credit cards will be given,
If during my life on Jesus I have relied.

Chorus or Refrain:

I won't need any credit cards in Heaven.
On the Cross of Calvary my precious Jesus died.
He paid it all; my debts are freely forgiven.
With His blood on the cross He cried.

There will be plenty of food at God's table.
A feast is already being prepared.
I'll be worthy to partake because I'll be able.
There will be enough with all believers to be shared.

Chorus or Refrain

I will be robed in garments of pure white.
With never a soiled spot of dirt again,
If on earth to the Lord I've given my life.
Because with His blood Jesus rid me from my sin.

Chorus or Refrain

One day I'll rest in that city of pure gold.
There with all my friends I will be,
Where goods are not bought or sold.
Don't miss Heaven by not relying on thee.

Chorus or Refrain

All believers in Christ will attend the concert free
To hear the Heavenly choirs singing.
Everyone will sing in the Gospel Jubilee.
The melodious praises to Him will be ringing.

Chorus or Refrain.

—Dr. L. Marvin Marion

THE EAGLE SOARS

See the eagle as he flies,
High up in the clear blue sky,
He dives and soars,
And floats on high.

His wings are spread in majestic grace,
He never fails to show his strength,
How does he continue to show
The awe of God in nature?

He makes his nest high on the rocks,
He protects his young with food and care.
He chases man and predator alike,
From his home that's out of sight.

He glides, he soars, he dives for fish,
Man can only wish,
To feel the wind beneath the wings of life.
Flying, soaring the eagle flies,
High up in the clear blue sky.

—Ginny Ogline

LIFE'S BEAUTY

Come take a wonderful trip with me,
There's many beautiful things to see.
Squirrels flittering among the trees,
Leaves drifting with the whispering breeze.

Beautiful horses so free and wild,
A loving smile from a trusting child.
Deer stop by a babbling brook,
Beautiful to see, just stop and look.

Snow covered fields so shiny and bright,
An eagle soaring softly in flight.
A friendly smile to brighten the day,
A loving hand extended your way.

Sleeping out under clear starry skies,
Seeing nature's world through watchful eyes.
The twinkling stars that glisten above,
Indicate the power of God's love.

Children of God share in His praises,
A joyful look on all their faces.
Praise the Lord for the gift of living,
Make someone glad by simply giving.

—Sandra Ann Moore

OUT OF THE HURT

Out of the hurt you must now come
Out of the depths it's over and done
Out of the past you must now move
Time to go forward and get in the groove
Bury the fear and turn off the pain
Cast off depression it's time to gain
Get rid of the hate and start to love
All of your help comes from above
Jesus is the way, the truth, and the life
Thru Him you can conquer all of the strife
Reach out to Him He's there for you
And He is so faithful and very true
Bury yourself in the word of God
Time to start feeding your spiritual bod
Learn from the past and live in the now
Trust in the Lord and He'll show you how
God works thru people and places them there
They'll help you out because they care
Receive God's love as He gives you some
And out of the hurt you will now come.

—Martin Fick

MY LAST ROAD

When I come to my
last road,
How gladn, I'll be, to
see my departed,
I fought the battle
of life,
Now the task is done,
Fame or fortune I
did not seek,
Only in my humble way,
I held fast to my dream,
to find love that would
last for all time,
this I did do,
without shame or fear,
I come before our lord,
Knowing I found love,
And left love behind,
on his great earth.

—Norma V. Jones

EXISTENCE

The bed looked large,
the pale, sunken face
on the white pillow,
looking out
from a white sea
of destruction.
At the bedside I sit,
overwhelmed with feeling.
We are just
people.
We are not
eternal.
In that face
only the eyes
tell all.
You, Sir,
have lived so much,
a blue spread
will brighten
your white sea.

—Alexis Upright

HIGHLIGHTS OF LIFE

Precious metals,
Pools of gold,
Flower petals,
And stories told.

Nostalgic dolls,
Pasture hills,
Shopping malls,
And dollar bills.

Summer beaches,
Tall sand castles,
Sweet, ripe peaches,
And graduation tassels.

Beautiful girls,
Cloudless skies,
Expensive pearls,
And apple pies.

Classic cars,
Pizza whenever,
Midnight stars,
And love forever.

—Te-Te Connaway

WARM LOVE, THE LIFE WISH, AND ONENESS

The difference between having nothing, and having everything, is love:

Without warm love, we have nothing:
we have no happiness;
we have no friends;
we have no home;
we have no work;
Without warm love, we eventually have no life;

But with warm love, we have everything:
we have happiness;
we have friends;
we have a home;
we have a job or work;
And with warm love, we have abundant life;

Without warm love, we are isolated and divided;
With warm love, we become Altogether One.

—Paul Bollman, Jr.

LEGACY

Within the shadows of her mind live memories from another time
of when she was a child.

"Why were things so simple then?" she once inquired of the friend
she had as a child.

He'd wink and slowly turn around then sit with her upon the ground
and smile at the child.

When things didn't go her way her friend would look at her and say,
"Have patience my child. Enjoy the beauty of life each day. Then tuck the
memories away to savor, dear child."

He'd comfort her with happy song, he taught her what was right and
wrong. She learned as a child.

No longer does she have this friend to chat with time and time again
about being a child.

She longs for the warm and witty ways of the one who filled her
carefree days with love as a child.

Living deep in the shadows of my mind are memories of the love and time
Grandpa gave me, I was that child.

—Bonita Winifred

MY NEPHEW BUDDY

In memory of Angelo James Lamitina
(Sept. 17, 1954,-Aug.7, 1977)

My nephew Buddy, was three, when he fell and broke his little arm
Doing his little odd chores up on the farm
I cried when I saw his little arm all fixed up in a cast
But to Buddy, it all seemed like a great big blast

Twas the fourth of July, the carnival was in town that day
But that cast wasn't going to stand in our way
I picked him up and we were off to the park
And we stayed there until it was nearly dark

The merry-go-round, went around and around
The ferris wheel so high, we couldn't see the ground
We rode all the rides and ate everything in sight
Getting tired, we decided to call it a night
"I had a lot of fun 'Jo Jo' he said
I think it's time to go home and to bed"

Buddy was killed by a drunken driver, one sad August night
He was only twenty two, so handsome, caring, loving, his future so bright
He now resides with our Lord, in the heavens above
I miss him so, we shared so much love
Our lives will never, ever, be the same
We all called him "Buddy" but "Angelo" was his name.

—Josephine Lamitina Johnson

OH! WHY NOT A CHILD FOR ME?

She was just a child herself and she loved other Children for them-
selves.
She would run up to strangers and ask, May I see and talk to your
baby?
Oh, Oh Mother she would cry out loud, Oh! What a darling Baby is
she and he. May I take it home with me?
Oh. Oh! No said her Mother You may not take it home Because
It does not belong to thee.

As she grew into womanhood and loved and married, she hoped she
would be blessed one day with a darling Baby.

But as time grew on and she got older, still no child
upon her shoulder.
She was happy as could be but saddened because she didn't have a he and she
But she understood it wasn't meant to be for thee.

—Patricia Shirk Burke

MEMORIES OF YESTERDAY UNFOLD TODAY

I sit by the window and see memories through the pane of yesterday.

I see you in your little mud-caked form running to me
seeking the glistening sprinkler and laughing in childish glee
ending a day of fun in the summer sun.
Autumn comes with leaves of color, crisp and cool
as with family you rake and romp in a high and bouncy pool.
Winter in its wondrous dress, sparkling and so pure
takes you by your warmly-clad hand
as you slide and sculpt with others strong and so sure.
Apple blossoms spring forth and you eagerly dance o'er the greening field
embracing the warming delight serving you as a caressing shield.

I long for you to know, again, the happiness of loving family and a friend
tho, at times, you express fragmented thoughts of joyousness
of your fragile mind trying to mend.
Time and season pass as you emerge from troubled teens to mid-life hours
waiting and wanting acceptance by society
still in search of a key to your locked-in space.
Now you sit clothed in womanhood dignity and special grace
hoping to unfold and forever end for all
the familiar pain of your loneliness of today.

—Ellen Astrid Laitila

TRUE COURAGE

Please tell me dear, what did the doctor say?
In her steady gaze, I met true courage, that day.

We hugged and loved each other, had a good cry;
Softly she said, "Don't worry Momma, I'm not going to die."

I saw her in her shock, a loving comfort, to her family be;
Lord, I questioned, would I have the same courage, if it were me.

She questioned, why not someone else, 'tis not fair a bit;
Then, "Forgive me Father, I guess you knew I could take it.

I have M.S., I'll meet each crisis as it comes along;
Good days or bad, in my heart, to my God, I'll sing a song."

We sat in silence, laughed, giggled, we talked;
I saw childish delight, when without pain she walked.

When others talked of crutches, braces and such things;
Quietly she said, "I'll meet each day whatever it brings.

I don't want people's sympathy or pity, just their love."
I saw quiet courage, true courage, that comes from Heaven above.

I ache for her, pray to our Heavenly Father, in Jesus' name;
Dear Lord, give us, her family and friends, courage that is the same.

To Jeanie Bagge, with all my love . . . Mother

—Ruth E. Holsten

SEIZE THE DAY

Now it's my turn
To stop,
Look around,
    Think what I want,
Realize what I want,
    Dream if I want,
And Seize The Day . . .

—Deana T. Potts

STREET CORNER

So much to life,
Just look and see.
So much more
Of what is to be.

The simple sights
Always seem to show,
The hardest ways
We choose to go.

Take a moment,
A breath, a sigh.
Let a dream
Refuse to die.

—Leah E. Epps

CHILD OF MINE

In your blue eyes
I see clear skies
Bumble bees
And skinned knees
While asking whys.

In your fleeting sighs
I hear happy ties
On long kite tails
Flying silvery veils
between our eyes.

In your first speech
I'll touch a sandy beach
The dawn of time
an endless rhyme
between our sighs.

—James P. Rudolph

Every candle
Across the world
Has been lit
A beautiful sight

Every angel
In the heavens
Sings a song
A wonderful sound

Every child
In all lands
Dances and plays
A great carefreeness

Every colour
Within the spectrum
Skips around
A terrific sight

Every candle
Across the world
Is being blown out
A terrifying darkness.

—Anne Michel Sayre

I wish for you a sunny day
And children's laughter while at play;

The soft sweet kiss of a summer breeze
And bluebirds in the willow trees;

Peaceful times and quiet hours;
Sparkling stars and cool spring showers;

Wildest joy! And deepest hope —
A world of bright kaleidoscope;

A dog to love, and lick your hand;
A lazy sea upon the sand.

I wish a winter snow for you
And snowflakes, delicate and new;

Autumn fires and crunching leaves
And God to help you to believe

That life is good and Earth is sweet,
And Jesus loves His every sheep.

  —Susan R. Pappan

FAREWELL

I never thought the time would come
to say "good-bye" at last,
it hurts a lot, you'll understand,
'cause you had all my trust.

To lose you tears away from me
a portion of my heart,
for all you leave are memories
of which you were a part.

It was so easy to rely
on you, when things got tough,
you always knew just what to do —
your being there was good enough.

You taught me well and patiently,
it will pay off, I'll say,
I thank you for the help you gave
to me in every way.

So long, dear friend, I wish you luck,
go on, and be your boss,
I'll always treasure knowing you —
your future is my loss.

  —Gertrude M. Altrichter

WHEN LOVE DIES

When love dies, it leaves an empty place
it can't be filled with any ole face
you're reminded by the love you knew before
the feelings that pop up just can't be ignored
I knew a love for many years
it faced a lot of bitter tears
so much has happened in the space of time
many times I've nearly lost my mind
but now inside is an emptiness so wide
I just can't pretend anymore
and I just can't hide
Somewhere out there
is a new love for me
I just have to learn to trust
and care and that I may see
that love when it's showing
will make you feel like glowing
cause love is the greatest gift in life
so let's have a lot of love
and no more strife.

  —Sandra Blomberg

WISH

I make a wish, when I look into your eyes,
That my dreams will come true.
It's like a ghost, that eludes the morning light____
My love's forever bound to you.

We are two ships, that sail upon the night,
Upon our journey home.
Safe on the course, your compass toward the light____
Will you sail away alone?

Don't you need someone
To hold you close at night____?
Don't you need someone
To make your burdens light____?

Each time we turn a page and spend another day____
Are moments shed away like tears?
I make a wish when I look into your eyes____
That you'll be my love tonight.

  —Eric R. Lawson

RESTLESS

Restless eyes wander to the perfect ocean view
I see the dunes
And the cottage
And the birds
And you
Restless feet wander to the place by your side
The place that stands alone
Only invaded by the tide
Restless voice wanders and asks, "Who are you?"
The girl only smiles
This girl of the ocean view
Restless hand wanders to caress her soft face
One as soft as silk
And as dainty as lace
Restless heart wanders and you say, "I love you"
I remember I am dreaming
This is too good to be true
Restless eyes wander and you fade just out of view
Reality comes back
And I miss seeing you.

  —John P. Watters

MARRIED LOVE

I fear the end is near, soon or now.
Just when I thought we began to know each other well,
And the hurts were nearly gone,
And the future was forever—
What went wrong?

Was love too blind to reveal each other's shortcomings?
Was the painting on the canvas too rosy to be real?
Have we changed, or grown, or merely drifted apart?

We need to search in order to know—
Is it love or convenience keeping us together now?
Is it easier just to stay than to go?
Is love enough to accept the bad with the good?

Life is for living, each day consumed with happiness—
Or close to it.

Can we make it? Do you know?
Is there left the desire, the passion for love that
 once was so strong?
Can it smother the doubts or fear of separation?

Is it strong? Is it real? Is it love?

Love is eternal.

  —Christy Tebbetts-Gorski

GENTLE LOVE

At the ocean's edge, there's a peace to be found
Though waves roar in from the sea.
For the sea and the waves make not one demand,
But they say, "If you like, come to me."

And if at the beach I pick up some sand
And hold it gently, at ease,
The sand in my hand escapes not at all
Like it would if I'd give it a squeeze.

Love is the same when gently it's given
It neither will choke nor demand,
But humbly it comes to a heart's doorstep
And there it will silently stand.

—Millie Sparks

TO MY HUSBAND

Together we are one, apart we are none.
You are the rising sun that gives me strength
To grow and blossom.
You are the gentle sculptor, taking a
Worthless stone and creating a sparkling
Diamond.
You dry my tears when the world closes in.
You share my burdens when the road gets rough.
You've seen me in my darkest moments when I
Felt no one cared; yet you've always stood by me.
So many things you've done; and all I have to
Repay you are three simple words . . .

I LOVE YOU !!

—Lise C. B. Page

SMILES

As the sun shines onto the world,
so does your smile.
As the rain was made to fall, and birds to sing,
so were you for me to love.
As people share their life in work or play,
it's sad for me to sit here with you so far away.

I long not for enjoyment nor lust,
but for companionship, love, and trust.
But as good and bad times have come to be,
so will you, someday return to me.

As the moon lights up the night when it shines,
so will I, when someday again,
you'll be mine.

—Juan Verdeja

Marry me, Mister, in the dark of me night.
Capture me heart it's a lover's delight.
No distance will find us when empty space breathes.
Save, ye fill another heart's yielding need.
Then ye forget me name and face
lest ye etch my silhouette without haste upon
ye heart and mind and soul.
Do it now, me sweet.
Now . . .
With stone or mace.
Don't let this image leave ye heart's embrace.
With luck and desire our paths may meet when
shadows are long and dreams are all reached.
It's then we'll fit the silhouette that stayed
etched in heart and mind and soul.
Never let it go.
Never let it go.

—Linda O'Toole

SMILED

Yesterday you passed by my window's view
While walking your non-chantily way.
As you passed — you waved hello,
Smiled.
Then proceeded to walk on into the night.

Today again but faster now
You strolled again into view.
Looked straight my way — had a hello to say,
Smiled.
Then proceeded to walk on into the night.

Tomorrow you'll stop and chat with me
And the minutes will turn into hours.
Before I know it — you'll decide to stay
And say hello forever.
Smile
And we'll proceed to walk on into the
Night — together.

—Maureen McNeil

SINCE I MET YOU

Since I met you
it's always spring.
Warm and new
fresh and alive.
Reality commands.
(I reluctantly comply)
Leaving the safe cocoon of your warm embrace
—fantasy wrapped all around me—
into the cold,
cruel,
winter of a world.
But my heart
stays with you.
The ecstacy of sweet chocolate kisses
and tomorrow dreams
held tightly in my arms.
And all the love songs
ever written
are talking about me
Since I met you . . . .

—Karen Louise Minick

MY DAD'S SMILE

A smile is such a special thing.
Joy and love it can bring.
When it's from your own dad's face
It's from a very special place.

Dad smiled on me with love and pride,
I often failed, but he knew I tried.
On children, some his own, some were not,
He smiled lovingly, he smiled a lot.

Never a stranger did he meet,
No one did he ever mistreat.
He never had fortune, he never had fame,
But, oh that smile was always the same.

A part of his smile I still see
Everytime I smile at me.
That smile I see everyday
When my son sends a smile my way.

Yes, my dad's gone, his life is done,
But that smile lives on—
In my little son.

In memory: Stevie Rosson
—Connie Rosson Hicks

Dear great grandfather,
You are 96 and you are dying.
I don't know where you
are going.
But wherever it is,
I hope you will be happy
This is from your
great granddaughter Laura
And I love you very much

—Laura Ann Judge

MY FATHER

Do you know the Son?
You and He are one
in my Father
God divine,
maker of all.
Many worlds,
sheep are driven
to find riches
within our King
my Father, your Father,
our Father in us.
Come into the kingdom
of wedding bliss.
Father of Love,
sons and daughters,
mild honey and
laughter by the tons
in heaven sought,
already bought
with happy ending
and our blending into one.
Father Love and a holy dove
within us from up above.
My Father elate.

—Ms. Bonnie Simmons Peter

DADDY I LOVE YOU

This little boy sits quietly
beside his dad,
With his tiny little hands pressed
against his face,
With his curious eyes, he watches
every move his dad makes.
He gently turns his timid head,
looks into his daddy's eyes,
and softly says,
"Daddy, I love you, and that is
the way it will be forever and
ever."
Then his daddy embraces his precious
little one, his first and only
son.
He speaks only kind words of
encouragement, for him to understand.
"You will be my son now and forever,
even when you grow up and find
your true love and others.
Then at that time, you will grow
as one. Then someday you will
have a son.
Then he will sit quietly beside
you and say,
'Daddy I love you, and that is
the way it will be forever and
ever'."

—Katherine E. Couch

MY GRANDFATHER

My Grandfather was an Englishman
With golden hair and a beard of tan.
When my Mother was eight or nine
He'd take her for walks, when the day was fine.
They'd stop at a farm and buy "High Tea."
Toast and a salad, and vegetables three.
Tomatoes, cheese and lettuce green,
With great dignity, it would seem.
One pretty day, as they ate formally,
My Grandfather, as he ate his "tea."
Gave a gulp, and putting down his mug,
With a fork took off a two horned slug!!
And put it on the edge of his plate.
Ate his salad, so they wouldn't be late.
As he finished his lettuce, and wiped his mouth,
Again he gulped, and turned due south!
That cute little two horned slimy slug,
Was chewed up well, by that gentleman's mug!!
And his face turned green and then bright red,
When he realized how he had been fed!!!
    Shh! Not a Word!!

—Valentine Taggart

JUST AN OLD MAN

Just an old man I knew left this world the other day
No bands, no shouts, no fanfare, he just quietly slipped
away.
He was thoughtful and kind, a man who was very proud
A simple man of taste, not much less than a face in
the crowd.
Just an old man who talked endlessly of living the olden
ways
Of great steamships, wars, and bootlegged scotch, reminders
of by-gone days.
He lived in a small house with his small dog and his ailing
bedridden wife
No riches or fame, no rewards were his, just a hard, hard life.
He escaped to the solitude of his little workshop, it helped
pass the time away
I guess he dreamed of the bridges he built, and of the days
he earned his pay.
He recalled the days he worked with a pick-ax, No, a man
couldn't get by with just talk
And the cold windy days he went fishing for Blues in the
seas off Montauk.
And of his sweet days of youth when his hair was still
dark and he stood tall and straight
Back when youth lived forever the world was still his, he
never thought of heaven's gate.
But now his time had come and gone and he's gone to that
promised land
Now still and life-less the old man laid, beneath the cold,
cold sand.
Just an old man of little consequence, he never did anything
great
The castles he built were in the air, Walter Mitty dreams and
empty pockets were to be his fate.
Just an old man who wasn't much to look at, slightly built
with a craggy weathered face
This testimony to this old man sounds a little sad, it seems
so, but I can make a better case
Just one grain of sand of the mortar that helped make strong
the base
Just an old man I knew and loved, that sure made this world
a better place!

—Dro Ostenhagen

THOSE GOLDEN YEARS

Time long ago when we were young
and had so much fun.
Time long passed as it flickered through the glass
and your time couldn't last.
Time is on the run and one has passed on,
so those Golden Years are gone.
So use the time at hand
and put it in God's plan.
Then those Golden Years will stay in a special land,
in the back of your mind locked for all time.
But you can bring them back
if your memory does not lack.
Time is a fading thing, but the good memories of the past
will stay for you and always last.
To lift you up when you are down
and help remove that frown, those Golden Years.

—Walter Mark Houseman

THE OLD MAN

I saw an old man walking, just the other day.
But what he was thinking, I couldn't say.
Maybe he was thinking, about that day.
Maybe he was thinking, about some other day.
I went up and asked him, if there was something I could do.
He just smiled and said, not that he knew.
So I walked along beside him, and we didn't even talk.
But somehow I knew, it was his last walk.
We walked for what seemed, to me like a week.
But in all that time, he didn't even speak.
Shortly after that, we came to a halt.
I think he was crying, but it wasn't my fault.
I think he said something, about not wanting to go.
But even till this day, I still don't know.
I don't even know his name, but I loved him just the same.
We both knew he was dying, but no one was to blame.
But it was time to go back, from where he came.
He mumbled something, under his breath.
Then started walking, back into the west.
I know some day, my time will come.
I too will have to go back, where I came from.
I know I won't want to, but I'm not afraid.

—Jeffrey G. Carrick

AN ELDERLY GENT

An elderly gent in a chair with wheels
Totally disoriented and unable to eat his meals.
A sad, lonely face with many wrinkles,
And stringy gray hair in little crinkles.
Calling out to whoever will hear,
Sometimes not even realizing his family is near.
This nice old man the world will never know,
But he did his part and suffered many woes.
In a plane he flew across the ocean blue,
And fought for his country, for me, and for you.
Now in a bed he sleeps the time away
Occasionally remembering things happy and gay.
He loves his family and only wants the best,
But because of a disease in the bed he must rest.
Friends of remembered days come by to see
Unfortunately, they don't realize the severity.
They talk and chat, trying to get a smile,
But he just sits and listens for awhile.
He can't speak clearly and he can't comprehend,
And deep down inside we know this illness should end.

Dedicated to my father who has been a victim of Alzheimers Disease
for six years and is currently in a nursing home.

—Deborah K. Heckman

GROWN AND GONE

Older, always older,
day by month by year,
gone, but never always,
young voices all you hear.

Advice once only given,
now returns twofold,
meaning they did listen
to every truth you told.

Their shoulders have grown broader,
conversations seem more real,
but you remember chicken pox,
they, the homemade meals.

So return they do to match memories,
to fill more than their minds,
to carry on tradition,
that links all humankind.

—Nancy K. Goodwin

TEACHINGS OF A BLIND MAN

I saw a blind man on the street
and felt sadness for him
and pity.

He made his way quite easily
with great determination
and little uncertainty.

I walked beside him
and asked him how he managed
to be so sure where he was going.

He kept walking
and told me that he needed only
his heart to see.

I stopped walking
and watched him pass and realized
that I was more blind than he
for I saw only with my eyes.

—M.E. Painter

Gone—
They say
I say not quite.
You live again with me each and
every night—
Dancing and singing, work and play—
We do each night since you went
away—
Your birthday-my birthday?
We have a ball!
Thanksgiving and Christmas?
No trouble at all—
Romping with grandchildren
You have never seen—
My—what a good life—
You live in my dream!
Gone! They say—
Just a knowing smile to them
I give—
Never! My Dear
Not as long as I live:

In memory of my husband
who died Dec. 17th, 1985
Ralph Edward Wright
'A loving husband and Father.'

—Sue O. Wright

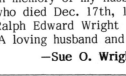

WATERGLASS

Has a rainy day ever mellowed your mind?
Has the drip and splash falling on idle thoughts
caused them to run together and blend
pasteled and glistening before they're caught
by a sonorous desire to ramble?
Foreign policy fuses with fancy
while droplets of memory confuse
with ever so serious ideas while advancing
images of good and bad parade
across watery windows in your head.
Let the sunny rainbows wait.
Make way for the showery thinkers instead.

—Janet E. Kauker

SNOW

What happens to the snow when it melts?

Does it sink into the ground
Like your foot in the mud?

Or does it evaporate into the air —
Like whispers from your mouth?

Or maybe it hides —
Like a child from the monsters
In the dark?

Maybe we can't see it —
Like a breeze from a tree.

Or is it there!

—Gretchen L. Klingler

AUTUMN'S FALL

Though the weather remains most fair,
There is a taint in the lazy air,
That tells me Autumn has come at last,
To end Summer's dying grasp;
Allowing a hint of cool to creep,
Where soon in joy Winter will leap.
For Fall is but a passing moment —
Of quiet death and brilliant color,
A time of end, retiring, and ease,
When all but the most hearty will cease,
To walk the empty, harvested fields,
Till Spring once more makes Winter yield.
And then again to Summer and back —
Once more to Fall's color and damp.

—Denise Lynn Pax

RESTLESS OCEAN

There lies a restless ocean near
Me. In my breast I hear
An echo, the thrust and flow
As the crests form and go.

Black clouds with angry faces
Challenge. Uneven foam erases
The gulls' tracks and my own
From the sand. The gulls are flown.

But I stay, bent against the wind
While the clouds burst and send
Their off'ring, libation poured
From flashing cups in major chord.

The rocks take tongue and speak,
Strange voices wet and weak,
And my heart pounds its echo
As I, sighing benediction, turn and go.

—Mary Helen Owen

SEASON OF LOVE

Flaming leaves of antique red and gold
Fell brittle and brown under Winter's beckoning call.
A brisk, bitter wind swept the leaves away,
Leaving a hard, frozen feeling; dismal and gray.
The seasons shifted as ancient stories told.
A hard driven sleet erased remaining signs of Fall.
With the subtle warmth of Autumn a shadow of the past,
Icicles splintered a heart frozen fast.

The lonely season is a desert, desolate and bare,
Concealing Nature's love harboring beneath.
A death that is necessary to start anew,
Only to be resurrected by the Spring's sweet dew.
A wandering soul searching for a garden of care,
Has stumbled upon the first green leaf.
A heart is thawing with God's tender touch
For He is the Summer that we need so much.

—Laura L. Heckman

WINTER

The ground was covered by a blanket of snow
It was like the weather was letting you know
Winter is not many months but just a few
It makes everything look so clean, fresh and new
Children are wrapped in coats, gloves and hats
This isn't the season for baseball and bats
The sun shining on the snow makes it so bright
They are building snowmen and having snowball fights
The grass and the trees are no longer green
And you don't hear the birds in the trees sing
The air is so cold, it feels like ice
People stay in their homes where it's warm and nice
Fireplaces are burning with colors so bright
You just sit and watch this beautiful sight
You never get tired of watching the logs burn
To keep it on fire the logs have to be turned
We should be thankful for winter seasons
It brings families closer for all kinds of reasons
We learn to get along and how to share
We learn what it means to be close and care

—Marla Norton

THE HONEYSUCKLE

When I smell the honeysuckle around
my door,
I'm a little girl back on the farm
once more.

I hear the roosters crow as the
new day begins.
Smell the aroma of country ham in
Mama's black frying pan.

Twilight — oh so peaceful
and serene.
Daddy and his songbooks, how I
loved to hear him sing.

Singing the old hymns helped create a
hunger for God in my heart.
And today there is nothing that can
cause it to depart.

We'd all sit together outside and listen
to the whippoorwill.
I praise God for my family and childhood;
it's precious to me still!

—Betty Lou Elliot

THE HUNTER

On my last hunting trip I spied this big buck.
His horns were widespread as the back of my truck.

About nine feet tall I would judge him to be,
(and there's very few guys as honest as me).

I think t'was a twelve point, though I'd not say for sure,
Cause to get accurate count I'd have had to stir,
Then I know his large ears would pick up the sound,
And know a "sure-shot" like me was around.

I think I'm allergic to some of those trees,
For wouldn't you know it—just then that I'd sneeze?

Then all I heard was a crash in the brush
As that mammoth buck disappeared in a rush!

It was the last day of season and it just seemed my fate,
To be a minute too early — or two minutes late.

But now I know where he's hiding so you just have no fear,
I'll bag him for sure opening day of next year!

—Alyce M Duncan

A SILVER SUNSET WITH GLITTERING STARS.

Not a cloud in sight!
I can see the moon.
It glistens and glows.
The brisk breeze tingles my senses,
As nature reveals her most beautiful thoughts to me.
I wish I could be swept away by the wind,
Into a deep, vast field far, far away.
A field stuffed with wild daises
The glorious smells of Spring.
Where no one can be hurt by anything.
My imagination runs over the hills,
Across the mountains and through the valleys.
To a city full of beauty,
A city where everyone notices a small sunrise or sunset.
A silent touch or glance, a perfect flower or weed,
Oh nature's beauty is revealed to everyone,
In its own special way.
All we have to do is look
It is different to each of us.

—Judy Anderson Greene

STOLEN FROM ME

I used to love to walk in the woods
Crackling branches beneath my feet
Looking for something, I'm not sure what
The treasures I found were there.

Maybe a chipmunk scurried away
Not sure my presence would harm
A small yellow bird, looking for food
Would land a few paces ahead.

The cobwebs across the path ahead
Told me that noone had passed
I was alone in the woods with just creatures around
The stillness and quiet like food.

My cathedral is a special place
Where the sun shines through the trees
On a jagged rock covered with moss
A shrine to noone but me.

Now there is progress; too many people
Guns, dogs and strangers
I can't walk in the woods and feel safe and secure
They've stolen that from me.

—Virginia Hladki

REFLECTIONS

When the nights are long and dreary
and the days are cold and weary,
take a moment to reflect
on several things you can expect.

Looking forward to the day
when birds no longer fly away,
but build their nests in yonder trees
without a thought of wintry breeze.

Look forward also to the clatter
of the ducks as they scatter,
and the ripples on the pond
begging nature to respond.

And don't forget the morning sun
and all the chores that must be done.
The barn door swaying to and fro
reminds us that we need to go
and latch it tight against the wind.
Wake up! Wake up! It's spring again.

—Jane L. Zoll

THE SKIES HAIKU

Jet patterns crisscross.
The evening sky shows sundown.
Universe broadens.

The skies are lofty.
Slow are the floating pillows.
Clouds float lazily.

Skies reflect oceans.
Endless space is so extreme.
The skies are blue fields.

Earth and sky collide.
Predominantly is moon.
Moon and sun are high.

Heaven lights twinkle.
Sometimes, the stars look like eyes.
The sky watches down.

Unlimited skies.
Sky is an endless pocket.
Long space seems lengthy.

—Audrey F. Brown

SUMMER

I hate summer
Boring bummer
Neighborhood children in my kitchen
Everybody out! Screamin, Bitchin,
A mother genius, but nobody knows
Cuz I'm in the laundry room
Washin' clothes

My husband is home
He's a working necessity
(All I do is dream incessantly)
He's the mechanic and pays the bills
(I only create for thrills)
He says his work comes first
(So my feminine brain can die of thirst)
He says, "Just remember honey,
your work doesn't make no money."

A mother genius
but nobody knows
cuz I'm coolin' off kids
with a green garden hose

—Tanno

MY SOUL
is a deep color
of ashes left from a campfire
burned out long before.

It's the color of the
deepest, darkest ocean.
The color of a giant rainstorm
engulfing people into its strong arms.

It is as cold as a freezing winter day,
the kind people bury their bodies
in many layers to stay warm.

Only my soul is never warm.

It's like a shivering sensation
running along my spine,
over and over.

The laughter coming from deep within me
is bitter, dry, sarcastic.
It is deep, cold, and eerie.

—Andrea Rinkel

INNER PEACE
Stepping ever so lightly
so as not to disturb
the crumpled figure lying there

I crept forward
across the light ridden room
to gather in the comfort of her arms
and be peaceful once again

Softly I give a kiss upon
her forehead and wish a
goodnight

Lazily staring into black
nothingness I feel
compassion well up once
again within me

Sense of security is strong now
and I feel peace beside her

Ever growing is the feeling
that I am not Dead!

—Andrew J. Brutsman

BURNT TOAST MORNING
Should I scrape it,
or should I pitch it?
Should I go to work today,
or should I ditch it?
I could toss it,
and drive to work like a half-crazed jerk,
and give everybody a big fat piece
of my grumpy burnt toast mind.
Or maybe . . .
I could spread,
that piece of scraped, burnt bread,
with a glob of Grandma's jam.
Yes!
I'd conquer my burnt toast morning.
Then,
knowing how I am,
I'd decide
that my post-burnt toast day
would be O.K.
Now my coffee's cold.

—Dawn Campbell

GOOD DAY
My life is dull, I can't do a thing.
The dog won't bark, the canary won't sing.
The cat won't chase, the mice in the house,
and I can't get along with my spouse.
The car won't run, the battery is down.
The engine's broke, it won't make a sound.
It rained all day, and the ceiling leaks.
I'm sop and wet, and the carpet creeps.
The rent is due, I don't have a dime.
My t.v.'s broke, and my clock won't chime.
My hair won't curl, my kids won't mind.
The corn won't pop, and the mill won't grind.
The stove won't burn, the bacon won't fry.
My neck won't turn, and my eyes won't cry.
My rooster won't crow, the hens won't lay,
but other than that I'll have a good day.

—Virginia Anne Koenig

THE OTHER SIDE OF NIGHT
Waking up on the other side of night,
The world looked out on a ghost
Chasing me down the street
Running far and wide.

I was a pig in my last life
And this time I was going to
Play it straight.

No holy-rollers, no too-tight jeans,
No dirty make-up. No cancellations.
Only pick me up at the top
And put me down safely at your knees.

Next time it happens
That I get so scared
I ruin toothpaste all over my mouth
And run the carpet sweeper over and over
It.
The Dead Give-a-way.

Why sell your jeans for a pocket,
When you can take this baby and Be Mine.

—Mary Anne Haas

A WING IN THE DUST
A wing in the dust, how long has it been there?
Alone in the deep, how did it get there?
A wing that at one time held such beauty of life,
the delicate weaving of air and light.
A wing that can fly into infinitesimal skies and beyond,
where no one hears the lonely cry from the dust.

So why, can you tell me?
A wing that belonged to the greater whole
but yet it lies within my soul, like Cronus,
awaiting for its golden age to return.

Waiting . . . waiting for a chance to break free
into the light among the sea. The aqua-blue, a lovely hue.
Isn't it due? Will someone break through?
To reach the depths inside of you and retrieve
what once was, life and love, the gifts from above.
Oh, but there it will remain, he says he must refrain.
So linger on dear pain.
A familiar face will take its place; Alone . . .
If I must, a wing in the dust,
Getting deeper and deeper, a thicker crust.
Harder and harder, a loveless lust.

—Francine Rosenzweig Robertson

DEATH

If I died tomorrow,
how would you react?
Would you be filled with sorrow,
or would you just go on living?

If I died tomorrow,
how many people would remember me,
long after I'm gone?
Would no one show up to say goodbye,
Will no one say farewell?

I know you don't want to discuss this,
but it's best to think of it now.
Because I could always have died
today.

—Bekki

JUST BRIAN

Each day he came
Each day he went
A smile upon his face
A little joke, a little fun
Just Brian, his way of life

A gentle way, a loving way
A trail of friends along the way
A stranger to him was never met
A good friend to all was he
Just Brian, his way of life.

A son, grandson and a friend
A memory on our minds and in our dreams
A ray of hope given, we'll meet again one day
A greater place than here on Earth,
    sun's forever shining
A gleaming smile with a twinkle in his eye
Just Brian, his way of life

—Janis Jensen

UNTIL WE MEET AGAIN

The tears have subsided
    But the hearts have been stained
Of all the loved ones
That have remained.

The storm is over
And the dark clouds are gone
Lori, is no longer with us
But she's singing our song.

I have a void
And I'm feeling the pain
Of an empty space inside me
That won't ever be the same

She knows she's loved
And is surely missed
But, she is at Rest
And our peace she would insist

Her voice can be heard
Her smile can be seen
And her warmth can be felt
In all of our dreams

So, The Happiness that was shared
With such a special friend,
Will simply be put aside . . .
Until we meet again.

This poem was in memory of my dearest friend
who has passed away tragically from a car
accident when she was nineteen years old.

—Lisa M. Pishko

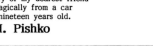

TO HIM — MY DEARLY BELOVED HUSBAND

I've never asked for fortune or fame,
Smooth sailing seas or sunlit cloudless weather,
I simply hoped that when I called his name,
That he would come, and we could be together.

So far my dreams of love have all come true,
For this my humble heart responds with prayer,
Yet, would I plead that all my lifetime through,
He will be there, dear God, he will be there.

Perhaps, I seek too much in fewer tears,
In days made brief beneath a setting sun,
But, how could I bear the long and lonely years
Without him? Yet, if it is God's will, His will be done.

—Dorothy P. Eldredge

HE WAS

He was my rock and my foundation
He was a one of a kind creation
He was my friend and confidante
He was always near, never distant
He was the image of a real man
He was always able to understand
He was my hero, as well as my friend
He was the one person on whom I could depend
He was my summer's breeze that cooled the heat
He was not one to easily succumb to defeat
He was my raindrop that cleanses the soul
He was the man who showed me my life's goal
He was the center of my world as I was to his
He was able to soothe all pain with one kiss
He was an eagle in flight soaring the blue skies
He was a free spirit able to hear my cries
He was the one who gave me the reason to live
He was the person who showed me that it is better to give
He was my everything before he left me
He was my father and I love him dearly.

—Alice M. Roberson

THE SOUND OF A MEMORY

The tenderness of your touch filled my heart,
    And the warmth of your incessant friendship during the
        summer and through the autumn
Surrounded and protected my life like a security blanket,
Never to let me experience darkness or despair—
    as long as you walked beside me.

What a small community it was in which we lived.
So small, even, that we humored at being able
To hear the cheerful shout of the arrival of the train
In every corner of our town as it often passed.

How ironic that with the approach of winter
Came the tragic clash of the train's metal against metal.
And suddenly cold bitterness seared through me
As my security blanket was lifted—
    and your life made its departure.

Why, oh Lord, is my head swimming in an ocean—
Blacker than the night, freezing like ice?
Why are my steps unsure, my thoughts opaque,
    and my actions like that of a timid mouse—
Even though my heart screams out in anguish,
    louder than a lion's roar?

Now the forlorn scream of the train
Brings a tear to the eye . . . a catch to the throat . . .
    a sharp pain to the heart.
A sad reminder of your departure always—
Although you still walk beside me.

—Emily D. Graham

MY DOG BUTTONS

My dog Buttons was cute as could be
He came when I called, and he played with me.
Now he's grown old and can hardly see.
I could never love another as much as he.
For he was such a good friend to me
I cried so hard when we laid him to rest
My dog Buttons was one of the Best.

—**Inez A. Pitts**

GRANNY

Come take my wrinkled, blue-veined hand in yours,
    and walk this way with me.
Through green fields and up tall mountains,
    never forgetting what we see.
Always remember the good times we have had,
    and promise me to never let memories make you sad.
Please accept this knowledge without a sigh,
    for I can show you how to live,
    but you can't teach me how to die.

—**Holly Victoria Pearson**

DEATH

Death is so very painful.
Why did you leave?
You could have fought that pain,
That awful disease.
The memories still linger,
But so does the pain.
But Dear Grandma, nothing is
Really the same.
It has been a year, and you haven't come home,
I guess it's decided the pain never goes.
I remember that day, that awful day—
I went in your room and nothing
Remained, but a box full of pictures
That seemed to bring nothing but pain.
I have cried for a year, and it's still
Not the same, but Grandma if you
Are listening, just remember I will
Always feel the same. I will love you forever and nothing
Will change, but memories of your
Caring love just isn't the same.

—**Dawn M. Mathias**

MY OWN DEATH

The voice is my own I hear!
Why can't it be still?
For it's him I fear.

You see, all I have on my mind is death.
The blackness, the coldness, the stillness, the sense of not
knowing what awaits me, the awareness of death.

But, it's not death I fear it's me!
My thoughts.
At birth I cry!
At kindergarden I wish I could die.
In elementary I am very withdrawn.
In high school I'm weakly
What's on your mind?
It's only the fear of the murder that happened!

It can be him.
The mystery man in God's image!
Again today, another death!
It's him again. The Murderer!
It's the horizon!

—**Mary Jean Noles**

STRADER

God took her from this mortal place,
The best is not always provided by
    the human race.

One day my friend you will understand,
The best is not always provided by
    the human hand.

—**Jennifer Toranto**

TILL WE MEET AGAIN

I'm thinking of you, Grandpa,
    each and every single day.
I cannot say that you are gone,
    cause I believe you're just away.
I believe that in the future,
    our paths will cross once more.
And the place that we shall meet,
    is right next to Heaven's door.
But since we cannot set a time,
    for that very special day.
I'll just keep on believing that,
    you're not gone but just away.

—**Debra Buck**

ROOMS IN MY HEART

Each loved one
has a room in my heart.
Where we meet to
laugh
talk
cry
and grow.
Rooms filled with joy and sadness
shared memories so important
that is life.
Now so many empty rooms
filled with those things
now behind a veil of grief
cannot see them clearly
shadowed sights and
muffled sounds
cannot go into them yet,
sadness prevails.

—**Caroline Hall**

NO RETURN

My aunt is now in peace
Her farmhouse up for sale
The warmth that radiated
From her soul and that land
Has turned to cold, distant memories.

It is not yet a reality
I empty out her bureau drawers;
Packing heirlooms into retired milkcrates,
Wondering why she never enjoyed life,
Not one vacation or whimsical purchase.

I will never run through those fields,
Help feed her chickens and rabbits,
Or see her clicking the backdoor
To attract the thirteen barn cats,
Who wait anxiously for their "reward."

It is not yet a reality
That my aunt is resting,
She will never return, but someday
I will join her.

—**Lisa Marie Weiss**

PLEASE, LET HIM IN

Do you believe there is a God
Above the world today?
Do you each moment his pardon seek
or don't you even pray?

The Lord today is waiting
To claim you as his own.
So won't you open up your heart
And give the Lord a home.

Dedicated to Jessie Rae Miner, granddaughter
—Nellie Lohr

ANGEL-HEART!

You are my
Angel-heart! . . .
Swept me
off my feet
right from
the Start!
Caressed and carried me
in such a Special way
that We share
Heaven on Earth every day!

—!AVIVA! Argonaut

NO EXCUSE

The day has gone
And darkness falls
What will I say
If Jesus calls
I didn't have time to work for you.
There will be no excuse
For what I didn't do
Please Dear Lord take my heart
And hold it tight
Thru this long and stormy night
And if I live to see another day
Help me walk closer in Thy way
And before I go to my lowly grave
Let me tell lost souls that
Jesus saves and
That God loves us everyone
Because he gave His only
Son,

—Leona England

OUR HERITAGE

A tender and soft embrace
that comes from above.
Can be found in a baby's love.

Quiet, yet sometimes loud
they're always something to
make you proud.

Receiving our gifts, Our Lord
did provide.
In hopes to train, with God's
knowledge far and wide.

Our prayers at night and
prayers in day.
Are that they grow in a special
mighty way.

Not like us or friends we know,
but like the one who blessed us so.

—Robin Cowart

WHEN ANGELS CRY

Tears slowly roll down heavenly cheeks
Incessantly dropping from a dark night sky
Creatures cower from the deluge of pain
That stalks their souls when angels cry

Torrential winds howl out the questions
Thunder rumbles its fierce reply
Lightning adds a bright reminder
That all's not bleak when angels cry

Children laugh the morning after
Splashing God-sent puddles dry
Sun adds warmth to cold November
Tears of joy when angels cry

—Lydell Reed

CONSOLATION

Like the flowers of Springtime, life unfolds.
It grows, matures, and God's beauty, beholds.
Then, after it has displayed its petals of beauty,
    And has given to the world, its products of duty,
God calls us home to take a rest in peace.
    He causes the turmoils of this life to cease.
He hath promised to be with us through the shadows of
    death.
He has prepared a room for us, the Bible saith.

May we trust, and rest, on the promises given to man.
    May we have much faith, as a Christian can.
May we all strive, while our breath doth last
    To rely on God, and our every burden, on Him, cast.
Let us try to live our lives as He doth guide.
    May we feel His Companionship by our side.
Let us anticipate meeting our loved ones on "The Golden
    Shore."
There, pain, and suffering, will be no more.
    May the permanent healing be a grand release.
May we all respect God's calling, and, be at peace.

**This poem was written after the demise of my cousin,
several days before.**
—Leona Ruth Jones

GRANDMA'S APPLICATION TO GOD

Dear Lord,
When I come home to be with Thee,
    I have one request, I pray, might be —
Will you accept my application, Lord
    To be placed in the department where —
I could never be bored?

I wish to be a nanny to your children up there.
    I would fix the braids in the little girls' hair.
I would brush their curls and their golden wings
    And rock the babies 'til my heart actually sings.

I would wash the faces of the little boys,
    Give them hugs and kisses and mend their toys.
I'll send you references if you want me to.
    I've been a mother, grandmother and a nurse, it's true.

Their mommies and daddies, whom they left behind,
    Will rest easy to know their care is so fine,
That each one is hugged and kissed every night.
    And a tiny star lit to shine its soft light.

As I cross over Jordan on my way home
    Please meet me there, Lord, so I won't be alone.
And take me to the children, to reside within.
    That's the position I wish for, dear Lord.
                                        Amen

—Nell C. Smith

THE GARDEN

The first garden on the earth was filled with splendor
and grace.
It had only a small amount of the human race.

The trees full of fruit and the grass so bright and green.
The rivers and streams so pure and clean.

The air so crisp and fresh as the taste of mint.
All the animals so peaceful and content.

Then mankind chose to disobey God and eat of the tree
of life.
In doing so they chose war and strife.

They were taken out of the wonderful place.
Now Eden is gone without a trace.

The world has searched but couldn't find
that beautiful garden Adam and Eve left behind.

—**Lesa Hise Meier**

ME

Me's awaken, the first thing on their mind...
What pleasure for 'Me' today might I find?
Me's putter through each and every day of their lives
Having no thought of other's needs, unhappiness or strife.

Me's first thought upon arising, and the last thing before
Lying down to sleep
Is what this great big world owes Me,
Never, what can I do for thee?

Me uses people selfishly, taking, never giving.
If one ceases to be of service to Me, they are tossed aside,
For newer and greener pastures, you see.
For who is more important...than Me!

Oh what a wonderful world, Me thinks so full of fools.
None at all so 'cool' as Me.
Or, is it possible, could it be...Me is sad, lonely and
Confused.

Such a waste of God created mind credentials...
When beneath the surface lurks potential!

—**Sandra Carol Butcher**

THE STEPS OF CHRIST

The night was well laden—so the dew must have already fell—I
-wonder if his footprints were left there to dwell?

I am speaking of the garden—where my Jesus wept and fell—on His
knees there in sorrow—for our sins his heart did swell.

And then came soldiers marching—their sandals mash the sod—For
they have come to take him—this Christ—The Son of God.

They rushed him stumbling onward—to the courts they held His fate
—His path was cast—His time was near—the night was so-so late.

It must have been so lonely—that time he spent alone—though men
were all about him—God had sent Him on His own.

Then up Calvary's mountain—His legs—His feet—they ached—there
He left humble footprints—God's plan—now he was to make.

His last prints were there—just before the cross—where they
thrust Him down to nail them—his feet—blood from them freely
loss.

But bless His name He is risen—His prints I clearly now can see—
even on the mountains—yes, in the hearts of thee and me.

How are you now walking—on your earthly trip you are—in his
steps—the Saviour—or wandering lost—from his footprints so far?

—**Michael E. Hoyle**

ABSOLUTION

Silent tears
Cleanse my soul...
Like the rain washed earth.
   Reborn,
      Purified,
         Renewed...
All the bitterness
   Washed away.

—**Janet Pinkley**

COMMUNICABLE

Dear God I pray
each and everyday,
we your people follow —
your way.

Why do we not listen to
the cries of the earth?

Without its forest, water,
and sky, it will all
one day die.

We humans will take over
the tears, facing even
more tragic years.

—**Faye Dyerwilkins**

MY SACRIFICE

I presented my body
To you, Father,
A living sacrifice
Such as it was,
Scarred by sin
Because of my lust
For things of the world,
Broken and bereaved
Of loved ones
By Satan's cruel hands.
Shattered dreams,
Shattered life
Were all I brought You,
Sorry pieces
Placed on Your altar,
But in Your infinite mercy
You said, "That's all I want."

—**Fawn Fulton**

LOVE IN THE SON

On an old rugged cross
Hung a man kind and brave
He hung in love and anguish
For a soul so cold and dim

On that old battered tree
With love so intent
Hung God's only Son
In anguish — and bent

To the soul that is dying
He is Life evermore.
For the one that is grieving
He is peace, love, and joy!!

This is the answer
For the love that you need.
Look to The Lord—
For He is the answer indeed.

—**SuEllen Davis**

DEATH

My son has cancer.
He is a child.
He's had it since before birth.

He's one year old,
He is a man.
I have not gauged his worth.

His skills are small,
And growing fast:
Like the cancer deep within

Which consumes his nerves,
Wilts his lymph;
Gives cause to discolor his skin.

Yes, He's just a youth of only one
The hair's gone from his head.
His playmates? Some are dead.

—Dennis Coffey

SHEILA

My little Sheila is a child
Who isn't timid, weak, or mild.
She can wrestle all the boys
Live her life in greatest joy.

She has charm like burning fire
Her pains are real and always dire
A certain sparkle in her eyes
Can mean "Use Caution," I advise.

But once I held a tiny girl
Dark and helpless with not a curl
She had some pains I couldn't mend
I didn't know it wouldn't end.

I love this kid with all my might
And try for her to do what's right.
Independence is what she wants
My teenage years come back to haunt.

I see myself inside her soul
Oh, what fate has yet to dole
Let her find the will to be
The best she can in spite of me.

—Denise Powell

BRONX

Oh, God! oh, God!
Will I ever sleep at all?
I hold my babies to me
Is the "Torch" there in the hall . . .!

Children look old, never smile—
Ghostly burnouts all around
Just one building stands beside us—
Oh, Lord, protect this ground!

I dream of sun and clean air
And think back to my homeland
With bare feet on warm sand . . . .
My heart cries . . . . "it isn't fair!"

My children have no future—
No place to escape, no money—
I wish I could have my babes
In a world of milk and honey.

See us through the night, Lord—
I promise I will try once more
Although my mind keeps saying
"Foolish woman, you'll try, what for!"

—Alyce "Lisa" Gehrling

MAKE A DIFFERENCE

Why don't people listen to the crying of a heart
and lift up a lonely spirit held prisoner in the dark?
Pain is all around us in the children's hungry eyes
a multitude of homeless in despair, alone, they die.

Don't let the dreams of children die for lack of hope
let's teach all of the children to "Just Say No" to dope.
Children bearing children are doomed right from the start
we must teach them all to let their head control their heart.

We can stop this horror if we will only do our part
just by lifting up a spirit held prisoner in the dark.
Words, alone, are empty it's deeds they need to see
then a difference we can make but it begins with charity.

Children are our future in their hands our futures lie
we must save these children or the price we'll pay is high.
If we each can help just one child regain his dignity,
then we will have made a difference for all humanity.

—Julie Westbrook Keith

A CHILD

A child — so innocent, too young to know,
This pain they're feeling just doesn't show.
Give me a reason — please, tell me why,
How can you hit this child, so shy?
They're crying inside; afraid to show tears.
Their hatred grows deeper all through the years.
They feel life is fading, they wish it would end.
They're looking for someone — in search of a friend.
Don't hurt these poor children, so rich with despair.
They want you to hold them, want you to care.
Please, help these sad children with their young, tender heart.
How can you hurt them? Tear them apart?
Your child so sweet, refreshing, like rain,
Lifts up its arms and takes hold of pain.
This child, this life you nourished so long;
How can you feel you're doing no wrong?
Please, don't turn away, and please, don't wait.
Open your heart before it's too late.
Please, hide angry eyes; don't be so wild.
They're only so young, so innocent — a child.

—Angela M. Serio

A CHILD'S PARADISE

Dawn
        comes
                upon a frosty window, the snow is deep.
All is quiet save the murmur of the wind.
Coffee's a steep near the fire.
A table is set and waiting for hungry mouths.
Suddenly! Like a clap of thunder a stampede of little feet.
Bouncing in to chairs, squabbles break out over the jar of honey.
Plates are cleaned
                dishes
                        are
                        washed.
Then the ritual of winter begins anew.
Coats are buttoned,
                boots are pulled,
                        hats are grabbed,
                                mittens are on.
Out the door with a mighty bolt!
Into the wonderful world of icy bliss.

— A Child's Paradise Winter —

—Tonya Massey

PAST PERFECT

So much of time is spent remembering
A winding country road—a village green
With the first sweet breath of early Spring.
The violet and dogwood tree—and then I knew
A spot where partridge berry grew—and woods
Tipped with the strong, bold hand of Autumn's glow.
A well-worn path, a creek, and snow
Which turned dark yesterday into a crystal world.

A store—a church quite near
A home that held a voice so dear.
Tears and the laughter spent, now slumbering
Would make exquisite pain recapturing
To question, can a world gone mad forever bring
My village back—to cease remembering.

—Jay Oliver Ewing

A THOUGHT

I dreamed a dream so very long ago
That this world was a beautiful place to grow.
I could see it in the forest with the flowers and the trees
I could see it in the animals, the birds and the bees.

I could see it in a sunrise, in the lakes and oceans too
I could see it in a sunset and the sky that is so blue.
Then I looked at its people and found it wasn't true
They all had made their plans with many things to do.

They were growing wild and crooked in almost everyplace
They pushed and clawed and scrambled, to establish a base.
They only thought of greed and pleasure, no love or happiness
They kept going, taking always more never less.

The time did come of which it's neither day or night
The land is stripped, the oceans out of sight.
The blackness covers the entire globe
We're wrapped, as if in the devil's robe.

It all could be prevented, if only we would care
Change the way we're growing and take only what is fair.
Stop and think a minute, people wherever you may be
Can this be a better place? It's up to you and me.

—Kathryn Daley

CIRCA ZERO

The sun lies in the sky, a pierced black heart
we sit here in silence as each plays their part
light drips down on a forgotten place
we're just close enough to tell we've lost the race

Here I sit in a small square box
surrounded by walls and protected by locks
the light filters down a forgotten blood red
we've just enough life left to see we are dead

The future and past are all frozen in now
a skeletal hand inside a deep cowl
it's too late to turn and there's nowhere to run
we've just enough time we can tell we have none

Care so much about what will, no one cares what has been
what has happened before will happen again
so busy with aiming don't see he's moved the mark
there's just enough light we can see it is dark

I've stayed here so long it is too late to move
What we've accomplished we're trying to prove
Chained to our station in body and mind
There's just enough color we know we are blind.

—David Ross Bearden

LIFE TO ME

Oh what is life to me
But a candle burning out
For the flame that used to be there
Like my life is just a doubt
It flickers in the moonlight
As a soft breeze makes it small
Until the strong winds start to blow
And the flame is not at all

—Amy Laviolette

Dark,
Darker . . .
Darkest.
The Cold Isolation From Feeling.
Numbness, So Chilling.
Absent From The Mind.
Defeated In Battle.
The Quest Was Over . . .
He Has Failed.
The Wounded Knight
Leans Sadly Upon His Steed.
His Blood Spilling Forth . . .
Turning The White Beast
To Crimson Red.
"Gallager, Take Me Home."
"Take Me Home, Dear Friend."

—The Butterfly

black lung

He sits in a rocker
    on the sagging porch
        watching the trucks
            rumble by —
He waves, and coughs

He thinks of the boys
    down in the mines,
        how things used to be,
            and he rocks
and coughs

He dreads the nights
    when he cannot rest —
        like a mine without a lantern
            and he coughs and coughs
and coughs . . .

—Harriette Mooring Horner

RED ORE GROUND

Up there we walked upon
the red ore ground.
Everywhere you saw it,
it sifts its way into the soil
and your soul.
Tracks like blood dried to dust,
the grit and taste of iron
always on your tongue
acrid and metallic,
as if you had bit into the
living flesh of the land.
When I am away I feel its pull
embracing, tugging at me
with a fierce desire
like the vampire craving
and I need the blood-red dust
upon the red ore ground.

—Janell Oelrich-Church

145

OUR LIVES

Life is when you move for
the first time
When you open your eyes to the world
and look around
When you learn to take steps without
falling
When you learn to really live
Be a real person
When you fall in love
You feel your life changing, it
feels better
Worth living
When your life is in its peak
When you never want to give up
That is life

—Nicole Mitchell

HAPPINESS

The sweet warmth of a smile
The pure adorning warmth from the eyes
His for her, hers for him
Happiness is in two people in love.

Two hearts beating as one
The quickening pulse when they meet
His for her, hers for him
Happiness is in two people in love.

Two minds thinking and dreaming as one
Mutual thoughts and wants at peace again
His for her, hers for him
Happiness is in two people in Love.

Lips that meet in a blissful kiss
Wanting, sweet, and moist for each
His for her, hers for him
Happiness is in two people in love.

Two souls that want to be one
To act on their dreams as one
His for her, hers for him
Yes, these are two people happily in love.

—Ronald C. Thompson

She walks with me in
The middle of the night

Where dreams separate
The darkness from light

Our hands entwine
When by the sea

As the world lies asleep
I whisper to thee

Of many lives and loves
We've known

Far reaching horizons
Yet to be shown

She holds me close
Before the morning mist

Erase the touch of
One warm kiss

I awaken now, the sun
I feel

A fleeting thought so unveiled

For one brief moment, my soul and I
Have tried where reality and dreams now lie

—E. Glenn Hickey

JAMES

Life was pretty empty
Until you came along,
Now my heart is happy,
Singing our love song.

You've filled my life with meaning
You've taught me how to care,
More than that my darling,
It's become a life we share.

—Anne Mae Roberts

THE SYMPHONY OF LIFE

The symphony of life
All the instruments can play so sweetly
Some are baritone, base, tenor, alto, and soprano
All the ups and downs combined
Put together the symphony of life
It gives us our song to sing.

Sweet, sweet concerto
Taking me home once again
Take me where I need to be
And return again I will
To sing an even sweeter concerto.

—Gloria M. White

JUST BECAUSE I CRY

Just because I cry
Does not mean that I am sad
Just because I cry
The whole world should be glad
Because frustrations now spent
While rages now vent
Releasing a most joyous and happy feeling

And just because this man cries
Should cause no one to enter the realm of surprise
For I shed these tears of mine
For a most beautiful Love lost in time
Be it that we are destined Love
Just you and I
Just because I cry

—Karin Sabu

YOU

The way I feel with you in my arms
A marvelous explosion of fireworks and bombs
A personality majestic, unique in its style
Your lips so shapely outline a smile

As you lay under my body
Your head nestled in my arms
I'm a prince with his princess
Engulfed in your charms

You have an intense desire
So I know you'll succeed
In all you want
And think you need

You have a harmonious blend of heart and mind
That keeps you searching and hoping all the time
You have a compassionate understanding for all to see
You've unleashed a power trapped inside of me

As it flows round my heart
Shout out from my soul
I feel surrounded by love
Finally part of a whole

—Gary Hopp

A LOVE TO CALL MY OWN

I knew from the beginning that you were just a flirt
and yet I fell in love with you, knowing I'd be hurt.

I thought I could tie you down, and make you love
just one, but how could I do something no one else
has done?

I knew you'd never love me. I'm trying not to cry,
for I must find the strength to kiss your lips good-bye.

When you ask for me again, you'll find that I won't
be there. I want a love to call my own, not one
I have to share.

So I will hide my broken heart beneath a smiling
face, and though you think I don't care, no one else
could ever take your place.

—Kimberly K. Clark

OVER MY SHOULDER

Let me start off by saying, "I love you." That seems to be
the most difficult part. I just wanted you to know that since
things are changing. I'm moving on, while you stay behind. I
think of the way we've been and smile. I look at you and see
I've become a shadow in your life. Now and again you'll notice
me, like we do our shadow, and you'll ponder how I've been
and what's keeping me busy. Soon however these thoughts give
way to more pressing matters. "But Heart I'll always be with
you. Like the shadow without the sun you won't always see me.
Our time together we both will remember, forever captured on the
film of our lives. Somewhere during our brief time together I've
learned the lesson of time. "Heart, it moves on if we pay
attention to it or not." We came to each other in adolescent
wonder. "Heart!!... Learn from me, take each day as a gift from
God." How I remember with smiles our days of joy. Do not let
time be a thief Heart! Let it be a guide to lead you on the
right. "Hurry along now Heart, I have a bit of a lead...Where
are you dear?...There now I see you. Come along now, we have
a great deal to share. I won't go too fast, I'll wait just up
ahead. Do hurry though Heart, I miss you love. It does get
so much easier to say.

—Kevin Stapish

WHAT MAKES A RELATIONSHIP?

A relationship is a special bond,
A bond shared between two people.
A bond that, when enriched with certain items,
Grows into something beautiful and everlasting.

The foundation of this bond is trust.
A trust that each other can depend on.
Without this common trust,
This bond will deteriorate.

Upon the foundation is caring.
When each person is there for the other,
Be it in time of joy or
be it in time of sorrow.

Along with caring is sharing.
One must share with the other
In order to Harmonize a Relationship
Both must be willing to give to the other.

A relationship also needs warmth and compassion
It's the tender, quiet moments that blend everything together.
May it be the snuggling by a warm fire on a cold winter night
or just a peaceful stroll through the park.

The last portion of a relationship is understanding.
One has to understand the other's needs and desires,
without understanding, you can't put the others into effect.

—Steven R. Wellman

HIM

Whispery curtains blow and sway
in the wind
feeling as if they were in my
mind.
I sit and think of how long it's
been
thinking of all the lost time.
My past, it comes back and
haunts me.
I think of what once was
or could have been.
If only the future I could
have seen
then I'd, now, be with him.

—Catherine Conn

BUT THEN...

But then...
There is hope,
Taking me by surprise
With a twinkle in her eyes,
And a tender smile
Making me feel worthwhile.

But then...
I met hope before,
And found the apple's core
Filled with wiggling deceit,
And not quite so sweet.

But then...
Who is he that knows
Which is wind and which is whistle?
Perhaps this is "The Rose,"
And not "The Thistle;"

But then...

—Gene Rhem

VISIONS OF LOVE

As pure as soft, silky snow,
clear as a beautiful stream's
flow,

Like the white of a unicorn's
eye,
Like a cloud floating up in
the sky,

The tip of an ocean's wave,
Precious things in life you
can't save,

A raindrop on a petal wet,
The sweet sun about to
set,

Like a bright, shining star,
A colorful rainbow from
afar,

Floating lilypads on a
glistening pond,
Dawn and day about
to bond,

A grain of loose sand,
The symbolism of a
wedding band.

—Denise Y. Moore

SUNNY

My Dear brother "Dave"
Rosy as grace!
Gloria his sis
her smiling face
Like a sunny kiss
for the race!

—Gloria Callaham

MY CHILD

String, string in a Wing,
this link, this treasure
this ecstasy of connection.
Linking the life of
light...
My child never doubt
my love for you.
Thou hast no father
but thy hast love—
then treasure
this string in
a wing—
of love...

—Sissú Pálsdóttir

OUR DAUGHTER SMILE

The day we brought you home
We did not want to let you go
But now—
You are all grown
And
You are on your own

We want to let you know
You fill our hearts with pride
The man that you have chosen
Is now by your side
Today we are not losing you
But gaining someone new

It seems like yesterday
We were holding you in our arms
Now leading you down the aisle—
We hold our tears for awhile
Just watching our daughter smile

—Eugene Chiarello

MOTHER

You were always there,
When I needed you.
You comforted me,
When I was sick.
You held me close,
When I cried.
You taught me,
The difference,
Between right and wrong.
You encouraged me,
To follow my dreams.
And you were always there,
When it came out right.
Or when I fell on my face,
You always let me know,
You loved me.
No matter what,
You are more,
Than just my mother.
You are also, my friend.

—D. A. Briand

ROSES

The rose, so safe in perfection, so fragrant.
Blue bred by tender hands in greenhouses, under watchful eyes,
Nurtured and pampered, they hold forth an arrogant head,
and grow painful thorns to nip the very hand that loves them so.

Beaus flock to seek the most beautiful for their ladies,
wrapping them tenderly in paper and ribbon worthy of the blossom.
The ladies display pridefully the blooms in crystal vases
for all to admire.

Alas, I do not desire the rose, with a proud stiff neck.
Far more I love the daisy, bending its head with the soft winds.
Being less sought after, even though just as bright of color,
taking her chance with life.

Yes, bring me the daisy!
Gathered up by my three year old in laughter and discovery.
Brought to Ma Ma in the first of spring, given with a hug.
My daisy will be just as loved in a mason jar!

—Cheryl L. McClure

MY ANGEL

I used to think of angels in a grand and glorious way
Bearing feathered wings and halos, watching over us each day.
And on a few occasions I would look up in the sky
to try to catch a glimpse of one that might be flying by.
Of course it never happened, and I think that now I know
they aren't up in the sky at all, but on the Earth below.
They're people all around us who give selflessly each day
Although we don't appreciate their warm and gentle way.
But I am very grateful to have known one in my time
And even though she's far away, she's always on my mind.
My angel was around me at my birth and as I grew
And when I had my own child she was there beside me, too.
When life is grey and cloudy she's the sunshine from above
And when I'm feeling cold and dry she warms me with her love.
The world's been done a favor just by having her on Earth
for a million golden halos couldn't equal what she's worth.
I thank the Lord above me for opening my eyes
and showing me that angels are the people in our lives.
So, if you're looking for one don't consider flying things,
Just look upon my grandma. She's an Angel without wings.

—Kelly R. Johnson-Terrill

A SPECIAL LADY

In my life I have known a very special person
Who was ever loving.
Her eyes would smile at me
And she was always giving.

This very special lady
Always spoke in a gentle, kind way.
When I was a little child,
There was so much about love, life and nature she would say.

She was gentle, kind and yet quick witted
There was an inner peacefulness about her
That no one else has really fitted,
For she was ever-loving, never boastful, harsh nor a bother.

I have always loved her, my Grandmother
Ever since I can remember.
There will never, ever be another
For she is so special—like no other.

Now I have a son, of my own, who has never seen her
And I do my best to teach him what she taught me.
For somehow we encounter her lessons of
Love, patience, kindness and a strong belief in God for all eternity!

—Kathleen Cullen Weisenborn

RAINDROPS

Once when I was very ill
I heard a pitter-patter upon my windowsill.
I opened the shutter
And what a surprise!
From the sky fell raindrops of every color and size;
Big ones and small ones all fell down;
Green, yellow, red and brown.
Oh, what an absolutely wonderful sight!
It made my day sunny and bright!

—S.A. Hickam

THE BEST OF FRIENDS

The best times in life were meant to be shared,
with family and friends and those who have cared.
As we part my dearest friend, I hope someday we
meet again.
We now travel along separate paths, yours to the
future, mine to the past.
So to you my dearest pal, I say to you a long farewell.
I will remember my dearest friend, who was there
for me through thick and thin.
But if that day when next we meet, just as we pass
along the street, please don't just walk on by,
stop and converse, even if to just say hi.
At least I know you remembered when, you and I
were the best of friends.

—Carrie Seffernick, age 14

A SMILE

A smile is a gesture, that's simply understood.
A smile means you're happy, and feel the way you should.

A smile is contagious, and can be spread around.
Everywhere in this whole world, a smile can be found.

A smile spreads a feeling, full of warmth and cheer.
A smile is in everyone, a message that is clear.

It seems a smile is pleasant, is comfortable and kind.
A smile does a world of good, and helps you to unwind.

A smile picks you up, when you're feeling down.
A smile is the perfect cure to wipe away a frown.

Start today off with a smile, and spread it everywhere.
A smile is a special gift, everyone should share.

—Amanda Davis

MY PARENTS' LOVE

Parents are a gift from God up above;
To teach us, to guide us, to shower us with love.

God gave us parents, to show us the way,
to handle our own lives, day after day.

It seems we forget that they need some time too;
To be just together, no problems from you.

We should not depend on them solely alone;
For they've got their own problems with
themselves on their own.

We need to start using the wisdom they've taught,
As the knowledge they gave, we know can't be bought.

All the time and the love they have given everyday;
From childhood to now, we could never repay.

I thank the Lord Jesus for that gift from above;
As nothing could replace that gift—My Parents' Love!
Your Loving Daughter,
Susie

—Susie

A RAINBOW IN THE SKY

There was a rainbow in the sky
The day that you did die.

It reached way up high
The beauty of it made you sigh.

On the ground both ends did lie
Its shape was perfect in the sky.

That rainbow seemed to say good-bye
To you Grandma,
The day that you did die.

—Charlotte Sue Hunter

SON

You're a part of me
For everyone to see.
My very first son
And although I wasn't done—
My very first love
The first one so special.
Then came your brother,
A second time mother.
You were so sweet
To let him crawl at your feet.
He certainly had his place
That darling baby face.
Then a third — — —
And your cry I hardly heard.
Even though you were still a baby,
There was so little time
For that first man of mine.
But Son, surely you must know,
No matter where you go
First, I Love You — Then the other two.

Mom

—Vickie C. White

A TRIBUTE TO MY MOM

You were born into hardship
But held your head high
You worked hard to make life better
So we wouldn't go without
You made us respect
Ourselves and others too
You taught us to work
And not to complain
To feel rich in our blessings
And thank God for them all
We worked hard together
But we played and laughed too

Then we were grown
And out on our own
But you always kept open
The door and an ear
You heard all our troubles
And gave advice when we asked

Then in the midst of our joys
And before all our sorrows
You were gone

Though your laughter
Lingers on
And your love
Is still felt
I pray a silent prayer
Of tribute to you, Mom
On this your Mother's Day.

—Vicki Shamhart

OCTOBER

October sun upon my face,
Golden leaves fall into place.

A tantalizing bit of breeze
Gently stirs the restless trees.

Upon October's placid face,
A veil of lovely priceless lace.

The beauty of her deep blue skies
Is photographed within my eyes.

How ever long upon this earth,
I find content in October's birth.

—Lynn H. Johnson

WEAVERS

Yesterday and tomorrow
Weave chains around today,
Forming an endless circle
In which we have to stay.

Time's loom is ever weaving
Designs in the changing years,
Intermingling hope and courage
With a mist of falling tears.

New hopes in a glad tomorrow
Regrets for the mistaken way,
Into intricate patterns are woven
From threads selected today.

—Shirley Woodring

A MAGICAL WEED

Today
A big, puffy, yellow sun
growing without love.
Cut down by some
but just to return.
Pulled by children
to give to mother
Or put under someone's chin.

Tomorrow
A big, puffy, white cloud
with no silver lining.
Not here for long
because dandelions blow away.

—Melanie Grant

LOOKING AT LIFE

Life can be, a total blunder
If you only, sit and wonder
But to take, a look at life
All its joys, and all its strife
It will give, an understanding
As to what, your life's demanding
Then to take, a cautious peek
Of the things, in life you seek
Never live your life, in haste
That will only, your life waste
Stop and think, a little while
Before you proceed, another mile
Try life's true and treasured tool
It is known, as the golden rule
A life of love, always extending
Takes the sting, out of the ending

—Reid P. Bowers

SERENITY

Walking alone on a winding country road on a winter afternoon
Calms the noises and hustle of the city in the background.
The bubbling of a partly frozen stream,
And the chirping of a tiny snowbird
Seem to form the treble voices for a small choir.
The harmony of a song the wind hums,
Whistling from time to time, it seems at me,
Resounds as mellow voices blending,
Or as that of a majestic organ, with tones unmatched.
And yes, even the rumble of only one car
Is a pleasant sound to my alert and tuned in ear,
As I plunge along on the soft new fallen powder.
"The world is a beautiful place," I think to myself,
"And tomorrow if blessed with one more chance
I may walk this road again,
And rediscover the aesthetic sights and sounds around me,
And feel once more that I am beholding them for the first time."

—Arline M. Hofland

LONESOME WANDERER

Drifting above the high mountains, is a huge white cloud,
In the village below, the noise is very loud.
I'm getting tired and weary, and no longer want to roam,
I'm just a lonesome wanderer, looking for a home.
The huge white cloud, has now turned black,
And I see up ahead, a lonely dark shack.
But where does one stop, when one has roamed so long,
I'm just a lonesome wanderer, looking for a home.
The rain has now started, it's pounding hard outside,
I'll rest in this old shack, till the morning light.
Another day is coming, another I will roam,
I'm just a lonesome wanderer, looking for a home.
The grass outside is wet and cold, from the evening rain,
My bones are tired and weary, and yet so full of pain,
One more mile to wander, one more mile to roam,
I'm just a lonesome wanderer, looking for a home.
Another day has ended, just one more mile to walk,
In this little village square, the people stop to talk,
The folks here are so friendly, and I no longer roam,
For now I'm not a wanderer, I have found a home.

—Lenora B. Rice

THE HOUSE ON THE HILL

Walking up the broken steps, on the porch I see
The old swing is hanging there, blowing in the breeze.
Opening the door . . . I enter, my steps are getting slow.
Could it have been, I wonder, ever so long ago,
When as a young man, my wife and child lived here?
Is that the sound of laughter? Their presence seems so near.
On the mantle a picture . . . A child I loved so well.
One of a fair young lady; of my Anna Belle.

All that's left of the home place is more than money can buy.
One day I know that I won't ask the reason, or why.
But I'll not let it bother me, they're free from pain, I know.
Still have I my memories that nothing can destroy.
The house on the hill is empty . . . standing there still . . .
Overlooking a meadow, there's the flour mill.

Many years it's been there strong but very old.
And many nights it sheltered someone from the cold.

It's evening now. I'm tired and worn. The sun is sinking low.
With one more look at the old house, it is best I should go.

The old oak tree is standing, the branches hanging low.
As if to say, "I wonder, where did everyone go?"

—Mrs. Evelyn Peters

FORGOTTEN HERO

His feet drop to earth like a soft snow
leaving small prints only few will know.
Spring soon comes and washes away
his small forgettable deeds of a yesterday.

His warm words blow soft like wind through trees
strengthening their limbs and turning their leaves.
Soon some leaves must fall to the ground
but before they wilt they're cradled by his sound.

Soon it's time for his soft steps to end;
his song is over and the voice he'd lend.
So with a soft whisper he breathes for last;
it warms our souls as it blows slowly past.

No songs do we sing in honor of small deeds,
though our hero has spoken and planted his seeds.

—Ron Papile

THE GHOST OF THE SIEGFRIED LINE

I have a story to tell you of World War Two—
And all the GI's that saw it say it's true—
It's about a ghost that would walk up and down
The Siegfried Line—
And the artillery shells and bullets he paid them no mind—

The ghost seemed to have a real story to tell—
About mankind starting wars that we all know is hell—
Night after night this ghost would walk his post—
And the bullets would go through him so we knew
He was a ghost—

The moon would shine bright so we could see him alright—
As he walked his post night after night—
Back in the rest area when the battles were o'er—
The GI's would talk and then talk some more—

They all agreed the ghost had a real story to tell—
That all mankind must stop raising this hell—
Ask the GI's and they will all say—
This ghost walked his post in a military way—
Trying to get his message across—
Before this old world is completely lost—

—Wistar Freeman

THE CURSE OF WAR

Light brown fine hair, brown eyes, light complexion,
Six feet one inches tall, weight of one hundred eighty lbs.,
No health problems and no deformities

An average high school graduate, co-captain in football;
No, he wasn't against the draft;
He was doing his duty for his country.

Once he was in the plane, our eyes swelled with tears.
Once he returned home, he was awarded The Bronze Star Medal.
Once, he witnessed a soldier's recognition of an arm lost in
    Battle by the ring still left on its finger. The
    Soldier kept the arm for days and wouldn't part with it.

He now lives for the dead;
Parties for the dead.
You see, he is the living dead.

The curse of war is endured by the men who have returned
    Home, as well as their families.
Families of the dead must live a life without their soldier.
The curse of the families of returning soldiers is to watch
    One, strong and healthy, die a slow, self-destructive
    Death from the guilt of still being alive, while so
    Many are dead.

—Helena Marsh

MOUNTAIN STREAM

Making its humble beginnings
In a bubbling mountain spring.
Gurgling and splashing
Up and over the edge.

Water crashes down the mountain
In an elegant endless waterfall,
Cascading through the cliffs of destiny,
Smashing against the rocks below.

Tumbling from rock to rock,
Weaving the twisted web of fate.
Such a simple thing;
Yet so complex.

Clean and crisp
Crystal clear liquid.
Only to be colored
By man's wicked hand.

—Adam D. Grantz

A STEP TOWARDS HELP

Stop for just a moment
and take a look at yourself,
you have a serious problem
and you need to get some help.
You've hurt a lot of people
who care for you very much,
and with each tip of the bottle
you drift further out of touch.
You may feel so alone
but you have your loved-ones' support,
the next move is yours, —
the ball is in your court.
You're admitting you have a problem
and that's no simple task,
grab a hold of that self-confidence
and don't ever look back.
The first step was the hardest
but now that it's been done,
each step will get easier
and the best is yet to come!

—Jean Marie Fulford

A PRAYER FOR ALL THE CHILDREN

Blue sky and trees of green;
O Let me dream.
Warm sun and damp grass
Where my soul may lie;
And in your hands I fit.

But no dream can keep out those
Cries for help that children whisper
In the night. No warm sun will
Fill the loss; for in their souls
The whisper stays.
For we, Oh God, have achieved so much,
So much in this world and share
It with so few.

Today my son has joy;
Tomorrow I will see his pain; for
Today I saw a child dying for his joy.
Why can't we see
What our children will have to see?
Let us feel the pain before they do;
So that they may have a dream.

—Michael F. Hammond

INTERLOCKING LIKENESSES

The rush of anxiety
overshadows the mind
to one, love is a form
of anxiety toward another
to have the love of
a beyond earthly explanation
the interlocking likenesses
bring two in bond as one
imagine — the beauty
on a fresh, sunny morning,
the fragrance of those silky
roses that send a sensation to
your nose
that anxiety rushes
throughout and what better
way to bring love and nature
together than with the velvety
petals of a rose.

—Asena Fugate, age 18

ALWAYS

You're always in my thoughts,
always on my mind.
I just wish I could
take the time,
to find your heart
and give
a piece of mine.

I wish I could
say the things I feel,
but my tear will say
my love is real.

You always share
the pain in me.
I just wish we
could both believe,
that love is more
than what **we** have,
love is a commitment
both should have.

—Cheryl Faas, grade 11

FLEETING MOMENTS

Starlight shines
on mooncasted shadow
a haunting refrain
accompanies the wind.

Copper days
violet nights full
of bittersweet splendor
spin golden threads.

Picturesque
tapestries and paintings
intricately woven
colors slowly fade.

Romances for
those who find them
unlock the secrets
look with your heart.

Starlight shines
on copper days
of picturesque
romances.

—Debra Calvanese

GIVING AND EXPECTING ALL

No more tears for things of the past
No more worries about what the future may hold
Concentrate on the here and now make the moment last
For this day in the present will soon become as a moment
in the past

Because of yesterday, today should always be better and brighter
We are more aware of who and what we are
Unsatisfied with the status quo, and the way things were before
We impatiently await daybreak, for this day tomorrow will bring
so much more

I love you more today than yesterday
And though it feels I'm giving my all, it is not as much as I'll
give tomorrow
For tomorrow I will know more of me, and you more of you
Each having more to share, more to offer, more love to carry us
The Curious Dignified Aquarian   through

—Aletha Denise Foster

MEMORIES

When all the guttural backwash implodes in a nasty end.

And the one that meant so much to you, is nary but a friend.

Like anything, and everything and so many things left to die,

There will always be small traces left to remind me of you and I.

A cool, summer breeze which sifts through the trees,

A warm, friendly smile which I cherish awhile.

A ring upon the finger, a band of endless gold,

set there to remind oneself of feelings left untold.

But all the endless treasure, and countless riches galore,

mean little to a man who hath love no more.

Faded pictures of a jaded past,
a lifelong sentence served at last.

Now gone in the ashes and lingering smoke,
of life's painful lesson; love's twisted joke.

—Jody Mansavage

IS ALWAYS FOREVER

If you are ALWAYS afraid, are you FOREVER in fear
If you are ALWAYS close, are you FOREVER near

If you ALWAYS forget, are you FOREVER trying to remember
If you are ALWAYS loose, are you FOREVER limber

If you are ALWAYS selfish, are you FOREVER thinking of you
If you are ALWAYS sad, are you FOREVER blue

If you ALWAYS do bad, are you FOREVER mean
If you ALWAYS want attention, are you FOREVER seen

If you are ALWAYS down, are you FOREVER getting up
If you ALWAYS have coffee, are you FOREVER drinking from a cup

If you are ALWAYS speaking, are you FOREVER talking
If you are ALWAYS in step, are you FOREVER walking

If you ALWAYS make an error, are you FOREVER wrong
If you are ALWAYS tough, are you FOREVER strong

If you are ALWAYS punctual, are you FOREVER on time
If you ALWAYS have ten cents, are you FOREVER holding a dime

If you are ALWAYS eating, are you FOREVER full
If you are ALWAYS boring, are you FOREVER dull

If you are ALWAYS smart, are you FOREVER clever
If you ALWAYS didn't, are you FOREVER never

Not ALWAYS is ALWAYS FOREVER

—Nancy Esarey

THE WITNESS

You left with her and there was loneliness,
The signs of senseless struggle littered her bed.
I removed them,
Wondering,
Bloodstains smearing the Christmas spread.
His and Hers,
Dexterity.
Brandishing his blade he cut himself.
Unable to sever her bondage,
His blood I saw mingle with hers leaving his imprint.
Vision bulged, aching to assure
It was not her the animal slit.
But as his hand shot up his thumb exposed the blood source.
Unwantonly I smiled.
No more No less.
Frantic gauzy searches arched his body to and fro,
While I watched his dance,
Impatience.

—Joaquin Ferreira

SEEKING REFUGE

Where could I go, when the beatings began?
Or when harsh words were spoken;
By the step-father man . . .
Who was there to tell me,
That his words were untrue?
Or to soften the blows,
His fists made on you.

Who could I run to, when my mother walked away?
Pretending not to see;
My sadness and pain . . .
Who was going to tell me,
That her love was still there?
How was I to know,
When she didn't seem to care.

And where did God go, so powerful and true?
When my big brother raped me;
Did he turn his back too?

Oh, where can you go; when you're small and afraid?
The answer is uncertain,
To a child, who's in pain . . .

—Rhonda K. Pfalzgraf

ET TŪ BRUTĒ?[1]

Et tū, Brutē?
Pain, pain of betrayal
My soul taken from me by one I loved
Death, I beseech you now, take me.
My love, my soul, both are gone
What good is life to me now?
Et tū, Brutē?

Et tū, Brutē.
I am healed, healed by strength I knew not I had.
Scars remain, never to disappear.
You pass by, eyes of fire and ice.
I burn with anger, yet my heart is cold.
Et tū, Brutē.

Yet to live, I must love
And so I know deep inside me
Somewhere, beyond the scars
I can say with truth:
Amō tē, Brutē[2]
Amō tē.

[1]Latin: "And you Brutus?" from Julius Caesar. Caesar submits to his assassins when
he sees that Brutus, one he dearly loved, is one of them.
[2]Latin: "I love you, Brutus."

—Merry Luedtke

THE VICEMASTER

You take your diamonds flung sky wide,
For just another stone.
You let your pictures fall as they will,
History has shone.
My pleasure gained, the halls resound
To cries of ecstasy;
But what mirror cracks and shatters,
In this funhouse I call me?

—Bruce I.W. Edwards

LIVE OR DIE?

I think that I should kill myself,
It seems completely clear,
All my life has ever been,
Is suffering and fear.
It's so very scary,
Living life with sin,
It's not actually grief,
But fright I'm really in.
Why does God let this happen,
To the nicest people 'round,
And let them live and suffer,
'Till they're six feet under ground.
All I have,
Is just this poem,
I have no one,
I am ALONE!

—Jennifer J. Herrewig

TOMBSTONE EPITAPH

Cover the marks where the rope
was bound,
Place him in the box, and put
the lid down.
Now bring the black wagon in which
he will ride,
Pick up the coffin, and slide it
inside.
Then out to the cemetery for six
feet of ground.
The gentleman's taking a trip out
of town.
Carve him a tombstone, and let his
epitaph say,
"They hung the wrong man at the
gallows today."

—L. English

KEVIN JUSTICE

As I sit among the demons
At a party that has no end
I think of the reason I left my home
Was it because I had lost my friend

So here I sit and wonder
While I do the fire burns hot
The pain will last forever
Because of the bullet I shot

I watch the demons start their work
They pass a cup of sin
One by one they take their turn
Each putting an evil deed in

Soon the cup is in my hand
I know not what to do
I close my eyes as though in thought
And all I see is you

—Abby Fontenot

INCOMPLETE THOUGHT

Lions came dancing in the weeping night;
The Abyss opened forth its unlit shadows;
Congested, the cities deceived the dancers;
And lame fell the truth, "We are as we think."

Illusions drink in the unshrivened dark;
Abstractions lope blindly their shallow errors;
Drunk intellect, reincarnated, sue visions
Of belief; lost silences exist; fornicated
With deception, they come home to philosophers
                dumb,

while

LIONS CAME DANCING IN THE WEEPING NIGHT;
THE ABYSS OPENED FORTH ITS UNLIT SHADOWS;
CONGESTED, THE CITIES DECEIVED THE DANCERS;
AND LAME FELL THE TRUTH, "WE ARE AS WE THINK."

          —Vonda Faye Pelow

REMEMBRANCE

Fleeting fantasies of
  Your head cradled in the valley of my lap,
Honest Face upturned.

Long liquid gaze from crystal eyes,
    soaring through my senseless flesh,
        entwined about the fiber of solid truth,
           that which is my reality, my entirety.

My eyes cascade the long torment of
    emptiness now forgotten,
Baptizing you in my fluid sorrow,
And I gorge as a beggar on the fullness of this love.

We embrace, your golden veil
    establishing our tiny world,
        our oasis of peace,
           isolating us from the
              chill outside.
The truth fills me . . .
I am complete, for I know now

This is all I need.
          —Raymond E. Cullins

i pour your still

i pour your still
warm coffee down
the sink

words hang in the cobwebs
like so many
dead flies

           they'll later fall
           to be swept into linoleum cracks
           forgotten specks

i never remember
the what or why   only
the sun's cold touch through
tear streaked windows   the empty
hum of the driveway

           i feel your ghost words
           stir the dust   the final
           curtain's drawn

i pour your still
warm coffee down
the sink
        —Suzanne F. Waters

THE SAME OLD STORY

The boy pushed his hand out,
  groping to reach the light.

They slit his fingers in the dark.

And when he stumbled, he wasn't helped.
He was walked on.

Finally, the hurt grew.

He asked to be heard.
They were too busy.

The boy turns man, the hurt to bitter.
The bitter turns to the streets, fighting.

. . . and prisons grow like fire
    in yesterday's oily rags.
        —John F. Hom-Ball

IMAGES

Glancing at a reflection one day
I thought the image was familiar
Clouded not with finger prints or spots
The form was still quite unclear

People all around me pushing and shoving
Keeping up with life's fast pace
No one noticing this stranger behind me
No one noticing the saddened face

Countless years of unhappiness it held
Tinged with disappointment for sure
Trying to blanket it all with a smile
No more could this one soul endure

Turning suddenly to extend my hand
Words of encouragement on my lips
I gasped in shocked disbelief
For the matter I touched was slick

Now the face bears a stronger resemblance
Just as a mirror will tell no lie
The image in the reflection that day
Was none other than I
        —Patricia A. Franklin

THE SHOELACE

Like my old sneakers
    So many times, . . .
Untied
  Much too long
    The laces were, . . .
      Dragging from either side
The ends becoming ragged
    And the holes between too wide

It came time
    To make them
Just my size
    And keep them
      . . . Tightly woven

Ah! . . . Yes!
      The lace in my shoe
The one that feels so right
    So pearly white

The one that ne'er be untied
    . . . Again
For not a lace alone it be
    But; A shoe I could sleep in
      . . . The one you gave to me
    —Sheila M. Lansing, Oct. 1987

As we walk the pathway of life
and you reach out your hand to me
I will touch it.
But you must remember
that you are only one among many
whom I will encounter
along this road.

—Vicki Kneeland

PROPHECY FULFILLED?
Love walked abroad
And knocked on doors
A-seeking understanding,
But none there were
Who said, "Come in!
Our land is yours, unstinting."
    Poor beggar Love!
    Be not dismayed
    By cruel politicians,
    'Ere long you'll be
    A welcome guest
    Within the mighty Kremlin.

—Alda J. Wild

EXPECTATIONS
I am tired of what should be—
    What would be if!
Tired of expectations and
    of ritual beauty dressing.
To be or not—
    What you expect of me.

Life consumed fitting into spaces,
Energy squandered on debate—
    Should I be light,
        or dark heavy night?
    Should I be fluted,
        or tied and suited?

I don't care to fit anymore;
The blame has grown old.
I'm staying put—
    I am flesh and bone
    spirit and soul.
    No more extras!

—Mary Ann Bourdo

CAN'T YOU SEE
Can't you hear me
    my crying
        in the wind
for a home and food to eat.
Can't you see me
    my figure,
            oh . . . so bleak.
It gets worn
        you know
        out on the street.
Don't you wonder
        what I think
    when I stand out here and see
all you people walk by me.
    Don't you wonder
            how I feel
    when you never
            stop to say hi.
    Don't you know I'm just like you
        inside?

—Lisa Hedrick

THE BOSS
As a boss, I give orders to others, telling them what, when and where.

Never considering my tone of voice but others were aware.

Then one day, I too was appointed a boss.

One who acted just like me.

It was as though I saw for the first time, the real unpleasant me.

It was because I didn't like what I saw that I decided to change.

All of a sudden, professionalism, productivity and accuracy began to interchange.

Employer, employee together achieved in the cooperated land.

Just by rendering to Caesar what is actually due.

Remember to be kind, show love and respect others, as you'll have them do you.

—LdyJoy

THE HOMELESS
From across the world, to next to me . . .
I've witnessed a sadness, I'd rather not see.
It's about a people without a home . . .
People that are hungry, penniless and all alone.
In the East and in the West, to our back door . . .
Many lack a ceiling, a wall and a floor.
There's no zip code, mail box nor an address . . .
They don't even have a room to leave a mess.
They have a bedroom which is the cold night . . .
And the moon is their night table light.
A garbage can fire is their source of heat . . .
And a parkbench is their bed, their seat.
They celebrate Thanksgiving and Christmas Eve . . .
By just remembering how it used to be.
The Homeless Foundation does not discriminate . . .
It is an open membership for all in every state.
We have come across them, we know they're around . . .
But we just walk away without making a sound.
There has to be an avenue, a path or a way . . .
To resolve this problem of today.

—Maria Eugenia Barba

SIXTEEN
Sixteen is a time between.
Not young enough, not old enough.
I'm trapped between child and adult.
Confused about responsibility.
Learning to deal with the birds and the bees.
Discovering myself for the first time.
High expectations placed on me.
Trying to grow up without letting go of youth.
Excited about the world around me; but unable to explore.
Expected to be mature yet treated like
        a child.
Wondering where life's paths will lead me.
What do you want to do with your life?
Is the question most frequently asked;
Where do you want to go to college?
What do you want to do when you get out?
Wait a minute! What am I doing this
        weekend?
Always wishing to be a little older.
        The old want to be young
        The young want to be old
        Where do I fit in?

—J. Andrew LaMantia

VICTIMLESS CRIME

It's a fine blue line,
I serve my country, and I get off late,
This year I've given back,
Uncle Sam a quarter what he's paid me.
I study hard, and it's the same hard line—
That's why I was blinded,
as the red, blue, red of a blue and white fazed me.
My tags were new, my inspection sticker's gum still fresh,
'Your license, your insurance . . ., boy . . .'
My seatbelt tight across my thumping chest.
He 'paced me at 61' just when his lights called for me, 'No Joy!'
I pull away, gluing my needle to the red five-five,
I soon took my exit '. . . no ticket this time,'
off of MoPac, Loop 1, Austin, TX,
This side of a thin grey line:
as a blue and white passes me at something near forty-plus,
in a zone clearly 'thirty-five . . .'

  —Joseph M. Collins

HISTORY

I pray for the kid down the street.
He's put together so incomplete . . .
Or is he?

He's fighting God, he's fighting the world, he's fighting
Himself.
He has no pictures on the wall, and that's sad.

Down on his knees he wants to cry,
But all the tear ducts have long run dry.

He can't sleep at night cause tomorrow's another day.
He can't relax, the fear won't go away.

Someday, he just wants someone to know that he wasn't bad.
He wants them to know the hurt that he had.
He wants them to know that he was living,
That he was loving, caring, and giving.
He wants them to know that his life mattered.
He wants them to know his life was shattered
Looking for love.

In a world so hard, in a world so cruel
He was looking for love. Oh what a fool!

  —Richard Jay Bowles

WHITE MAN'S DREAM

Who is to blame
While others hide in shame
Being pawns of others' games
with labels given to each name.

He came across the sea
An immigrant to a land fresh and clear
Made claim and called it Free
So others would let him be.

But he destroyed nations and people
who dared come so near
with a religion fostering fear.

He used guns killing indiscriminately
with disregard to tears
and conquered by violence with welcome cheers.

Onward he marched calling it new frontiers
destroying cultures not yet known
and calling it progress through technology.

White Man's Dream is measured by stealing ideas for his own.
White Man's Dream, where will you take your troubles today.
White Man's Dream locked in an ego complex scheme.

  —Paul We Pol Wilusz

How can a man
Have the strength to fight
Public battles
Unwavering in his stance
Stronger than steel
And yet . . .
A silent battle
With an inner demon
Brings him crashing to his knees
Weakness, lack of will
Being beaten each time
No longer resisting
Only inside, the pain
The knowledge
That a brave man
Lacks courage
When courage counts
Unable to turn away.

  —Michael Garner

SCREAM LOUDER

red man cried
Quietly as Whiteman
Locked his pride
In a tall, tall fence
Of submission.

yellow man ached
Quietly as Whiteman
Saw him baked
In a mushroom oven
Of submission.

brown man pained
Quietly as Whiteman
Had him chained
In an iron shackle
Of submission.

And still Whiteman knew no joy
For there was no man
Left to destroy
Except white man
With submission.

  —Shauna Thompson

LONELY VIGIL

I sit in a guardshack
Awake for the night
A vigil I'll keep
Alone 'til daylight . . .

I sit and watch
The things in my view
My questions are many
My answers are few . . .

My loneliness goes on
And on like a fight
It keeps me awake
eight hours a night.

When my time is up
I cannot say.
For all I can do
is count the day.

How can I tell you
Just how I feel
Because I'm the M.P.
And yes, This is Real.

  —Carlton Adams

WINDS OF CHANGE

The decade's ended — I realize
Ten years older — a bit more wise

The wisdom that I do impart
Comes to you directly from my heart

Each precious day — you must expect
A little knowledge — to collect

Some small kindness, you should bestow
So winds of change begin to blow

In all your dealings, please take heed
To be aware of a person's need

If you can ease another's pain
You'll know your life is not in vain

If each will share in some degree
The World a better place will be

   —Pauline Unger

I judge not your character,
but your personality.

I fear not your ways,
but your love.

I love you for yourself,
not for what I can make you.

I will accept your love,
and not refuse it.

I will let you guide me,
and not me guiding you.

For life is treasured each day,
thru my eyes and yours.

We share what we have,
not what we do not.

We must love one another,
not condemn.

For life holds many options,
and I chose the one to love you.

   —Helen Robinson

NO TIME . . .

Don't leave any sonnets unfinished —
Don't leave any lyrics unsung;
Our hours are borrowed
And not ours to keep —
Silent carillons wait to be rung.

Don't leave any kind words unuttered;
Your friend who may need them today
May be gone tomorrow
And deprived of the balm
And comfort only **your** lips can say.

Don't leave loving letters unwritten.
Don't leave any canvasses bare.
While the sentiment's fresh —
And the oil is undried —
Now's the time your creation to share.

So, empty your palette of colors —
Capture now each beautiful thing!
Only Art will endure —
When the artist is gone —
Like the poet whose sonnets still sing.

   —Mary Antil Lederman

THE BRIGHTEST STAR

I have seen the light in my loved one's eyes,
a shine so bright, it clears the darkest skies.
A sense of warmth and complete devotion,
it's something more powerful than a mere emotion.
It is a sense of being complete and whole,
making your life more than just a role.
Growing together in all of life's details,
the chance of being in love is something we all should hail.
You should not be scared because you may miss the chance,
to revel in life's most promising circumstance.
It is the magnitude of that shining bright star,
that makes life worth living and it's not too hard.
Know what's important in this age of life,
for only true love eases the every day stride.
Caring, sharing, the loving of family and friends,
keep on giving, true love never ends.
Learn what's important, give them all of your heart,
for each new day brings a loving new start.

   —Robert M. Block

WITHOUT LOVE . . .

. . . there could be no hate.
Without hate, there could be no war.
Without war, there could be no peace.

Without life, there could be no death.
Without death, there could be no end.
Without end, there could be no beginning.

Without darkness, there could be no light.
Without morning, there could be no night.
Without black, there could be no white.

Without today, there could be no tomorrow.
Without tomorrow, there could be no yesterday.
But what is that you say?

You believe my words are a silly game I've written
But, ah, my friend, you are mistaken.

For without these words life would have no
meaning.

And without meaning what would be the
point in life.

   —Cratus Thompson

PAINT YOUR OWN RAINBOW

Painting a rainbow takes courage and pain.
You may have to do it again and again.

Gold from the sunshine will brighten your day.
Your rainbow needs color, so paint it that way.

Maybe it just needs a small dab of blue,
From tears that you've shed of dreams not come true.

Get rid of a color when it starts to fade
Or stand in the way of the progress you've made.

A color worth saving may need some more light.
Work with it lovingly till you make it right.

Although advice and suggestions others may give,
Remember this rainbow is just yours to live.

So paint it yourself, and when you are done
Stand back and admire the triumphs you've won.

Think not of life's losses, but what you can gain.
The rainbow comes out — only after the rain.

Never give up till your life is through.
Keep painting your rainbow till it's right for you.

   —Dolores Perry

There are thoughts milling around in my head,
and I close my eyes every now and then to keep
them from escaping.

Emotions are rummaging through my gut. What
right have they to be there?

Here and there I come across an exceptionally
greedy one that wants to have its own place; as
if to dispense the others along to another
inhabitant.

Sometimes the feelings begin to take over,
and then there seems to be nothing left of my
sanity.

—Miss Kim A. Perry

DYING EMBERS

My mind remains in a constant state of reverie;
Searching . . . always searching;
Trying to find its identity.

And what does my heart do,
Now that it has been beguiled?
Why must my face be painted with an illusive smile?

I'm bemused with visions . . .
. . . the way it could have been . . .
. . . our future, now darkened by events unforeseen.

His gentleness, alike a summer breeze,
Has changed into a storm.
His character has now taken on a strange, new form.

Once he had a glow that shone all about him.
Now, even his brightness has suddenly grown dim.

All promise is gone and chance seems slimmer still.
I can only pray that time will heal . . .
. . . as I have been told it will.

Upon my death, my flesh bemired;
Will then my love decrease?
No . . . it's unlikely that I will ever know such peace.

—Helen Carletti

ONE MORE DAY TO WAIT

Today, being a new day
yet, thoughts of you remain the same.

How can I continue to Love you, when you refuse
to relate to what feelings you once knew.

"Me," I wait daily to hear,
and although I feel the loneliness within,
my love remains for you.

You can never destroy it, nor will any other,
But you do make my life confused if ever I
were to love another.

I would let go, if only you would tell me so.

But no words spoken from you to me,
Leave the feelings in my heart for only me to see.

I can't understand why you will not let me know
the truth that's in your heart.

It's your silence that keeps me torn apart.

Are you too afraid to love me or just too afraid
to tell me?

If fear is your reason, then I want you to know,
That there's "nothing to fear but fear itself"
At least that's what I've been told.

So tomorrow will be another day to wait,
I suppose, as with time I will dissipate.

—Rebecca Cruse DeWitt

MY EVERYTHING

There goes my everything walking away
Never looking back and nothing to say
I'll never forget the wonderful times we had
And I'm trying hard not to be sad
But loving you was simply divine
And now I'm sad because you're no longer mine.

—Debbie Stewart

IT'S OVER

Brass bed,
Never wed,
Rusting on the porch of times past,
Circled by a lover's almost touch;
And remembered from a time of uncertainty,
And a moments understanding.

—Sharon Elich

ENLIGHTENED

Bad memories fade like the darkening sky,
I remember the best without asking why.
Our lives too precious to dwell on defeat,
I look for the good things in all those I meet,
Life then surrounds me and as I reflect,
I build self-esteem and gain self-respect.

—Brian M. Mowrer

OUT THE DOOR

Staring out the window, I wondered why,
All the people were rushing by.

They were laughing or smiling as they passed.
Why are you so happy I wanted to ask.

As I sat alone,
Waiting patiently for anyone to phone.

I realized I was the only one,
Who could make my life fun.

As I jumped to my feet,
I knocked over my seat.

Grabbing my sweater,
I knew I was going to make my life better.

I rushed out the door,
Because I wanted more.

—Julie Huff

PURGATORY

Does she love me or does she not?
How mocking is that game of hers,
Of yes-no, yes-no, on and on—
Oh whimsical chameleon!

When her pretty head nods yes,
I'll give you odds at two to one,
She's flirting in her charming way,
Amused at my naiveté.

But when her tresses wave no-no,
The note they really bear is this:
Don't give up like lesser men—
I might reverse myself again.

Thus I lie upon the rack,
A soul consigned to purgatory,
Ever haunted by the thought—
Does she love me or does she not?

—Douglas Smeaton

159

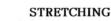

STRETCHING

I stepped forth and helped a soul
And found a value done.
I stepped forth and helped a child
And found a friendship won.

I stretched my hand and lifted one up
To greater heights I knew,
To see my God as I see Him
Where there are those too few.

I looked beyond the lonesome road
We travel here on earth
To joy in God who leads us on
From natural to new birth.

I listened to my Lord above
To put these words in rhyme.
He guides my hand as I let Him,
A special place in time.

—Mary E. Cox

HOPE IN DEATH

A good friend's son
died today;
It wasn't God's will
the boy wanted it that way.

He was a follower of Jesus
but I guess he couldn't wait;
To see what God had for him
beyond the Pearly Gate!

When the devil gets you going
he keeps you on the run;
Telling you all those fables
about having so much fun.

He forgot about the suffering
of those he left behind;
But oh the thoughts of loved ones
sometimes they are not too kind.

In his haste to leave
a world of hate and strife;
He thought it best to go see Jesus
and begin a brand new life.

—Mayola Holder

VINCENT

Vincent was a special man
So kind and good to me,
He always had a smile
For everyone to see.

Beauty was in everything
For Vincent, day by day
He knew the Lord was with him
In every single way.

From one week to the next,
He never remembered my name,
But always remembered to ask
"Would I be back again?"

He never forgot to wish me well,
What Joy he brought to me;
He did much more for me, I felt
Than I ever did for him.

Vincent was a special man
For all the world to see,
The Lord has taken him away
For all ETERNITY!

—Shirley Fetch

Why oh why I asked the Lord
Did you take him from me?
Was it because of things I did
Or things I couldn't see?
The pain that I am feeling
Is really hard to bear,
Even tho I know there are others who really care.
I see it in the way they look
And in their helping hands,
There are so many of them
In this beautiful land.
Thank you for the many years
That we had to share,
But taking him away from me
Do you think that's fair?
Why oh why I asked the Lord
Did you take him from me?
Then came the words of a little girl
"Now Grandpa's an angel isn't he!"

—Sandy Baltzell

"FOR MY LOVED ONES"
GOING QUIETLY

Don't look for me in an open grave, or near the
sea, or an ocean wave.

The sea is restless with its wind and sand, and
I'm at peace much more on land.

Perhaps I'll be on a mountain high, where the tall
pines grow and the Eagles fly.

So look for me near a mountain stream, with an
open book and a place to dream.

Or, look for me where the wild flowers grow, and
the air is quiet, with the falling snow.

And when your life brings a smile or tear, just
call my name, and I'll be near. So look for me in a
star-lit sky, when the night is still I'll be nearby.
I'll be nearby, to hold your hand and walk with
you, to the "Promised Land."

To greet the ones who have gone before,
and share our love, forevermore

—Edna Judd Selby

YAHWEH'S GIFT

Yahweh's gift came wrapped in burlap,
a flawless diamond among lumps of coal.
Our gift to Him was a feed trough,
a cradle filled with thorny hay.

Yahweh's gift came—a twelve year old boy,
listening to the teachers in the temple courts,
soaking up wisdom like a sponge in water.
Our gift to Him was a mother's scolding, a father's reproach.

Yahweh's gift came—a perfect man of thirty,
teaching in the synagogues of Nazareth,
healing leprosy in Capernaum, calming sea storms in Galilee.
Our gift to Him was a locked door to our heart.

Yahweh's gift came as a light of hope.
Our gift to Him was a bloody crown of thorns,
hatred-driven nails for His hands, a
wooden cross for a death bed.

Yahweh's gift came from the grave—three days later,
defeating death like a warrior striking the victory blow.
Our gift to Him is a heart of granite, hardened to His love.
His gift is never ending life—will we accept?

—Belinda A. Roper

A CHRISTMAS GATHERING

The toys are all purchased and the baking is done
and we're settling in for the real Christmas fun.
But as we gather together for some Holiday cheer,
let's recall for a moment just why we are here.

The love that we feel in this home here today
was expressed long ago in a similar way.
On a night, cold and quiet, in a faraway land,
a Baby was born — the Savior of man.

A star soon appeared and the angels began to sing,
as creatures, great and small, surrounded the tiny King.
They came bearing gifts and they pledged their devotion,
as He, in turn, offered love and salvation.

Sometimes the true meaning of Christmas slips away.
We should all take a moment to quietly pray.
So, let's join hands in a gesture of true family love,
and lift our hearts unto Heaven — to our Creator above.

—Lorna Hicks Ford

THE GOLD STAR MOTHER

Memorial Day is here again
Other mothers stand here with me
As we pause to remember our babies
Who died to keep us all free

How I remember the day that they told me
They saw him killed, his body never found
Never will I be able to bring him home
And lay him in home town ground

Yet here at my county's War Memorial
There stands a small cross with his name
And though he rests not here in silent peace
His spirit is here just the same

But I can not say I know not where he is
For in Heaven he waits patiently
And when I pass from this vail of tears
I'll again hold my son next to me

So please leave me alone for the moment
While I stand in the silence of grief
And stare at the small cross before me
And let the tears fall from my cheeks

—Janis Brunn

FOR JONATHAN

Though time may be the great healer
it doesn't keep the hurt locked in.
Each time I see your picture
I wonder how things might have been.

It's easy to say all the words
that everyone wants to hear.
But it doesn't make me miss you any less
for I still wish you were near.

I have so many precious memories
of a darling little boy.
Who was my ray of sunshine
and brought me so much joy.

It's all like a bad dream
and I wish I'd wake to find.
My special little angel
smiling at me one more time.

It's still hard for mama to believe
that I won't see you here anymore.
So I'll try to tell you with these few words
that I still love you even more.

—Karen Powell

THE BIBLE

The Bible is a wonderful book,
If you will open it and begin to look.
Turn each page and begin to read,
And you will find in it just what you need,

Strength for disappointment and strife,
And also the plan for eternal life.
It will be easier to avoid the wrong,
And in your heart you will be strong.

For God says in this Bible,
Seek and you shall find.
So obey the Bible,
And you will not be left behind.

—Curtis Garrison Long
At the age of 14 years old.

TO MY HUSBAND

I see you everywhere, Beloved,
In the softness of summer clouds,
The crimson flame of sunset
That kindles the western sea.

In the green of the cloistered forest,
The song of birds at dawn,
Dance of the changing seasons,
I see you everywhere.

You are in the laughter of children,
The innocence of their smiles,
Children who loved you and came to you,
For they knew you were one of them.

Death came from the cavern of darkness
And took you inexorably,
The grim, relentless buzzard
Destroyed your beautiful flesh.

Yet, you shall live forever
Above this tarnished world;
The essence of your truth and goodness
Bears seeds of immortality.

—Ruth Turkenich

A YOUNG WIDOW'S POEM

As day turns into night,
Night turns into day.
My husband wakes me from my sleep
in such a loving way.
Although not here in body and flesh
I feel him oh so near,
When I cry I feel his spirit
gently wash away my tears.

Oh God, my God
you are so great!
Through the good in my life
and the bad.
I thank you for the man you gave me,
the brief time on earth we had.

Though my sorrows are many
and my joys have been few,
I know my husband you now have,
will follow your will through.

That fact alone gives me strength
to wake up each new morn.
Yet it is so true what your prophets
wrote:
"Better the day of one's death,
than the day one's born."

—Shantay Al-Kassir

An Eclipse,
a shadow of the mind;
a forgotten portion,
of a little world;
A memory,
that has long since
been left behind;
then suddenly becomes,
unfurled.

—Rhonda L. Nunes

OLD QUILT

Under the covers
up to my ears
Pondering memories
of other years
Before me a painting
worked in cloth
Her brush a needle,
thimble and floss.
A scrap of yellow,
patches of blue
Lovingly placed
for just the right hue.
She lives on
it's plain to see
In the quilt my mother
made for me.

—Mary Joe French

SOUND/SILENCE

The screeching of cars
whizzing by, and the harsh
chatter of people, stops
dead at the hour.
It's like midnight triggers
an invisible button,
to turn off all sounds
so that the Earth can
catch up with the rushing
people,
and the tired ground
that the cities rest
upon can hear dead
silence that it heard
when the Earth was
being born.

—Mike Torocco

THE NEW DAY

The sweet, fresh
taste
of a spring morn
whispers by,
dancing
in the gentle breeze,
embracing
the delicate aroma
of dew-laden flowers,
softly kissing
each sleepy tree,
as the lazy sun
y a w n s
over the horizon,
smiling
upon the new day.

—Kellie Wirth

MY INNER STRENGTH

The sun is slowly going down, to end another day.
The light is gone but the warmth shines on to help us find our way.
We are all searching for some meaning in our life,
Struggling beyond our problems and pushing above our strife.
Each day is a new promise of better things to come,
A renewed spirit for many, a chance to grow for some.
We each have our hopes and dreams we want to share each day,
Looking for an inner strength to help us along the way.
For me God is my inner strength; my joy and peace beyond.
To Him I give my life; to Him I now belong.

—Gladys Ditmer

POETRY

Poetry, an expression of one's desires, thoughts and hopes;
Music to one's emotions,
Casting shadows upon the tides,
Evoking memories of bitter-sweetness,
Tantalizing the senses in awe.

Poetry, a word . . . a phrase . . . a reflection of one's inner soul;
Counting the moments,
Awaiting the freshness of a child's tender kiss,
Or the fire of lover's embrace,
And the joy of co-creation in God's universe.

Poetry, is the beginning of dreams and the idealism of reality.
Poetry is today!

—Kathy Ann Challis

A PLEA OF A CHILD

Oh Mommy, my Daddy, Our Plea to you is this
When teaching us the facts of life, just tell it like it is.
You are the one we come to, to learn the right from wrong
Don't hand out bad excuses, or make your words to twist
Oh Mom-my, my Daddy, just tell it like it is

Tell us that there is no gap, between the young and old,
It's only in the minds of man, who doubt what has been told
Tell the facts about the drugs, and all the harm they do
And talk about the wars, that kill the black and white alike
Oh Mom-my, Daddy because we love you so
Be sure your words are right

Teach us how to love and pray and how to stand up tall,
In case the road is rough and we do slip and fall
Yes tell us of the "Love of God" so we won't err forget.
Oh Mom-my — my Daddy, pray tell it like it is.

—Deloris Ballinger

MOTHER

Her great love rose from deep within, for children, one and all
Her work just never seemed to cease thru Winter, Spring, or Fall.
She'd build the fire and bake the bread and on the washboard scrub,
She'd clean the house and mend the clothes and soak us in the tub.

Though busy, busy, she might be, the time she'd always find
To pat this little towhead kid and ease his hurt and mind.
When the day was ended, and she got a chance to rest,
She'd tell us stories and sing us song: Oh, Mom! You were the best.

But, now you're gone; an emptiness is felt within my soul
The tears stream down my face tonite, my life's no longer whole:
No longer can I gaze at you and think in wondrous awe, of how
You loved us little kids and how we called you Maw!

I gaze at you as you lie there, soon covered by the sod,
And know without a single doubt you'll soon be home with God.
They tell me there's a place on high, a place that's for the best:
They saved a place for you, dear Mom, at last you'll get some rest!

—Leon R. Tinker

TIMED LOVE

Time, in essence has no measure.
 It is and always will be.
One cannot stop it,
Nor can it be turned back.
 It moves, it increases,
It develops into many things.
You cannot see it,
 but hence, it is there.
It can neither be bought nor sold,
And is true to all extents.
To go against it is foolish,
To be appreciative of it is; Dear.
 Time is a gift; not to be exchanged for anything less;
Not to be misused or overused, not to be abused
 In any way.
It is to be used wisely,
And not in defense as a weapon.
It is graceful and enduring,
 And precious to the wise.
Like all these things of time; So is my love with you . . .

    —Tami McCoy

SORROW PAST

Sorrow past — carved deep into my heart,
 With pain, without mercy,
 Leaving me in despair,
 Alone and hurting, again and again.

But, for some reason greater than I,
 Bitterness did not come
 And build her walls of cold stone
 Unfeeling within the chambers of my heart —
 Nor did the warm sun of life
 Cease to shine, and heal and rebirth
 The trampled garden of my heart!

For there, where tears had fallen
 Like oceans of rain
 To drown my weeping soul . . .
There, where tears overflowed,
 The pain carved chambers of my heart . . .
 There is now room to hold
 All the tender love
 That has blossomed there for you!

    —R.J. Lovelace-McClure

THE SECRETS OF MY HEART

My eyes that once danced, now drown in weary tears
 Confessing the secrets of my heart, admitting all my fears.
Yet you make me laugh, when I want to cry
You are honest with me, you'd never lie.
So much of you is still here with me now
And still the questions come to mind . . . When? Where? How?
You've given so much to me in ways you'll never know
Yet there are feelings still hidden that one day we'll show
What can I give you to show that I care?
The times I haven't been with you, have been hard to bear
I'd like to give you something special, a real part of me.
I have a gift in mind, but I wonder if it will appeal to thee.
My gift is as delicate as glass, yet durable too!
I wouldn't give it to anyone else, only you.
This gift that I'm giving you is quite frail you see,
But it's real special and comes only from me.
My heart is my gift and this I'll never regret
And as long as it's with you, don't ever forget
Friendship matures over a long, long time.
And from the very start, it seems ours was one-of-a-kind.

    —Mr. M.A.G. Wilson

LOST LOVE

On a long and lonely
 winter's night, I stared across
the sky,
 Searching for that love I'd
lost, the love lost in my life.
Yearning for the answer to the
question, alway's — Why?
It seems the things in life
we tend to love, always seem
to die.
 I wonder why the souls
we love always have to fly?
Leaving behind a shattered heart,
that never had a chance to say —
 Good-bye.

    —J.J. Johnson

FRIENDS

Friendship never questions you
 It doesn't have to ask
It shows in what you say and do
 No matter what the task

You can not see it with your eyes
 Or hold it in your hand
Together we must work and try
 To keep God's simple plan

A man named Jesus shows the way
 He teaches us what to do
"Love one another everyday
 As much as I love you"

When trials and troubles challenge you
 And life seems so unfair
Hand in hand we'll see them through
 together we can bear

Over the years as we grow
It may be put to the test
It's truly up to us you know
As friends we are the best.

    —Renee Dvojack

A SAD AND LONELY LOVE

A sad and lonely love is mine
 I slowly sip my glass of wine
The memories still bring the tears
For days gone by and wasted years.

I thought we had a life divine
A sad and lonely love is mine
Though we're apart and you are gone
The portrait of our love lives on.

And though it hurts for me to say
I love you more and more each day
I wouldn't have you back again
To live a lie would be a sin.

The best is what I'd wish for you
Although I know you're far from blue.
I know I used you as a crutch
I needed love so very much.

I know I'll make it thru the pain
To take you back would be in vain
So I'll just sit and sip my wine
For sad and lonely loves like mine!

    —Linda Brewer

COUNTRY MORNINGS

The sun shines
on the dew
Revealing hidden jewels
in the grass

Birds sing their
morning prayers
Thanking God for
another day

Coffee tastes best
at this time
Especially shared with
someone you love

—**Elizabeth Phillippi**

MARBLES

The circle is drawn
each child holds his marbles
in greedy, sweaty palms.
Down they go on bended knee
to start the age old ritual.

Clink! Those deceptively fragile
orbs full of colorful visions
future and past, hit.
The game has begun
each child for himself.
The circle becomes impenetrable
and the winner takes home
his trophies.

—**Amy E.R. Lang**

As a child,
My father took my hand.
He showed me the world,
And taught me to be strong.
He showered his love
On this earth —
Its people — its bounty.
Now on this day,
My hand is at my side,
And my father's in God's.
Knowing this I feel strong.
In God's hands he's safe,
In my heart,
His love and teachings
Are also safe.

—**Skip Sweeney**

TIME FLIES

Time flies, they say
As day turns to night
And night turns to day
Like soldiers in cadence
Time marches on
In the wink of an eye
It seems, a lifetime is gone

I look back and wonder
Can this be so?
My skin is wrinkled
My hair turned to snow!
It seems moments before
I had children at play
How much, I wonder
Did I miss on the way?

—**Wilma J. Houston**

THE PASSING OF THE OPEN HEARTH

Across this great land a legend was made
of the "Open Hearth Man" plying his trade.

First, second, third helpers and the slagging crew
crane operators, pitmen and the melter too.

From the mixer house to the main office you could see and feel
the historical saga of men making steel.

It's gone now, automation has taken its place.
It's been left behind as the world quickens its pace.

But, those who know will never forget
the noise, the heat, the face covered with sweat.

He has put down his shovel, his tapping rod at rest
and history will show it took a steel man to pass that test.

—**James M. Murphy**

AN EMPTY HOUSE

An empty house is a most formidable place. It is
unforgivable to the nostalgia that lies within its
walls. As one stands within the emptiness. The memories
concourse through the mind, at such a rapid rate, the house
seems to take on life again.

The laughing of children at play can be heard again from
the upstairs. The slamming of the screen door as mother
comes in. The aroma of cherry tobacco as daddy lights his
pipe. The barking of the dog still has an irritating sound
lingering in the silence.

Each step upon the hardwood creates a thundering echo of
nothingness, and a tear moistens the eye. Emotions engulf
the soul, and it is hard to stand.

An empty house is never empty, when it is filled with
memories of the one who lived there.

—**John Wright**

WE WERE THERE

I opened up my scrap book, just the other day,
and a thousand remember when's came at me from all directions.

When the world was young and full of surprises, we were there,
exploring, sharing, loving and caring.

During the good and bad times, we were there,
hoping, wishing, praying, dreaming.

Looking back, it surprises me how we got through it all without
being separated, but we did. The bond between us is unbreakable,
and those times only strengthened it somehow.

In the years to come, I know I will look over the added pages,
and once again, remember when . . . we were there.

—**Melva Gail Smith**

MEMORIES OF HOME

As I journey back to North Carolina,
it brings back memories when I was younger
though the mountains and the hills,
look a lot smaller now
than when I was a boy walking down the holler.

I remember the hill where I went sledding in the winter,
and hoed corn on the same hill, dern near all summer.
We had no money way back then,
when I'd go to the store, I'd take one of Mom's old sitting hens.
They would tell me right away how much she was worth,
the best I can remember, it wasn't very much.
A bag of smoking tobbaco and chewing gum,
and a Baby Ruth candy bar yum yum!

—**Thomas E. Reeves**

MODERN MAN

Early childhood memories of things to come—
    So dear.
The passion, the love, the riches—
    Thinking about it all without fear.
Wishing you were older—
    Life seems so dreary and boring.
When at a tender young age—
    Your dreams are a sea gull soaring.
Over an ocean, in clouds so blue—
    To do the things you can't yet do.
Year by year your wings sustain—
    What life has taught you in bitter pain.
To turn back time and soar no more—
    To return to the tranquility beyond your bedroom door.
To want each day to last as long as it can—
    For childhood is majestic compared to the burdens
of
Modern Man.

    —Reta J. Robinson Smartt

THE IMPORTANT

Unhurried time, unhurried time,
Nobody has any unhurried time.

I have to rush here!
I have to rush there!
Can't stop to talk, I have to go!
Go where? Can't say — haven't time!
Call you when I get back!
Back from where? Tell you later — must hurry, no time!

Unhurried time, unhurried time,
Nobody has any unhurried time.

Must keep rushing, rushing on,
Rushing to who knows where?
It doesn't matter to where we rush,
As long as we just keep rushing.
Rushing's the thing — that's what's important!
That's what life's all about.

Unhurried time, unhurried time,
Nobody has any unhurried time.

—Except, the Unimportant!

    —Cynthia A. Stockton

YOUNG AT HEART

This morning as I crossed the street
    I heard a young voice say
"If you'll take my arm, I'll help you
    and then be on my way."

I looked around astonished
    and turned my head to see
Two bright, expectant, caring eyes
    looking back at me.

In those seconds before I answered
    my eyes did fill with tears
As many memories came back to me
    each passing moment seemed like years.

My carefree days of childhood
    graduations, wedding day
Joys of motherhood and sorrow
    when grown children moved away.

With a sigh I took the offered arm
    and as our ways did part
Realized though I may seem old and frail
    inside I'm young at heart.

    —Cheryl Berger

GRAVEYARD

Nothing better suits the eye
than a graveyard 'gainst a moonlit sky
and that is where I want to be
in midst of all that majesty.
I once felt, or so it seemed
I'd grasped the great American dream;
But now those dreams are lost and torn
blown apart like a North Dakota storm
I'd welcome peace once more again
If on a tombstone was my name.

    —Lois Miller

OLD FOLKS' HOME

There she sat, for many days
    They tried and tried in many ways
To mend her heart that was broke in two
To give her Love and things to do.

But it was too late to start to give
She didn't have the will to live
She only started to get old and moan
When they put her in an Old Folks' Home

Some people there, I know
have a guest, almost everyday
But for many, many, others
They're just, Put out of the way.

    —Cookie

I got my license to drive at 25
    And I've been driving for 50 years.
        When the Doc. told me to quit
        I nearly had a fit
And that was the day that my spirit died.
I was so disappointed I think I cried.
        I couldn't go here
        And I couldn't go there
    In fact I couldn't go anywhere
        Alone.!!
    So here I am in a nursing home
    And the nurses are so nice
        But they don't know how
        I feel.
    And I still say my spirit
        DIED
    The day I lost my wheels!!!

    —Warren Webb

SPRINGTIME IN THE MEADOW

Take a stroll in the meadow
    In the Springtime of the year.
Walk along and visit some friends—
    The fox, the squirrel and the deer.

Capture the crispness of the morning
    As you admire all of nature — God's gift.
Enjoy the beauty of the flowers
    As they give your spirits a lift.

Feel the freedom of the butterfly
    As it flutters in the air.
Listen to the bird's song
    As he sings without a care.

Take a stroll in the meadow
    And realize all of its essence.
The most important of all is
    To know God and to feel his presence.

    —Charlotte I. Hoosac

RONDEVOUS

Come sit with me and talk awhile
Upon this hill of flowers
We'll track the clouds across the sky
We could be here for hours

We'll get to know each other
And dream the time away
I brought a picnic lunch
We could be here all day

When the sun goes down beyond the hill
And the night birds begin to gather
We'll smile, and remember this sunny day
In all inclement weather.

—Janet Donovan

SOUL MATE

I love you fascinating friend,
Unfathomable and wild:
Exciting as a shooting-star;
Yet gentle as a child.

I've loved you since before we met:
Before the world began.
Accept my love from first to last,
Be it holy or be damned.

Envelop me within your light,
Possess me soul and mind.
I pledge this heart that sings your name;
Oath sacred . . . beyond time.

—N. J. Beddingfield

And then through the mist,
A knight appeared,
And broke the shackles,
Of her loneliness,
With a sword,
Made of love,
   And passion

   Was it she,
Who needed him,
Or he,
Who needed her,
Through the ages,
All of history,
No one,
   Can e'er be sure

—Joseph G. Kressley

THE ROSE

The rose sat withered in the vase
Its color faded with the dawn
I threw it out into the rain
I never thought it'd root again
But then one day I saw a bud
Springing forth beneath the soil
A tiny leaf but yet so strong
It soon became a rose.
The rose did bud and then did bloom
I watched it from my upstairs room
I cut the stem so I could share
The beauty with someone who cares
For me.
The rose within the crystal vase
Reminds me of him now because
A precious gift I shared with him
The beauty of a rose on stem.

—Anita Norris Clower

LOVE IS —

Caring enough to be honest.
The warmth to reach out with a gentle touch.
That tingle of excitement in a first love.
Hanging in there when romance starts to fade
Bolstering your mate's sagging ego.
Sitting up all night with a sick child.
Letting go when it's time your fledging leaves the nest.
Having grandchildren to spoil — moderately of course.
The silent understanding of a beloved pet.
Making a house into a home.
One very special friend to confide in.
Quiet times spent with God
A mystery never completely solved!

—Emma Frencik

THE CRY OF LOVE

Is it so wrong to love one so?
Is it right even though
The future lies so uncertain
Veiled as by a phantom curtain?

How much time does one have to live?
Will all that love one has to give
Only be found in the tears of future years
That wash the gound amidst the sighs
Of sweet good-byes?

Enough! No more talk of teary eyes,
Of labored sighs
Enjoy full measure, the encapturing pleasure
Of new found love.

Love, warmed by the morning light,
Guided by the moon on the darkest night,
Travels at a quickening pace
Not deterred by obstacles it must face.

Two hearts—worlds apart; meeting first as strangers
Now face together every danger
So as each passing day is done—they learn to beat as one.

—Philip A. Moran

ECSTASY

This time wasn't meant to be,
I'm just sitting here living in ecstasy,
And everything's so unreal,
It makes me wish time could just stand still.

You see, I was living my life with a failure to see,
Never really being who I wanted to be,
I was younger then, and I didn't care,
For anything in life, however rare . . .

But now things have changed
In the moments we share,
As we sit here breathing in ecstasy.

I remember a dream I'd long forgot,
Where children played and seldom fought,
And music echoed through the dream,
It meant something then, I do believe.

I was living my life, I was blind to see,
Never really being who I wanted to be,
I was younger then, and I didn't care,
For life at all, however rare . . .

Because I never knew what it meant to be,
To live a life in ecstasy,
And my mind never saw the things it sees . . .
When I'm with you . . . In ecstasy

—Bryan Wisnoski

PRAYER

Most of us were taught our prayers by Father or Mother
And perhaps some got extra help from sister and brother

We were taught especially to pray morning, noon, and night
Sometimes when busy we missed and said that's all right

We should remember to teach our children to pray
Just as our parents did in the olden days

Some ask you to help win a ball game
Some ask you to cure the sick and heal the lame

Others Pray for good luck or good crops
When you keep praying faith never stops

Many prayers can be said while working or playing
Tune your mind into God, it will help when praying.

Whatever the favors you ask are
When you ask God they cannot be afar.

Please God will you answer our prayers
That will help us climb those heavenly stairs.

— **Joe Schumer**

DON'T GO ASTRAY
THE LORD WILL MAKE A WAY

There are times when things don't go your way
Please be patient and don't go astray.
The Lord is standing there by your side,
Just trust in him and he'll be your Guide.

The Lord will show you the right way to go
If you knock he will open the door.
If you seek he said ye shall find,
There will be joy, happiness and peace of mind.

Now you don't have to worry because the
Lord is your Guide,
He'll always be there by your side.
You just call him morning, noon, or night,
He will always make everything alright.

Please be patient and wait on the Lord.
He is always there even when you're having
it hard.
He wants you to trust him and truly believe,
And all of his blessing you will receive.

— **Arvester E. Lindsey**

MY FRIEND

I have a friend that cheers me
And makes my life worthwhile
He brightens up my darkest days
And then I have to smile
He's there when I'm in trouble
And need a helping hand
He tells me, "there's a brighter day, and on my
feet to stand"
He says, "Get up and face your problems, and don't
ever frown,
'Cause I'll be there to help you, I'll never let
you down"
I'll stand through all the storms of life
Yes, I'll make it through the tide
I'm not afraid of anything, with my friend
by my side
He'll never, ever leave me, on this I can
depend
I love Him, with all my heart
For Jesus is my friend

— **Faye Golden**

AN ODE TO FATHER FRAWLEY

Am I getting older Lord?
Am I getting gray?
Must I go thru priestly life
sharing everyday?

Was my mission in this world
to comfort everyone?
Will my work not be complete
until each day is done?

Must I always solace others
and think of myself last?
Must I always be the captain
standing at the mast?

You brought me to St. John's, Dear Lord,
you made me comforter of all!
I listened to you Jesus
I listened to your call!

There are 40 stairs that I must climb
Somehow they're getting steeper
But I look forward to each new day,
I am truly — my brother's keeper!

— **Shirley A. Dennis**

A HIGHER POWER

Lord, You have been with me
every step of the way.
You have been by my side
both night and day.
Without your love and
guiding light,
I could not find the strength
to stand and fight.

Lord, Most of my feelings are
hidden within.
But no one knows that as
well as you; My friend.
When I need you, all I have
to do is pray.
And believe in my heart you
will show me the way.

Lord, I was lost and all alone
when you found me,
You held me close and made
me feel like somebody.
Tears of joy fill my eyes
as I pray to you,
Expressing my thankfulness
for everything you do.

Lord, I try my best not to
stumble and fall,
Yet I am impatient, I want
to walk before I can crawl.
So calm my heart that
I may hear,
Your precious words I
hold so dear.

At Last, I give you all that
I have within me,
And ask that you use me
in your will of what is to be.
I thank you for the love
I would have never known,
and the life of Christianity
in which I have so richly grown.

— **Teresa E. Ralston**

When others see a thread
    dangling from your coat,
they warn you not to pull it
    for fear you'll lose a button
        or open a gap of protection
or they tell you that once you
    pull it, you'll never be done
with the pulling.
I saw your dangling thread
    and bade you let me pull and
        unravel till we had found
the end of it.
The difference is, as I unravel,
    Jesus is there with needle and thread;
        remaking your coat of protection
    into one of many colors.

—Kerry A. Reinhackel

ENEMY OR FRIEND?

Man looks upon the outward appearance,
    But Jesus looks upon the heart.
He needs not that any should testify.
He has seen each life from its start.

All things are open before His eyes
Which each of us have done.
The life of no man escaped His eyes
Since life on earth was begun.

He searches the depth of each heart
And knows the true affections of each man.
He knows each choosing friendship with the
    world
And—each—who with Jesus takes a stand.

According to our fruits, He knows us.
He knows each enemy and each friend.
He knows that destruction is awaiting
Each of His enemies at life's end.

Heaven shall be the dwelling place
Of His friends with affections true.
Are you His enemy or His friend—?
That decision—He leaves up to you!

—Florence Lillian Davis

FINDING "YOU."—A CHRISTIAN THOUGHT.

It's sometimes hard to stop yourself
    from going spiritually blind,
    And keep that eternal goal in mind
"What to do?" . . . "Where to turn?"
. . . "What am I supposed to learn?"

"Will it come after my work is done?"
"Will my joy be as bright as the sun?"
"Please let me know so these feelings
will cease,
and let my heart rest in peace."

I can see I've grown in these last few
months . . .
and pulled out of these problems and ruts
through faith and prayer I've broken
through the ice.
My tool?—the gospel of Jesus Christ.

So some may ask—"What's the deal?"
"How can I change those things I feel?"
My friend—the most important thing
to do—
is apply the principles of God in finding
the real "You!"

—Neal E. Smith

WHEN YOU ARE LONELY

When you are lonely and feel no one cares,
    Then take courage and don't despair;
The Lord has promised to watch over his own,
To never forsake or leave us alone;
On his Word we can depend,
Over and over he's a proven friend;
One who sticketh closer than a brother,
To provide all our needs like no other.
I ever thank him for his presence near,
When I feel lonely and need some cheer;
Sometime he will send a little bird to sing,
Or a reminder of pretty flowers of Spring,
Some beautiful thing he always brings in view,
And to him alone is my praises due!
I thank him for family and neighbors, near and afar,
And pray his protection and blessings, wherever they are.

—Dorothy Fallin Prescott

GOD'S GREATEST MASTERPIECE

We were made for you, Lord,
    To walk and talk with you;
To know your love and love you, too,
Made to enjoy you!
Created by your loving hand,
By you, Lord, we were planned.
You knew us while yet in the womb.
Enfolding as buds in bloom:
Adorable blessings from heaven above
Gift-wrapped in the Father's love,
Your precious sons . . . chosen ones,
We were made for you!
Equipped with talent and ability,
We can become all you meant us to be.
You said our sterling worth is "greater than gold,"
Our value beyond compare;
How sweet (as a honeycomb!) to be told,
We're special, priceless, and rare!
You've placed a treasure in our souls—
Like a diamond in the sun: beautiful!
You cherish and delight us, too,
We were made for you!

—C. Marie Metzger

ALONE

We at times feel so alone,
    Whether we walk in the park or we stay at home.
    He's by our side not far away,
He's with us as long as we want Him to stay.

At times we feel He doesn't hear our cries,
It's only Satan telling us those lies.
    In life He reaches out with much caring,
Hoping we'll listen and tell of His sharing.

He's ready and willing anytime of the day,
He's just watching and waiting for us only to say.
    He's just and forgiving no matter what the cause,
If we'll only trust Him and obey His Commandment
laws.

He died on the cross for all of our sins,
Could we be so humble for family or friends.
    So each day I feel alone or empty inside,
I will remember what Jesus did for me when
He died.

    I will pick my head up and look to the
heavens up above,
    Praise Him and Thank Him for all of His Love.

—Sue Estepp

168

SO ALL ALONE

All by myself, thinking of you
So alone, don't know what to do
Feelings of despair, I start to sink
Getting so lost, I can't think
Nights spent alone in misery
Wishing you were here with me
But we both know that that can't be
Conversations are now by phone
That is what I wait for when I am alone
Or via air mail from the heart
The millions of miles that keep us apart
I keep wishing for you, you my dear
I keep wishing that you were here
A long day at work and an empty home
Without you here, I am so all alone

—Dierdre Washington

IT'S BEEN __ YEARS

Well dear, it's been __ years,
    And we're still fighting back the tears.
Contrary to what people say,
When it's your child, the pain and hurt
    never go away.
We know in our hearts this will never
    change;
The years we can never rearrange.
We pray that other parents will never
    have to know
The heart-break and pain,
    "Oh God we're suffering so!"
We look at your picture every day
And to God "Please let this be a dream"
    we say,
We must realize that God has a plan
    for us all
It was just your turn to answer His
    beckoned call.
At least it's a comfort to know
That we need just to look up above
    to see your glow.

—Linda Larson

YESTERDAY

Who am I? Without my cause?
    Without my quest
        To change the past?

Would I but wake, to only future?
Without the fuel of hatred . . . pure?

No pounding heart or whirling senses,
Alert to sound . . .
    To touch . . . to smell?

To see the fear my eyes reflect,
My spirit withered by neglect.

But, forced to see my mirror image,
With all its flaws,
    Uncertainties.

When faced with my own insanity,
My past obese, with my vanity.

My battle and I have grown to one,
Each painfully lost,
    Inside the other.

I rage! Against the path I walk,
And yet . . . the ghosts within . . . I stalk.

—Margaret Lang Handler

THE RETURN OF AN OLD LOVE

Alone, I walk along paths we once walked
Alone, I go into cafes where we once talked.
Bittersweet the memories of things once shared
I loved her deeply, but she never really cared.

She lied, she cheated, she broke promises, and yet—
She was so beautiful I'd forgive and forget.
Then, without warning, with a grin on her face
She told me somebody new had taken my place.

No touch of the hand, no gentle good-bys
So cavalier, so indifferent, to tears in my eyes.
Her new love was waiting, I was important no more
Without a backward glance, she walked out the door.

In time, he used and abused her, she came back to me.
Too late she wanted the love that once used to be.
Now we live in regret for what might have been
She's the saddest of women; I, the saddest of men.

—Minnie Infelise

AWAY

While telling you, so, baby, I love you;
    Trouble leaks that you aren't here.
Revealing lonely, darkness speaks
What it seems your body seeks.

I'll do you right, I'll do you kind.
Won't do you at all, I'll do you fine.
And is coming end of time.
Without you, babe, is out of line.

Should I have shown more feeling before?
Where is more, now, for me from you?
Or is my name unheard, instead?
And will the words remain unsaid?

One thing for sure, I need some more
Of certain stuff, 'cause times are rough.
There's not enough mercy here.
Don't tell me now that you don't hear.

She said she'd been hurt, so, why not hurt.
She said this had been done, 'twas, now, her turn.
I seem to love, reject her, too.
Time never told what came over "who."

—Steven Eckols

NIGHTFALL

I sit here and
Patiently watch the sun set,
Watch while twilight falls
Upon the land.

Night fell so quickly, so quietly.
No beams from the new moon.
The stars are hidden by the clouds, and
Darkness has consumed the sky.

I see only the false light
Of street lamps, neon signs, and a bum's fire.
I see it reflected from feral eyes and junkies' needles,
And I close my eyes to it.

Though I walk through the valley of the shadow,
I should fear no evil,
Nor the black shadow itself
As it eclipses the bright flares of my soul.

I can't keep the fire burning,
With its spark smothered by the void.
I need someone, anyone, to save me from Nothing.
I can't make it through the night into the dawn alone.

—Kimberley Montgomery

ABODE OF THE BEREAVED

What deep, dark cavern is this,
Into which no thin shaft of light enters
To dispel the gloom which envelops my being?
Who would dwell here, alone and untended,
If choice were his? What power has driven me here
To this place devoid of life and love?
Time suspended — nights and days all one;
Dreams forgotten; plans unmade; desire gone.
O silent, endless wasteland of Grief!

—Mary R. Gaul

OPENING DAY

The forest is cold, quiet and serene,
Bitter and frosty with no touch of green.

The hunter is waiting to test his luck
Hoping this year for that big trophy buck.

As he stands in the cold, he remembers when
He was sitting back home in his comfortable den.

He remembers the stories, excitement and thrill
Hunters have told him regarding the kill.

There he was dreaming of this exciting trip
But he'd forgotten how deep the cold could grip.

His hands were froze; his feet were numb.
He'd have to start moving if that deer didn't come.

He looks at his watch and frowns in dismay
Only minutes have passed since he started this day.

He packs up his gun, his supplies and desires
And heads for his home and its warm cozy fires.

He stumbles through snow, the cold and the wind
Seeing his failures, knowing he didn't win.

After hours of strain, he falls to his truck
And watching him run is his big trophy buck.

—Karen L. Frey

THE PERFECT CHILD

Why can't you understand the turmoil and pain that
inundates my body?

You tell me to unleash the demon within. When I do,
however, it is humiliating

If I abstain from admitting my pain, then I am wrong

If I utter the painful words that I am finally
releasing, then I am a fool!

Moreover, if I declare my turmoil like a maelstrom,
then I am over-reacting

WHAT do you want from me??

You do not know the deep secrets that lay in the swamp
of my heart

I PLAY A FACADE

Do you see my tears that kiss me good night before I
sleep?

Do you feel the frost bite on your perfect fingers as
they touch my heart?

PERFECT children don't have fears, pain, frustration,
vengeance . . . .

OR feelings?

—Brandie Lipinsky

THE GOLDEN KEY

A golden key
so fragile and small
opens the door of childhood dreams.

The brass gate
looms ominously above.
A tightened fist holds the key.

Beyond that gate
lies a treasure in waiting
full of wondrous dreams.

A stance like a pirate in front of a booty,
closed eyes imagining a bountiful treasure.

With a sigh of expectation
the lock is turned,
the key breaking in half.

The gate swings open wide
to reveal what lay behind
the brass gate.

A wounded cry echoes
and the key clatters to the ground
resounding in the empty halls.

—Tehani Tuitele

THE STORM

Oh God, how long, how far, how deep,
a cloud of darkness comes for me,
there's no beginning and no end
I stand forever helplessly.

It strikes me like a force of wind
that pulls and spins and blows me free,
I know not where I go from here
forever gone security.

Away, beyond all hope and claim,
my life blows from me bit by bit,
oh night so dark, so cold, so long,
I scream in silence for the dawn.

I hear a moaning low and deep,
a sound that grows into a roar
of agony so dark and long
save hell alone can know its song.

Oh God, it's I whose sounds I hear,
the groans and wails of hell unleashed,
I'm trapped within this gulf of pain,
so black, intense and all complete.

How greedy are the gaping jaws
that pull and tug my bleeding soul,
take what you will ignoble guest,
I'm here to serve at your behest.

I'm twisted, pulled and broken down,
oh low, what's to become of me
when once this storm has blown its course
and seeks to find its destiny.

I'm tired, I'm done . . you've had it all,
oh mighty force I surely fall,
all innocence within is gone
from shreds of life that linger on.

Both torn and broken spirit and bone,
beyond the realm of pain I've borne,
I see a light, I hear a call
as slowly downward I do fall,
oh God, has this storm had its all.

—Grace R. Dalzell

THE SONG OF THE STARS

Listen closely, quietly now
From up high in the sky
Comes the sweet, tinkling sounds the stars are making
As they sing you their lullaby.

It's soft, and sad, and lonely, too
Like the sound of a faraway train
And the song of a solitary little bird
Searching for love in the misty rain.

They shine softly in the heavens above
As they drift along their way
Singing to you of life and love
And the stories of yesterday.

—Amy L. Bauman

SKY CHILD

On a small grass plain in the middle of the wild
stood a young boy — Devon's sky child.
Hair the color of wheat
Eyes the essence of myrrh
His brilliance outshone
the most radiant star

Intellect of the galaxy
Nothing outweighed his heart
He was the most beautiful human being
Ever to depart

But the boy could not stay
the wind swept away his tears
The sky child departed
To face infinite years

Such a young death
Cheats the world of a gift
But such sensitivity
Can not bear its own grief

—Frances Garrety

LIFE IN THE 20th CENTURY
THE LITTLE RAG DOLL

The little rag doll is faded and worn,
    For hard is the long toll of years.
Her little red dress is tattered and torn
    And her eyes seem brimming with tears.
Once was the time she was fancy and new
    And loved by her little friend,
But the little rag doll, so faithful and true,
    Never knew that life must end.

"It's beddy-bye time," her little friend said,
    "Kneel down and say a prayer."
Then with a hug she tucked her in bed
    And kissed her with tender care.
And snuggling close to her little rag doll
    Dreamt of an angel holding her hand;
Then awakened to hear the angel's sweet call
    And arose to a heavenly land.

Oh, the little rag doll, through years that are long,
    Still waits for her little friend;
For a hug or a kiss or a happy song,
    Not knowing that life must end,
And dreams of the time, in the gathering dust,
    When both were happy and gay;
And of the sweet little girl's true love and trust
    That someone has taken away.

—Joseph A. King

AMANDA

My Grandmama loved me.
I know, because she took care of me.
I did not know the meaning of the words
    or what the sweet sounds were
    that came from her lips.
I heard the softness of her voice and
    felt the caring in her touch.
She kept me full and warm, and
    clean and soft,
And made the pain go away.
Wonder and joy pulsed in my weakened heart
    that felt her love surround me.
Though I did not know the words—
I was too young
    and did not even make
    half a trip around the sun.

—June M. Clow

THE STORAGE SHED

Who searched the shack for loot or cash,
Found not treasure there but trash,
Relics of great granny's day
Flung about in disarray,

Tarnished trinkets, pots of paint,
Cross-stitched mottos queer and quaint,
Garments hanging patched and rotten
Worn with pride once, now forgotten.

Carpet remnants, paperbacks,
Fortune-telling almanacs,
Against a wall, a broom awry
The sort that wicked witches fly,

An old rag doll on a broken stool,
An empty, beaded reticule,
A yellowed news sheet on the floor
Dated eighteen ninety four,

A battered chest, a hob-nailed glass
And here a baby boot in brass,
Some verses tied in faded blue
With one entitled, "I Love You."

—Artemis Quint

MY FRIEND TEDDY

I'm talking to you Teddy 'cause I just don't
    understand.
I must have been just awful to make Mommy
    hurt my hand.
Mom and Dad — they get so angry, I don't know
    what makes it start.
But really Teddy, more than skin, it mostly hurts
    my heart.
I try to say "I love you" and sometimes they're
    really glad.
But then something will happen and I only
    make them mad
Tonight, before I go to sleep, I'll pray with all
    my might
And maybe in the morning things will change
    and be all right.
I can't tell other people, or they might think
    they're bad.
So when I'm hurt I tell a lie, "It's an accident
    I had."
Oh Teddy, I get so scared and very, very lonely.
    I'm glad I have you as a friend —
Sometimes the one and only.

—Cody Rainer

I've painted a water color picture of you in my mind,
I remember you the way I loved you best.
But as countless days go by, my water color picture fades.
Each passing day I think of you less and less until someday my
water color picture will fade completely away . . .
Maybe that day I'll stop loving you.

—**Debbie Jenkins**

He's big and strong; and I think my guy.
And tho' I never say it, I love him so much.
For words seem cheap, when emotions are strong.
And I wish I could show him with temples and gardens,
Like ancient lovers of the past.
But instead I go back into my room and dream.
For I am weak and so afraid I'll lose my catch.
And the days go on, and I see him more,
And I want to be with him.
But the fear grows. The fear of being discarded,
And once more alone.

—**Bonnie Hildreth**

WAITING

There is a voice I long to hear
There is a name I'm dared to know;
There is a step sounds to my ear,
There is a love I dare not show,
An ache that only you can ease,
A hurt that only you can heal.
Every night upon my knees —
A prayer for your lips to seal.
No one else can ease the pain,
Nor give me back my will to live.

Had I never looked into your eyes,
Nor ever held within the circle of your arms
Never to have heard the murmur of your heart.
Rather, my love, to go as the crow flies.
The beauty of your mind was like the soul of a violet,
The strength of your heart gave courage to mine.
Together — we will conquer the world, and all in it,
Unto my lips, all drink will be wine!

—**Gertrude N. Darling**

ON . . .

Over and over again
your image returns to the turntable of my mind.
You play like a worn record
but, my memory keeps you alive.

You drift in and out of my life
Just as the pain comes and goes
from the years we once shared.

What is to become of a dying love?
Can it be renewed?
Or is it forever lost
amongst the fears and tears we bury
in order to survive.

I've survived and have struggled
to find a new love
while you went on
to the first love you could find.

I hope that your life has turned out
well
and I trust mine will now begin
since the melody I once longed for
I no longer need to hear.

off.

—**Janet Gane**

NO ONE

No one steals your love,
If you have no love to take,
No one can break your heart,
If there is no heart to break.
There is no chance of failure,
For the one who doesn't try,
If one is all alone,
No one can say goodbye.
No one can guess your weakness,
If you never let them see,
Vulnerabilities never flourish,
If you never let them be.
No one can make you cry,
If there's not another tear,
It's a barren existence,
For the one who loves in fear.

—**Rebecca Joseph**

INDECISION

Indecision
is driving me insane
There are times
when I don't know my name

Undecided about love
which one's right, which one's wrong?
Who should I be running from?
And to whom do I belong?

One loves me too much
the other, not enough
Which one should I choose?
The decision's too tough

Why can't I love both?
I can't choose just one
Whose heart will be broken
when the choosing is done?

I love one
the other loves me
I'm caught in a triangle
never to be free

—**Janet R. Martin**

THE PAIN OF A LOVE UNREQUITED

A stone is heavy in my chest.
From this I cannot heal.
Oh, pain! Oh, precious pain
that teaches us the valuables
in this vale of tears.

She is a full, ripe woman now.
But I can still see her and
feel her in my arms.

I see her toddling across the street
to visit her cousins.
She turns, confident that I am
at the window.

Now she is grown.
She says I am a bitch.
Perhaps I am.
But the pain was so severe
when She Left Today.

She is headstrong, foolish
and wild.
I wait for her to learn to love again.

—**Arleen Marshall**

REQUIEM

Ambassador of mourning, bereaved, bereft,
offer Odinn precious life
victim's god of hanged.
Distant echoes speak of time, wearing
black the mantel of that left and lost,
cries the witch, ancient days bygone.

Softly goes the willow's wind across the whitened branch
coming tides approach the sands, to
murmur secrets of forgotten Brân
his vanquished warriors left running.

In hidden groves of blackened nights, nocturnal mystic feast
naked gathered midst the mists, mortals all they come to serve
past kings of death. Ecstasy, possession near, Phrygian Cybele
Overhead the echo of aforedoomed time hangs motionless
in patterned skies.
Below the earth dark blood ran down, lover's embrace the crucible end
in history's aged sepulcher.

—Jennifer Lynne Anastasia Walker

SEASONS . . .

As season passes, inhabitants find only very few pure companions
For seasons are a test of pure companionships.
Be it a beau or an acquaintance, endurance and sincerity are the leading certainties.
The devotion to another, is a way to unfold one's pure self
The devotion given to one so far away is the true way to test the seasons and the companion.
Though the seasons may be long, tedious and cold,
The feasible outcome and the present importances and the unforgettable remembrances
  are the vindication to grasp onto the devotion present.
Season presents what devotion purely is.

—Kathleen Spottiswoode

A FLEEING MEMORY

An old man set in his rocking chair, with a zither across his knee. While his two great
grandkids set close beside, with looks of eager glee. In his voice, though racked with age
there was a whisper so soft, as he spoke to them of some memories of the zither he had bought.

One little girl and boy stared softly at the man they loved. While the tunes from the
strings, as the old man played, showed a trace of love.

Even their mongrel pet crawled up close as could be, as lazily he was; right below the
old man's feet.

The old rocking chair, though sitting still, with arms showing weathered signs, as if
they too had tried to grasp feelings from the old man's inside.

His glasses set low on his nose, yet in his blue eyes there was a twinkling of a smile.
While his greying hair fell softly down and the beard he wore showed a trace of grey and
white.

Though his hands would tremble ever so slightly, as he struck the strings so tight; no
flaw was in the sounds which came to the children's delight.

No doubt this man throughout his years must have led a joyous life. I could not see
where any worry lines had embraced his brow on sight.

Much wisdom he must have gained throughout his youth and latter years. A humbleness
he also showed without a trace of fear.

The echoes of the words which came as a flawless mind let go; to share with them a dream of
hope, and a love of long ago. Such a measure of strength he had; as his cheeks began to glow.

His features for an aged old man still held a marvelous hue. The things this man would
leave these kids, will surely remain in their hearts forever true.

—Edith Faye Coots

174

THE TYROS

I spoke with an old man who told me of a great war,
great flags, and leaders, men had killed and died for.
And he spoke softly of one near endless night
  How fighting hand to hand he had lost his sight.

He sadly told me how the war had left him without descendents,
  How those great leaders had merely turned men into ravaging decadents,
How soldiers had raped and pillaged the now concrete scarred earth.
  He took a deep breath, smiled so slightly, he whispered . . . "Birth . . ."

"You," he said, "you're young. You have time.
  Live your life for things more worthy than mine.
Love your woman, raise your children. The love in you must swell
  Or . . . like me . . . you'll burn in hell."

        —Kevin Jepsen

GOLDEN AGE TRUCK DRIVER

He was a young man when he climbed in the cab of a great big truck
Tho he traveled many miles each day, he always had good luck.
He drove through many little towns and through big cities too
But when he got in a traffic jam, he always knew just what to do.
  He knew where all the truck stops were, and that's where he'd stop in
He would down a cup of coffee, then he'd hit the road again.
He was a very happy man with a wife and kids at home
Because he knew how they loved him, he never felt like he was alone.
  Years passed and he reached sixty-five, he said he'd retire then
So he laid his log to one side, he'd never drive that truck again
But there was sadness on his face, there were big tears in his eyes
When he became a golden ager and told his big truck good-bye.
  Now he is a grandfather, a great-grandfather, too
He's a very busy man, there's lots of things that he can do.
He has a little dog and cat, and there's children all around
So every once in a while, I see his smile turn up-side down.
  Then in a little while, he smiles again and turns the T.V. on
He loves gospel music and calling friends on the telephone
Then it's time to go to bed and have a restful night
He prays for God to keep him safe and then turns out the light.

        —"Sparkie" Vinnie Harper

THERE'S AN OLD TRAIN

There's an old hobo nobody knows, an old train whistle no longer blows
  There's a longing to feel the roar of her wheels though time has made
Them her own.

There's a loneliness it seems of forgotten dreams that lie in these rusted
Rails, like a lonesome sailor stares out to sea longing for the wind
In his sails.

There's time honored memories of an old freight train with her black
Coal smoke and white driven steam; you can almost hear the faded echo
Of her lonesome whistle blow, the essence of a childhood dream.

The new river rolls neath the old iron bridge on her majestic path
To the sea, and the mountains like a cradle guide her along, a flowing
Blue ribbon, she's free.

The memories still linger in this old river ville, they rest about
Her like a shadow, silent and still. With only the stories left to be
Told of old days and old trains and mountains of coal.

Although these times are past and gone, the memories play the part
To rekindle the fire of a hidden desire deep within the heart.

There's an old hobo nobody knows, an old train whistle no longer blows
There's a longing to feel the roar of her wheels, though time has made
Them her own.

There's a loneliness it seems of long forgotten dreams that lie in
Those rusted rails.

        —Matthew B. Baldwin

I AM
Most
of what i am

i am

uncontrollably

i am

uncontrollably

me
—D. J. Lewis

As you walk
through life's paths
you pass many dangers
seen and unseen
Along the way
are many choices
you make and change
but,
In the end
it was already
Destiny
—Kaye-Lincoln-Davila

UNKNOWN SOLDIER
You are the spark of
Patriotism in the
Star-spangled eyes of
Bright young soldiers;
You are the
Old glory of
Experienced veterans;
You are an eternal
Flame that lives on in
Our hearts.
Although the
Stone says
"Unknown Soldier,"
Your spirit lives on in
Those who know
Freedom.

—Debra Brown

JUST ONE WORD
A blank page,
waiting silently,
stares at me.

"What do you
want of me?"
I ask it.

"Cover me,
fill me with words"
it replies.

"Just like
that?" I ask
the page.

"Yes, just
like that.
It's simple.

Go ahead.
Try.
Just one word."
—Barbara Enright

TRUST

I heard a bird this morning
    He sang so merrily,
He did not mind the heat at all
    Just fluttered in my tree.
I saw that same bird after
    A storm had come our way,
He flew down from his little perch,
    And ate a meal that day.
I trust the Lord for many things,
    And yet I know not how
To trust God like a warbling bird
    Through weather calm or fowl.

        —Opal A. Elliott

GRIN TYME

Poe-tree in Moshun

From the Ark to the Rock in the Bible
    The Old Testament into the New
        66 books to instruct us
    And every word of it's true

    4 Gospel writers inform us—
King James writes with "Thou and Thee"—
I'd write a 5th—the one I'd like best
It's the Gospel according to Dorothy

Meetings are scheduled in evenings
    I try to attend when I can
I mean—there's Dallas, Cosby, and Starwars
    And how can I miss Roseanne

Christ wants us with utter devotion
Or He'll spew us out of his mouth
He expects us as dedicated followers
East—West—North—and South

    He's laid rules for us to follow
    With nothing left to surmise
His eyes of concern are upon us
Let's keep our eyes on the Prize

        —DOT/dot

NEW DAY

When dawn lifts the eyelids of morning
    to a bright new day,

Will you bask in sunlight?
    Pick a flower along the way?

Will a burdened face seem brighter,
    when lighted by your smile?

Will you refrain from quick retort?
    Rest your tongue a while?

Will you use your ability, talent
    to help your fellow man?

Will you take time to stoop,
    and help another stand?

Will you lift your voice,
    to sing some happy melody?

Will you give thanks
    for a land so rich and free?

Then, when the eyelids of evening
    close again in rest,

Can you say, truly say,
    I have done my best?

        —J. L. Jacobs

TREMENDOUS

My life is tremendous, I live it for my Lord;
    And each day I'm drawn closer,
Through the study of His Word.

His blessings are tremendous, innumerable as the stars;
    I cast all my cares on Him,
He knows just what they are!

Tremendous was His sacrifice that was given at Calvary;
    "Whosoever will" that comes confessing,
Can be a soul set free!

His love is tremendous, His voice is oh, so sweet;
    'Twill make your life shine forth,
To those whom you will meet!

Life can be tremendous, for you if you will give,
    A consecrated life to Him;
Then, you've just begun to live!

        —Arlene Deckard

REVENGE

O' sweet revenge beget from bitter pain!
    Strike out for justice! Inflict pain again!
What victory is won? What evil wrought?
    Exchanging blow for blow! All for naught!

Beware! Lest your innocence begone
    And leave you with revenge now to atone;
Triumph o'er offenders gained with spite
    Yet leaves your heart to sadly ponder right.

And so you win, but then exact too much;
    Pray! Who of us has Allah's righteous touch?
"Vengeance is mine!" our Lord loudly proclaims
    And wise men hear; the fool, a mortal blames.

Compound the human debt! Heap flame on fire!
    Damn the wretched knave that raised your ire.
Death to the one who dares insult your honor.
    Have your revenge; replenish evil's garner.

But when the truth is out and all is known,
    All have transgressed and have some evil sown.
It's all in vain — revenge; 'tis human fate
    That only love at last shall conquer hate!

        —Damu Sudi Alii

HELPING EACH OTHER

Helping each other— That's the name of this game.
    Learning to love all, as one in the same.

    Treating everyone as you wish to be treated,
And lending a hand— It's how happiness is created.

    For helping each other is such an easy demand.
And the rewards that it reaps would overflow in your hand.

    So give of yourself in money, knowledge or time.
    There are so many ways in which to be kind.

    Help others to do the things they're unable.
    Or be there to listen, when they feel unstable.

    If they need help in some other way,
    Do what you can, to help make their day.

    If they need a favor, or maybe a friend,
    It will be worth your while to make time to lend.

    In the law of attraction, what you give you get back.
So if you give help and love— That's what you'll attract.

    If you want true happiness, just keep in mind—
    The way to achieve it is to be unselfishly kind.

        —Cindy Curit

GOD'S CHILDREN

So many countries at war with each other
Don't they know they are destroying their brother
If countries would only instead of war seek peace
Maybe anger and hatred would finally cease
If each individual followed the golden rule
Destructive forces of anger would have to cool
We are all God's children and His next of kin
No matter what our race or color of skin
Each race has beauty for the world as a whole
It could enhance our world and enrich our soul
All our customs, costumes, our music and art
Should bring us together and never apart
Isn't it better to love instead of fight
The world would be richer if we all lived right

—Mary D. Price

THE STRANGER

He came into our life so suddenly,
Bringing with him love and kindness.
He brought sunlight into this gloomy world,
And gave our hearts such a twirl.

He stepped in, to help and care.
And even though we know not where,
We gave our hearts to him to share
We'll always love that stranger there.

"Who is he?" you ask, looking here and there,
"We want to give him our lives to share."
Well, he might be your neighbor or
Just someone you pass by one day.
This is something we can not say.

We can not say where or even who your stranger is
All we can tell you is, be kind to everyone that
Passes your way, for someone might turn as you
Walk by and say "We Love that Stranger that came
Our way!"

For we do love and miss the greatest friend we
Have ever had, that stranger that showed He Cares.

—Anne Clarren

LIPS

Whispers of revelation
Herald the moment of the soul's recreation

Loving and gentle corrections
Of the Father's patience a clear reflection

A simple confession
Frees the soul from every secret transgression

Benedictions of forgiveness breathe the message of Grace
And from the soul all traces of guilt erase

Consolation in sorrow
Encouragement and hope for tomorrow

Confidences shared in quiet conversation
Prayers uplifted in heartfelt supplication

Problems explored
Tattered self-confidence restored

Partners in mutual endeavors
Whose fruits Faith in God restores.

Thankful affirmations
Fruits of prayerful meditations.

August, 1983
January, 1967

—Irene Warner

THE VOICE OF GOD

I heard the voice of God today
When I awoke at dawn;
The birds were singing in the trees
And chirping on the lawn.

I heard His voice again this noon
When children came to play;
I heard them laughing in the yard;
The sound was light and gay.

I heard His voice again tonight
Upon the evening breeze;
It rustled in the aspen leaves
And sifted through the trees.

I heard His voice within my soul
When I lay down to sleep;
His voice was peace within my heart,
And I am His to keep.

—Delphine LeDoux

GOD'S WONDROUS LOVE

The glistening of the waters
as the morning sun appears
whispers quietly to me
that God is standing near.

The peaceful song of the wind
as it roams about the land
gives me comfort and lets me know
all is in Jesus' hands.

The gentle fingers of God's moon
and his stars that shine so bright
reach down to wipe my brow
as I slumber through the night.

No, I can never doubt God's love.
It lingers through and through.
Just like the moon, the stars,
the sunshine, and rain —

It's so real and very true!

By inspiration of God,

—Antqualene Brandon

RELAXATION

When my troubles over come me,
and I just can't seem to rest.
I go to my lake for relaxation,
this place I like the best.

I sit and look out my window,
at my lake way down below.
Like a mirror I see all God's beauty,
as it reflects in the lake with a glow.

The light of the moon shines brightly,
nature's beauty is every where.
I see the moon's reflection,
from the window by my chair.

I love to watch nature display its color,
as it changes from time to time.
And I can watch from my window,
down on the lake of mine.

For only when I see God's beauty,
can peace enter into my heart.
And all my troubles and worries,
soon just seem to depart.

—Jannie Clark

I lay here and wonder
As time passes by
I think about us
And I lay here and cry
There's tears on my pillow
There's pain in my heart
We still love each other
So why are we apart
I sleep with your picture
'Cause you're not here
I lay here and worry
And live with the fear
That we won't find our way back
And will lose our true love
So I did the only thing left
I asked God above
To help us make it
To help us day by day
Until we can be together
Until we can find a way.

—Ruth Ann Anderson

FINISHED WITH PERMISSION
It is finished
    and so, with the writing
    ended a life
And slowly, memories good and bad.
Picking up threads
    a new life begins,
    reality settles.
What was done, was done
    with permission.
One willing to do
    the other permitting.
Departure, meaningless
    without feeling.
Torn and shredded
    shattering dreams.
How does one person
    dare do this to another?
    because of permission.
Now, it is finished,
    and slowly memories fade.

—Brenda J. Housler

WHEN YOU'VE GONE
The nights are long and dreary
    The hours pass away.
The time goes by so slowly
As the night turns into day.
No sooner does the first snow fall
When the sun comes out to glow.
And slowly with its radiant heat
It melts away the snow.
So it is, when I am dreary
And my heart is full of gloom,
That you come as does the sun
And brighten up my room.
You melt away my troubles
And warm my yearning heart.
And give to me your tender love
Before you must depart.
So again the nights are dreary
The hours seem so long.
The time goes by so slowly
My Darling, when you've gone.

—Judy Melvin

SECRET LOVE
Words pleading to be spoken remain quietly unsaid
    That special one they are meant for . . . is not here
I stare into that part of my life I've yet to live
My eyes come to rest on a sense of loss and fear

Existence, if this facade could be but a memory
This life that I confront and survive each day
Unfair consequence of searching through spent years
At last I find the one, and then I must stay away

A secret love can be a punishing and torturous burden
If it cannot be given life nor allowed to breathe free
And until stones turn into sand, this profound caring
Shall rest quietly upon my heart, that is not up to me

Please remember . . . true love that cannot be expressed or given
Is but a fragile flower lying in the shade of a tree
Sorely it struggles to flourish and bloom
But sadly, it never becomes what it could come to be

—Edgar James Haney

HOW DO YOU SAY TO SOMEONE
How do you say to someone,
    That you want to spend the rest of your life with them?
That you will always love and cherish them?
That you will try with all your heart and soul
to accept him without change?

How do you say to someone,
That he is your being?
That he makes your life full of joy?
That he is the one that makes you smile when you are down?
Or laugh when you feel like crying?

How do you say to someone,
Please forgive me for my mistakes?
Or can we accept each other for what we are?
And please, if humanly possible,
can we try to be open with another?

How do you say to someone,
That you wish you could make things easier to accept?
That if you could, you would always be beside him in every way?
And maybe with God's love and grace it would be that way.

—Burdean Briscoe

TOMORROW NEVER COMES
All of those promises will never be kept,
    Because upon us, the end of today has secretly crept.
Everything we've got, has blown away in the dust,
We never had love — we never had trust.
Our future, we thought, would be wonderfully great,
And to be with you forever, I could hardly wait.
But I've always heard, and found out that it's true,
That tomorrow never comes, I've had only one day with you.
We've had some good times, I've gotta' admit,
But now I look back, and was it worth it to try? I've so
many things to attempt to forget.
I've tried to love you and let it be known,
But we hadn't enough time, or enough faith did I own.
Our relationship wasn't special, like I thought it to be,
Nor did it blossom, to ripe from the green.
We were so young, too young for it all,
The day is now over, it's here the curtain must fall.
Maybe we'll find another, only time will tell.
But always remember, if you try to fall in love, you're
headed straight to hell.
Because there is no tomorrow, there's only today.
And you can't fall in love in time, Babe, there's just
no way!!!!

—Ashley R. Bumpers

LOVE IS LOVE

Love is such an easy word, but sometimes hard to say,
It can really make a difference in a very special way.
Love has as many meanings as there are pebbles on the beach,
You can sometimes hide love in your heart never to repeat.
Love can be a tender smile, a touch, a warm embrace or
even anger spent at someone else in haste.
Love could be a season, maybe rain or summer heat,
What about the job we have or the home that's our retreat,
The trees we climbed as children, the flowers, a bed of
grass, a butterfly in solo these loves will never pass.
Love is God, Mom and Dad, lots of family too
Love can tie us together or tear us apart
It comes from a thought and then from the heart.
We can't throw it away like that old sock that we wore
or buy it at any price and I know of no person as yet
in my life, Love has not touched or helped through strife.
Man is Man, Woman is Woman, but Love is Love is Love.

— **Dorre Kauffman**

SWEET DREAMS

Sweet dreams, my love, I wish to you,
Many of happiness; sad ones few.
'Twas upon this night a very long time ago,
You had loved me and I also loved you so.
But as time went by, because of many reasons, we drifted
apart.
And then it seemed nothing could mend my broken heart.
You had your life to lead; you had dreams of your own.
Without even a single "goodbye" you had left me all alone.
Just once I wish I could see you again;
For once to see you just as a friend.
It causes me great pain knowing that's all we can be.
Of course my feelings are too deep for anyone else to see.
And for all that you put me through and all of the tears
that I have cried,
To this day, there is not a bit of hate for you that lingers
on inside.
The memories of you are all still there.
I loved you too much and I will always care.
For this reason I bid you sweet dreams, my love,
And happiness by far,
And tonight may you think of me
Wherever you are.

— **Judy Iannazzo**

WHEN I THINK OF YOU

When I think of you,
I think of a Constable painting; an unspoiled landscape,
and as I look across your hills and valleys
I see magnificent beauty—
let me gaze—until my eyes will see no more.

When I think of you,
I think of fine wine; whose color and bouquet
I must savor; over and over again,
such flavor and quality unequaled—
let me drink—until I can hold no more.

When I think of you,
I think of a spring morning:
clean, crisp, fresh, and new; so beautifully untouched.
I wish I might experience—
mornings like these—everyday of my life.

When I think of you, I think of uncharted seas;
a wide expanse of endless ocean: let me ride
your raging surf or drift on still, silent blue:
oh, let me feel—all this and more—
each time—I think of you!

— **Sylvia E. Diffey**

SOUL FOOD

My love is a happy love
For your love has made it so.
The yielding of the fruit
and the budding of the flower
Gives me strength for my body
and strength for my soul.

The sun warms my heart
while the melting snow keeps
the rivers flowing to cool
the fire. While I may have
grief and you will be with me
I will later have joy
because of my love.

Amid grief and frustrations
come happy times of great love.
These restore my soul
and liven my body.

— **Rosetta Lowry Veasey**

YOU . . .

my poem was not cast off in scorn—
it was just trying to elude me.
but i had patience
and i waited for it—
my poem.
i waited for *you*
but
you are not a poem
you are not my poem

you are not so easily understood.

my poem.
i wrote this poem
i know how it ends
but
you are not a poem
you are not my poem
i know that too well
but i have patience
and i *still*
wait for *you*.

— **Carolyn Reilly**

DO YOU REMEMBER

It's hard to love someone
Whom you don't know
You see me everyday
But still you can't see
What's inside of me—

Inside of me is my heart
My soul's there too
Ever since the very start
They've both belonged to you—
But I can't seem to please you
No matter what I do
So I've left you alone
Alone to think—

I'll give you all I can
And most of what you want
I'd do most anything
To win back your heart—

Do you remember
When we shared that special Love
Do you remember—

— **Lee Bowen**

179

BIRD THAT SINGS

Oft times we're too involved with—
The many hassles that life brings—
We fail to see things as they are—
And turn a deaf ear to the bird that
Sings—

We tend to live our lives each day—
At a pace that defies tomorrow—
So busy we are getting ahead—
We don't hear the bird song of sorrow—

We finally reach that stage in life—
Where we understand and seem to
Know—
To enjoy life requires that we
Listen more—
A little bird that sings has
Told us so—

      —Peggy Vaughn

IF

If I had 3 good wishes
And they would all be granted,
I would wish I were a large oak tree
On the White House lawn be planted.

Now you may think me silly,
And at me laugh and scorn,
But what is any more prosperous
Than the wee, tiny acorn.

Wish #2 I would want to be
A great huge silver jet.
I'd fly off in the sky so blue
And my worries I'd soon forget.

Now #3 I'd want to be
My plain old self, I guess.
Made in God's own image
Striving to do my best.

But I don't have 3 wishes
And they can not be spent.
So I'll just live with what I have
And be very well content.

      —Annie A. Smith

A BOY'S FANCY

I know where luscious berries grow
And flows the coolest stream—
And fields of clover make a bed
   Where I may lie and dream.

I know where trouts the biggest
   And the apples reddest too—
Where pumpkins are more yellow
   The sky a deeper blue.

I know a wood of pine trees
   Where birds sing all the day
And squirrels scamper all about
   And rabbits come to play.

I know where I can gather nuts
   And store them in a cave
And just outside there is a pond,
   Where I can swim or bathe.

I know where there's a bird's nest
   And a house up in a tree—
I know where I can find a boat
   I bet you wish that you were me.

      —Helen M. Weston Govaya

LET THERE BE SOMEONE

Let there be someone to hear the children cry,
   Let there be someone to sing a lullaby,
   And when the shadows on the wall become
monsters in the night . . . .
   Let there be someone to turn on a light.

   For love and understanding is what we must give
to help our children keep their will to live.

   And when it's time for us to send them off to school,
where there is knowledge to seek . . .
   Let there be someone to excel their abilities,
to its highest peak.

   For one day that very same knowledge will enable
them to put their lives on the right track,
   And when that happens, please let there be
someone to give a pat on the back.

   For love and understanding is what we must give
to help our children keep their will to live.

      —Stan Boyer

LAMENT

When children come to you and your wife
   They make a big change in the pace of your life
You have feedings and diapers and not much sleep
They sit up, then crawl and finally, they creep
You coax forth small steps and, at last, they try it
You teach them to talk; then they won't be quiet
Then school—peer adjustment—the opposite sex
Overcoming their problems, however complex
You guide; make decisions—some hit and some miss
And you long for the day you'll be free of all this
Now the children have gone—they have fled the nest
I didn't know then how well I was blessed
I sit in a silence that hangs wall-to-wall
And my once crowded home isn't like that at all
A loud shout would seem like a lover's caress
The peace that I wanted just seems to depress
No loud music or squabbles; no accusing "That's mine!"
The bathroom is empty and you don't wait in line
Each small noise by silence is magnified
And I can't say I'm happy unless I lied

      —Mel Kintz

PARENTS TO CHILDREN

Listen children while we tell you:
   Morals and ethical values we teach you.
These come first from us,
From our hearts to yours,
To give you a start.
Later, your school will reinforce—
Strengthen.

Express your feelings
All the time appropriately,
Listen carefully and then heed—
And when you don't
There will be consequences
Strong and stringent.

Attitudes, skills and techniques
We give you to meet your challenges
Because we want the very best for you.
Your character will speak for you with honor.
The insight and solutions we give you.
The responsibility is yours
Accept it and make your path a success.

      —Dr. Anne B. Smith Cunningham

THE POLLIWOG

The polliwog is small and harmless,
     Not only footless, but also armless,
But soon he'll hop across the bog,
     When he becomes a full-fledged frog!

—Tommy C.

JOY OF LIFE

I stopped the minute the other day
 I stood and watched my children at play
Seeing the past in each special child
Sitting back remembering my babies a while
One day they're little and can be held in your hand
Next day they're telling you where they stand
The holding, the scolding, giving each a part
Of all the love you hold in your heart
Sharing a world of wonder and life
Protecting them from all its strife
Giving a smile and childish laughter
They're giving you the joy of life now and forever after

—Sharon Elyea Gray

BECOMING A TEEN

I know you feel so insecure
 But believe me, there is no cure
You're a teenager now, have no fear
We have all gone through the same, my dear.
One minute you're told "you're all grown up"
The next "you're so immature."

You feel confused "am I too young or too old?"
As you get a bit older you'll know, without being told.
Your emotions are as wild as can be
And unpredictable they are, we know you see
An identity of your own is what you seek
It'll take years, not just a few weeks.

Quiet one minute, but not for long
Soon you'll be jumping and singing a song
You start wanting more privacy
I guess that means you're also maturing physically
Yes, parents all know what teens go through
We may be old, but we have memories too.

—Nancy Spoerke

EVILS OF THE NIGHT

They protect me from the evils of the night,
     Two bodies that hide my vulnerability.
She sleeps on my left and he sleeps on my right.

A moon beam pierces the darkness with its light.
     As dark shadows disturb my tranquility,
     They protect me from the evils of the night.

A distant sound creaks, the fearsome flame ignites.
     Danger cloaked in invisibility.
She sleeps on my left and he sleeps on my right.

I lay quiet and wide-eyed from my fright.
     What is their responsibility to me?
     They protect me from the evils of the night.

Her voice, a low growl and his movement is slight,
     Danger knows not my invincibility.
She sleeps on my left and he sleeps on my right.

And through the window, breaks a new day's light.
     The full circle brings me my tranquility.
     They protect me from the evils of the night.
She sleeps on my left and he sleeps on my right.

—Mark A. Bender

MAKE YOUR MARK UNDER THE SUN

Don't just take up space
 Make this world a better place

Talents are in us, everyone
Make your mark under the sun

If you'll only look inside your mind
All the wonders there you'll find

Make this world a better place
Don't just take up space

Anything you put your mind to can be done
Make your mark under the sun

Ah, the wonders you can attain
If you remember this little refrain

I think I can
I think I can

Anything you put your mind to can be done
Make your mark under the sun

—Joyce M. Kress

TREASURE THE MOMENTS

Today you are growing,
     Things in life you are knowing.

     It is not easy.

Parents say it is for your own good.
A brother has his own mood.
A sister tries to show she cares.
Friends come and go,
Some you think you know.

     Treasure the moments
     one by one.

Some are good, some are bad,
Others memorable, others sad.

     Treasure the moments,
     I always try,
     For you'll never know
When a tomorrow will bring . . . a Good-bye.

In Memory of my brother, Roberto R. Mesa
     —Martina M. Cardenas

HEAVYWEIGHT CHAMPION

Small children love to romp and roam,
 Until they grow up and drift from home.
Small children have the laugh of love,
God has given us from up above.
Small children do sometimes cry,
About small tasks they do try.
Life is filled with much ups and downs,
Like the boxer in several rounds.
You keep on fighting with all your might,
Until you get through the tunnel to light.
There are many things for you to see,
And much more out there for you to be.
Take heed to what this message brings,
You need to listen for the bell that rings.
Put on your gloves and take control,
Searching down deep within your soul.
Life is always worthy of one more round,
Even if you are knocked to the ground.
Get up holding your head with great pride,
Walking through life with an enormous stride.

—Judith Knight

NOVEMBER

Leaves,
Aimlessly falling
To the frozen, sleeping
Ground;
Withering and lifeless
Like my lost desires.

Rain,
Wildly beating
Against the windowpane;
Flooding the earth like
My tears;
Drowning my love.

Snow,
Madly whirling
Mercifully covering all
The desolation;
Drifting like an ermine mantle
Warming my grief.

—Beverly L. Mabee

SEASONS

Spring

Fields of violets
A cool crisp day—newborn lambs
Rest in the warm sun.

Summer

A velvet-soft night
Whir of wings, a cricket's song
Fireflies light their lamps.

Autumn

Mountains, color-splashed
A cool breeze ascends the heights
Gently a leaf falls.

Winter

Little gray squirrel
Asleep, snug in his burrow
Snow drifts to the ground.

—Joan Attaway

'Tis good to plow behind a knowing team of horses.
Oxen can move along with greater strength,
But that is often all they give.
Good horses gain a knowledge
With the passing work of every day.
A tractor moves along with greater speed,
And men can do more in a day with spinning motors
Than with beating heart.
But with an engine always pushing on,
There is no time to watch the passing of a cloud
Through lace of trees;
No time to catch that extra dip of blue
That seems like sky, but is the jay instead.
No chance to listen to the song of larks
Or even to the raucous call of crows
Unless you stop that chugging motor.
Then the work stops, too.
To plow behind a team of horses
Lets a man live with his heart, not just his head and hands.

—Doris S. Brennan

METAMORPHOSIS

Each spring. . .I blossom with each flower.
My cheeks. . .put on the blush of a rose petal.
Free. . .as the wind. . .is my hair.
Each step I take is of vining ivy. . .

strong,
secure. . .
always reaching out. . .

In the summer. . .I feel with my heart,
the morning birds' songs.

My spirit. . .flies graceful
as the butterflies.

The fragrance. . .that adorns me,
is of the lily.

My eyes. . .are the color of the earth.
The gentle breeze. . .becomes my very soul.

Summer. . .like a true friend. . .
will be back again. . .
until then. . .I will await. . .
like the caterpillar. . .

—Mary Louise Warren

SUNFLOWERS

This is the story of two Sunflowers;
Sadie Sunflower, who lived on a window sill,
and Sandy Sunflower, who lived in a field.

Sadie would look out her window to Sandy in the field and would laugh and say; "How crazy you are to live in that field, when 'Someone' will water and feed you, so that you don't have to do a thing but look pretty, here on this sill."

But Sandy would say, "I love it here in the field swaying in the sun and rain, although the birds feed on my seed and I'm sometimes trampled to the ground, fierce winds scatter my seed and cold winter snow covers me deep in the ground."

So Sadie sat day after day on her window sill. Her seeds grew fat and fell at her feet, but had no room to grow, so they just faded away. One day "Someone" never came to feed and water Sadie. She waited and waited, all in vain; so Sadie grew weak and died there on her window sill.

Sandy, although trampled and blown rose up each day to catch the sun and rain, and to share her seed with the birds. One spring Sandy rose from the cold winter ground and saw the field covered with sunflowers, thus Sandy and her seed stand year after year in that field, their seeds are scattered near and far, so that there will always be sunflowers to sway in the sun and to feed the birds.

—Bernice M. Abshire

ESCAPE

Sun-dried sheets on a summer's day
Rising yeast and new mown hay
Fresh picked apples and lilac blooms
Stove-black polish and new straw brooms.
Cinnamon, nutmeg, ginger and cloves
Incense, lamp oil and pot-bellied stove—
My Grandmother's house is a vague memory
But the scents it held are still with me.
And when life grows grim and the world turns sour,
I go back through that gate neath the red rose bower
Down through the grape arbor, sweet and cool
To the straw-strewn stalls and the milking stool
Out through the pasture — on to the hill
And there on its crest
I stand very still
To drink in all the sweetness
My soul can contain
To last 'til the day I can come back again.

—Alice S. Griffiths

AS I GLORY IN THE SUN

Crusty white remnants of snow,
Unwanted,
Out of place
On the dry brown grass.
I see them as I leave in the morning,
With Spring imaginings swelling in my head
They seep
Into my wintered heart, and fill it
Expanding like the clear, warm, azure ocean waters
that quietly crash on the shore.
The yellow breeze feathers my face
And undulates my lightening hair.

Glorious rays toss bright the afternoon
As I step on the bus returning home
My soul excited by the sweetened air of
Warm memories past—
Home, I clutch my 10-speed
As I glory in the sun.

—Tracy L. Hauppa

THE BRANCH

Looking at the waterfall
As I walk through the snow,
Ice is at the edges
Of its solid rock bed as it flows.

The branch runs swift
Past the dogwood tree,
Past the redbud
Past the buttercups of Spring.

It rolls through the Summer
Clear as crystal it flows,
It offers a cold drink of water
To thirsty creatures as they go.

The branch keeps rushing
During the Fall,
While the leaves change colors
In the trees both short and tall.

It rushes down off the mountain
Crashing through the rocky wooded hollows as it goes,
It rolls through all seasons
In Spring rain, Summer heat, Autumn frost, and Winter snow.

—John R. Baker

CLOUDS

The Clouds in the Sky
are
Like Ballerinas
Wearing White Fluffy Tutus
as
They Dance across the Sky
In their Costumes,
Which get Dirty and Turn Gray
When these Costumes get Washed
and
Become White, as ever,
These Ballerinas Dance
across
The Sky once Again.

—Katie Haynes, 10 years old

THE MOST BEAUTIFUL PICTURES OF ALL

I've seen the galleries of art
that hands of men have wrought.
Pictures of the earth and sky
or of battles they have fought.

The things we see from day to day
like city streets, or lakes,
whatever strikes our fancy
are the pictures an artist makes.

The vast beauty all around us
that spreads from earth to sky,
we move too fast to see it,
we're so busy, you and I.

We have at our convenience the
greatest canvas ever spread
and painted, oh so beautifully
in greens and blues and red.

With many other colors,
God made them all, you see.
He placed them all around us
for the joy of you and me.

—Doris Griffin Autry

SAYING GOODBYE TO WINTER

And as the Winter melts away,
I feel that Spring is on its way
The leaves are slowly taking shape.
as we make a final effort—
to escape—
the coldness.

Bitter-cold, rough winds
I once felt,
have vanished under
what the sun does melt.
Frozen roads and highways
are now paved;
the icicles on branches
have all been shaved—
it's clear.

Buds spring newly gained warmth
on the scene.
Earth is adorned with green.
Fruitful sights appear
within reach.
Birds to us their songs will teach—
Spring's Lesson.

—Diane Troncone

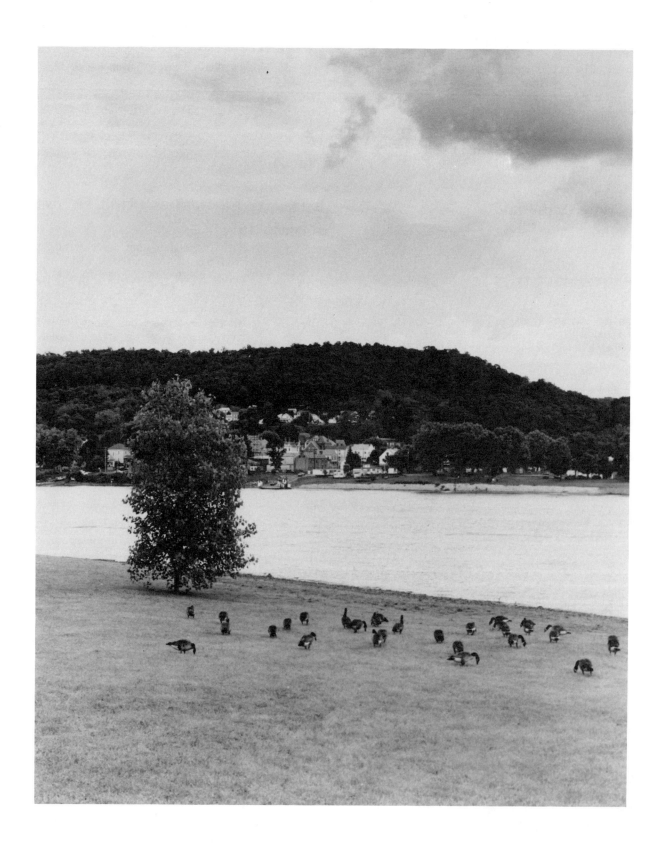

TODAY IS BUT A MEMORY TOMORROW

Today is but a memory tomorrow of laughter,
of pain, of joy and of sorrow, to dream of the things
we'd like to do, to hope and to pray and courage renew.

Tomorrow is but a dream today with the undetermined just hours away.

When our eyes awaken into another day, who
do we thank and what do we say?

For many lay on their beds last night and never
awakened to see today's light.

If tomorrow was today what would we do? Would
we love, and hope as we plan to, or would we keep on
dreaming while time passes on.

Waiting to live and life is gone.

—**Mary McKenzie**

HE IS BLIND

He hates darkness
yet without darkness
how would he enjoy the radiant light?

He despises winter
yet without winter
how would he cherish the spring?

He detests thunder
yet without thunder
how would he appreciate quietness?

He loathes the ordinary
yet without the ordinary
how would he treasure the unpredictable?

He abhors loneliness
yet without loneliness
how would he relish the moments spent together?

He condemns her presence
yet without her
who would he have to love him?

He is blind, for though he can see with his eyes
He cannot see with his heart

—**Irene Thomas**

LIFE

Can you ever recall the love and joy in your life?
Or must you go on living each day in a lonely strife,
Forgetting about the good things that God imparts
And never feeling them down in your heart?

Or can you face tomorrow with a smile
And know that life marches on mile after mile?
It is not what we think that we must do,
But realizing that in all things life is very true.

Never look for the gloomy and the side that's dark
Set your eyes upon that heavenly mark
And love all mankind in this life,
Never letting the deeds of sorrow cut you like a knife.

Love is a gift that we all can receive
And learn it's better to accept than to leave
Because love and joy is only for a while,
So share it in your life and wear it with a smile!

Then walk in this world with your head up high
Reaching the loftier things that race through the sky,
For it is there for all of us to take
And mold it and use it for it will never break.

—**Juanita Ruth Burns Sanders**

LIFE

I used to wonder, why was I born?
What am I destined to be?
Why was I put on this earth, anyhow?
Many other creatures could be me.

How do I know what my future holds,
And how can I prevent the worst?
I used to ponder these questions so hard,
Out of anxiety, I thought I would burst.

What if I fail life's big test,
And turn to drugs and that stuff?
I used to think life was an impassable maze,
Unless I knew enough.

Now I know that life is straight forward,
Like a freeway, with dangerous exits.
As long as I stay on the beaten path,
Life for me, will be a success.

—**Danella Hafeman**

ALWAYS NOW

Now is here and always will be,
Close to you and close to me.
'Tis one thing all share alike,
Be great or small or just a tyke.

Now is here and always will be,
Seasons cannot make it flee.
Summer, winter, spring or fall,
Cannot make it flee at all.

Now is here and always will be,
On mountains peak or by the sea.
Dusk to dawn and through the day,
Now, besets us all the way.

Now is here and always will be,
This is but a fact, you see.
To think, feel, walk or sit,
No one dare try deny it.

Now is here and always will be,
Through ALL eternity.
Each passing day, hour, minute, second,
Brings the NOW that bids us reckon.

—**Linda Harwood Herron**

NOW IS THE TIME

Help me through each day, oh God—
And help me be the best I can.
Let me walk the righteous road
And do good for my fellow man.

If some sad soul should pass my way
Make me more Conscious and aware.
Forgetting the little problems I have,
So I can let others know I care.

Today is here for once to live
And is a precious gift from God above,
But many times I waste my day
Not showing others I care and love.

Now is the time to do what I can,
To help, to give, and to share.
Later my body could be weak
And I could be filled with despair.

So while I'm well and richly blessed,
I realize I can't waste another minute.
Right now I will do all the things I should
And put my heart and soul in it.

—**Anne B. Simpson**

185

ONLY A WHISPER AWAY

The sorrow that is in my heart
Is impossible to bear
Without His Comfort and His Love
There is no-one to care
I cannot hear the voices near
Only those who share these tears
Though farther than my eyes can see
I know that He is pressing me
Ever closer to His Loving Fold

—**Carol Koehler Hebert**

GOD BROUGHT TO LIFE . . .

God brought to life this earth of ours
to cherish and to hold.
He thought we would be kind to it,
but instead, are we not cold?

The sun, He gave to keep us warm,
the stars, to glow above.
The rain, to wash our wicked lips,
and to peace, one small, white dove.

The earth, it spins on moral lies,
on lust and sinful ways.
The Lord just could've given up,
but why waste seven days?

—**Sheri Fussell-Smith**

Why am I
Never Scared!
  Never Quiet!
    Never, oh never Tired!
But always courageous
  with continuous shouts of Praise
    and
  Always, yes, always full of Joy!
Never Dirty
  Never unworthy
    Never, oh never, ashamed
But Always, yes always, proud
  to be called
  a child of the
           KING!

—**Joyce M. Robinson**

SOMEWHERE IN THE DARKNESS

Somewhere in the Darkness—I stand
on a wall, not knowing how to land,
or how to fall.

I have no light, no way to see.
No place to go, or to be.

Many times life seems high, yet so
low, still having no daylight or a
place to go.

I think over my laughters, my sorrows,
my todays, and all of my tomorrows.

I smile of relief, I give no grief.

I realize, in the darkness, on that
wall, I do have a place to land,
and a place to fall.

Then a light was shown this is
true, I still remember "Lord I
am thankful, because; Somewhere
In the Darkness, I still have you."

—**Lisa Ann Warner**

We live in this world, beautiful by sight,
  But sometimes we all have a certain fright.
When you feel this way, you should look up above,
And ask, "Dear Lord, please show me your love?"
  The Lord may not answer verbally to you,
  But you will notice by the things you say and do.
That he's always there, to lend a helping hand,
To Men, Women, and Children of this beautiful land.
  Too bad you have to watch your shoulder so you
                              don't get hurt,
  Cause some in this world will treat you like dirt.
Not everyone, will treat you this way,
There are some, that care about today,
  About tomorrow and the future to come,
  If you look real hard, you'll see you're not the only One.
So if you feel insecure and you have a fear,
You can look afar or around you, but he's always
                              near!

—**Lisa Crawford**

HE LISTENS TO ME

He made the whole world in only one week.
He heals the sick, and causes the dumb to speak.
He makes the lame walk, and causes blind men to see.
And yet when I pray — He listens to me.

He makes clouds to give rain when the ground becomes dry.
He makes flowers bloom, and birds to fly.
When the sun becomes hot, we have shade from His trees.
And yet when I'm lonely — He listens to me.

He sees the way clear for those who may fall,
And works out each problem, no matter how small.
His work He is doing continuously,
And yet when I praise Him — He listens to me.

The Lord must be busy each second of the day,
Guiding his people as they go on their way.
But no matter how busy our Lord seems to be,
He always takes time to listen to me.

—**Jan Bomar**

HE'S COMING BACK

Some time in the night, not so far away.
The Lord is gonna tell him to come back
to me and stay.
It's been so lonely without him
ever since he went away, but my good
Lord always tells me, he's coming back to stay.

Eleven years since he left me, and why I do not know
I think the pressure got to him and he
Just had to go.
I still love him dearly and I know he loves me too
When it's time for the Lord to tell him, He'll be
Coming back, wouldn't you?

The good Lord shows me daily, in all kinds of
ways, That he's coming home some day, and
He's coming back to stay
So Thank You dear Lord for helping me
through these lonely years, and thank you
dear Lord for wiping away most of the tears.

Five minutes or less with him, will wipe
away all pain for with the good Lord's
help he's coming back again.
We will spend our lives together
and be in each other's hearts,
Until death takes one of us
and then we'll have to part.

—**Helen Goins**

A GOD BREAK

How often during the day do I think of the God around me . . . When pressures and troubles are too much; do I think of those rolling, soothing waves heaving on to the hot sand; do I think of the spider's web carefully and intricately knitted in the corner; do I think of the gentle laughing eyes of a child when I'm sad; do I think of the comforting hand, lending support when I need it.

Do I think of the hiss of the gentle snow kissing the warm earth, the vibrant leaves colored red, yellow and burnt orange, of the sound of my voice on a mountain top, the power to forgive when trouble arises between friends and family, the power to understand when things are confused, the power of love when problems are too big to handle.

How often do I breathe in the salty, sea air and breathe out frustration, and thank God for all the gifts he has given me. Today and everyday, I will take a God break, and thank God for the God within me and the God around me.

—Patricia Strader

WITH HIM LIFE GOES ON

When your world seems rattled and about to fall;
Don't have a pity party or sit down and squawl.
You've got to snap out of it and open your eyes;
And talk to that friend up above in the sky.
    Because with Him life goes on.
When you feel the mistakes you've made can never be righted;
Talk to the man upstairs, I know He'll be delighted.
He'll listen and comfort you and help with your sorrow;
And give you strength and hope for a brighter tomorrow.
    Because with Him life goes on.
Sometimes we put Him to the back of the shelf;
It's times like these when we're thinking only of ourself.
But He's patient and kind and always there for us;
A relationship with Him must be nurtured with trust.
    Because with Him life goes on.
It seems most of us only call Him in times of need;
But He'll be our best friend if we'll only follow His lead.
The sacrifice He made for us is one we can never repay;
So we must always believe in Him and give thanks every day.
    Because with Him life goes on!

—Carrie Galigher Newton

THE EASTER STORY

If I said I saw an Easter Bunny many hearts would jump with joy for he would bring me lots of jelly beans, pretty flowers, colored eggs and furry toys.

Now let's talk of Heavenly Father's most dear and precious Son, will that make the same kind of joy jump in your hearts with all your inner LOVE.

JESUS was resurrected not just his own soul to save but to remind all the world that at some future date we will all come forth from our dark and cold damp graves.

JESUS tried to teach mankind of his Father's eternal plan the one of repentance the only way to reach that Promised Land.

The oddest part of Christian history that is hard to understand is that most people remember the Crucifixion and not the impact of the Resurrection of the Universe's purest Man.

Was he real?, Did he Live?, that's up to each one of us to decide but if He lived then every EASTER, GOD THE FATHER must go off into a corner of HEAVEN and sit down and cry.

So when you take an Easter Lily and hold it in your hand please stop and ponder for a moment which EASTER is more Beautiful the one created by GOD the Father or the one created by the imagination of man.

—James M. Kerr

COMMUNION

I received my Lord,
My soul grew calm,
A kiss so soft, as from Angel
lips was felt upon my cheek,
We were infused, we were
one.
For a moment so sweet,
with love, hope and peace,
My Lord, my child, and I.

—Katherine M. Wicklander

NO APPOINTMENT NEEDED

Make sure your path is open,
and clean of all debris!
Your hall-ways unobstructed,
and entry ways are clean.
Make sure your heart is full
of good.
Your temple light to shine,
For Jesus, needs no appoint-
ment.
He may come at any time.

—Rita G. Cole

REMEMBER ME

Lord, remember me?
"Now I lay me down
    to sleep;
God bless mommy and
    God bless dad,
Make me good, take
    away the bad."
The prayer of a child
    so long ago;
Well Lord I'm back
but a child no more,
I need you now like
    never before.
Make me strong now,
Oh Lord I pray
To make Life good
For each coming day.

—Janet M. Harper

WITHIN OUR SOULS

What great sacrifices
we mortals bear
Our laughter creates such
a stir within ourselves
What great master was
there
Taking time to care
we bare ourselves completely
naked and cold
Our souls reaching out
to God
Speaking to him
Searching for the voice
within
Once we had, now gone
Down deep in our
inner mind
Wanting for someone,
anyone to care

—Lea

THOUGHTS OF A DYING MAN

Here I lie down in bed, the
angel of death upon me. I look
to heaven for support, yet there's
no response. Why in death do I
look for him, when in life I
only sought, the riches of earth
I never got? If only I could
receive him now, the power that I
needed, to help me through life,
and then in death his love I could
achieve. Now I see what I have
done, and this I must accept.
For the time of judgment has
finally come. And for me the
judgment is Death.

—Douglas D. Sherlock Jr.

TIMEPIECE OF LIFE

Life contains a divine time clock
sealed securely by padlock.
We arrive, study, work, depart,
many leave quickly,
some distressfully slow,
when pains of body, stabs to mind
turn life into shadows
minus warmth of sunshine.
Hope allows light
to filter through;
love bestows strength
to encouragingly renew
insight to restore faith
with will to overcome
weakness to succumb
to despondent delirium.
Wisdom, power, infuse one to strive
to conquer catastrophic problems,
employing wisely, noble stratagem
to survive, thrive — 'till time expires.

—Clarice A. Merswolke

FREE PEACE

When I die don't cry for me,
just let my soul run free.

For I have loved and been given love,
so much from you to me.

My life was never boring, my days
were filled with pride.

Because I did the best of things
I lived, I loved, I tried.

So when you look upon me, just look
at me and smile.

And, tell yourself you're happy
we were together for awhile.

Don't look back on our memories,
don't let stray tears escape.

Look on them with a grateful smile
and let your life reshape.

Although, I am not with you
and, again I'll never be.

Rejoice at all the progress made
between just you and me.

—Annette Hall-Roegiers

YOU HAD TO GO

You came to us so young and energetic. It seemed that
playing was your only goal. And you would eat — most
everything in sight — til you could hold no more. Your
tiny limbs strengthened and your body grew. And still you
played. More serious now, but life was still a game. It
was all a challenge — a playing field — and you were
young. You knew not of fear or terror or pain. You were
secure within the perimeters of home. But the challenge came
— and you had to go. You had to cross the road from safety,
warmth and security to the unknown ravages of the world. It
mattered not that ones who loved you begged you stay. You
had to go. And go you did. But you'll not come back. Your
body lies still — tangled, shattered dreams — your hair
blowing in the breeze as life passes by you.

—C.M. Douglass

MOM AND DAD WILL ALWAYS BE THERE

We take for granted Mom and Dad will always be there
As we go our own way and do as we please
Never a thought of our parents and their needs

As the years roll by, we all grow older
We think Mom and Dad will always be there
At our weddings they cry, our graduations they beam with pride
Hoping in their hearts that everything will be all right.

Did you call your Mom or Dad today?
I pray they are alive to say "Hello"
Today I picked up the phone, to make a call
When I realized, they were not there at all

My inspiration
My reason for being
No longer could I pour out my troubles
Share a funny story or laugh about everyday life

Someday the phone will ring
and I will hear
the most beautiful voices
on earth.

—Ann Hodge

PARENTS AND FEELINGS

With them my feelings I try to share, but it doesn't matter,
they don't listen, they don't care.

I keep my feelings locked away; when I try to tell them
they don't listen anyway.

They always say I'm wrong, their excuse is I'm too young.

What can I do to get my point across, when somewhere within
them all my words get lost.

I think they are scared I will forget everything we have
shared.

Why can't they see? I realize they are forever there for
me.

It really seems they've made come true my finest dreams.

This is my final wish — may it come true, because they must
realize long ago my toys I outgrew.

Just because I grow doesn't mean I'm letting them go.

I am older, but like everyone, I need a shoulder.

I only hope they can see, they'll have to remove the bars
and set me free.

I think they should know, they have got to let me go,
because no matter how small I am, my mind will grow.

—Samantha Asmus

AS TIME GOES BY

It occurred to me the other day, as I read through her letter
That Grandma must look back sometimes, to days when life was better.
Her writing now so difficult, her spirit yet unbroken
I wonder of the things she feels, the thoughts she keeps unspoken.
Though her body weakens daily, and her features change with age
She seems to take it all in stride, instead of bitterness or rage.
She has a million memories, of so many wondrous years
She's lived through days I cannot know, with her dreams and joys and tears.
Her contributions in this world, have not won her a prize
But her victories are evident, in her laugh, her smile, her eyes.
None of us can ever know, what it feels like in her shoes
To see the changes in this world, each time she hears the news.
A lifetime spent in sharing, her devotion given to others
God's greatest gift to all mankind . . . was surely our Grandmothers.

       —Mary Degenhart

THE MIND'S EYE

The family is gone now.
   I walk this earth alone
The land I used to trod lies fallow
Memories of the past linger on,
To fill the mind like grain gathered by the sparrow.

Vivid pictures are recalled in the mind's eye
Of meeting friends down the lane on the old wooden bridge
Of dancing in the moonlight, our feet would feel they could fly.

Climbing the big walnut tree
Crawling down a limb slowly to catch a locust
Fearful of breaking a limb, and losing our focus.

Riding stick horses, pretending we were cowboys
We ran through the ravines in the field,
Gathered tumbleweeds to make houses,
Checking the watermelon patch for what it would yield.

Many events come to the mind's eye from time to time
Bringing a touch of joy with a touch of sadness
Knowing God meant for it to be this way,
And we accept with gladness.

       —Murieldean Hammond

DEAR MOM AND DAD

Down through the years,
   You have helped me face my fears;
From teaching me to swim in a pool,
To meeting new friends my first day of school.

Remember the oddly colored pictures from kindergarten?
Kindly forget those rotten grades I have gotten.
But no matter what it was I did right or wrong,
You loved and cherished me despite them all.

You were always willing to help me up from a fall,
Or to scold me when you knew I hadn't given it my all.
You have always been there,
With your love and your care.

The years have come,
And the years have gone.
Now it is time I spread my wings, said goodbye, and were gone.

But never fear,
I won't be gone forever.
You are a precious tie I never want to sever.

Goodbye, Mom and Dad.
P.S. I Love You.

       —J.C. Brown

LOSING DREAMS

Once I said if I should die
   I don't expect anyone to cry.
Then I thought how silly that
would be because that would mean
nobody loved me.
I once thought that was true
until the day that I met you.
You came into my life and
made all my dreams come true.
Now as I sit here all alone
I wonder how I let my dreams
slip by.
You were the dream that I
let go.
But now I know that
should I die you of all people
you will be there to cry.

       —Lisa C. Trask

BENJAMIN

He was born into the limelight
   And found it suited him
His life is good and easy
His stage is never dim

Things come easy to him
People seek him out
He is popular and handsome
He's what charisma is about

He has an inborn sense of justice
Will he be a diplomat?
He can set a goal and reach it
Gladys would say "A Democrat!"

He confides with his mother
Her opinions shape his mind
He sees his Dad as strong and smart
And slow and quite resigned

He adjusted when life's fairy tales
Were all replaced with Truth
He will make a difference
This vine produces fruit.

       —Donna Cantrell

SAY GOODBYE

Say goodbye to Emerald Ridge
   But not for very long
Look upon her mountains
And capture them in song.

Look upon her houses
That tower to the sky
And those that dwell within them
On whom you can rely.

Look upon her children
Who make this place so rare
And of their happy faces
That are beyond compare.

Look upon her landscape
The hillsides and the park
Where one can hear the singing
Of the meadowlark.

Look upon the full moon
That rises from the bridge
And know someday you will return
To stay in Emerald Ridge.

Dedicated to Miss Robyn Phillips and Emerald Ridge
       —David Alan Nankin

LOVE IS SPIRITUAL

Love is spiritual.
It is beyond physical
destruction.
It cannot waste away or die
for it originates within the soul.

It denotes all feeling
makes one whole.
And hurt, sadness, longing,
will not destroy it;
but strengthen it.

Love is carried in one's soul
and as such lives forever.
And not time or age or eternity
can destroy it;
for God is love.

—Janice Walsh

THE LIGHT OF THE WAY

My serenity had become lost
    in life's daily problems
thrusting me against a tide
    carrying me under

My lonely excursion into the world
    to find myself turned into joy
for I found peace and goodness
    in Nature, Mankind and God

Walking an abandoned country road
    I came upon a church in decadence
waiting to serve its purpose
    as despairingly I walked in

The old Pulpit stood at the Altar
    still solid as a rock
holding an open, dusty Bible
    which became my salvation

Slowly I turned the fragile pages
    hungrily reading words
which became my bread and wine
    and road map to Eternal Life

—Willard Lee Skelton

AN INSTRUMENT

I want to be like the violin
To be tuned to do my best
And play along with all the others
To sing my praise like the rest!

I want to be like the grand piano
To lift my voice so high
That even the angels in heaven hear
My music float thru the sky!

But like these noble instruments
I need the Master's touch
To tune me to perfection
And polish the strings and such

O, but when I'm finally ready
He'll call me center stage
I'll bow down to His majesty
And play thru golden days!

And when my song has ended
The last note finally played
He'll lift me up and smile
For at last my journey's made!

                        Amen.

—Ruth Pate

THE BEAUTY OF THE WEEPING WILLOW TREE

I see you all as the ones who are me,
living your lives the way only you and I can see.

We don't know of our true destiny;
we only know of the weeping willow tree.

Sad do you think that to be?
Those who truly know that weeping willow tree,
are those who know that sorrow sometimes sets us free.

So let our tears flow out to the sea,
where they may be lost til all eternity;
Til all of us find our reason to be . . . .

To see through those tears that lie deep in the sea.

—Tina Nicholson

DON'T WEEP FOR ME

Don't weep now, don't weep for me
    For I am gone, gone to be free,
For I will suffer no more pain or sorrow
    Nor worry about what will happen tomorrow.

Don't weep now, don't weep for me
    For I am free, for eternal life to see,
No more disappointments will I find
    No more troubles to confuse my mind.

Don't weep now, don't weep for me
    For I am not here, that's plain to see,
If a friend you were, then a friend you are
    Remember the good times for they'll take you far.

Don't weep now, don't weep for me
    A good friend should always be a good friend, you see,
Time heals all wounds, no matter the pain
    Through years it will still hurt, but not the same.

Don't weep now, don't weep for me
    For I am happy and eternally free,
Remember me and I'll always be with you
    But don't weep now for me, weep for you.

—Kristine Stratman McCoy

THE BLOOD

In the dark hours, while a world slept, He entered
the garden to pray.
He knew, when He entered, the Father's will, and He
knew this was the day.
As sweat drops fell on garden ground, His blood was
already spilling.
God loved His Son as Son loved Father, and for
this He was willing.

The agony then continued as thorns pierced His brow.
Again the blood trickled down the Lamb's face, dripping
from His cruel crown.
His body battered but His Spirit undaunted, His
accusers continue their hate.
They could break down His silent stand, then mocking
they sent Him away.
A spectacle to see as the nails were driven,
Suspended between earth and sky.
And then the blood flowed from the Lamb that was given
Yes, for you and I.

Oh Saviour, I see Thee, and I see myself, and the stain
I cannot hide.
Oh with Thy Blood, cover me with that crimson tide.

The Blood — it took the blood — shed in agony
To make His joy — to gain His prize.
Praise God! He wanted me!

—Andréa Svaren

WHY SHOULD OUR HEARTS SING?

In His own time,
In every place and clime,
God has made beautiful everything
That can make the human heart sing.

To show that He is just,
He gave us His Son as a trust
To bring peace on earth
To those who want to experience rebirth.

To show that God is embodied grace,
Christ's blood hides our sins without a trace,
To give forgiveness to those who repent,
To those who accept salvation, heaven-sent.

So let us all freely sing
and our devotions freely bring.
God is still making beautiful everything
For which our hearts should sing.

—Orien Chafin

A MACHINIST'S HANDS

A machinist's hands are strong and firm;
from lifting a thousand and one steel bars,
and from measuring a thousand and one parts;
from cutting, shaping cold steel for the productions
needed in the backbone of industry.

A machinist's hands are loving and caring;
from taking care of the tools of the trade, and
making sure the equipment does its job;
from honing and filing to grinding and shaping,
with care and appreciation of machinery.

A machinist's hands are gentle and kind;
from helping people and his family and holding his
wife's hand with love and affection;
from teaching his family the way of life, and setting
the examples of patience and exactness.

A machinist's hands are strong and firm;
from daily walks with God, an expression of trust
in a power greater than himself.
Today another Machinist, the Creator of All is giving
new skills to his craftsman's caring hands.

—Dr. George H. Mullins

THE MUSIC KINGDOM

Enter into my Music Kingdom;
Where you can strike the bass drum,
Or the black and white piano keys,
To create melodious harmonies.

Pluck the strings of a violin cello
To hear the deep pizzicato.
Hark! The clarinets and oboes
Playing chromatic scales and arpeggios.

Blow! Blow! Brass trumpets,
Quarter notes, half notes, and triplets.
Listen to the high-pitched piccolo trill;
And the angelic harp, so tranquil.

If you listen carefully, you just may hear
The sweet sound of a Mozart Air,
Or the enchanting Chopin Fantasia
Performed by a symphonic orchestra.

In the distance the sound of the glockenspiels ring;
They bring an end to the lullaby I sing.
From now and into eternity, wherever you may go,
You will always carry the Music Land deep within your soul.

—Jennifer Sze-Wan Ho

THE RAINBOW

God made the rainbow
With His infinite love,
By spraying a ray of color
In the Heavens above.
This is His way of saying,
After a rain,
"See, it's all over,
The sun will shine again."
He chose the favorite color,
Blue and gold, with a touch of white,
He added green and red,
Then surveyed it with delight.
"The rainbow will be a prophesy,
In the upper room,
It will appear to frighten
And chase away the gloom!"

—Sylvia J. Houston

Take a ride to an island
Warm wind through the mind
Clouds over rainbows
Bridges from end to end
Forever in your heart
Will peace be settled in.

Impounded without bondage
And released from tensions grip
Drifting waves over rocks
Rooted in the sand
That time could not replace
And progress could not destroy.

An island of treasure
Priceless and free
And the sun paints your eyes
Where the sky meets the sea.

—Bill Johnson

THANK YOU DEAR LORD

Thank you God for the
golden finches, singing
their delightful song
and the sheep, grazing
on the hillside by the
pool.
The flowers that
blossom, all day long,
first, crocuses, tulips,
tiger lilies, with
colors, so bright.
The blue jays, singing
they are such a pretty sight.
It's breakfast time
and the ham is
frying on the old
wood stove.
The choke cherries
are now ripening
in the cove.
The black berries and
wild grapes are ripe
and sweet.
The children are playing
in the street, there
is an apple tree close
by, apples for the children
to eat.
Thank you Jesus.

—Alice Sires

THE BACKRUB

A drowsy butterfly
silhouetted against the window
reaches out to dance
ever so lightly
touching the smooth warm skin
that lays stretched before it:
Sweeping the softness
circling around tickle spots
climbing its spine
to drift
back down
side to side
to rest gently
after flight
and sleep.

for M.M.B.
—Heather J. Bennett

BIRTH

A little flower pale and dry,
lay deep beneath the sod,
unseen by those who passed it by
unknown except for God.

Its beauty was yet hidden,
its fragrance still contained,
the sun could not awake its sleep
before the kiss of rain.

Now time had made a promise,
and soon the time would be,
when barren ground would give to life,
and beauty would be seen.

The sun did send its warming rays,
the rain did kiss the earth,
and soon a lovely blossom,
the earth had given birth.

Now all could see the beauty
that no one knew was there,
and breathe the lovely fragrance,
that lingers in the air.

—Linda R. Myers

AS AN EAGLE

Driving swiftly down the highway
In the heat of middle summer,
I saw him in the distance
And slowed to view him as I passed.

A golden eagle
Holding dominion over the
Wind-swept Wyoming plain.

Regal, majestic, powerful—
The feathered sovereign
Of tor and tableland.

The words of the prophet
Sang in my heart—
"They that wait upon the Lord
Shall renew their strength,
They shall mount up with wings
As eagles."

Oh Lord, may I wait upon You,
That I might renew my strength,
Mounting up with golden-eagle-wings
To overcome the world.

—Lonnie C. Crowe

LIFE OF A GOLFER

I stepped up to the figure, it was white and it was round
I grabbed my mighty driver and nailed it in the ground.
The ball went flying high and landed with such grace
It landed in the fairway about 400 pace.
I looked down in the grass and there lay my ball
I looked down the fairway the flag was so so very small.
I grabbed my metal 3 wood, I lined it to the pin
I raised my club with a smile, I raised it with a grin.
I hit the ball with such style, it flew right toward the cup
I saw the ball hit the green, where there it did check up.
It laid about 3 feet from the little hole
I grabbed my trusty putter for the last and final blow.
I lined it up so carefully, I tried to see the break
The gallery stood watching, I could not make a mistake.
I hit the little ball it rolled right above the great pit
If I had missed the hole I would have had a fit.
But the lord above was with me, as you well know
For that little ball fell in the hole, Due to the mighty wind
That started to blow.

—Gregory Phillip Anderson

ONE MOMENT IN TIME

The deer that is silent, prancing on air,
his pleading-filled eyes instinctively aware.

His knowing look, superior to all,
sheds light on the scene, of capture and fall.

He runs like the wind, passing on distance,
his determination fierce, with pursuing insistence.

The corners that round, walls that close in,
send panic throughout, time again and again.

His hope is shattered, his prayers left erased,
he staggers and twitches, faith not yet replaced.

And when aim is mastered, and nature stands still,
he inhales his fear, and regains his strong will.

A dash through a crack, a sprint through the air,
that deer remains free, and sheds his despair.

Once more he is alone, and stalks like a mime,
he owns a solitary life, living one moment in time.

—Stephanie Welborn

THE WILD GEESE.

In the still of the night I hear a cry,
It is not the cock's crow, or the passing by,
Of a lonesome hound on the trail of a coon.
Hark! there it is again,
And across the moon.
A V shaped wedge spreads.
And the haunting cry,
Of the wild geese. as they northward fly.
To a home in the wild for a little while.
Until it's time to return south in the fall,
I hear the call of a soul mate in their call,
If only I too could rise and fly,
And follow the wild both north and south.
But my wings are tied by household cares,
And often at night, as I listen for the cry,
Of the wild geese,
I too can fly, if only for a moment,
My soul takes wings,
And a haunting answer to the wild it sings.
As back to the northward land they go,
To rest among the ice and snow.
To stay rooted here, more will power takes,
I miss them so.

—Ada Mae Davis

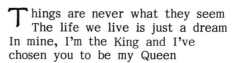

YOUR DAY IN MAY

On your day in May you will stand and say I love you.
On your day in May you will stand and say I do.
You will pledge your love for the world to see.
Oh, what a wonderful wedding there will be.
Bells will chime, your hearts will glow.
Your love will grow and grow.
God in heaven above,
Looks down on your love.
Happy is the couple that the sun shines on today.
May the sun brighten your love and light your way.
May your love shine so brightly,
That it will bind you tightly.
You can face the future without fear,
Because your love will always be near.
On your day in May
Look at each other and say,
"Come travel life's highway with me.
The best is yet to be."

—Bertha Coleman-Downs

MY DARLING

Ever since the day we first met,
My eyes upon you, they will always set.
My fantasies are gone,
My dreams are here,
But to you, My Darling, my love is dear.
The sun is shining,
The sky is Blue,
But for you, My Darling, my love is true.
May God be with you always and forever.
Don't fear My Darling, I'll leave you never.
May the lights shine upon us today and tomorrow,
Now that I'm with you my heart feels no sorrow.
May our house be blessed and pure,
I shall be by your side of that I'm sure.
When you need me, I will be there,
For between our sons there's lots of love to share.
Time is running out by day and by night,
I love you so much, but there is no fright.
My Darling, ever since the day we first met,
My eyes upon you they will always set.

—Angela Hoover Wallace

NEW LIFE

How does one know when she's losing her mind,
She feels that she must turn and run,
But where does she go, and how does she know,
That things can be better for some?

She feels not a care for the beat of her heart,
Nor the life that her body contains,
How can she wait, depicting her fate,
While loneliness runs through her veins.

Then down on her knees, she prays to the Lord,
"Please help me, I need much more strength,"
A tear from her eye, an unfiltered cry,
He listens to her, at great length.

And what did he do to relieve her,
To let this young woman start new,
He sent her a friend, to help her heart mend,
A person who needed her too.

Now they have learned about laughter,
And sharing in every small way,
He gave them new life, as husband and wife,
Together, they conquer each day.

—Debbie Adams

Things are never what they seem
The life we live is just a dream
In mine, I'm the King and I've
chosen you to be my Queen

And in my realm, I rule
There isn't a jester, there aren't any fools
No hate. No lies
Peace and harmony abides

Fantasy becomes reality
No place for anger or hostility
No values placed on inability
All that matters is compatability
There aren't any fears
No one ever cries a tear
It's a never-never land
Only wishes, never a demand

A world of sheer delight
Always day, never night
        —Timothy J. Hartmann

The night was coming nearer
    with promises of rain.
We sat and talked of the past,
    the heartaches and the pain.

Sitting side by side, the rain began
    to pour and the pain subside,
We realized we could trust each other,
    and we had nothing to hide.

You took me in your arms, kissed
    me and held me tight.
You said to me, "Just hold me and let
    me love you tonight."

I held you in the dark of the
    cool rainy night.
Somehow I knew everything
    would be alright.

The love we shared, no other
    two have known,
We know in our hearts we'll
    never, again, be alone.

        —Lisa Coutu

MY BIRTHDAY GIFT

Out of all the gifts that I received,
    One stood out from the rest.
It was the gift you sent to me,
    that I really loved the best.

It wasn't a diamond ring,
    that sparkled like a star.
Or even a new Ferrari,
    so that I could drive fast and far.

Not a Gucci watch, or a black mink coat,
    or a CD Stereo.
No, it wasn't even a trip to a place
    like Mexico.

Your gift cannot be found at Macy's
    or Bloomingdale's,
And certainly cannot be found on a
    rack, marked down, on sale.

Your birthday gift was nothing like
    anything listed above,
Yet it was more priceless than anything
    because you sent your love . . . .
        —Jill Joswick

400 YARD DASH

On your mark!
Get set!
Go!
I'm off!
Sprint this first curve.
100 yards; 300 more to go.
Stride this out.
DON'T slow down!
I almost got her.
Curve . . . lean into it.
100 more yards.
Sprint.
Is she getting closer?
No matter, here's the finish line.
I'm finished.
First Place — Gold Medal — #1!
THANK GOD!
Now maybe my family will leave me alone.
I won. I did my best. I quit.

—Teresa L. Presley

CAMPING WITH UNCLE VERNON'S

Under the stars we did camp

Never a fear did we have.

Cause we always knew Uncle Vernon
        would be there
Listening to us tell, that we
        thought we heard a Bear.
Eager to calm us, he'd say all is
        clear go back to sleep.

Very well we said, as we dove
        back under the covers.
Even though we still had thoughts
        of creatures around us.
Rhythm of the creek near by, we heard

Never fear as we knew we were
        in good hands.
Often I think of our camping trips
        with Uncle Vernon's.
Now, he's safe with Jesus.

—Sara Louise Weirich

BEDTIME

Now you know it's lullaby time
So put your toys away
You can lay on Mommy's lap
and hear what I have to say.

I know you miss Daddy tonight
But he has to be gone awhile.
He loves us both and wants you to know
He thinks of us every mile.

Go to sleep, my little child.
It's time to close your eyes
And dream of Daddy holding you tight.
He'll be here when you arise.

You look at me with those big, blue eyes
that say you do know love.
I want to tell you what's in my heart,
But, sometimes, a look speaks above.

The time has slipped into a very late hour,
So little ones must go to bed.
Good night, my sleepy baby child.
Remember what I've said.

—Bobbi Thompson Grende

LIFE WITH A TEEN

You have never lived till you've lived with a teen
I'm sure you who have one know what I mean
You're never right, they're never wrong
Little do they know that won't last for long
I love the one where they ask for the car
Come on Mom and Dad I won't go very far
Six hours later when they're still not home
You wonder where it is they decided to roam
Things were so different when I was a child
We wore socks with shoes that was the style
Now it's not cool to wear socks with shoes
I was surprised when my teen gave me this news
You also poof your hair so high on top of your head
And then spray it with hairspray till it feels like lead
With the boys it's the arrows and the lines on the side
Carved in their hair some narrow some wide
I don't remember doing these things when I was a kid
But I'm sure that my parents would say that I did

—Karen St. Clair

ACORNS

Two little acorns were tossed my way.
    So tiny, cute, fragile and helpless.
The recipe says with constant care, loving
nutrients, and guidance — these little acorns
Can grow big, powerful and strong.
The recipe was hard to follow — sometimes the
acorns swayed between weak and strong.
Sometimes the boughs would bend — even break
in striving toward growth.
At times, we did not know if we could make it.
As the acorns grow bigger, they reach out
toward the sun growing the way they want.
Why can't I always dominate and control?
I want them to grow the way I think is right —
but what is right?
Maybe a combination — my way — their way.
Through the years,
We put all the ingredients together —
Struggles, heartaches, tears, joys and fights
Shaped molded and formed — when completed
my two tiny acorns became two strong wonderful oaks!

—Joan S. Parker

GREGORY

He's our Son. He's our pride and joy
A bundle of sunshine, He's all Boy

His boots are worn out leaning to the side
It's from running, jumping, then he'll slide

Blonde hair blowing as he plays as hard as he can
Whatever he's playing "He's got a plan"

His friend kissed him on the cheek, he said
They thought it was funny, But what's ahead?

He's God's special gift created just for us to love
Only a child like him comes from heaven above.

He has a dog, a parakeet and a small gray cat
Tons of toys, guns, and even a cowboy hat

He's making A's on most of his school tests
but his "following teachers' instructions" aren't the best

As a first grader he thinks he's grown
before we know it Dad and I will be alone

Without adoption this "Miracle" could never be
Thank You God for the Son You gave my husband and me

—Jean Palmer

THORNS

The rose a flower intriguing, beautiful beyond degree,
In it lies a lesson for all the world to see.
Petals of royal velvet, aroma so sweet,
But in all its splendor a thorn makes it complete.
As we grow our roses, tend them every day.
There will be many times a thorn gets in our way.
It may prick our finger, even break the skin.
Soon we pass it over never think of it again.
Life can be beautiful, filled with joy and glee.
When it is the flower and not the thorns we see.
As we grow our roses, as our lives go by,
Always feed the flower let the thorns die.
For the thorns will hurt us, cause us misery.
When it is the thorns, and not the flowers we see.

    —Perry O. Worley

Once I was young and had dreams like others
Then I met drugs and found some new brothers

I thought I knew everything to me none could say
Advice was for others my own game I would play

Trouble I've had plenty of this you can be sure
For this life I lead there just ain't no cure

They tied off my arm and filled up a point
The rush that it gave me my first step to the joint

The pain was no longer, this drug that I use
It cured all my problems until I learned to abuse

The pain that was life so hard and so mean
It washed all my problems but was only a dream

How long will I suffer, how long can this be
No help from no others it must come from me

Respect for no others not even myself
Now I have nothing, not even my health

I've learned to be bitter, I've learned to be mean
For me there's no changing, I will never be clean

Life is a trip, when you're young you don't care
For you that are young I caution BEWARE

    —Raul E. Gastelo

PHARAOH

In dreams I hear you tell me no,
So I did not want to love you anymore.

You held on to me like Pharaoh of old,
Who would not let God's people go.
The god of my desires cried, "Let my people go."
"Let my dreams grow."

Unclench white-knuckled fingers from around my throat.
I begged for mercy as I began to choke.

I cannot you whispered for my grip is too tight,
So you swallowed disease and committed suicide.
I do not say this was for me,
For you yourself were lost and tossed by the sea.

You escaped from a life you could not bear,
I escaped from a love that shreds and tears.

I speak up from the ancient well,
Of tears, hope, and despair.
But finally you did let go,
So I'll forgive that's only fair.

Though I did not want to love you anymore,
You are part of me so I must care.

    —Jennifer L. Matthews

SUICIDE

A mirror killed by reflections.
A candle killed by the flame.
A man killed by the woman,
he did not know her name.
The notes brought death to the music.
The grapes soured the wine.
The inventor killed the machine
because of a flaw in the design.
The ship was sunken by the sailors.
The army defeated itself.
The book that was written by the author
now lies untouched on the shelf.
A government killed by The People.
A family killed by its kin.
We blame outside forces
but our death comes from within.

    —Randall Chancellor

WITH HER DRINK

Liquid finds its way to her glass
As usually it tends to do
Ice cubes clink-a stirrer is stirred
With her drink, her thoughts can come through

Much maligned feet find way to chair
As usually they tend to do
Cigarette lit-a puff inhaled
With her drink, her thoughts can come through

Cruel words find way straight to her tongue
As usually they tend to do
Bitterness here-sarcasm there
With her drink, her thoughts can come through

Barbs find targets, then sleep lends a hand
As usually it tends to do
Cigarette put out-glass turned up
With her drink, her thoughts can come through

New sun finds sky-new day has come
As usually it tends to do
She rises fresh-last night a dream
With her drink, her thoughts did come through

    —W. Tod Gibbs

THIRTY YEAR LAMENT
(1960-1990)

Give me this and give me that

    But don't send me to Vietnam
and let me demonstrate against the bureaucrat

Give me alcohol and give me drugs

But don't send me to jail
with other types of thugs

Give me money, food stamps and commodities
give me education and housing
but not responsibilities

Give me America and all the
freedoms that I want

Never mind those who died for her
or their graves
that my deeds will haunt

All of this I must have
while the government I shall spurn

But I warn you
expect nothing from me in return

    —Billy G. Selby

MY GRANDPA

My Grandpa's eyes sparkle with the light.
They never turn gray with hate.
He gives me treats every time we meet.
His bright blue eyes gleam at me
When I look in them.
I can see right through his eyes
and see the love.
He takes me fishing all summer round.
I like books. He likes to hear them read.
I Love him, he Loves me too.
I like to be with him not just
to have the treats but to be
with him.
I Love him.
   Grandpa.

—Elizabeth Corine Hirsch

GRANDMA'S HOUSE

I remember Grandma's house
Weather-beaten and old
With traps set to catch a mouse
It was drafty and sometimes cold

There were plenty of toys
To make the children smile
Both for girls and boys
Behind a door in a pile

She always gave us a treat
From the refrigerator near the sink
Ice cream and other goodies to eat
And a cold glass of juice to drink

Grandad was always there when we came
Sitting in his living room chair
Ready to play a make-believe game
Making sure the rules were fair

Now they are both gone
Even the house is no longer there
But they left a family to carry on
Their ideas of give and share

Dedicated to my grandparents, Mr. and Mrs. A.C.B. Honn

—Lora L. Coslet

HAPPY ANNIVERSARY

I'm just a woman, and you just a man
But "remember" when we first met?
I was just a girl, and you a boy
And now, years later, we are a "set."

We've been blessed with a daughter and son
We thank God for what He's done.
Lord, help us to lead them "Your" way
Help us to know when and what to say.

Now I think back to all the times
When we counted our pennies and dimes.
And now we have 'real' treasures
It's when we together share our pleasures.

My how the times do go
We've been together for almost 10 years.
We've had times that were high and low
Which have to me become more dear!

I do love you, Oh my Sweetheart!
And don't you forget it, ever
"Til death do us part"
But until then, we are together.

   P.S. "I Love You!"

—Glenda Cunningham

THE GOLDEN YEARS

Seems like the Golden Years are always on my mind
Contemplating on what I hope to find.
Seeking for the advantages of the Golden Age,
Trying not to look back, but on to a new page.

Time labeled past are memories cherished well,
What's in the future — only time will tell.
If lucky, there will be a feeling of security,
This is how I pray that it will be.

One could just sit back and do nothing but dwell,
Or keep busy with thoughts of staying well.
In the Golden Years we all need an incentive,
To boost our ego and to be more attentive.

Time does not stand still as we journey through the
      years,
We try to be brave and conquer our fears.
Be it ever so humble, be it ever so sweet,
Growing old gracefully is to make our life complete.

—Helen Barrante

SIEGE

The beauty of your soul
Is shining through the walls you've built.
It glows through the cracks you consider weaknesses.
Its brilliance awes me and fills me with wonder
As to the majesty of the whole.
What warmth I find in these bits of you!
What can the source be like?!
I yearn to bathe in its entirety!

I wait outside this barrier.
I seek the hollows.
I climb to exhaustion.
I take my fists and pound at the granite.
I scrape at the mortar and dig at the foundation.
I moisten the earth with my tears of hope
Which are dried only when the golden rays touch me.

I walk the circumference of your being,
Stopping to absorb the warmth I find as I come upon
Those blessed, radiant, falterings of your fortress,
Searching for a gate.

—Carla Gallagher

A NEW BEGINNING

When we first met I didn't pay attention
to your name. As the days passed I found
myself stealing glances your way. I had
to ask your name.

The girls at work, we talk. You heard.
Then came the dreaded question. "What about
the ring." I drew in a breath, with pain came
time to explain.

I was hurting. You saw through the pain, then
came the note you wrote. I was confused. I
looked to you for a signal of some kind, while
you were on my mind. I asked you out, you accepted.
It wasn't what I expected. I couldn't explain the
way I felt, but when your arm went around me I started
to melt.

I was scared, I couldn't explain the security I felt.
As time went on and we were together the pain eased.
I wanted to say I need a hug please. You read my mind.
Then came that hug! When you were gone I felt alone.
I thought of you and I wasn't blue. Thank You!

—Barbara Bazoff

AGORAPHOBIA

No words, movements, mimes or tears
    will allow your mind to know my fears.

I know them well, but they have not names,
    and before I'm ready they start their games.

Are they inside or outside, in the world or in me?
Are they from ignorance, by choice, or are they destiny?

        —Deborah Ann Quinley

SUBSTANCE

There is a place inside my skull
    that no one has the time or inclination
        to discover:
It is my last vestige of hope
    sealed off from the world
    so that it may not be withered
    by the mundane existence
    which is forcefully produced.
It fears the godless capitalists
    whose control is adored by the world
    while my skull's other facets
    play the game of life:
    Get a Job/Pay Taxes/Support Spouse
    Be a Good Boy and Obey the Rules.
Where is that haunting, lilting world
    I once so loved
    where each new experience
    was a thrill to be enjoyed?
Have I cast aside my humanity
    in order to survive?
How many others have accomplished this task
    in order to be driven by a desire
    for what they have already lost?
When the game is over, who wins?

        —John Bridges

FROM PRESENT TO FUTURE

Just suppose you were on the other side of the world,
Where starvation existed each and every day,

And how would you like to be among the millions,
Not knowing if help was really on the way,

In a land where the water supply is polluted,
And disease is as rampant as the ones who die,

Just stop for a moment and let us come to reason,
That this situation could very well be you and I,

Have you ever cried because you were so hungry,
So much that the tears refused to come anymore?

Or been unable just to take an extra step,
Because your health and limbs were much too poor,

Have you every seen a little baby dying?
Or their stomach swollen as though it would suddenly burst?

Have you ever seen their little hands reach out,
Unable to ask for water to quench their thirst?

I am certain the poor will be with us for always,
Just like I am certain together we can ease their pain,

We just can't overlook this critical problem,
After all we, civilized, are supposed to be humane,

We must unite and join our forces together,
No matter how the opposition arise,

I am confident that when we stand together,
It would more than enough be sufficient to turn the tide.

        —Bobbie E. Teague

THOU SHALT NOT . . . SAYS WHO?

Don't Ever STEAL a Loaf of Bread—
    Grab the WHOLE BAKERY Instead.
    Very Soon You'll be in CLOVER!
    It's SIMPLE—Just Yell TAKEOVER!

    —Robert Emmett Clarke

THE TRUE BEASTS

The beastly lion attacks his
    prey,
and savagely rips the tender
flesh.
    He takes his prey's life away,
    to nourish and satisfy himself.
    But we are the true beasts,
    the ones who rob, harm and
kill.
    So that we may enjoy our
feasts,
    of money, distinction and
power.
    We hang and admire a trophy,
    that was gained by jealousy
and greed.
    While never paying a just fee,
    for all we have viciously
reaped.
    But we will be identified by
fate,
    with a deep cut mark on our
souls.
    As the ones of scorn and hate,
    and the true beasts of the world.

        —Lisa Lovgren

NOBODY CARES

The birds aren't flying in
    the sky.
    The trees aren't full and green.
    Children aren't playing in
the park.
    The stars aren't shining in
the dark.
    The air doesn't smell fresh
and clean.
    The sun isn't as bright as
it use to be.
    The tap of the rain nobody
hears.
    The ocean doesn't refresh us
anymore.
    The wind doesn't whistle its
famous tune.
    The mountains just stand there
waiting to be seen.
    What happened to our once
amazing moon.
    The snow isn't so beautiful
anymore.
    The flowers aren't bright and
colorful.
    Who really notices how our
world is.
    Nobody looks, Nobody cares.
    What would you do if all
this was gone?
    Then would you notice?
    Then would you care?

        —Christi Miller

HEART AT HOME

Home is where the heart is
    Such a beautiful phrase to say
It becomes an inspiring guideline
    In our lives every day.

Sending cards and letters to loved ones
    Far across the seas
The many things that were left undone
    Touches, both you and me.

Skies are cloudy, the days are long
    Living far across the miles
So many things have already gone wrong
    But I remember the friendly smiles.

When you feel ill and so forlorn
    And your heart begins to roam
Follow the gleam in your mother's eyes
    And touch the "heart at home."

       —"Mlgo"

A MOTHER'S LOVE

I'm growing up to be someone great,
'cause you've taught me how to love,
not hate.

It's wonderful to know,
that I'll be guided by your love,
wherever I go.

The laughter, the smiles, the tears I've cried,
your caring ways have always kept me
by your side.

Knowing that sometimes you're sad,
but, still making me smile,
cause you're the best friend I've ever had.

You've taught me that I'm someone special too,
given me all you could;
It's for all of this, Mother, that
I LOVE YOU!!

       —Connie Beseda

GRANDMOTHER'S LOVE

**(To Crystal Amber Britton, on her first Birthday,
August 11, 1989 from Gamama Jones-Steidle)**

When sometimes life has no good reason
or meaning, or rhythm, or rhyme . . .
I find myself, once again, returning
To the day of your birth, YOUR tyme.

I think of the lives that gave you yours
and all that you give in return . . .
And somehow, then, I can understand
The lessons we're put here to learn.

The laughter you put in everyone's heart,
The smiles on everyone's faces . . .
The simple joy you give, unaware
That nothing . . . ever . . . replaces.

Your smile is the envy of Sunlit rays,
Your laughter, the light of the moon . . .
Whimsical expressions convey to the world
The miraculous wonder of life, in bloom!

But most of all, in your "Gamama's" heart,
The seed of a song that you've planted
A song that perhaps only we two shall hear
Yet we know of the blessings we're granted!

       —"Roxanne"

THE INEVITABLE

How can I ever face it—
This change from the old to the new?
I knew that it <u>must</u> happen
But the time just simply <u>flew</u>!
He's on his way to <u>manhood</u>—
My tears are quite profuse!
—Today I just discovered—
His first baby tooth — is <u>loose</u>!!!

       —Marguerite C. Sherry

SUEFAWN

A little girl, the joy she brings from
the moment of birth is indescribable

Enchanted — literally wrapped up in her life
living her highs and lows
Heart pounding fast — desperately trying
to soften any hurt
    Years rushing by like seconds
Filled with wonder at her inner beauty
    So elegant and collected
        yet friendly and sweet
    So composed and in order
        yet lively beaming with joy

Catching sight of her walking toward me . . .

    Is this gorgeous woman that little
    girl I love so much?

    I wonder at the Beautiful person
    you've become.

       —Sandra E. Cancino

MY MOM

Little things I remember:
Your warm safe hands,
to pick me up and brush me off.

The soft caring lips to kiss
my cheek or my mortal wounds.

The long strong arms to hold
me away from all the bad.

The glowing eyes to drink
in my happiness or rub out my pain.

The fragile shoulders to carry
my burdens.

The tireless legs to chase
after your wayward child.

The prestigious cologne,
behind each ear to fragrance my dreams.

The quick brain for
the endless questions.

The attentive ears
to detect my moods.

The soft words to pacify
my heart.

The witty tongue to erase
my frown.

The tireless back, to work to make my life filled
with things I'd just "die" without.

The pain, joy, pride and fear,
when you let me go.

       —Melanie Myer

FRAGILITY

A bubble shimmers in the air
But soon—too—soon — it is not there
A butterfly with gossamer wings —
A monarch from a tribe of kings —
But life for it is very short
For life is easy to abort
A rainbow in the eastern sky
Gives just a glimpse to human eye
Then like all beauty it will die
Love glowing from an ancient face
That's touched with gentleness and grace
No credence gives but does belie
All proof that beauty soon must die

—**Dorothy Howard Adler**

WHAT ARE THE LOVELIEST THINGS I KNOW?

"What are the loveliest things I know?
Trees bowing 'neath silent snow,
The gallant red of a cardinal bird,
The distant tinkle of lowing herd, —
Smoke from a cabin in the wild,
Companionship with a beautiful child,
A river winding through canyons wide,
The rumble and roar of an incoming tide, —
The wondering thrill of a seagull's cry,
One lone bird's flight across the sky,
A foghorn sounding in the mist,
The silver surf and all the rest, —
A lighted church on Christmas Eve,
A steadfast look of firm belief,
The smile of trust in two friend's eyes,
And mounting faith as each day dies, —
A ship, full sail on the bounding main,
The freshening smell of an April's rain,
A splendid horse, a loving dog,
A valiant knight in stories bold, —
On cents the motto of our nation —
Most precious thing of all creation,
Lives as pure as driven snow —
These are the loveliest things I know."

—**Grayce I. Cunningham**

A PAINTING BY CHAGALL

For her wedding bed she chose silky,
               orange sheet.
Little did she know that before the day
               was done,
She and her groom would travel,
entering heaven —
She in her white bridal gown,
he, handsome in black —
hit by a lightning in front of the reverend
next to the altar.
"I pronounce you man and wife . . ."
and then the end came.
Hand in hand and side by side, floating
             through the Pearly Gates,
They met the angels,
Snow was falling and it rained,
but they did not care —
They only felt the warm Sun.
Three white doves were being chased
          by a big, black hawk,
and a purple Pegasus,
eyes of emeralds,
was moving his way upwards
trying to reach the rainbow.

—**Solveig Creato**

WILDFLOWERS

Wildflowers we. Like abandoned children;
   our beginnings borne on a random hand,
sown in a furrow unplanned.

Earth Mother, with gentle hands nurture us
  with sun drenched days, with rains scooped
from the deep seas; so frail, a wind and away.

Palette our colors true, that though our span
  brief, joy to the eye and heart we bestow.
And finally — glory over death —
  as in Flanders' red profusion we grow.

—**Anne Porter Moore**

AN ODE TO A WHIPPOORWILL

Oh Whippoorwill, you bird of night
   You fill my heart with sheer delight.
When in early spring your voice is heard
  I say Thank You Jesus, there's my bird.

When moonlight glows, and nightwinds sigh
  Among the pines, his perch is high.
His call is blythe and full of cheer
  For all the weary world to hear.

His eyes are red, his coat is brown
  A plainer bird cannot be found.
But for melody and music sweet
  All other birds just can't compete.

So—Whippoorwill, you bird of night
  Call out, call out with all your might.
Call from the wildwood, sing on the hill
  For when you sing the world listens
And with contentment is filled.

An afterthought

I hope that when I old have grown
  I still can get around— And that I will
always be—Where Whippoorwills are found.

—**Kathleen Godwin Boney**

SIX SENSES

Take time to SMELL the flowers
   in their variety of fragrances.
Take time to HEAR the rain
   as the drops hit upon the earth.
Take time to See the stars
   twinkling in the vast universe.
Take time to TOUCH a tree
   and wonder at its growth.
Take time to TASTE hot coffee
   as you visit with a friend.
Take time to SPEAK a kind word
   to someone you love.

BECAUSE*—
When you're put beneath the earth,

The flowers will still be fragrant,
  but you no longer will be able to SMELL.
The rain will still fall,
  but you no longer will be able to HEAR.
The stars will still twinkle,
  but you no longer will be able to SEE
The trees will still be growing,
  but you no longer will be able to TOUCH.
The coffee will still be hot,
  but you no longer will be able to TASTE.
The loved one will still be—
  but you no longer will be able to SPEAK.

—**Carol Freitag**

MY FATHER'S HOMELAND

I have walked the hillside and
looked out his window to the ocean
and mountains.
   The wonders I have felt and seen,
the hopes of a young boy were once
only in my dream.
   I am content to say good-bye and yet
somehow a strange, sweet sadness
surrounds my heart.
   Here the reality is more like a dream
than the dream itself, apart.
   Today touched by yesterday and given to
me in all that I have experienced and
deeply felt; Beautiful hours, now dear.
   In a moment I will be far away, this
mountain, in the distance too, leaving behind
that lost part I found here.
   The beauty I have realized in the majestic
mountains, the smiles, the laughter,
the acceptance, the picturesque villages,
the colorful countryside and the magic
of this moment belong to me.
   I think as I look ahead to tomorrow, how
close, but so far away.
   I wonder, do I belong to these mountains?
To the sea?
   And who that has looked into himself
and to God and Heaven, can truly
answer and say.

—Carol A. Piscetelli

FOLDERS

Moving on is the only way for me,
sitting in my muck is a waste, you see.

So I'll take my moments of despair and
   grief,
knowing the pains will give me relief.

Hoping for an easy way seems to be the
   trend,
when it is time for the truth, my soul
   is my only friend.

Reflect upon yourself, your only true
   love,
and realize all that you have is from
   above.

Life is a test to see who is the best,
when all you have to do is satisfy your
   ego by knowing you are blessed.

My father, don't you understand you taught
   me well,
my simple devotion will keep me out of
   hell,
I owe no one, yet my debts seem to swell.

The weight of the world is on my shoulders,
I can walk among the debtors, holding my
   folders.

My only payment is to be honest and
   nothing more,
my weaknesses become my strength, for they
   are my core.

So, when you despair and life seems at a
   loss,
you hold your own folder . . . you are the boss.

—William R. Thies

lives

Forever as we live our lives,
We go and take each other in time.
We shan't not live, we shan't not die,
We shan't not see the days go by.
As we take our troubles and put them away,
As we take our troubles and leave them to stay.
We've paid our dues and that's the end,
We'll go together and still be friends.
Eternally yours, and faithfully mine,
We'll live our lives and that's just fine.

—Jill René Cornett

REFLECTIONS AT THE LAUNDROMAT

I took some clothes to the laundromat.
While the washer ran, I observed and sat.

In came a grandmother with a large box
Filled with children's dirty jeans and socks.

Next came a laborer with grimey hands.
Life for him must have many demands.

The new bride entered with stars in her eyes.
Marriage for her was still a surprise.

A Navy lieutenant did laundry with care.
He had six white shirts and some underwear.

The young mother came with baby's layette,
And her baby too, in a carrying basket.

A housewife with many children to tend,
Made a pile of clean clothes she had to mend.

The old man came last, his clothes in rags.
All his possessions he carried in bags.

I reflected as I observed and sat,
Many people meet at the laundromat.

I wished that problems of life everyday,
Could go down the drain and be washed away.

—Jean G. Curtis

NOT HONOR DR. KING'S BIRTHDAY?

Not honor Dr. King's Birthday?
What did you say?
Treat it just like any other day.
Surely you jest.
Have you forgotten how long it took?
To get recognition and for the day to
get on the books.

Men pleaded and cried after Dr. King died
HONOR HIM!!!   HONOR HIM!!!
Let's CELEBRATE, the life of one who did so
great.
Time passed, we had to wait.
Finally the bells began to ring.
State after state began to honor Dr. King.

A few are still lagging . . . it's such a shame
They don't want to honor him.
They think he gets too much fame.
And you with your Black face, dare to say,
"Too much is being said and done," poor us.
How could we forget so soon, the back of
the bus?
The colored and white water fountains.
The worst jobs for us.
Oh, Now you will say . . .
"COME ON, LET'S CELEBRATE DR. KING'S
BIRTHDAY!!!!"

—Mrs. Mattie J. Coleman

PAST, PRESENT, FUTURE . . .

The past has brought me so much confusion,
Happiness was only an illusion.
The past seemed like a drawn out nightmare,
Not knowing if anyone ever did care.

The present has brought happiness back,
And other feelings that I once did lack.
The present is now the beginning of a dream,
Allowing me to lift my self-esteem.

The future will begin tomorrow,
A time of very little sorrow.
The future has so much in store for me,
Making it as happy as it possibly can be.

—Becky Ptacek

LIFE IS WHAT YOU MAKE IT

No matter what course you choose,
Be you wise or be you a fool,
Fate deals, win, draw, or lose,
    Life is what you make it.

No matter what is your life's goal,
Be you young or be you old,
Your destiny is your own to hold,
    Life is what you make it.

No matter what is your journey's end,
If you leave behind not one true friend,
What good has your living been?
    Life is what you make it.

No matter what success you have gain,
If you have lived your life in vain,
You alone must reap the pain,
    Life is what you make it.

No matter what is your life's theme,
It is not impossible as it seems,
You can accomplish all your dreams,
    Life is what you make it.

—Bettye Jo Dabbs (Cox) Tarkington

UPON THE SEA

Upon the sea the light reposed
The edges curled a rhyme

From swells that imperceptibly rose
And fell, the sound of time.

Crinkles on the sand where water
Lined a salty purse

Who the parent, who the daughter
That gives this universe?

A murmur line drew on the shore
And whispered, lost, was THIS—

Then pressed upon the curve of dune
A ghost that was a kiss

A moon from somewhere rose from out—
Its dripping silvery-ground

Here praise would never make a shout
Or sand hills cup a sound

As of a picture, wherein the frame
Around is thickly drawn

The curtain falls, confusing time
Shall it be dusk—or dawn?

—Charles Brown Cooper

JOY AND SORROW

As we all well know
With time we all must go
But the family will remain and grow
Though we all feel pain and sorrow
Remember the one thing we all must show
Is the Love and Joy that makes all of us glow

—Billy Dean

CHARACTER

There are men who are brave,
There are men who are strong,
There are those who know right,
And those who know wrong.

True character must all be sought,
And not be held in just one's thoughts.
For each should keep his honor bright,
And hold himself with head upright.

As we respect our country's flag,
We'll make our character flame, not drag.
Heroes of today should be strong,
And help our country right every wrong.

A bit of patience fills our need,
For it will grow just like a seed.
Charity should be in every heart,
So let it live and not depart.

Honesty, courage, faith, kindness of heart,
Are some of the traits that play a great part—
And as we go along, day by day,
We'll develop a character that will lead the way.

—Amy Ruth Levin

I'M GETTING THERE

I used to climb hills with ease,
But now somebody added 50 feet more
        to the top.
I climb the same stairways I used to
But now there are six more steps
        added to the top.
I walk the same mile to get where I used to
But now it is 200 feet longer.
I used to pick up 100 lbs. with ease
But now I look at it as if it were a bad,
        bad disease.
I used to say, "I'm getting there."
But now I wonder — getting where?
I used to say bedtime is when I get in
        tomorrow morning
Now it's no later than 10 p.m.
I used to love getting up at the crack
        of dawn,
Now there are creaks and groans if I
        get up at eight.
I used to hit the floor and dash through
        the door
Now I find the floor and feel for the door.
I used to eagerly hurry to a large
        breakfast
But now I slowly take my pills and
        prunes.
Tell me, is something wrong?
That once sharp mind had it all figured out
But now there lingers that little bit of
        doubt.
Tell me, is something changing?
Am I getting there?

—Robert E. Carrig

LITTLE BABE OF STAINED GLASS

The Poverello of composure and exposure
Creates imagery
Design and beauty.
Tints, shades and hues
Fashion reality
To expose one's soul
To open one's heart
To giftedness and grace,
All by the touch
Of a Babe, lying on straw.

—Sister Mary Valenta

TRAVELING TO THE LORD

Come, let us build a highway to the Lord . . .
By praying.
Life's journey need not seem so hard.
Through prayer.
O, to build a highway to the Lord!
Let's build a highway to the Lord.
Let's find a skyway to the Lord.

My load is heavy, Lord I tire.
I would rest by some fire.
Let me rest, surrender by the fire!
Must I travel on?
Come, let us build a highway to the Lord.

Saints trod this road before . . .
Their path then was not broad.
I must journey to the Lord.
The way can not be far — not as hard.
By praying.

I fear death, Lord, death's flat breath near.
The way ahead's not clear!
I will build a highway to the Lord.
By praying
I will climb, I shall find . . . let me mind . . .
That high road winding to our Lord.

—Eva M. Fanning

INSPIRATION

May God's love be with you
all the days of your life and forever —
May Christ's words guide you
when you go astray —
May you always find strength
in Christ and never be weak —
May you always find happiness
in Christ and never be blue —
May you always look to Jesus
in crisis and in health —
May Christ dry all your tears;
set aside all your fears —
May the Lord be with you
every step you take and may He always
be by your side and keep you happy and
joyous —
Everyday of your life may
you see God's wonders and may you
see a miracle everyday —
May Christ's blessings be many
and your heart feel warm —
In Christ, may all your dreams
come true —
And may God's steadfast love
show you His righteousness the rest of
your days and forever

—Kenn McFarland

YOU ARE EVERYTHING TO ME

Lord, without you where would I be?
Tossed upon life's stormy sea
Wondering what serving you really means.
But you looked down upon me with love in your heart
You brushed me off and gave me a brand new start.
Lord, I love you, I want you to know
You are everything to me, how can I show?
Wonderful, Counselor, Prince of Peace
Lord of all my stormy seas.
I give to you all my life — good times, bad times
joy and strife
I give to you all my sickness and pain
Let you turn everything to peace again.
Lord, look down upon me with your smiling face
Let me bless you with heartfelt praise
For you are everything I want to be
Lord, you truly are everything to me.

—Lisa Hargis

THERE IS NO GOD

I gazed into the small, angelic face
And scarcely could take in all the beauty.
I counted the tiny toes neatly curled
And the fingers as they slowly unfurled.
Looking for the magic ten in number
As she gently slept in peaceful slumber.

This miracle I held so close to me
Was living proof for me to see
His creation — who could even dare to say,
"There is no God."

I gazed into the dawning morning sky
And scarcely could take in all the beauty.
Rich colors of orange and yellow and pink
The golden brightness forced my eyes to blink.
Looking around me at nature's work of art
Tears of wonderment trickled from my heart.

This miracle of nature had to be
The living proof for all to see
His creation — who could even dare to say,
"There is no God."

—Carol J. Wells

HE AROSE

Our Lord was crucified on the cross,
Our sins to save at this awful cost.
On the cruel cross, He hung and died;
Between two thieves — one on either side.

Now that the scriptures might be fulfilled,
On the cross He hung, silent and still.
Then they took his body to suffice,
And wound it in linen with the spice.

Some came on the first day of the week,
To the Sepulchre, their Lord to seek.
Christ had risen, the scriptures say,
For Lo' the stone had been rolled away.

Some told the Disciples all they could,
Then in the Upper Room, there Christ stood.
He said to them, "Peace be unto you —
Go Feed my sheep, Filling Souls anew."

Reflecting back — He hung on Calvary —
He suffered and bled for you and me.
He died our Salvation He bestows,
And on that Promised day, Christ Arose.

—Marcell Meldrum

THE SOLDIERS GROUND

At first I thought it was only the wind,
But then I heard it quite clearly once again,
Rising up from the ground on which I stood,
Came the cries of many men,
The soil was stained from the bloodshed,
Sickeningly sweet, it smelled of the dying,
Through the cries, and gunfire, and explosions,
I could hear their mothers crying,
The faces of the soldiers were hazy,
But even through the mist I saw their pride,
Souls march eternally, this old battlefield,
On the soil where they died,
I stood and said a prayer for the brave dead,
Nothing could ever erase those many cries,
How proud I was to have felt these many men,
Where forever on this soldiers ground,
Their memory never dies.

(Dedicated to David A. Quinlan, 2-89)
—Debra Kesterson

WHEREIN LIES THE MEANING

The young man bent and pat his dog,
    closed the gate and walked toward town.
He traveled lone each day to work
    and back the same dirt road.
The young girl always spoke good morn
    each day as he came by
and waved good eve on each return;
    the young man always smiled.

A word, a wave as friends began;
A walk, then touch of loving hands.

Together then they loved two sons
    for many "so few" years.
The eldest liked to venture some
    and died for Country's cause;
The youngest with his zest for Life
    just waved and closed the door.
They lived alone together then
    until the day she died.

The old man bent and pat his dog
    and closed the gate and cried.

—Robin L. Cook

WAR BRINGS BRIEF: GOD BRINGS RELIEF

The glow was there upon his face,
    He was touched by The Mighty Hand.
This was the day; so full of grace,
    That he became a free man.

His father had taught him very well,
    Show not your fear, my son.
Be not ashamed if you should fail,
    Stand up and never run.

His mother stood off to one side,
    Her job cut short; incomplete.
Tears she could no longer hide,
    Fell silent to her feet.

The fruit of this old couple fell,
    To leave only an empty place.
Can you truly say there is no Hell,
    When you look upon their face?

Man on earth thinks nothing about
    All God's great and wonderful plans,
For a foolish war takes another son out,
    To rest now in God's Mighty Hands.

—Nancy H. Christain

THE WAR

The soldier walks a weary path,
    in Blood and sweat and bodies of ash.
In the distance he can hear a baby cry,
Ten paces away a village of people
is waiting to die.
He stumbles on waiting for his prey, it doesn't
matter, night or day, killing is killing in any way.
He thinks he hears voices, he stops, he waits,
he must have imagined it, it was getting late.
He dug a hole the Army called fox, he
wanted to sleep but his mind like a clock,
would sound alarms for warning.
He thought to himself as he faded
into slumber, "How many more do
I kill to even the number?"

—Carla A. Beaber

FORGOTTEN

I am a ghost that nobody sees,
A memory in someone's mind.
A M.I.A. of flesh and blood,
A P.O.W. with nothing but time.

You say that I am missing,
Perhaps a prisoner of war.
I think you got it backwards,
It's my country that's unaccounted for.

Will I ever taste the fruits of freedom?
To walk again in the land of the free?
To see Old Glory flying proudly in the wind.
To be returned to the shores of my country.

Hear me, America! You know where I'm at!
Or is it that you just don't care?
When are you going to rescue me?
It's not too late to take that dare!

As my thoughts of freedom slowly slip away,
While I dream the dreams I hope come true.
For all I have left are my memories,
As I sit here, dying, waiting for you.

—Joseph Guzman

THE UNWANTED LETTER

It came one day, all edged in black
    My heart, in pain, began to pound,
I knew that there was only grief
    Inside that letter, darkly bound.

It had the seal of government
    Official stamps, were all in place,
I looked at it then, held it close
    As tears were running down my face.

"We are sorry," are the words I read
    It tore my heart apart,
I read it over, once again
    The pain so great, inside my heart.

Then, slowly, those dark words sank in
    As I looked from one to another,
This was no simple message here
    Oh! Missing in action, was my brother.

The years have passed, the war is gone
    They never brought my brother back,
To lay his body in home soil
    Just the UNWANTED LETTER edged in black.

In memory of my only brother Sgt.1st. Class
Joseph Arthur Wooten Somewhere in Korea
Dec. 1950 Never was found.

—Wanda (Wooten) Baugess

REFLECTIONS UPON A DEEP LAKE

Does the sun glow because I touched him?
I don't think any more leaves fell.
Scared like a rabbit freezing,
Thrilled like spring in the hearts of
   life.
No mountain rock tumbled to the
   crater's bowl.
No day was more felt by me.

—Kate McCord

AN EARLY MOMENT

A warm cream color yellow
   awakens the day.
A field of tiny pink flowers
   lift their heads to the morning sun.
A pair of birds
   dart gayly in the new day's air.
A lazy black cat meows a friendly hello
   as he curls himself around my legs.
All the sounds of a new day
   begin to filter through my screen door.

—Lisa MacKenzie

SWAYING BREEZE IN SPRINGTIME

Palm fronds dance
   Rhythmically to the gentle breeze
   Swaying costumed in green attire
   Trunks rooted in the marina's sand
Borders overseeing the Gulf of Mexico
   Moving happily underneath Springtimes
Sun throwing shadows of themselves
   A hundred different ways
Pelicans roosting on a piling
   Grooming themselves with flapping wings
Landing gently in the water going for a swim
   Pleasure craft roll slightly tied
Securely in their slips mast flags waving
   Proudly in the gentle breeze
White coatings above the water line
   Zigzag patterns reflecting the sun's
Shimmering effect on the Gulf's water

—Joe & Eleanor D'Ambrosio

TAKE A WALK

Take a walk down the walking trail
   Up a hill, down a hill
You can make it, never fail.

Take a walk alongside the lake
   I know you'll see some ducks
And if you're wide awake
Look into the sky, thru the trees
   You can't miss seeing wild geese.

Try walking in the nearby mall
   One lap, two laps, count them all.

Take a walk down a country road!
   Don't stop to pick wild flowers
They'll stay fresher in the moat.

Take a walk on the beach and let
   The ocean breeze touch your hands
And underneath your feet, there's the sand.

Take a walk and feel the summer heat
   Or the fall and winter wind
No matter the season, take a walk
   You'll be glad you did, it's neat!

—Sue Fletcher

ODE TO THE THISTLE

Warrior of weeds —
   barbed symbol of the ancient Celts,
how proud you wear your glories past
in tender hues upon your brow.

In victory and defeat you thrived
through feudal wars of noble clans
upon parched battlefields
with naught but blood
to slake your thirst.

How can such puffs
in tones of softest mauve
in comfort rest
upon a bed of thorns?

Perhaps
your verdant swords of pain
long to atone
and humbly offer clouds of royal purple down
in sweet apology.

—Guri Henderson

NATURE'S BEAUTY

Time to say goodbye.
We'll be all right.
The time has come when we have to go,
Even though I will miss this place so.
This is such a beautiful place to be,
Being at Champion makes you want to feel free.
Free from frustrations and pressures.
A place to enjoy the nature and to be free.
A place to enjoy life.
The gorgeous beauty of nature.
Nature's beauty
Lake Champion is a place
Where you see nature's beauty,
Life is worth fulfilling,
And where you can feel free
Of all life's frustrations.
We really have to go,
Even though I will miss this place so.
This is a beautiful place to be.
Being at Champion makes you want to be free.

—Valerie Agro

AUTUMN IS

Autumn Is — pumpkins in the cornfield.
   Blackeyed-Susans along the road.
Purple Asters and Golden Rod
Looks like someone had just sowed
Them in lovely patches
For the world to see
For all who loved Nature's Beauty—
My Jesse and me.
Autumn Is the Maple Trees of
Orange, red, green, copper and gold.
Makes us realize, it's getting very cold.
The coon hunters are out in full
Just hear those Blue Ticks howl—
Mr. Raccoon is in the cornfield—
Listen! Hear that hooty owl?
Autumn brings these things and more—
Especially Common Ground Fairs—
If you want to enjoy Autumn in Maine
Make sure that you are there.
Autumn Is.

—Norma Claflin-Trask

EVE IN EDEN

She was a small, shy elf.
A wood nymph, my childhood self
Who sat and picked woodland flowers
Lifted her face to sun-sprinkled showers.

No wild dreams entered her head
Nature, held her heart instead
She heard her lullabies in trees
That moved with a gently blowing breeze.

Time would not let her stay
To dream her precious life away
So this small Eve from Eden was thrown
And made to face the world alone.

Now this older Eve has turned
Away from the world; lessons learned
To follow that innate guide
The spiritual self, that never dies.

—Nora Salvo

A WINK AND A SMILE

While all the world and time sails by
    and people wink and smile a lie.
Children hunger for more than food.
    Eyes are wandering, thoughts are lewd.

While the weak reach out for false illusions,
    the lawless live their weird delusions.
The rich get richer and workers go broke.
    Justice for all is a paid-off joke.

While wondrous creatures die in vain,
    brokers scramble to catch a gain.
And progress robs our ground and air;
    shattered dreams a vacant stare.

While nations race to build more arms,
    lifetimes are auctioned on bankrupt farms.
The wise and gray are tucked away.
    In silence they waste for their black day.

While all that was wrong is now all right.
    People rush to catch a flight.
And all the world and time sails by
    while people wink and smile a lie.

—Kathleen L. Hilty

COLD

I met a strange man many years ago
A bearded one, with a cloven toe.
I still remember that dark, December day
When he tried to lead me astray.

He gave me a chill up my spine
When he icily invited me to dine.
Goose bumps developed on my skin
When he laughed at Original Sin.

The man looked me dead straight in the eye
And told me that not every man must die.
Then he informed me of my ultimate fate:
It would be determined by a measurement of hate.

He asked me to trade my beloved morality
For the wonderful gift of immortality.
I turned away and softly spoke "no"
Just before he disappeared into the snow.

But many years have since gone by
And finally I understand who, how and why.
No longer do I believe in what I once was told
That hell is hot, for I know it to be cold!

—Thomas J. Quinn

SIX WHITE HORSES

Magnificent! Their eyes ablaze.
Running in the morning haze.
Their black hooves pounding on the ground.
What a mighty, thundering sound.
Down through the meadow and past the trees,
Then, by the water's edge they be.
These messengers, from God, are sent
To carry those who do repent.
They're off again, no rest for them,
Out of the meadow and up the rise.
Then lightning, bright, almost to blinding.
Nostrils flared and white manes flying.
The storm clouds now these horses see.
God called them, Come home to me.
Another mission is at hand!
A young lad, hurting, needs to see you.
Let Ronnie know he's in My keeping,
That all who seek the Lord shall find Him.
When his life on earth is through,
You six will be there two by two.

—Ron E. Mangel

THE WEB

Like chiffon kerchiefs spread to dry
    on fields of stubbled hay
Weaver spiders work at night
    their silken webs to lay;
Then dawn takes every drop of dew
    and strings it on a chain—
Nature's necklace shines like gems,
    spiders' traps are lain.
Small insects lured by tinseled light
    are caught in sparkling glow—
Bodies stilled forevermore,
    drawn to traps below.
Life weaves ITS web of golden dreams
    and spreads it out bejeweled—
Blinds the eyes of human greed,
    laughs when Man is fooled.

For he who weaves the web at night
    is deadly in the baiting—
Tensed beneath the silken threads
    Reality lies waiting!

—Barbara S. Weppener

THE PARTY

Last night as I went to bed,
The Lord came into my head.
He heard me thinking about a party,
That would serve drugs for them and me.
During the party I said "No" to them,
And told them what I thought of 'em.
They gave me dirty looks,
And said that I was nuts.
But all I did was stand up and walk away.
After that half of the group walked my way
While the others said that we were rats.
The group that came with me could now see,
The other half were not what friends should be.
Then we walked out the door,
Saying we were bored.
And sick of being near
All that smelly beer.
Then I heard the Lord say,
"That is the way"
After that I've never left,
The safety of listening to the Lord in my chest.

—Tammy Chapin

AMERICA IS DYING

How long, my friend,
How long will you be silent?
America is sick—
She is sick unto death.
Will you do nothing to help her?
Do you fail to hear her cries?
They are the cries of the sick and dying.
Her cancerous growths are spreading.
Will you do nothing to stop them?
Will you wait until it's too late—
Too late to save America?
Will you hide your face in shame
When your children ask you,
"Why did you let it happen?"
"Why didn't you save America?"
"Why did you wait so long to help her?"
"Why did you wait until it was too late?"
How long mister? How long miss?
How long before you do something?
America is dying.

—Eugenia Lovedahl Johnson

I WONDER

When I see all the love in my family,
And I know that God is near,
It causes me to wonder why
People think there's not a God here.
When I look on the fields and the flowers,
And I see the birds are in flight;
I wonder why people aren't thankful
For God, who gave them their sight.
Yes I think, and I pray, and I wonder,
And my head I sometimes nod;
For I just can't see how people
Can think there's not a God.
When I look on a newborn baby,
And I see all the love in its eyes;
I marvel at the wonder
That God can be so wise.
But at night when I look to the heavens,
And I behold the beautiful stars;
Then I know God made the world perfect,
And man provided its scars.

—Catherine Cosmato Richburg

THE ROSE CHILDREN

I never saw your baby form
nor heard your infant cry,
but your spilled blood cries out to me
louder each day that goes by.
Reminded of your tragedy
by the sweetness of the gift of life to me,
by my own growing awareness of God's love
man's hate — without Him we're reprobate.
Reminded of you each time the babe
stirs in my womb
you who were not counted worthy of life
too weak and unprotected
are now received by the Lord of Love
who came as a babe and went to the cross
whose blood was spilled for each one of you
and for the ones who killed you.
And every time I see a red rose
I'm reminded of the blooms
that were picked before they blossomed
and the blood that flowed down Calvary
that takes the sin and shame from me.

—Christine Noonan Funnell

THE LOST CHILDREN

During the time of which I sit,
neglected children's faces stare me down
the walls crumbled down to fit,
all the deep, dark trenches they found
to lay in while their life passes,
eating them away to extinction.
Such the time for these masses
to sit at their own mistrial protection
and I am one of them.
There I sit years before—
away from all the turmoil.
While I know one day what I was a part of.
But yet it was canvas and oil
and suffering much like time my heart,
I'll never know of life I speak,
until yet I turn my other cheek,
deny the rest of my careless feats
until I become a child of no more.

—Jennifer Lee Duke

WHERE'D MY BROTHER GO

Where'd my brother go
They sent him over seas
To fight someone he don't know
Our country will never learn
Maybe his plane will crash and burn

We keep starting these wars
When we should be opening doors . . . to peace
He's too young to be over there
But we don't care
People keep dying
Women and children keep crying
But our bombs keep rolling off the assembly line

I haven't heard his voice in so long
Something must be wrong
He went over to defend our flag
Now he's in a body bag

Now can we lay down our guns
Or kiss our children good-bye
As they go off to war
And prepare to die

—Aaron

SAFE PLACE

I walked into a donut shop
saw sitting next to me
Two girls, both with long stringy hair
and holes in both their sleeves.

They sat there staring at the floor
and wouldn't look at me.
And then, I noticed on the wall
a sign read "Safe Place to be."

I couldn't help but wonder
what kind of life they led!
The story of their running,
the reasons why they fled!

They both looked so unhappy,
like life was such a bore,
It made me think of my two kids
and how I knew where they both were!

Next time I go to say my prayers,
I'll get down on my knees
And thank God for my happiness
and "Safe Places" like these.

—Theresa L. Cummings

MOTHER NATURE'S TOWN

Sun turning clouds to gold,
Eagles flying high and bold,
Mountains protecting the valley below,
Silver streams swiftly flow.
Deer grazing in the meadow green,
Wildflowers breaking upon the scene,
Squirrels are seeking their winter fare,
Insects buzzing in the air.
Pine trees standing green and tall,
Breezes whispering through it all,
Birds are singing in the trees,
Flowers are flirting with the bees.
Ants are building their own little hills,
Porcupines holding onto their quills,
Frogs are croaking from the pond,
Crickets chirping out beyond.
Rabbits hopping all around . . .
This looks like Mother Nature's Town.

—Donna R. Lindblom

MARCH WIND

The March wind howls and gusts and roars,
bending low the tree tops as it soars,
It plunders the dark and ominous sky,
seeking revenge with a maddening cry,
It gives my oak a mighty shake
scattering dead leaves in its awful wake;
and, yet, at times, so mellow soft,
it sings a song in the old church loft,
such a bitter-sweet and sad refrain—
something about an angel's wing.
It whistles and rattles my window pane,
then quiets down, but comes again,
It sends mighty breakers against the shore,
and beats poor sailors with a heavy oar.
I cannot see or understand
its many moods on sea and land.
I only know this much matters,
I'm thankful for the seed it scatters.

—Mary Faye Brumby Sherwood

LEAVES

Swirl of maple, elm and oak,
Expressive last identity,
Before autumnal colors cloak,
The earth in anonymity.

Six careless months in shaped structure,
They danced in light mobility,
Within their purposed role secure,
In innocent fragility.

Once torn from their accustomed place,
To winds, the leaves their course adjust,
And replicate with slavish grace,
Conflicting puffs of every gust.

Illusive flash of freedom passed,
The remnants rest upon the ground,
In dull passivity contrast,
Arboreal life that once they crowned.

When winter's whiteness leaves conceals,
And snows the foliage inter,
The dullness of their end reveals:
It matters not what once they were.

—Richard Lydecker

THE POND

Your waters lay so calm and tranquil,
Your surface glimmers like a star in the sky,
You liked me for what I was,
You didn't care what I did,
I would skip a rock on your surface,
and wonder what was deep beneath.
You kept many things a secret,
But much was to be told.
You would hum as the birds would sing;
A smooth harmonious tone.
When I came, you gave me your attention.
Somehow, I knew you were listening.
Why must you leave me,
you were such a friend.
I must say goodbye.
Mustn't I forget you
You are there no more,
There is nothing to see.

—Jason M. Insalaco

DOWN AT THE FARM

One sees a glass-smooth looking pond
Offering a mirror image of Autumn,
Reflecting scarlet, russet and golden leaves
Creating a view that's awesome!

Hardworking hands that have maintained
And burnished the farmstead
Are probably hard at work to sustain
And gather in another year's harvest!

As they work they're reaping another crop.
Memories of gorgeous fall days such as this
Does not make their labor stop.
They reap on — nothing goes amiss!

From the album of their minds comes an
    inner flashing beam,
Enjoying once more beautiful leaves, azure
    sky and memories so fond!
Come Winter once more they'll think of
    the glorious colorful scene
Such as the beautiful mirror-like pond!

—Harriet Ahmels

WIND

The wind, moving like hands
Reaching, reaching for you
Twirling you, spinning you
A dance
A dance of
Joy
Pride
A dance which evil cannot destroy
A dance that is there, a dance that is here
Whether strong or soft, pleasant or painful
It's there
Ready to play, ready to sing, ready to haunt

The wind, it is powerful
Swaying, swinging
Its enemies
Blowing harder, harder
Ever-lasting
Gusts
Sipping you, tasting you, holding you
This is the dance of the wind
Dancing

—Meghan Simpson

THE EMERALD ISLE

The Ring of Kerry is not a dance,
And Waterford is not a race track,
Now Shannon is not some celestial body,
Or Donegual a group of girls;

Lisdonvarnia is not a place of confinement,
Connemara is not just a factory,
DuBlin is not some new cleaning agent,
Or Dingle some unusual sound,

Killarney is not a new salutation,
Or Galway a new medical procedure,
These constitute those towns,
Having a strong back hand,
With top hats, shillelaghs and walking canes
swinging with time,

All in a proud heritage,
Some fully can not understand,
For these alone belong to—IRELAND

—Charles R. Eskew

HERE TODAY, GONE TOMORROW

The house sits alone in the morning dew
It's always been there
Ever since I've been here
Everyday I pass it without a flicker of the eye
Not looking at it as I walk by
It will always be here I thought
The wood will never rot
There came a day when I walked by
To see that the house had indeed gone
Only then did I stop to take a second glance
I tried to remember it sitting in the dew
Its roof wet the siding pale blue,
Or was it grey, I really couldn't say,
This time I really wasn't sure
Even though it had been there so long,
I felt empty seeing it wasn't there
And wished that somehow I'd open my eyes
To see it carved in the blue of the sky
But never was it to be,
Knowing now that taking the glance then
Would make the difference today.

—Tracey Monahan

TRAVELOGUE

East Interstate 80 Nebraska,
Exit 145, No Hitchhiking No U turn.
Travelers information
Radio 970 1240 1410 AM.

Entering Central Time Zone.
Entering Lincoln City,
Ramada Inn, Kearny— Indoor Pool,
117 Miles, Exit 272

Next exit Sutherland, Lodging fuel and food;
Exit 158, Sutherland.
Bridges may be icy, icy road not salted,
Rest area two miles, Applecreek Down.

Buffalo Bills Ranch next two exits
Cody go carts family fun.
Sinclair Tomahawk truckstop
Exit 177 North Platte.

End Construction Thank You,
Drive safely speed limit 65.
Pony Express Station Gaithersburg, 30 miles;
East interstate 80, Nebraska.

—James Karr

COASTAL WINTER

Winter fog descends like greedy Death
Clutching at a weary landscape;
Enclosing earth and sky
In a dark and clammy shroud.
Familiar shrubs and trees
Become but grotesque shadows.
My footsteps grope an unreal pathway
In a weird and sullen world.
I am chilled in isolated loneliness.
The muffled sounds of church bells
And unsure traffic slowed
Reinforce a sense of deep depression.
I shiver in a cloistral capsule;
Lost in time and space.

—Jessie R. Roberts

HILLBILLY OKIE

A Hillbilly Okie, that's what I am
HEE HAW!!! and a Howdy Mam
I'll fry some taters, catfish galore
Give me a bucket and I'll scrub
the old wood floor!
Crawdad hunten here I go
barefooten doe-see-doe!
Me and my banjo, Flatt and Scruggs
can't play too much, I gotta clean my rugs.
From Oklahoma flat land to the Arkansas hills,
this ain't California, no time for thrills,
Hogs to slop, cows to feed
hard work is all I need
Washen and a scrubben and clothes to mend,
Well I'll be here comes my kin.
the sky is blue and it's a full moon
we's all gonna get us a big fat coon
Hamhocks and beans, possem stew
gotta get up before the morning dew
Can't chew the fat it's time to go
It'll be morning before I know

—Linda Diane Trathen

THE CHESAPEAKE BAY

The Bay — Oh how pretty and sweet she
may be, with an everlasting row of lights
that glitter continuously.

Whose waters work so hard each day to
carry our ships from shore to shore.
Each day as she works she'll stop to take
a break, and every ship that floats upon
her soul will sit still.

Oh, how they rejoice in harmony to
celebrate a hard day's work, by decorating
her waters with lights that will shine
amongst her soul throughout eternity.

The Bay — with each and every shore
she has made, we have come to build our
homes upon her banks where we now stand
to see the lights that sparkle amongst
her soul with peace and harmony.

The Bay — as the night falls, her
waters will begin to speak to all of us,
asking of us to please help secure the
beauty for which she stands, which is
peace and harmony to all living things
that life has to offer for the world
to see.

—Theresa Pollock

Little ragdolls and animals
Being dragged to and fro.
For the comfort of a little one
Someone snuggly to know.

Then comes books and schoolwork,
Hard for little guys to do.
But thought and preparation
Will eventually see him through.

Stuffed play animals are forgotten
and girls are begotten.
With love and tender care,
he goes to a dance with an important air.

Later on comes marriage
to the special woman he has found.
And he bears a child of his own
To carry an old ragged bear around.

—Reagan Asher

FOR JODIE

Sitting here alone
Just thinking about the past;
The best years of my life
That slipped away too fast.

Growing up with you
Was the best thing for me;
You told me just to be myself
And the best poet and singer I could possibly be.

I remember all our fights
That most of the time you would lose;
About whose room was cleaner
And whose clothes were whose.

But all those old days are gone now
They're just a good memory;
Of me and my little sister
Together faithfully.

So! please take all my love
And a great big hug and kiss;
'Cause you deserve the best in life
My one and only little sis.

—Shannon M. Chapman, age 19

MY SPECIAL MESSAGE TO JOE:

I wonder every moment of every day
Whether I tell you enough or in the right way
Just exactly how much I love you
How much I need, trust and believe in you too.

You are the biggest thing in my life
With you I can overcome any trouble or strife.
I promise to be here for you
For whatever you need and whatever you do.

Forever and always
Together through all days.
I'll be right here by your side
No matter how rough or smooth the ride.

I will always try to listen and hear
I'll never be far, I'll always be near.
I will be everything you need me to be,
I want it to be forever you and me.

Don't ever doubt or ask me why
Just know that it will always be you and I.
You and me together forever
You and me forever and ever.

—Nicole A. Anthony

SWEET—SWEET

A growing child in Mother's arms
Sends to Grandma her laser charms.
Though miles apart
And years could gap,
Granny misses the child on her lap.

The ring of the telephone . . . "Who can it be?"
A tiny voice babbles confidently.
"Is this my precious Sweet—sweet?"
The elder's voice rejuvenates.
Her wrinkled face does radiate.

What a blessing to realize
That youth and age can compromise
To make a forceful love alloy,
Priming hearts
With sunshine and joy.

—Joyce Lund

ODE TO A NEW GRANDSON
(Born 1-15-80) George Burton Dodge, Jr.

Like the coming of the Christ Child
We anxiously waited for you;
Thinking you'd arrive in December,
But you were long overdue!

The event we shall always remember—
Mid-January you made your debut.
On the fifteenth of the first month
We welcomed our new "little you."

The day that Heaven sent you
Was a blessing from above,
For it's Grandma's birthday, also,
So we'll celebrate with love.

George, you've many years before you
And mine are all behind,
May you grow strong and sturdy,
In body and in mind.

God bless you and protect you,
Dear little Birthday Boy;
May your days be always blessed
With Love and Peace and Joy.

—Helen L. Dodge

GRANDMA LISTENS

Timothy called and was eager to say,
"What a day this Thursday has been!
The first two times were not really much
But then a boy from my second grade stepped in.
He knew how to hit, and he moved very fast,
But I didn't let my guard down a bit.
I knew I had won, and I sat down to rest
When a fifth grader said, 'This is it!'

What chance does a second grader have?
What chance does a second grader have?

I thought to myself, this is going to be tough,
But I will do the best that I can.
I fought that fifth grader; and, Grandma,
I won!

I won and I feel like a champ!
I won and I feel like a champ!

I'll talk to you after karate next week,
But right now I'd better go.
Mamma is coming home before long,
And I still have homework to do."

—Blanche Pinion

REFLECTIONS OF A PARENT

You are my Son, I experience you today.
I feel your heartbeat, it's seconds away.

I see your face, it's a mirror of mine.
I feel your birth and its limitless time.

I hear you speak, don't ask me how.
I feel your pain through our connectedness now.

I gave you birth, a warm place inside.
Your journey to earth we shared side by side.

You were a gift, not someone to own.
But I had forgotten you were a loan.

I've given you back, it wasn't easy you know.
And when I did that, you returned home.

Releasing is hard, but when I let go,
I gave you to Him to find and to know.

—Jan Wright

JESSI

When I know that the sands of
time have taken wing,
And this lonely, broken, heart has
forgotten how to sing.

Solace may be found, perhaps,
in recalling past golden days
When happiness reigned supreme,
appearing often in many ways.

Ignoring reality, I see two eyes
of brown, a twinkling delight,
And long wavy hair, darker
than the darkest night.

A child seeing beauty in everything
she touched or gazed upon,
Radiant as the morning sunrise,
sharing her joys with everyone.

A perplexing nymph, ever riant,
walking among the flowers in awe,
Oh! to once more hear that soft, sweet
voice saying, "Walk with me Grandpa."

—James H. McGowen, Jr.

LIFE'S CIRCLE

Life forever runs its course;
It's very confusing to us.
Testing our stability—
Never with a cause that's just.

God's there to help all of us
When searching for comfort somewhere.
He sends friends and family
To aid in our time of despair.

We found strength in our numbers
With the loss of a dear loved one;
Expecting a new grandchild
To be born to his youngest son.

Life's miracle did return
Soon after he went to Our Lord.
Our grief began to subside
As our beautiful child was born.

She's never met her grandfather;
Her father sees him each day.
Within her actions or smile
Returns all the pain—back from May.

—Heidi Krause

Today our hearts are heavy
We have lost someone we love
We have always had her with us
God's gift from up above.

She laughed with us thru sunshine
She cried with us thru rain
She guided us when happy
And eased our heart thru pain.

She grew up thru the hard times
She toiled for what she had
But God blessed her in the last years
Which made up for all the bad.

She's now with Dad in Heaven
Just as they were before
They're waiting for us to join them
At God's precious Golden Door.

—Lavon Spangler Johnson

A TRIBUTE TO MINNIE PETERSON

The harmonica is now stilled for'er,
Our loved one's passed away.
But in our hearts we all know well
That the mem-ories will stay.
    She started at the age of three,
And music from her flowed.
On through the many years ahead,
Her talent ever glowed.
    The joy of life was hers to give,
And that she did so well.
Our town will miss this dear old friend,
We bid our fond fare-well.
    That grand old lady's left us now,
And sad her friends will be.
But God knew what was best for her,
And bid her come with Him.
    'Tis but a few short years on Earth,
That all of us shall dwell,
Then God will call us home to Him,
And hymns of praise will swell.

—Lenore M. Triplett

MATHEW RAY

There once was a little boy,
who was happy and gay.
He had dark brown hair,
and was named Mathew Ray!!

He was my favorite cousin,
and we would always play,
pretending we were pirates,
and big monsters we would slay,

The summer nights would find us,
looking up at the stars!
Pretending we were rockets,
and flying up to Mars!

When I came home from playing,
for it happened the next day.
They told me about the accident,
that killed poor Mathew Ray!!!

And now I sit here crying
for I miss him and I'm all alone.
There's nobody to play with the pirates,
and the rockets to Mars have all gone!

Dedicated to in Memory: Mathew Ray Deleon,
Born—August 30, 1975 Died—October 23, 1982
Seven years old

—Raquel Martinez

BECOMING A CARE BEAR

The important thing about a Care Bear,
Is the fact that he'll always share!
He doesn't believe in push or shove,
He just believes in lots of love!
So in the cold month of December,
You can become a Royal Member!
All you have to do you see,
Is follow this very important plea!
Share your things with your sister and brother,
And give lots of love to your father and mother!

—Mary H. DeMoure

JULY FOURTH

Sitting on my mother's lap
I watched the stars in fey
with brilliant colors of illumination
the stars would glow and expand
into fictional patterns
then disappear in a roar of anger
the sky was tenuous with this amusement
until darkness conquered it
then I was carried away
in total confusion

—"Rocky" McNickle

MARY ANN'S SONG

Time has no meaning with my bundle of joy,
Especially at those gentle times we share.
And in my lap she wriggles and cries,
    when mealtime is near.
Then Jessica sounds like music to my ears,
As she sighs and drifts off to sleep.
There were many times that I've dreamed
    of this day.
But my wishes never came as close,
Because she's more than could be imagined.
To share, to touch, to love to caress.
Yes, there's more we'll give to each other!

—Theresa J.

MY BABY DAUGHTER

I love you with all my heart
When I think of you my tear drops start
You're like an angel from up above
I come to you when I need love

We've had our troubles here and there
But to me there is no one else I can compare
Your love to me is like a dream
That comes to me in mid stream

We've both done each other wrong in the past
But I am glad that it didn't last
We've got to go forward with a smile
Because I think it is worthwhile

I am happy to say from now on
We'll think of each other and not want to roam
We're satisfied with each other like a dream
It's a wonderful feeling it does seem

I'll close this poem with a dream
That we'll be together in our dream
That we've got to cope with life on earth
Cause one of these days we'll have a new birth

—Dorothy Lee Lewis

MOMS

Moms tuck you in at night,
Moms make you dinner and make sure
you eat right.
Moms give you kisses and hug you tight
Moms can be mean or nice.
Some kids aren't as lucky as others
Some don't live with their mothers
That's why I thank the Lord everyday for
giving me a mother who Loves me in a
very special way.

—Chelisa Jackson, age 11

MY LITTLE ANGELS

My little angels as you sleep I hold you near.
In your slumber, it's no wonder the sweet
dreams you dream.
    With each night you grow so much more,
before my eyes.
    In the night you may cry out, don't worry
I'll be there to dry your eyes.
    As I sit and watch you sleep I thank
God for my angels so dear.
    When you've grown and I'm alone
I'll think of you when you were small.

—Deanna McCarty

BABY DEAR

To me your birth's the greatest thing
That my life will ever know.
I'll care for you the best I can
    And I'll daily watch you grow.

I'll ever strive to use all means
    And ever watch the things I say,
That will support a better life
    That's yours to live on down the way.

I'll careful be of how I live
    And give much thought to what I do.
I'll think of you throughout my life
    And I'll keep this poem for you.

—Ross Wyatt

A MOTHER'S EYES

A mother's eyes see everything
The good, the bad that life will bring
A mother's eyes will watch them grow
As they fill with tears, they will glow

A mother's eyes show joy and pride
As she feels her love deep inside
A mother's eyes will fill with tears
As she chases away all their fears

A mother's eyes will teach and guide
To make them feel strong and brave inside
A mother's eyes show the love and pain
The good times, the bad times, lose or gain

A mother's eyes will learn and share
She taught them love and how to care
A mother's eyes show joy and sorrow
Yesterday's gone, but we have tomorrow

A mother's eyes that show the laughter
We shared the fun that we were after
A mother's eyes will always be there
To see the love that we all share

—Janice F. Morton

LIVE FOR TODAY

There will be many days in my lifetime
I will not feel so good, but today I
feel fine.

Tomorrow I can't count on, for nobody
can foresee, so I'll enjoy this day to
its fullest before it's taken far
from me.

Many roads will be traveled, a lot
will have dead ends, but if I can
keep faith I'll find the strength to
always begin again.

For today I will not worry about any
roads mistaken, the sun is out, the
sky is blue, a brand new day is
breaking through, and I feel just
fine.

—Roger M. Reynolds

FORGOTTEN FINGERS

Nursery Rhymes;
    How I long to hear them again.
Playing Pat-a-Cake;
    How I long to touch your hands again,
Do we adults realize how long it's been?

Ring-Around-the-Rosy;
    How we laughed and all fell down;
Hide-n-Seek;
    How we grabbed a partner and ran around.
Do we realize all these things took place
        so long ago?

Spud, and Dodge Ball;
    A game where the ball was it,
Night Swimming at midnight;
        thought those romantic nights wouldn't quit;

And since those days have all been gone,
My childhood and I have built a bond,
Between the past and the future;
Not knowing if I'll ever really let go;
    or really ever be sure.

—"Darlin"

Outside my window the snow falls
in downy flakes, adrift in the December air.

Before me lie my yesterdays, sprawling
on the carpet, adrift in the boxes that linger
and mock. The passages of my life
tumble in a flurry of comings and goings.

Memories sift in my gaze from the window,
a blue jay flits into view, and I dawn
to the amazement that she too is new.

Good-byes give birth to unknown treasure.
What has gone before, what is to be,
materialize like a blue jay
searching for scraps in the newfallen snow.

The passages of life defy definition:
they are the rings that stretch to Redwood glory,
they are the grapes that age to wine,
they change farewells to benedictions
and trust that endings are beginnings.

Outside my window the snow is falling,
and the glass sends back a warming smile.

—Cheri Farr Keipper

GOD CARES FOR ALL

Out under the canopy of heaven —
I see the beautiful skies
God in the wonder of creation
    Has given love for the living our lives.

Go tell the world how I love them
    Show people the way to take
How God in great glory and splendor
    Has given His love for our sake.

'Tis not the land that He loves
    'Tis not the splendor He made
It is rather the soul within us
    That brings God cause to give aid.

O happy ones and holy
    O joy beyond compare
How great and faithful God is
    To lift us above all care.

—L. George Hostetter

OUR DREAM

The sun arises around your face
    and sets behind your smile.
The whispering winds leave a trace
of your voice, and of a child's.
A gentle voice, that of the babes,
So calm, and yet it sounds,
as if the child's words are from
the bundle your arms surround.

I look inside this ball of cloth
So lovingly you hold
the child looks up and smiles at me
(it makes me feel old.)

And then I realize
just what I have seen.
The beauty that the future holds
The power of our dream.

For the child that's held within your arms
Who smiles so sure and fine.
Can only be one hope of ours
This child is yours and mine.

—Roger Bowers

DADDY'S HANDS

As a little girl I can remember holding
Daddy's strong and calloused hands,
Watching him at hard work farming tomatoes
in the soft white Florida sand.

He worked so hard to provide for a family
of four, But not once did he complain,
unless it was behind my Mother's bedroom door.

He has always been there for me
that quiet gentle man,
with so much love to give
So proud of him I am.

I'm all grown up and married now and
have long since moved away,
but my Daddy's little girl I will always stay.

I don't see Daddy as much as I would
like, but go home every chance I can,
cause one thing I still love to do
is hold my Daddy's hand.

I LOVE YOU DADDY!

—Sandie Foster

213

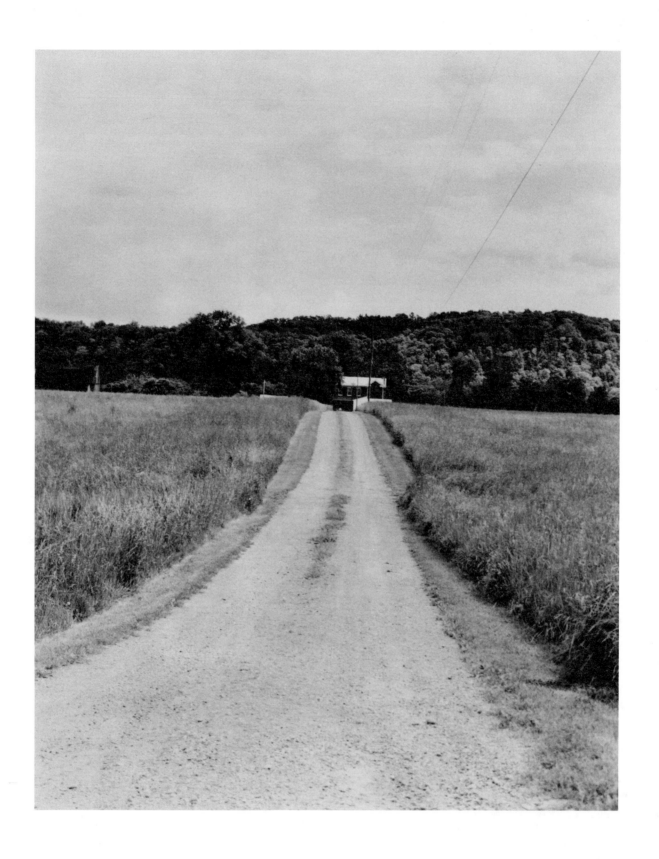

A FRIEND LIKE YOU

I'd like to have more friends like you
to cheer my thoughts each day,
to spread the kind of sunshine
that you have along my way.
I'd like to be a friend like you
so other folks could see,
your very special brand of warmth
and thoughtfulness in me.
At many times and seasons
through many changing scenes,
I often think about you
and all our friendship means.
I feel a sense of gratitude
as I realize anew,
how fortunate I am
to have a friend like you.

—Kayle Jeffery

"DESTINY" — MY GRANDCHILD

Guess who comes to see me
two or three times every day,
A cute little darling Angel
    a laughing all the way.

She has four long fat pigtails
    with babbles on the end,
They bob this way and that way
    as she flashes her lovely grin.

She rushes into my bedroom
    and stops me right in my tracks,
"Guess what I've got for you Mom-Mom?"
    with both arms behind her back.

I greatly act surprised you see
    and kiss her lovely nose,
For in her hand that dandelion
    seems like a lovely rose.

This lovely little grandchild
    means all the world to me,
I often wonder everyday
    what she'll grow up to be.

—Elizabeth "Bettye" Thompson

"For Margaret Elder, a Very Special Person"

(Director and Pianist of our Turlock Senior Citizens Chorus)

Sweet and melodious is your voice,
Loving and touching,
    And filled with grace and lilt,
While leading our chorus in song.

Joyous music ripples the air
    As your fingers dance upon the keys,
And the old piano bursts
    In glorious beauty and magnificent sounds,
And your rolling music flows
    Like a refreshing and soothing river.

Our singing soars.
Our joys awaken.
Our tenderness and kindness bloom,
    All because of you.

Our compassions are stirred
    As longing hearts revive.
Our varied pains softly and gently subside,
    And melody, harmony, and love abundantly abide,
    All because of you.

—Mary N. Kamiya

MY DAUGHTER JILL

My daughter is a precious gem
A gift of love, heaven sent
Kind, thoughtful, forever dear
In my thoughts, so sincere

My wish for her, I pray each day
That life be kind in every way
For the joy she gives to me
Will be hers forever

Forever young may she be
A ray of light and beauty
Her very voice, I hear each day
Makes me know she is ok

The pride I feel, that Jill has given me
Is the joy I have in a daughter such as she
Though we are miles apart
We are forever in each other's hearts.

—Pauline Rentner

CLARA

Such a wonderful name
I'm blessed, as it is mine.
To do it justice, that will be hard,
A special lady had it before my time.

She was a lovely lady,
Kind in heart, mind and soul.
You didn't have far to search,
To find her heart was pure gold.

She taught throughout her life
Far beyond her school teaching days.
She taught love, honesty and justice,
If you listened and learned her ways.

She had respect from deep within
And from everyone who knew her well.
She is taken from us with love,
Thus we know with whom she'll dwell.

Grieve not for me, she would say to you,
With her smile and her grace,
Grieve not for me, you should know
I've passed on to a wondrous place.

—Clara J. Henderson

A SINGLE ROSE

A single rose I give to you.
It is for your heart that is so true.
Your love is a special kind.
One that is so hard to find.

When I am down, you are there.
Always showing that you care.
You give a meaning to my days.
You do things in special ways.

Our time together seems to go so fast.
Sometimes I wonder if we will last.
You seem to always be there.
You make life seem so fair.

No requirements do you put on our love.
Sometimes I think you were sent from above.
Your presence is all that I need.
From your love I want to feed.

You make my day so bright.
Your lovely face is a precious sight.
You make me want to live.
To you, a single rose I do give.

—Robert L. Gregory

MORNING

It's the best thing,
The beauty of the sunrise.
Peacefully, we watch,
And can't picture anything more golden.

—Katie J. Stockton

A tear is so minutely small
It hardly seems worth while at all.
Yet each tear of pain and sorrow
Increases the weight of tomorrow.
So, too, each tear of joyousness
Contributes to life's happiness.

—Eleanor Pillsbury

THE ARTIST'S MASTERPIECE

It seemed as though the hand of God
Had taken up a paint brush
And artfully dabbed the sky
With brilliant glowing colors.

He dipped from His palette
A flaming shade of orange,
Touching it to the horizon
To form a burning sphere.

Close to the sphere He cast
Billowing clouds of crimson.
Then, drawing outward from the globe,
He added strokes of warm rose.

Higher in the heavens still
He painted deep purple puffs
Laid against shades of azure blue
And a ceiling of soft gray.

With all the sky for His canvas,
He created a masterpiece
In ever-changing tints and hues,
And called it simply, "Sunrise."

—Linda Jay

HEART TIMES

The heart and mind, two worlds
apart,
Like paint and canvas, becomes
an art.
Apply one to the latter. What
do you find?
A person of love, both wise
and kind.
They work in harmony, like
lovers in love.
For were we not created by
God above?
The mind is used to rule in
the land we live,
But where's the heart in which
to forgive?
We wonder why our nation is
falling apart
And we search the mind, but
not the heart.
We'll search and search, but
search in vain,
Until we apply the heart to
the mind again.

—Duke Palmer

There is a gentleness to spring approaching.
The way she taps you on the shoulder
With a familiar light, as if to say,
"Remember me?"

How it is that that light
Reminds us of another time.
The way things used to be.
We were younger then.
Happier or sadder?

But some things do not change.
The instant of the light
That does not change.
It is seen in the same way,
With the same sudden flash
Of recognition and response
Year after year.
As if for an instant
Not an instant had passed.

—John Gioffre

REFLECTIONS

It is a quiet October day,
The sky is azure blue,
The trees are resplendent
In colors of every hue.
It is a day to enjoy—
To appreciate and reflect,
It is a day to remember—
To look back in retrospect.
It is a day for walking down country lanes
As I am doing now,
This autumn wonderland is God's cathedral,
And to Him I humbly bow.
It is the kind of day
My mom would love,
But, on this day, her birthday
She's with our Father above.
I miss her so much,
But today she seems very near—
As through the rustling leaves she whispers,
"Honey, I'm right here."

—Mildred J. Worster

DREAM AWAY THE HOURS

How nice to dream away one's hours
Lost among the trees and flowers,

To breathe the scented air with ease
And dwell with butterflies and bees,

Where song birds chant their sweet refrain
In fields of hay and golden grain,

The chipmunks scatter here and there
So freely without woe or care,

A host of crickets oft' respond
To croaks of frogs from nature's pond,

Green blades of grass that whisper low
And dance as gentle breezes blow,

The sunlight peeks behind the clouds,
Far from the city's life and crowds,

It's here where nature sports her powers,
Hidden from life's dread and showers,

Where dreams come true in solitude,
Devoured with awe and pensive mood.

—Anton J. Stoffle

TO BE IN LOVE

To be in love is to have a special feeling
 That special feeling must be true,
To express your love in many ways
It can be quiet, out loud or in a romantic way.
True love is way deep inside of you
Like in orbit, it floats in darkness,
But that darkness of love is a special place
Like the love in your heart always to embrace . . .
. . . . . YOUR SPECIAL LOVE . . . . .

　　　　—Marie D. Piris Robert

WHEN THE TIME COMES

When the time comes to say good-bye,
　　　　　　　　I will not cry.
　　　　　　　　At least, I'll try.
For you **only** asked to make love to me,
　　　　　　　　and I agreed.

　　Falling in love came after the passion
　　　　　healed my broken heart
　　　　　　from another love.
　　And I believe you love me too, as much
　　　　　　as you say you do;
　　　　but love affairs with married men
　　　　　　must always end.

There is someone out there who wants to give me
　　　　what you're afraid to give.
　　　　　　I will find him
　　　　　when the time comes.
Then our stolen moments will be gone forever,
　　and the sadness will be the realization of
　　　how fleeting love really is —
　　　　　　if love really is.

　　When the time comes to say good-bye,
　　　　　　　　I will not cry.
　　For you **only** asked to make love to me,
　　　　　　　　and I agreed.

　　　　　　　—Glenda F. Mink

DOTH ONE BUT KNOW THIS HEART?

I have waited . . . Oh prayed! for Spring,
 for the Monarch's return.
The Winter hath pierced me like a knife
　. . . leaving only an empty shell
　. . . waiting for the hungry birds.

I should feed them after their long journey
　. . . but I have nothing to give.

I see them return . . . but coldness has
　. . . left me cold in the ground.
Alone . . . so alone . . . all the giving done;
and to those given . . . all has been flight.
　That is my epitaph.

For is it not enough — to give life where there is none?
　To give back a spark to a dying one?
　To give a crumb of bread to a bird slow in flight?

Who is there to give in return . . .
　I will rest until my giving time shall come again.
In deep sleep until Morning comes, and GOD shall rise
　a giving heart from its sleep.
Forgive the death that gave only — until death.

The heart shall live in glory and brightness, and see the
　goodness of its deeds.
　To love beyond love . . .
　To give beyond give . . .
Doth one but not know this heart.

　　　　—Kathleen Rogers

VOWS OF LOVE AND TRUST

Promise me darling you will always be true
 then my heart will never be blue.
Our lives together are entwined;
　The vows we made really do bind.
To honor and cherish till death do we part,
　Our vows that we made from our hearts.
Together we'll stay, our love will endure,
　Of each other we will always be sure.
Life may not be easy, it may even be hard;
　but of each other we will never be tired.
Our love has grown from Day to Day
　and will continue if we stay,
　close in spirit and in mind
　and never let our selves be blind.
An open mind, a trusting heart
　will never let us drift apart.

　　　　—Betty R. Sledge

WHAT IS LOVE

Love is like a flower in Winter
 Laying dormant, but always there,
Then comes the warmth of a lovely smile
And love is blooming every where.

A parent's love comes naturally,
But when a wee one says, "I love you,"
Your heart is filled to overflowing
And a special love comes shining through.

A friendship should be filled with love
And willingness to help in time of need,
A friend is someone you can trust,
To have one is a Joy indeed.

Then comes that very special person,
Sent to you from God above,
Sent to be a friend and helpmate,
With an ever blossoming love.

All these loves, like the flower
Need ever tender loving care,
So thank your lord for all these gifts,
And know His love is every where.

　　　　—Doris Graham

reasons

because i was lonely,
　　and you were a traveling Berkeley man,
　　　　i smiled with you.

because i like to dance,
　　and you played the beat,
　　　　i went with you.

because i like to drink,
　　and you bought the wine,
　　　　i got high with you.

because i liked your softness,
　　and you liked my lips,
　　　　i kissed you to death.

because i was cold,
　　and your bed was small,
　　　　i slept with you.

　　and,

because i needed someone that night,
　　and you were there,
　　　　i loved you.

　　　　—marjorie anne wallace

217

MY MOM AND DAD

Years ago when I was born;
    My mom and dad lived on a farm.

I was the second for my dad and mom;
Then came their third, this time a son.

We were loved and very well fed;
They were always there to put us to bed.

Then came the time when I was five;
My dad who I loved so much died.

Back then it was hard to survive;
Sometimes you were lucky to be alive.

Then my mother had to leave the farm;
She left us with my aunt to keep us from harm.

She then married again, and sent for us three;
Our hearts were happy, we were full of glee.

But now my mom is also gone;
And once more I am all alone.

—Fern Brewer

MY SWEET DADDY

I once had a precious mama and
    a sweet daddy too . . .
    But Jesus took my mama and
it left us sad and blue . . .
    The Devil took my daddy and
led him by the hand.
    He took him thru a dark and
very troublesome land.
    My heart aches and hurts so much,
it seems I can't stand the pain,
    With every new day dawning,
it's always just the same!
    To think of losing Mother, I'm oh!
So! Sad! and blue . . .!
    And . . . think, I've even lost my
daddy, is even worse too . . .
    But . . . oh! how very much I
loved him, If only he could see . . .
    He'll always be my "sweet daddy,"
and oh so dear to me!

—Corinne Rushing

WHAT SHOULD'VE BEEN SAID

Waking up that cold, dreary morning,
    I knew it had come to an end.
That struggle and fight,
You'd kept for so long,
Finally took your life.
They say you went so fast,
that it's all for the better,
for now you lay in peace and eternal rest.
I lay awake at night crying,
Not knowing why God did this to me.
Guilt and selfishness are all I feel inside.
I want you back with me,
Another chance for you to see,
the love I hide inside for you.
Now it's too late,
though they say
you knew.
This dear, Grandma, is for you,
To say what should've been said,
so long ago—I Love You!

—Christine La Pierre

ALWAYS MY SON

This is a poem to my son Zack
    who has hurt me a thousand times.
My eyes fill with tears
and my chest constricts with pain
when I picture your face.
Where are you now? Do you think about me?
Do you miss the joys we shared?
There's a lump in my throat but words won't come.
All I feel is anguish for the distance between us.
To hold you in my arms again . . .
To tell you I love you . . .
To hear you tell me you love me.
It's only a dream.
Mothers don't have all the answers
but your happiness was always my goal.
Sometimes "No" means I love you.
I can't remember the bad times
I just remember the love . . . and I miss you.
I write this to bridge the distance between us.
May love heal the wounds, my son, Zack.

—Linda S. Shaw

THE STORY OF JOHN

In 1947 my brother was born
    Like a star from the heavens
We named him John.
He was a darling baby
With brown curly hair
And each day his laughter
Rang thru the air.
As he grew older he was not content
Although many hours together we spent
Walking, biking, swimming and shopping
To all his energy—there was no stopping.
Closer we grew as life went on
Oh! How I loved my brother John!
Overnight he changed from a boy to a man
But the power of life is not in our hand.
The Lord took John from us
He was only eighteen
And left us all with dear memories.
That star from heaven is where it belongs
And his spirit is with us—We're not alone.

—Kathleen A. Collins

LAURA

Flowing blonde hair against dark smooth skin
    To share your love is a dream
Those soft lovely eyes and smooth pretty lips
It's a shame that our love cannot be
Falling in love with you
But only too late
Giving up my freedom
My foolishness I hate
My love for you Laura
I certainly must hide
For this love is forbidden
I must keep it inside
For we could have such fun
Sharing little things
Playfully teasing each other
And making clover chains
But we won't share any love
Or lay in clover fields
And now
I cry.

—John Michael White

218

MOM, I LOVE YOU

When I would be in bed sick,
She knew just what story to pick,
When I start off to school I couldn't say good-bye.
And mom would wipe a tear from my eye.

When I was down and feeling rather sad,
She knew what to say to make me glad.
When I would have a terrible day,
She knew exactly what to say.

She would take me out and do special things,
Boy! What joy to my heart that it brings,
She is more than a mom to me.
She is closer than any friend could be.

She is always there for me,
To help me to understand and to see,
I don't know what else to say or do,
But just to say. Mom I love you . . . .

        —Michael D. Bell

JAMES E. CRAWFORD (MY DAD)

I close my eyes and see your face,
Patrician features, leathered skin.
Reverent awe stood in our place,
Honorable man above all men.

The world around you knew your hand,
Respected your values, admired your stand,
Quiet, strong, stable and still,
Walking with God in the fields you'd till.

Pedestal high — I kept you there,
Treasuring you beyond compare,
But you opened my eyes — forced me to see.
You too had clay feet — you set me free.

You were a man — God knew that too,
But you, like David, returned anew.
You bent your twigs, spared not the rod,
Mended your fences, carried your hod.

Steel gray eyes held humor and wit,
Flashed instant judgement, mirrored true grit.
Man to be trusted, turned to again,
Honorable man above all men.

        —Audrie C. Bennett

MOTHER . . . THE ESSENCE OF LOVE

My Mother is a figure of wisdom untold.
Her humbleness is more valuable than fine gold.
She's truly a peacemaker, by which I should learn —
To be precious like her, I earnestly yearn.

She is the best example to me.
World's greatest mother, she'll always be.
Her prize patience is never ending;
Broken hearts she is always mending.

Love to others she constantly shows;
Love she freely gives wherever she goes.
A wonderful woman, where virtues abound
And in her heart, sincerity is found.

To me her beauty is beyond compare —
Her bright eyes full of spark, her skin so fair.
Hands so affectionate, gentle and kind
A more graceful woman you will not find.

I love my dear Mother with all my heart.
In my life she's played a very big part.
She did her best, as a widow you see,
To be both Mother and Daddy to me.

        —Verna Ollis McKinney

MY GREAT-GREAT GRANDPA

My grandpa died today.
And I had only seen him yesterday,
Lying there in his bed,
He looked up to me and said,
"I will get better, you just wait and see."
I had my doubts; he was one-hundred and three.
He had only been sick a few days of the year,
And now he could not even get his lungs clear.
His coughs rumbled like thunder across the sky.
I looked into his eyes and saw him say goodbye.
Holding his hand, I wanted not to let go.
But I had to, and did, ever so slow.
I walked out of his room, a tear in my eye.
We will never again meet, until I, too, also die.
It is a miracle, I thought, to live to be
As old as he, one-hundred and three.

        —Kathy Nachazel

TO MY DAUGHTER . . .

My daughter — how could that be?
Why, only moments ago, I was the child,
laying my head in my mother's lap, to dream.
How does it happen — that we stop
    Being a child, to create a child.

You were just a heartbeat within a heartbeat.
  A nudge in the side — a hiccup —
Doing somersaults to let me know
    you were alive.
  I patted the roundness and in touching me —
    I touched you.
You were me — my child.

Now, as I stand in the shadows of your room,
I ache — for your love —
For you to know — my love.
You are so young, yet so grown —
Tonite you even walked to me and
fell into my arms.
Looking up with eyes of love
    my love . . . my child.

        —Ida S. Hill

GRANDPA

Grandpa has a gentle face
With an expression, oh so kind.
He sits in his old easy chair
And lets thoughts wonder through his mind.

He thinks about the good old days
When he was just a kid,
Of all the fun he used to have
And other things he did.

Grandpa now has a bald spot
Where his hair once use to be,
He has the nicest gray-blue eyes
When he looks out at me.

His occupation is farming.
He loves to till the soil.
Watching the little plants come up
Rewards his earnest toil.

He says farming isn't profitable
No matter what he seems to do,
But we know Grandpa will keep farming
Until his Social Security check comes through.

        —Darlene Wichers

A LOVING RELATIONSHIP

I find comfort in the silent presence of
you, through words as well as body language
I share mutual trust, honesty, admiration,
devotion, and that special thrill of happiness
simply in being together.

You are "home" for my soul — a
place to be myself and explore my
deepest inner yearnings, hopes, fears
and joys without fear of rejection or
being abandoned. You are an environment
in which I can be relaxed and
comfortable, and able to gain strength
to fight life's battle.

I find our relationship mystical,
a dynamic experience. There are no
expectations, but appreciation of the
relationship because of its unique value,
and its wonder of being experienced
with you.

—Tina L. Sadowski

BIRTH

My heart is filled with joy as I
Gaze in awe at the creature before me.

The skin, a soft peach, reflects the delicacy
And innocence of birth like that of
Petals of a rose. The hands are
Delicate and tiny that the slightest
Pressure could shatter.

Being around such a small, little
Creature makes you feel like protecting
Them from the troubles and the worries
Of the world.

With trepidation, you watch as they
Grow from that helpless little bundle
Into a toddler full of mischief, then into
A rebellious teen and finally into a
Responsible adult and you know that
You have to let go, to let them
Experience the cruelties of life.

—Rebecca Holmes

KITTEN

From the moment I met her I knew
I had been stricken, for she has
great style and is as lovely as a kitten.

Sometimes she says I flatter her, and
that may be the case, but I can't help but
say nice things to such a pretty face.

I'm not sure why she loves me, but she
must think that I'm swell, and surely
as she sees me I see her just as well.

Some tell me she can be vicious, but so
far I've few complaints, I only hope her
love for me is given without restraints.

She has a special smile and I truly think
she's hot, so she never needs to change her
ways or be anything she's not.

She's the sweetest one I know, so believe
what I have written, for it was done with
love for the girl that I call kitten.

—Gary J. Voichoski

I REMEMBER LOVE

I remember the comfort inside Mommy's womb,
Curled into a ball floating in my cocoon.
The sounds were so soothing, like soft falling rain,
The steady low rhythm — her heartbeat's refrain.
A world of my own, secure as could be;
Yes Mommy was always so careful with me!
She spoke to me softly, and all through the day,
She sang to me sweetly, and then she would pray.
I knew that she loved me with all of her heart,
Caressing me gently — giving love was her part.
Though reluctant to leave my safe, warm cocoon,
My mommy compelled me — I had to leave soon.
I burst forth with tears at the strangeness around —
The lights, the masked people, the funny new sounds
Then through the confusion, my Daddy took hold,

His voice was familiar — so strong and so bold.
He held me — he loved me — his touch said, "I care."
I'm here to protect you — and now Mommy's there . . .
Her voice was the same — so loving and true
I snuggled up close as she sang and I cooed.

—W. Lois Crim

MOTHER, I KNOW!

Mother, I see you now as a child, after many
years away, in a wistful photograph, glazed but
faded, a frozen snap of intent and pose dated 1911.
In candid moment, perhaps from summer play in
warm July, you are thin beneath the close gingham
and behind your soft smile, raven hair is drawn
severe and capped with a flared bow.
You shade your dark eyes with a narrow hand,
but I know you could not see me here, this
feather instant. I see you there again with a
clarity of twice reflection: you were eleven and
so was I, and you knew yourself and me, in later
years and space from a further planting amid my
tears and burned eyes. Yet in length of view,
we shall never catch your parents or their's in
membrane layers of eternity — they have known us
all from a broader frame. Still, in all, I am
glad to be young in knowing you knew yourself
and me in later years, since now I know us both,
entwined, from where I grow.

—John K. Mulliken

I remember carrying you
And while inside you never reached out to me
Little did I know that your moods are so subtle and pure
That it takes me by surprise everytime

The sweet way you smile
The way you wrap everyone around your little finger

I am amazed at how much having you in my life
Has changed me forever
The fight we had for your life
A battle you won in your sweet quiet way
With the strength of a thousand armies
How your courage has braced me up
And shown me how to keep fighting

You have taught me how to trust again
And that it's OK to be gentle and loving
But still stay strong

You are my best friend
I love you with all my heart
And I pray that when I grow up
I can be just like you.

—Sandra Kozlowski

THE LAWN

By the window in the late afternoon I sit
And look out on the cloudless sky
The promised rain has since gone by
We didn't get a drop or even a little bit.
The grass has just been cut to show
The green was all on top but down below
It looks a faded kind of spread
To accent flowers and trees
It looks so dry and so forlorn
Grow back fast so I'll again have a lawn.
To look upon and for birds to strut,
Until you need another cut.

—Betty Perotti

AUTUMN

I wandered down the road through the lea,
    But when I stopped and turned to see,
I saw the maple as a dainty maid
    Who lights the dusky forest glade.

The elm in shimmering robes of gold
    That catch the sunlight glistening fold on fold.
A monarch the proud and princely oak
    Towering high above the woods in his yellow cloak.

The gypsy sumac flaunts its crimson dress,
    Wild along the roadside red blossoms on her breast.
On down the dark windy dale I now go
    To these autumn fancies I bow low.

—Blanche Hall

fall promise

the last warm kiss of a summer wind is brushing
    my cheek

the kelly green on the shore line has turned a
    dull, black avocado

the brilliant sapphire blue of the river, hints
    winter in its slate quiet gray

the birds are gathering for their annual flight
    south; only the leaders chattering

even i sit quietly thinking of the coming
    winter; reflecting on summer colors unused

i must promise myself a winter white
    a rainbow spring

—Patti Myers

A SUMMER MORN

There is a mist between the House and the Barn
    in the early morn.
There is Dew on the blades of grass
that are still warm
From the Sun that shone on the day before
and now is arising, to repeat once more
Its daily arc from dawn til dusk.
The fragrance of Roses mingle
with the scent of musk
Akin to the rich pungent aroma of the Earth
present since its birth.
The Birds chirp their songs of melody
with a note of mirth
While ever so gentle a cooling breeze
begins to stir in the top of the trees
And all is well on a Summer Morn
At the start of a new day about to be born.

—Margie Roemele

SECRET SUNRISE

Though delphin dawn with peaceful pace
    Greets the world with golden grace,
    Casts gilded glow on land and sea,
    Sings ancient anthems silently,
    And spreads its smile across the earth
    In tribute to the day's re-birth,

Its breathless beauty, clear and bright,
    Becomes a spark beside your light
    That sears away the haunting haze
    Of my life's disenchanted days.

My secret sunrise; my cherished one;
    My shadowed soul's own rising sun!
    Although our paths were drawn apart
    Upon that vast unearthly chart,
    I sparkle with your spirit's touch
    And thank my God who's granted much.

—Aileen Hutton

TREES

Standing tall on a hill
naked trees stretch
waiting for spring
the air warms, buds form
color brightens the hill

Leaves of different green
emerald, olive, pea
thick, thin, long, short
oak, birch, maple, hickory
all with leaves of green

Multi-coloured crowned hill
draws eyes to its beauty
one then many fall until
leaves brown and withered
lay in deep piles on the hill

Through winter's ice, wind and snow
bare brown branches
wait for spring
roots warm underneath
outlast the snow

—Kathleen J. Miller

WINTER

Winter
        is nearing very soon.
Frigid
        winds are blowing.
A
        warm fire burns in the fire place.
Out
        the small window snow softly falls.
Hot
        cocoa rests in two large mugs.
Big,
        soft, pillows are thrown on the floor.
You
        and I sit together by the fire.
The
        warmth in the room,
Sets
        a romantic mood in our hearts.
Hold
        me close, my love, til dawn.
The
        sunrise will warm the new day.

—Louise Dove

SUMMERTIME

Yonder in a yellow pine, a woodpecker
　　leaves his mark.
Down below, in a secret retreat, a
　　frisky squirrel begins to bark.

In the thick pine wood, a mockingbird
　　warbles her notes sublime.
There is a spring in my step and a song
　　in my heart; it must be summertime!

The river is softly calling, as a steamboat
　　rounds the bend.
It is moving very leisurely, as it whistles
　　in the wind.

If my timing is right, the fish will bite.
　　If not, I will not mind.
There is a fragrance in the air, and the sky
　　is fair. It must be summertime!

　　　　—Ramona L. Smith

ETERNAL LIFE . . .

Through winter winds of ice and snow
　　and storms of rain and sleet—
When golden rays and winter's haze
reflect giant shadows as silhouettes
meet, one leaf still clings as if
in quiet defiance . . . waits and abides
the hour, knowing well

That the Hand that holds it safely on
the bough, will reach out to every living
thing and once again, reveal itself,
In the Lovely beauty and majesty of Spring.

　　　　—Delfina Casillas

SPRING MIST

I love to walk with mist on my face
　In the early spring. The clouds are lace
Hung on an unseen string.

The earth is covered with new-born grass,
A tree is now a thin, green flash
Of the love that is the spring.

The mist falls gently from the clouds above
On the trees, the grass, and me,
And nothing is left in all the world
But sky, mist, grass, and tree.

　　　　—Gladys L. Doak

FEELINGS OF SPRINGTIME

There's a feeling of springtime in the air,
　And Spring's beauties will soon appear;
There's a promise of all things fresh and new
In the mornings that dawn sunny and clear.

The beautiful flowers will soon reawaken
With their blossoms bright and gay,
The trees are once again greening and budding,
For Springtime's on its way.

The brilliant golden forsythia,
Its sunshine will uninhibitedly spray,
While the fragrance of lilacs and roses
Will soon greet each happy new day.

Hopes are reborn in the Springtime,
When all things are lovely and new,
For Springtime's the season of miracles,
And faith in God's promises are renewed.

　　　　—Mary Lee Dauer

A CHRISTMAS THANKS

　　Christmas time has come and gone, but friends
and memories linger on;

　　Twinkling lights and goodies sweet, a Christmas
tree and friends to greet;

　　These are all part of the Christmas past, but
what does the new year hold I ask?

　　Health and happiness we wish for you, and thank
you for our Christmas too!!

　　　　—Jana Lea Holman

WINTER BEAUTY

Dashing through the snow
　On a cold wintry day,
Vibrates the body with excitement,
As the graceful, snowy white flakes
Float lazily to the ground.
Trees dressed in their wintry coats
Of white, glisten as the ice graces
Their branches with beauty.
Truly a winter wonderland of beauty
To be seen and admired by all.
A great peace is felt within
As the snow creates its own fantasies.

　　　　—Ann Swan

HOLIDAY THOUGHTS

The beauty of Christmas with so many lights,
　That sparkle and glisten, like jewels in the night.

Houses are decorated, gables aglow,
It surely is, a spectacular show.

Children's excitement remembered through life,
Though some are torn, with sadness and strife.

Some people are lucky, and grow to be old,
While others are homeless, and out in the cold.

Let's strive to bring joy like Santa, the man,
If we all try I'm sure that we can.

A gift and a smile, may save many a tear,
'Merry Christmas,' to all, and to all a 'Good Year.'

　　　　—Stella Gill

EASTER

Easter comes but once a year
　It's named for the Saviour we hold dear
Born in a stable not an inn
He came to earth our love to win
He started his task at an early age
With doctors in the temple—he did engage
When he grew older he began his mission
To carry out God's commission
For him to heal the sick the blind
And cast out evil from their mind
His loving work he did so well
He was known from plain to dell
But man's hatred had him crucified
Because his love they all denied
But hate could not keep him in the tomb
For love delivered him from doom
He came forth on the third day
And talked with friends along the way
We all rejoice that we can say
He arose—God Bless—Easter Day

　　　　—Della Moran, age 93

FRIENDS

Friendship is not bought with silver or gold,
Faithfulness and honesty can not be sold.
To be with a friend is most often a pleasure.
But having a true friend is a real treasure.

Good friends stick by you when things get bad.
Or they are not the best friends you've had.
Husband and parents can be your good friends,
But when they are gone, true friendship ne'er ends.

Think not of money and all of those worldly things,
On the journey to heaven they're not worth a thing.
Just a convenience down here on this earth,
Things of beauty and power, but of no real worth.

God is the best friend we can ever find,
He can always help us to have peace of mind.
If we walk the narrow path with Him at our side,
He will surely guide us whatever betide.

—Joyce Lenk

FRIENDSHIP

How can we explain friendship
and say exactly what it seems?
It would be the hardest thing for me
to say just what it means.
It has so many meanings
that change from heart to heart.
Is a true friendship
something that will never part?
Is there anything in life
that really lasts forever?
Love?   Hate?
Or even the word never?
Should we love a friendship
not knowing how long it will last?
All we can do is pray
that it won't be put in the past.
So I will treasure my friendships
as each day goes by
because you never know if our friendships are true
or when they will die.

—LeeAnn Hilligoss

BUTTONS MY FRIEND

I have a friend who is always there.
He is always beside me, no matter where.
If only everyone, could see his love,
They would say, he must be from above.

He never asks for much at all.
He makes me feel, like I'm ten feet tall.
He's my constant companion, thru thick or thin,
No matter how many problems, I have within.

I'm sure, by now, you are asking, Who can this be?
How could I find such a friend for me?
Where would I go to get such a friend?
Is it just a passing fancy, or maybe a trend?

Well, I guess I can tell you, right from the start,
Is the first thing you will need, is a big loving heart.
Next, comes the patience, to find the right one,
That will stay by your side, no matter what's done.

This friend that I have, is much better than most,
Because he's a Dachshund, I feel I can boast.
His colors, are black and tan, with just a little white.
That's why I named him Buttons, my friend, my delight.

—Mary Ellen Walther

FRIEND-SHIP

Friendship brings special things
to people who really care,
and when there's a special friend around
there's always something to share.

Friendship is a priceless gift,
with special moments untold.
For friendships blossom many things
that never could be sold!

Friendship is a meaningful word
that most can understand.
To hold a very strong friendship
goes together hand in hand.

So, think of friendships now and then,
and look what you may find.
That friends are very special
and forever being kind!

—Lauri-Young-Halm

RICKETY ROAD

There's an old road called Rickety Road,
Named for an old man's farm.
The farm and the road are rickety,
But they still do hold a charm.

They both can tell a story,
Of a time long ago,
When an old man, his horse and wagon,
Used to come and go.

He and his faithful horse Joey,
Worked the whole day long,
The old man had Joey for company,
And a cheerful, old-time song.

In the cold and the rain;
Or the heat of the sun,
Man and horse worked hard,
Although their work was never done.

They say the old man's Spirit,
Along with Joey pulling her load,
Still sing and work together,
As they travel the old Rickety Road.

—Jenny Lynne Becker

MY MASTER

My master got on the train one day
I waited, looking this way and that way;
I watched every train coming in the depot
I watched diligently for my master to show.

I would go and lay down, eat when need be
Waiting so patiently for my master to see;
We were great pals for so many years
We worked together, we're always real near.

Why did my master leave me this way?
Laying in that box, leaving to stay;
I will keep watch for my master, my friend
I will keep watch, until the very end.

One day I accidently slipped and fell
Right on the train track, and well;
Now I know where my master went
Dying that day, to him I was sent.

I drove his sheep, was his very best pal
Whenever I saw him, I'd wag my tail;
My master was the best in all the land
And he thought I was really grand.

—Donna Dyer

SACRIFICE

When one has to do what is best—
It really puts one to the test.
To give up something for another one—
Isn't so bad when all is said and done.
The end result is clear to see—
For all concerned we all are free
To continue life with all its glory
Forget the pain, forget the worry—
Treasure our win and we can afford
To leave what is behind and remember
                    our reward.
Is to give one another the love and
                    caring,
That has always been there and never-
                    ending.

                    —Rebecca J. Evans

SWEETHEART OF MY DREAMS

Sweetheart, oh how I miss you.
     Just to kiss you
Would make things seem right
For I'm lonely tonight.

Sweetheart, just to hold you again tenderly
Would mean this world to me.
     Just to see the sunlight of your smile
Would be my greatest consolation
For you are my everything.

The birds don't sing so sweet,
     When you're not neigh
Every star in the night
     Sends your message of love

And its far shining light tells me
You're up above

I can see sunlight streaming
From heaven above
And I hear you calling to me
Now it seems
     Oh how I miss you
     Sweetheart of my dreams

                    —Marlene Dittenber Shook

PERFECT WEEKEND

It was a feeling I just can't
                    describe.
A smile across my face I could not
                    hide.
As you held me in your warm
                    embrace,
You began slowly caressing my
                    face.
It was like in the beginning it felt
                    brand new.
You made me feel loved and wanted
                    too.
As we took the floor, everybody
                    glanced.
But you just held me closer as we
                    danced.
Your touch was like magic, it made me
                    melt
But I don't have to explain just how
                    I felt.
The feelings we share, I know will last
                    forever,
And for me to stop loving you will happen,
                    never.

                    —Angie Reda

LOST LOVE

As I lay thinking
There are two things I keep linking,
     love and despair.
After awhile one learns that the two go hand in hand
     because neither are ever fair.
When two people fall in love they are still two people
     with two minds. However, there is
     something that binds. That is the heart.
As two hearts become one, it is at that moment
     that love is found and forever bound.
The heart that feels the joys of tomorrow
     will also feel the pain and sorrow.
It is also the one thing that forgives all failings.

Just as you think you are beginning to
     accept your defeats with the grace of a woman,
     the emptiness returns and that small
     spark inside still burns.
And so you look into the beam of light,
     hoping your only dream is still in flight.

                    —Dawn Pace

ONLY LOVE

You are my only love;
     You remind me of a beautiful dove.
No one has ever cared before;
You give me confidence more and more.
You brighten each day;
How could you not stay?
With your golden blond hair and big blue eyes,
You never could tell me any lies.
You bring me so much happiness;
How life would be without you I could never guess.
Through good times and bad,
Nothing could ever make you mad.
I solved your problems you solved mine;
Together we worked things out just fine.
How could you leave me here;
Now who will know my fear?
You've gone away,
Never to return another day.
Now I kneel next to you on the ground;
To be with you someday I am bound.

                    —Lisa Pickett

WE LOVED

We loved,
     as love knew how.

Our not knowing hurt the other.
Full, yet empty
     we trod the path of souls imperceptively withering.

I KNOW YOU.

The mind, good hider that it is
     did not know,
     yet thinking knowing hurt the more.

The other danced in phantom form,
     but would not leave the soul quite alone,
until in rage the other said,
     I AM HERE.
     YOU DO NOT LOVE ME AS I AM,
     BUT I WILL BE AS I AM.

Wrenched from the grasp of that unknowing,
     the phantom form joined soul once more
     and soared.

                    —Kathleen Schuler

ONE OF A KIND

Love has found me once again
But this time it's for real
Now he's my lover and my friend
And nothing can change the way we feel

I tremble with every touch
It's the only one that makes me feel good
Is it possible to love too much
It'll only happen if it should

Our souls have combined
We grow closer each day
While our bodies interwind
In every single way

We are as radiant as the sun
And brighter than the morning dew
This feeling, I believe, is the one
That will eternally shine and remain anew.

—Tina Tischer

LOVE IS GREAT AND GRAND

Love is one of the greatest things
that can happen to man in his life,
Love can help him in choosing
a woman for a lovely wife.

Sometimes they don't court too long until
he will put the woman on the spot,
He will ask her to wear his ring,
and talk about getting the preacher
to tie the wedding knot.

Love will cause them to work real fast,
they will start planning for a church wedding
that will be first class.

They will start contacting flower girls
and someone to carry the wedding ring.
They are so deeply in love,
they are sure they are doing the right thing!

Marriage was in God's plan for woman and man,
if you will always look to Him
He will guide and bless you with a
helping hand.

—Dee Johnson

TRULY

What I must say, I can not.
Love is without words of mouth nor mind.
I shall say my love not with words,
but with this gentle touch of fingertips
to thy sweet, soft cheek.

To let you know that what fate brings forth,
my honest and wholesomely, pure love will surpass.
And it will be here in my eyes,
as you now see it.

For another time may not come
for me to take you in arms tightly
and whisper godly words.
I love thee beautiful one,
without fault to my eyes.

Love is much more than these heartfelt words,
and I will only and truly be able to tell you
from a final resting place,
in your precious memory,
memory that scans back and shows you that
I truly love you.

—Jervas J. Hyde

MY LOVE

My love,
Oh how cold would be
our home without love,
How warm our hearth
with hearts that fit like hand and glove.

My love,
How heaven sent
is a love well spent,
Never is it a waste
for love needs not haste.

My love,
Marrying for money
does not bring honey,
But to be as busy as a bee
will bring me close to thee.

—Sherrie L. Owen

SONG OF LOVE

Ah, love of mine awake my soul
from slumber low and deep,
Your vibrant song stir in my breast
a melody rich and sweet.

Awake within me chords of peace
to ring out through the night,
Create an endless beam of joy
that gives its ray of light.

And one day when my eyes shall close
in the deep, deep sleep of death,
Know also that my love for you
still beats within your breast.

For when our hearts were joined as one
while in us they did thrill,
Our destiny said they'd e'er be so
'till both in us were stilled!¶¶

—Barbara B. Frye

BECAUSE

Because you melted my heart and made
me love again.

Because you looked into my eyes and
took away the pain.

Because you make me smile when there
is no reason to.

Because my world has no sadness, as
long as I'm with you.

Because I know your love is mine and
you think mine is a treasure.

Because being in your arms is my
life's only pleasure.

Because you see that I'm imperfect
and can forgive my mistakes.

Because you believe our love is worth
the highest of all stakes.

Because the world was against us and
you said we wouldn't budge.

Our love is too beautiful and only
God should be our judge.

You asked why I love you?
Just Because Babe, Just Because.

—Carmen L. Rosario

A SINGLE APRIL ROSE

It begins to grow in early Spring
And takes away my woes,
A special, beautiful, wonderful thing,
A single April rose.

When it is time for birds to sing
Along the winding roads,
You can be sure your lover will bring
A single April rose.

My sweetheart gave me a beautiful ring
With a loving heart he chose,
Then plucked from a bush, for me his darling,
A single April rose.

A child will be coming to me in the Spring
And if it's a girl with bows,
I'll give her a name, that sweet little thing,
My baby April Rose.

—Barbara Farr Kelley

ODE TO AN OLD OAK

There is a large forested park
on the eastern edge of our town.
This morning I went out in the dark
and beneath an old oak sat down.

I remembered a warm July day
when beneath the old oak's boughs
two old friends, now lovers, lay
and to each other pledged their vows.

If the wise old oak could talk
of things seen 'neath its branches.
Do you think the old oak would balk
at telling of knowing glances?

A loving picnic was spread
with grapes and wine and cheese.
And the woman laughed and was glad
when the man gave her a kiss and a squeeze.

The day sped by as they talked and
before they knew it, it was time to go.
They declared to each other what old oaks know,
"We'll be back."

—John Weber Webb

MY APPLE TREE

When the hoary frost of winter
        Relaxed its hold possessive,
My apple tree began to bloom,
        Arrayed in dress quite festive.

By the wafting of the fragrance
        From the blooms, both pink and white,
Scores of bees were then attracted,
        Wings a-buzz in bright sunlight.

All collecting golden pollen,
        Making honey for their young,
Unaware of service rendered,
        Pollination had begun.

When the tree's first little apples
        Turned to red and grew so sweet,
A ravaging pair of Blue Jays
        Had themselves a daily treat.

But, God, in his omnipotence,
        Perceiving the diversion,
Sent "bride and groom" brave Cardinals,
        And stopped the Jay incursion.

—Bernice Yeoman

SILENT MELODY

Soft as a whisper it calls in the night
Sprightly it bounces from the dark to the light
Singing a song with no words to hear
Lovers alone lend it an ear

Sleeping realms unfold their bounteous sweets
Ripened and ready for sumptuous feasts
Soft and warm as it slides through the trees
Striking earth's orchestral strings
Heralding loudly and ever so proudly
It's time for the rites of spring

—Shawna Black

IRAZÚ*

We came up from the sea to Irazú
For mountains of feeling drew us
To summits and higher metaphors of our love.

Perfections spread from the ascending vistas;
And we knew that every problem yields to perspective
And the last summit is God.

Essences and eternities touched us
As we kissed in the silence, in the ice-cold winds.

Irazú! We who love understand you!
The depths and heights and red-hot power
That burns the night,
That cracks the world,
The geometry of ancient love and longing,
The deep source of searing death and life
Hidden in the mystery of the Center.

But also there were flowers in the bleakness,
Red and yellow in the sun's last touch,
Reconciling grandeur and grace,
Harmonizing Irazú's majestic drama
With the modest melody of our love.

*Semi-dormant Central American volcano

—Harold Raley

MAGNOLIAS ON THE BAYOU

In deep slumber lies acadiana.
December has arrived in South Louisiana.
Mother Nature's cold and silent hand,
has gently touched on cajun land.

There's a copper-tarnish on the cypress trees,
amber waters softly flow around their knees.
Of raven body and limb bearded oaks sigh at rest.
While ghostly egrets flow across the misty sky,
guided only by their past.

A peaceful silence fills the air.
Feast your eye, then cast a sign.
But wait! look there, beyond the marshy meadow.
Over there where light rendezvous with shadow.

Clouds part to a sunlit sky,
heaven's beacon come to visit.
in the sunlit-grayish haze — What is it?

A stately cone of emerald green,
a golden light coming from within.
Bathed in raindrops blue and silver bright
Twinkling in that heaven's light.

A giant Magnolia Tree,
A single blossom I can see.
A late bloom, I can't believe . . .
What is today???
                It's   Christmas Eve.

—Andy Garza, sr.

WE LOST

We're saying our final goodbye this morning;
the tears have ceased to flow.
Did this come upon us without any warning,
or did each of us secretly know?

We've been together for many years;
Shared a lot of times, good and bad;
But there came less laughter, then more tears,
And we found ourselves too often mad.

We just grew apart. No one to blame;
Long ago, you made my heart melt.
We've left only ashes where once there was flame;
We've played out the cards we once dealt.

We can't continue to play this game
At such a terrific cost.
Maybe both of us will forget the pain
Of the wonderful love that we lost.

— Diane E. Jones

IN MEMORIAM TO MY BELOVED FATHER, LEON SNIDER

Here's to you,
Daddy.

To continue to mourn for you would,
In essence, do injustice to your memory.

Rather, in gratitude and blessings,
Do I celebrate
You.

Your being,
Your life,
Our connection
Eternal.

It is my sincerest hope that
I do you
Honor.

My love and respect for you are
Timeless.

Here's to you,
Daddy.

— Penny Snider Gaffin

NANA'S FAREWELL

Logan and Stephanie what can I do?
I know I'll be only a phantom to you
Only a picture that hangs on a wall
With no loving memories you can recall

No rock a bye baby and no creepy mouse
No dressed up kings and queens marching
proudly through the house
But maybe there's something that we can share
Besides the color of eyes and hair

When you call a make believe friend to play
Could it be me? I know such games to play!
Or when you're wishing upon a star
Could you say one wish instead, to Nana
And I will wink back at you
Tho time is a curtain
And grant all the wishes I can,
That's for certain

If you need a friend to speak in God's ear
I'll be more than happy to volunteer
He owes us a blessing, you and this grandmother
For we didn't have time to get to know each other

— Barbara J. Morrison

A MOTHER'S LOVE

A cloud engulfs the sun,
will it rain or will it pass?
No one knows what lies within
this dark mysterious mass.
Some predict and try to warn others,
Then there are those who shelter
and protect,
People we call Mothers.
Whether it be the bright sun, or
the cloud's darkest shade,
There's only one thing for certain,
A Mother's love will never fade.

— Troy Jarrett

SHE DIED OLD

— remembering Grandma

She aged too soon.
She wasn't supposed to —
grow old.

This woman in a wheelchair —
unrecognizable.
Her brown hair turned gray.
The once laughing face
now sad, mad.

It wasn't fair!
Her spirit once young, now weary.
The years had turned on her.
Betrayed her!

Gone were parents, husband, friends.
Remaining were only —
those younger.

They wanted her to
be the same.
She couldn't.
Her body said no.
Her spirit died.

— Rita Ginger-Miller

THE OLD CEMETERY

The pioneer men and women
stood with bowed heads,
In unison the Lord's Prayer
was reverently said.
The babies, the elderly,
each person laid to rest,
Under the stately oak trees
ending their adventure West.

Over one hundred years later
at this same location,
This small abandoned cemetery
is in need of restoration,
Where the cattle once grazed
now a deep thicket grows,
And a single monument base
amid the grave-sunken rows.

The tombstones have fallen
into the ravine below,
But if you look closely
they sometimes still show.
Their records are long lost
from the pages of time,
They're somebody's ancestors
perhaps yours or mine.

— Amy C. Kirchhoff

SUMMER WIND

The summer wind rolls off the sea
and laughing, stings my eyes;
it strokes my hair with playful hands
and to our mutual surprise
I kiss its salt-tinged mouth.

The summer wind slips through the vines
and sighing, strokes my face
with loving honeysuckle hands,
and in its gentlest embrace,
I kiss its satin mouth.

The summer wind skims through the trees
and singing, takes my hand;
we dance until we trip on stars,
until we make the sky expand —
I kiss its moonlight mouth.

—Bianca Covelli Stewart

FROM THE WINDOW

The parlor window open wide,
A pillow on the sill,
Gram and I would lean outside
To watch the people mill.

Up from the subway they'd ascend
Half blinded by the light.
Daily News in hand, they'd wend
Their ways home for the night.

On windy days men's hats would fly;
Fedoras filled the air.
With the breeze the men would vie,
But seldom won the tear.

On days when Mother Nature failed
To exercise her clout:
As the passengers derailed,
Their lives we'd figure out.

Our pleasures were so simple then;
We had a clearer view
Of the things we needed when
The T.V.'s still were few.

—Mary F. Walker

CONSTANCY

We sat by a campfire
My friend and I
Waiting for nothing
But time to go by

It was quiet and still
As we sat neath the stars
We liked how we felt
The whole universe ours

We pondered the stars
Dotting up space
Ever widening circles
Of God's evening grace

Stars being so stable
They stay where they're born
Ne'r leaving anyone
Lost and forlorn

My hope rose as I sat there
That my friend might be
Like a star in the heavens
Constant to me

—Peggy Jean Mason

THE HIGH PLACES

After many years and much searching,
I think I have found my mountain,
For life holds many a hooded peak
Above childhood's gushing fountain.
I started up this rocky slope,
A survival kit strapped to my back,
But I hadn't reckoned with biting snow,
Or the strength of sneaky downdrafts.
I hadn't known of sudden drops,
I must place my feet with care.
But all about as I upward went,
Above the snow were wheels of prayer
Forever turning in the rarefied air.
    The peak looms above, a few feet away,
    But my gaze is riveted down below
    Where a silver ribbon of remembrance flows,
    The place of beginnings never touched by the snow.

—Dorothy Faye Osner

THE OLD VIOLIN

The old violin was resting near the wall.
Yes, it was old, but aren't we all?
All in the era when its strings were in tune,
As only its master knew how to do.

It travelled to villages, lakes, and towns,
Always ready to make its rounds.
The tango, the two-step, and the gentle waltz
Were deftly fingered by its waiting boss.

It supplied a meaning to a family of five.
They often accompanied it on a ride
And were thrilled by its music, so quick and so sweet,
That its requirements had to fulfill and meet.

But a violin is just like man:
The older it gets, the longer its span,
The more love on both is easily given,
And we long for the music it gave to us living.

Such music seems very hard to recapture,
And nostalgia creeps in to a very high fraction.
We realize that the beauty, the music, and grace
Of the old violin just can't be replaced.

—Edelia Jenson

SEWING MEMORIES

Me and my well-used sewing machine
With many bright spools of thread,
Sit amid many yards of cloth
While a table with prints now is spread.

Many patterns are stacked just waiting
Neatly, everywhere you can see,
While I sit and ponder, which one to use
Or what color or shape it will be.

As I sew, I think of the many times
When a child how I watched Mother sew,
Bright dresses so pretty, came from her machine
Far into the night, while her lamps burned low.

She sewed every color and piece of cloth
Into dresses and shirts, just anything,
Just for us children, we were every size,
Her nimble fingers, happy smiles did bring.

So as I sew my thoughts wonder back
Just for a little while,
To Mother, as she sat, where I sit now
With her machine and a happy smile.

—Dorothy Behringer

God is the pearl
In the oyster of life.
Will we love Him or cast Him aside
And spend our lives searching
For something unknown
To ease the longing inside?

—**Margaret Peterson**

WHO IS THIS MAN?

Who is this man who healed the sick,
 and caused the blind to see?
Who is this man with so much love,
He died for you and me?

Who is this man, who took my sins,
and washed them white as snow?
Who is this man who takes my hand,
and directs the path I go?

Who is this man, who raised the dead,
and walked upon the sea?
Who is this man, the only man,
who can set all people free?

Who is this man, with just His voice,
can calm a stormy wind?
Who is this man who died, and then,
returned to life again?

His name is called Emmanuel,
the Blessed Holy One;
Prince of Peace, All-Mighty God,
the Father's only Son.

Nature's storms or man-made wars,
or an evil man's device;
can't separate the love I have,
for this man called Jesus Christ.

—**Linda Meche**

Lift up your eyes on high, and
behold who hath created these things.
Isaiah 40:26

Truly our fellowship is with the Father,
and with His Son, Jesus Christ.
I John 1:3

INCREDIBLE

How wonderful it is to think
 That I His voice have heard,
Who the glorious universe
 Fashioned with a word.

Majestic, lofty, sovereign,
 God the Holy One;
Yet to a simple heart made known
 Through Jesus Christ, His Son.

Comprehension of my God
 Is so very dim:
He's far beyond my highest thoughts,
 Yet I may walk with Him.

So much of the Omnipotent
 Is in mystery sealed,
Yet now His burning heart of love
 To me has been revealed.

Oh most great God, I worship Thee,
 In silence do I bow,
Who hast been, art, and will be
 In the eternal now.

—**Marjory Windsor**

CHRISTIAN RECIPE

The Word	Prayer
Understanding	Tears
Repentance	Fear
Baptism	Teaching
Faith	Bible Studies
Holy Ghost	Minister's Preaching

Begin with the word and with understanding keep it steady
Add sincere repentance and baptism when ready
Now a dash of faith can be used at anytime
And the Holy Ghost is a must as you'll find
Cover the dish with prayer and tears
And humble it with Godly fear
Then simmer it with lots of teaching
Bible studies and a Minister's preaching
Now turn up the fire and keep it hot
For cold Christian is a spoiled pot.
Now serve with determination and desire.
Last reminder: Keep it on fire!

—**Deb Pogue**

CRUCIFIED WITH CHRIST

"Once upon a cruel tree,"
 "Died our Lord,"—"for you,"—"for me;"
"Caring not the shame "He" knew,"
"Nor the pain that "He" went through!"
"His heart's desire was to do the will,"
"Of God,"—"His Father,"—"on that hill!"
"He said"—"Not my will,"—"but "Thine" be done,"
"Then "God's Divine" "will" "was done,"—"through His Son!"
"He said,"—"It is finished,"—"on that day;"
"And "His" "Precious" "Blood" "washed our sins away;"
"If we will but "Repent" of "Sin,"
"And let our "Precious" "Saviour" "In"!"
"Oh!"—"Dear Lord,"—"that we" might be,"
"Crucified,"—"Dear Christ,"—"with Thee;"
"Dead to self,"—"and worldly gain,"
"Willing,"—"Lord,"—"to bear the pain!"
"For," "if for Jesus," "we do stand,"
"We'll "suffer much" at the "hands" of "man;"
"But at the "End,"—"we'll "See" "His" "Face,"
"And "Know" "Complete,"—"Amazing Grace!"

—**Naomi Chandler**

RISEN INDEED

With sorrowful hearts they went to His tomb
 Not understanding how they could go on
There was not even a glimmer of hope
 Only fear and despair
Who would roll away the heavy stone?

Mary, the first at the tomb
 Could not believe her tearful eyes
For behold; the stone had been rolled away
 She knelt and looked in where her Lord had been
Joy beyond belief
 Swept over her heart where once there was utter grief

The Lord is not here but is risen indeed
 Were the words she heard from the young men in white
The Lord is not here but is risen indeed
 Were the words her Lord spake as He appeared

Risen indeed!
 Just as He had promised He would
Now there was reason to believe
 Every prayer would be heard
Risen indeed!
 To fulfill God's Holy word!

—**Faye Riley**

In the beginning did darkness prevail
No creatures were seen, neither large nor small;
When the sky tore open releasing the hail
With creatures abundant, both short and tall.
From out of the mist man soon strode
Commanding the land, leader of all.
Then horses sprang forth and man soon rode
To the center of life — the Creator's great hall.
Then the Creator weighed out the pros and the cons
Judging their worth — rating His work;
But seeing his creature — clothes did he don
He knew in an instant man's single-most quirk.
    From the garden emerged a figleaf-clad female
    The devil, He knew, had told quite a tale.

    —Deborah Moore

DID GOD MAKE A MISTAKE?

God makes no mistakes, it's true.
But after spending many hours with you,
Did the Great Creator who brings the rain
Make a mistake when He made the brain?

It's hard to explain just how I feel,
Seeing a loved one whose brain won't heal.
Broken bones and scratches seem to mend.
"Why not the brain?" I say over and over again.
Oh, it's not just our family, but others as well,
That have experienced this "earthly" Hell.

Driving thirty miles is no big chore;
It's having the strength to open his door.
When Rex says, "I don't know and I don't know why,"
I reach for his hand and look to the sky.
"Things just happen" and "It was meant to be"
Are not very good answers to me.

So, I guess I'll just keep wondering why
Until the day I join Him in the sky.
I know others are wondering the same:
God, did You make a mistake when You made the brain?

    —Joy Smith

I WONDER

I wonder if it would be right
For very young girls to sneak out at night
When one should really be in bed
And listening to what their mother said.

Stay home for now
Just don't say "how."
The time isn't here
But stay home, stay near.

You're old enough to understand
Yet you're not, on the other hand,
Listening is a part of growing
So just keep trying and the knowing,

Will grow with you and become a part
Of a very pure and trusting heart
That everyone is bound to Love
Even the good great God up above.

    —Clara Rosinsky

A THOUGHT ON DEATH

When Life's curtain begins to close for me
And my final hour draws near,
When the end of my earthly journey I see
    With time no longer here.

Will my anguished soul cry: "Not yet,
    Just a few more years, I pray,
I've much to do ere Life's sun is set."
    Are these the words I would say?

May I live each day that's given to me
    For the work I was meant to do,
Being the best person that I can be
    Spreading joy and gladness too.

So when the time comes for me to go.
    Laying my unfinished tasks aside,
May I willingly leave this world below
    Forever with Him to abide.

    —Minnie F. Harris

FEAR NOT . . . THE TEENAGERS BELIEVE

We believe in God, and the trueness of his words and deeds,
even among the mob that obstructs the paths of our daily needs.

We believe in God, despite the disbelief in today's worlds by others,
for this Earth was greatly cared for and respected by the ancestors of our fathers and mothers.

We believe in God, because we know, somewhere he is there,
and will be with us to comfort us, through all of life's despair.

We believe in God, despite whatever your tongue may say,
because we see, and hear, and feel his presence, each and every day.

We believe in God, in the midst of all of the material possessions that are,
for all one has to do when in disbelief is to gaze upon a star.

We believe in God, although this may be hard for you to digest,
for despite our belief, we still put many Commandments to the test.

We believe in God, for he holds the answer to internal freedom,
and because it is the only way to his eternal kingdom.

We believe in God, even in this Godforsaken world,
because he has given to us, a flower of love, unfurled.

We believe in God, because of all of the things he gives to us,
and so that one day, he, us, and our love shall be set free in trust.

We believe in God, no matter what you or you or you may say,
for we shall believe in God, until our last Earth liven day.

    —Scott B. Malice

DARCI

She carried the crown
And she looked so sweet,
This tiny red haired child.

Long gingham dress
That swished at her feet,
As she sort of danced
                down the aisle.
Look at me folks,
She almost seemed to say,
As she bestowed each with a
                generous smile,
I'm the star of this show.
And I guess you know,
Born this month, I'm Granny's
                only GRANDCHILD.

—Mabel E. Ward

SOMETIMES

Sometimes what I want to be
Is the little girl you see in me.
With little girl fears and little girl tears
And you there to hold me and wipe them away.

Sometimes what I want to be
Is the good friend you see in me.
To be there for you, for whatever you need,
Is my one goal in life and I will succeed.

Sometimes what I want to be
Is the lover that you see in me.
Each time we make love outshines before
And I could hardly ask for more.

You're quite a person, as many know
And I have learned to love you so.
So take me as all . . . all rolled into one,
Little girl, best friend, lover and then,
Someday maybe even your wife,
That's what I want for the rest of my life.

—Caitlin Woods

MY GRANNY

A Granny is a lot of fun,
And even though I'm only one,
She does the nicest things for me.
(She'll be worn out by the time I'm three.)
    She sings a lot and dances, too.
    She teaches me to eat a few
    Vegetables and things like that.
    She won't get mad when I'm a brat.
She stays so sweet and good and kind.
She always knows what's on my mind.
She seems to know that her granddaughter
Would really like a glass of water.
    There's here no generation gap
    'Cause Granny holds me on her lap
    And tells me that she loves me, too,
    And rocks me when the day is through.
When Daddy and Mommy must go out,
They ask you to stay, and without a doubt
You'll pick me up and hold me tight
And answer, "Yes, I'll sit tonight."
    This poem really means to say,
    "Have a happy, happy day!
    And please remember little Annette
    Has the best Granny a girl could get!"

—Annie Simonini

On behalf of her tiny daughter, to
"Granny" (Mrs. E.J. Simonini)

YOU ARE THE ONE WHO MADE ME; ME

As a young girl when things were strange and new,
You were always the one that I could go to.

Now that I am older and grown,
I realize you made the morals that are now my own.

I hope you understand Grandma, that it is you,
Who made me what I have grown into.

After all of these years I have had to see,
You are the one who made me; me.

—Jason Hannam

SUMMER'S GIRL

Summer's girl, with the sun caught in your hair,
You walk the beach, while the gulls soar above,
Shading your eyes from the glare.
You, who are touched with the gold of the sun,
Feel the breeze off the sea, and laugh your delight
as you run.
The beach calls to you, Summer's girl, with its treasure
of glistening shells,
You answer its call, with a song in your heart,
A song that you know so well.
Twilight is a time to reflect, as you pause at the
end of the day,
Pink turns to grey, as day fades into night, and the
clouds go drifting away.
The moon sends its beam, from the Heavens above,
With a sheen in the water below, and you call out
his name,
As you think of the one, whom you love.
Summer's girl, you live for your day in the sun,
And when the chill's on the air and Summer's long gone,
You'll hold this day close, when you and your love
were one.

—Barbara W. Fleming

THE CHILD

You imagine a world of innocence,
 With your young mind naive to the real world.
With everyday that is filled with nonsense,
Nighttime is secured with a blanket furled.
Dreams complete with boundless exaggeration,
Thought's "running wild" inside of your mind,
Eyes filled with vivid imagination,
And yet to reality, you are blind.
Living in a world of simplicity;
Lucky to live the life in which you do,
Lost in a world of creativity,
Carefree, courageous, and spirited too.
Jealous I am, for I no longer can
Live in a world in which I lived in then.

—Jeff Wendt

THE DREAM OF A CHILD

There once lived a child who hadn't a toy,
 but he dreamed of them nightly in all of his joy.
And off in his slumber into his toy land
he dreamt of castles built in the sand.
Inside of the castles were toys great and small.
The tin soldiers indeed were the greatest of all.
They stood tall in their glory and strong in their pride
awaiting the battle marching in stride.
Onward my men the child would say
go forth and win this battle today.
So off they went and the battle was won.
Good work my men your job is done.
Then he'd shake their hands and say good bye
I'll see you in my dreams another night.
And off he slept in a soundless sleep
Til the angels awakened him to take him to keep.
You are a brave soldier they said to the boy.
We'll take you with us to a land full of toys.

—Theresa M. Schott

A TRIBUTE TO ALL LITTLE LEAGUERS

It is with pride that we watch these leaguers.
 As they parade around.
And we are proud because we can say,
"These boys are representatives of our town."
On the baseball diamond, the boys learn sportsmanship
And other traits which earn them recognition.
And will someday help them become good citizens
And merit them a good position.
We can all rest assured as we watch the game,
From our seats in the stands,
That these Little Leaguers under the
 coaches and managers.
Are in mighty capable hands.
Yes, congratulations should certainly be given,
To each and every Little Leaguer.
Don't get me wrong, the credit due to the parents
 Is much more than meager.
The father surely deserves acclaim,
 For teaching his boy tactics of being a winner.
And orchids to the mother,
 Who warms over a dinner.
True sometimes these little guys
 get on dad's nerves.
But, when all is said and done,
You can often hear dad, yell at the
game,
"That Boy out there,
 He's my son."
—Stanley Pavlick

REMEMBER AND LOVE THE SOUND

I remember and love the sound of evil
 the breaking glass of the windowpane
and Mrs. Collins'
                    Naughty boy no
                    Naughty boy no
Momma would be in her
blue print dress
when I got spanked
and the belt
would crack
like the complaint of that fallen tree
in the woods
where my yellowed baseball lies now
I was gonna be
an old timer
with a pitcher of lemonade and
stories on a honeyed back porch
but I was a naughty boy.

—Kwana A.L. Martinez

UPSY DOWN

Upsy down, bouncing all around
 My daddy held me
  upon his knee,
  tossing into the
  air, then caught me.

Upsy down, bouncing all around
 My Grandpa, held me
  upon his knee,
  threw me in the air,
  then said wee.

Mommy put me in my crib, to sleep.
 I tumbled, tossed then wept.
 My tummy felt wishy washy.
Upsy down bouncing all around
 playing maybe fun for some
 but not for me,
 upon my daddy's knee.
Upsy down and all around.
 Oh! Mommy, Please help Me.

—Ethel J. Morsey

THE LOFT

In the loft,
 I can have fun,
Sitting in my little
Hideout,
Made out of
Walls of straw, and
An old blanket,
Thinking of things
To do, on a
Hot summer's day,
Jumping off the loft's
Edge, landing in
The bed of straw,
Seeing the straw
Come down like yellow
Yarn falling,
Walking on the wooden plank,
Bouncing up and down,
Jumping in the old
Grain wagon,
And falling on
The hard ground.

—Jennifer Conboy, age 11

OLDUVAI
Life is. Older than Olduvai.
Granite gods fall
Like rain from a leaden sky.
Time is eternal.
Man stands out in time
As on glass do the tracks of a fly.

    —Kris Paul Killingsworth

MY SONG
Childish excitement kept me blind.
The world would be mine forever.
Futile expectations led me on,
But failure answered every endeavor.

All I've ever wanted — ever dreamed
    could be mine
Seems to have vanished in the
    tarnished pages of time.
My world now is empty —
    I own not a thing.
Just hope in tomorrow and
    what it might bring.

    —Becke Resor

FATHER TIME
We watch, we watch old Father Time
His old hands move so slow
They falter on the clock of time
He suffers pain and woe.

He limps toward the new year
His back is bent with age
The conflicts of the past year
Have ravaged the old sage.

He travels down the path of life
From new year to the old
He's greeted by the winter's chill
Which makes his blood run cold.

He never laments, never gripes
Regarding his sad fate
He's cheerful when the new year starts
But, downcast when it grows late.

His passage leads through hail and rain
Biting winds that never cease
He staggers through the blinding snow
To year's end and final peace.

    —Raymond Le Rendu

LIFE
What sense can we make of this life?
We rush about hurry—skurry,
Life passes so quickly,
But can we mortals not enjoy
    a moment in all of the flurry?

What is life but many moments?
Are they treasured memories?
Do they fill your soul with
    happiness or with torment?

We must savor each moment,
For life will not linger.
Joy and grief will become one,
When with no final farewell, we meet
    our Redeemer.

    —Linda French

STILL ON THE GROUND
Who in the world can control their emotions
unhindered control, rendering not their anger fierce
Who in the world can say with the motion
the lack of control should make my heart pierce

Perhaps in the eyes of an infant the answer can truly be seen
their unspoken language can be so complex
their gurgled expression can be unexplainably clean
Yet closed minded disenlightened adults can
surely tell what they want next

Who knows? Do you? How I feel about this situation?
About how a child can let it flow and let it go
and give us all mental rehabilitation
Is it something the world will never know

The babe cries for a bottle, in getting it is contempt
then goes to sleep without a sound
in trying to understand we are exempt
We look to the sky for answers and yet we can't see
that they are still on the ground.

    —Scott Allen Beatty

THE CYCLE OF LIFE
Sometimes I feel . . .
    I'm spinning, it's a never ending cycle.
    A spiral of emotions, every revolution takes me lower.
    No way to move up, just down.
    Directions change, things remain the same.
    I'm pulled lower, the force is too strong.
    I try to get free, they entangle me.
    There is no way out, I cry for help.

Someone says . . .
    "This is life, the cycle is never ending.
    He will come in time, He will set you free.
    Stop searching for an end that can never be.
    He is the only one who can set you free."

Still . . .
    The cycle continues. There is no way out.
    No way to move up, just down.
    I'm drowning.
    I want to be free.
    Please Lord, come for me!

    —Mary Pershall

LIFE'S SEASONS
Spring of childhood
Fair of face,
Growing and learning
Life to taste.

Summer of youth
The world's yours to take,
Planning and dreaming, not a minute to waste.
Meaning of life you constantly seek,
Stand tall youth, the world's at your feet!

Fall of maturity
Constantly striving within,
Taking stock of life; where you're going, where you've been.
Working and toiling, burning candles at both ends,
Summer's dreams you can now see just around the bend.

Winter of old age
Weak and frail,
Unfinished dreams now of little avail.
Soon the body to dust will return,
But the soul of spring's childhood will eternally burn.

    —Judy McLamb Smith

BIRTH TO DEATH

Fluffy quilts cover a baby-plump body
  as two tiny lungs emit a robust cry.
Midget toes wriggle tirelessly;
then the hairless head nods sleepily.
All is well.
Slowly, the little body s t r e t c h e s
and makes room for BIGNESS.
Soon, little hands are writing numbers
and hiding baby snakes in apron pockets.
Then, one by one,
the jonquil moments fade away.
Tulip kisses and daisy days are replaced
with peeling potatoes and mowing the hay.
After many stars have lost their twinkle,
and a jillion moons have slid behind the horizon,
the threadbare quilts cover a slightly bent frame.
Breaths come in short, labored wisps.
The bald head nods slowly and
finally
all is well.

—Ruth L. Spaugh

THE WEB

As we walk through life
We are surrounded by an unseen web
This web is the bonds of thought
The bonds of emotion, love, hate, fear
I just call them strings
The strings that make you care
The strings that make you cry
The strings between two people
That almost make you high
The strings of trust, love and hope
But beware of the strings that make you dance
To another person's song
The strings that wear your heart out
If you hang from them too long
The strings we ought to have
Are the ones we weave ourself
Strings that make us happy
Strings that make us sing
Strings that make us smile
In the web that is unseen

—Henry Michael Jones

PRESENT TENSE WISHING

I gazed out over the melancholy shades of winter
 and wished for spring;
    rebirth, recycle.
Spring danced about me in hues of green and blue
and I wished for summer;
    growing, blooming.
Summer splashed itself across my windowpane
and I wished for fall;
    turning, changing.
Fall traipsed across the fields leaving trails of brown
and I wished to be older;
    adult, responsible.
Mid-year I stared across my cluttered desk
and wished for middle age;
    stability, domestication.
Mid-life I watched my children fight
and wished for retirement;
    wisdom, respect.
I lay on my deathbed and wish for my youth, spring;

I never got what I wanted.

—Sonora A. Quick

WHAT'S IN A DREAM?

Hopes.
  Desires.
Wishes.
Needs.
Ideals. Hopes. Desires. Wishes. Needs.
Energy that moves you through a day.
Energy that inspires you through a night.
Visions.
Shady figures. Shadows.
You.
Reflections of an inner self.
Smiles. Twinkling eyes. Floating thoughts.
Your true self.
Hope.
What's in a dream?
Life.

—Kris M. Eiring

APPEARANCES

I stand on a mountain and look below,
 And watch a river as it flows.
It seems so small from where I stand,
Yet that river is oh, so grand.

I stand in a valley and look above,
And wonder how people ever find love.

From where I stand, the world seems vast,
Yet love will come, and love will last.

I stand on a rock and look ahead,
And see a journey I have to tread.

It seems so long from where I stand,
Yet the end will come, sooner than planned.

I stand by a mirror and look and see,
The image that everyone thinks is me.
Yet the real me has feelings and also dreams,
And I know things aren't what they
always seem.

—Melissa Wenczkowski

WHAT LIFE IS

Life is like a roller coaster,
 With all its ups and downs.

I always thought things would look better,
But it's been forever.

It seems that things have been
Worse for me than for the others.

Now I have a dreadful disease
That's filled me with sorrow,
They say hope for the cure tomorrow,
But they don't know how I feel,
I just wish I could heal.

With all the love from my mother,
And all the pain from my brother,
It's driving me insane.

I have a broken heart that's never healed,
I wish it could be sealed.
I wish I would have never lost him,
Now I realize it has cost me.
Maybe he'll be back someday,
And love me the way he did before he left me.

I know one day things will be better,
So now I just take it day by day,
And hope toward then — when it's better.

—Karla Lee Griffin

HOME

Home is where the living is easy
And the warmth and the presence
Of the people there is all
That is needed.

—Dennis J. Mullins

LOVES RELEASE

Lost in a wicked wilderness.
Ominous storm clouds filled the
bleak sky. Does anyone hear
my silenced cry?

Every hope choked by unconquerable
fear. Journeys throughout the
wilderness prove peace does not
exist here.

Then Love looked down and saw
my pain. For me, and the
wilderness he became flesh
with an omnipotent name.

Scorned—Jesus endured all—
including the heartrending
shame. For every soul he
took a blame.

On a rugged cross he hung.
Yet death defeated; sin washed
clean. Oh, how the cherubims
sung!

Alive, a king he rules
and reigns—his order is
charity. Unspeakable joys
now never cease. Love is released.

—Ginger Clark

MY FATHER

My father is very sweet and caring,
He loves me very much.
His hands are big and strong, yet
Gentle to the touch.

He praises me when I'm good.
He punishes me when I'm bad.
He even tries to cheer me up,
Whenever I am sad.

Though every man has his bad points,
My father has but few.
He just wants me to be careful
In what I say and do.

I know what he wants for me
Is just what is right.
I know that I am special
In my father's sight.

He wants me to act like a lady
And not like a child.
He wants me to be good,
And not run off wild.

He says "NO" to smoking and drinking
And such things.
But even my father knows,
"It takes an angel to grow wings."

He doesn't expect miracles,
All he wants is my best,
And as long as I behave,
His mind will be at rest.

—Sylvia Jo Tevepaugh

ONE LIFE TO GIVE

Way up on Golgotha's hill—
Everything seemed to be calm and still.
The clouds were hovering dark and low
As three crosses stood there in a row.

The man on the middle cross wore a crown of thorns—
The two men on each side looked rugged and worn.
On the face of the middle man I saw grief and sorrow—
Heavy on his shoulders were the sins of tomorrow.

From his crown of thorns the blood was dripping—
With the sword in his side, his life was slipping.
The nails were a symbol of the world in his hands
His mission on earth, victory over sin, was finished.

—Frances D. Knight

MARTIN LUTHER KING JR.

His choice was one for all,
He followed his heart and was true.
He was proud to be who he was,
He did what he had to do.

A man of courage, bravery, and strength,
He watched the injustice of the world around him.
Black men beat, Indian women hurt,
He decided it was time to do something to save them.

There were two ways for him to go,
Violently or with peace.
This decision was the biggest he would make,
He took action, but prejudice didn't decrease.

White power people became more and more enraged,
They shunned other races without a thought.
The cruelty they inflicted upon others,
Did not end with just a bullet shot.

Just because of the color of skin and of customs,
White power felt they were supreme.
This is when a great man, Martin Luther King Jr.,
Exclaimed the words, "I have a dream!"

—Sharon Holwick

CONVICTIONS AGAINST EVIL

I just want to live—as God intended,
Not as the world dictates, but with love blended.

I just want to be relieved—from life's strife and battles,
And just love, as was meant to be.

I just want to be me—Goodhearted and Kind;
Not intending to hurt, just caring and allowing.

I just want to be free—as we were born to be;
No man should command another, not family, or said kin,
    And certainly not me!

I just want to live—in respect and fairness,
Not of bitterness and un-truths.

I have seen the Devil's loathsome face!
His stab, leaving scars of distaste!

Giving into the Devil as his wanton mate,
Would determine a horrible fate!

I just want to love—to be loved;
My heart sings this song, hoping and waiting.

I just want to die knowing—
I hadn't just lived for the Devil's pleasure!

I believe that "Good" will triumph over "Bad!"
And by example—show courage and strength,
    To end in a Victorious Fight!

—Nancy D. Rice

THE AGE OF DISENCHANTMENT

America, please know that we're all insecure,
　　Frustrated by panic and doubt,
While politicians righteously insist to us,
　　That they have all our problems worked out.

To stop murderers from murdering we imprison ourselves
　　Behind deadbolts and safelocked doors.
To stop rapists from raping, we lock women inside
　　And tell them "the fault is all yours."

It's alright to seize houses and property of thugs,
　　Because criminals make us so mad.
We pay actors and athletes incredible money
　　And say about teachers "how sad."

Small justice is excercised in this world we accept,
　　Behind an anger apparent.
Pursuit of happiness? We're destroying ourselves,
　　In the Age of Disenchantment.

　　　　　—K. V. Dannis

RUNNIN' AWAY

Don't run away
From those problems you've had today.
I know it may be hard
For I've had some myself these days.

Oh, don't run away, don't turn your back,
For if you do they will grow on you and may start
to haunt you.

Tryin' to put the key in the ignition so fast,
Turnin' up the volume on your radio to full blast

Oh, don't run away, don't turn your back,
For if you do they will grow on you and may start
to haunt you.

You come back home, bills are due,
Your house is a mess,
Children cryin', your patience is dyin'.

Oh, don't run away, don't turn your back,
For if you do they will grow on you and may start
to haunt you.

　　　　　—Marissa L. Dray

HOMELESS

He stood on the corner clutching the Book in his hand,
Pulled it to his chest and prayed he'd understand.
The road that lay before him was not of his choosing,
The tears in his eyes — life, a gamble for the losing.

"A nickel? . . . a dime? . . . a dollar?" he would cry.
But they couldn't feel his hurting; they didn't even try.
Considering only the garments in which he was clothed,
A beggar and his stench they openly loathed.

He wandered aimlessly by day and even by night,
Seeking a kindred being to share in his fright.
Chastised by demands of existing, if only day to day,
The urgency of the present, he knew he'd find his way.

The gaunt man slowly knelt at the foot of the bed
Offering thanks once again — a place to lay his head.
Never stopping the struggle with impending doom
Until now — a calm Spirit moves quietly about the room.

His mind in a stupor as he slips 'tween the sheets,
Pangs of hunger, kissed by numbness, his body now meets
As the pillow cradles 'round him — a gentle, bearded face —
Now christened in comfort with the Lord's unfailing grace.

　　　　　—Jeana Celeste Ferguson

YOU MAY ASK WHAT IS PEACE?

Some have found it in a garden . . .
Some have found it in a stream
For the Peace of true contentment
Is the depth of every dream;
Some have found it on the hilltops
And the search is ages old.
But no man has ever found it
In a selfish strife for gold . . .

You will never rest contented
If you serve yourself alone
From your comrades, from your neighbors
Come the peace that you would own
It is born of love and friendship
In a thousand ways tis told
But no man has ever found it
In a selfish strife for gold . . . .

　　　　　—Joan Malone

WHITE POWDER

An evil villain monster
stalks a proud strong land.
He lures away our children
White powder's killing them.

The monster has no boundaries
He knows you'll sell your soul.
Wasted moments of sheer pleasure
this deadly poison takes its toll.

Lurking in the school yard
Hovering in cover of night;
He takes from golden satchels
White powder to give flight.

In ebony steel he makes his exit
Reaped of blood and bitter tears.
Satan is the dealers sentry;
Their reward our babies souls.

Harvest your sleazy profits
Pyre the tainted gold.
Hell fires will soon consume you.
Tell me; was it worth your soul?

　　　　　—Linda A. Hicks

THE RACE

I cry for you because I see . . .
the sick and the dying,
the fallen and the lame,
the old and the forgotten.

I cry for you because I hear . . .
the moans of wounded soldiers,
the cries of hungry children,
the yells of the unjust.

I cry for you because I feel . . .
the pain of the abused,
the sorrow of the old,
the pity of the desperate.

I cry for you because I know . . .
love can exist,
peace can ring true,
and hope can grow.

I cry for you because these
are the elements that make you whole.

I cry for you . . .
Mankind.

　　　　　—Gregory S. Costner

I DREAMT . . .

I dreamt of a world
full of happiness,
while the rain pitter-patted
on my blue and white umbrella.

I dreamt of a world
full of peace and joy,
while the thunder clouds roared
with jubilant cries.

I dreamt of a world
full of good not bad,
while the lightning flashed bright
saying it was alright.

I dreamt of a world
that afternoon day,
as I sat on my swing
in our imperfect world.

—Brigid A. Elliott

NO LULLABY

As she passes by the alleys,
Her bright eyes scan the street.
She clutches a small teddy bear
With torn and tattered feet.

As they cuddle close together
Beside a hard, brick wall
She softly sings a lullaby
To the matted, little ball

She finds a crude, old shelter
To keep them from the storm—
Her head is throbbing worse today
Her skin is damp and warm.

Again she sings the lullaby,
But this time tears appear.
She kisses her precious teddy good-bye
And escapes her pain and fear.

On a lonely corner of the street,
Lies a battered little bear,
With no one to sing a lullaby
Or to give it love and care.

—Lori J. Ryder, age 15

FEAST OF THE LIVING

Out in the desert
Where life is for the few
I met up with a strange old man
Who taught me a thing or two

He's old and he's wrinkled
But he's still wise beyond his years
I glimpsed into his happy times
I saw into his tears

There's so much more to life, my son
Than money and its strings
No one tells you of the loneliness
Or the sorrow that it brings

It takes you to its highest point
Then drops you without warning
It grabs your soul just twice a day
In the night time and the morning

I will never understand
This taking without giving
Or that money is the God they call
The Feast of the Living

—Dorothy Sondgeroth

A DREAMY KNIGHT

We have a great uncle of indisputable fame,
A knight with a mission, we're proud to acclaim.
He emerged as an adult, missing growth as a boy,
A symbolic relative with a promise of joy.

Always swift and willing, to cut us some slack,
Even cutting our taxes, a really good whack.
Compassionate by nature, helping those who need,
Scorning evil others, conniving in greed.

An imposing figure full of radiant charm,
Treating things equal, without cause for alarm.
Forthright and fair, with impeccable class,
Seeking one thing only, from his relative mass.

Now, we are at fault, letting his system look bad,
It's a puzzle to me, why uncle, doesn't seem to be mad.
The way we hurt uncle, is by electing his tools,
The ones serving him, in Congressional pools.

—Wealthy J. Kortz

A VERDICT BEFORE SUNSET

In these stormy dark times our hearts race with fear.
How many more lives will be stolen this year?
Morale at rock bottom; not a smile or laugh one.
Their project is failing; there's more torment to come.
I've toiled long hours to discover a way
To end the crime and the killing in our country some day.
I hold the solution to put "Good" at its peak;
To rescue the weary, the starving, the weak.
At best it's a gamble, but aside from the risks,
Away from the terror and beyond all the myths;
It has to be tested and could save your life
From discharge of machine-gun or quick thrust of a knife.
As the clouds drift away and eyes gleam with warm light,
It's the dawn of emotion, to abort panic and fright.
From the street corner pusher to the King of the Crop,
There's one positive answer to make all of this stop!
Just like prohibition, with the Mob and Capone;
If drugs are deemed legal, it will conquer crime's throne.
Is your mind still myopic, one sided and closed?
Then study your history, it's written in prose!

—David B. Yancey

AHA! KANSAS

Just think, the buffalo used to
roam here free;
Now when you look, highways
and houses are all you see.

They've torn down the hills and
landfilled the creeks;
Now, house rooftops and machines
make up the mystique.

The western plains are irrigated fields
with towns springing up here and there.
The eastern hills are crowded with
plants and factories, polluting the air.

The summer rains and winter snows still cover
and preserve the immense of the Flint Hills;
Thank God, they've been spared the dozers,
cranes, dirt movers and drills!

You still find some section wheat fields, a few
pheasants, deer and sunflowers by the roadside;
But, you don't see any buffalo. The white man
came; killed them off, and sold their hides!

—C. Dian Worley Chambers

A CANDLE FELL

When at first a candle is lit, the flame is bright, it's strong and eager to stand up tall, waiting to light the entire world. Sharing its warmth, waiting for its chance to do the great deeds that were intended.

As the flame sways back and forth through its burning life, a trickle of wax flows down its cheeks as though it crys as its life grows shorter, as time goes by. The ever ending flame grows small as the wax continues to flow, but now for only a short distance, for now its life is over and it's time for the candle to fall.

—**Richard L. Wood Jr.**

SOUTHBOUND TRAIN FOR HOME

Taking that southbound train for Georgia,
   taking that southbound train for home.
Taking that southbound train home to my wife,
   taking that train to my kids.
Gotta take that southbound train home.

Tired of taking that plane home,
   tired of taking the bus home to the wife and kids.
Tired of traveling cross the country and living
   out of a suitcase.
Tired of living in hotel rooms.
Gonna take that southbound train home.

Gonna do some fishing while I'm home, gonna play ball
   with my kids, gonna take long walks with my wife.
Going home, gonna take that southbound train home to Georgia,
   taking that southbound train home.

Gonna take that southbound train home.
Tired of taking taxis,
   tired of taking limos.
Gonna take that southbound train home.
Gonna spend some time relaxing,
   gonna spend time with neighbors and friends.
Gonna take that southbound train home to Georgia,
   taking that southbound train for home.

—**Jeff Campbell**

CLASS REUNION

We stare at each other
   with impenetrable faces

Wondering what became of us
   even as we look

Trying not to show
   the sadness the years have brought
   . . . or the pain

Faces in the room —
   familiar faces that dust off old feelings —
   anger, shame, affection, pity

I wonder why we come

Is it to find our past again
   To look at it from farther away and accept it more easily

. . . Away from those years
   when admitting error or weakness is too risky

Maybe it's to see those people as they really were —
   just children
   growing, learning, failing, trying the same as we

We haven't all turned out so very different
   . . . We've just grown up

—**Ann Kungel**

DREAMS

How can I hope to tell you
What is on my mind?
You — at the beginning of your life,
Me — near the end of mine . . .

. . . Or so it sometimes seems to me,
When I look at you,
Facing your tomorrows,
With hope for dreams come true.

The dreams I followed yesterday,
For me, could not come true,
So I have packed each one away,
And send them now with you.

I wish for you the happiness,
That seeking dreams can bring,
With choices — yours alone to make—
And never ending Spring.

—**Kristie Lynn Beavers**

MY SOUL AND I

My soul and I have traveled
together a lifetime.
Side by side, but never as one.

We've bathed in the quiet
waters of life,
but never to touch.

Strange — the soul is patient
and waits.
But, I have never been able
to put my hand out and say,
come, be part of me.

Now, as we reach into the ocean
of life, energies create a
pull and a force that bring us
close.

We touch, and we are one.

And so, my soul and I go
hand in hand, as the richness
of life comes to greet us.

—**Ruth Gates**

SOMETIMES

Sometimes,
When I'm just sitting around,
I think about life.
I get scared
Just wondering
Where I am,
Who I am,
And
When I will die.
It's like going
Into a scary dream.
While
I'm in a daze-dream,
It's like
Nothing's real.
Like
I'm not really
Supposed to be here,
And any minute
Someone will come and take me
To where
I'm supposed to be.

—**Angela Grow**

COPING WITH LIFE

Daily schedules demand, People command.
I stand—and delay
To start my list of things to do.
I'd rather sit and think things through
So much can be done at once
So much can be finished after lunch.
Soaking in sights, sounds and such
Must be done whenever they abound.
Sunshine is here! — I can be found
In the swing, looking down on the town.

—Gloria Greiner

BEING A KID

I enjoy fun things like cartoons.
And playing outside on sunny afternoons.
Or swimming with Jill in the neighbor's
  pool.
And making jewelry out of old thread
  spools.
I like kool-aid with lots of ice.
But I don't like little white mice.
I can jump higher than my brother Tim.
But I can't run as fast as him.
I loved these things I really did.
It was a lot of fun being a kid.

—Margaret (Peggy) Goodrich

THE CHALK BOARD'S POINT OF VIEW

We get used from year to year
Kids write, draw, mess, and smear

Get away from us is what we'd like to shout
But then they'd walk away ready to pout.

What we'd really like to hear
Is they're moving away not very near.

Then the bell rings and all the students sit
That's when we'd like to yell I quit!

Then we see all those smiling faces
Even all those untied shoelaces.

It makes us want to stay
And never ever go away.

—Leslie Smith

DEATH OF "MO"

Dear Mo: There are many songs about
old dogs and poems written too.
But I'd not be able to write a good
enough song or poem describing anyone
as sweet as you.
Your personality was so humble and
kind—for you grew up with children
playing and rolling over you.
With your 4 by 6 plank you were happy
to play as if you were a child too.
You nuzzled knees to let folks know you
were there and pancakes you ate by the
dozen. You walked in snow—Will
there be snowflakes in Heaven?
It's nice to think that when we all go
you'll be waiting somewhere too, to
watch out for us there like you did here—
Somewhere beyond the blue.
Goodby Mo

—Betty Merritt Lee

THE PIANO MAN
For Andy

Out there through the darkness,
Flowed a tender melody.
As the piano man began to play,
A song to set him free.
I turned to see his handsome face,
Through the shadows of the room.
It was serious and deep in thought,
But shone brightly through the gloom.
He saw none of our faces,
And heard no other sound.
His only care was staying in,
The musicland he'd found.
I couldn't tear my eyes from him,
I was afraid he'd fade away.
When I could have stayed forever there,
Just listening to him play.

—Heather Fouts

WHAT KIND OF WORLD

What kind of world would it be if the sky was green
  and the trees were blue?
What kind of world would it be if the clouds
  were brown and earth was white?
What kind of world indeed . . . what a sight!
What kind of world would it be if time stood still
  and the future had past?
What kind of world would it be if day was night,
  the sun shining bright, the stars nowhere
  in sight?
What kind of world indeed . . . imagine if you might!
What kind of world would it be if love didn't hurt
  and pain brought a smile, with every adult
  as innocent as a child?
What kind of world would it be if I were you
  and you were me, what kind of world would we
  both see?
What kind of world indeed . . . what kind of world
  that would be!

—Michael Noland

SLEEP

Sleep, slumber sleep, where dreams begin
Of huge castles and princesses, dragons,
Dungeons, and serenades and lost maidens.
Things that fantasies are made of.

Sleep, don't stop sleeping
About cowboys and Indians, heroes and villans,
And legends that never die.
About people who existed long ago.

Sleep, sweet and happy
About what you want to be.
Striving for goodness and justice
In all you plan to be and do.

Sleep, where good overcomes evil,
Of victorious battles, and reigning kingdoms,
Of loving romances, and friendships that last forever.
About happy endings.

Sleep, where dreams end,
Of impossible journeys and what could be,
About unrealistic ideas about the future,
And about the little CHILD in all of us.

—Jane Carey

THE SWEETEST SONG

There she sits amidst the anguish of the street,
    playing her melodious tune
Her fingers weave an invisible web
    upon the broken harp
She murmurs a soft song,
    a mother's lullaby
        So gentle,
         so sweet
The chime of coins upon the cobblestone
    joins in harmony
The relentless torture of the world
    is broken
    for just an instant
The music swells and fills my soul
as the sweetness of her song
    echoes through my heart

        —Kathryn M. Burke

THE DREAM SONG

Close your eyes, sleep.
Let your worries and your pain
drift away . . .

. . . and soon you'll be
Greeted on the sea of dreams
by the moon and stars
like children, come to play.

And all that you've been, becomes just memories.
And all that you've seen, was never there.
And all that's to be, becomes a part of reality
And all of the world is yours to share.

When at last
You find your way
To the sandy shores
Of a new and better sunny day . . .

. . . Through your eyes
I know you'll see
That it only takes one small dream
  to set you free.

        —Eugene Sebastion B.

THE RAIN ON THE OLD TIN ROOF

So dear to my heart are the memories that come
Pardon me if I reminisce
About scenes in our home by the railroad track
And one of the best is this: The Rain.
The sound of the rain on our old tin roof.

Pop was a man with twinkling eyes
Who gently dried my tears
When I went to him with my childish woes,
Skinned-up knees and unnamed fears;
Pop knew how to make the hurt go away
And to show me his love with more proof
He'd open wide the attic door
And we'd listen to the rain on the old tin roof.

Many years have passed and Pop's gone away
But sometimes I still feel him near;
His warm, gentle strength like a blanket of love
Surrounding me yet — and I hear
His dear voice saying, just like he used to do
Sister, remember how we'd listen to
The rain on the old tin roof?

        —Jane Blair

CHOCOLATE CHIP COOKIE

Oh my chocolate chip cookie,
  how you captivate me!
My nose is deliciously hypnotized
    by your cinnamon fragrance.
Like a dark phantom thriving upon
a child's curiosity, you beckon me to come,
to behold your sweet glory,
      and yes,
my starving eyes worship you.
      those round jagged edges
      your buttery bumpy surface
      that umber hue
You luscious creation
Endowed with monuments of chocolate delight!
    Like a vicious beast,
    drooling over its prey
  I now know
    the destiny
of my appetite.

        —Richard A. May III

WHERE MAN GOETH

Man Goeth Daily Into Fantasy Land
Oftimes Only For A Step Or Two
He Dreams Of Places He'd Like To Go
And Marvels At Things He'd Like To Do
He May Climb Upon A Snow Clad Mountain
Feeling The Gale Upon His Face
Or Fly A Balloon To Yonder Places
Or Win The Masters Cup In A Sail Boat Race
Maybe A Trip Back Into His Childhood Days
Realizing It Will Never Be The Same
Suddenly He Sees His Old Schoolhouse
And His Long Left Home At The End Of The Lane
He May Visit In Out Of Bound Places
And See Good, Plain People, Who Wear No Disguise
That Shake Hands With Heartfelt Emotions
As They Smile With Kind, Love Hungry Eyes
Suddenly His Thoughts Arise From The Past
From The Distant Horizon He Directeth His Stare
A Smile Radiantly Covereth His Face
How Wonderful The Time He Spendeth There

        —Rudy Lane

KIDS SPIRIT

The rain is pouring down
  It's beating on my crown
Oh, what a dreary blue day
This last day of May

Hark! I see a rainbow
And the end of the Winter snow
The warm sunny days to come
Time to put away the hot toddy rum

Soon school will recess
The kids' hearts are filled with bliss
Parents wonder whether to laugh or moan
The lively spirits so near "Oh groan"

Summer always makes you feel younger
Kids make you yearn for youth with hunger
The strength for the games we would play
Would make my body beat again lite-n-gay

As the saying goes we all have our seasons
I wish mine wasn't gone for many reasons
But the kids I'll watch all spry-n-tart
And still know youth and happiness in my heart

        —Candy Moore

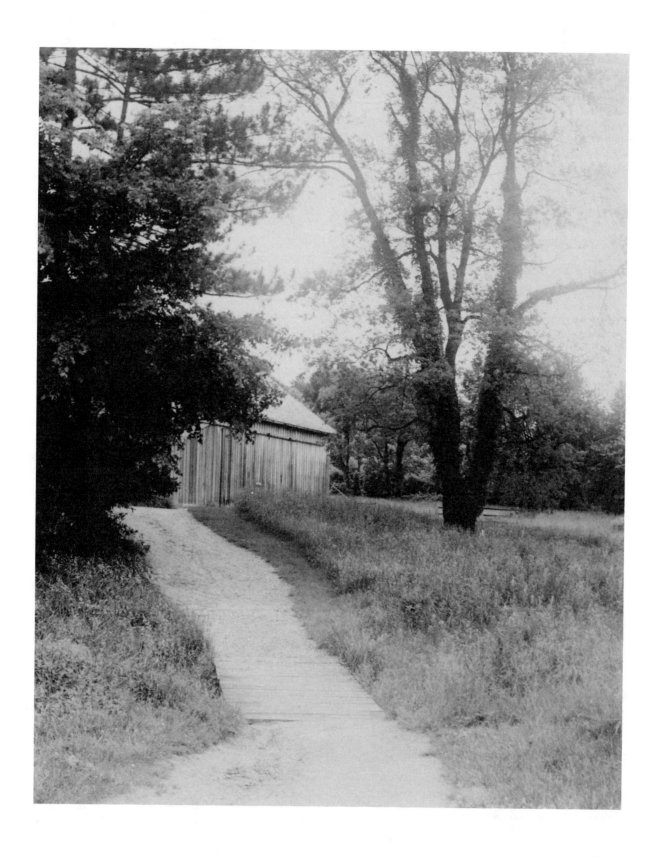

LIFE GOES ON

The great old oak tree
   that grew in the front yard
with its long, wide-spread branches
cast its regal shadow upon the house.

Winters came and winters went
years of snow and ice had taken its toll.
For one spring day, the birds sang
but no new sprouts or sprigs of leaves grew.

The great old oak had given up.
There would be no nests for the birds,
no more hide 'n seek for the squirrels,
no regal shadow upon the house.

A crew came to take the great oak away.
The sound of thunder was heard and the rains came.
It rained for days suddenly from among the clouds appeared the sun
its rays of light and warmth gave life to a new oak tree.

— Marcia Brauer

I saw an old man today peering through a rain streaked window.
   His eyes were hollowed His face furrowed with time
He appeared to look, but not to see
   He had words on his lips but nothing to say

I thought to myself how far he must have been
   How much he must have seen How change had passed him by
How time had almost overtaken him
   I lowered my eyes with his silence

I saw a young boy today with eyes of wonder
   His face all aglow
He had not enough eyes to see all the new and wonderful things
he beheld
   He had so much to tell but not enough words to say
His heart raced with a blaze of excitement
   I smiled at his joy

Then the thought came to me
   Who were these people I had seen
Might they have been me
   The child of days gone by
The old man of days to come
   I sat and thought—then I wept

—Mike Smith

JOURNEY OF A RAINDROP

I saw a tiny raindrop, as it fell from the sky,
and I began to wonder, oh! what if it were I?
So just to make its journey, now I do pretend
Being a small drop of rain. Where does its journey end?

From many miles above the earth, I fell to the ground
Alas, I landed in a little stream, with a splashing sound.
There were millions of us there, and we began to roll.
As we moved swiftly along, the earth, she took her toll.

Now after a short fast journey, we joined a river wide
Rolling down the shore line, we seemed to make a tide
But I kept my eyes opened, saw many sights and sounds
I saw people, green fields and cattle, houses and many towns.

Beneath me I could see many fish both large and small
Saw many rocks, snakes, turtles and frogs, then a waterfall
on I traveled many days, there was beauty to a fault
then one day to my surprise, a taste of briny salt.

The sunlight began to shine, oh so hot you see
and then if by some magic touch, up it lifted me
once again, I was in a cloud, high above the land
would fall and journey once again, this was God's recycle Plan.

—Paul T. Sharpe

ETERNITY

One, hot
Scorching tear
Runs down, down my face
As I relieve myself of one,
One bit of sadness
One bit of sadness is gone.
If one more tear should fall,
That would make two,
Two bits of sadness, gone
It goes on forever!
Or until there is nothing left
But one empty heart,
Left to be filled with one,
One bit of love.
The cycle goes on,
And on,
Forever,
Eternity.

—Kari Pekarek, age 15

LEGACY

Take it for granted:

The air will be
pollution free very soon.

Rain forests will grow
back in our lifetime.

Ivory tusked elephants will
multiply on Africa's plains.

Oil can be easily
removed from rocky shores.

Fishermen's nets will not
diminish the majestic dolphins.

The hole in the
ozone layer's a myth.

Recycling trash is an
activity for spare time.

Tomorrow's children won't miss
what they don't have.

—Kathleen Wegener

LEARNING

Not much time was left:
Not much time to waste,
Not much time to wait around,
Not much time to live.
10,9,8

Less time was left:
Less time to waste,
Less time to wait around.
7,6,5

4 seconds were left:
4 seconds to waste.
4,3,2

1 second left.
1

Blastoff! We have lift off!
No time left:
No time to waste,
No time to wait around,
No time to live.
No time to learn.

—Elizabeth Miller

ANGEL IN DISGUISE

They call him "retarded;"
An "ugly child;"
And yet
Springtime hides in his smile.

Ladies at tea notice
Twisted limbs.
They fail to see
Uneven but graceful strides.

Playmates has he;
Stars, flowers, the smallest ant,
Kept in a warm loving place
For a moment.

He dwells where he shares
A warm embrace,
In an unknown world real to him,
An angel in disguise.

—Virginia L. Randall

A MESSAGE TO CARE GIVERS

I know that I'm old
and I often forget—
But I've worked all my life—
my mind is slow, I regret.
Now, don't get mad
if I loudly protest
Being rolled side to side—
my bones are far past their best!
My fingers and legs
and my back are cruelly bent—
It may be aggravating to you,
but I have to live with this torment!
So as you care for me
day after long day—
Think of what would be
Said IF I could say.
So please treat me
as if I were your friend—
I'd care for myself, if I could—
but on YOU I must depend!

—Debby Laferriere

THE SILENT CRY

I'd like to tell you a story,
Of someone that I know well,
They have a smile upon their face,
But their life is a living hell.

When as a helpless little child,
They were so badly abused,
And can't even remember,
All the methods that were used.

They had no one to talk to,
Because they were afraid to tell,
For who was going to believe them,
The adult was known so well.

So their cry was so silent,
And no one ever heard,
They kept it all down deep inside,
And never said a word.

This life has been destroyed,
By someone with an evil mind,
The past is there to haunt them,
And can never be put behind.

—Pat Sullivan

SILENT EXPLOSION

It wells up within me I am swollen with rage masked and
paraded no more,

Until I can hide it no more and it explodes, as a demon
would guard its lair, fierce and vicious I cry,

My body is wild, and is throwing, kicking away what will
not go, I can hide it no more what is within me, the anger
within me

Looks perceive and my body is strange, I cry sobs of
wounds deep within me, embedded in my soul, sobs rack me
uncontrolled by my body weak and scared

A cry for help, so small, so meek, unheard as
unspoken, bottled up, until the next
Silent
Explosion

—Jennifer Robyn Blott

ENVY IS A CANCER

She wished, Oh how she wished, to be like her.
She hated her because she was not.
The envy burned inside her,
She had an evil plot.
She thought about the girl's beauty,
How she was well-loved and respected by a lot.
All this flamed her fury, she was like a woman scorned.
"I'll get my revenge, she'll be sorry she was
Ever born!"
So she started a rumor, she knew it was a lie.
"I'll fix her, she'll be sorry until the day I die."
The rumor spread like wildfire!
She was soon to learn;
You shouldn't play with matches
If you don't want to get burned.
The rumor backfired, the truth was soon found out.
Everyone turned against her, and certainly there is no doubt,
She had learned a lesson—
Perhaps a little late—
Envy is a cancer, consuming you with hate.

—Kay Ray

THE TOWN OF CLICK

There are only two groups of people that live in the town of
Click, those who are in and those who are out. If you are
not in a click and your name doesn't make the clicking
sound; you may then have a rough time becoming involved with
the other click groups. One day a group came along that
changed the name of the town to Clack; this made the clicks
upset with the clacks for stirring up their little click
town.

The clicks thought everything should be done according to
their own selfish click ways. The clack people became angry
at this; nevertheless the clicks were equally upset over
control of the click name. Then one day another group
entered into the picture to challenge the click, clack name.

This group decided to change the town back to the way it had
been before the clicks and the clacks began. So the clicks
and the clacks formed a committee so as to revive their
clickish little town. They decided there would be equal
treatment for all; and that no one group would be superior
to the other group.

Everyone was happy that day as the little town of click,
clack, became a new town with new thoughts and ideas.
Centered on understanding for the other clicks, clacks, and
the town they call Click!

—Harry C. Clarke

FIRST SIGNS OF SPRING

Sleeping branches awaken the leaves
    Birds chirping in the trees
In the grass, hidden deep
    Something is stirring, what could it be?
A robin tugging on a worm
    From the ground that is still firm
Tug, little robin, don't give in
  Don't worry, be happy it's only the first day of Spring!

—**Helen Fish**

WINTER THAW

The trees have stood naked all winter long,
    Now new buds are growing beautiful and strong.
The birds are hard at work,
While their music flows without mistake nor quirk.
The last drops of snow are dripping to the ground,
Making puddles all around.
Mud is piled up everywhere,
Making everything look disgusting and bare.
But among all this it is obvious to me,
Spring is speedily passing over the sea.

—**Kathy Howe**

NUMBERS

Winter 1, Spring 2, Summer 3, Fall 4 — Numbers
    The seasons are all very beautiful:
1, Winter lays its blanket of snow on the land,
The cold air bites your skin;

Spring has come, 2, melting the snow and the cold,
Petals on pink flowers, green leaves,
Trees, once again, stand tall;

3, Summer sun, bees hum songs of laughter and joy,
Their happiness for summertime shows through;

4, Fall, mighty wind gusts through the trees, pulling off
    their leaves,
Colored by a small child using his favorite crayons,
The deciduous trees are bare again;

The divine seasons form a repetitive cycle,
Each one will last only three months,
Take advantage!

—**Cailin Rosemary Cannon**

THE SOUNDS OF WIND

The ocean wind gently surrounds me
  with the freedom of an eagle high above the sky.

The fullness of the wind rushes in,
while I walk into the treachery of the sea.

A narrow step downward destroys the courage
it takes to continue onward.

A rock is my only refuge;
latching on to the object, my soul is quickly
mounted.

A flawless plan to nurture the tired, worn body
is mastered by the wind.

The wind pierces my ears
with peaceful messages from far away lands.

The peaceful message is silent, yet clear.
The waves of the wind cannot lie and will not die.

An awesome wonder fills the air as the magical
surroundings bring forth great happiness and joy!

—**Martin G. Fraunces**

ON TOP OF THE HILL

I know for a place, on top of the hill —
Where you can see both near and far
But it's not until you get up to the top
That you see how — real things are!

To the north of me lies the horizon,
From the south balmy breezes blow —
In the early morn, if you look to the east
You catch a glimpse of the sun's first glow!

You toil all day long in the fields,
And at evening, it's time for a rest—
And as you sit and recline,
You watch the sun as he sinks in the west!

The evening shadows lengthen
And all is quiet and still —
For that's the way I see it
When you live "on top of the Hill!"

—**Rudy Jackopich**

GOLDEN MOMENTS

Golden moments are thankful times
    For God's mercy to everyone,
Because we're all so grateful to Him
    And rejoice for what He's done,
Golden moments are loving times
    Just praying for a friend,
We must share our love more freely
    And pray more than we intend,
Golden moments are forgiving times
    So be faithful to God above,
And in return He will forgive
    And bless you with His love,
Golden moments are sharing times
    Knowing we've planted a seed,
Sharing God's word to a lonely heart
    And giving hope to someone in need,
Golden moments in our life
    Are times God shines within,
And all these Golden Moments
    Are truly a gift from Him.

—**Charlotte J. Miller**

SOFTLY-SOFTLY MURMURING SEA

Softly, softly murmuring sea,
    Softly — softly lullaby sea,
My anguished heart prays to thee
    To cast its shackled hurt from me.

Softly, softly meandering waves,
Softly, softly cresting waves,
My soul from toil your whisper saves
Cobwebbed in anguished mental maize.

Softly, softly blanketing foam,
Softly, softly humming foam,
Reach out to calm my sandman's home
And cease my mind in constant roam.

Softly, softly soothing song,
Softly, softly tranquil song,
I sip, but slow, Neptune's tea,
    Which slowly mesmer's me.

Softly, softly gentle sleep,
Softly, softly dream-land sleep,
Enwrapped in aura of sublime rest
My soul — my mind, my heart knows best.

—**Bert Knowles**
    Brick, NJ

MORE THAN IT SEEMS

Living
    Dying
Laughing
    Crying
After life and after death
    Love is all that is left
Through the laughter and through
the tears
    Love will last year after year
I Love you, as you love me
    One day we'll be gone
But love will live on
    Growing Stronger
Lasting Longer
    than we could ever dream.
Love is much more than it seems

    —Jenny Lynn Mosley

THREAD OF TIME

I knew him many years ago
When I was just a boy.
I was young, he was so old,
Back home in Illinois.

An ancient, tattered thread of time,
He always seemed to be.
A recollection of the past,
He fascinated me.

A youngster bothered by old age,
I watched him everyday.
I guess I thought he'd never die,
That he was here to stay.

Tall, ungainly, walking slow,
With thoughtful, gentle eyes,
He gently smiled in passing,
Always peaceful, looked so wise.

And I missed school the day he left,
To stay at home and cry.
I started understanding life
The day that old man died.

    —Jerry Karr

THE POTTERS FIELD

I see that field upon the hill
And all that open ground;
It is that open potters field,
With all the trees around:

When I die I hope and pray
There be loved ones by my side;
Far away from potters field,
And all my foolish pride:

There's only some old wooden stakes
And markers cold and grey;
Take me away from potters field,
Up to God I pray:

To be alone or down and out,
Sure is hard to take;
Keep me from that potters field,
I ask you for my sake:

With out a friend or loved one
What would this life be?
Down in that old potters field,
By that old oak tree:

    —Paul Hugh Turner

THOUGH WE ARE PARTED . . .

Though we are parted, my beloved,
    your beauty lingers in my memory still.
Your eyes, that stared like dull, glass marbles into eternity,
    saw past us all, yet saw nothing.
Your lips, as soft as damp, gray clay,
    would have spoken of love eternal,
        yet remained silent.
Your skin, as pale as bleached bone and alabaster,
    was beyond mortal touch in its marble coldness.
Though we are parted by a veil of white,
    though the earth's embrace
        would keep you from me,
    I shall not forget your beauty.
I will always remember your visage
        as last I saw it.
            So calm,
                so cool,
    so lacking the confusion of life.

    —Matthew A. Richardson

FORGIVE ME MY FATHER

When a loved one dies, are they really, truly gone?
    Or is there a better place where they now live on.
Is there a place, a time, or a warm beautiful mist,
that they go on to rest, to reflect, to exist?
Their body is here, as are their family and friends,
but their souls are gone, are they with the winds?

Why don't we know, it would be worth all the cost,
to know that our loved ones are not really lost.
Be it a father, a mother, a brother or sis,
why can't we know that their souls are in bliss.
Why are we so tormented, it never seems to cease.
Is there some way to know that they are truly at peace?

But is all this concern all for those passed on?
Is this tormented feeling because of those now gone?
I wonder if it could be that we are feeling the strife
of not being loving enough to those people in life.
If this is true, then my heart will always carry grief
Forgive me my father, for I loved you beyond belief.

    —Jerry W. Bostwick

MY FATHER LIVES

A phone call. A scream, then my world went dark.
Grief enveloped me.

My days turned to weeks, the weeks into months—
and still no light to see.

I retrieved memories from a long forgotten past.
I sought out his friends. A martyred memory I sought to cast.

Life continued as if Dad had never died.
My days were filled with darkness; I found that I still cried.

My daughter was a saving grace — somewhere to place my cares.
I found myself repeating his warnings, wisdom, and prayers.

And then it all was clear to me:
Dad's spirit will never die.
He lives within my brothers, the grandchildren,
and always through my eyes.

Then I saw a ray of light
I thought it couldn't be.

But I have seen the sun;
The dawn has shone on me.

    —Helen M. Null

ONCE

Once, a strong and sturdy man,
With deep calloused hands.

By the age lines in his face,
A once hard life, could be traced.

His eyes, filled with intrigue and mystery.
Once beheld, a lifetime's history.

Once, a vital being filled with wit,
Now so empty, so silent.

Loved ones and friends thought, him eternally strong,
Once, couldn't conceive him gone.

—Bonnie K. Crockett

OUR PRECIOUS TIME

MY MOTHER, a precious woman, requires constant care,
It hurts inside, so little time with her to share.
Such a good example for me; when I became a wife,
Well earned 'Thank You' for all the good things in my life.
I'll care for her with love as she did for me . . .
Now that I'm the Mother, she is childlike you see.

Gingerly I bathe and wash her hair,
If she'd show recognition, all I get is a stare.
A promise kept, He would come for us all,
I'll love her faithfully and wait for death to call.
Reaching up I brush the tears from my eyes,
Lord, give me strength when it is time for Good-bye.

—Emma L. Valenteen

OUR BELOVED

Forget you — we will never
For our Love lasts forever;
Your Death brings us much sorrow,
But all we can do is hope for a better tomorrow
Even though you are gone
We all must carry on;
Our teardrops may dry
But for in Love we will cry
You've touched our hearts in many ways
That is why we've come to pray today;
In our hearts you will remain
Our Love for you is still the same
Not a day would go by —
That we won't silently cry;
Now as we all stand together
We will remember his Love for us, FOREVER . . .

—Patricia L. Semanik

LIFE FEAR

In the predawn stillness
before the first bird trills or movement begins
I grow small with fear because he's leaving today.
Last week my Mother died — 22 years ago my daughter.
The idea of fear came from that.

I looked at his face; his eyes, nose, profile;
Saw his chest rise and fall in sleep;
tried to memorize the breath between life and death.
Be brave! You're being silly with your thoughts.
He will be fine.

The first bird calls — first light — time to wake him.
Don't ever let him know this fear!
He's only twelve — he's going to camp — he'll come back.
Isn't the only thing to fear, fear itself?
Yes, but only of things that have taken away.

—Carol E. Shaul

UNNOTICED

Farewell to anyone out there
Who is willing to listen
To a voice that has gone unnoticed
For all these years.
Not to make you think
I've anything to say
That you could understand.
My life is—rather was
Trivial—therefore it seems logical
That my death should be as well.
The world holds many kinds of people.
Some happy, some sad
And some left behind by the rest.
Myself, I am one of the latter kind.
Unnoticed in life, unnoticed in death.

—James B. Pitcock

MISS YOU

Time heals they say,
and so it has to some degree.
A year's gone by,
since you passed away.

The tears, still there,
the loneliness a little less.
Friends helped with this,
they came from everywhere.

We miss those playful smiles,
beneath your fuzzy mustache.
Your gentle voice, a yodel,
heard over many miles.

Autumn leaves, blackberry brandy
the travels we so enjoyed.
The falls, mountains, rainbows,
sunsets, lakes—so sandy.

Golden gloves, roses, your Purple Heart,
all, cherished memories now.
We miss you, dearest Uncle
as we, go on, with life, apart.

—Clara A. Hamilton

LURE OF THE NIGHT

Listen to the night wind,
it calls my name.
The dark of the night,
the stars of the sky,
the moon has turned its face to cry.

And the dawn will bring
the evil sun back,
the stars will flee
on the cool wind's back.

Once more I'll have to endure
till dusk,
for freedom from life and,
an end to day's strife.

Someday I'll sleep, dawn to dawn
and dusk to dusk, the man will say
ashes to ashes and dust to dust,
they'll lower me down to the arms
of the cool dark ground.

The cruel sun will burn me never again,
I'll be safe from life forever.

—Bob Kelley Jr.

CHILDREN: OUR GARDEN OF LOVE

Sprinkle daily with love
and nurturing
Watch and guide their growth and
development
Do not let them go to seed
Provide for their many needs by
loving, caring and sharing
Weed out the negatives
Create positive self-esteem
Encourage high educational goals
Find time daily to listen to their
concerns about life
When they have reached maturity
and leave the garden of love,
A hug and a kiss to send them on
to their future
As productive citizens from your
garden of love.

—Delores Jean DaVané

IN HARMONY WITH TODAY

Today looked into my window,
While I still lay in bed;
I sensed a warm and gentle touch,
Where my pillow held my head.

Today came through my window pane,
And focused upon my eyes;
Right then I felt Today just stare,
With a bright new morning sunrise.

Today reached out and touched my hand,
And tickled me on my feet;
Then when I laughed and tried to stand,
Today snatched away my sheet.

Then no matter where I went — Today,
Just stayed right by my side;
Today was never out of my reach,
I couldn't even hide.

All the things I did — Today
Did right along with me;
And even when I sang a song,
Today was in harmony.

—Helen S. Perry

FOREVER

The beauty of the sun
Sinking into the ocean
The echo of a child's laughter
Ringing in your ears
The gentle touch of a lover's lips

These are forever

The whispering winds
The restless waves
The stars above on a moonlit night

These are forever

My love for you
And our future life together
The children we'll bear
The generations we'll see
The love in your eyes
The warmth in our hearts

These are forever.

—Michelle Zarate

A RED TOP SPINNING

A red top spinning on the floor,
was what I saw from an open door.
A child sitting so happy at play,
his eyes were shining so bright and gay.
The top was spinning round and round,
when it stopped, the child's smile became a frown.

—Myrtle D. Hubbard

HER SMILE

Her smile reminds me of the first day of spring.
With joy and happiness each day does it bring.
I look forward to seeing it every day.
And each time I see it like a school boy I play.
Her smile sends a chill that flutters my heart.
And makes me never want to see the day that we part.
Her smile is something that will never end.
Her smile is why she's my best friend.

—Yusef Perkins Kamakeeaina

EARLY MORNINGS

In the early mornings, I awake from my sleep
I look over memories as a child, so many I shall keep
The sunshine would hit my face to remove me from a dream
As I get up with a smile and show a bit of gleam
The dog would bark aloud, and the birds outside would sing
I'd sit in bed and wait, and think what the day may bring
From my window, I view birds spreading their wings and fly
And soar across this bright blue thing, which all
would call a sky
I'd hear a plane pass, the sound of a loud jet roar
Then I'd hear laughter from the children right next door
The aroma of Mama's morning meal brings me to a stop
It'd make me ask for second servings with food piling on top
I'd feel the morning heat, the summer sun touching my skin
Then I'd hear the morning noise, laughter from my kin
The T.V. would be on downstairs, cartoons on full blast
I'd run downstairs, and who's awake? Everyone . . .
I'm always last

—Melanie D. Dirige

AKIN

You have to love
a friend who always gives the best, expects the best,
makes no apologies, accepts no excuses
when the best is
a tuna fish sandwich.

We each share memories
edged in velvet and lace,
set beside rainbows and sunsets,
decked in crystal, fine china.

But our past is sealed in multi-grain conversations,
spread with low salt, water-packed
caring.

A sandwich connection is
cozy, sticky kitchen floors, holes in the socks:
Always there.

We still think of each other in
joy, crisis, beauty, defeat;
in every peanut butter and jelly,
grilled cheese bite:
Often.

—Ann Malokas

250

TWO MEs

If two me's should wake to the break of dawn,
One would be weak, the other one strong.
They'd face the task of the day ahead,
One with optimism, the other with dread.

The strong would spring forth, the face with a smile.
The weak would drag, wondering, "Is waking worthwhile?"

Comes a child with a problem, the weak would scream and shout,
While the strong would take the hand and say "Don't worry, we'll work
it out."

The wonder of God's nature, the strong would stop to see,
But the weak could not appreciate, for he's blinded to its beauty.

And at the close of day, the strong would feel complete,
But the weak would only agonize, feeling but defeat.

Inside I have the two of me, one of bondage, one of peace
And the choice becomes mine at break of dawn of which I choose to be.

      —Mrs. Janet Martin

AN OLD FRIEND

An old friend stands in the middle
Of the meadow—

               Still.

                   Quiet.
Out of the air — children come

                     Running,
                            Skipping
To their friend.

            Hanging.
                Clinging to his arms.
His strong body carrying all his
    Little children. Boys. Girls.

                 Laughing.
                     Screaming — cries of fun
          and happiness ring through the field.
Hugging their old friend and

           climbing

              higher and higher

                  until they touch the sky.

      —Bekah Malone

CARRY ME DADDY

They tell me not to pick him up, he's too big to carry around.
  Everyone is looking at you, why don't you put him down?
He's almost five and over three feet tall, let him walk for himself today.
He's too big for you to carry, but I don't hear a word they say.

He comes to me with his arms outstretched, "Oh Daddy please carry me"
and I gladly will as long as I can. I love him don't you see?
Those little arms around my neck, are this daddy's greatest thrill.
So when he asks me to pick him up, he knows I always will.

Our time together is all we have; Each moment I want to share;
So when I bend down and pick him up, it's a way to say I care.
A smile as payment for this ride, is all he has to give;
More precious to me than silver or gold, my treasure as long as I live.

Give me the strength in this right arm, to carry him while he'll let.
Someday he'll say "Dad I'm too big." But he hasn't said it yet.
So I'll pick him up and hold him close, and hope it's not the last time I can.
I faintly remember being a boy, but a long time I've been a man.

And when he is a man with his own son, please grant that he may recall,
these wonderful days that I carried him, when he was over three feet tall.
So in my arms he'll probably be when you see us in town,
please do us one small kindness,—Don't tell me to put him down.

**Dedicated to my husband Bert, who is such a good Dad, he's made being Mom
wonderful.**
      —Barbara Davis

LONELY NIGHTS

At night—
  Silently,
Love comes—
Past my bed,
While loneliness
Echoes—
Across the room.

—Wondering Waters

THE DROP OF A...HAT

I used to
    Fall
  in Love
At the drop of a . . .
    Hat

  Until . . .
    One day,
  Much to my surprise,
  You reached
      down
To pick it up.

—Julina Froman

LOVE BALANCE

Relationships
  out of balance
are like
being on a
teeter-totter
One must
move
in towards
the center
or
out to the end
to correct
the imbalance
Being willing
to move
in or out
is Love
in action.

—Helen G. Brubaker

WHY

We wonder why
  the baby cries,
yet we never take
the time.

We wonder why
the child hides,
yet we never take
the time.

We wonder why
the men fight,
yet we never take
the time.

We wonder why
the people die,
yet we never take
the time.

    Why?
—Denise M. Dudzik

THE QUESTION

The candle burns low at the bedside
The gold of the sunrise steals through
The curtain that hangs at my window
My thoughts, once again, turn to you

All night, in my mind, I've been drifting
To the place where our lives once meshed
But the weight of some memories can crush you
And nightmares come real in the flesh

The good times we had for certain
The bad times weren't all in our minds
But that was enough, to scatter like dust
What we felt to the borders of time

Was it pretense, or were we true lovers?
Was it lust, or was the game lies?
When I see you again, will I know this?
Or will I get lost in your eyes?

     —Carol Prichard-Moffitt

SHARON

Be still my heart, it's only a voice!
But the melody lingers on echoing
  In the caverns
        of my mind.

Don't beat so hard at the song you hear!
  But the notes keep tinkling
  Like the first drops of rain in the spring
  Awakening my soul like leaves unfurling
  When catching drops
        as they fall.

Oh, the words we speak are not our thoughts,
  But the sounds we hear
  Are thunder in our ear
  Beating back the loneliness
        of years gone by.

Be still my heart, it's only a voice.
  But the emptiness is filled
        with your song.

     —John L. Hamilton

FAREWELL

We must have known from the start,
The day would come when we would part.
It seemed the dye had been cast,
The love we felt was not to last.

Everything seemed so special and right,
A moment in time was captured that night.
Ours was a joy for all to behold,
We gave to each other our very soul.

Then the differences grew so great,
Our timing in life seemed too late.
Within our hearts, enduring the pain,
Watching our sunshine turn to rain.

Knowing our love would not stand the test,
Parting and wishing each other the best.
Remembering the moments that we had shared,
Cherishing how much we both had cared.

In time to come our paths may cross,
Deep inside we will hide our loss.
Thru warm tears we'll extend a hand,
Knowing a love that was truly grand.

     —deMarigny Denis

LOVE, REMEMBERED

Your love haunts me
Like a spirit it fades through the door of Eternity
Never more to be wholly mine, and yet—
Ever present, like a lover's dreams.
I hold you in my heart, love
Like a little cherished kitten you slumber there
And in every summer's night you awaken and
Stir me to laughter and remembrance.
Your love is all around me, a silent sleepy echo
In a cavern called my Heart
Blossom's tufts fall from the sky
With a kiss of comfort and a whisper of sweetness
Yet all that is there
Is a tear
And a sigh that says
I will not forget.

     —Darlene T. Abston

KEY TO HAPPINESS

A sense of humor is a key to happiness
Always accepting things with a grin
Politely smile and count to 10,
When your patience starts running thin.

Instead of finding fault in others
Look for all the good that you can
Nothing works better to bring out the best,
Than to give someone a helping hand.

Enjoy the simpler things in life
An evening walk with a full moon above
Now what could bring more happiness
Than strolling hand in hand with the one you Love.

Smiles are very important keys
Believe me on this you can depend,
There isn't any nicer way of saying
I sure would like to be your friend.

The major keys to happiness are,
Kindness, sharing, friendship and love,
But there is still another you must always remember,
Don't ever lose your faith in the Lord above.

     —Ruth Heisler

THE WONDER DRUG

How wonderful I feel when this substance is in my
    presence.

Bewildered without it am I,
    acquiring emotions of loneliness,
        emptiness,
        frightfulness,
        and worthlessness.

No doubt in the mind an addiction is present.

The more I have the more I need!

This drug I seek does wonders.

Without it, it is clear, my mood swiftly changes.

It brings feeling of security, it brings reason
    to live, for in itself it is life.

Ah! But carefully I guide my path, for if taken
    a wrong turn this drug will betray me and
    leave me at lower status than before.

For this wonder drug I seek is LOVE!!!!!

     —Rebecca Malley

YOU

Sometimes I feel alone . . . For the Love that should be shown.
I try to understand waiting for the touch of your hand.
I try to change the way things are.
But I don't seem to go too far.
My Love is true, I don't want to be alone.
With or without you.

—Debra E. Wright

I KNOW

I know you are for me . . . Because in your eyes,
I can see . . . The gentle flow, of life you hold . . . The sound
of love, that you have told . . . A love, that I would never
lose . . . To be apart, I would never choose . . . A love
from you, I would hold . . . To turn away from me, would
be so cold . . . I know love sets us free . . . To unlock my
heart, you hold the key . . . My love feels as though, it's been
rolled . . . I have got to get back up, I have got to be bold . . .
I know that I do . . . Sincerely, honestly, hold on to you . . .
Laughing, Sharing . . . Loving, Caring . . .
"I Know"

—Cameron Poulos

ONE WISH

If I could wish upon a star and make a dream come true
I'd ask God for a miracle and send it off to you
I'd free you from those prison walls that keep us far apart
Not the white and solid kind but the walls within your heart

I'd crush them into tiny bits and take away your pain
I'd build your trust and honesty and free you from the blame
I'd vanish all the guilt and fear that haunts you in your sleep
I'd dry your tearing eyes so you would never weep

I'd help to show a part of you so few would ever know
A part of you so loving you're still afraid to show
I'd ease unpleasant memories dear and provide a second try
I'd give back the security that long ago ran dry

For you I'd wish serenity and happiness to live
And if I could send a miracle this is surely what I'd give
I never thought I'd love again til the day that I met you
I knew in one swift moment that you would say I do

—Dale Ray Cardinale

STORM WALK

I feel the magnet pull to brave the cold of blizzard night
As if some atavistic urge lures and compels exploring white
Horizontal lines of stinging snow.
Cap pulled low with collar high
I half turn as snow stabs cheeks and forces wry grimace.
Oh why did I take this nature powered stroll without goal?
I think of her, petite; she has the neat
Way of sensing what is pleasing, what is right,
But the sight of her saucy jaunty gait, her effervescent way
Validates the wait for her reserve to melt, so she may weigh
My attributes and let me stay
In her thoughts . . .
Oh I would pocket her this night
And protect her from the ice gnomes might!
I'd plant upon her storm red cheeks
A kiss of promise, one that seeks
A commitment, a yearning for long term lease
And never cease to treasure this blessing from above
This new found lady,
This new found love!

—Kenneth G. Place

Trying to hold you
Is like dancing with a dream
The feeling's so real
But all is not what it seems
I reach out to touch you
Just to find you're not there
I call out your name
You're not even aware
Your hair I do fondle
Your lips I caress
I reach for the velvet
In which you are dressed
But I rip through the fabric
Of that thin velveteen
Which acts as a border
For what's real and what is dream

—Michael J. Badach

I REMEMBER

I remember love.
I remember warmth and laughter,
And summer nights,
And spring days.
I remember winter storm,
And summer lightning.
I remember love.
I remember love
In all its phases—
Anger and joy,
Sorrow and laughter,
Good times,
And bad times,
And in-between times.
I remember firm and gentle hands,
Caressing lips.
I remember safe, strong arms,
I remember love.
I remember loving you.

—Joyce Freeman-Clark

FLAME

Life, and yes—Death;
Are but down to a flame,
The flame in my heart,
Which burns in your name,
Frigid, the winds;
Which blow in the night,
Cruel, the world;
Which extinguishes light.

Lay here beside me,
Kindle the fire,
The Night is so strong,
Yet so is desire,
Beautiful, the warmth;
Which melts ice in the heart,
Raging, the blaze;
And so soon it departs.

And so burns the fire,
Late into the night,
The flames last departed,
Silent wraiths taking flight,
Defiant, the ash;
Which glows brilliant red,
Defiant, are we;
Who embrace by its bed.

—R. David Fulcher

EPITAPH OF ONE GONE ON

As you stand there and look down on me
don't let your heart grieve
But take a moment to meditate
    on what I say before you leave

As you are now, so once was I
    full of laughter, hope, and dreams
Time flies by and comes to an end
    all too soon, or so it seems

Dying is a part of living,
    doesn't matter if you're rich or poor
It's each one's final destiny,
    a fact of life for sure

So, my friend, some good advice
    live each day as though your last
For soon you'll be as I am now
    someone's memory from the past

—Barbara Barnes Wright

Monuments cold to touch
    cover loved ones in death's repose.
Lonely people on marble benches
With saddened eyes await their fate.
Days go by without a hope.
To feel again the warmth of love,
    and see again those lost in death.
To touch their hand,
    and feel their breath.
Through all the seasons of the year,
    like doves of peace they sit and coo.
Watering flowers with their tears
    that roll down stones
    where they will lie.
Stones with spaces for the chiseler's hand
    to carve their names
    so they can lie
    and fill the places set aside.
To lie beside the love they lost,
    and whisper words of love again.

—Adelle R. Pitts

INTRUSION

Why would I intrude upon your thoughts?
    Why would I impose upon your day?
Why would I presume to tell you,
About the "Living Way?"

Many books have been written:
Many books have been read:
Multitudes still do not know,
What Jesus, the Son of God, said.

"I am the resurrection, and the life:
"He that believes in me, though dead,
Yet shall he live:"
These are words, that Jesus said.

"I am the living water:"
"I am the living bread:"
"He that eats, and drinks of me,
Shall live forever," Jesus said.

"He shall not walk in darkness,
Who follows me."
"He that has the Son, has life,
And has it abundantly."

—Bernice Robertson Winkler

BATTLE FIELDS

Battle fields dismal and grey
    Our dying men, let us pray.
Professional Soldiers are all around,
With an unlucky shot, they're on the ground.
A bright red flash and they hit the trench,
The common odors; dead body stench.
No one questioned who was right or wrong,
But they gave their lives with dedications strong.
Our men did die, left and right—
While at home, we could only fight.
We marched the streets and gave our views,
Then prayed to God, How many more will we lose?
They didn't ask to be sent to war,
And in American hearts this left a sore.
Our Soldiers came back, their spirits high
For THEY were willing to fight and die!
Some men came back from that hell far away,
But some "Americans" made life for them grey.
They did the job that they were trained to do,
Poor American Soldiers, their hearts were true.

—Julia Florence Hackett

THEY THOUGHT I WAS DEAD

I laid there not moving a muscle,
    Stone cold dead: ah yes!
They thought I was dead . . . They thought,
I fooled them, I fooled them,
Three hundred enemy marched right over me,
They thought I was dead but I fooled them,
Our platoon no more,
Eighty men wiped out, all but me,
My chances were maybe one in a million,
All dead but me,
I knew they would kill me if I moved,
So I waited . . . waited . . . waited,
Ten maybe fifteen minutes is all it was,
In those ten minutes ten thousand eternities had passed,
Then all was quiet,
As the last enemy had left I thanked the lord,
They all thought I was dead but we fooled them,
It was not yet time for me to die,
As I left, I prayed for the dead!
Thankful, that I wasn't one of them.

—Alan Charles Bard

WHEN THE BELL TOLLS

When day is through and night no more
    Twilight comes and sun bursts forth in
        flame,
On that day when Death first came.
To seal his crypt beneath the blackest
    door,
I would remember, shadows crept beneath
    the floor,
The flowers, lavender and lace in love-
    liness,
And I would feel in sleep, the fragrant
    press
Of rippling tides along the shore.
I would remember the littlest things:
The hum of music, and would hear alone,
The rush of rivers over stone.
And when in vision, from that spring of
    springs,
The toll of bells, which were meant to be,
Harps of Angels, calling me.

—Lee Fissori Wright

254

DO FENCES MAKE GOOD NEIGHBORS?

He died. Did she feel insecure?
I really don't know—I'm not sure.
But up went the fence with no knothole in sight.
The five-foot-high boards were ever so tight.
I miss the beauty of flowers so rare
That kept blooming all summer in her yard over there.

We used to wave and say "Hi,"
But that was in years gone by.
I wish, like the flowers, our friendship had flourished,
But she shut me out, and it could not be nourished.
'Tis sad to be almost a friend
And then to see it suddenly end.

    —Charlotte W. Wagner

SAD PEOPLE

Do you ever stop to think about the people who have no place to go?

These people might have to live through rain, sleet, or snow.

People don't care how sad, sick, or lonely these people are.

No, instead they drive with stereo blasting a new sports car.

Some people wish they could help some way.

I hope I can, when I'm older. I will one day.

    —Chelle LaBounty, age 13

LEGAL CRIMES

The so-called mighty jets tear across the sky.
Who would fight them or rather— why?
The pilots think it's all a joke,
As they fly away streaming black and white smoke.
Don't they think it is a crime
When they see all of those people die?
I see some people try and try,
And others just seem to cry.
I saw my father die
By a tree on a mountainside.
But he said goodbye,
And that helps me not to cry.
I see so many children weep.
There are those tears you cannot keep.
Don't die—at least let us say goodbye.

    —Hilary Clamage

THE UNFOLDING

Caged below a musterseed moon,
Under heavy current and hunchbacked river
Where movement lies unnoticed,
His heart grown over with histories
And scores of obsolete theories,
Oblique hours harass the unborn, as
Vacant strangers purchase memories made
Cheap by uninvited callers.
He, on surface of light, alone
With but survivors,
Prays who sees the first and final moment of kings
And gleaming eyes gone blind.
Bolts of incandescent light mark mirror seas,
As silence is beckoned from the Holy stare
And gleaming men no more removed
Vault reefs of fire into soul's preserve.

    —Leslie Hansen

FOOTPRINTS

Silver crystals bathe the world across
in careless, wind-swept drifts of down,
Taming land in all its dross
beneath a silver frosted crown.

A virgin cloak bedecks the earth
upon whose satin surface, heading home,
footprints ford the frozen firth
where none are seen or heard to roam.

A fragile grace adorns the scene
as though by Merlin scattered — these
the tracks of those that go unseen
and vanish soon in gusting breeze
or thaw that taints the season's song.
Lost the footprints beneath the moon,
forever gone and treasured long,
the fleeting tracks that died so soon.

    —Walt Rae

WOMAN

A Gift to Man
A Companion
A Helpmeet

At Her Best,	Tender and Loving Sweet and Charming A Source of Relief
At Her Worst,	Bitter and Vengeful Jealous and Cruel A Source of Grief
Her Best,	When Most Loved When Most Respected
Her Worst,	When Dominated When Neglected
A Victim of Man,	Used and Abused Rejected and Dejected

Her Worst Enemy is Man
Yet Man She Loves Most
Yet Man She Helps Most

    —George Nnoli

so

so who **are** you, anyway?

dig your probing eyes
beneath my mask
render it to shreds
in answer to your quest

swallow me whole
chew me up and spit me out
so you think you know
what i am about

you say you want to know
more about me well, then
come on inside
welcome to my dark side
crawl into the mind
of potential suicide

you thrust the gun of conformity
into my hand point it at my head
expect me to pull the trigger and
annihilate my security
something i cannot-willnot do

    —Susan Rodabaugh

YOUNG LOVERS

Walkin down the lane hand in hand,
wonderin what to say,
talkin about the love we once had,
then things got in our way

We were lovers so young and so brave,
seems as though things just got in our way,
then the young love that we had,
just began to all turn bad

But then it was as time went by,
things got better because we both tried,
and then the young love that we had,
began getting stronger every day,
no matter what, came in our way . . . .

—Malcolm Maxwell

EYE II EYE

Sometimes we yell
and sometimes we fight.
At times you can't tell
which of us is really right.

We make up our mind
and set our own course,
Not knowing what we'll find
or from what source.

I don't listen to you
and you don't listen to me
We each decide what to do
without asking what the other may see.

We need to work together
learn to see eye to eye
We need to trust each other
without asking why.

Only then can we be at peace
to get along
And find the release
to grow and admit when we're wrong.

—Karen Carranza

COMEDY OF HOUSE WORK

I see dust all over the house— — —
I feel just like I am going to bust,
to see dirt laughing at me— — —
like Circus Clowns jumping on my gown.

My floor needs sweeping, but work will
not make me start weeping.
For I am the Circus Master and I know
how to keep the show on the road.
With all the new gadgets, it is like
"Magic" to conquer the Clowns in my house.

Thank God for the brain of the man,
that make house cleaning as easy as
dreaming.
Too bad, the dream is so short, for it
is time again to enter the dust ring again.

Here comes the Circus Master to show the
dust and dirt that they make me laugh to
see the house clowns turn over a speedy
performance. But I have the platform and
I am the "Star of the Show," for I have
tasted the feeling of success— — —
can it be I am no longer the Queen of
Distress???????????

—Sally Hare

SHARING OUR LIVES AS ONE

Each moment we share is like a wondrous dream.
For we are best friends, supporting each other's
growth and exploring the depths inside each other.

We bring out the best in both of us.

We are lovers of great passion. As our bodies
combine as one, the softness of our skin and the
fiery of our lips touch, as we embrace our hearts,
body and soul.

As companions, we share so many things.
Our interests, beliefs and dreams,
Our compassion for life.

These things we instill within our relationship
for better, for worse, richer or poorer,
Til the heavens take us from the earth.

—Joyce Chavez

MY DEAR HUSBAND, WHERE HAVE YOU BEEN?

My dear husband, where have you been?
You seem like a stranger just walking in.
Where did I lose you? Was it in the hospital?
Antibiotics were the only answer.
At least you didn't have cancer.

The farm was sold. The auctioneer was there.
For 20 years you had been my farmer, my
carpenter, my painter, my husband.
As you stood on the hayrack, I was real proud;
As the auctioneer had chanted long and loud.

Your sickness was a shock I know.
The doctor prescribed warm climate, though.
Was it your sickness or mine, that we are parted?
I think we need a fresh new start.
Where did I lose you. Was it in the bus depot?

Now I push dishcarts and fix fancy salads.
What a letdown from fixing your meals;
and taking you cookies out to the field.
Someday you'll be back in answer to prayer;
and you can be sure, I'll always be there.

—Louise H. Runner

CHEESECAKE 'N CREAM

I'm not a tomato you chauvinist pig;
I'm not a tomato that is a mean dig.
I'm not a lot of things especially a peach.
I'm not a woman who's just for your reach.

But I am a wonderful and kindly dear,
Who won't dash to the fridge to fetch you a beer.
And I am a tremendously smashing good cook,
Who strongly resents receiving a nasty look.

You get so indifferent about "this and that;"
And never have inclination for a courting chat.
"Do what you want" isn't agreeableness.
Then it sometimes seems that more is less.

You get your comfort and in you know where;
Though sometimes you act like a grouchy bear.
There are times I'm irked by your, "I don't care."
Which rivals your stubborn pigheaded glare.

Now that I've stated it all most abundantly clear
You better handle me tender lest I might tear.
Some consideration for me from you on the go,
And now you are becoming a man in the know.

—Verna C. Weyl

PEOPLE ARE JUST LIKE EGGS

People are just like eggs
  Force them a little and they crack
    Push them a little more and they break.
      They are one thing on the outside,
      And another thing on the inside.
      You can never tell if an egg is
    Raw or hard-boiled.
  You can never tell about people
People are just like eggs.

—Carol Mccallum-Shockness

DIFFERENTIAL

With me you thought you could not live,
  As one accustomed to more than you could give;
You could not, would not, ask that I should bear
The lack of careless wealth within your care.
Ah, yes, you took another woman for your wife
To have, to hold, throughout an unknown life.
I wonder often if you've ever come to know
How wrong you were about the monied glow and show,
How much I yearned, and yet I yearn to be,
The one who shares with you your poverty.

—Lee Allen

Oh God . . . the pain
  I couldn't sleep at all last night
Everytime I closed my eyes
I saw you making-love to her
the way you used to with me
I cried
and then I couldn't cry anymore
I was angry
but the anger faded
all that remained was the pain
my body was numb, my mind confused, my heart broken
I wanted to hate you
but couldn't
I love you more than that
maybe
in time
I'll close my eyes and see you with me again
for now
I just won't close
my eyes

—Kymberly Richard

A friend in need
  Is a friend indeed
This is what we just might be
As you get your thoughts together
Just remember all men are not the same
Take me for who I am
When you go dancing
And have a good time
You are certainly free
To be able to see
Whom you well please,
But as for me I'll be here waiting for the phone to ring
Remember the long walks
Remember the good talks
Remember how much we cared
Remember what we shared
Just think of the way it could be
If it wasn't meant for you and me
I will be your friend until
The end

—Jeán Piérre

SEARCH FOR HAPPINESS

I'll tell you lies for my sake
  I'm not fancy I'm fake
I'm anger, I will destroy and damage
Without me you will manage
Leave me behind. Search for my brother
His name is Happiness and he is there
Look to the stars, breathe his air
Take him into your lung
Speak his language, it's on your tongue
This poem is not for anger
If you meet Happiness you're not in danger
The winner will eventually be Happiness
The heart and soul will always caress

—James K. Argurieo

GOODBYE

I'm going to start over again
  I've wasted enough paper and pen
That's if I can think
Getting my thoughts to ink.

It's hard to tell someone goodbye
But it's better than believing a lie
I thought it would be easy as pie
And now I can't bring myself to try.

I loved you with all my heart
I know I promised we'd never part
But I have to go my own way
I'm sorry you're the one to pay.

I need to spread my wings and fly
It's time I took to the sky
I really thought we'd grow together
And it would last forever.

Something happened somewhere in time
We both missed the sign
When "I love you" became just another line.

—Angela Fernandez Just

JUST SO LONG

I can keep my thoughts just so long
  From lingering with you,
Until violins play a rhapsody
And then all my restraint is through.

I can keep my dreams just so long
Protected from the image of you,
Until beauty beats upon my mind
And then what can I do?

I can keep my ideals just so long
From centering entirely on you
Until poetry awakens within me
The old worship, wilder than when new.

I can keep my desire just so long
Buried from the longing for you
Until I hold in my arms a blond baby boy
And feel his body's warmth thru and thru.

I can keep my hopes just so long
From living for the return of you
Until we exchange a warm hello
And all the answers to what's new.

I can keep my love just so long
Silent in my body and my brain
But every twenty-four hours I weaken
And the struggle starts all over again.

—Vi Dykins

BUILDING LOT

The stump — an amputation
The eye cannot abide —
Where is the leafy torso
In which the birds could hide?
This mutilated body,
With severed limbs beside,
Was once a rustling arbor
Where winds and breezes sighed.
Its arms held singing warblers
And baby birds that cried —
How can a heart stop weeping
When such a tree has died?

—Sally Belenardo

Whales are lying
Upon the shore,
And dolphins are dying,
By the score.
The human race,
With hopeless greed,
Can never replace,
All nature's seeds.

Otters and seals,
Hopelessly drown,
And birds whose wings,
Are oiled down.
We rape the land
And poison the air.
All at our command,
It's just not fair.

—Deborah L. Dershem

TROUBLE IN PARADISE

When the rivers flow black
The animals become violent
    little creatures,
Humans stay in their boats.

When the trees blow down
Hurricanes come to Florida
    blowing down beaches,
Humans stay in their houses.

When the rains flood Louisiana
The crops are threatened with
    rainfall,
Now humans care — costs them.

—Eric Mertens

LOOK AROUND

There is something very special,
    We just need to look around.
It is priceless,
    Yet has been given freely.
It can be found anywhere,
    Yet is often overlooked.
It can give new life,
    But is often stopped.
It is our Earth.
Her greens, her blues, her
    waters and skies, her
    temper and her soothingness.
It is something very special,
    We just need to look around.

—Pamela J. Holcombe

STOP: LOOK: AND LISTEN . . . .

Stop and reflect on life, when all was free, happy,
    and simple.
    Look at how it all has changed, at how nothing
is normal, and happy is an expression of the past.
    Listen to the cries of the impoverished, those
in pestilence, or stricken with disease, or famine.

    Stop and ponder, is this our destiny; one filled
with war and destruction.
    Look beyond the faces of the children, see their
hearts, see the building blocks, our future.
    Listen to the plea of the people, wanting peace and
harmony, from all nations and tongues.

    Stop and decide; is it not our right, as mankind,
to want freedom and peace, co-exist with our world,
belonging to all.
    Look at each dawn, see the splendor of a new beginning,
an example for all eons to come.
    Listen to the heart beating inside yourself, feel
how wonderful life can be, and enjoy a tranquility flowing
like the evening tide.

—Jesse Willis

THE SILENT MONSTER

Scientists all tell us that our very lives are doomed.
There is something called pollution, in which we'll be entombed.

This problem of pollution is more evident each day.
The animals are dying off, and yet, some people say;
"Oh, that's not true. Man's much too smart to kill off his
own kind.
The scientists exaggerate those silly things they find."

Meanwhile, poison sprays and radiation damages plants and soil.
Our waterways are filled with things like mercury and oil.
The smoke and fumes from car exhausts are filling up the air,
And factory wastes are flowing from the smokestacks everywhere.

The dying birds and animals are God's way of showing man
That we've got to work together if we're going to save this land.
God made this bounteous earth for us, it met our every need,
But, year by year, man's robbed the land to satisfy his greed.

It's time to look around us now, and make a resolution—
To clear the waters and the air of this monster called pollution.

—I. Best

CRY FOR THE REDWOODS

The Majestic Redwoods stood on a western shore.
They were supposed to exist forever more.
They stood, silent, graceful and majestically proud.
As their branches uplifting reached the cloud.
They stood silent witness when the pioneers came . . .
Riding their wagons across the Great Plain.
They watched in horror when the white man cut the Indians down.
They witnessed the prairies turn into a town.
They witnessed the slaughter of the buffalo herds.
They cried out, but no one could hear their words.
They stood silent as towns became a city.
What transpired thru time was such a pity.
They heard the echo from the cannons' roar,
When America fought the Civil War.
Pollution from smog turned their branches brown.
And the Redmen who worshipped them were no more around.
There is an insanity that precludes reason.
Even so they withstood time from season to season.
Death comes stalking with a tumultuous sound.
No one cries out, as they cut the Redwoods down.

—Florence Bailey

IN THE BALCONY

It is dark in the balcony,
high up here among the crowds,
where I sit watching you perform.
I sit amidst shadowed strangers
who, like I, have not merited
to be in the spotlight.
So many love who you are,
what you can do, and
all that you are becoming.
Yet I am unknown to all.
For you, the curtain opens,
the eyes adore, and
the applause echoes forth.
And I, your loyal faithful friend,
cheer for you loudest of all
from my cold vinyl seat
high up here
where it is dark in the balcony.

—Suzanne E. LaBonte

TRAUMATICUS

Dark stanced on the mountain
he prowls, grim smiler
of non smiles—
scythe resting lightly,
wound tight and restless.

When he
swings,
ripping the sunset
into bloody ribbon,

the sea writhes
and foams at the mouth

and the wind
gasps and shrieks
as the behemoth gears
rumble and growl
to another cosmic mesh . . .

and all is silent
but the whispers.

—James A. Hadsell

The Earth is swollen
And has swallowed me whole.
The sun no longer warms
My face
The stars no longer twinkle
in place . . .

Above my head . . .
With my hopes hidden in the haze—
Of the moon's
Iridescent glow . . .

This I have come to know . . .
   That the rain storm
      runs away
   And the echoes of the
      clapping sky
   Muffle and,
      Die
   And the darkness gives way
      To a green so alive
   That my senses can not
      fully master
   And then I
      AM.

—Christina L. Vaughn

ADRIFT

I'm cast adrift upon two oceans, one below and one above
The waves upon the water are like the clouds upon the air
rolling never ceasing

Their parallel paths move in separate circles
on their endless journey through time.

—Kevin Schamel

HELLO TODAY

Another day I woke up crying. Oh but I've learned so
well to put my pretend smile on, hoping that the day
will hurry on by so I can go home to hide behind the
walls and remove my painted on smile, that has been so
heavy on me all day.

Gloom, sadness, tears, they are the reality in me. The
energy of going from pretend to reality is becoming more
than I can generate.

What will I do when I no longer have the energy? Cry . . . .

—Beatrice Estella Strader

WEDDED BLISS

Delving into the depths of my self-remorse
I caress the despair of days foregone

His urgrund vindications of love devote and pure
But, Sabotage's vigor was only to endure

I thus sought the brawn of another for peace
But, conclusive to love was only degration, desecration and deceit

Now what is left is a mind vulcanized like stone
And a soul left completely alone

So I dam my heart, evading Reality
Protecting it from further vulnerability

No longer have I the strength
To pursue a love so dear

Only can I emerge like a vigilante
From those battlefields of Remorse

To repent and seek shelter
In self-pity's crooked course.

—May Katorji

NO REASON LEFT TO LIVE

She told me life's a fairy tale, that I would see come true,
I see them in my dreams at night, and fear the morning dew,
The horror of the hurt and pain I'll feel each coming day,
These nightmares that I have to live aren't fairy tales at all.
He told me love's a precious thing that I will one day feel,
No one can explain to you, you know it when it's real,
He tells me that he loves me as he kisses off the blood,
That splatter from my flesh each time he struck with love,
Ashes to ashes, that's how I really feel,
They tell me that I live in freedom, to do with as I choose,
Yet I sit here in this prison, in the middle of it all,
Stuck inside these barriers that can't be seen or touched,
What is the reason that I'm here? It couldn't be that much,
Cause there is no happiness that sits upon my heart,
I feel no passion, love, or glee flow through my body parts,
Inside a giant bubble looking out above it all,
No where can I find a spot to break between the walls,
There may be someone out there, that really cares for me,
But I couldn't wait for you to come and set me free,
Ashes to ashes it's time for me to go!

—P. Banks

REFLECTION INTERPRETATION

Person inside of me leave me alone,
I don't want you holding on,
Let my body and mind be free,
I deserve the liberty,
It's hard to comprehend,
The life you choose,
So let us not pretend,
Lets call it truce.
Hey you whats your name?
Living inside my brain,
Let me live the life I need,
Hey you take heed,
For I'am a soul with a gentlemens seed.
My weakness is real too real to confuse,
You failed to fullfill so now you lose.
Saying good-bye is like a cut deep in my heart,
But the wound will heal to keep it from falling apart.

—Mike L. Hernandez, Jr.

REFLECTIONS

I pass a glass and there I see
          a reflection quite familiar.
I've seen it change throughout the years,
          yet it remains the same.
The form I see is but the shell,
          the person hides within.
'Tis but a reflection greets me
          when into the glass I peer.
Yet some reflections that I glimpse
          are of a different kind:
In his strong face I see the form of
          wife and friend and lover,
In trusting eyes above plump cheeks
          the image is of mother,
In glistening tears on a friend's fair face
          I see one who is most trusted.

Each image captures a portion
          of the life within the shell,
But none holds more importance
          than the one seen from within.

—Sonya Barron

WHOSE VIEW?

Beautiful snow — whispering snow!
Lightly it falls; softly it glows.
Covering the ground with a blanket of "down" —
Creating a smile, instead of a frown.
Making each farmer and gardener rejoice;
"Welcome" the moisture, for crops of his choice.
Bringing fertility throughout the dry land —
Blessings to man from a Providential hand!

Yet, some will complain: wet roads are slick;
Cars, trucks and buses do many strange tricks!
Airplanes can't fly or schedules are changed.
All daily routines are slightly rearranged.
Schools may be closed; visibility is low.
Rush-hour traffic is horrendously slow.
Mom's patience ebbs as she tackles her chores;
The kids are now having a "track meet" indoors!

Considering the reasons for one's frame of mind,
Any situation may seem villainous or kind.
Personal perspective may not be all wrong;
But, one person laments and the other writes a song!

—Ruth Fowler

PATHS I'VE CHOSEN

The paths I've chosen weren't always right;
   I've strayed so many times.
Until one day I found a resting place;
The Lord has been so kind.

Little did I know the joys I'd find,
At times I didn't even care.
Then the Lord came in to live,
And I left my troubles there.

There've been so many roadblocks,
Along the winding paths,
But each time He has picked me up,
And my hand He did grasp.

He's walked beside me all the way;
At times I thought, "Why Me?"
He always had an answer,
And now my eyes can see.

—Charlotte A. Dowden

VISIONS 6

A vision of yesterday
Like sand through time
For it to be only yesterday
Precious times long sent away.

To a vision of tomorrow
How may things project
For only to remember yesterday
Nothing shall remain.

To the vision long ago
Not to see in so long
Gone to the time forgotten
Perhaps things lost.

To a vision of yesterday
Farewell to each and everyone
To travel a time long remembered
Not to say goodbye but to say hello.

—Jim Wells

THE MIRROR REVISITED

Between me and myself
is a widening gulf
and I am standing there looking at the mirror
Is that me?!
No!
Away from the mirror, I look alot myself!

I turned around, no body was there to ask
May be the mirror has been cheating
or me wearing a mask!
I tried to pull
Nothing came off, except dirt
And my poker face started to hurt!

That face in the mirror is supposed to be mine!
How come?!
Away from the mirror, I very often shine!

So that face is me
Me and I, could that be?
It is following me
I turn it turns
And it sees what I see!
That face became my picture
Is that meeeeeeeee?!

—A. Y. M. Nour

HEDY

Through days filled with the noise and movement of untamed youth,
With tensions ebbing and flowing like a great thunderstorm
Turbulence rolling internally, Fiercely! Clashes of minds and wills
A roller coaster ride of hypertension in a blackboard zoo
Then home to the peace and quiet of a well-kept, warm, and friendly home
To colors and sounds that relax the soul
To beauty of form and shape, neat and clean
And amid' this — my own goddess!! As goddesses of old with a
Temperament of paprika, a woman without comparison,
A mate with talents so numerous, a spirit defiant and indomitable
But kind and generous who during the quiet, loving time
Gives tenderness, passion, and joy, The paradise of love
My arms around the satin-skinned body, the loving touch, the curves
That warm my heart and passions a union priceless — My love
Grows greater day by day for
The love of my life, my Darling, my Sweetheart Hedy

      —Edward E. Jex

WHERE SOME PEOPLE . . .

Where some people refuse to dream, I dare to reach for those dreams
Where some are afraid of chances, I eagerly look forward to the risks in life
Where others are skeptical, I am a visionary
Where some sit back and watch, I get involved with gusto
Where others doubt, I believe
Where others are dependent on others, I am self-reliant
Where some merely "wish," I know I will achieve
Where some are fearful to love, I love whole heartedly
Where some hope to win the lottery, I write my own winning ticket
Where some read books of exotic lands, I live on the island
Where some are negative, I am positive
Where some are critical, I am encouraging
Where some just get by, I gather riches
Where some dread the morning, I awake before the alarm
Where some say I can't, I already have
Where some hoard their possessions, I keep what I give away
Where some are tired after 8 hours, I have energy after 20
Where some sit on the side-lines, I am an active player
Where some say "it will never fly," I am inventing the next model
Where some think dreams are for children, my dreams will become my children's reality.

      —Dawn M. Tielbar

KENNETH'S SONG

Though my body is young, my soul's seen many planes,
It's traveled many dimensions and experienced many things.

When Christ died on the cross I, too, felt his pain.
And when Napoleon met his match at Waterloo, I also felt his shame.

When thirteen little colonies fought for democracy,
I bled with all the dead men, though no one's eyes could see.

When brothers met on the battlefield dressed in blue and gray,
I shed tears, the taste of salt, I still can taste today.

When hell broke out over there and Americans went to war,
To fight in trenches of mud and sweat, my bones too, were sore.

But to me nothing can compare to the suffering that you beared
By the Japs who took you, and by God you were spared.
For though you did not see me, truly I was there.

I was the soldier who carried you, half-conscious, nearly dead
Along the "Death March" roadway, as I watched them slay our fall-behind comrades.

When you were cold and hungry, I froze and starved with you.
And I gave you courage, to help you make it through.

But, too, with you I suffered those long, lonely years.
And though you could not see me, truly I was there.

      —Patti Patrick

MOTHER

Mother, you've raised me to
   be the best that I can.
Hard times, smooth times,
   you lend the helping hand.

You've never, ever let me down.
And when I need you, you're
   always around.

Daytime, nightime, any hour of
   the day.
You comfort and hold me,
   by my side you stay.

A relationship never to be torn
   apart.
Mother, I love you with
   all my heart.

—Amy Jo Starr, age 13

MY SON

Kendall my son
   I love you don't you know
Your every hope and every dream
I wanted for so long.

All the emptiness I felt
All the years that passed me by
Were worth every moment
When you came into my life.

You have no idea the joy
You've brought into our lives
You have no idea the love
I feel for you inside.

I hope you always know my son
How much you mean to me
For God answered all my prayers
When he gave you to me.

You're a special little boy
And growing far too fast for me
And I'm so glad you know
You're the son God gave to me.

Mommie

—Lois Findley

MY SONS AND MUSIC

My sons have been a blessing
   To me throughout the years—
We've shared our joy and sorrow,
Our laughter and our tears.

Life has a richer meaning
And little things mean much;
Tho' miles may separate us,
We always stay in touch.

They're both involved in music
—To higher goals aspire,
Each time they play the organ
As well as lead the choir.

Their music is inspiring
—It lifts the spirit high;
The sounds are so majestic,
They seem to reach the sky!

Their talents are God-given
So they could others bless;
We share, because of music,
Much peace and happiness.

—Anna M. Matthews

I watch our children run gleefully through the warm sunshine
   the wind gently blowing their soft shiny hair.

The feeling of immortality mixed with love and pride and joy.
Watching tiny pieces of one another grow and change and learn.

Our love shining like bright lights
through the eyes of our children.
As the last of winter's leaves gently swirl around me,
Gliding to the ground . .

—Tammy L. Byrns

FOREVER FRIENDS

Forever Friends stick together in even the worst of times,
   and you have always been there for me, and I in return will
always be here for you. We have been through so much together,
and no matter good or bad, we always seem to work things out.

   I have other friends, but you're so special. You have
seen me off to school for quite a few years now, and I
always miss you while I'm gone. You are still in my thoughts
all through the day.

   We have such a unique relationship, that only a mother,
and daughter could have. I'm so glad that God gave me the
wonderful gift of a friend like you; mom.

Dedicated to: Sherril Lowe with love, your daughter.

—Leeann Gribbins

CHILDREN

Children are a special gift to a family made of love,
   they warm the hearts of all mankind under heaven above.

All through their lives children will bring,
a feeling much like the first day of spring.

A feeling of sharing their hopes and their dreams,
and getting them over life's first giant streams.

Always being there through good times and bad,
and helping them feel better when they're feeling sad.

Children are a lot of hard work, but through it all they say,
there is no greater happiness than that received from a child
   each day.

They are a special kind of people, that need a special kind of
   care,
and they will never fall astray as long as love is always
   there.

—Sandra Lyons

A CHILD'S EMOTIONS

She was four years old then as she stood by my chair,
   and asked, "Mom, would you please put a braid in my hair?"
   I agreed but then asked for a brush for this task;
she seemed bothered that I would even think to ask.
   "Why me? Always me! It's your turn!" she exclaimed,
in a voice so assertive that I should be ashamed.
   I replied, "Here's a deal. You first look over there,
and if you can't find it, I'll go look way upstairs."
   She thought I was brilliant to make up such a plan,
and without delay, to the cabinet she ran.
   But she returned in a moment with her face drooping low,
the brush clutched in her hand, and her eyes downcast below.
   She felt cheated, betrayed and was sure I was not
the most wonderful mother as she'd previously thought.
   Her hair was then pampered as I held back my grin
from this child I had wounded and tortured within.
   She quietly waited, then she turned and she smiled
with her face bright, her eyes glowing, and her hair neatly styled.

—Elaine Beal Howes

MOVE ON WATER

"Move on Water"
Move on.
Flat stream down slope.
Decay bank tied boat.
"Move on Water"
Move on.
Catch twig and leaves.
Rush around trees.
"Move on Water"
Move on.
Spread over the land.
Soak in yonder sand.
"Move on Water"
Move on.

—Lillie Marshall

FOREVER AND BEYOND

Forever and beyond
my love for you
shall linger . . .
long after this
world we now know
fades into naught —
when the sun's rays
cease to sparkle iridescent
upon peaceful lochs —
when the moon's
pale beams dance
no more upon
the lonely moors —
when shadows lie
cold upon this
desolate land
my love shall
transcend the void
and find you
in the darkness.

—Lizabeth Cox

MY GIFT

Feel my presence
See my light
Focus on me
Look inside

Feel my power
Feel my peace
Feel my love
Feel my strength

I was told I must hurry
I now understand
This is my message
as real as I can

Live in the moment
Live in the truth
Live in yourself
Live in your youth

Feel my power
Feel my peace
Feel my love
Feel my strength

My gift is myself
I give me to you
I invite you to love me
For I will always love you.

—Kim L. Evans

MY CORNER OF THE EARTH

The seagulls breeze by, their majesty unveiling,
    as the gentle breeze sweeps waves of blue upon the shoreline.
            God is present.
Excited, carefree children play in the green, tree-lined park,
    their sun-kissed faces gleaming.
            Moments to treasure.
Contented fishermen display their prize catches,
    with pride and fulfillment, oblivious to time.
            All is at peace.
The "Vikings" conquer, happy fans cheer, the town glows.
            All is right with the world.
O, how I long for days past,
    when cares were few and memories were being made.
Where innocence abounded, with disregard to ever increasing pressures,
    and world-induced turmoil.
            To go home again . . .

—Jane Harmon Jakubiak

STEPS TAKEN (D.J.)

We all have decisions in this life that we must face.
    Some change your life dramatically.
Others are so insignificant,
That they leave not a trace.

Your mind can become clouded,
Your eyes blinded by fear.
But if you reach down deep inside,
And listen to your heart, it might become clear.

Self doubt and indecision,
Will leave you confused.
Your spirit in agony,
Not sure if you have been abused.

But there are times in your life when you must make the long hard run.
Stand up, take the reins.
Forget what consequence it might bring.
Sometimes you must take care of number one.

    You will survive, I know this to be true.
    Because even decisions my friend may be reversed too.

—Greyy

TAKE TIME TO LIVE

Take time to drink freely of the waters that flow from the Fountain
    of Life.
Take time to listen with deep feeling to the Music of the Masters.
Take time to dream and to think of new ideas; you may be the builder
of a better world—your mind is the greatest possession you have.
Take time to play, and thereby refresh your mind with quiet pleasure
and laughter—all work only stifles your being—and takes from you
your creative energy—but when you work, do your work willing and with
great care.
Take time to give a smile of encouragement to a passerby, or wipe a
tear from a child's eye—your life will be greatly enriched by these little
acts of kindness. This is the essence of living.
Take time to meditate, and experience the peace that you find within
your heart.
Take time to know yourself, it will enable you to know your strengths
as well as your weaknesses, and to gain insight into others.
Take time to be quiet, there is much to hear and to learn in stillness.
Take time to read—reading requires quietness, and books can be best
friends.
Take time to appreciate the beauty and the aroma of a rose—the life
of a rose is so fleeting—soon it withers and fades, and is no more.
Take time to love—it is only by loving that we are loved.
Take time to live. Death has no age.

—Frances Ann Gardiner

THERE'S A PLACE ON EARTH JUST WAITING FOR ME.

Somewhere underneath the Rainbow, somewhere over the Sea.
There's a place on earth just waiting for me. A time for peace
a time for Love. Like the flowers, rain, the sky above. Life
is not to fear when your heart has been broken, cause death
is so near when your words are out spoken. Open your eyes
and see the light. Listen to the words of wisdom as
I say Goodnight. Listen to the wind as it blows soft
towards the south. Is it sirens and guns going off or is it
just the birds chirping when they open their mouths. We have the freedom,
the right to choose. We can fight to stay alive, or we can die and lose.
Whatever we decide in Life, is alright with me. Because what
we make of it, is for the world to see. We have its beauty,
that comes within. Some call it passion, others call it sin.
We have four seasons that go by very fast. That means time
never slows down, when you come in Last. I guess what I'm trying
to say, no matter where you go or what you do. There's someone
always watching you. Where every eye can see, there's a
place on earth just waiting for me.

— Randy Lynn Keatts

REMEMBERING

You brought home a bundle wrapped in down
How fondly you huddled this little clown.
He laughed, he cried, you lived, you died.
When he toddled and fell, you were under his spell.
Seems it was only yesterday, he was wrapped in down,
Now he struts all over town.
All the kids have 'bikes' so you buy one for this little tyke.
He goes off on his own to join the race, want to shout "slow your pace"
But refrain as, he should himself train.
Years are jetting by as he goes out on his own,
School, dates he's free to roam.
Now you watch as down the aisle they come, each and every one
Handsome and full of hope, that they will all cope,
With the hazards of life and no strife.
Another era you sigh, as it starts all over again, college is nigh.
Another graduation, he sure is handsome, wouldn't change all this
For a king's ransom.
Now he's on his own, his wild seeds sown.
Children of his own as the cycle starts over again.
You are remembering again no end: Eon.

— Dot Luria Nadler

THE DREAM

The sweet liquid from the lip of my glass,
Touched me and a drop rolled from my mouth,
Adventurously exploring the curvatures of my dismayed chin.
I brought the half defeated cigarette to meet its awaiting hunger,
Before it had left my grasp the mysterious smoke began to billow out of me.

Somewhere within the smoke I became lost
At once my mind drifted endlessly
Taking meaningless turns on forbidden passages,
Those which had been cast deep into an endless hell,
Never to be uncovered.

I became motionless, my mind lost sense of time,
My body lost sense of reality,
I felt the ocean, the waves carried me
The soothing sounds sent me deeper,
At once I felt at peace, calling out never to return.

Suddenly the drop fell and time became forever,
It seemed like a heavenly eternity,
When a lifeless second struck,
And I returned
The drop had come to a peaceful rest upon my hand.

— Pamela Fimognari Koch

ONENESS HAPPINESS

Running through the night
Turning on a candle
You and I strain to rise
Once upon a morning sun

— Peter Graham

VANISHED CIVILIZATION

A small babe cries
flustered with heat
His mother rushes to him
carrying a basket
of stone ground corn.

The hunt,
the men's hunt
rages
on the mountain
to bring to the
people
life giving food.

Children
climb, shout
and holler
and laugh
and laugh.

Everywhere there
was life,
Now there is
silent beauty.

— Brenna Renee Mead

THE GRAVEYARD

Dark,
Misty,
Whispering,
Gloomy,
Graveyard.

Keep your eternal
hands off me.
Let me walk by,
And keep my soul
within my young
body.

But it's Halloween,
And I feel like some
one,
Something,
Is watching me.

As my shoes are jogging
faster,
It's like this walk is
everlasting!

Seems like I've been
running,
But the moon hasn't
moved,
Nor have I.

In a moment's time,
I realize with fright,
That I'm forever stuck
in this night!

— Anna Thompson

265

FOR MY MOTHER

In a garden filled with roses
I know she walks today
Down a path that's bright and shining
No weeds along the way.

In life the way might have been rocky
But she never did complain.
Singing hymns of glory
As the years went rolling by.
Now her day has ended
And I'm sure she's found contentment.

Her face so fair and peaceful
Shows no trace of pain and care.
While she walks among the roses
In that garden over there.

—Lillie B. Garner

DEAREST JOE DON

If only I could hold you,
And rock you once again.
And see your lovely smile,
And touch your precious hand.

I'd give my life to have you
Here, where you should be,
With all the ones that love you
And hold tight your memory.

It's so hard to keep going,
Life doesn't seem worthwhile.
I miss you so much, Joe Don.
You're Mommy's Special Child.

You know, it's almost Christmas,
I hope that God will do
The things I would have done,
If I could be with you.

You'll always be here with me,
I can almost feel your touch.
You're in my heart Sweet Baby.
I love you so, so much.
Always and Forever, Love, Mommy

In memory of Joe Don Nathan Ezzo
Sept. 22, 1989 — Oct. 11, 1989
—Teri Ezzo

A PRAYER FOR JOE DON NATHAN EZZO

Dear God,
Do you have a rocking chair
To rock our little baby there?
And, will you sing him a lullabye,
Like, hush little baby, don't you cry?
And will you teach him to patty cake?
Do this Lord, for Pap-pa's sake.
Will you tickle him under the chin,
Just to see that lopsided grin?
Will you play with him peek-a-boo?
And teach him to make faces too?
These are things that we would do,
But now God, it's all up to you.
We have these memories to enjoy
Of our tiny, precious baby boy.
This is the deepest pain
We could ever know.
So give us strength Lord
To just let go. We thank you.
Amen
Joe Don's Gramma

—JoAnn Olds

THE CHILDREN

Soon the children will be off to school,
Books in arms and lunch pails swinging,
To learn and live by the Golden Rule,
Their spirits free—new joy bringing.

Soon the children will be grown;
They will leave this home—their nest.
Their seeds of life will have to be sown;
They will settle after their restlessness.

Soon the children will grow old;
They'll have gone through life's course.
They'll tell of times—just as they were told,
When times were better, when times were worse.

Soon the children will come to death,
And the child will be no more.
So it is of life—just a fleeting breath,
Just a step inside the door.

—Barbara J. Wiggins

SAD . . .

I am so sad
and I don't know why.
Tears run down my face
as I sit here and cry.
My life is so confusing,
like the lines on this paper.
I don't know where I am heading,
I feel so blind.
I feel like running, so very far,
to get lost in the clouds and find
my life again.
But I don't know what to do, until
I get lost in the clouds to find my life.
I am so lonely and sad, I wish I could smile,
but it seems like I don't even remember how!
I dream so many dreams, but I have
one dream I wish to come true, that
is that I could find someone who can
teach me how to smile, once more . . .

—Deb Nachazel

THE GATHERING

Moonbeams pour and trickle down
heavy-bent pines laden with snowy white,
while men below in the quiet town
restlessly slumber throughout the night,
their heavy breathing the only sound.

Brightened cathedral, white from the moon
stands sincere in the forest dark.
Pillars erected by God all too soon,
this place in the woodland park
appears all too different in the dead of noon.

Here, animals come from the earth and sky
all things which creep or crawl,
to gather in church and to reason why
man cannot worship outside the walls
not knowing, or seeing that He is nigh.

Sparkling crystals dance and glow
whilst He above observes this Mass
and their love for the natural world they know.
Can man's infinite wisdom ever surpass
that which the animals already know?

—John Smelcer

MASTERPIECE

As I'm laying here
My thoughts absorbing your absence
The interior space within my world
    motionless, noiseless
Loneliness consuming the element essential
    for my existence
Falling off into a faint state
    reminiscing, remembering
Each occurrence
    vivid, so obvious
Wakening from a state that's, more than, true to life
Exhausted from the overwhelming emotions,
    dried tears outlining my face
My masterpiece, the greatest of all
Empty without another, lonely, waiting,
    anxious for the void to be filled, waiting
Soon will be together,
    the thoughts being replaced by reality

      —S. M. Ashby

A RETREAT

There was a time when I cried for my mother,
But she did not hear me.
There was a time when I cried for my friend,
But she did not care for me
There was a time when I cried for my darling
But he could not help me.

Today first time in my life I cried for my Saviour,
I regretted for my ingratitude;
He had followed me — all my years,
He had directed me — all through the days.
He consoled and encouraged me — all my life,
He never failed me, in any of my moments.
Oh my everloving friend,
I thank you.

I need you
You are close to me
As close or as far as
A red rose in a blind woman's hand.
I can feel your presence
But cannot enjoy you fully!

      —B. Puthur

Thinking of all the people I've ever known when I was a
    child, or now that I'm grown.
Not one in my life can ever compare to my grandma who was
    always there.
In ten short years she gave me a beginning, all money could
    never buy.
Number one was the Love of God and a better life after we
    die.
She taught me so much, day after day, when we went to the
    old tree stump to pray.
We walked to the graveyard high on the hill, it was
    beautiful there, so quiet and still.
We picked wild flowers to place on the graves, and talked
    for hours about past summer days.
She talked of her children now grown and away, and the ones
    who lay sleeping alone in the clay.
She wasn't sad, for she would see them again, she often sang
    "When We All Get To Heaven."
Many years have gone by since way back then, and she's still
    the best grandma that has ever been.

      —Jean Gordon

MY HEAVEN

When I get to heaven I'll dance
over the world.
I'll swing from the moon-beams,
and shine like a pearl.

I'll converse with the authors and
poets of old, and paint with
the artist who painted the World.

I'll lay down with the lions
in meadows of gold, and sleep
in a straw-bed like the father I know.

I'll fly with the ravens, and
swim in the sea, and before
God in heaven I'll bend my knee.

      —Mattie Lowe

FOR THE LOVE OF JEREMY

The tiny little heart inside
Tried hard to keep beating
You knew no matter how you tried,
The hurt was too defeating.

Finally, the hurt stopped
Peace became your friend
No one could replace the smile
You wore until the end.

As you entered into the Gates,
You were not afraid
Because you knew within your heart
The plans that God had made.

You worried about your mom and dad
How would they be?
God looked at you and said,
"They know you're with me."

You received your tiny little wings
A tiny halo too
Then you took your place in Heaven
That God made just for you.

      —Kathy Reynolds

A BUD IN GOD'S BOUQUET

It seems but just a day or two
Since we held you in our arms,
And thrilled so much in new delight
With each of your baby charms.

We remember your funny, charming way
Of tottering at our side,
And chattering a language all your own,
You filled our hearts with pride.

We're thankful for the years gone by,
Tho much too short they seem,
So much so that at times we feel
You were really just a dream.

Just "yesterday" our dearest one,
Your smiling face gazed into ours,
As together we picked a bouquet
Of God's beautiful flowers.

Suddenly I understand
And tears flow like a flood,
God too loves a beautiful bouquet,
Now he's added you, a tiny bud.

      —Ardiss M. Laughery

BLACK ROSES

The roses in the vase
Are black with decay.
Our love is dead and
I'm telling him so today.

I don't want to hurt him.
He never did hurt me.
But everything just crumbled
And now I have to flee.

Too many actions
Too soon and too fast.
I should have known sooner
That desire wouldn't last.

So now the oceans
I've stored in my eyes
Are flooding my face.
I hope it never dries.

—Tammy-Lynn Clason,
age 15

FANTASY

The hour's late.
A voice from long ago
lingers in my memory.

This shadow floats
in misty mountain scenes
a cabin
quails grouping
to gossip news
of lovers locked together
damp as the dew
clinging to dawn blossoms.

Was this scene
a fantasy
a past life remembrance
or a longing dream
of love

gone

spent?

—Lisa Ferris Rubin
In collaboration with Carmen M. Pursifull

DREAMS DIE HARD

Dreams die hard,
when of the heart.
Mine all died,
when we fell apart.

Young and foolish,
that was me.
Only believing
what I wanted to see.

A little girl who,
grew up too fast.
Thank God it's over,
and in the past.

Someone new,
has come along,
and filled my heart,
with a beautiful song.

Dreams die hard,
when of the heart.
But new ones arise,
for a brand new start.

—Susan V. Adams

TEARY EYES

Look into my eyes and you will see
Straight into my heart,
For that is where you will always be.
I placed you there in 1962 and yet I knew
There were just too many clues.
I always thought we were meant to be until we married in November,
Perhaps it should have been December.
The Drugs, the Pot, and your family were your number one priorities.
I will never forget how much that hurt,
The loss I felt, the lifelessness,
For I had no self-worth.
You filed for divorce and now you are free
And I have never felt so lonely.
My eyes fill with tears so much of the time,
Because the one man I loved
Chose not to be mine.
Oh yes, my dear, you are still here, deep within my heart,
Along with the scars you left for me
Until my day of eternity.

—Pam Hoyle

Tonight —
you have gone.
I am empty as I sit and stare attentively at nothing.
For there is nothing left.
You were everything and you are gone.
The rain beats rhythmically against my window.
There is no more sun in my life.
This weather is fitting —
This noose is fitting —
securely about my neck.
It is the first feeling of security I've had in a long time.
It must be right.
Of course it's not hard to pick the right answer when
there's only one choice.
Yes, this is the right answer.
It was a trick question though.
There were so many other answers that seemed so right for so long —
but together we eliminated them —
it is so clear now,
so easy,
so peaceful,

so long . . .

—Mary Kay Lanzafame

BROKEN ROSE

A rose, withered, and faded lay faceless against the table's edge, waiting for the next breeze, to blow it from existence. From the window, remorsefully, the petals recall the brush of a woman's lips, that so passionately, cherished it.

But its deliverance, was of harder substance, whose intent bruised its velvety velour. For he is gone, and the broken remains of this flowery form, are all that's left to her.

She lives on better than the broken rose without summer's sun. But this summer has lied to her, with foretellings of warmth, stemming from summer's love.

Now, however, like the rose her aura has lost some pigment, and some inside parts have died. As this summer's love, lost radiance through manipulation, and lies.

The rose, in its last days, turns toward the window's glass. And secretly wishes for a strong north wind, to blow its shameful existence away . . . .

AT LAST.

—Carman Smith

HOBBY AIRPORT HILTON 3:00 a.m. BLUES

As I sat in the dark looking out the window, it occurred to me that the airport seemed very lonely at night. Almost as lonely as me.

The cool blue lights made it feel distant and aloof.

I watched a single plane with its blinking red tail light, for what seemed like a long time, directly across from me. It slowly turned and taxied out of sight.

I didn't notice the truck until the plane began to move.

When I saw the truck drive away in the opposite direction, I wanted to cry. I'm not sure why, exactly.

I think because it was like saying goodbye to a friend that you know you'll never see again. It gave me an emptiness inside.

Now the sun is rising and with its light I am able to see the mist hovering above the runway. The shuttle buses are beginning to scurry up and down Airport Blvd. The roar from the airplanes taking off break the silence and the blue lights are fading into the background. The airport doesn't seem lonely anymore.

Why do I?

—Czarina Crystal

ABANDONED GARDEN

Away out on the prairie, far from any town, stands an old abandoned farm house where once a family and their laughter did abound.

Many years have come and gone and time did take its toll. Still, I think about the mother and the hard times (bless her soul.)

Each spring, as I pass by in caring for the land, I see a miracle happening that's hard to understand. For beside the house as the snow lets go to spring there are daffodils a'blooming and no one's tended there.

Then comes May, the lilacs do profusely bloom. I think about the flowers and why they flourish so. The land is often dry and harsh winds do surely blow. There's iris, lilies, woodvine and others I don't know all clinging tenaciously to life all on their own.

What keeps them thriving in this so hard and bitter land?

Many years have passed since the family tended there with hoe and rake and surely a silent prayer.

I sometimes think I'll dig those daffodils and take them with home with me and plant them in my garden to enjoy them patiently.

Then a small voice seems to say, "Don't touch them! Don't you see, they are striving as a living memory to a scattered family."

I truly think that mother is looking from above and, maybe, still tending her garden with a spiritual hand of love.

—Roy M. Andersen

LIVE

As time passed, I wondered if time even existed at all.
Yet, after life had passed me by, I knew it had.
As days went by, my eyes became unaware
of the beauty of the Earth.
The sun seemed to bear down upon me as if I was a barren desert.
In despair, I asked if water ever fell from the vast sky . . .
only to find that my eyes failed to notice
that rain came yesterday.
Time wore on, and my heart became weak; my flesh grew apathetic,
and my toil seemed useless . . . so I failed to put forth effort.
There I stood, upon a weary garden,
wondering if roses had ever found pleasure
in that flowerbed . . . only to receive the reply,
"Yes, they did, until you trampled them in carelessness."
As morning arrived, I cringed at the thought
of facing the world again.
And as my life continued, I wondered if death even existed at all.
Unfortunately, I wasn't able to hear a reply . . .
for life had surely
passed me by.

—Melanie E. Miller

GRAY

Gray rain
Slumbered into evening.

Raindrops monologued
The river.

While I to my gray heart
Attended.

—Lily Beth Appleton

OUR AMERICAN FLAG

Here stands our Flag,
It's no rag.
Stand by it with pride,
For it many have died.
Red, white and blue,
It's ours that is true.
Win or lose,
You're the one to choose.
Let's keep it flying high,
Way up in the sky.
For all to see,
From sea to sea.

—Anita T. Swensen

PARTS OF A MACHINE

They move with grace
Across the field.
Each a separate part
Of a giant machine.

If one breaks
Others are there
To take its place
'Till they break.

Each must work
Together as one
To fulfill the duty
To its fullest potential.

For without
Teamwork
The machine
No longer functions.

—Jess Drennan

VIETNAM

There once was a war
On a distant shore
With bombs in the sky
Many soldiers would die
Why they were there
They did not care
For they had to go
Someone told them so
All the women would cry
All the children ask why
Because man killing man
They did not understand
We learn from these years
And from all our tears
To solve a dispute
We don't have to shoot
For a problem to end
We should just be a friend

—R. M. Reed

EMPTINESS

A sweat-stained hat hanging from a hook;
A worn shirt stored away in its own little nook;
A workman's boots lying abandoned near the door;
A crumpled pair of jeans discarded on the floor;
All are reminders of a man who was cherished.
All are reminders of a man who has perished.

The memory of the unmoving, lifeless form;
The drifts of snow left by yesterday's storm;
The nightmares and insomnia which consume each night;
The fact that things will never again be all right;
Each is a reminder of the emptiness within my mind.
Each is a reminder of the emptiness left behind.

—Mary Jo Cocking

ALL OUR HEROES DIDN'T DIE IN THE WAR

All our heroes didn't die in the war;
                          the storekeeper
stashes death in a cluttered arrangement of ancient apothecary jars,
precariously juggled upon cobwebbed shelves hidden in the back ante room
of his shop.

All our heroes didn't die in the war;
                          the storekeeper
chooses carefully the next apothecary jar he will uncork.
Which dusty label will carry out his timeless mission?

All our heroes didn't die in the war;
                    some before,   some after,
their last chapter the quotes of a lifetime, unheard.
                          Without a word the
gnarled hand hovers, wanting no mistakes, and then with deliberation,
one apothecary jar judiciously leaves the shelf.

And, the empty space screams . . . .

The scream is the silence.
The silence the scream.
Which is reality?
Which is the dream?

—Versey A. Chapelle

BROTHER DEAR

Cannot understand why it should be,
You went away so quick like a ship out to sea,
Your birthday is so very near,
We miss you so very much, Brother Dear.

We remember when you marched with the rest,
To receive your high school diploma when you did your best,
You were so young when Uncle Sam took you away,
We prayed often that you would return some day.

When the 71st Fighter Wing landed at Normandy in France,
Didn't seem like none of the fellows had a chance,
What with all the fighting all around,
Everyone was praying to make it safely to the ground.

It was such a surprise when I received the pink, plastic locket with the
P-38 Fighter Plane.
Then 19 out of 23 were killed in the Billings, Montana plane crash and
Dad rode all night with you on the train,
One young man gave his life for you and another young man,
God gave you 40 more years, a college degree, a Master's Degree,
a Christian woman.

You have surely left your fine marks along your merry way,
Like a ship going out in the bay,
And the time seems so very near,
That we'll all be reunited, Brother Dear.

—Lois Barnes Willson

NEAR TIME

I have seen you for the first time in years.
Your body was like a tree in the cold winter months.
Your face seemed cracked and shattered, not that it
Mattered.
Your eyes dazed with distress, not that you were a mess.
You lost track of time, but not your mind.
Through the years there has been many tears.
You struggled and suffered enough pain now it's time
To loosen the chains.
I knew you had the strength to go the full length.
Your day is near and soon, things will be clear.

—Mi Mi

SEAWIND

Miles and miles of an unending ocean,
The sunrise reflects off the open water.
The lone ship is just awakening.
The hull creaking as if it is yawning.
The Seawind wanders restlessly about,
Looking for its lost comrades.
For they have been taken, Prisoners of War.
A war where peace is a word from faraway shores.
Where life and death walk hand in hand.
The life is lost, but death lives on.
For every life lost, another is spared.
And that life spared is so precious,
As precious as the ocean is to the SeaWind.

—Amanda L. Smith

DESERTED CEMETERY

Deserted cemetery
Strewn about are many bones,
And broken head stones.
In the wind, can be heard human cries and moans.

II
The weeds have grown tall.
The graveled paths are gone.
Graffiti is scrawled on a wall.
A pall hangs in the smoky dawn.

III
Rusted—sagging fences and gates—
On the stones, you can't read the dates,
Or know who were their children or who were their mates.
For a caretaker, the desecrated graveyard waits and waits.

—Jane Pierritz

IN THE COURSE OF BATTLE . . .

A soldier floats above his dead body
in the midst of a lonely battlefield;
his lingering spirit waiting to see
an allotted companion keep his oath.

Through the dead the living soldier wanders
seeking his comrade, divorced by the lot.
He had heard the horn, the signal of death,
and came to put the soul to final rest.

The trumpet was still clutched in the hand
of his friend's hewn body when he found him.
Grey stones soon found their place on the deceased—
granting body and soul infinite peace.

The soul ascends looking down to bless his
comrade, then smiles—content with life at last.

—Jonathan W. Neske

LOSING

Losing is never easy,
It seems to hurt so bad.
Often it makes one queazy,
And wonder what he had.

One loses at games,
And sometimes at life.
Losing never has any claims.
Just an endless trail of strife.

But, when one loses at love,
He loses a part of his soul.
Like the clouds up above,
He has no destiny, no goal.

So why must we ever lose,
It's such a meaningless trend.
But, I guess we all must sometimes lose,
If we ever expect to win.

—Rebecca C. Cowan

SHADOWS OF NIGHT

Shadows of night are creeping around
Dimming the sun's golden light
All the joys of summer's sound
Seem to have taken sudden flight.

Why can't you stay? Why did you leave?
Oh: what a tangled web we weave.

Why come at all to gladden the heart?
That labored so long to be free
Then take it with you as you depart
On your fateful journey to eternity.

To that illusive land of dreams
Where none can follow—or so it seems.

Life must go on—that is the plan
Till the sands of time run out
Ride with the tide as best you can
That's what life is all about.

So gather round you shadows of night
Protect me from love's tender light.

—Emma Pletcher

AMERICA WE LOVE

America the land we love,
Was given to us from God above.
We shall never forget the ones before,
That taught us to love forevermore.

America, the land of freedom,
To worship God as we choose,
Go where we want to go,
And do what we want to do.

America, a land of beauty,
Of many wonderful places,
Will make tears in our eyes,
And joyful smiling faces.

America, the land we love,
No matter what color, race, or creed.
We will never forget you America,
Because you are the land we need.

We want to thank you, America,
For this wonderful land of ours,
And we shall always be grateful,
As we bow our heads in prayer.

—Emily S. McCormick

SOLO

I saw you last night
Stars all around your face
A fast falling comet
On a solo flight.

You burned so bright
And lit up my tears
They sparkled like fireflies
In the cold desert night.

—Kati Schnaufer

AN UNFEELING HEART

My love was lost
my heart closed up
and refused to feel anymore.

I'd been hurt one too
many times
my heart couldn't take
any more pain.

Someday a tear will fall,
the pain will wash away,
and my heart
will open up
once more.

—Catherine M. Ruen

VIVISECTION

With every gesture
The slash of knife
Whispered arrows fly
Words through my heart
Callous, careless
Want and need foremost
Love, less understanding
Foundations rock in fault

Crooning cat claws
Slice and slip in deep
Reiterate the point
Another lesson quickly taught
Hurtful, spiteful
Tenderness victim to the self
Fear not the future
For it's only love again

—J. Fannell

WIDOW

No sweet surprises for this
Widow.
Only quiet longings
Rememberings
Wishes.

No voices but her own
No comparisons
No exchanges.

How long before the voices
are heard again?
Hold fast, Widow.
Time will let you go—
Changed
but
somehow
More.

—Paulette M. Barry

TREASURES

I have no silver or gold, no trunks of priceless treasure
No precious sheets of silk to hold, no material objects of measure.

But I have a sky of sapphire blue, my gold is in the sun above
Shining stars of silver hue, the only gift I have is love.

My emerald green is in the leaves, my ruby the firelight
My soft as silk the gentle breeze, my ebony the velvet night.

You can have your treasures, the status it brings,
The temporary pleasures of material things.

For wretched the mind and shallow the soul
Thru death shall find there's nothing to show.

But I'll give you my sunrise, my diamonds of dew.
My gold in the sunshine, my love for you,

Across the universe till the edge of time.
My treasures are memories what treasures are thine?

—Vickie Bright

ALONE

The evening shadows lengthen and creep slowly 'cross the floor.
The howling wind is blowing in, cold air beneath the door.
On the wall the clock keeps ticking; tick, tick, tick, the seconds fly;
But he doesn't seem to notice for the tears dim his eyes
As he gazes out the window at the grave upon the hill;
And his old white head rests wearily against the window sill.

His eyes never blinking, a smile steals across his face,
As his mind goes back in years to another time, another place.
Then he stands alert, lifts his head and listens very hard.
Was that the sound of children playing outside in the yard?
In his mind's eye he sees them, running carefree like the wind;
And his heart is warm and glowing as he beckons them "come in."

He hears her in the kitchen cooking supper, like she should.
What is that she's cooking? It sure smells mighty good.
He hears the clatter of the dishes as the evening table's spread;
And he hears the creak of the oven door as she takes out the bread.
The family is all together for this evening meal;
But then his eyes move slowly to the grave upon the hill.

The evening shadows lengthen and creep slowly 'cross the floor.
The howling wind is blowing in, cold air beneath the door . . . .

—Linda Picklesimer Collins

EMPTY MOMENTS

No dirty workboots outside the door,
Listening for footsteps on the kitchen floor.
Sunshine to darkness, work over long ago,
Stopped for a drink, visit friends or so.
Where are you, Empty Moments?

Candles on a table, drowned in time,
A special dinner, tender moments, lost never to find.
My heart so insignificant on your list of stops,
I try closing my eyes, but the anger won't drop.
Where are you, Empty Moments?

A folded newspaper beside your favorite chair,
Hurt eyes from a child who wonders, "Where."
Passing headlights send silent messages through my window pane;
Worry and questions are making me insane.
Where are you, Empty Moments?

If waiting moments were measured in love,
My timepiece would reflect a person cherished above.
Will the clock softly keep ticking away, or fail to start?
When it seems senseless to measure empty moments on an empty heart.
Where are you, Empty Moments?

—Jeanne L. Aderholt

THE LOSS

Why was it that we trapped each day and caged it
    behind walls of words,
Making prisons of our minds and eyes?
We fostered jealousy with our suspicious hearts,
    clung too selfishly to what we hoped was love,
Just to find that all we ever shared was fear.

Why was it that we bought and sold each precious hour
    with threats and vows,
Snaring promises with bonds of guilt and shame?
We locked ourselves together in a lonely cell, and
    somehow lost the keys,
And Love, in trembling desperation, slipped away.

—**Moranda C. Hamer**

TO BE WITHOUT YOU

To be without you, . . . is a fate worse than death,
    to slowly die and heave my final breath.
Succumbing to depressed kind of loneliness,
    and withdrawing into a hollow state of emptiness.
To be without you, . . . is to gradually fade away,
    to become a morsel on Misery's silver tray.
Wandering aimlessly down Sorrow's barren halls,
    and locked-up within Pain's gripping walls.
To be without you, . . . is to shed my last tear,
    to fall victim to my greatest fear.
Forever seeking someone to take your place,
    and help me endure the hardships of the human race.
To be without you, . . . is to be without life,
    cruelly cut down by Society's fatal knife.
Looted and pillaged by the Vikings of lore,
    until my heart can take it no more.
To be without you, . . . is to be without hope,
    reaching the end of my emotional rope.
To be without you, . . . is to be cast into the fire,
    because you alone, woman, . . . are my greatest desire.

I love you.

—**Micky Edinger**

SLOWLY COPING

Thinking back over, through all the years. Brings back to me
nothing, but a stream of tears.

The reason for this, is I missed it all. Now it's too late,
for I have built a wall.

The wall I built was not by hand, but in my mind and heart, I had
made my own land.

For nobody could enter, because I had the key. Lies and
deceptions, who needs it? not me!

She broke my heart, which she did not care. In my heart though, we had
made a good pair.

Within myself, I hoped she'd be back but I was wrong so I began
to pack.

I figured I'd leave to sort some things out, I knew I still
loved her, without any doubt.

I reached the age to understand, that my life will go on, not
holding her hand.

I broke down my wall and started to cry. For the girl I "loved,"
I had said good-bye.

I loved you, I really did, I tried. Forever Yours, in a dream
forever I'll remember.

—**Jim Pavelchak**

TEARS BEYOND REPAIR

Gazing into a mirror
of loneliness,
I look past the vision
of singularity
And sink, mind deep
Into the eye of despair;
Fenced fast
By heart linked chains
Of yesterday,
Golden wheated dreams
Drop as chaff
On tears beyond repair.

—**Marie Joudrey**

SILENCE

I sit in my room
And try to remember
The last time
I saw your face,
But I cannot even recall
The sound of your voice.
You were my best friend,
But now you are a
Memory.

Did I say good-bye
That last time?

I do not remember.

—**Christine Grosz**

As I lay in bed,
I dream of the times
That we've had.
I can't forget them.
I want more,
But I'm uncertain
About you.
You are a dark forest
And I cannot see within.
As I travel
In search of your heart,
You surround me.
I'm lost within you.
Lost,
And never to be found.

—**Susan L. Wintzell**

ALONE IN THE RAIN

The fire that keeps us
    feeling so warm
is the light that blinds us
    from seeing the storm
The love that leads us
    into the pain
is the hurt that leaves us
    alone in the rain
The pride that assures us
    that alone we'll prevail
is the fool within us
who brought down the hail
The fear that keeps us
    from loving again
is the heart that left us
    alone in the rain

—**Haley Groth**

DAWN

The world is new and young again.
Hummingbirds dance in the breeze.
A dual of doves coo a sad song.
Spiders trail invisible webs in the mist.
Rabbits nibble sweet clover 'neath foggy trees.
Magic dawn wakes over earth's rim.
With bare feet I scamper through dewy grass,
Laughing, forgetting
The troubled war and death of yesterday.

—Ann G. Howard

PHOENIX FOR A NEW AGE

We drifted silently into the machine
where we hope our hopes and dream our dreams.

The younger ones guessed but only a few.
And down they forgot as up they grew.

We saw and we did not understand
that in this reflection was a void and barren land.

But there is hope there must be hope if only in a few.
That we may rise from the ashes and create anew.

—Scott Deane

THE BRIDGE

The river at night
Under the bridge
Light dances on the rippled platform.
No trolls of hate and anger.
Just the echos of the sky breathing.
The breath that rustles the leaves
And blows water finely onto the shore
Closer to the leaves that fall back and forth
. . . Into the air.

If only the whole world was sitting under the bridge,
If only every human could taste what I taste now,
If all could sit together under the bridge
And experience the power at this moment,
All would realize they know not what power is,
All would utter, "I've been a fool."
All would find and embrace their enemy.
If only all knew what real power is,
All would make love emotionally . . .
And set their watches
To the clock under the bridge.

—RB

IT IS OUR WORLD NOW
**(after reading "Reflections (The End of Nature)"
in the New Yorker, 9/11/89)**

If you would follow me through holes in space
We shall be landing on an asteroid.
We may look back; I'd rather though avoid
The scene, the startled look upon your face.
Creation has been altered so and thus
The view. The land and water, atmosphere
Are not as we were taught, but it is clear
The Earth we see is labelled MADE BY US.

We shudder; how could that have happened when
We only sought a better world for all?
Inventions fell as rain but did not fall
On all alike. It is destruction then
Which will be shared. What follows has begun,
That Nature as we know it could be done.

—W. Robert Scott

A HIGHER VISION

When you're riding with the clouds
and you're looking down below.
The earth seems very peaceful
without a single foe.
The land is laid so perfectly
with squares of brown and green;
With splashes of blue where lakes and
ponds are scattered in between.

Everything is so much nicer
when viewed up in the air.
The world's at peace, with love and hope
and contentment everywhere.
If only things could be below
as they seem from up above.
There'd be no war, no hunger, no hate;
just happiness and love.

—Donna Daniels Wade

A CHILD

I see the pain that these children bear,
I want to hold them in my arms and share,
Their feelings of frustration,
Their youth and its mutation.
Their eyes should never see,
the abusive life, we've led it to be.
Their bodies should never know,
the painful cringe of a mighty blow.
Children should not shudder at a fond caress,
or feel the despair of loneliness.
Children are precious, innocent and clean,
let us not teach them to be bitter or mean.
Put the children first you see,
they are the tomorrow, that's yet to be.
Give them morals, values and love,
and you will be rewarded from above.
Let us not rob this child of childhood,
let us love him and show him what's good.
If chaos, from your child is brought,
he will do what he was taught.
If from love, your child has come,
he will do as you have done.

—Wendy Borowski

IS THERE A FUTURE?

The kids of the future have a lot to do
They blame it on me and on you.

We polluted our Earth without a care
To the kids of the future it isn't fair.

They have to undo what we have already done
We did it all, we had our fun.

Now it's up to them to make it right
They are the ones who have to fight.

Now they are the ones who have to care
A world like ours is very rare.

It's all our fault, we are to blame
To all of us it was just a game.

The kids of the future are the only hope
They are the ones who have to cope.

What have we created, what have we done
Please try to help, don't try to run.

Do what you can, give the future a start
Help them out, find it in your heart.

—Kristine K. Davis

GIFT OF LOVE

As I lay in bed, sit at my desk, or walk in the park, I am not alone. For the gift of love has been given.

Now I have the chance to give it all back, and it's amazing because I still get to keep it.·

Keep it I shall, Cherish it I will,
In love I am.

—Shelia Renee Armstrong

LOVE

Love is forever love is like treasure, you can feel it all over. Love is something you can not keep what good is it if you don't give it away. To someone special, that you can share things with, someone to laugh with someone to love. Love is like gold love is like silver love is like treasure something forever.

—Kashonda Lynn Carter

FACES

We greet each day the same.
A lonely vigil holds us at bay.
A smile, kiss, and embrace—
Who really knows beyond the face?

Self travels alone through life.
Touching flesh, muscle, and bone—
carrying within a mournful strife—
has anyone ever really known?

A lonely tear caresses the cheek.
Such sighs of agony—
All this transpires unseen
Lost within a gentle flutter.

Moving about day and night—
Speaking and doing what others deem right.
A moment unguarded slips by—
LOOK! Did anyone see the light?

—Sandra L. Wooten

TO KISS A ROSE

To be alone would drag out my day
And make my nights seem long
But to be with you
Gives me reason to live
And birds to sing song
All my life I waited
All my days counted down
For every smile you give
Seeking a promise to bind
Gives me no reason to frown
They say every sparkle has its tear
When your sad grey eyes turn a loving blue
Makes my heart sing out in joy
A world of only you and I, I find
When I say I Love You
The love we share
Only God knows
How together we are
Like the romance on my lips
To kiss a wilted rose.

—Missy Currie

GHOST THAT WALKS

That moody night of ocean salt and spray,
I tossed my ring into your swirling grave.
Burying a love that came close to burying me.
But your ghost keeps haunting me.
And our memories take away my breath.
Sad endings eat at my heart.
And each month, each year without you,
makes me remember til death do us part.
I wish that I could die now; I'd stop missing you.
But would a sad soul stop loving you?
Salt water burns an open wound.
With my ring, I drowned my wounds in the sea.
No element of pain can burn you out of me.
Not when I can still see your hollow, loveless eyes.
The eyes that only briefly held my face in them.
Death will be the ending of us.
We must die to ourselves to kill our vows.
No vow can make us love forever.

—Katherine Daniel

I LONG TO BE FREE

I long to be free, free to be me.
To soar as do birds with my actions and words.

To say what I feel, just as free as I will.
To be who I am, to break down the dam.

To let the tide rush in, to let my life begin.
To tell you the truth, share with you my youth.

To be honest in all things, to open my heart.
To tell you my feelings, in full, not in part.

To tell you I love you, to make you believe.
To laugh when you're happy, and cry when you grieve.

To share your plans, your hopes, your schemes.
To gaze at the stars, and to live all your dreams.

I long to be free, free to be me.
Me loving you, for an eternity.

—Angela K. Hobbs

FEELINGS

My love for you grows stronger day by day,
And upon this hour I don't know what to say.
I want to hold you and kiss you ever so light,
Cause your heart glows and your smile is ever so bright.
One day soon I hope to hold your hand,
And upon your ring finger shall be a golden band.
You shall have everything that I can give.
And if it comes down to it, not I, but you shall live.
For on my last breath and dying moan,
I will shout my love for you, and let it be known.

—Sheldon Herrington

THOUGHTS OF YOU

I behold your image before my eyes,
comparable only to the beauty of a morning sunrise.
A love within my soul, shall never die,
heaven or hell you're by my side,
with head held high, so full of pride.
Believe me my love, to you I cannot lie,
on bended knee, on sacred land,
I will speak my heart and hold your hand.
Unending days as grains of sand,
will come to be with one gold band.

—Billy E. Moore, Jr.

ONCE IN A LIFETIME

Once in a lifetime that man comes along,
He loves you no matter, if right or if wrong.
He helps you, he guides you, he lets you know,
Whatever he thinks, his feelings will show.

Once in a lifetime, that man comes your way,
And you know you're in love, no matter what may.
He's gentle, he's loving, he's one of a kind,
He's that special someone that's so hard to find.

Once in a lifetime has happened to me,
You're all of these things, and much more to me.

—Lisa Wing

OUR WEDDED YEARS TOGETHER

This is no hard-trodden path we travel,
No barren wilderness made waste by the blazing sun;
This is no desolate plain where sand and gravel
Are trod upon and ground to senseless dust.

This is, instead, the beautiful meadow of life,
Where you and I spend many precious hours;
Where we bestow affection and no strife,
And are giving our love as husband and wife.

Our romance is perfect—our life together is pleasure,
A kindly sun sheds its abundant beams from above;
We've reaped many a year of priceless treasure,
For we'll always be rich, with one another's love.

—Randy Louvier

TOGETHER FOREVER

You must be magic with all your charms
The way that you move me
The pleasure of your arms, wrapped tightly around me
Or softly by my side
The way you ignite me, the way we collide
As if we were seabirds high in the sky
Not knowing the answers not questioning why
The gift of our joining we don't take for granted
We treasure each moment for firmly we're planted
Together forever, here side by side
Lost in each other, together we'll ride
The heights of our passion
The depths of our love
Together forever, together in love.

—Cornelia E. Bates

MARY LOU,

Thirty-four years ago today
I took you for my bride
No one could be happier
As we stood side by side.
You were a vision of loveliness
That no one could deny.
Such a day of happiness for me
One that no money could buy.
Now it's thirty-four years later and
We have had our share of laughter and tears.
But I needed someone like you
To share those wonder years.
God blessed us with five beautiful children
Who to our hearts gave us joy and love;
A beautiful daughter-in-law and wonderful grandchildren,
Another gift from the man up above!
So you see, my love, what I am trying to say . . .
I loved you thirty-four years ago,
But I am in love with you more and more today.

—Hugh B. Griffith

APART

I am standing here alone,
I wonder where he has gone.
I pretend things are the way they were,
I dream of times to come.
I am standing here alone.

—Mikaela Martin

DRY ICE

We are, at times, dry ice.
Steam rolls up, the illusion of warmth
In the chill of the day.

Yet light flowed
Through the cracks and fissures
Bathing our wounds in something like glory,
Not precisely the balm of Gilead,
But good enough for the moment.

Winter still.
Can there be so much tenderness
With so little warmth?
The silver of your hair glinting
In the gray of my eyes
Reflecting off the tears
I refuse to let flow
In the wake of love.

—Catherine Bliss Rudolph

FATE

She slumps in a worn, overstuffed chair,
Wisps of hair drooping about her face,
Slip showing beneath her cotton dress,
Tired eyes brimming with frustration.

Unable to endure the burden
Of loneliness . . . dreams unfulfilled . . .
She struggles like a wounded sparrow.
"I was a good wife . . . a good mother,"
She sighs, pairing her perfect efforts
With those of her less perfect husband—
The man she loved "At first sight."
The man she trusted . . . rock of her life.

Fate . . . how ironic . . . senseless . . .
A fragile, full-blown rose withers,
Petal by petal. Her luster
Gone, she lingers on . . . defenseless.

—Kathryn Bosch Thompson

THE OPERA GHOST PT: TWO*

Hark! What's This I Hear, Can It Be?!?
Yes! The Angel, She Has Sung To Me.
It's Time To Rise From This Place,
Oh How I Must See Her Face.
When I Give Her The World She'll Know
To Her My Heart I Have Shown.
Brought To Me From The Dove
I Will Make Her My True Love.

No! My Face She Has Seen
Now She's Afraid Of Me.
Christine, My True Heart You Didn't See
When You Gazed Upon Poor Wretched Me.
Now You're In Raoul's Arms
Receiving All His Fine Charms.
Because You Were Shocked By My Face
Alone I Will Die In This Accursed Place!

*Inspired by Gaston Lesoux's novel "The Phantom of the Opera."

—Randall J. Fortunato

Sadly lay the rock upon the ground
for in it, life had ceased to abound.
The sun did shine for it to warm.
The rock refused, for fear of harm.
The rock relaxed, the rays increased;
the rock relaxed, there was a peace.
A piece of life in it did form.
A life, the healing light had born.

—Jonathan D. Turner

OF NELSON

He touched my life but once or twice,
And yet, each time was full of spice;
For thru his humor came his love
To comfort like a well-worn glove.
His peaceful, unassuming way
Would brighten any gloomy day.
His charming wit could soon fast knit
Another's heart with his to fit
Together in a harmony
Brought on thru truthful charity.
Altho he's left ahead of me,
I know I once again will see
His twinkling, tender gaiety.

—David G. Cruse

BABY ASLEEP . . . .

Baby asleep don't make a peep.
If we walk too close to the door,
the floor will creek.

We don't want to disturb a
baby who is asleep.

A baby doesn't really like to be
woken up by those mysterious foot steps.

A baby can also feel us trying
to creep up to watch them sleeping.
One should treat a baby as they
would like to be treated themselves.

We all know if we wake a baby
in the daylight, what might happen
in the night!

—Patricia Durkin

URBAN AND RURAL

Gathering and Scattering,
Pod and Seed,
Perennial in Irregular Winds,

We Collect in Corners,
Until Densely Strangers,
Dreaming Space With Paradoxical Hunger.

Dreams and Visions,
Faith and Promised Lands,
Tearing Us From Our Tangled Roots,

We Scatter East and West,
Invisibly Strewn To and From Jerusalem,
Journeying With Enigmatic Purpose.

Circling, Cycling, Eternity's Cadence,
Nothing New Made New Again,
Repetitious Rhythms of Seasons Repeating,

We Migrate,
Reaching and Releasing,
Still Seeking.

—M. Patterson

LOOKING BACK

If there comes a time that we all should meet,
Be it a class reunion or somewhere on the street.

We will reminisce and look back at our schooling years,
We'll shed many peals of laughter or many cries and tears.

And if this time is to come we should be able to say,
It was good to see you, call me soon, and seeing you
brightened my day!!

—Chandra Mattiece Coleman

MY MOST TREASURED BOUQUET

I was doing my work just as busy as could be
When in came my son who was not quite three.
He opened the door quickly and noisily walked in.
He looked at me shyly and said with a grin,
"I know you love flowers so I picked these for you, Mom."
In my hands he placed six dandelions and then he was gone.

They were withered and wilted and nothing much to see.
But the love they represented made them beautiful to me.
I once received an orchid from an audience after a play.
I carried yellow roses on my wedding day.
I picked daisies in a meadow, grew hollyhocks so tall.
Tulips and chrysanthemums, I've really loved them all.
But my most treasured bouquet I know will always be
Those dandelions from my son when he was not quite three.

—Mae S. Fleming

A STRANGE, YET DELIGHTFUL, DREAM

I dreamed I opened up the door—
Upon the porch's floor was a basket
Cradling a child, just lying there.
He opened his eyes and smiled—
A smile that burst my heart.
The teardrops began to start.
How could a mother part
With such a darling child?
Beneath the blankets piled
He raised his hand to mine
And softly cooed. Barely six months old
He lay there in the cold, without a cry.
I wonder why she left him in my care?
Life is not always fair. Her burdens, great,
Perhaps there was no mate to help along the way.
To this very day I wonder about that strange dream.
What does it mean? What a strange, yet delightful, dream.

—Gladys Mae Olsen

FIRST BORN

Son, you are my First Born,
The day you were Born it was Christmas Eve morn.
I knew then we would have many years together,
I'd Raise you up Right and Love you Forever.

You've been my Best Friend, you've always Been there,
And our Bond of Love is what we Both share.
There are some things we have not done,
Don't worry there's still time I Promise you Son.

I want to give a Better life to you,
I will succeed, and work hard at everything I do.
I'll be here to Love you, as you sleep at night,
I'll send you to college so your Future is Bright.

I'll always be here to guide you through Life,
And help you with Any Problem or strife.
Because of a Broken Family, I know your heart's torn,
But, I'll Always Love you Son, you are my First Born.

—Ronald G. Bingham

THE GREEN HORNET

With a ding ding, we're on our way
To the Yellow Islands, and the ball parks, per se!
The Clark Street Wall, at 60 you see
Was the speed at the time, and a catch up to me, but,
As we pass thru the portals of time
Toronto can tell you, we're not far behind.

—The Streetcar Man

A CHILDHOOD MEMORY

The sturdy treehouse stands hard and fast
in the summer downpour,
Out in the middle of nowhere in a suburban backyard,
serenity with its tin roof,
and tidalwave legs of support,
is a place of escape.

Symbolic of a time similar, but a generation ago,
this is an emblem to someone.
As I peer through the foggy droplet-covered
pane of my window,
I see a thoughtful figure inside that is
present now . . . and in a generation to come.

—Kimberly A. Warren

MY GRANDMOTHER KNEW

When I was young, I did not care,
Who lived here, or who lived there.

How I wish I could recall,
Every detail of them all.

When granny could tell me everything,
I ran away to play and sing.

Now I am old, and Oh, how I yearn,
For facts never heard, and now cannot learn.

It is sad, so sad, but never too late,
To tell what I know, with no time to wait.

My family will know all that I do,
And will learn even more, for now they yearn too.

—Susie E. Toal

HOUSE FOR SALE

This is a house that has known love and laughter,
Warm is her heart like the firelight that glows,
Strong are her beams and sturdy her rafter.
Mellow and wise in the things that she knows.

Many the crises her stout heart has weathered,
Warm are the friendships embraced by her walls,
Tender the love songs to which she has listened,
Happy the children who raced through her halls.

Dancing and feasting and gay voices calling,
Christmas and Easter and Fourth of July,
Days' bright dawning and darkness falling,
Swiftly and sweetly the years going by.

But now our journey together is over,
Old friends who must part at the end of the trail,
Sad circumstance has made us a rover,
The house, to our sorrow, is now up for sale.

Soon we will seek other climes other faces,
Destination unknown, for the future's not clear,
But love of home, time nor tide ne'er displaces,
Infinitely precious, inexpressively dear.

—Margaret Kyle

SHADOWS OF THE PAST

Days of happy, carefree fun
Happiness should be yours but never done.
Shadows of the past
Shining eyes and haunting smile
Lingering thoughts of you with graceful style.
Shadows of the past
Soft warm lips speaking out with truth
Of beauty and love, you are proof.
Shadows of the past
Dreams of life so full of worth
Should be yours from birth.
Shadows of the past
Missing you, I know not why.
However, to stop I shall not try.
Shadows of the past
Maybe . . .

—Vonita White Dandridge, Ph.D.

THE STORY TELLERS

I always sat and listened
In the shimmering summer haze
To the stories that my elders told
About the good old bygone days.

For their lives went back to the time
When our hometown was so new
And all the stories that they told
Were personal and were true.

For everyone knew everyone
The old, the newly rich, and the very poor,
And all the tales wound 'round and round
And bound them together evermore.

From them I learned the history
Of our hometown's early days
And how the happenings of the bygone past
Influenced my life in so many ways.

The stories were like pieces of a puzzle
That made a picture clear and bold
And it seemed to me these stories
Were some of the greatest ever told.

—Florence Reid Riemann

THE BED

The crib was down, something was different
You got it in your head
"I'm not sleeping in this thing
that mommy called a 'Big Bed'."

You screamed as I was leaving
Your eyes were filled with fright
I had an inkling feeling
I was in for a Lo-o-o-ng night.

Just as I predicted
You got back out of bed
All I saw was "Boppy"
And the shape of your little head

It was dark and you were scared
Your little voice said "Mommy"
I reached down to pick you up
Both you and faithful boppy.

I picked you up, it was getting late
I knew that it was wrong
But — the fight was over, you were asleep
In our bed all night long.
Boppy=Blanket

—Sheri L. Salavitch

279

WIDOW LADY
She waits behind the willow tree,
Our widow neighbor.

Grays and greens play shadows
Across her face and heart.

Her tilted, frozen smile conceals the pain
And the wrenching fright.

How does one go on . . .?

—Eleanor Bassman

ELVENA
Sometimes, when all is still, and
twilight shadows close around to ease
my fears, and grant the peace denied
by day. I walk once more through
memory's halls and see again, as clear
as yesterday, my own sweet girl, in
all her loving ways—and down those
many years, her kind and tender
care, defined more clearly still by
Time's bequest of sweet recall.

—Gordon Straub

YOURS AND MINE
Was it so long ago, or only yesterday,
When we were both so young and gay.
We lived in a dream world so divine,
But then the world was yours and mine.

Nothing could go wrong,
For our love was a song.
Every day the sun would shine,
But then the world was yours and mine.
Was it so long ago, or only yesterday,
When you went away,
And my world fell apart,
With it went my heart.
Now I hope and pray
We will be forever together each day.
Then the sun once again will shine,
And the world will be
Forever yours and mine.

—Helen M. Avelis

MY ANGEL
As I sit here, oh so lonely,
Cold and still is my home.
Trouble faces me around every corner,
Why won't it leave me alone?

As I look in front of me,
I see many ways to end my trouble:
Some pills, a razor, a gun.
It all looks and seems so easily done.

My angel no longer sits upon my shoulder,
The devil has made her leave.
Taking me on his side,
Only, for selfish greed.

I turn around to the sound of a voice,
To see my angel there,
Fighting it out with the devil,
I knew that she cared.

Thank you for saving me, angel.
My true, eternal friend.
Thanks to you, I realize,
Life is too precious to end.

—Brandi Potter

SUNRISE
Your eyes are like the sunrise;
You bring my day to a beautiful start;
As I see your outline on the rising sun;
I look into your eyes and I can tell no lies;
Your body is so fabulous some call it art;
And you light up my life until the day is done;
Then I can hold you again in my warm embrace;
And our love will last until the end of time and space.

—John L Darrett

I OFTEN WONDER
I often wonder, lying here alone,
Intently staring and yet seeing not
What lies before me but images gone
Yet forever in my memory caught,
How often is it you read the sonnet
That I labored with love to write for you?
D'you know of the stains my tears left on it?
Are there stains of your own tears on it too?
I still see those beautiful eyes of yours,
Those very em'ralds that inspired the poem
And I wonder if they still read my verse
Did my words e'er save you from being alone?
      And more painfully: were they understood?
      Did they reach your heart, as I'd hoped they would?

—James Daniel

LET ME BE THERE
You are the one,
The one in my dreams . . .
I finally realize.
I can't express it in a song . . .
Or tell you on the phone . . .
Just look into my eyes, my dear . . .
And you will never be alone.
Even if you just call me friend,
Or say you love me through and through . . .
Just call my name . . . I am always there for you.
I will be by your side through thick and thin . . .
In good times and in bad . . .
Doing the best that I can do,
To keep your life from being sad.
Just give me a chance to show you who I am . . .
And you will never have to face the world alone again.

—Robert A. Lebo

PEACE
How can we find peace in a world shaken by fear
where each person fights to defend his own?

When will we see the futility of war
and fighting a battle that no one can win?

Strife carries a pain that no one can ease away
and fighting only shows where we are weak.

Love is the answer and only we can show the world that
Peace comes from sharing our lives with each other.

If our brothers and sisters are struggling to survive
we must be the hand that gives them hope to go on.

Where is that hope if we only share in hate
competing for a power that belongs to no man?

Love is the answer and only we can show the world that
Peace comes from sharing our lives with each other.

—Nita Pollock

THE HEAVENS

The days of disparity are numbered,
each day seems as though it's your last
and you often wonder will this troubled time ever pass.
Things seem so dim, and so far away,
that there is no justice and everything is in a bad way.
You wonder sometimes, is this for real,
or is this just the way you feel?
So you just close your eyes,
and keep reaching for the sky.
Remember, beyond the clouds, the moon, the stars and the sun,
there's a place where dreams never die.

—C. J. Detiege

PORTRAIT OF A MAN

A kindness as beautiful as a field of flowers
splashing their vibrant colors against the blue sky.

Compassion to build a warm shelter
that protects from the cold of a dark winter night.

The wisdom to journey through life's shadows
leading courage into the strength of the sun.

A heart impassioned by the beauty of the universe
and a spirit that dances to the melody of a gentle wind.

Energy to fill a treasure chest full of hopes and dreams
and inspiration to perpetuate eternal wealth.

—Ann Halloran

I SEE THE LIGHT

I see the light through the forest shining down through the
    trees;
I see the light through the forest shining down to the seas;
I see the light from the heavens shining down, calling me;
Calling me to His side, up in Heaven I'll be.

I hear His voice in the daytime telling me, "Do what you should;"
I hear His voice in the nighttime telling me He understood;
I hear His voice in the morning asking me to be good;
Asking me to be good, . . . Lord, I did what I could.

I feel His presence in my life, and in the sky above;
I feel His truth, I feel His warmth, I feel His never-dying love.
I feel His faith, and I feel His touch, gentle as a dove;
And I'll try to be with Him in eternal life above.

—Franklin Roberts

HE LOVED ME SO

He loved me so, He died for me,
    That I might enter in;
It was on the Cross at Calvary,
    That He paid for my sin!

He is the Saviour of my soul,
    To Him I give my all;
I know He will return for me;
    And I await His call!

He watches over me day by day,
    And through the lonely night;
And He sees that I do not stray,
    Far from His guiding light!

And when it's time for me to go,
    I will find Him waiting there;
To welcome me into that home,
    That He went to prepare!

—Eileen Albert

DREAMS

World spinning inward,
dreams constantly collide.
Phantom lovers changing faces,
sliding into a kaleidoscope.

Princes becoming monsters
Knights not riding horses,
but nightmarish screams.
Days sliding into darkness,

Darkness into dust.
Frantic, faceless lovers
mingling truth with lies
and seducing minds to emptiness.

Dreams seeping over
reality's collapsing gates
and fantasies lasting forever
when the dreamer never wakes.

—Anne Wilson

DREAMS

If you have a dream
Don't let it go;
Don't forget it;
Just reach for your goal.
No matter what people tell you,
No matter what they will say;
If it is your dream,
Don't let it stray.
Practice makes perfect,
It's all up to you;
There's nothing that anyone
Can do, except you.
Through hardship and turmoil,
Through times that are rough;
Only you can achieve it
If you stay tough.
So no matter how far away
Your accomplishments may seem
If you want it enough,
Just follow your dream.

—Karie M. Phillips

THE RAIN

Soft — the raindrops fall
On hard, gray, crusty earth,
Drops of soothing balm
Healing parched earth's skin.

Firm — the raindrops fall
Quenching dry soil's thirst,
Softening rigid mounds
To sculptor's cool wet clay.

Hard — the raindrops fall
Cooling burned flesh wounds
Inflicted on the soil
By red hot baking sun.

Slow — the raindrops fall
Loosening earth below,
Arousing the passing gods
With fertile scents released

The earth sighs sweet relief . . .
Grateful for this gift—
Cool spray of holy water
Anointing her fertility.

—Janice Maroney Bzura

A THOUGHT

All but are a reflection,
within the imagination of time.
Floating through the remnants
of creation.
Riding smoothly beside its tail,
doomed to ceaseless wandering,
left in the illusion of ignorance.

—**Kim Rednour**

The violet crash of thunder
is a match,
made unbroken
by the suffocating feelings
of torment,
that drives me
to your side,
to hide my eyes,
that are blinded
by the lightning,
to reality,
and the gentle rain
of life.

—**Gloria LeBeau**

GARDEN OF FRIENDSHIP

Within the garden of my heart,
a friendship flower grows true,
Its blossoms bring fond memories,
of moments spent with you.

The fragrance of the flower,
is filled with hints of pleasure,
for the growth of true friendship
is beauty beyond measure.

Like the flowers, it will bloom,
and decorate my heart.
I will cherish all the moments,
While we're near, when we're apart.

With time the flower will grow,
It will endure any weather,
And with gentle tender care,
We will share its growth together.

—**Sara Dee Moore**

SUNSET

The artist's palette
Fell upon
The backdrop of blue.
He sighed in frustration
As the colors blended
Into streaks
Of fiery orange and pink.
They spread
And spread
Until, with an angry sigh,
He began to put them
Back onto his palette.
The colors faded.
Stripped away
Along with the backdrop of blue.
Darkness is left behind
Until tomorrow,
When the clumsy artist
Once again drops
His palette.

—**Tanisha Alanna Wealot**

SPRING

Spring forward is the saying we use in March,
To anticipate warm weather after winters were harsh,
May the flowers and freshness of the cool spring air,
Not contain pollens that could cause us to care.

As we turn our clocks forward to gain an extra hour,
Let's handle our frustrations with more confidence and power,
As new leaves appear on all the bare trees,
May it help us to accept each day like a breeze.

—**Melodee Botts**

THE HEART IS A LONELY HUNTER

The heart is a lonely hunter. The mind searching endlessly
for what the heart cannot find.

Mother love I've never known. Father love so swiftly gone.
Looking here and looking there for the elusive butterfly.
This thing called love.

Like dew that falls upon the grass, it vanishes quickly with
the rays of the sun. The elusive butterfly this thing called
love.

The heart is a lonely hunter. Some are blessed to find it,
others let it get away. The elusive butterfly this thing called
love.

The heart is a lonely hunter. The mind searching endlessly
for what the heart cannot find.

—**Juanita Guy**

STRAWBERRIES

Berries are sweet, like my children's excitement on our annual
trip to the "Pik-yor-self" ranch.
Berries are sour, like the death of my father one October night.
Berries are red, like the rose that represents love and the blood
that represents life.
Berries are white and orange, like the sherbert in a cup I used
to eat, as a child on Brennan Street.
Berries are firm, like the migrant fieldworker telling his child
he must pick faster.
Berries are mushy, like the letter that says "I love you" 28
times.
Berries are ripe, like a woman in her ninth month of pregnancy.
Berries are rotten, like hatred, greed and envy.
Berries are big, like my love for family, culture and life.
Berries are small, like this poem.
But most of all, Berries are Watsonville . . . a part of me.

—**Rebecca Valdivia-Godoy**

BLUE BIRD OF HAPPINESS

I walked along a country road, the sky was clear and blue
The air was so sweet smelling and the birds were singing too.

My heart had been so lonely since my lovely wife had died,
And I had been unhappy with bitterness inside.

But then I saw a little bird perched up in a tree
He sounded so sweet and cheery; it seemed he sang to me.

He said you've lost your true love, but please don't be so sad.
Something good will happen to make your heart so glad.

I am the bird of happiness with coat so fine and blue;
And if you'll stop and listen, I'll sing my song for you.

He said I've been around the world and I've seen many things;
And you just cannot realize the change time always brings.

So if you're sad and blue today it will not linger long,
You will find true joy again and sing a brand new song.

—**Millie Marie Gilbert**

ARMAGEDDON

Nuclear disaster is feared.
People wandering the streets.
Fear, anger, and depression.
Genocide, homicide, and suicide take so many lives.
Music exploding, people exposing.
Sick of religion, politics, and living for holidays.
We're being eaten up with our own vices.
Smoking, drinking, and intolerance of those things.
Lawlessness by those who uphold the law.
Protesting, molesting, and conquesting.
Abortion, pollution, and aids.
Fear of hurting ourselves or others physically, morally, and verbally.
Fanatical and senseless belief in all kinds of schemes,
A lot of this unknowingly.
Sketchy and nonexistent claims of satan's uninvolvement in world affairs.
Depreciation of Jehovah's commands;
"Thou shall have no other Gods in place of me."
"Love thy neighbor as thyself."

— Joyce L. Utne

FOR NIGHT IS NOT PEACEFUL

The light fades,
emptiness lingers on,
the still of the night is praised,
why is this wondrous thing so alluding to him who hath called
the still of the night peaceful,
Damned be to him, for the evil smothers the world when all
of the shadows are gone,
When the wind can blow and be so alone,
the birds, horrid to break the silence hide under their mother's wings,
The wind has only one friend on its midnight journey,
It shall be forever horrid and kill this planet,
When all of the shadows are gone it stalks out its prey
like a hungry lion, searching, then biting off the heads of
their young for food,
brittle frailness of one another makes them look away,
not boldly at each other,
damned be to him who hath said the night is peaceful,
for at night,
man has only begun to hunt.

— Jennifer L. Pownall

THE HISPANIC WOMAN

The Hispanic woman has had a lifetime of tears,
She has been held back by society, her own family, and her peers,

She has had to deal with prejudice of more than just one kind,
She has had to deal with prejudice of her color, her sex, and her
mind,

But all this has only served to give the Hispana more ambition,
Because she knows she can do anything in order to accomplish her
mission,

I do believe things are getting better and they are opening up
more doors,
The Hispana no longer has to be content to just scrub floors,

We have the choice to pick the field in which we want to work,
But work is the key to reaching our goals, our duties we cannot
shirk,

So when you see a Hispana who has reached her goal, she is worth
her weight in gold,
Because when God made our Hispanic woman, He used a very special
mold!

— Pauline J. Davalos

THE SHIFT

The rulers smile
Their evil smiles
Steeped in useless
Paradigms
Uncomprehending, blind
Chaos reigns
Dreams stir
Deep in people's minds
Shadowy outlines
of new visions
Reaching toward the light
Will these myriad fragments
Unite
Will freedom reign
Will love and harmony
Abound
Dare we dwell
In this rare air
Everyone
Everywhere

— Darl E. Wittmer

CAMPAIGN NOW

Package small will travel
Illegal yet steady
Holding power over
Rich, famous, poor, youth.
Laughable when
Results — open
Destructive for sure
Stop the travel —
How? What Cure?
Beginning before birth?
Homes, Churches, Schools
Steeples of all
Civilizations, past,
Present, Future —
Fathers, mothers, teachers,
Ministers, writers, artist
Join Campaign Now —
Fight to win over drugs —
A Must or leave heritage
Deterioration or dust.

— Nina Mason

THE QUEST

Unclear relationships
Of underlying potentials
Puzzling manifestations
Yearn for comprehension
Mystical perception
Material rejection
Advancement or
Circumnavigational
Tail chasing
Back to zero?

Searching for
Or fleeing from
Leads to
Similar sanctuaries
Rejecting
The surface values
Probing for
Elusive realities
Quixotesque
Intellectual hero.

— R. Austin Baker

PAIN

Sores on me
ache with pain.
I need to feel
    warmth and love
from someone
    who cares,
but you insist on
    picking off the scabs.

—Nikki West

GOING MY WAY

Going my way
    I saw a man.
He was carrying a cross.
He looked sad.
I said a little prayer.
Then I looked at him.
I went up to him,
and said, "thank you
for your prayer."
Then he smiled and
closed his eyes.
Going my way . . .

—Christina Jakubiec

Wide black eyes.
    Pain.   Confusion.
Child-like in intensity.
Trust.   Sorrow.
A dimple.
Chin, cheek.
A pointed tail.
Cloven hoof.
Heat.   Flame.
A high-pitched screech.
Whimpers.   Tears.
A strong presence.
Feel.   Clutching.
Support.
Strength, calm.
Wide black eyes.
Close.

—Kristee L. Allen

SEEING OURSELVES

He sees himself with
    This light curly hair
Eyes clear, skin soft
And his nose is over
A gate of pink lips
To fine white teeth
And long tapered neck
On tall straight spine
While flat hardened gut
Fits his slim hips

But this other guy
Has mousy gray hair
And rummy eyed stare
Above crooked nose;
Double chin rests
On short flapjack stack
While big shoulders sag
And flab over belt
Has homesteader rights
Each day he shaves.

—Ralph E. Martin

LOVE ME FOR TODAY

The memories I once treasured — I treasure no more
    The thoughts I think today — are not those which I thought before

My past is now buried — 'neath the ever shifting sand
For I now hold — another true love's hand

I think no more of "forever" — for the word has somehow died
Replaced by a "perhaps" or "maybe" — all torn by waves of pride

Living is day-to-day — for today is all I can cope
Tomorrow is an undreamt facade — with just a touch of hope

So bless those around me — who love me for "today"
As I blindly rush — through time's uncertain way

—Dianne E. Lade

I AM AN ANIMAL-LOVING GIRL . . .

I am an animal-loving girl who loves the wonders of the universe.
I wonder how old I will be and how I will die.
I hear stars exploding in the far corners of space.
I see heaven as a place of eternal peace.
I want to have front row center tickets to the "New Kids on the Block"
concert!
I am an animal-loving girl who loves the wonders of the universe.

I pretend that all the world is peaceful, just for the night.
I feel that anything can be accomplished if you keep at it long
enough!
I touch the stars and reach into space for all the answers.
I worry what will become of me in the future.
I cry for all the animals being slaughtered for their skins and
parts or just to be rid of.
I am an animal-loving girl who loves the wonders of the universe.

I understand that all the world is being torn apart by man.
I say that if the world would only stop fighting, we could have
a long needed peace and comfort and friendship.
I try to be the best person I can be, and I hope that someday I
will go to heaven.
I am an animal-loving girl who loves the wonders of the universe.

—Reagan Elizabeth Boyce, age 12

ECONOMICS OF A SMALL BUSINESSMAN

I am a small businessman, that you can plainly see.
    I work on locks, tons of locks, I'm busy as a bee.

My valued customers are from far and wide, their needs are most diverse.
    Some jobs are simple, some cantankerous, troublesome, even cursed.

The urgent request for my prompt service, or work to be done,
    All receive my utmost attention, honesty . . . bar none.

All charges and fees charged are used to keep,
    My bills paid, even next winter's oil heat.

But when my work is finally done, with charges carefully explained,
    I feel hesitation, hear excuses, with payment often feigned.

"We're leaving at 6 a.m. sharp, for a much needed vacation.
    We'll mail it from Katonah, or another postal station."

Then 10 days, two weeks, 30 days, 60 days or more,
    Have passed, now one month, perhaps even four.

So, now you can plainly see,
    How simple economics effects both you and me.

Although I love you as a valued customer and friend,
    Small Claims Court, will no doubt shortly send,

A summons, a decree, your presence is urgently requested!
    I'm a small businessman who needs cash . . I won't . . by you be bested.

—Donald M. Foulke

284

New mahogany for her hull with which to plow the water
A tall spruce stick to furl her sails he named her for his daughter
The finest fittings to be found rigged her for the ocean
The dreams of flying new frontiers were now more than a notion
Setting sail from New Cape Town a heading for the Tropics
A million dreams set sail that day with stories of a million topics
The drama played on many years and many ports of fame
Upon the wooden sailing ship which bore his daughter's name
With weathers fair and oceans calm the ship grew ripe with age
The stories and the ports of call were written by the sage
They tell the ship does fares for hire for tourists from afar
Who wish to ride on a sailing ship beneath the Southern star
The man who made the dreams begin has long since passed away
But left behind his sailing ship to sail another day

—Joseph Phelps Carter

RESTLESS SOUL

I see a radiant sunset, I am a sunset. I can feel the soft clouds
as I gently shine with deep mingled saddening colors.
Being a sunset I feel the loss of whatever might have been today
will never be as I slowly slide farther and farther away.
I see a calm ocean as it turns quickly into an angry rage of swirls.
I am calm waters on the outside but a raging storm of waves inside.
I feel the slow provocative movements of blue green waters as I watch
with tender feelings of people in love all around me. Yet I feel the
waves swell within me as I reach ever so far attempting to find the
answers to my own lost love so . . . so angry as the white capping ocean
tosses me and no answer for the restlessness seems to be found within.
I hear the wind because I am the wind rushing to and fro as it blows
through my hair and my soul. My blowing wind is not a gentle wind
whispering in my hair, it is a howling raging and mocking wind,
waiting to be calmed. I know now I am a saddened sunset, a tormented
ocean of waves and a rushing swirl of wind because I am searching for
that lasting love of my own. Waiting for that special moment when I am
no longer a wandering lost soul in search of that special enigma of love.

—J.C. Perry

REFLECTIONS

The Moving Wall came to the city, bringing with it hurt and pain,
It held the names of many young people, some of them were my friends.
It brought back memories of times I'd put aside, of sleepness nights
and frightening days when comrades fell and died.

But with the pain came peace, and as I bid a last farewell,
I felt a strange new strength, something words can never tell.

They've taken down the wall now, and sent it on its way,
It may bring peace to others, to help them through each day.
As for me I feel a calmness coming from within, my trip to the wall
brought needed reflection, now it's on with my life again.

—Hubby Clement

A FRIEND

As life travels through the days,
        And you feel you're in a haze;
As time passes through your mind,
        And you feel an answer—you'll
                never find.
Then think back to a familiar face,
        And recall you'll have a place;
To spend your time and you know—
        You'll always have a friend—not
                a foe.
Take the time to shout or cry,
        Sharing feelings you'll know why—
I am your friend and I always will care,
        No matter what feelings you want
                to share.

—Renda R. Maxwell

A FALL DAY

The leaves are falling,
    I am calling,
Come out and play,
Play all day
In the clay-colored leaves.
    —Emily H. Stricker

FLOWERS

Flowers will grow,
    After the snow,
When spring is here
And the sun is near.

Flowers will grow,
When the cold does go,
When the rain comes down
And falls to the ground.
    —Joni Weller, age 8

LEAVES' FOLLY

Fall's advancing;
    Leaves are dancing—
Gaily prancing
To and fro.
Days are colder—
Breezes bolder.
Clouds presage
An early snow.

Should we tell them,
Break the spell,
Then ring the knell
To end their ball?
Bother's needless.
Leaves will, heedless,
Cavort and sport
Until they fall!
    —Kathleen R. Brumage

THE YEAR OF SURPRISES

January winters bring
February hearts,
February hearts bring
March clovers,
March clovers bring
April showers,
April showers bring
May flowers,
May flowers bring
June winds,
June winds bring
July summers,
July summers bring
August peaches,
August peaches bring
September falls,
September falls bring
October pumpkins,
October pumpkins bring
November turkeys,
November turkeys bring
December presents,
December presents bring
A Year full of Surprises!
    —Hether Phillips, age 11

THE LAKE

Out the window,
the world shines today.
Across the lake
the ice glows yellow,
and blinds this way.
I look to the dark
and calmer patches.
A scene flashes.
Three men and a dog,
the figures skate and play.
The dog runs, skids away.
Gone now,
the end of the game.
The window remains
my impermanent frame.

—**Kerry J. Leclair**

THE BIRD

I watched a bird today
Soaring high, and free
And I envied it
For I wished it was me

It circled, and again, hunting,
For what, I don't know,
A flap of its wings
And higher would go

Streamlined, and gracious
A ballet of art
Casting a play
With all of its heart

Gently it darted
As it caught a wind's brush
Then up it would curl
And climb in a rush

I gazed in wondrous awe
As it slowly by went
Leaving me peaceful
And feeling content

—**Willard Anderson**

SAX APPEAL

It starts with a gust,
Air pumped from the lungs.
Just the beginning,
A ladder's first rung.

The airstream travels up,
Reaching his cheeks.
In just an instant,
His instrument speaks.

The blending of breath, flesh,
Plastic, and wood.
All form the beautiful sound,
It feels so good.

The tone hits the walls,
The floor, the ceiling.
Bouncing in vibrations,
It sends his head reeling.

Melodies, rhythms,
Etudes attacked with a zeal.
It's hard to deny,
The man has "sax appeal."

—**Gary Eizenwasser**

A FRIEND

The depth of a friend is heard in their silence
The heart of a friend is felt in one's laughter
The soul of a friend is measured in teardrops
The need for a friend is seen in our smiles.

—**Linda Griffith**

SAM

The first time I saw Samantha, I knew I'd call her Sam.
She looked at me as if to say, "If you want me here I am."
We got her in the early spring on a bright and sunny morn,
Just about three months before our baby son was born.
Although they grew up together, Sam and our little boy
She knew somehow instinctively she was my own pride and joy.
We spent a lot of time together and we had a lot of "talks."
We had quiet times together and a lot of dusty walks.
She'd always run to meet me whenever I drove up,
She'd prance around and lick my hand like any playful pup.
But time went by as well it must, and Sam did older grow
But years made her more dear to me, than I would ever know.
And then one day, somehow, I knew her time was drawing near
And Oh, it hurt me through and through and I shed a shameless tear.
But Sam slept peacefully away in the sun's warm after glow,
But I know—I'll always think of her when the warm winds softly blow.

—**Eileen Zachary Vice**

SCOTT

My warm one
Witty and gay
With eyes aglow

How I wish for you the good things in life

For you I would tackle all the pains and frustrations I know are
coming your way

Your innocence I would keep intact
Preserving your warm responses to affection
Never allowing you to feel the fire that burns at my heart even now.

Scotty, so anxious to please
so impulsive
yet so loving
May life lie open to your probing, spreading itself like a red carpet
before you, welcoming your eagerness and presenting you with the
happiness that I wish for you

—**Penny Brickman**

As we slip silently through the smooth velvet of our galaxy,
aboard spaceship Earth within our crystal dome, we glance oc-
casionally outward, at the trillions of other celestial ships crewing
afar, on all sides upon the endless sea of forever, among the billions
of passengers aboard the mighty ship, incredibly only a small number are a-
ware, of an area in the ship, where on a sunny October day there are
mountains towering up from green valleys, the smell of autumn hangs
heavy in the fresh fall air, at night while the country-side is at rest,
a sister ship pulls along side, golden in the night, she reflects her glow
up-on the black humps of the mountains, of the area of the ship
known as Eastern Kentucky, standing boldly in the moonlite night
against a back drop of endless space, their feet adorned in the white
cotton mist of cool freshness blanketing the valley below
without doubt, from the upper deck view,
of the universe,
Just off the bow of spaceship Earth,
above the fog-mist laden valleys and Butcher Hollow
far below, the great builder used a little extra touch
IN THE BEGINNING

—**deMart Bowling**

THE QUIET BEACH

The beach is cold and lonely again, the waves slap at the shore
A lone gull soars o'er the ocean, As I walk in the stillness once more.
This is my favorite time of year, the chill keeps the crowds away
The peace and quiet are for dreaming of the long-ago peaceful day.

The water was clean and untouched, the sand on the beach was for play,
God was in charge of our ocean then, His methods kept destruction away.
Then greed entered the picture, As it has all over the place
And man put his waste in the water, for a time God stepped out of the pace.

Now God has decided to show us that His way was better before
He decided to churn up the ocean, throwing mammals and junk on the shore.
We now need people who really care, not groups who scream and shout
Fighting each other will not get results, That's not what reform is about.

Everyone wants what we once had
            A beach that is healthy and clean
                    Our children deserve what we once had
                            Then they will continue the dream.

    —Eileen Trofi

GREY MOURNING

How ironic, a day that matches my state of being.
            Surrounded in fog, thick fog,
            it's hard to determine what I can see,
            difficult to look for the right direction.
            Thick as pea soup is the phrase oft used;
            no smell of garlic here, tho, only salty sea air.
            A nondescript soft, soft, floating grey,
            opaque in nature — a full reminder of an ectoplasm
                    that has eeked from my existence.
            An emptiness, an infinite void within my body..........

My body..........a shell, a thin veneer for my weeping soul, ...my fragile heart.
It took years for the indefinite number of broken pieces to repair themselves.
        The healed lines barely showing, the heart seemed so strong again,
                        and now —
            it beats tiny quiet beats, barely heard
in the torrent of tears that accumulate in the weakening scars.

Outside, a golden warmth has burned through the dense cool grey mist.
        That fog is lifting, dissipating into the heavens.

        Wistfully, my heart fantasizes about sprouting wings.
                My soul echos the desire.............

    —C.E. LaRiviere

IMPRESSIONS

Yesterday morning, while getting in the shower,
        I glanced over my shoulder into the mirror.
Imagine my surprise when I discovered the print of your hand
            on the small of my back,
            with your thumb resting in that small hollow.
I looked at my face and found your lips adorning my cheekbone and my chin.
Then, I saw a thin, straight trail left by your tongue running down my neck.
The trail ended just below my collarbone in a print of your teeth.
It occurred to me that perhaps I am too easily reached
            That it is too simple to leave impressions on my
                body and my soul.
            But I pushed that fear away.
So last night, after we had finished, and you
            were resting peacefully, your breath coming
            in a slow, heavy rhythm—
I studied your body to see where I had
            left prints, tracks, and signs.
But your body was empty, save for the paper
            cut on your finger from the day before.

    —Monica A. Cawvey

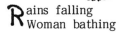

Rains falling
Woman bathing

Earth cleansing
She singing
    —Vanessa Brown

GUARDED OPINION

pillar of light
you bray you
are right
when unblinded his
right leaves you
right on the floor
perhaps the next time
if so compelled
to rise up
to preach
you might save yourself
from con-descending
by first divining
the truth
in his reach.

    —Steve Finley

THOUGHTS OF MINES

    Time is travel.
Space is time.
    true to the worlds,
are the thoughts.
    of our mines,
Shake a hand.
    touch a soul,
look at the object,
    far below.
Open your eyes.
    to the birds,
of the sky.
walk don't run,
    put your face,
to the sun.
    One to one,
      or maybe,
None.

    —Barry R. Collins

THE MOTHERS

Mothers in twos
Come to the park
And watch their
Children at play.

Mothers in twos
and threes will watch
and see what
they'll be someday.

The hopes and dreams
of the future lie
with the hearts that
watch and see.

We watch the world
in a sand pile,
and you see what
we must be . . . .

The Mothers
    —S. Setzler

WHAT ARE YOU?

Your hair is brown, your eyes are true,
tell me are they, brown or blue?

Your lips are soft, with a touch of pink,
who could say, that they stink?

Your face is tan, with rosy cheeks,
is it true, they really reek?

Your nose is short, and really cute,
when people see it, they almost puke.

Your body is fat, and sometimes skinny,
about your friends, do you have many?

The reason why, I'm asking questions,
people don't like, to often mention . . .

                    You!
          —Kathryn L. Parker

THE WRITER

Nightbeams link the trailing day,
Where fantasies and realities
Share exalting displays.
Know not what horse the rider
Comes? For glory, he charges
Against the setting sun.

Heat endured in this darkest night;
The flame is feeble that gives light.
Sweet enchantments bubble and
Burst. Elusive vapors ride the wind,
As the striped serpent slithers
Within.

The quills' of Masters
                    pen accusing rhymes
Of prose evoked, "time after time."
Yet when dawn breaks the night-holds'
Grasp, the father delivers his beloved
Child,
              and lays it on the altar.
          —Brenda Newton

MYTHICAL IRISH MEN

In the Dark-Tall Irish forests
Live Mythical Irish Men,
They hide from all who seek them
Then slip into their yearly den.

The leprechaun has a secret in his mind
He has hid his pot of gold,
Try to catch him if you can
For he is very hard to hold.

He is as sly as a silver fox
and as quick as a rabbit,
He jumps and skips and plays dirty tricks
and has a lot of bad habits.

He will make you look just like a fool
When you look the other way,
He is never really cruel
Because he is always gay.

If he is caught and gets free
His secret will remain untold,
Because of his sneaky and snobbish ways
No one has found his gold.
          —Deborah K. Cassidy-Beck

THE BOOGIE MAN
(By Dawns Early Light)

He dances in the street
  To an unheard beat,

  His feet tapping lightly
    His face smiling slightly,

  Every week on the very same day
    A bit of soul comes into play,

  Swinging cans to and fro from the ground
    The world is his — oblivious to anyone around,

  With a whirl he glides turns spins
    Earphones snapped over his ragged cap — he grins,

Inching his way down the street emptying cans
    Doing his job and being the "Boogie" Man,

He never even glimpses the lady — nor her envious stare
    Silently watching with pink rollers in her hair.
          —Wilda M. Goldberg

I AM

I am the girl with chameleon eyes
I wonder how they change
I hear they are magical by the give of a wink
I see they are changing blink after blink
I want you to know, I'm not telling you lies
I am the girl with chameleon eyes

I pretend I am normal by covering them up
I feel kind of fake when they're not themselves
I teach them to see if they are still there
I worry to think they're not taken with care
I cry at the thought if one of them dies
I am the girl with chameleon eyes

I understand they are precious and specially given to me
I say they are pretty, could I be wrong
I dream about everyone liking them so
I try to make them reflect off the snow
I hope they are liked by all of you guys
I am the girl with chameleon eyes
          —Amy Marth

BARN BLOSSOMS

The Wind said to the Farmer
              The stink of rot is upon your stables.

Nevertheless,
      Replied the man,
I will sow painted blossoms against its walls.

A cow will not tend to its shed
              while the worms molder the timber, old man.
The decay is your own.

Nevertheless,
      Replied the knowing smile,
The Book of Good Growing
              states otherwise.
The barn is not my harvest.

I am curious, said The Wind, What will
              You Do
      when the Stalls are Spoiled?

Pluck up the blossoms,
      Laughed the Farmer,
                    They are very Colorful!
          —C. Joseph Cadle

UTOPIA

Watching the tide come rolling in
Thoughts given birth emerge from within.
Of a place only in my mind
A place which, no one else can find.
Where there is no pain or power to be sought
A place of peace, where no war is fought.
Where broken is no law
Perfection without flaw.
Utopia, some did call
Spring and summer without winter and fall.
All stays the same
There is no need for shame.
Nothing dies, everything born
There is no danger, of which to warn.
Utopia is the solace I seek
I need not of explanation speak.
All the time I wish to flee
To that Utopia by the sea.

—Craig Spratt

ODE TO THE TREE

I stood before the Tree of Life
Its branches twisting with age
How perfect is thou demeanor.

Tree you old majestic one
Leaves of golden-green
Winding weathered mossy trunk
Like canvas I've never seen.

Give birth to saplings every year
Spread life across the land,
How quietly you smile.

In depth I've pondered your quiet resolve
In forests I've heard gossip not
How proud and bold your stance.

I stand alone
With lips to speak
Tis' your wisdom, only,
I seek.

—Edward E. Share, Jr.

THE LOST SUNDAY GENTLEMAN

Wayfarer, on the frost bound plain
pulling the black stallions rein.
Recalling the summery bed once claimed,
as though a dream obtaining.

His words are captive within a cloud,
as frigid air shivers the whispering calm.
Asserting the path before is yet beyond,
and I am a man scourned.

Through snow covered birches, wherever
the eyes may wander, hibernating trees lay
in slumber. Alone in cover, alone and serene.
Shrouding the life beheld in old, to become
a reminder of love untold.

Quietness bellows

The ebony stallions ears pierce the still air.
May it be the clear crisp chime in call?
Beckoning to lead,
their enchanted gaze,
their enchanted walk.

—Andrew Walter Crandall

SECRET LOVE

You live in my thoughts day by day,
You ease my pain and make it go away.
You are there for the good times as well as the bad,
You are there for the happy times as well as the sad.
To think of you always makes me smile,
To think of you makes life somewhat worthwhile.
You have me now in heart and soul,
Unspoken words never to be told.
Only a fantasy, a wish on the moon,
To be mine forever—not anytime soon.

—Brenda L. Nolen

FLIGHT

Oh, Red Tailed Hawk, circling above, how I envy you
as I take my morning walk.

Oh if I could only fly, but not like the 747 that
flies so high,

Oh what freedom you have; and I; and you don't leave
the white scratches in the sky.

Oh I hear an occasional cry, but it's your mate you're
trying to reach on the other mountain nearby.

Oh I hope you stay in our valley so green and we'll
continue to fly together only in my dreams.

—Richard A. Dahl

SOUL'S TRAVEL

In days of old
When last we met
There never was any so bold,
of the few we were quite a set,
and the eternal end was yet.

When next we set
Our foot to ground,
There we were when again we met,
there was many more around,
that are never more bound.

In future times I see
Of all the souls alive
There is only one besides thee,
we shall be the eternal bride,
never more to have died.

—Wanda L. vonSeeberg

ALONE

Alone in the dark,
Not a person to stand by me,
No one to lean on,
No one to hold,
I feel like a weed in a garden of beautiful flowers.

What's to do I ask myself,
No where to go, no one to see,
Not a single person who really loves me.
But wait—I hear a voice in the distance,

It's just my voice echoing in the night.

Maybe someday, some one who really cares,
Will come my way.
There's always hope I tell myself,
For life isn't over,
Until I breathe my last breath.

—Matthew Geromi, age 14

RAINDROPS

A raindrop glistens in the sun.
I like watching raindrops fall one by one.
Yes I know there is homework to be done.
But you see my friend when a raindrop hits the ground,
You will notice when you look around,
There is none left to be around.

—Cynthia Ann Collins

SLEEPLESS NIGHTS

Turn out the lights and so to bed
My thoughts go racing round my head
Of things undone and words unsaid
The poem unpublished the song unsung
The many plans I left undone
It's three o'clock in this long night
While I wait and wait for the morning light
I wear that same old memory thin
And write those letters again and again
And think of my life as it might have been
None of this brings sleep for sure
It never has in those nights before
I face the day with broken dreams and nothing more.

—Alice Stoddard

THE ETERNAL QUEST

Ever since the beginning of Time,
souls have searched for this which is Divine.
from Socrates to Voltaire to the modern day Man,
in venture of finding what they may not Understand.
a bird's chirp, a soft red rose, a sparkling white Glacier,
or a fleeting blue sky for the lovers of Nature.
a living Scripture, a majestic hymn, a heavenly Sight,
or a fiery sermon for the lovers of Christ.
a candlelight dinner, a sweet perfume, a starry night Above,
or a moist kiss for the lovers of Love.
every person thinks that he has the perfect plan or Remedy,
but I cannot find a solution which is right for Me.
is there a common panacea? is it simple or Complex?
to this question that keeps mortal men Vexed.
who knows the answer which has caused so much Strife,
for "What is the Meaning of Life?"

—John Thomas McPherson

GLASS ROSES

Candy promises and liquid dreams
glass roses are like that
A lonely Christmas, a separate team
a glass rose is like that
A breath of fire, endearing hate
thoughts of steel, predictable fate
holy lies, a silent mate
are all a glass rose
A pulsing stone, a piece of fear
shattered hope, walls that hear
an ebony sun, a wooden tear
are so unto a glass rose
Eyes of ice, a heart of night
a will of air, an iron kite
a spoon of time, loving fights
are simply a rose of glass
Intelligent madness, feelings spoken
a pool of space, forgotten tokens
an empty mirror and vows that have been broken:
as irreplaceable as a glass rose.

—Loren Craig-Young

THE HOSTILE BEE

The Bee is a beautiful creature
Collecting honey is an added feature
Pollinating the veggies and flowers
It never seems to tire
Even after laboring many hours
On the other hand
You have to be wary
That contact with the Bee
Won't be scary
I caution you, never near flowers linger
Or you may find yourself
With a stinger in your finger
That's exactly what happened to me
I got stung with a vengeance
By a delicate insect, called the "Bee"

—Anna Gregos

GULLIBILITY

We have all been duped, tis sad but true
At some given time along life's way,
And most of us have felt the sting
More times than we would care to say.

A few of us have learned to be
A tad more wise next time around.
We've taken pains, pulled back the reins,
Feet firmly planted on the ground.

But others of us trusting fools
Would rather think the best of men.
We take the chance, as in romance,
And so, we're duped again.

A simple way I've yet to find
For weeding out deceiving fakes.
How rich I'd be if I were paid
For each of my mistakes.

—Carla McCloud

PYRAMIDS

Geometric shapes
Solid
Stacked high
Practically shaking hands with the sky

Like an arrow
Pointed
In space
Settled on sands, somewhere, someplace

Impossible?
Maybe
But how?
Who ever did it, please take a bow

You've fooled the best
Somehow
Strange myth
Or just the million slaves you were with

A lost secret
Misplaced?
Hidden?
Mankind is puzzled, we quit you win

Pyranoidal
Sweet home
Kings tomb
Preserved in an atmospheric womb

—Stephen Fallon

SHADOWS

Consider the gifts we've been given
Account for the time we've shared,
What of the struggle within us
When all we have left is scarred.
Token memories, balanced against life's odds
We've all separate reasons for living
Where is the balance in life?
What of the struggle within us
Born of a false sense of pride
Blind to the total existence
What of the struggle within us
Why do we shade it in shadows?
Revealed at a chance in our lives
Are we judged by our own importance
Or merely the passage of time.

—Patricia Herrnkind

THE CANDLE GOES OUT

Slowly a candle burns
Burns into the night
It burns some more
Past twilight

No one is home
Everyone is away
Candle may just burn into infinity
All night and day

It gets lower and lower
Lower some more
Not a sound in the house
Nobody's at the door

But what do I see
What do I see
Who kept that candle lit
It wasn't me

No one is home
Everyone is out
Finally now
The candle goes out

—Craig A. Whitney

AS THE WORLD TURNS

As the world turns
My life is at a standstill
Not knowing exactly where to go
Or what to do.

As the world turns
watching a handful of people jumping off
wondering if I'm slipping also.
What am I to do?

As the world turns
watching an assortment just hanging around
wondering if I should just join the crowd
What am I to do?

As the world turns
watching a group doing what turns them on
wondering what I could be doing now
What am I to do?

As the world turns
watching only a few surviving
wondering if I might be a survivor
What am I to do?

—Lorraine Blanchard

PERSPECTIVE

I blinked a silky teardrop from my eye
That rolled along the contours of my cheek,
Exposing a compelling need to cry,
Though, looking back, things weren't all that bleak.
An opaque film of warmth beneath each lid,
Like liquid window shades upon my eyes.
The sensitivities that I once hid—
those streaming tears negated my disguise.
My lashes, dampened, stuck in clumps of two's;
A little sip of wine, a perfect crutch.
Ah! Wond'rous ways we manifest the blues
Of broken hearts, abandonment and such.
Those tears dried up around me all too well,
But I remember every one that fell.

—Robin E. Wening

FILLING PALE BOXES OF TIME

Pine needles gathering tremors
Of eternity, silent gestures
Of sibylline caravans convert
Soft tourniquets of gold to carmine lulls
And amber trespasses of fragile moons,
Carillon-jade epitaphs carving sceptered
Calyxes of masonic omens on white-mortared grails,
Whispering knights rolling Harlech stones
Across transomed moats, papyrus murmurs
Calling mullioned lethargies of time
Into sandstone lagoons, fallow martyrs filling
Pale boxes of time with wet-stone crosses
And bane-silences of pandora-winds.

—Hugo Walter

A LONELY STREET

Walking down a lonely, street at night.
Not another soul, at all in sight.
The noise from the quiet, will soon overcome.
The mental stability, it will take from some.
Things not really there, that may be seen.
Although all your senses, are clear and keen.
The moon glowing high, is above you now.
Throws light into your path, you can see somehow.
The more light that's shed, the faster you walk.
Wishing for someone else there, so you could talk.
Constantly trying to recollect, things of fun.
Then you hear a snap, you break into a run.
Promptly you awaken, from out of the dream.
As afraid as you were, it wasn't as it seemed.
Yet, you lay and ponder, in total dismay.
For the reasoning behind it, what can you say?
Suddenly you realize, it's your way in daylight.
Recalling that lonely, street in the night.

—Amy L. Darnell

ECHOES OF WIND

Wind whistles through the trees
carrying away the sad echoes of a few
some try so hard to flee
from the little that they knew
a dying flower reaches its petals
for the sunlight that can sometimes be a precious metal.
A lonely drop of rain drops down like a tear
rolling down the cheek of
an innocent child crying for her life
a leaf floats in the breeze like
a soul reaching for the heavens.

—Coleen Hannan

TAKING FOR GRANTED

Nothing lasts forever and you know what they say,
you don't know what ya got until it's gone away.
We take for granted something,
something very dear,
and we never really treasure all the love and cheer.
We don't really mean to,
we know it means a lot,
but when it goes away,
it leaves an empty spot.
So it isn't very wise to it like I,
and take for granted something before it says good-bye.
So next time you have something that means a lot to you,
before it goes away,
make sure you treasure it more and more each and every day!

—Lydia Ricci

DEAR LOVELORN

What is love?
Love is undefined. It is cruel, it is kind,
Men and women without intellectual minds.
It's survival of a species. It's so unprecise, yet so very refined.
Love can end with death, desertion or divorce.
Here's the story of a lover's discourse:
They only got to know each other much to fast,
Passion without love will only pass,
Forever freedom a love does not last,
Death's-head at the feast,
Tears of discontent to say the least,
Fallen prey to Jonah jinx,
Empty glasses, no more spirits, no more wine,
Still love stands the test of time.

—Nicholas Dean Pierro

SHADOWS ON THE SAND

The ocean may divide us, and keep us miles apart,
But, thoughts of you and I, just linger in my heart.
We have a common language; it's known throughout the land,
OUR love affair is shared by two, OUR shadows on the sand.
When day is done and night appears; OUR shadows never sleep,
OUR images never fade my love; they're yours and mine to keep.
We're simply destined lovers; "MY" love please take my hand.
I'll return one day soon, to OUR shadows on the sand.
So till we meet again "MY" love; I'll love you from afar;
I'll dream of you at night, I'll wonder how you are.
My lips will gently "brush your cheek,"
I'll kiss OUR "wedding band,"
And we will love, side by side,
Like OUR shadows on the sand.

—Evelyn Farrell

FARAWAY THOUGHTS

Since the day I first met you, my life has really changed,
Somethings I put in order, somethings I rearranged.
I've put you in the middle, and built my dreams around,
Someone who means so much to me, the special one I've found.

Before you came into my life, my skies were not as blue,
Then one day you came along, and the sun came shining through.
Although we may be far apart   the miles cannot erase,
The precious memories that I have, of sparkling blue eyes
and a smiling face.

So now I'm waiting patiently, for the day when you'll come home,
I'll not regret one moment spent, of reminiscing while you're gone.
Some say you're where your thoughts are, now if that's really true,
You don't ever have to be alone, for I'll always be with you.
Dedicated to a very special couple in my life.

—Deana L. McNew

WORDS

Many words are written
Many words are read
Many words forgotten
That should have been said
But words of love live on and on
And we never seem to tire
Of hearing one short phrase
That is our hearts desire
"I Love You"

—Martha Ratliff

LOVE: A MANDATORY CHOICE

Acceptance, then
Blinding Lights,
Companionship,
Oh, Passion—
Hold me in Arms,
Caressing.
It's over, yes,
Even now.
Control the soul,
I listen—
Electric waves
Sound as built;
Rushing water,
Restored Hope.

—E.W. Daring

SWEET TREASURES

Hold dear to the heart all
sweet treasures.
Hold dear to the heart all
that's rather.
When the sperm hit its mark,
it begins a breath of hope.
Life has so many things
that has to cope.
Must give back to life all
that is taught, with the first
beat of the heart.
Be ready for all the many
busy times.
For faith is what's needed in
all our finds.
Hold dear to the heart all
sweet treasures.
Hold dear to the heart
all that's rather.
Turn loose of all the lost
yesterdays, for there were
some.
While tomorrow will surely
come.
Hold tight to love and
nurture it good.
Every creature will return
what it can.
Let not a moment go by
without a grateful glance.
Life was given on earth
only to enhance.
Hold dear to the heart all
sweet treasures.
Hold dear to the heart all
that's rather.

—Emily Piazza

KAREN

Rosy cheeks, blue of eye
And golden are her curls;
My angel-faced imp
Laughs and gurgles and
Smiles her baby smile.

She dreams her dreams
Of whatever babies dream
And sighs her baby sighs.

She held my hand and said
So much without saying a
Word—laughter was all around.

Then one night an angel came
And took my baby away.
And every day I pray to God
She dreams her dreams and
Smiles her smile that
Says so much without
Saying a word.

—Margaret Arnett

TIME REMAINS

As time Goes
So I go

I real; no, I reel
Flung Past Far-futured Fancy

In Mind
In My tied up, I unwind
In Mine: solarium bright
I close eyes I Sigh
Society Scythes, Shakes high —
headed imbedded view, Blundering
In their unfair but unaware
Smiles

Smiles; similes simplicit.
Subject to scrutiny.
Unpenetrated.

My room is my room
my leaving? Won't be soon
Won't for some be soon enough

Time remains
my gain, my gain.

—Stanley Bowers

dad

i'll never know
the pain
but can only imagine
through the tremor of your hand

i'll never know
the love
but i can see the living of love
through you and mom

i'll never know
the thoughts
for your wisdom is so full
and my mind is so shallow

i only know
that in my solitude
i care and love you
even though it may not show

—Erika Sauer

Across the sky I see my life. The things that have been and the things that will be. I see laughter and tears, good times and bad. I see times when there seemed to be no tomorrow, but there was always a today. I see hope and love, but never quitting. I see times when no one is there, but I am never alone. I see a life, a full life. I see things that if I could, I would change and things I would never change. But the one thing I always see is today, and as long as I have today things can change.

—Donna E. Dennis

SONNET TO A SMALL BOY'S MOTHER

Shall I compare thee to a new tube of toothpaste?
Thou art more fair than the unsoiled cap:
As smooth and unwrinkled as the new tube,
    When it first comes out of the box:
Ah, but rough hands do squeeze the tube right away,
    and a fragile tube hath all too short a stay;
And with every use he takes his toll,
    Upon the unsuspecting cylinder;
But thy eternal patience shall not fade,
    Nor shall thee lose possession of thy temper,
Nor shall frustration cast thee in distress,
    When instructions go unheard;
        So long as small arms around thy neck goeth adoringly,
        So long lives love, and this gives new life to thee.

—Sandra Greenman

THOSE TWO AND THEIR MOTHER

They started out so small. I couldn't touch them yet, but I could feel them. I couldn't see them, but I knew that these two were no ordinary two. I saw the joy in their mother's eyes, I felt their tenderness in her skin.

These two were sent from above only to a mother with her kind of love. She's done so much for me, but now she's filled our whole house with glee.

When I met her, my life started for real. Now with these little ones, my life's been fulfilled.

Our love started with you and me. Then we thought, "Why not three?" But you know, with four, I love you just that much more.

The future is bright, I can't wait to squeeze them tight. Yes, you could say I really love those two, but I first loved you.

—Ricky L. Paul

MOTHER I FOUND IT JUST THE OTHER DAY

Mother I want you to know that I have it
But I found it just the other day.
Hidden behind all of my busyness, yet right in plain view.
Everyone around me could see it
But I found it just the other day.
After I found it, I realized it had been there all the time
Always growing, taking new shapes, yet never really changing
But I found it just the other day.
That's when I stopped all of my busyness,
And took a really good look at it.
Then I realized it was yours, oh mine too, you give it to me
But I found it just the other day.
Sometimes you gave it to me knowingly,
Othertimes by God's divine plan.
I know you haven't missed it, you kept as much as you gave away,
But Mother, I found just the other day.
That's it, that's right, that's exactly what I found
I FOUND YOUR BEST, THE VERY BEST OF YOU MOTHER,
I FOUND IT, I FOUND IT IN ME.

THANK YOU

—Marylea Monroe

AN ISLAND

I am an island;
Silence my sand.

People the sea;
Smiles they broke with glee.

But silence sipped these smiles —
Till back they'll flow — for some whiles.

—**Michael Leland C. Baradi**

FLYING

Flowing through the emptiness of space
On wings not meant for beings like ourselves to possess.
Turning and gliding
As graceful as a fledgling bird
Out of the way of an invisible predator.
Then, arch your way up and feel the cool wind against your face,
As you stretch your flexed muscles behind you,
And begin your euphoric ascent towards the heavens,
Like an eager child.
Then, after you explore the outer reaches of the unknown,
You begin your slow, spiraling descent downward,
Like a feather thrown carelessly to the wind.

—**Katren Munstock, age 14**

A TALK WITH DAD

Hi Dad, I miss you Dad, I wish that you were here.
  I need a hug, your strong embrace, to wipe away a tear.
Even as I talk to you I start to feel much better.
  I have to talk to you this way 'cause you can't answer my letter.

And Mom is doing very good, she sends her love as I do
  Your other two sons do as they should and your daughter too.
Vines of love still bind us all and will until we die
  Watered by the tears we shed, no, I'm not ashamed to cry.

Even as we laugh with joy, a tear expresses grief
  And all of these emotions grant us some relief.
Now as I depart, with lighter heart, to see you I do crave
  'Til later then, as He decides, I'll talk to you at your grave.

  I miss you Dad
    I love you Dad
      Thanks Dad.

—**Ralph T. Stoermer, Jr.**

DADDY

Daddy, I just want to say that I enjoy the games we play.
  Going fishing, on hikes, swimming, dancing, and riding bikes.

Daddy, do you know that I copy you and all the things I
    see you do?
I tag along behind your back putting my footsteps in your tracks.

Daddy, you are so strong and yet, the softest touch I've
    ever met.
When I need help I know that you will be right there
    to see me through.

Daddy, you are the best. You are tops over all the rest.
When I grow up I want to be like you are, as I see.

Daddy, you are my stone. The very rock I lean upon.
You give me support in the things I do and you comfort
    me when I am blue.

Daddy, you have such gentle hands. I think that
    you are the greatest man.
And daddy, I just want you to know "I love you so!"

—**Evelynn Musick Cassady**

AS I WALK THROUGH THE FOG

As I walk through the fog
I see clouds surrounding me.
It's a mystical place.
You have fun,
For you don't know what's ahead.
As I walk through the fog,
I hear, but I don't see.

—**Sara E. Rinehart, age 10**

CITY SNOW

High above the building tops
Snow falls from the sky.
It tumbles gently on the wind,
  Gracefully gliding in the air.
But suddenly then it is stopped—
  On man's own cold, dark street.
And like man's hopes of yesterday
  It melts upon his heart.

—**Chris Rodenbeck**

CHANGES

The times we spent together,
  The times we were apart.
I'll never forget them,
They're embedded in my heart.
Like when I was two,
And just beginning to understand.
You were always there,
To offer your caring hand.
And then when I was ten,
And feeling all alone.
You took me out for ice cream,
To help to calm the tone.
Later, at age fifteen,
When you got very ill.
I was never at school,
I was always at the hospital.
Then the dreaded day came,
When you passed away.
Oh, dear grandmother,
I'll never be the same.

—**Kaci L. Orton**

FOOL'S GOLD

Oh, listen to the hootin' owl
Tell his tale of woe,
Listen to the miser
A'countin' out his gold.

Hoo-Hoo, Hoo-Hoo,
The owl doth screech
Throughout the night,
Tee-Hee, laughs the miser
As he toils by candlelight.

Oh, envy not the miser
That heavy bag of gold,
Without the warmth of caring
The world is bleak and cold.

Tis far better to have
One star filled night,
A lover's hand in thine.
Then the heart can go a'dancin'
On the merry sands of time.

—**Pat Calhoun**

MOTHER

Mom, I really love you
You are the greatest, too.
If you really love me,
I'll be happy with glee!
You help me when I'm ill.
You give me help at will,
Since I was a small tot,
So really thanks a lot!
You helped me with a broken toy.
You'll help me with a troubled boy.

—Denise Gilman

OUR FAMILY TREE

I think that I should never see [1]
A family as great as thee.
A family whose mouths are fed
By earth's fruits and daily bread.
A family that looks so good today,
I hope it will always be that way.
A family that may in summertime
Join in a picnic so sublime.
As we look upon this family tree
Someday we may all agree,
If only God can make a tree
Then God has blessed our family tree.
[1]"TREES" by Joyce Kilmer

—Ronald F. Pfleegor

From the time I felt the first kick
Until the time I saw your face
I knew you'd be a wonder
    That no one could replace

A beautiful little baby girl
    My darling Kristen Leigh
Beauty and grace; an angel face
For all the world to see

No mom could ever be more proud
Or love you like I do
For in this world God's greatest gift
To me my daughter . . . is you.

—Karen L. Scarpaci

GOOD-BYE

Please tell me Lord
        why must I cry
Please tell me Lord
        why can't I say good-bye
It was on my lips
        I almost said it yesterday
It was on my lips
        and there it seemed to stay
It's been eight months
        eight months today
It's been eight months
        he's far away
You took him Lord
        away from me,
You took him Lord,
        couldn't let him be.
I know Lord,
        you must have loved him so
I know Lord,
        it was his time to go.
        Bye — John.

—Barbara J. Howard (Mrs. John)

SWEET RELIEF

Rainbow flesh emerges, explodes
Quick and sweet inside (peanut or plain?)
Intense and wonderful, but so insane!
Deciding which is best, and getting sick . . .
Removing melted prisms with a lick.
Amazing! This melange of dyes and cane
is potent for relief of life mundane . . .
A dose of Nitro for the heart that makes us tick!

A sweet narcotic for a neurotic nation,
Destroying tension, twisting turmoils-GONE!

—Therese M. Frischolz

DON'T GIVE UP

It is a crazy thing this life we live.
It is a little take and a little give.
One minute you are up and then you are down.
You wonder how it all happened as you look around.
For we make this life what it is.
The fault is not always hers or always his.
To define happiness is a point of view.
I believe it is understanding and compassion, old and nothing new.
If you try real hard and with all your might,
You will find most things in life turn out right.
So do not give up on today for tomorrow who knows,
What you thought was a weed is really a rose.

—Jack Morris

GRANDMA'S LITTLE SUNSHINE BOY

So very still you lay in that strange bed.
As I reach through the bars and gently rub your forehead.
You do not wake but remain very still.
The heat from your flesh tells me you are very ill.
Your mom faithfully stays at your side day and night.
Her loving eyes for not one minute will let you out of her sight.
My eyes follow the tubes with clear liquids running into your arm.
A prayer fills my heart asking God to keep you from harm.
The tears start quickly flowing down my cheeks.
I turn my back for your mom's eyes I did not want to meet.
After what seemed like endless time had passed.
The doctor finally came to speak to us at last.
He gently took hold of your mom's hand and also mine.
Reassurance in his voice, telling us you soon would be fine.
This grandma's heart is filled with such joy.
God answered my prayer for grandma's Little Sunshine Boy.

—Carol A. Bergantzel

TO WHOM IT MAY CONCERN:

Softly she sleeps, wrapped in her dreams—
Better for her, reality is too cruel.
She awakens, unaware and unsure of today's experiences.
Lost in her world, surrounded by a handmade cocoon,
Refusing to see life as the puzzle it must be.
This tightly circled existence has its many rewards,
No loneliness, no misery for her.
Her soul is too fragile—she knows this and is wise to keep it safe.
Her figure denotes womanhood—her mind a child's, yielding to the
                    tender thoughts within.
I love her so, and cannot begin to shield her from the light of day
Or the inevitable darkness that must come.
Walking slowly towards a future that holds no certainty,
I unknowingly grasp her hand to pull her back to the warmth
                    of what is me.
She is a woman, but she is my child—
Be gentle with her heart.

—Lisa Sine Parks

LIFE'S MYSTERIES

A cool breeze on a cloudless night,
A cry from a newborn baby's tongue,
A delicate sapling standing erect,
These are mysteries of life.

A hurricane ripping a town to shreds,
A screaming, lonely, orphaned child,
A wilting, stomped-on flower bed,
These are mysteries of life.

The mysteries of life cannot be explained.
Only hypothesized by men well-trained.
Everything experienced in life has wonder,
From the beauty of a spectrum to a clap of thunder.

Man was created with a free will and mind.
To challenge these phenomena and find,
Clues that bring us close to an answer,
For these "mysterious" questions of our time.

—Mary Anne Sauer

SCHOOL

The Students . . .
    behavior . . .
        talking loudly,
        hitting and punching,
        daydreaming about after school activities,
        exhibiting a rude behavior.

The Teachers . . .
    behavior . . .
        teaching subject matter,
        shaping children's minds with knowledge,
        scolding the absent-minded children,
        returning ink blemished tests.

The Principal . . .
    behavior . . .
        punishing the punished,
        announcing school days events,
        planning school activities,
        admiring the work of students.

—Sarah Elizabeth Steinbarger

SCHOOL

Oh, Lord, why is it my sad fate
To sit in school, both early and late,
To study from books till the page looks red,
Knowing that I have an ache in my head?

Yet knowledge still is wondrous bait;
I get it from books, if I concentrate
On History and English of an obsolete age;
But it makes me wish I were back on the sage.

I prefer a bronc to the school's hard desk
That confines my movements, though this is the west;
For I was built with a healthy stature,
And this type of life just isn't my nature!

'Twould rather I'd be back out on the plain,
A second of kin to the wind and the rain.
Why, rather than school I'd rather fix fence,
But Math is a must, and Science makes sense.

So I'll go on to school, and study each day
On problems with fractions, and Panama Bay.
Though typing is hard, I may possibly learn
From the works of writers as eccentric as Hearn.

—Brother John

SPRING FEVER

The sky is blue, the sun so bright
A February morning sure to delight
Springtime bulbs just breaking through
Our snow has melted, and showers are due
To help the grass turn green, and grow
Another season's lawn to mow

—Phyllis M. Path

THE TEACHER

Perfect in every way,
I tell you she's here to stay.

Her skills will help you learn,
which will help you earn.

She helps you to study,
there-for you won't be an old fuddy-duddy!

Some say she's mean and cruel,
please, don't be a fool!

Even though she works us to the bone,
she is always willing to loan.

So don't say mean things about her,
because, what would we do without her?

—Jessica Bekech

FALL REFLECTIONS

The sights, sounds and smells of a fall day
are wonderful.
When light winds blow the fallen leaves appear
to be skipping along.
As you walk the leaves underfoot make a
delightful crunching sound;
Their fragrance carried in the air is
indescribable.
A beautifully colored quilt is formed by leaves
lying on the ground;
And, looking across the fields clusters of woods
look like mixed bouquets of reds, oranges and
yellows.
Rays of sunlight touching the yellow leaves
bounce back as if the leaves were gold.
Oh, the reflections of a fall day are truly
lovely to behold.

—Dorothy M. Smith

PILGRIMAGE

I am a foreigner on a journey.
Don't know when I'll arrive.
I know where I'm going.
Won't get out of this world alive!

The road signs are so obscure.
You'll have to look carefully to see,
Many beautiful shams which lure.
Try as it may, they won't fool me.

The journey lasts a lifetime.
It's very trying, when you can, sit and rest.
Then run awhile to just the first climb.
The spirit tires, after I reach the top,
But I know I've done my best.

As the journeys' end comes into view,
(I can hardly wait to get there!)
I'll be sure to look for you;
In those delightful mountains, so fair!

—Jenny Stewart

REFLECTIONS OF LIFE

As one looks in a shimmering stream;
back to our eyes reflections beam;
but distorted is the image that our eyes see;
maybe the way we see ourselves is wrong;
and the waters reflect the way we be.

—Dan Ragsdale

FALLING

I once took a walk in a wood by the sea
And watched a woodsman fell a tree.
After it was fair cut through
It seemed to know not what to do.

It only stood for quite a spell,
then slowly . . . slowly then, it fell.
A massive tree with lofty crown;
I watched it topple to the ground

America is grand, but seems to me
To be somehow just like that tree.
Near cut through with evil and greed . .
She falls, oh yes. She falls indeed.

—William R. Meador

JUST SAY NO

People try to take my soul away
But I don't hear the drugs they say
This is my life and I'm proud
I love you and I'll say it for-ever out loud.

I don't see no reason for drugs at all
There's no future in it from what I saw
Take all your drugs and please just go
No use in asking me, I'll just say no.

Inject the needles, inhale the coke
Go ahead and laugh, to me it's no joke
We see it every where even at school
They just smile, "Hey, Dude it's cool."

Life's too precious to throw away
Don't offer any to me I'll be O.K.
Do what you want it's your decision to do
I see no reason in it for me or you.

—Michael

IF TOMORROW NEVER COMES

You know that He is waiting there
but you always say tomorrow
what if tomorrow never comes
and there's no more time to borrow
think about what happens
when our world comes to an end
and think about how you would feel
when friends start killing friends
what would you say if just to eat
you had to have a number
and you're standing in the driving rain
and thought that sound was thunder
you turn your head up to the air
and see the Lord on high
and now tomorrow never comes
but you'll never know just why
so you see the Lord is asking you
to follow Him today
'cause He'd rather see you smile forever
than to laugh for just one day

—Peter J. King

CRY OF AN ANGUISHED HEART . . .

Who is this? Trying to poison the world . . .
Destroying it.
Who is hurling hatred amongst brotherhood?
Who placed monsters in the human hearts?
Hunters set the traps in the sweet lands.
Enemies heard, in the veneer of friends.
Venomous these winds, blowing day and night.
Masses burnt, hell is let loose.
A handful of villains, nurturing their dreams.
Strangling innocence—love—humanity.
Who made enemies of brothers?
Tried to break apart our heartland.
Speak up! Open up sealed lips.
Innocence is being butchered
Speak up—
You are being used.
Don't be the pawns.
Don't let the devil be victorious.
Don't sell your soul, to fallacious.

—Renu Mahajan

I WAS CONCERNED ABOUT MY HEALTH
(A poem about criminals. Each one has a
$1,000,000 reward for their capture.)

One day as I was walking down the street,
I saw the Masked Avenger with crocodile feet.
If I told where he was I would receive a lot of wealth,
But, I was concerned about my health.

One day as I was riding in a car,
I saw the Skunk Ape with a Chinese star.
If I told where he was I would receive a lot of wealth,
But as usual, I was concerned about my health.

One day as I was riding on the bus,
I saw the Caped Avenger, making up a fuss.
If I told where he was I would receive a lot of wealth,
But as usual, I was concerned about my health.

One day in China, as I was riding on my bike,
I saw the Sundance Woman, standing on a dike.
If I told where she was I would receive a lot of wealth,
But as usual I was concerned about my health.

—Takeshia L. Brooks

THINK AGAIN, MR. DOPE MAN

Mr. Dope Man, you think you've got it made
Your car looks nice and your pad is laid.
Your pocket is full, but your mind is through
Wake up and take heed—those drugs are killing you!

Listen, Dope Man, you'd better think again
Death is the price that you pay for sin.
You won't have a choice; in the end, you'll pay
So don't count on tomorrow, it's too far away.

To steal, kill and destroy is Satan's ultimate goal
He'll let you gain the world, while you lose your soul.
You should reconsider, Man, and count the cost
The one thing that's eternal, your soul, is lost.

You are now accountable for all you've heard
So give your life to God and help spread his word.
Please, young people, wake up and see
That you, through Christ, can have the victory.

Mr. Dope Man, let Jesus change your name
Before a drug bust rocks and shocks your fame!

—Cherese L. Moore

NICK AND RICK

Once upon a time there was a man named Nick who had a brother named Rick who he liked to pick on with his wooden stick. You see, Rick thought he was something slick when he picked on his brother Rick with his wooden stick.

—Scott Stinespring

OFF TO THE RACES

One morning at eight o'clock
M.J.B. got into his MAXWELL HOUSE car
Went two blocks and picked up the HILLS BROTHERS
Drove on to SUNRISE City
And picked up several CHOCK FULL OF NUTS.

Now, with a MAXIM of speed
He was on his way
Coming to a HIGH POINT in the road
He FOLGERS his car on
But a SPOTLIGHT blinded him.
He hit the BRIM at the side of the road
And rolled over in SANKA sand.

A tow truck pulled them out
And took them to a NESCAFE truck stop
Where they enjoyed several cups of hot TASTERS CHOICE.

—Florence I. McEckron

THREE HAPPY MAIDENS

There was Olly, Polly and Marly,
three happy maidens; lovely, ripe and ready to go,
Their grandpa said they should go, and get married
Their mother said is that so.

Their father had a word or two
The preacher said, mach schnell,
and I shall bless all three of you
on your wedding day,
but where are the future grooms I say.

Bless you the girls procrastinated another year,
Growing older and bolder, like Paul Revere,
They rode off in to the country side
carring a sighn, available future bride,
and men folk gathered, had fun galore
now all three girls are happily married,
not maidens any more.

—Karl Fischer

THE WORM, WHO ON THE SIDEWALK LAY

A worm on the sidewalk caught my eye
As I was walking by
In the rain that was coming down fast.
I just stepped over the worm as I walked past.
I was in a hurry.
I had no time to worry
About a worm who on the sidewalk lay,
That one dreary day.
But that worm I would see again
In the same place, that on the previous day, he had been.
It appeared that in his struggle to survive
He was unable to remain alive.
A rainy day, that to us is boring,
Was to the worm, a life-ending warning.
So, the next time you are bored on a dreary day,
Think about the worm,
Who on the sidewalk lay.

—Elaine M. Houska

DECEMBER DREAMS

Deer darting thru the night,
Every package in paper bright.
Kris Kringle is in his sleigh,
Elves have helped him on his way.
Mothers tuck and kiss on the cheek
Babes hoping for a peek.
Every Scrooge is mellow and mild,
Remembering the birth of the Christ child.

—Richard A. Muraska

ENGAGEMENT RING

I'm wearing your Engagement Ring.
And I know my heart should sing.
You give me sweet tender kisses.
But I'm not ready to be your Mrs.
And you give me the truest love.
But it's not what I'm worthy of.
I'm sorry if this breaks your heart.
But it's best for us to part.
Go sow your oats, and have a fling
Goodbye, Here's your Engagement Ring.

—Zelma N. Speer

THE LAFARGE WINDOW

My friend shuddered,
"There is the Angel of Death,
Symbol of destruction, catastrophe,
and bitter finality.
All are included with no escape."

The sun rose behind the window.
Colors filtered through the transept.
Rays of pink and green, yellow and purple
Illuminated the Angel's inscription:
"Death with the might of his sunbeam
Touches the flesh and the soul awakes."

Then the Angel spoke,
"The Beginning and the End are One.
Alpha and Omega are forever united.
I, the Angel, am the Messenger of Life.
For all eternity, an unbroken circle."

—Jane C. Whitten

HELL'S GATES

Death awaits at hell's gates.
You can't escape it now. It's here to
stay, no time to pray, you've gone
too far this time. As the children
burn, the families yearn for one
more chance to be, the ones who
look outside the door and see the
children who played there once before.
But, as you know it's all too late as
one more day goes by. When you sit
there all alone with no more tears
to cry. The fire flames a blazing
high, almost reaching to the sky.
But, when you cry or when you mourn
the lives of kids are ripped and torn.
The flame sparks, the fire starts to
take another life. And you my friend
don't turn away. This happens in real
life.

—Aimée Denson

SUMMER PARADISE

Maui — Forever Summer
Rainbow Hues
Majestic Verdant Mountains
Sugarcane, Pineapple Grows.

Pristine Waters Shimmer Azure
Brilliant Golden Orb Sizzles Pure.

—Vivien Bellamy

INTERGALACTIC

I asked but all was silent.
Questions fell and dried the rain.
Life crumbled right before me.
I searched but found lonely pain.

How can a heart keep beating?
Like the earth just spin around.
On some suspended planet.
Feeling each tear's dying sound.

—Rani Luria

MOURNING DAWN, SILENT DUSK

Eyes to fate, I've met myself,
My voice I've yet to hear.
The tides of age,
The shouts of life,
My eyes I beg of sight.
But this story's done,
I breathe, I'm gone.
I've yet to live,
I've still to die,
These hands behold my fate.
I beg of life,
And know my end,
This is the depth of my passion.
Beyond the vision,
An empty voice
Foretells a shadow dawn.
I hear the dusk
Whisper oblivion.

—R. L. Comstock

WINTER'S IMAGES

I looked out thru the window
I guess in late December
I'm really not too sure
It might have been November.

I saw that it was snowing
It caused my heart to sing
The snow machines of heaven
Released their icy sting.

White fluffy clouds up yonder
A treat for any eye
To me they really look like
Meringue on lemon pie.

Our Lord arouses nature
He causes birds to sing
Just how much rejoicing
Can a snowflake bring.

Let me end to make a point
This all tells a story
Someday we'll all pull the rope
That rings the bells of glory.

—Harry Kerstetter

THE WONDER OF THE NIGHT

I went out to see and listen to the wonders of the night.
A galaxy of stars glittered in the vastness of the sky.
A full moon bathed the land in a silvery light,
And a cooling breeze wafted the fragrance of flowers near by.

Far in the distance some animal gave a plaintive cry,
And I heard the faintest of barking from a dog.
A sleeping bird was awakened and arose to fly,
And a small creature scurried for its nest in a log.

Fireflies flitted about, katydids and crickets all chirped together.
As I watched the antics of a squirrel, and a playful young coon,
I heard a night bird call to its mate down in the heather,
And a pack of wolves yelping and mournfully howling at the moon.

Some of wild life were sleeping, and some were seeking prey,
And there was an ancient turtle resting in its shell.
A hoot owl hooted, and a frightened rabbit scampered away.
Nature has formed the habits of life, and all is well.

All these things happen in the stillness of the night,
While man is safely sleeping in a soft warm bed.
I stand in awe at such a wondrous beautiful sight,
Knowing God spoke, and things came to be, just as He said.

—Bertha Fite

THE MOUNTAINS IN ME

The mountains are within me.
I mentally drive through them everyday.

I cherish the treasures they share,
And the majesty they display.

I gain such strength from those magnificent boulders,
As I ponder their greatness and strength.

They give me strength to carry the burdens upon my shoulders
Each day, often of extremely long length.

But wait!
Is there a greater lesson here to be seen?

Those beautiful mountains upon their shoulders do not bear
Years of hopelessness, doubt or tears of despair

They are free and wonderful
Because their nature is of God.

And if my nature is of the same,
Am I not free and full of majesty
Without burden, without blame?

—Bonnie Boulton

UNFOLDING

The sun on Maple Island looks warm on its blanket of snow
With blue skies above and zero below
But spring not far off with warm winds and showers
Will unearth a garden of fragrant spring flowers.

Maple Island is a joyful place
Its rivers and lake provide it grace
The warmth from its homes appears so inviting
And the pleasures it offers are so exciting.

You may boat, you may fish and swim as a bird is free
With family, friends and neighbors upon its crystal sea
The night sky brings the stars so close
And breezes caress the evening's repose.

Winter, spring, summer and fall
Has atmospheric pleasure geared to all
Maple Island is an oasis upon the sea of life
Away from the clamor of the city's strife.

—Muriel Zieman

SHADED DREAMS

We Begin Our Lives Quite Worry Free, of What Life Holds for Us.
   Then As We Get Older Day by Day,
      We Start to Wonder What's All the Fuss?
So We Spend Some Time in Dreamland, Dreaming of Bright Sunny Days.
   Then Along Comes Some Rain and Thunder,
      To Wash All Those Dreams Right Away.
Now All that We Have Left are Memories, of Good Times Now Gone By.
   Then We Try to Pick Up Life's Pieces,
      But Once Again We Begin to Cry.
Well We Know that We Must Go On, to Keep the Sweet Memories Alive.
   To Show the World We Won't Give Up,
      Even Though Our Dreams Did Not Survive.
So Once Again We Must Start Over, Wondering What Else Life Holds for Us.
   Day by Day We are Getting Older,
      So It's Harder to Understand What's All The Fuss.
Should We Again Spend Some Time in Dreamland? Well No One Can Really Say.
   But We Remember After the Rain and Thunder,
      There Can Still Be Many Bright Sunny Days. *****

In Memory of A Friend
   —Kim Emanuel

REMEMBER

Outside it's a winter wonderland,
  There are signs all around, God touched earth with His very hand.
As a little bird searches for a crumb or a seed,
Somewhere someone has a valid need.
It's Christmas Eve and families have this time to share,
But let us not forget, this is a time to care.
We have children, we have loved ones, we have families, we have friends,
So let us remember one another before this Blessed season ends.
To a man who has no home, no where to place his head,
There's not much life in that man, and at times he wishes he were dead.
There are babies with no hope in sight,
Cold, hungry and crying through the night.
There are mothers who for their babies say a silent prayer inside,
For God to keep them safe, in his arms so warm and wide.
There are fathers who for their families always try to give them more,
But often times he's kicked, before he can get even to the door.
But most of all, let us not forget the man who has no one,
He lives in total darkness, for him there is no rising sun.
So always do your best, to each other be a friend,
And the one who gains the most, you'll find yourself rewarded in the end.

   —Faye Rouse

THE SMILE

I watched an old woman rummaging through a battered trash can
  Searching amid the broken glass and dented beer and soda cans
For stale and moldy crusts of bread.
I stared in amazement as she carefully peeked into each plastic bag,
Looking for remnants of food from yesterday's litter.
A ragged shawl, that had lost all of its original color,
Only partially covered the disheveled strands of graying hair.
What had destined her to such poverty; had she strayed as a young girl,
And was now cast aside, neglected, alone and forgotten.

I could not stop myself from wanting to help in some small way.
If I offered her a little money would she look at me with scorn;
Or would she patronize the nearest saloon.
I walked over to her, stepping around the hills of bulging trash bags.
As I touched the sleeve of the tattered garment
I felt the trembling of her cold and bony arm.
For just a fleeting moment a smile appeared on her wrinkled face
As I dropped the few silver coins into her gnarled out-stretched hand.
With a saddened heart I hurried away from the filth and stench.
I did not want to see where her shuffling feet directed her.
Only God would know.

   —Ruth V. Shillito

UNDERSTANDING LIFE

As I walked by a grave
  I happened to see,
A very old man
Who looked like me.

He had a cane,
And a little top hat.
His coat was torn,
His heels were flat.

I walked on over
And stood by his side.
He just sort of stood there,
And started to cry.

He began to speak,
Said his soul was free.
I looked at the marker
And it was for me!

   —Kenneth Dunlap

THE GOING

Here lie the bones
  of Jeramia Heath.
Died one night
  in the middle of sleep.
Hope he's in Heaven
  and not Below.
He wasn't ready but
  had to go.
Was no time for
  speculation,
Even less for
  reparation.
Let this be a
  warning.
Don't wait till the
  End.
Death seldom comes
  in the guise of a
  friend.

   —A.R. Miller

PRETTY FLOWERS

In an empty room
  On the window sill
Pretty Flowers
Cured the ill

Near an empty bed
On the table
Pretty Flowers
Who is able

The empty rain
On the grass
Pretty Flowers
Who no one asked

An empty heart
In mournful minds
Pretty Flowers
Behind the times

Empty eyes
With no hope in sight
Pretty Flowers
Have lost their might

   —Sandra Bennett

LADYFOOL

Kiss no longer, my eager lips.
Sleep no more, content beside me.
Taste not, the salty tears I cry.
Eat no more, the fruit of my toil.
Feel no more, the pain of my endeavor.
Smell not, the fragrance of my being.
Smile not, at the happiness known.
Share no more, the ecstasy of oneness.

And with all thy sweet essence,
Hate me wholly with much fervor.
Let thine anger brood deep within
so it will consume your whole mind.
For some bright, early morning,
You will awaken early and find,
'Tis thyself you've been hating
And for a decade, you've been blind.

—Harvey D. Wright

Tears and rain
Fall the same
Both distorting images
Through windows to observe
Memories of happy times I see
Pictures of you and me.

Seeing the truth
And our love
Forever washed away.
I couldn't stop the tide of lies
Controlled by what we happened to say.

As I watched the rain again
Staining my face
And smearing the window pane
Realizing how ironic
How they both fall the same.
My tears and the rain.

—Amy A. Seyller

LOOKING IN THE MIRROR

Looking in the mirror
shattering glass
blows before her eyes
terror of love ungiven
she hears the cries
they come from way inside
mirrors of life.

Faulty impressions upon the face
somehow the shatter cannot erase.
Broken pieces laying there
upon the floor, she sits and stares.

Mirrors of life
seeing only what she will
one for hate, one for love.

Looking in the mirror
shattering before her eyes.
The life of love is held inside.

She reaches out to grasp it,
but only gets the pain
she's inflicted upon the body,
upon the shattered face she sees again.
Broken pieces of glass lay upon her
she'll stare and wait and wonder
what it told her
in the . . . mirror of life.

—Cheryl J. Morris

******* ABRACADABRA *******

One is constantly seeking wisdom and truth,
Yet all one has to do is to go in the chamber within.

—Charles R. Linton Jr.

Look into my eyes my sweet savior.
Hear and feel my heart pounding against your
very breast as you embrace me.
Do what you will with me.
Run with me, ravage my dreams, love me and
make love to me.
My breath is hot on your neck as I rest it there
to tell you these things.
My hands might be an evil drug that makes
you lose your mind.
My mouth will make you writhe in the sweet pain
that you have become a slave to.
Decide what your life shall hold for you,
I will be your provider.
Take me under your wing and make me your personal secret.
I will only do what you don't ask of me
my love.

—Kelley R. Long

SHADOWS

So mysterious,
So many different types.
Some are shadows from the sun,
Some are shadows from the past,
All are dark and lonely, forbidding your presence,
Making you feel cold and unloved
Without saying a word.
Putting forth the image of heartlessness,
Yet calling out for the warmth of the sun,
Or the forgiveness of the past.
Shadows,
So mysterious,
Saying, "Come see what I am hiding."
They beckon you, "Come if you dare."
Sometimes they seem to beg,
"Bring in the warmth and light."
But more often than not,
Their coldness overshadows those few glimpses of warmth.

Don't be a shadow.

—Deborah Anne Kent

THE JUDGEMENT

It is so simple now, looking down from this tower.
I mock the people's foolish mistakes.
As an inhabitant among the hills matters seemed superlative.
Now the pettiness overwhelms.
Recalling people observing the color of skin
Bronze, ochre or ivory.
This place only houses transparencies
A thin, silky film as personification of the soul.
No longer caring for the tables of time
Looking from my turret for eternity
Eagerly searching for random trivialities.
What scenes I have witnessed.
The achievements
The horrors.
No longer justifying former actions
Mortals blindly grasping their way
Through the tumultuously demon infested seas
As terror is unleashed uncontrollably
Above we may only revel in the wisdom of Epimetheus
Weeping for the unnoticed obscurities of time.

—Karen Stern

TO WHOM IT MAY CONCERN:

I do believe that it is time to express all of the
total emotions that I may share, with the one I share
my free time with.
It is extremely important that I be given freedom,
not to do what I want when I want. To do what I want
when the thought comes around to be creative.
If given the opportunity to explore I'll invent.
If held back I'll still invent without sharing what
I have to offer.
This only means if you want it . . . whatever it may be!
Then let it be me.

—Kenneth D. Younger

WHEN WILL THESE THINGS BE?

When shall the human mind perform the brain-stymieing feat
Grasping the infinite ends of space to meet?
When shall the lion and the lamb by a child be led
And all life sustained on grace and bread?

When shall the folly of wars be understood
And all nations and men aim all to the good?
When shall the time come for the last trumpet to sound
And herald an end to this mortal round?

When shall the Book of Life be opened and read
And the myriads of souls be raised from the dead?
When shall the destiny of creation come abreast
And every soul, atom and star be joyously blest?

—Anthony Russello

CAN YOU MEND A BROKEN HEART?

Pardon me sir, but can you mend a broken heart?
You see, my heart is slowly breaking apart.
    See, my trouble is, every time I find true love,
they always end up hurting me. How can it be?
I'll need it done right away, I don't think I can
wait.
        "I've got a major case. Can't you tell by the
    look on my face?" "Where did I go wrong? Why can't
love be strong?"
        So do you think you can mend a broken heart? . . .
right away? Oh, you're not that kind of person. Well,
thank you anyway . . .
        Pardon me, sir, but can you mend a broken
heart? . . . .

—Melissa Grundmeyer, age 13

WHO CARES?

Here I sit waiting for a call or visit
            Who cares?
Time passes by, day and night, I sit alone
            Who cares?
Often times I cry myself to sleep with fear of loneliness
            Who cares?

Many holidays have come and gone
            Who cares?
Someday someone will come to my rescue of loneliness
            Who cares?
The pain and hurt I feel, not only from illness, now shows
            Who cares?

Who cares? I care
If only you would put yourself in my place
            You would then care.
The want of love and caring of a loved one
            Hurts when no one cares
            Please care.

—Beverly Ann (Andrade) Gonsalves

LOVE'S SUNSHINE

I've seen you in a thousand mornings,
Within the red sunrise,
Every day a brand new wonder,
To appear before my eyes.
The sun, just like my love for you,
Grows stronger with the day.
In everything I say and do,
Our love falls in the way.
But if it be an obstacle,
It's one that I embrace,
Just as I hold you now,
Seeing sunshine on your face.
And as the sun is setting down,
And you walk me to my door,
I think about tomorrow's sunrise,
And love you all the more.
For the love we have does not fade,
Along with the daylight,
For just as strong as through the day,
Is our love all through the night.

—Jackie Biltoft

FOREVER AND A DAY

To you I give my love, my life,
Forever to be your faithful wife.
To take care of you
Is my true virtue,
Together, forever for life.
Through the years of joy and pain
Our children of love they came,
Us, into our new lives form
Our children I have borne.
And into our time, then you parted
From my soul and broken-hearted.
Alone by myself,
No more is your presence,
Depression is my only essence.
Until my own time, my dear spouse,
I sit inside our empty house.
Our children — all away,
How I miss you and I pray
That soon together we may be
Forever and a day.

—Katherine Ann Downes

MY ONLY LOVE

The feelings we once shared are
deep within me,
Though you have been gone for
quite a long time.
Still my skin yearns for your
loving touch.
I loved you once, and I
always shall.

When I first saw you, my
heart wept with pity.
You were a poor, starving artist,
begging for shelter and food.

But then I took you under
my wing,
feeding, clothing, and petting you.
Then my love for you grew
until it could grow no more.

You died with the coming
of Spring.

—Starr Wilmoth

BE MY GUEST.

I know a place
Where violets grow
Close by a city street.
Come, treat your eyes
To glad surprise
And slow your hurrying feet.

—Dorothy Pinkerton

THE MYZER

If I could capture the sheen
From the trees
Or insnare the faintly pungent
Breeze of an autumn day,
Or clip a sample from the
Turquoise sky
Of merchandise rare
For mortals to buy
I'd hold them fast
A myzer at last

—Lola B. Branch

VALENTINE'S DAY.

Valentine's day is a very
special day. It's a time to
share your feeling, It's a time
to say I love you, Valentine's
Day is the most wonderful
day of the year.

—Jennifer Steele

CRYSTAL BEAUTY

In realms of crystal beauty, this splendid earth lay now,
    In all majestic paradise, like jewels on bush and bough:
And midst this earthly splendor, the sparrows on the wing,
    While in their flight of magic love, their praise and homage sing.

Raindrops like shimmering diamonds, He scattered on the trees,
    And twittering birds are singing, while swaying on the breeze.
So open now, your eyes, so blind, and see the earth so fair.
    And know God's love is keeping us in His eternal care.

—Anna W. Palm

EXTREMITIES (THE RUSSIANS)

I heard the news today and it left me numb.
It said that the Russians want to blow us to Kingdom Come!
Now, I don't want to be incinerated, do you?
So, I wrote my congressman to ask what to do.
He said:
    Send me tax money to build more arms to defeat the Red Peril
    From across the sea.
That sounded pretty stupid to me:
Build more arms?
I already got two . . . I don't need three!
Why don't we take that money and build more heads.
Then, we would have more brains than those terrible Reds.
Or, build more eyes for those who can't see.
This is a better idea to me.
Or, build more hearts (we can always use more).
Then, we could love each other and we wouldn't need war.

—Shawn Micheal Pearson

FUEL FOR LIFE

Love and Dreams, Truth and Trust,
Are all the things you mean to me,
Love is how you understand me,
Dreams help you believe in what you seek,
Truth will keep your heart free,
Trust comes from all the times we've shared,
Without the Love, Without the Dreams,
Without the Truth, without the Trust,
All the Love we feel would never be,
All Life as we know becomes empty and lonely.

—Nand Samuel Guerrero

THE BIG ROUND BOX

The gentle little girl delights in playing with buttons, and grand ma ma has many in the big round box. The buttons are all shapes, sizes, and colours from ages past that have many stories to tell of people, and places they have known, and have seen in the big round box.

Securely they are kept in the silence of their place as the gentle little girl wants to look, and run her tiny fingers through their many colours, and shapes in the big round box.

Grand ma ma, may I have this one, or that one? Which ever catches her eye. She carts them home in a safe little box to have and to look at, and see from the ages past of buttons that can tell stories of people, places, and times, from the big round box.

—Addy M

AUTUMN

Autumn is here, as you can see
And the trees are as pretty as can be.
Covered with color from head to toe.
Soon Jack Frost will come, and the leaves will have to go.
Falling from the trees and covering the ground.
Pretty soon not a pretty leaf can be found.

All the trees will be bare,
All the pretty colors gone,
And all the birds will fly south,
To a warmer home.

All the crops have been gathered,
And the grass has turned brown,
Soon old man winter will appear, and cover the ground
With a blanket of lace, so white and so pure,
But God willing autumn will come again
next year.

—Virginia R. Williams

ANNE FRANK'S DIARY

I sit still with my diary, I can't make a move carelessly.
I feel like I want to cry, but my eyes must stay dry
Or else I might be heard, I can't even whistle like a
bluebird.
I wish this was a dream, how wonderful that would
seem.
It isn't true I feel blue
I am scared and angry not to mention hungry.
All because of a cruel monster, he's a hunter
I don't want this book dirtied by his name, he causes fear.
He thinks of this as a game.
Oh lord save us from this cruelty, you have the
highest nobility.
My life gets darker, I wish some one would
make the monster's life harder.
When he catches me, the killing will be done hastily.
The war shall end, I shall not descend.

—Zehra Naqvi

FALL

Fall is a time to set me wondering,
from where I have come, and
the direction I will follow.

It is an in-between time, beauteous
in its own right, but saddening
because the gay and glittering summer
has passed; sobering because of
the impending Winter.

Oh, Fall, if you could just emulate
Spring, with its spirit of hope,
and not preface the bitter winds
as the year closes, you would
be one of my first loves.

—Ethel M. Powers

OUTER SPACE

There's nothing new that's under sun
Or, so the story goes.
Then we have finished 'fore begun
Whichever, heaven knows!

But, let's consider outer space
It's under sun and o'er.
Frontiers are boundless for the race—
We've not been there before!

We'll end this rat race—tail 'n all,
And other problems, too;
Then zoom away and have a ball,
Where skies are always blue!

A stop by MERCURY for mail
And travel hints 'n trade,
Then JUPITER for laws 'n bail—
Aha! we've got it made!

We'll bypass MARS—we've got it here!
There's VENUS just above.
Her shining beauty makes it clear
To us—from GOD with love!

—Marjorie Squires

THE SHADOWS OF SAINT MARY'S

In the shadows of Saint Mary's
I ventured one day
Not caring or thinking
How long I would stay.

No, I'm not a member
Of the Catholic Church
But I am sure my God will say
They are the salt of the earth.

Many good things have happened
Some not so good too
But I keep counting my blessings
All the day through.

God has sure blessed me
With a family so fine
It's a wonderful feeling
To know they are mine.

Soon the sun will be setting
And to God I humbly say,
Thanks for sending me to the shadows
Of Saint Mary's that day.

—Brown Johnson

A WINTER NIGHT

A wolf howls in the wind.
It lets out its sorrow and says
How cold it's been.
It's been a long winter
And the trees are in splinters
From the weight of the ice
That has doubled them thrice.
The place is barren
On a long winter's night.
—David Phillips

KITTENS

Kittens are nice
they're also funny
when they chase a frog
they'll hop like a bunny.
Kittens are playful,
little creatures
with their small paws
and other cute features.
They'll play all day
and sleep all night
they might be small
but they can be a joyful sight.

—Tracy Munson

MONARCH BUTTERFLY

The Monarch Butterfly,
So regal and so free;
It is a wondrous symbol,
Of love and life to me.

I hear the gentle rustle,
Of gorgeous velvet wings;
Of movements softly waving,
As it rests and quiet brings.

I find my faith uplifted,
As its loveliness I see;
And I would wing my way,
To the Heavens and to Thee.

Could I become so regal,
So loved and yet so free;
I'd set my course aloft,
And then a Monarch be.

—Jessamine B. Borst

SEAGULLS

Shades
spread across the sky
flapping the sun
circle in silence.

Sparks
of the fire winged
set the heart
a seething moment.

Sizzling
the sensations burn
flaking the embers
of cindered lament.

Scattered
my emotions fly
reflecting the light
of lost content.

—Philip Horky

ON FAITHFULNESS

She came into my life with five years of trauma behind her.
She was like a baglady, taking what was left.
She had two redeeming qualities when first I saw her:
Her brown eyes were expressive,
with a complexity of sadness and hope.
Her mouth curved into a smile,
when approached and acknowledged.
She came home with me timidly.
She misunderstood kindness.
She remained quiet, but her eyes sparkled: she smiled.

After a year together she has become a faithful companion,
Adapting to our unique lifestyle.
Into a constant pleasure she has evolved,
Displaying a pleasant sense of humor.
How grateful she is: how thrilled am I!

Her little ears pick up intruders around our cozy home.
Her little white tail wags with any type of conversation.

How could I have almost overlooked her when
She was silently crying for a chance
To prove her faithfulness?

—J.S. Ritter

"THE BIRD"

There is a singer everyone has heard,
It is the charming and elegant Cardinal red bird.
This bird makes the spring time come again,
The Cardinal is to spring as foil is to tin.
The Cardinal says that leaves are old and it's time for flowers.
But in order for flowers to grow, there must be showers.
The Cardinal is such an exquisite bird to see,
Flying through the air so cheerfully.
The bird is a magical bird—only on certain days,
It has healed the sick to make people sing songs of praise.
The Cardinal doesn't stay in one place too long,
It has other places to go where these people need a song.
But as you watch it fly away,
It's true that you're sad.
You know that you'll see it some other day,
And with this thought you are glad.
So if you hear a sound, quite like you've never heard,
You'll know it's the sound of the Cardinal red bird.

—Ryan Hassani-Sadi

DUCKLING

He's shedding his feathers for new ones:
All summer it's said that he sheds.
He must get rather uncomfortable,
For I see that he scratches sometimes.
Constantly it seems that he's cleaning his feathers,
Removing some that are loosely connected.
Bathing himself is usually private,
Yet today he just doesn't know I am watching.

The cleaner water surrounded by mud is helpful to him,
His bathing a painstakingly long task.
He covers his bill with the feathers on his wings,
To prevent his mouth from getting too cold in this night-time air.
His eye closes when he sees I am safe.
Almost I would wish to provide him a blanket for his neck,
But that would be too much cover for him I know,
For his movements must be quick when that's called for.

I must leave the night air to animals with coating provided already,
For it seems a bit chilly to me, too, with no coat.

—Arlene M. Babb

VISIONS

Imagine a place:
Where the air is as clear as glass
      Where children can play.
      Where work has no stress.
Now go into this place, step into a new world
      Where there is little sickness,
      Where happiness is everywhere.
      Where sadness comes only with death.
There is no prejudice, no hate. everyone loves everyone.
But then you wake and the visions are gone.
You're a child of nuclear age.
      Where the air is so dirty,
      Where there is no room for kids.
      Where life is filled with hell and stress.
 You live here. Step into your world
      Where epidemics kill everyday.
      Where happiness comes only to some. Sadness is abundant.
Meet your neighbor. the one who ridicules and hates you.
        These are real visions.

      —Jeniece Yvonne

BUT THE GREATEST OF THESE IS LOVE

In the Oval Office, the Red Phone hot line gangles the warning;
A nuclear missile attack is imminent:
We have only minutes to remember; the World Series, bread baking;
Puccini's aria La Boheme, The Rose Bowl, movie clips,
Christmas, Passover, a Rembrandt painting:
Rock-group-REO Speedwagon, a first snowfall, micro-chips;
We will not have to worry about—
Drugs, crime, the homeless, terrorism,
Bigotry, child abuse, and racism—
In the Oval Office, there is a key marked SPLC 13:13
Emanating from this key are four deterents to nuclear war;
Faith, hope, charity and love;
Faith is trust that the world's leaders corps—
Will honor the arms limitations treaties;
Hope, that we see the strong banner of the peace dove,
Charity, sharing our blessings unstintingly,
God's supreme gift to us, love, which is mightier than a two
Edged sword, its power is awesome, and can slash nuclear weaponry;
SPLC 13:13-St. Paul's Love to the Corinthians, Chapter 13: Verse
13: faith, hope, charity, love, but the greatest of these is love.

      —Reené George

THE MEMORY ROCK

The "Rock" where we use to play,
  In memory of my childhood day;
was big and round and full of wonder,
The holes and moss made for such grand plunder
for four little girls in make believe,
Just to be outside—what a relief.

      How warm you were on a bright spring day,
      "Time to go barefoot," mommy would say.
      "Clean your shoes and put them away,
        you will need them come Sunday."

If your feet get cold and your knees start to knock,
Warm them upon the "Rock."
Grandpa is plowing today on the hill,
Careful of the Horses, "Old Maude and Bill."

      Years fled by as busy ones do,
      Then another spring day I saw you;
      So full of memories of days gone by,
      But you were so small, "my oh my—I wonder why."

The rock was at Snake Run Hollow, Greenbrier County, West Virginia, 1930's

      —Hope Midkiff Wright

MESMERIZED

Summer rolls in,
  Off the New England coast,
My rock awaits,
A private sitting-place,
To view tranquility,
Of a low tide,
A soft breeze,
Bringing fragrance,
Of the blueness,
Before me,
That's laced with foam,
And tickles the rock,
Only too quickly,
Bounces back,
Into that blueness,
That keeps me,
And my rock,
    Mesmerized.

    —Pauline Piechota

HOPE

When certain times are
  changing;
And you do not understand,
The shift in your surroundings,
Or you need a helping hand.

When you need someone to
    talk to,
'cause things don't look too
    bright;
Or some advice would help
    you,
To try to make things right.

If matters seem too doubtful,
When you don't think you
    can cope,
Keep searching till you find
    it
The only answer—HOPE!

    —Jeana Marie Grace

DEEP MIND

There is a place
  deep in my mind
that no one ever sees.
While it's only one of many,
it's the one I like the best.
In this room
I make all the rules,
the world works like it should.
There are no wars,
no one kills or steals.
Everyone's polite,
considerate and kind,
just like in story books,
and in this room of mine.
This room is full of hope,
with my most powerful wishes.
Every one has rooms like mine,
with many different plans,
but don't you wish,
the world would visit,
and steal my magic plan.

    —R. C. Van Meter

ADDICTED TO YOUR LOVE

The desire to feel all emotion
emerge from your body
professing your unbound love;
an undying need to fulfill all
inconsistencies
in my life. I relish in your love
worn and drained of emotion
my heart pounds restlessly
through my flesh. My love profusely
protrudes from within my body;
through my eyes a passion filled sea.

—Caroline Price

MY ANGEL

God had an angel
and he sent her to me.
Directly from heaven
how lucky can I be.

She doesn't have wings
but her halo's still there.
Her eyes sparkle like stars
she's the answer to my prayer.

With her by my side
there's nothing I can't do.
You can accomplish a lot
when you have a love that's true.

Yes, she's the foundation
of my entire life.
If you haven't guessed by now
the angel's my wife.

—Rick James

HERE WE STAND, FACE TO FACE

Here we stand face to face,
your eyes stare into mine,
our days ahead we may not
know,
but in our memories are
the days behind.

Our love is always growing,
it goes on and on forever,
and as long as the wind goes
on blowing,
we'll always be together.

As long as the sun shines on
so bright,
and the moon beams down so
clear,
I'll feel this love in my
heart,
so true, so faithful and dear.

Now we stand here hand
in hand, this feels so right
inside,
and tonight I'll always
remember,
that your love is forever mine.

My heart is overflowing,
our love goes on forever,
and the wind is always
blowing,
thank God, we'll always
be together.

—Matthew Rusk

random encounter

stalking me with hungry knives that rip and tear and
watching me with piercing eyes that raze my disguise and
i see you over and over and over watching your hair cascading
down the beauty the wonder the prison i want you i need you
pressed close to my aching body passion succumbing shivering
down my spine through space and time and your mind perceptive
keen but yet so subtle and you taunt and taunt and stalk me and
cut me and love me

—todd polenberg

FIFTY—MINUS ONE

Darling—

Today—I think quite hard about our snow-capped apple tree,
Leafless, silent, kept alive by deep, warm, stubborn roots
Planted hopefully so very many years ago by you and me—
No thought of freezing winter days which menace growing shoots

Or even blight that sometimes cuts the output of its fruit.
Yet this tree, so like our marriage (years at number forty nine)
Still stands straight—firm, prepared and always resolute
To take the best, or very worst—a stance like yours and mine.

The cold rains, the angry winds may often thrash its leaves
And sometimes thwart the caliber of fruit it bears—
Or even worse may crack the sturdy bark that it conceives
To balk the hurts which nature deals to cut its years.

So we too resist the threats—still staunch to love, to touch,
To emulate our apple tree that indicates so very much.

—Maury Krasner

A POEM FOR YOU AND ONLY YOU

Sweetheart this poem is for you and only
you because you are one of God's greatest
creations given to earth for me to love.

Sweetheart this poem is for you and
only you because your love to me is a
fountain of hope and a river that flows with
eternal love that will last until the end of
time.

Sweetheart this poem is for you and
only you because your love to me is more than
a mountain, and stronger than the seven seas,
and the wind which has no end.

Sweetheart this poem is for you and only
you because your lips to me are like flowers that
have been sprinkled with heaven's dew.

Sweetheart this poem is for you and only
you because your kisses to me are like fine wine
that has been aged with time.

Sweetheart this poem is for you and only
you because your beautiful smile to me is a
flame of love that will burn forever.

Sweetheart this poem is for you and only
you because your eyes to me are like stars that
twinkle with heaven's love, and to hold
your lovely hand is a touch of paradise.

Sweetheart this poem is for you and only
you because your love to me is sweeter than all of
the flowers that this earth has ever produced,
and more kinder than the gentlest lamb on this planet
earth, and my prayers for you my love will always be that
God keep you safe, loving and free for me to love.

—Reuben Oglesby

MY ROSE

Sometimes all that's left of the rose is the thorns.

Its color has darkened and the petals
begin to decompose.

Emitting the sickly sweet scent of the past.

The rose was magnificent with its crimson splendor.

Unfolding in the light of day
casting a rosy glow of beauty.

But this rose's day is gone
and its beauty now laid to rest.

—Jill Marie McCormick Bensyl

LEARNING TO COPE

When we were young, and danced warmly together in the sun,
always busy with our family, travels, and friends;
no one thought then, it could ever end.
But time was passing, quietly on its way
just like the tide, for no man does it stay.
We had the golden warmth of the sunrises
that now gave way to the sunset's chill;
and with it, a dear familiar, loving voice was stilled.
Never again, to answer a question, call my name, or give me hope.
So now alone, and with God's help,
I must learn to cope.

Charles
In memory 1/7/14 — 1/6/90
—Constance K. Richardson

REFLECTIONS

The bed that I sleep in is hard and cold.
The only thing that keeps me warm is last week's
news and the only thing that feeds me is yesterday's
mold. This morning I found a mirror someone must have
thrown away. I looked in the mirror hoping to see a reflection
of my youth. Instead I was horrified at the sight of my faded
face and sappy eyes. In torment, I dropped the mirror and
the pieces shattered just as my heart did. That can't
really be me. God what have I become? Oh! how can
I live in this cruel world full of poverty and
sickness? Everyday a child cries and every
day somebody dies. Why can't people see
that the reflection in the mirror isn't
just a reflection of me, but of the
way the world shouldn't be!

—Cynthia Badger

I get up in the morning, brush my teeth
and comb my hair, go to work and once I'm there,
try to act as if I care, I don't get anywhere,
I'm going through the motions of life.
Going through the motions of life,
since I lost you as my wife,
can't imagine living without you, oh no.
I'm going through the motions of life.
The days go by, the tears I cry, I just can't
count them all. I sit around just starin' at the wall.
Hopin' you'll walk through that door and love me like before,
I just don't wanna' make it without you
Going through the motions of life,
since I lost you my dear wife,
can't go on living without you, oh no.
I'm going through the motions of life.

—Mr. Tracy John Delosh

FEELINGS

Feelings
Playing hide-and-seek
In my mind
Never lost yet never found
The rules keep changing
Yet are never fully understood
Like my feelings

—Jenel Stelton

THE WAR WITHIN

There may not be a war
of the worlds, but a war
lives within the body of
ourselves that seems to
be the bloodiest of all.

Tears that are shed with
a thought of hope . . .
of understanding.

Dry my tears and I'll
never forget how we
won the war.

—Ame Louise Range

RECOVERY

Riding on a sea of discontent
I turn my face
upwards
in hopes of some enlightenment.
My alcoholic fits now gone
replaced by still
another fear not faced.
Repercussions of my past
Can I now save myself at last?
Can I now salvage years of dread?
Of money spent, of feelings dead?
To rid myself of horrid ghosts
And finally become a host
of calm and quiet revelry.
This is my hope.
This is my plea.
To someday find serenity.

—Denise Merat

It is over, it is done!
They are gone.
Only pain lingers,
And my fingers.
Folding to pray,
And I say:
Thank you heavenly blesser.
Everyday lesser
Is the fear
Here
Round me.
But will we
Have made it for sure?
May other tears of misery lurk
Just round the corner?
I am too long a mourner
To be an easy believer.
Hopeful after
It is laughter
We will remember.

—Irma Yrene

AGING

I look in the mirror and who is this I see?
An old woman is looking back at me.
Her wrinkled face shows great surprise
As she looks at me with my own eyes.
My mind is young, my dreams are too
How did I become like you?
Looking at me, she says with a grin,
"I'm but the shell, you're the one within."

—**Lois A. Reaves**

SPOKEN WORDS

There are times when words fast spoken
Sink beneath a heart of gold
And the scar it leaves remains unhealed
Not even when you are old.

And if one knew the heartache
A harsh word has oft' times done
It has broken all the heart strings
That led to a life of fun.

The pain is so great
That mere words can't relate
For after it's all said and done
The only true thing in life itself
Are words spoken soft—then you've WON!

—**Alice Mulcahy**

THE REFLECTION

When I look into the sky,
I see your eyes.
The reflection of my life.
A sad memory of a time gone by,
And so it goes.
Just as a cloud drifts away,
And disappears into the horizon,
So have you.
Gone from me, but not forgotten.
A shapeless form within my mind.
A darkened overcast whispering of the past,
Leaving the sunshine far behind.
And as the pastels of the sunset,
Cry bleeding in vain across a pale blue sky,
I see your eyes;
The reflection of my life . . .

—**Linda Patterson**

ONLY YESTERDAY

Tomorrow, she said, is gone when the sun
goes down.
And no one is the wiser.
For all their toiling and drudgeries—
Do they ever find any answers?

Tomorrow, she said, is a day beyond our
imaginings.
When we will find our dreams
And make ourselves happier—
But that too will pass.

For tomorrow, like all todays, will become
a yesterday.
When dreams take us from bad to worse—
And tomorrow's hopes
Become yesterday's sorrows.

—**Jessica McNamara**

MY SHELTER

You give me strength to keep on trying
To keep on living when I feel like dying
You are always there with tender words
To make my biggest worries seem absurd
You keep me believing tomorrow will be a better day
Because your love is constant, here to stay
So darling, thank you for being my safety in the storm
Thank you for giving this fragile heart of mine a home

—**Teresa Steffenson**

SWEETSONG OF BEAUTY

There's a ripple effect in all that we
do. What you do touches me; what I do
touches you.
There is a pleasure in the pathless
woods. There is a rapture on the
lonely shore. There is society where
none have walked. If you walk hand in
hand with me I'll walk hand in hand
with you.

—**Heather Hemesath**

A MESSAGE FROM MOM ON YOUR WEDDING DAY

I don't think there could ever be
A Mother and Daughter closer than we
Not quite twenty years ago
Something was missing in my heart and soul
So God in his infinite wisdom and grace
Sent me a bundle of joy with a sweet smiling face
To nurture and love and help to grow
Into the beautiful young lady that we now all know
I thought this day would make me sad
But instead I find I am really glad
Glad you found Tom to share your life
Love you and keep you as his wife
He's very special, I'm sure you'll agree
And we already include him in our family tree
So as you begin your life together
I know it will only get better and better
My only wish today for you
Is that all of your hopes and dreams come true!

—**Flo Johnson**

MOTHER/DAUGHTER

Mom . . . can it be that I too am one?
Incredible to me how fast time has passed on

Mom . . . always knowing, so strong and so brave
Always knowing the answers, always knowing the way

I . . . on the other hand, don't feel so secure
Not always knowing the answers or the right way to go

Daughter . . . dear to my heart, being and soul
I didn't always feel so sure of myself

Scared at the unknown I charged on like the wind
Since I couldn't just stop
And call it quits

I'm glad I accomplished all that I did
That I seemed so strong and sure
To your little eyes and ears

Because that's what I tried to be . . . to do . . .
All for a small child . . .
All because of you.

—**Teresa Proano**

MRS. TRUESDALE

Eyes dance like a web in the wind;
A voice bathed richly in resonance conquers the strong;
Hair neatly curled
Shines like a dew touched flower on an early morn.

Pisces swim to all depths of the seas;
Aves soar to fill the skies with song;
Terrestrials intermingle in uncommon harmony;
All paying homage to the day you were born.

Your abode, neat and stylish, bulges with remnants
of then and now.

In your bosom lies the treasure of a race;
Let all the world come to you and bow.

—Alexander W. Jones, Jr.

(TO RICHARD, in memory of mother, Margaret Weed Murphy — December 1988)

GOSSAMER REALITY

It was made of the ethereal, like a wispy stirring of the air;
A first-light glimpse of something there, a fleeting glance to say, "We care."

What is this thing that calls, that turns our heads around to stare?
Who? Who is causing us to bare our tired will to reach and care?

Surely we no longer fall on long gone feelings that are not there?
Yet . . . here awakening fresh and fair is that thought long eldered, like silver hair.

And here emerging above all, gathering strength to boldly dare,
a metamorphasis so pure and rare, to reach and say, "My friend, we care."

There it is, the key word to fall; that wintered over so long in lair.
"Friend!" Our friend, that is where our hearts do yearn to stay. We care.

—Samuel P. Smith

THE HANDS OF HANS

Twice in a decade—just ten short years,
Bad news again had come to my ears.

A problem in my heart was the cause of my ills,
And could not be cured with shots and pills.

If I was to live any kind of a life,
Again I would have to go under the knife.

Now, the ace of spades is the card of death.
I knew it could soon take away my breath.

I looked the ace over, looked at it hard.
Said I know a man that can outdraw this card.

I come to this man—weak, sick and near dead.
Sometimes a great effort just to hold up my head.

Now I lay cold and straight, stiff on the table.
His hands are steady and his mind is able.

With razor sharp knife and tools of his trade,
He cuts and sews 'til repairs are all made.

Now, with tender care from skilled caring nurses,
There will be no need for those long, black hearses.

May your music be clear and sweet in your ears.
Good luck. Long life. Many, many years.

—Arvie L. Sheets

TO THE SPIDER IN MY WINDOW SILL SUMMER OF 1989

Sticky silken
Spider threads,
Strands of broken white
Entrap the flies
that dangle there, dead.

Sticky silver threads
Woven with cleaver skill
Strands of broken white
gleam in rain,
sparkle in light

Hides the Spider
Traps the fly —
(Enchants
          I.)
—Bethany J. Lucien

GERMAN SHEPARD

German Shepard, what do you see?
I hope you know you mean the world to me.
As we go through life together, with laughter and fun.
We'll learn life's treasures together, one by one.
With you by my side, my heart is filled with great pride.
You'll stick by me when I'm sick or in pain.
And I'll be by your side just the same.
Watching you grow as time goes by.
Puts a joyful twinkle in my eye.
For you're a part of my life and so close to me.
You're not a pet, you're my family.
And now you're full grown. It was only a matter of time.
But that's o.k. Because I'm so glad you're mine.

—Victoria A. Brand

A MATTER OF EQUILIBRIUM

That fly is quite well balanced,
I decided watching him.
He looked at me as on he came
walking slowly 'round the rim.

My cup was full of coffee—
a deep pool for the fly.
Quite casually he came around.
What a daring guy!

Then all of a sudden in he fell,
splashing all around.
I stuck my spoon in; up he climbed
'til he was safe and sound.

He sat there on the edge of my cup
looking wet and quite dejected.
I said to him, "Well, little fly,
isn't this what you expected?"

After a while, he flexed his wings
as in the air he flew.
And calling back he said to me,
"By the way, ma'am, thank you!"
—Mary O'Beirne Rebstock

LIFE

Life —
is a fleeting of moments in which
you live, love, die.

Life —
is swift.
When least expected, it is gone.

Life —
is to be lived,
every moment utilized.

Life —
is mine, yours,
meant to be shared.

Life —
rushes by in a flurry of
hellos, goodbys, I love yous.

Life.

—DD Turner

PHYSICALLY GONE

She and I smiled . . .
A greeting to each new rain.
Which at the time,
Seemed to us completely sane.

Then the noon sun . . .
Came to warm our love again.
Now I have found,
Weather. as time brings a change.

The morning light . . .
Clothes me now only with pain.
Evening's stillness,
Finds me with mere dreams to claim.

Does she realize . . .
Her image still haunts my brain?
Forever my thoughts,
Shall see her the same.
I stumble on,
Lost in self-made rain.

—Robert G. Smith

IN MEMORY

Sometimes someone passes by,
In life, time doesn't matter;
The impact of their presence
And all illusions shatter.

Faith, Hope and Charity,
They base their lives on these;
Trust and confidence in God
And Him alone to please.

The world looks at them
And turns its eyes away;
Poor, afflicted, timid souls
And yet for us they pray.

God blesses and enriches them
Gives courage, strength and fear;
When He comes to take them home
He'll brush away each tear.

Good-bye for now, we loved you;
The years were all too few.
We know Our Lord will comfort us
Because you asked Him to.

—Betty McGovern

SON OF WILLIAM

The sky darkened as the native son came home to die.
Instead of open arms, the Son of William found
clenched fists.

Son carried a disease, a plague, some said. Others said a
curse from heaven.

He came home to die in a quiet place.
But his childhood haven changed to a personal prison.
People shunned their native born.

"If this is the Christian town from my childhood, where
is your Christian love?" the son pleaded.

"We take care of our own and you are no longer one of
us," they coldly stated.

Exiled not by disease, but by ignorance.
As he waited for merciful death, Son of William weeps,
not for his torment, but his tormentors.

Welcome home Son of William, welcome home.

—Brent Hadden Smith

MEMORIES

At night, when the sun sets and the wind begins to blow,
Vivid memories appear of a loved one long ago.
I remember trips meaning much
Along with grandfather's special touch—
My first trips to Disneyland
And Huntington Beach barefoot in the sand.
Even before the day I was born,
He was racing Mom to the hospital with one broken arm,
beeping the horn.
Who was more excited? The grandfather to be
Or his daughter alone—husband at war overseas.
I still recall the day when grandfather was tucked away.
All I could think of were words lost in memory that I could
never say.
"I love you, grandfather!" were the only words I remember
from that warm July day.
Memories of you will NEVER fade away!

—Christina L. Sudweeks, age 18

This Poem is for You Dad,
It's About Fishing and Searching for a Better Life

father forgive me
            for not stopping time
in youthful days we floated silently on a morning lake
while beneath us another world swam with the speed of
            survival
we cast a line and broke the smooth ceiling of the watery
            world
trying to hook into the heart and soul of the mysterious life
            below
we laughed at the sunfish that took me for food, biting me on
            the nose
as I leaned over the boat to catch a glimpse of the swimming
            miracles
we watched with wonder as quick fish leapt into the air,
            another existence
then came crashing down again to the home they belonged
we were two thrilled souls when we reeled in the beautiful
            bodies
sleek and glistening; thrashing for life on the end of a
            wormed hook
then without regret we threw them back into the water
we couldn't eat them, they gave us so much
while the noon sun baked us we rowed back to shore
leaving the search for meaning a catch for another day
father forgive me
            for you are the one that got away

—Heather Ann Hillier

T-E-A-C-H-E-R-S

T Touch a child; it shows the child you care.

E Excite the child; it causes learning to be fun

A Admit you are wrong; it tells a child it is acceptable to make a mistake

C Create with a child; it encourages the child to be creative.

H Help a child willingly; it lets the child know you care

E Enrich beyond the purple dittos and workbooks; it causes the child to think.

R Reinforce the positive; it teaches the child respect for others.

S Smile often; it is a silent way of saying, "I care."

—JoAnn Marion

UNDERSTAND THEM

Some people are harder to love than others,
Friends, casual acquaintances, sisters, brothers
But that does not mean we should quit trying
Leaving people in a rut and sadly crying;
We, all of us, need just as much love as we can get
And when you give love freely, you'll receive it, you can bet!
Some lives are filled with utter consternation
And so, if to these lives your love you ration
'Twill only serve to cause more pain and doubt
Causing them to wonder how they'll do without;
In such a situation I would give you this advice
Overlook his faults and try to treat him nice,
Think of how 'twould be were the shoe on the other foot,
And you were hurting badly with a friend who did not give a hoot.

—Gloria Stagi Stopford

FRIENDS

We've been friends now for quite awhile,
You taught me to laugh, and even to smile.
we met when we were little,
And then you moved away.
And even though the miles divide us,
our friendship is just as strong today.
Whenever I needed to talk, you were always there for me,
And if you need someone to talk to, I'm always here you see.
So if you are upset, or maybe a little confused,
Just pick up the phone, or write a letter and I'll see what I can do.
For you see my friend I owe it all to you,
without the friendship you gave me, I wouldn't have known what to do.

—Ronae Busch

GRATITUDE FOR FIVE SENSES

Thank you, God for eyes to see
The splendor of a tree;
For ears to hear the ripple of a brook
In a quiet nook;
For the privilege of smelling the
pungent air of a new morning
You have given it birth;
For the ability to taste the fruits
of the earth;
For the touch of a friend's hand
Giving assurance they understand
Thank you God, it's such a small
thing to say,
Just help me to use what you've
given me
To bless some soul to-day. Amen

—Rebecca Kennel Beiler

SHARING DREAMS AND LIFE

In our recent acquisitions,
We have progressed in life.
Through these transitions,
We must overcome strife.

My love is deep and true;
No words to express my feelings,
Only comprehension in you,
Seen in all our hurts and healings.

By looking outward as one,
We shall share the nature of man.
Our love will remain as the sun;
The sustaining feature of the plan.

Each day we share on Earth,
There may be no conversation
Of the magnitude of your worth.
Our love is fortification!

—David L. Peeler, Jr.

THE EDGE

Muted by the light
voices
rise and whine
at the window of my consciousness
writhing
struggling to pass through
Untold horrors beckoning
"come play with me"
tease
and taunt
my battered self control
Please
they say
open the window just a little
let us in
let us join with you
A siren song
growing sweeter
with each darkened moment

—Allen L. Jones

PROGRESSIVE SEVENS TRIAD FORM
TEACHER'S CHALLENGE

Children
So small,
Just turning six
Half smiling at me
With teary eyes,
Step softly
In.

Teacher
So great,
Awaits each one.
With a reassuring touch
And loving words,
Hearts to
Win.

School,
A place
For molding lives,
Future joys and greatness.
A new age
Ready to
Begin.

—Mrs. Robert L. Mason

FOREVER

We laughed and we loved
    together as one.
Beneath the moon,
    and beneath the sun.

Now you are gone,
    our words are few.
I want you to know,
    I will always love you.

—Tracy L. Carl

ROSES AND ASHES

Roses to ashes as the
    page turns.
Storybook novels the plot
    crumbles and burns.

Romance builds and takes
    a fall.
People in real life not much
    difference at all.

In a picture or in words,
    somehow we all can pose,
finding our dreams, turning the
    page from ashes to a Rose!

—Lynette Dausman

Rain paint for me a story
A story for one
A story for all
A new poem
An old rhyme

Wind sing for me a song
A song for one
A song for all
A new line
An old hymn

Paint and sing for me
Of the wonder of love
Old as yesterday
New as tomorrow
But with me always
In my heart

—Mark A. Smith

We all have our own,
    Separate pathways to take.
Our own destinations . . .
    To choose.

We all have our own,
    Contributions to make.
Our own special talents . . .
    To use.

We all have our own,
    Kind of life to pursue.
Our own kind of dreams,
    To be weaving.

And we all have the power,
    To make wishes come true;
        As long . . . .
    As we keep believing!

—Irene J. Hackman

A SUICIDE REGRET

I sit here and swallow, the wonder drug has not taken effect.
But then suddenly, the feeling is more well known.
The doors seem to be growing smaller, the windows the color of fog.
The walls begin to melt, the room shrinking.
But it's not over!
I see the darkness when I close my eyes.
The picture of gory blood enters through the open pores of my mind.
Then, all is calm and blank.
I know I am not dead yet, for my mind is still working.
Not thinking, but filling with memories.
Memories from when I was young, running, jumping, and playing.
Then my teen years, dances, parties, and guys.
And even still, the last of my life, the mistake I am making now.
Never wanting me to suffer is making me suffer the most.
I don't want to die anymore!
But it's too late, the drug has taken its effect.
I can no longer do what I did before,
My greed has taken me forever . . . .

—Kim

REAL LIFE

The world is a harsh, uncaring site, Don't expect to be
    assisted by others, for they wouldn't trouble themselves
    with you they don't care.

The world is indecent and unjust, it will let you wither away.
In this world, there is none to watch over you. People are
    cruel, adapted to their way of life. They neglect morals
    and ethics, even if it was the way you were nurtured.
    Nobody cares.

Talents you may have flaunted before others are now futile
    attempts at nothing. These ineffectual efforts are not
    worth the endeavor.

Your life on this earth is nothing, unless you are defiant of
    others and ward off others in their attempt to deter
    what you aspire for, and you, are as depraved as others.

But then, there is the circle, and as is from dust to dust, it
    is unavoidable. Everyone will end up as dispassionate as
    they started.

It will never end.

—Michelle A. Deerwester

BEFORE WE LEFT THE TOWN

Within a few minutes, we were back to the hotel room. Any other
day we would've spent the rest of our times somewhere, somewhere
in that city. But not then. Nothing had any attraction. Even the
short time we spent walking up and down the big market, the old
church and the train station was short of anything. I mean it. In
the room our presence was so dominant that the service man could
knock at the door and walk into our room and still we would not
have noticed him. We were sealed and a block or two further—the
heart of city with its shops and its lights completely ceased to
exist. Only silence stood around and the room was like a mirror
in front of us. Almost empty with its few pieces of furniture and
a large bed. We wanted to say something to each other but words
weren't coming out. I guess we didn't want to make it harder.
Neither of us, really. I was the first who threw myself on the
bed. Lying there for a while, then feeling her weight beside me.

Night was showing its face. A small plant was sitting near the
window. I took her in my arms. I wasn't thinking much except I
knew that when the morning would come, I had slept the night
beside her as if all were planned and nothing more could be done
and how each of us was going his (her) own way. Alone.

—Vahid Hamidi

SERENITY THROUGH PAIN (OF VIOLENCE)

Out of the pits of hell I rise to the light!
Unencumbered with remembrance of horror past
Enlightened, forgiving, I strive
To forget the paralyzing injury to mind, body and soul!
Demons beckon to remember and hold the bitter gall
Chains bind, but I break loose
I walk in the light pardoning all
Intentionally asking The One above me to "handle the pain"
Steadfastly I pursue good not evil
Unfettered and pure of heart, I seek the solace of unending grace,
Nevermore to remember — but to be free
For in forgiveness one loses the pain
And there comes gain for the soul
Silently I journey on through the maze
Welcoming Peace and Love forever!
I embrace a feeling of being healed!

—Donna M Crebbin

WHITE SENTIMENTS

They say I am like You.
    at U C We arrived,
        a lost school of fish, together in a sea of confusion.
    our assignments We finished,
        pushing stone after stone up Sisyphus' hill.
I think I am not like You.
    the rosy complexion of life My eyes see,
        set far into my skull.
    the sundry of city scents My nose smells,
        jutting out on a tall and narrow bridge.
I am not like You.
    from separate corners We were born,
        sitting on stools with hands wrapped and mouths filled.
    to come to U C We worked,
        now hearing our ten-after bells ring and touching gloves.
I am not like You.
    I remove my gloves and reach out with warm, supple hands.
    Crunch, my knuckles crack against the transparent shield.
    Unexpectedly, I am dead.

—Gary S Brown

NORTH SOUTH NORTH TRAIN

Walking; the fantasy streets of York—birth place of
    Fawkes
Then in Caithness we try to celebrate a guy . . .
Fawkes failure with our single sparkling rocket.
It would not ignite—so damn it!
The man from Indore spoke brokenly the Gita
on the Southbound train, "Accept it."
I do—reluctantly passing through
a spiring beautiful bleak air piercing Edinburgh.
On towards Stirling stop; the idiot still stands,
stands . . . smiling . . . smeared . . .
a smudged conversation left on the moist pane.
A baby wails—it's so dark inside this train.
Little children whisper . . . ghosts; in my soul a chill.
Later near the Dorset coast I will
find a green seeded apple, some rest.
Outside scattered points of light faintly show the path . . .
a path set centuries ago—those circles no one knows.
It's late I'm tired, having to wait and go on with more . . .
more of the same; to look for fossils, to walk the Cobb
    shore.
Walking; hearing the raw echo; piercing gulls; Fowles;
    Plath . . .

—Jan Ashmore

THE STORM

A cloud covered sky,
  Dark and threatening,
Signals The Storm.
Rain drops march
Down from the sky
Like patterned warriors.
Each time The Lightning
Shines a path,
They know The Thunder
Soon will be there
Shouting orders.
Each row of warriors,
Lined up farther than the eye
Can see, uniformly fall.
Row after row march
To their death until
No more rows,
No more drops of rain.

—Kristina Lee

THE OTHER

The demon lives
  in my mind's eye.
My breath is his very being;
my desires
the rich red life
pumping through his veins.

He grows mightier
as my thoughts nourish his dark,
unsettling presence.
He calls me to do great work,
makes folly of a Diligence
that has withstood all of time.

The demon plays
but will never win.
His promise is only an echo
of my birthright;
his hovering shadow,
my salvation.

—Lisa M. Lawrence

To Love Is To Remember
         KEVE

Your life
  You lived
Is a keepsake.

A feeling,
You imparted
Is a keepsake.

Your memory,
My treasure
Is a keepsake.

Your love
For me,
Is a keepsake.

Victory, you claimed
In death
Is a keepsake.

KEVE, my son
Forever
My keepsake.

—Jayne Guest

MOTHER'S GRIEF

Lord why not me?
I ask in silent prayer?
Instead of such a youth as he,
Who hadn't lived his share.

—Dorothy Feind

STUCK

Just plain stuck
oh-the thought of—
    the sleepless nights,—
    the feedings,—
    the diapers,—
    the etc., etc., etc.,
Then you wrapped
your tiny hand
around my finger.
Now, I'm Stuck—
Just Plain Stuck on
    You!
and I love it!!

—Kathleen Woodrum

THOUGHTS IN FLIGHT

A thought on the wing
    takes on a form
Like an owl in flight
Holding both wisdom and
    ideas in motion
Propelled by the sender.
Even upon its arrival
It cannot be separated
    from its source
Who like a scepter becomes
    one with that thought
As long as it lives.
And so it is with all
    those thoughts I send
On the wing to you,
Backed by the power
    of love for you,
And all that you represent.
Like the owl and the sender
We are joined by our love.

—Richard C. Motter

LOVE

Love is a feeling that
    two people share.
Love is a special feeling
    that can bring two
    people together.
Love is when you stay
    together forever.
When two people love
each other they bring a
    baby into the world.
Love and caring about
    others make them
    feel a whole lot better.
Love is something you feel
    deep inside your heart, it
    never breaks unless someone
    breaks it.
Love will last forever and
    ever.
Love will never go away.

—Tina Thompson

ANGELS

Our Angels come in snowy white their daily rounds to make.
To weave for us a grand facade of which we can partake.
They carry us to lofty heights with soft words and a smile.
With soothing tones they lift us high,
With eyes they do beguile.
How happy we who dwell within, this place which we have come.
We glory in the thought that there is an Angel for everyone.
But all too soon we realize that behind this veil of white,
toils a being, mechanically, far into the night.
They change the beds, they clean us up, administer to each need.
Marking down each filthy chore as a truly loving deed.
With hearts yet full they come to know they can not serve each one.
The work goes on, day by day, a battle never won.
For one or two a change takes place and tempered by the strain,
with hardened hearts they live each day to serve in mental pain.
Most endure the incessant chore of caring for the mob.
Knowing help will never come, Love becomes a Job.

—Landis D. Eans

FORTY

It's not quite as bad as you will see
the years rolling by, I think you'll agree,
we somehow mellow and set with time
all beauty and handsomeness is not left behind.
We now are quite settled in a different way
than the day of youth and frivolousness wouldn't you say
so sit back, relax and enjoy your birthday.
Forty's not the end of the world so they say,
forty's the beginning of a new beautiful way.
Be happy and cherish all of the past
you are lurking into a world that's quite fast
now there's pot, L.S.D., and drugs we didn't have
aren't you glad that's behind you it's really quite sad.
So look at it this way and take that step forward,
hello new world, hello forty and looking toward the new horizon
beyond the bend, distinguishing, graying, and sometimes on the mend.
Taking a twrill saying goodbye to "thirty-nine."
Say hello to that's right "forty-time!"

**Written on February 8, 1976
for my husband Joe on his fortieth birthday.**

—Jan Dosch

OF MY MOTHER

The love we share is so enormously great.
We share our love through give and take.
No matter what, unto us, that may befall,
Our love grows through it all.

Through my years of growing up,
You've been there for me and have never let me drop.
You've taught me the best lessons
To be proud, responsible, and to thrive on independence.

I want to make you proud.
So you can exclaim out loud
"My son is the best he can be."
"For I have given him all of me."

And if this should bring tears to your eyes,
Remember we have devoted both our lives,
To the love of God, and his son's holy face.
We will live together, forever by his grace.

I love you mom,
For now and for evermore.
And I know our love will continue to soar
For both now and forever more.

—Steven Conrad

A DREAM BY NIGHT

I dreamt of you on a hot summer's night,
While all of God's stars shone bright.
A wilted laurel rests by my bed,
While visions of you dance through my head.
A lark sings,
As I jump to my feet.
A wondering eye, a shining star,
For you are traveling off afar.
I wish my love to come to thee . . .
Alas, I just sit here with my tea.
—**Carey Butler**

EVERY ROSE

Every rose has perfect petals blooming
in the Spring.
Every dove brings peace and love as
it spreads its wings.
But every rose has piercing thorns cutting
through the warmest hearts.
And every dove soon dies tearing
people apart.
The world is filled with love as it is
with hate.
Some come together with love, some
come together with fate.
I know it is true, love never dies
When it is in her heart and in
his eyes.

—**Carrie Frances Connors**

CUPID

Chubby little god who flies in the heavens,
Unicorns are his companions.
Power in his search for love,
Images of lovers please his heart,
Doves surround him when he rests.

Gold dust sprinkled by the fairies
Over the clouds to filter
Down to make us surrender to his arrows.

Old love potions will energize
Fantasies that fill our dreams.

Love comes in many forms.
Orchids are the flowers of love.
Valentines are shared with loved ones as
Every heart seems to fill with joy.

—**Dee Overpeck**

MY LOVE,

You seem as the wind, come and gone—
a light brighter than the sun—
warmth stronger than the summer's heat.
Your eyes, dark and beautiful, pull me close.
Your hair, turned golden by the sun's rays,
reflects thy beauty.
Your lips, with soft, smooth touch and
rosy tint, send my mind afar.
You are sweet and humorous—
always full of cheer.
In your presence, I want to jump,
shout—caress you, a vision
of exquisite beauty.
My love for you shall continue forever
through dawn and eve—desiring
your touch and tender passion.

—**Thomas James Seurynck**

THE MOUNTAINS

A place, where beauty is held high.
A place, where I held beauty, by my side.

A place, where love once rode, between
the peaks in the sky.

Stopping and looking, at great valleys, far below.

Thanking God, for feeling, love everywhere we
go.
Stopping in a city, setting snugly down below.

A place called Gatlinburg, where lovers go.

Where, my loved one, and I felt such a glorious
glow.
I will, never forget her, no matter where I go.

"The Mountains," we loved, will always be there,
for me to go.

For the lady, I love, I will go alone.

Never to feel that glorious glow.

"The Mountains," a place where love once
growed.

—**Larry G. House**

REMEMBER AND FORGET

Remember and Forget, upon their way,
Had chanced upon some children at their play;
"Remember how it was?" Remember sighed;
"I've quite forgot," Forget replied.

"When Time was young and Love was new:"
Remember's Spirit swelled and grew;
Forget looked up for signs of rain:
"Remember, there was also Pain."

Remember paled: "Yes, I recall—
The Pain of Love—but, wherewithal,
A purse so meagre and so slim
That has no secret lining sewn for him."

The pair walked on, Forget forgetting,
Remember musing and regretting
The Pain which he could not forget;
Forget could not such Love remember.

—**Wayne E. Fuhrmann**

LOVE IS CLEAR

I Can See Love in The Distant Sky
I Reach—I Grasp—I fail—I Cry.

The Tears in My Eyes, Reflections of Tries
For The Love I Desire, To fuel Love's fire

My Love you Have faded, friends you Have Aided
in The Loss of A Lifetime, Gone for All Time.

Hatred, Anger, Disgust, These Things All I feel
I Just Can't Believe They All Are So Real

And Then Comes A Light, Shining So Bright
A Chance I now See, To Bring you To Me

My Words Are now Spoken, Marked with A
Tear, And now We Can See, for our
Love is Clear.

I Can See Love in The Distant
Sky—I Reach—I Grasp—I Hold, I Smile.
—**Jeff Carter**

I WONDER . . .

Did you ever sit and think or cry . . .
How many good times we let go on by . . .
Without realizing soon they would end . . .
And forever you'd be . . . just a long lost friend.

—Linda S. Govendo

TRANSITION

Bubbling up from deep within my mind
          old memories surface once again
carrying me back to my childhood days,
          when life was simple in many ways.
Catching crayfish, on a hot summer day,
          under an old broken-down bridge.
Watching a doe and her fawn feeding
          on the tree studded ridge.
Chickens, ducks and barking dogs,
a sturdy house made out of cement and logs,
We giggled at the fireflys clinging
          to the side of a stained fruit jar
and we made secret wishes
          on every falling star.
Faded blue jeans and a golden t-shirt tan,
all these things . . . are a part . . .
of an age-old metamorphosis . . . from boyhood
          into Modern Man.

—Milo Von Strom

THE ALBAUGH RANCH HOME

Where the Lazy Pit River Winds and flows
And the green lush pasture, waves and grows

Where the white-face cattle roam
On that Modoc range near home

Mt. Shasta stands out big and bold
And the snowy streams run clear and cold

The stars at night are close and bright
And the harvest moon is a golden light

The crisp cold wind from the mountain cries
Through the yellow pines, it blows and sighs

Where the summer breeze flows softly through
And the friendly skies are a deeper blue

That's where I have longed to be
For that's home sweet home to me

—Reuben Albaugh

AUNT NIN

I thought of you today, Aunt Nin
Memories bold and bright
And it reminded me of days
With you, when I was just a tike

Of cherry cobbler crisp and light
Of many kisses, with eyes shut tight
Of apple peels in your lap
Of cookies in the jar . . .

I walked with you again, Aunt Nin
As we did years ago.
My hand is older now
And yours is older still

I feel you slipping from my grasp
But I hold tight, to memories bold and bright
Of years of love that flowed from you to me
And now flows out of sight

—Judy Bonnette McCullough

THE QUIET SEASON

Glasses of wine swirling in time,
Neighborhood gossip that doesn't unwind,
Unfriendly glares and hollow stares
Outline the boundaries of time.

Children hide, confused yet snide,
Inside the yards of their parents' minds.
Nails of care, rust and lie there
Beside fences that never can bind.

Please bring back the days
When we smiled as we waved,
And we cried when the neighbor's dog died.

—Gale DiMartino

THE WAGONS IN BLACK

They sat there, thinking of the past,
     Faded and worn,
From not being touched in forgotten decades.
     The wooden wheels so dusty,
Like an old book never touched.
     The harnesses, crackled from the sun,
Like meat smoked for ages on end.
     Old and tattered,
Like wrinkles on a face.
     They have been swallowed up,
By the years that passed.
     Their time is almost gone,
But they will not be forgotten.
     Will they?

—Dan Bergman, age 13

AFTERMATH

The flies are still there
With no tails to swish them away
The tracks remain
With no trucks to forge them anew

The odor of manure
Once a fresh smell of life living
Hangs stale and heavy on the air

The gates hang lifeless on their sagging hinges
With nothing left to pen

The For Sale sign hangs sprightly and alive
With new wood and fresh paint
The auction is over
The math is done

—Pat Freeman

THE OLD WOODEN BRIDGE

Paint, long faded from wooden tread
Hints of an era long since past
Where freckled faced bare footed boys
Cavorted with stringed bamboo poles
Hoping to lure the elusive fish
That shimmered in the stream below
The old Model T trod the creaking boards
Lovers sat sparking in its rumble seat
Little girls tripped merrily schoolward bound
Time, ever vigilant, has etched indelible scars
Eroding this once proud stately fording span
Now reduced to but a fading memory
Hinting of a proud heritage of the past
The old wooden bridge offers a trip to yesterday
For those brave ones willing to take the voyage

—Dr. Stanley S. Reyburn

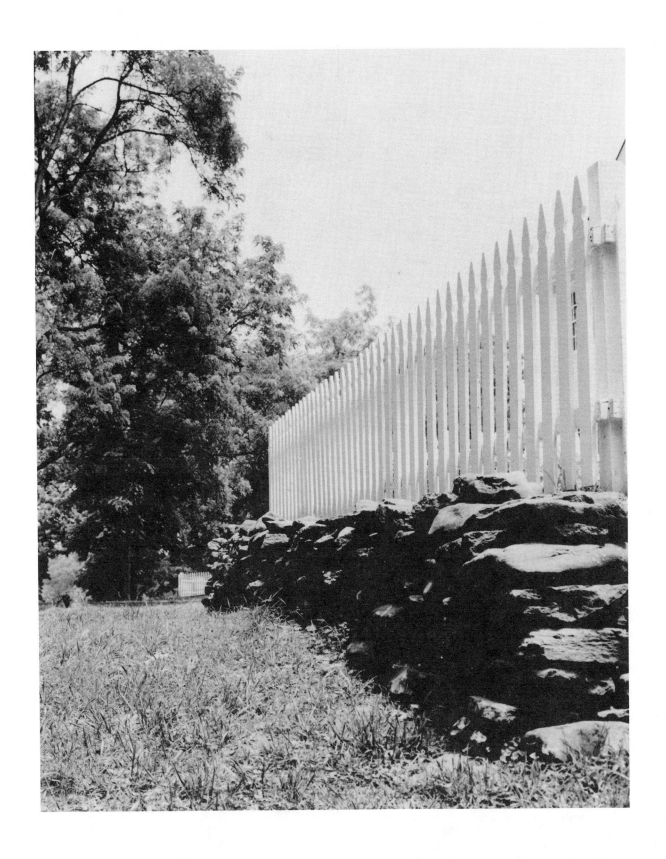

There is a God; He is alive.
If we live in Him, we will survive.

Be not afraid of what lies ahead.
God is your Aide; your daily bread.

Trust in Him; give Him your life.
He'll give you comfort in your toil and strife.

Love Him always . . . as He loves you;
That's all He wants us all to do.

—**Marcelle L. Walters**

GREAT MAN
Larger than life the picture stands
it shows a brother giving another a hand
Portraying hardship, suffering and pain
for his work wasn't done all in vain
He is a man many should know
but they glance and stare, just come and go
His life was hard I see it in his eyes
but there were many praises sung, bye and bye
God was his master this ambitious man
and now he's marble left to stand
You may think he has come and gone
but in me his memory lives on and on.

—**Kimberly M. Johnson**

LIFE'S MOUNTAINS
When we stumble and find ourselves falling,
When our mountains seem too high to climb,
When we wish we had wings to fly over,
When we long for, again, peace of mind . . .

God says to us, "Trust Me and listen.
Hand in hand we will face each new day.
I will strengthen you through all your struggles,
I will lovingly show you the way.

"I have plans for you—some day you'll see
How I weave your life daily with care,
How this mountain is there for a purpose . . .
Just lean on Me, knowing I'm there."

With God by our side we can face it,
Be it heartache, temptation, or pain.
And we know, in the end, we'll be stronger,
For He'll turn our great loss into gain.

—**Dianne Mischlich**

THE MEANING OF CHRISTMAS
It seems like nowadays everyone has forgotten
About when we were younger what our parents
                had taught us;
They taught us that giving was better than
                receiving
And that we should be happy because we
                were all living;
If only the people who are so downright
                greedy
Could just take the time to think of the
                lonely, sick, and needy;
Everyone should take just a minute for prayer
Maybe then loving God wouldn't be oh so rare;
God let us know so much about love
When he sent us, Jesus Christ from above;
So each day when I think about Our Dear Lord
To me loving him is my just reward;
        "This is"
        The Meaning of Christmas
—**Teresa Whalen**

THE MOUNTAINTOP
Joyfully we race across the meadow,
and leap from rock to rock.

The glittering sun fills our days,
for He sets our feet upon high places.

There to behold the beauty of His face,
and receive His many graces.

Mountaintops—where humanity meets divinity.
This poem is written to express that thought.

—**Alyce J. Smith**

In Memory Of Douglas Devon Bailey
February 26, 1952—March 3, 1981
What beautiful gifts God gave to Dad and me.
Three Boys—Three Girls for company
To love and to care for—to have and to hold
To raise and to tend too
        Gifts of pure Gold!
As the poem goes "they're just a loan"
"To love and cherish until called Home."
    You left us all with memories,
        to have and keep forever.
    We love you still and always will
until that someday we'll all be Home together.

—**Mrs. Alfred D. Bailey**

REDEEMED
The years sped by, the tears rolled down,
The sky and I still wept.
One day I prayed, "Thy will be done!"
And finally I slept.

The dawn was gray, the tears still fell,
But peace was in my soul.
Then, tears were gone, but loneliness
On me still took its toll.

One dawn, the sun; and raindrops ceased,
One by one, to fall;
In front of me, from God Himself—
A rainbeau, six feet tall!

—**Lochie Jo Allen**

HOW DO I KNOW THERE IS A GOD?
How do I know there is a God?
Why! I see him every day.
Is that a look of doubt I see?
You can't believe the words I say?

I wake in the morning in my husband's arms,
The gentlest man I know.
In his smile and love for me,
I see God from head to toe.

My children are a blessing to me,
A true gift from God above.
My grandchildren a blessing too,
An extension of his love.

The mountains, stars, deserts, trees,
The lakes, moon and sun so bright.
Are but a few of the wondrous things,
That places God within our sight.

If you will stop and look around,
Just take some time each day.
If you will open your eyes and heart,
You will see truth in the words I say.

—**Marlene Duran**

WARMTH

The leaves of summer
　　Have gone
　　　　Leaving trees and bushes
　　　　Bare and stark.
　　　　　　The days are cold and gray
　　　　　　But summer's in your heart.

When the pine-sweet fragrance
　　Of your sun-drenched soul is
　　　　Wafted on the air of a friendly
　　　　And sunny smile,
　　　　　　The cold days of winter
　　　　　　With their cares depart.

You may never know,
　　You cannot tell
　　　　How much cheer you give to weary souls
　　　　When you pass along to them
　　　　　　The God-given wealth of a
　　　　　　Summer-warmed joyful heart.

　　　　　—H. Barbara Tharp

SHOW ME THE LIGHT

Caught between torn feelings
A sky of blue emotions
A sea of blackened memories
A feeling being locked with no key
No truth in understanding why me
The reason being, the reason has no light
Endlessly crying blindly in the night
Something in the future, maybe a chance
Hoping for that something, even a glance
Time to act on mature responsibility
Time to rid of those built up feelings
Judging the present, forgetting the past
Wanting to relieve all morals, forgiving at last
A conflicting dilemma in my life
Oh, please Lord, help me decide
Good from the bad. Is this right?
I've lost control and stepped aside
Oh, please Lord, help me win this fight

　　　　—William G. Travis

HE KNOWS BEST

To abound in God's love
Can give you wings of a dove
He has an unconditional love
That comes from up above.

To admit to God's prerogative
Can take away the negative
He has a perfect right to do with me
As he plans, only he knows what is to be.

To appropriate God's provisions
Can give some great visions.
He has a home prepared for me
Where the cares of life will not be

To accept God's pardon
Can aid in accepting my own pardon
He paid the price in his own way
We all like sheep have gone astray

To surrender to God's will
Can aid in climbing the hill
He has a will for me so I can rest
Assured that all things work out for the best.

　　　　—Bonnie Stevens

ONE STEP CLOSER

It's not so much the mountain tops
As those lonely valleys we trod
That help us grow even beyond our dreams
And blossom in the eyes of God
Each step is one step closer
To the life that we desire
To do what God would have us do
The road that leads us higher

A heavy load we sometimes bear
The road seems rugged and long
But my friend there is a brighter day
So fill your heart and soul with a song
The sun will shine again as bright
As the days you laughed with glee
Look sweetly ahead with a smile
As that day unfolds and comes to be

　　—Beverley J. (Klarholm) Wolf

HIGH ON JESUS

I get a spiritual high whenever I think of him.
I get a spiritual high just praising his name.
Such a feeling that is never grim,
He sets my soul aflame.

I get a spiritual high whenever I sing
His love is never harmful.
I get a spiritual high just praising my king
Such a feeling that is so wonderful.

High on Jesus.
Day and Night,
He is one I trust
To make me feel all right.

High on Jesus
Everywhere I go
He treats me just
And to his words I can never say no.

I get a spiritual high just praising his name.
The wonderful name of Jesus
Such a feeling that I will never be the same,
High on the holy name of Jesus.

　　　　—Janice A. Edwards

NOTHING TOO HARD

There's nothing too hard for the Saviour.
　　There's nothing that He can't do.
But He is too wise to make a mistake
　　As He lovingly cares for you.

Sometimes He lets trouble assail us
　　So we can learn how to pray,
And show Him we love Him and trust Him
　　No matter what stands in the way.

So many things we just can't handle,
　　Some burdens seem too hard to bear;
But these we can lay at the Saviour's feet
　　And gratefully leave them there.

There's nothing too hard for the Saviour,
　　So why do we worry and fret?
If we take a moment to think of it—
　　He's never forsaken us yet!

We've nothing to fear for the future
　　As long as we follow our Lord,
And claim all the promises given
　　To us in His Holy Word.

　　　　—Vera B. Parker

321

BACKYARD HAPPINESS

Backyard Happiness
Flies in on wings
Flitters in the branches
Whispers to the leaves
"We love you"
"Protect our food"
"We love you"
"Morsels good"
"We love you"
They fly by
Backyard Happiness

—Jan Neville

PINE TREES

On the deep rolling mountains
Where the deer always go,
There's a little wee spot
Where the pine trees grow.

They don't grow too big
And they don't grow too small.
They just grow medium
And that's no lie at all!

They have a green bushy wig
And brown barky skin.
They smell like wintergreen
When they blow in the cool crisp wind.

—David Lee Brubaker, at age 9

SILENT FEAR

As lightning lit up the room
        and showed shadows of whipping trees
I lay, shaking, beneath my blankets
        with the thunder I would freeze.

I would pray, "Dear Lord, keep me safe
        please protect me from harm"
Still it seemed, to me,
        there would be no end to the storm.

Did the house move,
        is it falling down?!
I could not scream out,
        only lie there making not a sound.

I don't remember falling asleep
        only waking in the morning
To find both storm and fear gone
        just as they came; without warning.

—John G. Shady

WITHOUT FAITH

Fair, gentle butterfly;
        lying still as I stare.
We live and we die.
If we are lucky, we care.

There is no purpose to life;
no meaning, save pain.
We are held captive by our minds
in our own shackles and chains.

I say, my silent friend butterfly:
"Where have you gone?"
Has your soul died off with you,
or does it rage on.

May I call you "soil?"—my friend butterfly.
Because it is soil that you will soon be.
Carried away by the rain,
and washed to the sea.

—Raymond P. Glessner

AUTUMN

this is the season of the autobiography of visions . . .
                too beautiful
                        for —the naked eye of, Man!!!
as the orchestration of the forest and the florist fade
together,
they have composed a compelling aria . . .
we acclaim Her . . . the Empress . . . the Empire!!!!
with heaven's interpretation, we embark our heart.
into your journey . . . your splendor is our gift also.
we . . . shall maintain your place on earth,
waiting!!!
                excitement, shall reign once again,
as you return in your
spectacular
"spring wardrobe"
this is the moment of, my fond adieu to you.

—Patricia Mancini

BEFORE THE FALL OF DAY

The slow, rhythmic beating,
    The steady pulse,
Electrical nerve impulses
Giving rise to ozone
And the following thunderous applause
For the Lifebeat.

A million and more
Blades sing with exuberance
As their thirst is quenched,
As the blood drenches their parched souls;
They stand rigid like fingers
Stretching to grasp the source of their existence.

It betrays its promise,
It surpasses their bloated reach;
Before there is time to mourn,
Long, red shadows appear
And only the kiss of Iris remains
Before the fall of day.

—Stephanie Dreibelbis

NATURE

Nature Nature all around
from the sky to the ground

Nature is the stream trickling by
Nature is the big white clouds floating in the sky

Nature is the animals scampering around
Nature is the flowers growing in the ground

Nature is the valley down between the mountains
Nature makes the rivers run like fountains

Nature is the birds chirping in the tree
Nature is the bees going about freely

Nature is the leaves falling to the ground
Nature is the waves crashing with such a sound

Nature is the trees' mighty bark
Nature is the YELLOWSTONE NATIONAL PARK

Nature is the fox sly and free
Nature is the swan swimming gracefully

Nature is there to be enjoyed
So please take care, do not destroy!

—Denise M. Pagliarulo

SPRING KITE

Fly that kite high as you
please, into sky over the trees,
fill it with wind, color, with sun,
Let out the string and run, run,
run!

—Anne Glick

A TIME TO FLY

Under the gray skies of November's gloom
perched a dove upon an iron sundial,
whose shadow was not cast upon the face
of its cold metallic host.

And the bird sat with frozen feet grasping
the pointed edge of the timeless dial.
No feather or wing lifted that might carry
or protect it from the cold.

The dove merely sat watching the unchanging sky,
and finding no patch of blue
through which it could fly
chose to sit, and wait for a time to fly.

—Christopher B. Kypta

THE DANCE

It's late,
Midnight I think,
And the snow;
Has just started its dance.
Everyone is inside but me.
I am the audience.
Wind is her partner.
Together they merge,
And begin their moonlight dance.
They start off slowly,
Skipping down the street.
They stop every so often,
On nearby windshields and cracks in the street.
Gradually, they build momentum.
Climbing into the air.
Snow likes to climb the light poles,
So she can dance with the light.
Wind is tired.
He can't dance anymore tonight.
They both rest until it's time to perform again.

—Judy J. Miller

WILD AND FREE

The sun shines bright, as the eagle soars
Down below are a herd of boars.
The snow has fallen on cold winter ground
The echo of their hoofs can be heard all around,
As they run, wild and free.
With their spirits on fire,
Their mane drenched with sweat,
They gently play,
Keeping far from the net.
You can see them in the fields,
Both the young and the old.
They're safe there, for they won't be sold.
As they run, wild and free.
Dusk draws near as the coyote howls,
Watching their young devour a fowl.
The stream flows briskly as they drink
Dawn will rise again quick as a wink.
As they run, wild and free.

—Judith Ann Vela

SEASON'S LOVE

As I look upon the daytime sun,
I know that spring has just begun.
The flowers, the river, all step in time
to the rhythm of the old willow
that's been withered by this rhyme.

As I look upon the summernight sky,
the stars, the moon, they all pass by.
I hear them whisper, and call my name,
and I know that I'll be back here again.

As the leaves fall down in the autumn breeze,
the cries of the wind, they do not cease.
The old willow stands in the same old place,
with the same sad look of a weathered face.

As the snow drifts down,
I hear a soft swift song
of a snowflake,
a lonely snowflake,
alone and gone.

—Jaclyn Hayes

FOR EVERYTHING THERE IS A SEASON
SEASONS OF THE SOUL
As the Seasons of Nature
keep perfect time—
never too early nor late.

SPRINGTIME AND BLOSSOMS
harvest and fruit,
Summer for growing and—
Winter demands a rest.

OUR FINITE MINDS WONDER—
at the harshness of Winter.

WITH GREAT LONGING
our infinite souls look forward
to Spring!

(Ecc 3:1)

**This, God gave to me in comfort and
healing shortly after my younger brother
was tragically killed.**

—N. Jean Leas

TOKENS OF LOVE

I get so low when the North Winds blow
o'er the gray plains of Nebraska.

Every year I proclaim, "It will not be the same."
But, hard as I pray and try as I may,
it's always the same. My heart feels the pain
on the gray plains of Nebraska.

But, God up above always shows me His love
on the gray plains of Nebraska.
As the winters drag on He gives me a song
on the gray plains of Nebraska.

When I pray to my Lord He hears every word.
He says, "I have heard," in the trill of a bird.
He sends up a flower to attest to His power.
He wraps me in love with rays from above
on the gray plains of Nebraska.

The winters are cold and my body feels old
on the gray plains of Nebraska.
But, I thank God above for His tokens of love
on the gray plains of Nebraska.

—Caralee Meston Harkins

323

THE WATERFALL

A waterfall is only,
However majestic its flow,
One drop after another
Tumbling to levels below.

—Kathy Pelton

WAVES

Rolling hard
Crashing the rock
Birds flying over the waves
Man swimming in the roaring ocean
like a lion.

—Kong Ly

PAPER, PENCIL AND LIGHT

Shelly, Scott and Browning too
They were all poets
They knew what to do
They got their paper, pencil and light
And sometimes they sat there
And wrote all night
That gives us something to do
When our lives don't go right
We can sit here and read
What they wrote that night
Thank God for poets
All poets alike
God bless their paper, pencil and light.

—Rena R. Hester

Poetry is a funny thing.
It's a chance for my heart to sing.
It's a maple tree in spring.
It's the eaglet as it first takes wing.

Poetry is a way to speak
Even for a soul too meek.
It's a traveler's long road seek,
The abandoned house with a shutter's creak.

Poetry is my mind's rest
When tension is an unwelcome guest.
It turns my thoughts to the far wave's crest
Until once again I'm at my best.

—Becky L. Whited

Written Friday 05 August 1983

THE LEAF AND THE WRITER

A writer
a thought
for mankind
does pen
A leaf
to pluck
in its moment
GOLDEN
As a writer, a leaf
from green to yellow
to red to golden
to save before brown
and olden.
To seize the golden thought
to save, with symboled paper
the leaf
and the thought
forever.

—Ralph J. Ryan, III

BUTTERFLIES

Sometimes I sit and wonder why God
created the butterfly, but then after
watching it go from place to place so
peacefully, I know that they were
created for their beauty.

Butterflies are wonderful. They fly
around as free as can be and
somehow just watching them brings
a peaceful feeling over me. Because
if God could care so much about
creating beautiful butterflies, just
think how much more he cares about
you and I.

—Becky Patterson

LIGHTHOUSE

My lighthouse proudly stands
Against winds, high seas and sands.
I guide the weary seafarer to port
Through challenges of all sorts.

I was built in 1839.
And, I withstand the test of time.
In 1989, I became automated.
The keeper's dwelling was removed.

I feel sadness for my fate.
My keeper was my mate.
Lonely, I shall stand.
Protecting ships and man.

—Norma Carter

THE GREATEST RACE

You take off from the starting line,
In the greatest race of all,
Your coach has told you everything,
But did you hear his call?

If you keep your chin up,
And never look behind,
The opponent has no chance,
He'll never taint your mind.

You're running from the devil,
Avoiding any sin,
Just listen to your coach,
And you can only win.

—Victoria Lynn Machtig

A PLEA FROM THE HEART

I long for the sweet restraints
    Of meter, and rhythm, and rhyme—
But am cursed, for my sins, with . ." free verse . ."
    Born—oh God — out of my time.

O for a well-rounded sonnet!
    O Shakespeare! O Wordsworth! O Blake!
O blessed iambic pentameter!
    Return once again, for my sake.

My soul, my brain, and my senses
    Are simply unmoved by the lot
Of ". . . Twentieth Century Poets . . ."
    Void of beauty, of feeling, of thought—

O voices long stilled—where are you?
    A new century beckons—dare I hope?
Incipient bards, have pity and write
    More like Byron, and Shelley, and—Pope.

—Shelley Ellmann

THE LADY WITH A POEM ON HER MIND

The fingers of her heart
Search the attic in her mind
Through boxes of words,
New combinations to find.

Adjectives to describe
The ingredients of snow,
Adverbs to soothe
A grief-stricken soul.

Through trunks of tears and years
And threadbare poetry
The dust of time-worn dreams
And treasured memory.

Until the knowing shows.
Behind her blue, brown eyes,
She's always the lady
With a poem on her mind.

—Bonnie Colby

NEW FRIENDS

Many verses have been written
   of friendships tried and true,
but very few make comment
   on a friendship that is new.
Perhaps those poet-authors
   have long forgot the day
when old friends first spoke greeting
   in a very special way.
In an instant came a liking
   from which the friendship grew;
never again more exciting
   than when it was first new.
Together you discover
   joint philosophies;
together you explore
   life's vast mysteries.
You learn and grow together
   to friendship tried and true,
but, forget? Oh no, not ever
   the joy when it was new.

—Judith A. Wolf

THE BIRTH OF A POEM

As I sit here thinking
Of all I hear and see,
I thank the Lord above
For what He's given me.

As I gaze out through my window
At the gentle falling rain,
It's like Mother Nature's tear drops
Sliding down my window pane.

Then with the dawn the sun comes out
To brighten the new day,
And like a warm and gentle hand
It dries the tears away.

His works are all around us
Everywhere we look,
So many things to think about
Enough to write a book.

My mind is always filled with thoughts
Of things to write about,
So thus, there's always one more poem
Just waiting to come flowing out!

—Roma Menke

THE POET

The man who writes his lines of wit, of glamour, distress,
   tragedy and love.
A man seldom understood.
A man with a mind totally his own and answers to nothing
but his own Creative Soul.
Yes the noble bard, the writer of beautiful verse, with lines
that seem to come alive.
That elevate the soul, feeds the mind and increases the
senses.
The man whose words live on long after he dies.
This noble man they call the Poet.

—Albert Bruckelmeyer II

A POET'S LAST WORDS

White paper be my kingdom,
   my realm. A dictionary serves as my
   advisor. Pens stand guard, they are my
   soldiers and ink glides through my
   veins like blood . . .

I, creator of glorious words and quaint
   phrases, am willing to do battle with
   nouns, verbs, adjectives, and the like.
   I bend words to my will. I become
   master over them . . .

I scribble these words on bits and pieces
   of paper, and pray that one day
   the words and phrases I have created
   will endure centuries of readers, although
   I realize that I am no match for Shakespeare.

—Jacqueline Smith

MY POEM TO YOU

I wanted to write You a Poem that comes straight from My
Heart.
I feel Your Love for Me even when We're apart.
My Love for You "Buttercup" is warm and sincere even when
You're not near.
It's been Twenty Years since We've said Our I Do's, but, My
Love for You is still like new.
December 28, 1969, We were so young but our Love was so
Devine;
I looked in Your eyes and You in mine, there was a Special
Twinkle and I knew You were all mine.
Now, I'm as happy as I can be, Because I know You truly
Love Me!
We've had bad times and sad times that made our Love for
each other grow even Dearer.
We've had good times and fun times,
But, the best times are the times when We're Together.
Honey, I just wanted to take a minute to tell You how much
I do care.
My Love for You is Forever and Always and I know You will
always be there.
So, From My Heart to Your Heart a Special Love Entwines.
I'm in Love with You and I'M glad You're mine.
I see many more years of Wedded Bliss.
Our Love for each other will always carry us through to the
Golden Years with lots of Memories We'll hold so Dear;
This is the end of My Poem To You.
Hope You've enjoyed it like I have You.
I LOVE YOU!

LOVE FOREVER & ALWAYS,
YOUR BABYCAKES

—Theresa McEntire

SHOES

As I walk down the boardwalk,
my bare feet calloused and brown,
I notice the summer people,
the mass of endless clones.
They're here only for vacation
equipped with their umbrellas and sunblock,
Flip Flops and sneakers covering their feet.
It seems so strange to me
wearing shoes on the beach
And I don't see the point of it;
they only fill with sand.
I just laugh to myself
as if it were some inside joke.
The city people seem so peculiar,
afraid to put away their briefcases.
You don't need shoes on the beach
as a matter of fact,
I don't have a pair.

—Elizabeth Cornell

GOIN' FISHIN'

The morn has come, the sky is gray,
But I don't care, this is my day.
Cause—I'm goin fishin!

The boat is ready, the poles are set,
I've even got my biggest net.
Cause—I'm goin fishin!

The boats in motion, just movin' slow,
The down-riggers holdin the lines down low.
Cause—Now I'm fishin!

The pole just bobbed, I hope it's a fish,
Likely as not it's just a good wish.
Cause—That's fishin.

Now the day is done and I'm headin for shore,
Got a bad snag and lost my best lure.
But—That's fishin.

Another day it's sure to come,
No fish today but it's been fun.
Cause—That's Fishin!

—Leonard P. Long

LET ME GO — GERMS

You pesky, little pests,
You obnoxious pain producers,
You enter without knocking,
You're a trillion, billion Lucifers.

You're savage. You destroy.
You are prolific parasites.
You're a cruel hoard of vipers.
You've unsatiable appetites.

You take for your abode,
You invaders, my head and throat.
You've got to be evicted.
I'll not serve as your table d'hôte.

You ruthless savages,
You squanderers, you think it's free—
Your living will soon get tough
When there begins to be less of me.

You're warm now, well supplied.
You will not always find it so,
Before it's too late for us both,
Please —Let me go, let me go, let me go!

—Mary E. Higgins

A SPENSERIAN STANZA

To study poetry of history
We can't ignore Spenser who was so great.
After four hundred years we can still see
Why we must, of him, recapitulate.
Then why is it that modern students hate
To get assignments from that time between
Poets Chaucer and Shakespeare also great?
Because they will not let themselves be seen
With a book with a title like The Faerie Queene.

—Gene M. Royer

THE PIANO

The piano is a beautiful instrument,
Not only for pupils with a musical intent.
For her with bursitis, and bed ridden,
The musical talent of the player was hidden.
"Sweet Hour of Prayer" was a radio theme,
His rendition made her want to scream.
His musical knowledge
Sure never went to college.
With bursitis, and his help,
She couldn't squawk or yelp.
"Oh! Lord My God, How Great Thou Art"
When he and the piano had to part.

—Guy Jackman

FREE SPIRIT

You'd think an ordinary helium-filled balloon
had no alternative purpose in life
save perch haughtily atop a flower arrangement
emblazoned with glittering greetings of "Get Well,"
"Happy Birthday," or perhaps "Happy Mother's Day;"
yet for three weeks after Mother's Day
my silvery, free spirited friend
clung stubbornly to my kitchen ceiling
until one afternoon it decided to explore,
search, and float freely and gleefully
to each and every room in my house—
that is with the exception of the bathroom.
Perhaps that's the room it was searching for.
After all, what more appropriate place
could a silvery, free spirited balloon find
to expel its last ounce of gas before
falling helplessly to the floor?

—Pauline W. Elswick

WHO'S TURN

They are all stacked in a pile so big;
The only way to get to them is to dig.
On the cup lays the plate;
And the bowl used to grate.
On the plate, is something my mom likes to make;
From this and that and some steak.
In the sink is an old milk container;
Sitting next to the water drainer.
Next to it is an old soup tin can;
What a mess! man-o-man.
On the spoon was some soup;
And a little piece of a fruit loop.
Another thing I saw was a fork;
Stuck in a prong was some pork.
Stuck to a knife was some meat;
It didn't really look that neat.
I wish and hope with all my wishes,
That it isn't my turn to do the dishes.

—Jason Hackler, age 11

INCOME TAX TIME

Income Tax comes once a year,
But oh, how we hate for the time to be here.
It's not that we don't want to part with what we don't have,
It's not being there when you need it is what's so sad.

We may only owe just a little bit,
Or we may get to wait to see what we git.
Someone who knows how it's all done,
May fill out the form and say "Now look here son!"

You didn't do this, you didn't do that,
Unless you do it right you won't git nothin' back.
You'll owe Uncle Sam a heap bit more,
If you don't know how to even up the score.

Cheat you he won't but just wants what's due,
You've got to pull it right out of the blue.
If you can't git it just real fast,
Now, son, don't you ever give him no sass.

With the right kind of help you'll be O.K.,
No need waitin' for another day.
Do right by Uncle Sam and he'll do right by you,
Otherwise, he just might have to sue.

—Roberta Lee

CLOSING THE WEIGHT BOOKS FOR 1989

This closes the weight books for the end of 1989,
and this group of six, has all enjoyed the time.
We put on weight, we take off weight, and sometimes—
we stay the same, putting weight on and taking weight off,
is not supposed to be a game.
On TUESDAY mornings, we gather here—to have our
regular meetings, we are up and down on the scales each week,
but we still have our weekly greetings;
"Good Morning" here, "Good Morning" there, Our group
is quite a bunch, and so after most every meeting—we put on
weight with lunch.
Sometimes things have made us sad, but I know we
will always be glad, for the years together that we have
already had.
We talk and laugh and give our—THANKS to the
LORD O' MIGHTY,
I hope that we can all enjoy—THE NEW YEAR 1990.

—Hazel Firster

"THE ROCK"
OF
ATASCADERO

A bunch of the boys were laughing it up in Players TV
room.
"Did ya hear he was dead?" someone said, and down came a
curtain of gloom.
"Who's dead?" asked Jack, as he finished his beer.
"Heart Attack Hank? His time was real near."
"No, Muscles Malone, also known as 'The Rock'!
The health nut who'd never, never even been crocked!"
"The guy who took vitamins six times a day?"
"He was pushing 50 without any gray!"
"By himself he lifted a hog to the truck!"
"He'd work in his shorts in the rain and the muck."
"He ran ten miles every day of the week."
"For leisure he'd climb the most dangerous peak."
"He had a bad temper — it's been said many times
That would do him in — not one of his climbs!"
"Still, he fell off a ladder?" asked farmer O'Toole.
"It's even much sadder, he was kicked by a mule!"
"Jake, why are you smilin' — that couldn't be worse!"
"His neighbor reports that he kicked the mule first!"

—Ross Morgan

THE RATter

The little pitter patter
Of teeny tiny feet
To the chitter chatter
And screaming li'l squeek
My heart's a titter tatter
And fear, my knees so weak
The sounds of the RATter
Scare even as I speak.

—Victor Sowell

SASHAY

I'm waiting for the Spring, she said,
To shed this Winter gloom.
But, with the dawn of Spring, she
Hoped for Summer's bloom.
And, when the days of Summer,
Began to idly pass,
It seemed that Autumn leaves
Were kinder than the grass.
As Winter nodded knowingly,
And donned a graying sky,
She folded arms akimbo
And pled that time would fly!

—Helen M. Mikel

EASTER BUNNY

I saw an Easter bunny,
Hopping down the road.
It looked like he was carrying,
A very heavy load.

Your names were on the eggs I saw
So colorful and bright.
I'll bet that little bunny,
Has a very busy night.

So don't you see my children?
He is bringing eggs for you.
I saw your names, Jack and Mary,
And your little sister Sue.

So set your little baskets out,
Tuck away all snug and warm.
And see what big surprises,
You have on Easter morn.

—Ardith I. Holbert

FANTASY

To dream of unicorns
And dragons flying in the wind
To believe in the magic
of Merlin and Camelot
And castles in the sky

There are times I can almost
touch them
If I dare to dream
Because I believe in all that
is magical
I have been called a fool

If believing in unicorns is foolish
If believing in Knights of the
Round Table is impossible
Then I'd rather be a fool
Than live in a world without
unicorns

—Belen

ONE LAST QUESTION

My life is filled with music,
Tho the words don't always rhyme.
I look around and I see things,
I love the things in my life.
It's hard to see why people hate;
After all, we're made from love.
The love that God has given—
From His home so high above.
So why can't the world be happy?
For on His shore we'll someday meet;
What will you do when you get there,
Will you love or will you still hate?

—Jackie Face

JESUS

You could love someone like me
Who has made so many mistakes.
Live every day for You,
Die each day for Your sake.

Here's my hand
Help me up, to stand tall.
Use my life to help another
'cause my name, You have called.

So here's my life
Use me, to glorify Your name.
In everything I do
Give glory to Your name.

—Letha I. Graham

DEAR GOD

I prayed this weekend,
with open eyes,
because I knew you were there.

I prayed to you,
and waited for an answer,
because I knew you were there.

I prayed to you,
in faith, oh Lord,
because I knew you were there.

Why don't I always
pray like this,
since I know you are always there?

—James T. Parker

HIM

See the signs of wars
Gaze at the skies, see the stars
Call on Him, that creates
Pray for peace and keep the faith

Hunger and famine on the land
Believe in Him, the son of man
From above, his glory glows
As blessings, on the land flows

Feeling, the pain and suffering
Praise Him, rejoice and sing
With Him, all things are possible
His love for all, so comfortable

And in Him, there is hope
A plan in life, a way to cope
So, praise his name in fellowship
In his house of worship

—Joseph S. Boteilho

THE SON OF MAN

The Son of man was crucified,
Then Israel looked up and cried;
He loved them that much so they sighed;
Then He stretched out His arms and died.

"Father, into Your hands I commend My spirit."
Was uttered before but they did not hear it;
The curtain of the temple was torn in two;
When Jesus gave His life for me and you.
Mark 15: 38
"And the curtain of the temple was
torn in two from top to bottom."

—Barbara Lucia Farinella-Fritsch

A MOTHER'S PRAYER

A mother's prayer is for peace,
That her child may live without hurt.

A mother's prayer is for patience,
That she may not become angry without cause.

A mother's prayer is for guidance,
That she may lead her child right.

A mother's prayer is for stamina,
That she may survive the long years ahead.

A mother's prayer is above all,
A prayer for her young one,
That he may follow the righteous path.

—Marvella R. Nicodemus

BUILDERS

Jesus is the carpenter that builds
The apostles are the varnish that veneers

The finish is the sun casting its rays on the earth that shields

The hammers are the judges who judge the hearts by their eye that peers

The nails are the angel that guilds

The squares are prophets who foretell
the future

The rulers are the Davidic throne that rules by measurement of the suture

The bits are the layman who preach

The supports are the missionaries who care for the sick

The derricks are the elders that reach

The drills are the war chiefs who light the wick

The brick layers are the saints that protect from the storms

The columns are the foundation supports of the church which holds it together

The windows are the seers who enable us to see through the gospel clearly

The foundation or cornerstone is Jesus Christ whose eyes are blearly

The keystone or capstone is the harbinger.

The roof keeps the word warm in the winter and cool in the summer

The electrician is the lightbearer

The plumber unclogs the controversies in the church

—John H. Gum, Jr

the blackness seeps out now that you've gone
my heart is so heavy, the nights are so long
once sweet lullabies now funeral songs
memories of you laments in my head
mourning and grief now my only friends
then there you are up ahead at the bend
a soft kiss from you and the agony ends

—**Matthew Sailor**

THE LORD'S WILL

So precious is the gift of life.
Some may do away with a child and have it mechanically
removed.
Others lose it naturally.

To lose a child—
Is it the testing of our Faith?
Or, is it the Lord's way of protecting us from life's
other devastating news of our unborn child?

Through the tears, we know and feel only the sense of
loss and emptiness that is inside.
A child whom we've grown to love, will never be met by
our open arms.

Although, through the many tears and prayers of thankfulness
of having one child, we've grown to accept The Lord's Will.

—**Cheryl L. Ferrell**

THE OTHER SIDE

The other side of what you say, well let me tell the tale,
I'm talking of that very last day when your body parts
will fail.
No matter if you're rich or poor, the ride that you will take,
The ride that you must take alone; the ride that you'll
forsake.
The lighted tunnel, that I hear, is waiting for your soul,
The hollow shaft which you will go; your spirit will have no
control.
A light at the end, from what I hear, is blinding to the
sight,
A place where no cares will bother you, and there's no such
thing as night.
From what I hear you'll meet your friends, your parents and
your foe,
No matter how you put it off, on that faithful ride you'll go.
I really wonder if Saint Peter is waiting at the gate,
Your sole will anxiously race to wrestle with your destined
fate.
The ride is free, no tokens here; it's peaceful and it's calm,
Who knows for sure what waits for you, maybe a story or a
psalm.
For who knows what they will say when they write your
final story,
They'll say it's heaven or maybe hell; you may find out earth
was purgatory.
The earthly bounds we know of now; they may be good or
bad,
Your spirit will be free and calm; even though your family's
sad.
So don't just wait for that faithful day; for I know it will
arrive,
Just do the best your whole life through, and your spirit will
Survive.

**A poem to my departed mother by—Herb Dingfeld
I love you mom!**
—**Herbert A. Dingfeld**

THE SONG OF BATTLE

As they stood behind the bushes,
Chills ran down their spines.
Waiting for the trumpet,
That would form the battle line.
As the mocking bird began to sing,
Shots began to ring.
And in the still morning light,
The enemies began to fight.
If one listens, he will hear,
The sounds of fear.

—**Gregory Butcher**

FEARS

There's the fear of strange places
The fear of strange faces

The fear of cats
The fear of rats

The fear of heights
The fear of depths

But none so great as the fear
of Death.

—**Angelic M Hollander**

DESCENDING INTO A BRICK WALL

I look at God's creation,
I just stand . . . and I stare,
Hoping to drown my thoughts,
Bypass . . . despair!

I drink in the beauty,
I thirst for it . . . each day,

Even as the pain lingers on,
And darkness leads the way!

There is no future,
But why do I care . . . today?
Where . . . am I going
And which road is the way?

I struggle with my thoughts,
I . . . vision my fall,

I find myself descending,
Into . . . a brick wall!

—**Sandy Vossler**

SIERRA

Little clothes lie still on the bed
Where once her head was warm
The agony of loving without her
burns hot upon our faces
The smell of her person
Still lives in our souls
And every precious memory
Laughs with the angels of Heaven
The taste of kissing her face
Warms my blood intensely
And we wait with anticipation
The next sweet sensation
That will remind us of her
Our love now flows out into eternity
Rejoicing with our SIERRA
As the sound of Heaven rings
We hurt a little more
Just to hold her once again

—**David Stainback**

I LOOK UPON THE NIGHT SKY

I look upon the night sky
Wondering what might have become
For if my dream would be answered
Then I wouldn't have to wonder

I look upon the night sky
Wondering what I did wrong
For if I would have been more knowledgeable
Then I wouldn't have to wonder

I look upon the night sky
Wondering if it could be again
For maybe the time was just wrong
Then I wouldn't have to wonder

I look upon the night sky
With a star gleaming upon my tear filled face
For it speaks and says wonder no longer
For your dream has just become

—Michelle Haskins

EVERYTHING YOU WERE MEANT TO BE

Life will not always be what
you want it to, some even say that it's
cruel to you.

Your life is only as good you see,
as you are willing to make it be.

Count your blessings and you can
do, all the things you've wanted to.

You only get dealt life once around,
so don't waste your life in feeling down.

Fulfill your dreams while you are young,
for it is too late when your years are done.

Look deep inside and you will see,
that you're just as beautiful as you dreamed
you'd be.
Don't let life put you on the run,
just do what you have to and get it done.

Then pretty soon you will clearly see,
that you're everything you were meant to be.

—Jay W. Evans

REFLECTION

When you look in the mirror
Do you like who you see?
Is that person good and kind
The way you want to be?

Is there anything at all
You would like to change?
Or, anything within that life
That you should rearrange?

You are the best friend
That person will ever have.
You can mold and shape that life
Into a friend others would like to have.

As best friend it is your duty
To help that person each day
To grow tall and strong
And walk in the right way.

When you look in the mirror
Do you like who you see?
Are you helping that person become
Everything that you should be?

—Olivia Jean Helton Underwood

Climbing up a mountain
I feel the wind rushing by
Trying to keep me from reaching the top.
But I persevere and pull myself up
Grabbing at branches and rocks along the way.
Sweaty and brown I reach the top
And I take a deep breath in.
But I choke because of the thin air
And I trip over a rock
And I plummet to the ground
Like a pebble you kick off a hill.
And when I hit bottom
I wonder "Why?"

—Maura M. Madden

YOU ALONE

Lofty breezes brush through your hair
As in all the glory there about,
Looking into our lives so fair
Knowing what it's all about.

To this extent we are exposed
In all phrases too numerous to name
But know yourself well
And apologize not, for the person you retain.

The inner soul that's only you
And no one can compare
To you, yourself alone
The ingredients you inhere.

A tiny fragment, so hard to see
Passing along with the tide
Going almost unnoticed free
Our existence we abide.

Until the day when you will depart
To the earth where you are lain
For you will have left a legacy
For some to remember, more than just your name.

—Nancy Roeser

FREEDOM

I'm alive—
Neither dependent nor independent

I have a place to go
A place—though it's not my own

I'm covered . . .
No real cares. No real worries.

I can be—I can do—
ANYTHING

It is all out there
in the beginning of life as I will soon know it.

I see the flower garden . . .
I know not how
some would grow if picked and planted,
but—it's MY pick.

What I want is what I do.

It's up to me . . .

Now I realize,
THIS is FREEDOM . . .
The time is NOW
to LIVE . . . .

—Jolene Lovett

SELF-CONSCIOUS

Ripple in Time.
Epicenter Here.
Consciousness.
Consciousness of Time.
One shot.
Famished and Lost Child,
In a world of opportunities,
A nightmare of decisions,
History is made Here.
Moon-case.
Alien Landing Here.
Reality.
Shooting through the Cosmic Plazma of Life,
Steer the ship well Navigator.
True on a divine Course,
   on the path with Heart.

     —Ari B. Swartz

grey stains

Eyes that love; eyes that cry;
   the fragile heart; the mind can see;
the constant hoax; the love and lie;
   the cruel world in front of me.

Restless nature; tiresome turmoil;
   dark sunglasses; clouded sight;
nothing clean; all dirt and soil;
   grey stains on fictitious white.

Despair; the tear-stained pillow;
   alone and longing; an infant's view;
the questions; the answers never to know;
   the circles; the tightening of the screw.

Ceaseless circles of reason; a hopeless heart;
   society's exile; the mind's own slave;
a cripple pulling the horse and cart;
   the passing tear; blind beckoning grave.

Elusive illusion; hope's faint glimmer;
   tomorrow the sorrow; the day at an end;
vitality and vision; each hour yet dimmer;
   lacking the solace of one true friend.

     —Kent R. Jackson

LABOR FOR THE WIND

The story of life is an uncertain one,
   Evil hand-in-hand with good will often go,
We labor for things that have no worth
And in the end, no effort of our labors show.

We labor in vain for silver and gold,
And a house of mighty stone
And furniture and clothes and lots of furs,
But when we die, we go alone.

Let not the results of our labor on earth
Disappear like the wafting wind
But set our eyes on a spiritual goal,
Unlimited will be our riches then.

For earthly things tend to decay,
And cannot forever last,
Teach me to dwell in a future life,
And not to wail for that which is past.

Teach me to walk in the light of faith,
And to walk firmly on higher ground,
Teach me not to labor for the wind,
Then the riches of a true faith will be found.

     —Gracie Wittkohl

THE QUEEN

Why can't they understand
A teen-ager has feelings too?
Why the constant command
To stand straight and comb your hair?
Just the same old story—never anything new!
I don't think my room is messy
Everything is within reach.
I know just where to locate that blouse
And those shorts I wore last week to the beach.
All the rest of the kids are out until two
I'm the first to have to come home.
You should see the raised brows
When I have to leave alone!
Don't they realize I'm grown up now?
After all I am sixteen.
How old do you have to be
Before you're treated like a queen?

     —Betty L. Logsdon

WHAT IS A MAN?

What is a man? Who can say?
Burdened with sorrow, alone every day
Aware of what was and can never be
Wiser in mistrust and no longer free.

What is a man? A fleck of time on its way
A life of brief chance from day to day
Should he look back at paths not taken,
Tattered dreams destroyed and forever forsaken?

No! A man should not look back and enjoy
   his life to unfold
He should enjoy those he loves and carry
   his load
Be aware of his lack, his turn of the dice
Never jealous of those who chance gave a
   bigger slice.

But my friend it is easy to say, but hard to
   achieve
For man is mortal and slow to believe
Go on with your life and go on with your way
Aware that yesterday's dream unfurls to
   tomorrow's day.

     —Stanley Hymowech

HENRY SMILES

Henry lives across the street;
   no one knows how many years.
And Henry smiles.

His hair is almost gone,
   except for wisping cobwebs in his ears
 and a few forgotten strands
   fluttering, like banners after a parade.

Arms, blotched and blue veined,
   erupting into arthritic hands
 molded forever into the shapes of labor;
   folded over the head of an old cane.

Henry's fragile frame is bent,
   held on spindle legs and slippered feet.

His dimming eyes hold memories
   locked behind thick bifocals,

While dropped cigar ashes leave brown wounds
    upon his shirt.

And Henry smiles.

     —Jacki Freiberg

PRAIRIE SNOW

Snow makes majesty of weeds.
Thistle stalks and buffalo grass
      march, ermine-trimmed,
Across the prairie.
A royal procession.

      —Donna Johnson

SHEFFIELD 1991

The flash turned into darkness
   I was blind to the mushrooms
that sprouted in an endless chain
to turn the decay into dirt

The dust flew up so thick
my breath was lost in it
I thought about the shelves
I hadn't cleaned since September

And there was no water
And my house was no more
So when it started raining
My skin was my only shelter

And so I awoke
and fell asleep.

      —John L. Denslow

WINDS OF IDAHO

The desert wind unfurls its fury
    At the mid-day hour
It blows hot and wild
    With untamed power
I watch as it sweeps clean
    Earth's sandy face
Tossing carefree tumbleweeds
    Then giving chase

Little twisters spin
    And twirl with glee
Baring lava rock
    Black as ebony
Daydreams, gay
    As fantasies
Steal silently away
    On the desert breeze

      —Geneva Ervine Sherlock

YOU SEVEN

On the wings of gulls
    And the albatross
    Your spirits ride.
They flank the rocky shoreline,
    Blanket the rising tide.
You chanced to give and gave
    Your most prized
Possession, and for this
The moons of distant skies
    Are named for you.
For us you left your home
    Pioneering a way into
The strange and the unknown.
    And for this
We will think of you
    Each time we view
    The heavens,
    Or gaze into
The warm glow of a new
    And crackling fire.

      —McKenzie Patterson Ison

WHAT'S A CRIME?

Is it a crime to be naive?
   Is it a crime to feel fatigue?
Is it a crime to cry out loud?
Is it a crime to settle down?
I wonder and worry what life has to say.
Should I bother? Does it matter anyway?
Tears of pain are tears of joy.
Life uses them as a twisted toy.
A smile on your face, a knife in your hand.
I want me to be an honest man.

      —Daniel A. Rothwell

Rolling hills of fabric,
  the freedom of an entire nation—
destroyed with a single spark
              just a small flame.
Each stitch full with personification.
   Red, White, Blue.
Our pride,
   "Old Glory,"
           up in smoke.
Thread deeply woven into each traded soul.

Faceless apathy views the shameless cremation of our country.
God even looks on
         as dying stars melt away.

The flame is out.
But a fire will always be sewn in the hearts of those who carried
out this execution.

the thread of morality unravels—

      —Cati Diamond

FREEDOM'S FIREBRANDS

Freedom's firebrands are spreading throughout the Earth.
  People have a burning desire to be free, and it is not a
new feeling.
He may be Moslem or Christian OR Atheist or Catholic or
    Jew.
A woman or a man or boy or girl all crave for freedom.
Today, most have a never-ending desire for liberty and
    democracy!

Army bullets or tanks or swords or bayonets have never
    quenched freedom.
Many men were killed in Boston and New England they fell;
    others took their place.
In the middle 1770's, many fell, but the ranks filled back up
    rapidly.
The aringing firebrands were not ultimately quenched.
Nor will they be in China or the Eastern Bloc countries.

The Berlin wall was aringed with freedom's firebrands; and it
    is falling.
Force only fans the stinging smouldering of freedom's fire-
    brands.
Chinese and Russian citizens may die for freedom, but others
    rise.
Yes, others rise to forward freedom's blazing truth and its
    quest.
Freedom's firebrands are being lit by Modern Day Sampsons.
Some fall, but others rise up to carry on the firebrands of
    Freedom.
Take care oppressors! Some fall from the ranks; but the ranks
    are filling up fast!

      —Maynard Floyd John Krieg

OUTLOOK

All around me the world is changing.
Nothing ever stays the same.
People have lost all compassion
for the hungry, sick, and lame.

Conservation is lost again.
Water too dirty to drink.
Our parks and forests ever darken.
Our animals becoming extinct.

Terrorists bomb passenger planes.
Talks end up in riots.
Politicians create political scandals.
Freedom is ever quiet.

The war of words continues.
As nations talk of defense.
The world will finally realize
It is all at our own expense.

—Eric Matthews

ETHIOPIA

Listen to my plea, nations of the world,
Listen to my cry, leaders of the world,
I was once a land of fame
now, a land of shame.

I was once known for my fertility,
yearned and craved for my hospitality,
blessed with greens, fountains and river,
and, now, I am the land of grimmer.

I am now like a lofty tree;
devoid of its fruits and leaves.
My people are dying of hunger
struck to be lame and left to be languor.

Alas! Too hard to bear seeing my children dying,
hard to see countless skulls lying.
So, nations of the world,
ETHIOPIA is my name, the forgotten country
that once was the symbol of victory.

—(Sophie) Fisseha

PARADE

If only there was a "parade"
to show them that we care.
Coming home from Nam
would have been a lot easier to bear.

They never asked for much
it was plain to see.
Just getting on with their lives
made them as happy as they could be.

But how could we forget
all the torture and sorrow they've seen.
When they've been through it all
at a very young age of nineteen.

We're sorry for no "parade,"
you deserve much more than that.
We're proud of what you've done,
and our country's much better for that.

We've said so many times,
"How could it be."
If we had a chance to do it again,
a "parade" is what you would see.

—Phyllis Altomare

CRAZED WORLD-9/19/89

Through a mind of confusion
I see a crazed world
So involved one in itself
Through a mind disillusion
I hear a silenced scream
so bold are the chimes
Through a mind of insanity
I feel a penetrating blackness
so wrong in the context
Through a mind of versatility
I taste a horrible sour
so grotesque are the human
Through a mind of reality
I smell the rotting decay
so dead of one's heart.

—Esther M. Shaffer

NIGHT WATCH

A soldier patrols a desolate road,
Numb with the biting cold.
He questions his role in a violent world
Where lives are bought and sold.
A sound behind him makes him turn
And fire into the night.
He turns again and runs away
With death just out of sight.
A soldier lies bleeding a few feet away
From a wound in the side of his head.
The last sound he hears is the fading footsteps
Of the man who wished him dead.

—Thomas E. White

FLASHBACK NO. 2001

Here I sit at my desk,
watching the war and remembering . . .
The wet, hot, stinking death.

Seeing my friend in a O.D. shroud.
Saying to myself, be strong, be proud.

Then again it comes creeping
into my mind, things I will
remember for all time . . .

The wet, hot, stinking death,
those memories still bother me . . .

That is one sight I hope
and pray my son never sees.

—Michael Ainsworth

1989

Integrity.
Life has turned a page against
our planetary immaturity . . .
we're coming of age.
From deep within,
hearts smile like daisies
up through pavement cracks.
Freedom—warm like a hug
felt all the way around the equator . . .
the Wall is c
    o
      m
        i
          n
            g
              down!

—Mimi Alexander

THE MIGHTY OAK

The mighty oak stood silently as if it knew its fate.
    The many memories it beheld to be marked off the slate.
It looked down on the little girl that played beneath its branches,
    It laughed at the two little boys who took so many chances.
At climbing and swinging and frolicking around
    At forts and roads they made all over the ground.
It protected the stovewood fixed all in a pile.
    It shaded the farmer who many sickles filed.
The tree stored its memories as each year came and went.
    It grew older and bigger til its many branches bent.
The fierce lightning came from out of the sky
    Struck the mighty oak and caused it to die.
Then one day they came with their chainsaws and truck
    And began eating away at its branches and trunk.
Oh, what a sad day to see the mighty oak fall
    But this is the fate that faces us all.

      —Audrey Mumert

THE WOOD CUTTERS

man with the chainsaw
don't you know
the age of the woodfeller has passed
— slipped away with the passenger pigeon
that man pursued to extinction.

man with the bulldozer
have you not seen
the felling and death of the forests
—wiped away to deserts as chalk across a board

man with the chopping ax
have you no care
for our earth that was green and abundant
—its life eroded into streams of sewage

men with the sawmills
what will you do
when all the forests are gone
—your chainsaws and axes as silent
as the call of the wild?

      —Dee Haizlip

THE HIGHWAY MAN

Throughout the years I will remain the fear as eternal as
    the tears
The peasant and the king are my servants
I thrive in the shroud of humanity . . .

In the beginning the night was simple, to live was to survive
There was no greed, instinct supplied all
Through the eons, time was the only reaper
This is where it started, it was easy to rest
For in the crimson of the sunrise was the message of strife

The game did commence, the duels did come, for ages past
The roles were many, the highwayman was the start but not
    the end
For in the time of chivalry swords spoke for me often
Power and riches as sweet as the maidens
Foundations were set that made me immortal

Inventions of man changed the perceptions and uses
My allegiance grew, greed making puppets of them all
The lands bathed in sorrow and silence
No longer can the children claim innocence
Forever cursed to participate in the game
Knowledge, sought as a retreat, bites back
All offerings to me as if to a god

      —James Fecteau

Running
Feet touching Earth in Rhythm
Heart pounding in Unison
Air fornicating the Lungs
Hair fluxing wildly in Wind
Breeze fondling the face gently
Intercourse with the Universe

      —Joanne D. Lilgeberg

BUTTERFLIES

Yellow, green, orange, red,
    a flighty little spaceship
    landing in Mom's flowerbed.
Touching down for a moment,
    to refuel for the return trip.

Where did you come from?
I've seen none quite like you.
You've a special grace and beauty
    like something in a dream.

But in this little spaceship,
    there is no little man.
Just a small computer
    to take his place.

      —Jennifer L. Rubé

If there be lions . . . ROAR!

Back down, back down,
    little man of no spice.
You live in the dream
    of ongoing life.

Stand aside, stand aside,
    lost soul in the ice.
You bask in the gleam
    of your miserable strife.

Make room, make room,
    you doomed little man.
There are others like us
    who thrive in your strife.

Fall down, fall down,
    you creature so bland.
For we are the lions
    who feed on your life.

      —John E. Taylor, Jr.

HAVE YOU EVER DREAMED

Have you ever dreamed
You were an eagle,
Or think how it would seem
To soar the ocean like a seagull?

Have you ever dreamed
You were the deep blue sea,
With a cool breeze to breathe
Lulling lazily with glee?

Have you ever dreamed
the moon was you,
Full of light illumination
And nothing obstructing your view?

Have you ever dreamed
Your dreams came true?
I always wished they could,
And now I know, they do.

      —Carmen A. Rachal

THREE PHASES OF LIFE

Life in the past
Floating, feeling for love and laughter.
Life in the present
Soaring, seeping in hatred from my enemies.
Life in the future
Feeling the love and laughter.
Kicking away the hatred.
Lifting my life.
You're now here with me.

—Amanda Hope Langley

WE HAVE A POODLE

We have a poodle whose name is Boy,
He is a mini— and not a toy.
He likes to sleep on my bed at night,
He's not ferocious, and will never bite.
He prefers ice cream from a cone,
Over the original doggy bone.
Every night he stands his guard,
And looks for prowlers in the yard.
He was born in Scotland, a land not near,
And flew in a plane to live with us here.
Our grandmother loves him a little bit,
But never to this will she ever admit.
We'll love this dog forever and a day,
While he turns from black to silver gray.

—Sarah E. Gagne

DEAD PUPPIES TELL NO TALES

You see them walking across the street.
A hazard to every car they meet.
Inquisitive puppies who love to roam.
Many of them without a home.
Innocent victims who don't sense the dangers.
An easy target for heartless strangers.
All too often you know the result . . .
They're sacrificed in a satanic cult.
Perhaps a few will take a last breath
awaiting an injection of certain death.
Still others are used in the name of science
in laboratory tests for wealthy clients.
Captive puppies with tortured souls
have many stories to be told.
And yet they try through barks and wails.
But alas, dead puppies tell no tales.

—Kathy Gilbert

BLUE JAY

A peaceful blue jay comes
                    soaring
                         down
landing gracefully on the bird feeder.
Pitter patter
pitter patter along comes a little chipmunk
meaning no harm at all
to the BIG   black-eyed
bird who sits there staring
as still as could be. Then as quick—
as a flash   S P R E A D S
his BIG blue wings
                    soaring
                         to yet
                              another
                                   feeder.

—C. Beige Berryman

BEFORE YOU CAME

Before You Came the world was peaceful
It was joyous and the world was ONE
Before You Came WE BLACK PEOPLE HAD, HAD A LIFE
AND LOOK WHAT WE HAVE NOW.

—Tensía LaToya Hyde, age 10

ODYSSEY

Let us drink;
Let us drink to its lurid bonnet; its glowing awe
to the Western sun and Apollo's chariot.

Between the twinges of night and dusk, between
rainbows and mornings musk, is where I shall be . . .
Is where you shall find me.

Here in this valley far above Earth
Where the wind kiss the wild flower
Where I celebrate my rebirth . . .,

Here in this valley where soft gold leaf entwine, round
Waist of gods to feet sublime, here where
the emerald rivers flow, when the sun casts
its longest shadow,
Is where I shall be . . . Is where you . . .
Shall ever find me.

—Joseph A. Booth

A SIMPLE SMILE

A simple smile can make a perfect day
The glow of a smile can be seen far away

Smiling can make you feel good inside
Your deepest fears a smile can hide

The price of a smile is always cheap
An expression of love felt way down deep

To always wear a frown is no fun
Smiles will brighten a day like a ray of sun

To share a priceless gift just send a smile
A feeling of warmth that will last awhile

With a smile, a friend you can win
Overcome your enemy with a great big grin

Life will seem to move along at an easier pace
If you would just go through life with a smiling face

—Wanda M. Lackey

A CHILD UNFOLDS

Being a child must be a wonderful thing,
For life's just beginning and one learns to sing.
Tomorrows yet to unfold with new learning
And today's filled with parents' care and loving.

Learning who to call on for your daily care
And knowing when you call, they'll always be there,
Will make life a safe and loving place to be
And the child will say, "That's good enough for me."

Time passes and the child learns to work with others.
He learns to accept his sisters and brothers,
Each with a personality soon to unfold . . .
Patterns to begin before he's very old.

Years come and go as he grows up to be a man.
Patterns set when he was young, now help him to stand.
Life has been good to the child that once used to be.
Perhaps by his life, better times we all will see.

—Ida Louise Lee

METAMORPHOSIS

Swiftly, deftly, mercilessly, yet mercifully
The message comes.
Is knowledge better than ignorance?
Does uncertainty welcome finality?

Swirling, whirling, adrift in possibilities;
A kaleidoscope of thoughts blur and focus.
Answers beget questions.
Questions torture the imagination.

Retreat, denial, regrets pursue relentless speculation;
Yet steadily, new horizons beckon.
Survival the forerunner,
Plans, dreams, goals a luxury.

Center, balance, adapt, regroup;
Slowly born from within, resolve and ingenuity.
Unsolicited strategies clamor for their due.
I will build a castle from this carnage.

—Marci Williams

IT MIGHT

Rolling in snow
skiing down hills
Bounding—
               or jumping—
                              then flying . . .
What thrills!
Using small hands to shape
snow into balls,
It was truly too bad there was
no truth to it all . . . .

His alarm went off in the dark of the morn,
but he had a thought—he was thus less forlorn.
Then came a moment of sorrow,
of disgust
and of grief.
A moment of utter intense disbelief.
As he peered out the window,
he saw such a sight!
It had not snowed,
although Dad had said "it might."

—Jaime Fitzgerald

TERRA ALBA

What is it you want Holy Man,
For the way is crossed with your clan?
Speak truth now if ever you will,
Lest I command much blood to spill.

* This green world is my God's domain;
Do not the girdling fields of Rome stain.
Seek now instead a deed with honor great,
Turning aside to exhibit more than hate.

You fear my strength amid your God's realm;
Knowing your armies I can overwhelm.
Put forth a reason for my turning back,
This seat of learning I could easily sack.

* The birds incline in the heaven's blue high;
They fly in freedom not regarding your sigh.
You surely see where our roads all lead;
Let the scourge of this war go to seed.

Do the stars bespeak this call for charity?
Such courses my soul only in rarity.
Retire I will and thus lead my array;
Learn you so everlastingly upon this day!

—Conray Arris

THE PERFORMANCE

Thunder's solo commences the show while
Lightning excites the audience
awaiting the main performance.

Then, the soft sounds of Rain gently
fall from the sky with a quick and
steady rhythm backed by Thunder's
rolling overtures.

And Lightning reenters the scene by
brightening the stage; streaking,
cracking and flashing in accordance
with Thunder's loud music and Rain's
gentle melody.

When Rain is ready to end her song,
Thunder and Lightning rest, waiting
until the Clouds are willing to
sponsor another heavenly show.

—Debra Warren

REQUIEM . . .

Behold, O Lord! Our prince of fires prostrate
upon this scarred battlescape of pain
whereon, as holy ghosts, we emulate,
at random intervals you preordain,
our caring, sharing, husbanding of seed
aborning, yet unborn and still unheard . . .
fulfilled, yet unfulfilling to our need,
charged yet with propagation of thy word!

Empower him to summon healing rains
down on this fitful, profane interlude
to soothe and mitigate remembered pain
of endless hours of days and nights endured!

Perceive him not to call thine name in vain!
Absolve him, Lord, and make him whole again!

. . . Requiescat.   (JBMKII)
DHA Jr., Major, Artillery
05/06/21 — 01/17/90

—James B. Knight

I'LL BE THERE

Weep not for me, when I am gone,
someday you'll meet me there
and with each day remember,
no more pain and sorrow will I bear.

You may not see or hear me,
but in spirit, I'll be by your side
I'll be your guardian angel
through all, so do abide.

You may feel a warm breeze upon your face,
or an instant of bright light
I may lead you when your eyes can't see,
or guide you through the night.

A gentle touch or whisper
a twinkling star above
no matter how old, or where you are
you'll always be wrapped in love.

You will always be protected
no matter what, I will be there
so weep not for me my loved ones,
I'll be your wings up in the air.

—Janie M. Colella

MUSIC?

The music runs
 Roundaroundthru
My head, not allowing
 me to sleep.
  But this song is not my own.
  It belongs, I think,
  To someone else.
Someone whose song,
 Clashes
  With mine.
 Making
  Out of tune chords,
 And rhythmless
  beats.
So it drowns me
 And takes my freedom.
Binds me with melody,
 and holds me
  with love?

—Christa S. Chamberlin

OUR FEELINGS

We can't feel sad for letting the
 years go by—
We can't feel that we never did
try
With all the memories we some-
times want to cry.
But there are things we did
accomplish and we really did try
We must feel as sure as
there are four seasons
We were put here for our Lord's
reasons.
And each one has a part to do,
be it great or small
The strength and beauty of what we
build depends on the work of all
So when we think of all the work
there is left to do
We must once again Thank
God for workers such as you.

—Catherine Reader

ANGELS

There really are angels,
 I surely must say;
They're there right beside you
to keep you astray.

When you're first born,
They nudge that first cry;
With that first step,
They tell you "Just try."

There really are angels,
they help you through school;
A ride on a bicycle,
First strokes in a pool.

Friendship and kindness
they try to instill;
Fairness and honesty,
the ability and will.

There really are angels,
Best friend above others;
That's why our Lord made them,
that's why they're called mothers.

—Nancy A. Moreira

THE SEA

The Sea; it is filled with life,
  love, hate, anxiety, and all emotions.
The shore: a place where the sea fights, struggles, and rests.
When sea brings in her tides, hate, anxiety, and weariness
are washed away. When sea pushes out her tides, love, happiness,
and joy are brought in. Then there are the waves, sometimes
crashing against a bare rocky cliff, yet at other times they
gently and lovingly caress the shore. Perhaps the most important
of all: the shore. The very foundation of the sea; for without it
the sea would go on endlessly . . . tides never going in, nor out.

The tides that I speaketh of: the days passing by, with sunset,
and sunrise.
The waves: the hours passing by . . . sometimes ever so quickly,
yet at other times as slow as can be.
The shore: the very foundation of life.
The sea: the person dearest to you.

—Jason T. Hucks

CHRISTMAS

Ho, Ho, Ho, Christmas is here!
 A time for joy and Christmas cheer.
A time when Santa travels down the flue,
So don't burn a fire or there'll be nothing left for you.
Santa's wide around the middle, a jolly old chap;
Read off your Christmas list while you sit upon his lap.

Ho, Ho, Ho, Christmas at last.
Here come the ghosts of Christmases—future, present, past.
Everyone is singing with glee
As they decorate the Christmas tree.
Presents on the bottom, a star on the top,
Gee, I wish this Christmas season never would stop.

But Christmas is more than ribbons and bows—
More than a time when it snows and getting frozen toes.
It's more than decorations and Santa's Ho, Ho, Ho's.
It's loving and giving apple butter or jam.
Christmas is the day when Jesus was born in Bethlehem.
There is still one problem with Christmas you see;
We're as far away from next year's as we ever will be.

—Jase Abbott

TO: KIRK

Nine long months of growing inside, it was so hard to wait,
 The movements, the kicking and even the sickness is so
unbelievable, it's great!

Finally labor, oh, how it hurt, but it was pain combined with
joy,
The contractions, the pushing finally paid off — a brand new
baby boy!

Now at five months, you've grown so much, you're changing
every day
I love to play with you, hug you, watch you and the looks
you give my way.

Your eyes can melt me, your cry can wound me, your smile is
so sweet.
To hear you laugh, and the way you reach for me, every-
thing's so neat!

I never knew what it would be like, I only had my dreams
Day by day, the bond just grows, we make a perfect team!

I could go on explaining over and over until the end of
time—
'Cause no love has ever been so pure as ours — sweet child of
mine!

—Debi Rutherford

MY SPECIAL PLACE

There's a place in the trees out in the country where I go when I want to be alone. A wide rock where I sit and dream in the sun.

A brook flows by the place where I sit. A silver stide FULL OF LIFE as it sweeps on down to reach the sea.

The trees overhead partly BLOCK OUT Sun—Leaving many a shadow pattern on the ground. The Wind brushes by swiftly on its way to a place no one knows.

It is here alone among the giants who silently guard the quiet that I know what it is like to be FULLY ALIVE.

—Lisa Wersinger

When the sun rises in Africa
It leaps whole above the dark layered horizon
With a suddenness that
Startles in its absoluteness
And leaves no doubt of its power
To instill life by burning away
Darkness
Or to blast the earth with
Its purifying flames.
I wonder if those who live
Below feel its presence
In that way.

—Richard E. Gillespie

BLACK LACE

Shining brightly through the night
As it crosses overhead in the sky.
Luminating the way for man's sight,
Toward journey's end with nary a sigh!

Hiding in the clouds away from view
At times never to rein.
Places on earth to be seen by few
Until the time has come for it to wane.

Controlling tides and guiding seasons
As it journeys circular, in blackened space,
For which there are no earthly reasons.
Parting clouds softly luminating, representing beacons of lace.

Generation through generation
Testifying to all creation!

—Virginia A. Grecko

THAT COULD BE ME

I've seen him before
Once by my back door
He was lonely, standing in the rain.
By looking at him I could tell he was in pain
He was dressed in drab old clothes
Where he got them, nobody knows
He had nobody, nobody at all.
And though ashamed, he still managed to
walk tall.
I could tell he was starving
I looked down at the chicken I was carving
I thought "That could be me."
It could happen so easily
I opened my mouth to take my first bite
But I couldn't eat because of that sight
How could I let this happen to another
human being?
  Still I did nothing, nothing at all
Now I am the one who cannot walk Tall.

—Eva Escobedo

THE BEACH

Big waves, small waves
Tumbling along,

The wind in your hair,
Singing a song.

The sundrops dancing,
On the sand,

It's the Beach!
This Place Is Grand!

Smiling faces, wiggling toes,
Different families, all in rows.

Dogs running up, dogs running down,
Young children running all around.

First one raindrop, then two
and the sky is blackish-blue.

We all pack up our things to leave,
But the memory lives, happily.

—Addie Lueth

SUNSET

By the river in the valley,
There I stopped to watch the day
End its ever shorter hours
In its own spectacular way.
The rose-gold hues of sunset
Blent with blue across the sky,
Slowly fell behind the hilltop
As the day began to die.
In its beauty there was sadness,
For I wished that it could stay;
But I knew that naught could stop it,
That it had to go its way.
As I grieved day's end, O'er the hill
Slowly, softly crept the night,
With its moon and stars and splendor
And I gazed with great delight.
For each moment has its beauty
That becomes a memory, too
When the night is finally over;
And a day begins anew.

—Winnifred Gies

MEXICO

Mexico, magical name!
I repeat it with pride
Land of valiant men
and beautiful ladies

Of royal lineage
MEXICO, land of lights
and flashing colors
for artists; my brothers

With your hands
With your ideas
Create many, many works of art
to sell everywhere . . .

Your paths, your highways,
your songbirds and your joy,
nothing can compare with you.
For these reasons, I salute you

Loudly and Proudly . . .
Long live lovely MEXICO
LONG LIVE MY BELOVED COUNTRY!!

—Evelia Alcaraz

Within our reach
        lies every path
    we ever dream of taking.

Within our power
        lies every step
    we ever dream of making.

Within our range·
        lies every joy
    we ever dream of seeing.

Within ourselves
        lies everything
    we ever dream of being.

—Lisa Elaine Hines

THE IMPERATIVE

I found out the other day,
What they mean,
By the imperative,
"Grow Up!"
It means,
Do what they do,
Like what they like,
Think what they think,
Be like them.
All all along,
I thought,
It had something to do,
With becoming one's self.

—Anne M. Clingman

AFTERMATH

Lying broken on the ground
    crushed and mangled
    torn and bleeding
The blood runs like a stream
        and drips
                    drips
    Like tear drops
    from swollen crying eyes
    There is no sound
    There is no color
    and a small thin red line
    where the blood once ran

—Sallie J. McCollom

PARTS

This is the baby seeder
    in three parts
Him
This is the baby door
to its inside home
for waiting — growing
Her
These are the baby-feeders
drinky life
until the teeth can bite
Her pride
His mock
This is smellfinder
HerHimHimHer
together join and baby get
And humans much the same

—James McMenamin

ANGER

What is this beast that lurks behind this face I look upon
It fills a space where love once dwelled, but now that love is gone
There's anger now that fills this space, and love can not come in
When shall it cease, it eats away the me that I once knew
So take away this anger LORD, return this space to me
So I can be the me I knew, and love can see me thru

—Dawne Germann

I UNDERSTAND

We walked along a street one night
    And he tenderly took my hand
He said to me in a gentle voice,
"My daughter I'm in demand,
I've seen what this awful world can do and people will throw you aside.
Try not to lose sight of yourself or your dignity and pride.
And remember there's still another place to come if ever you're denied."

I looked into his teary blue eyes and finally understood,
That all this time he's been doing his job that they call fatherhood.
As we kept walking along the street, I tenderly squeezed his hand,
"I love you very much father, and this time . . . I understand."

—Susan Colosimo

THE MASK

I wear a mask, so none can see, the way I am inside,
        The way I think, and dream, and feel, all these I try to hide.
My joys and my disasters I bury way down deep,
        So none can see into me, at all the things I keep.
For, what man can sense the beauty, hidden in a heart,
        Of all the riches in the world, they are the lasting part.
Outside I am a calloused man, a fool, of no account,
        My speech is light and bubbly, like water from a font.
Yet deep within me is a well, a well of vast content,
        Full of ecstasy, and sorrow, too, at the way men's wills are bent.
It boils up in anger, to see my brother bruised,
        But, outwardly I'm cynical, and often act amused,
My actions may seem careless, and my work seem fancy-free,
        Yet a fool, unfeeling, hardhearted man, I fear I'll never be.
And so each day, as I wake up, I don my mask anew,
        To play my part, and hide the heart, within me all day through.
Yet, still not all, see the mask, this turtle shell I chose,
        And to those few with sunburst hearts, I open like the rose.

—Stephen Herbes

COUNTRY ROAD

Walk with me my dearest love, along the green country roads,
    Where blue butterflies flutter and crickets sing with many a croaking toad.
Walk with me love hand in hand down to the silvery stream,
Where fishes jump and polywogs swim of sights few have ever seen.

Walk with me sweetheart to clover banks, covered in wild flowers
of white, yellow, blue. Where large boulder stones red and brown
kissed by flocks sparking diamonds new. We jumped carefully
from each mossy stone until we reached the other side, then
sat beneath a wild plum tree to watch ebbs flowing tide.

The sky was a cloudy blue with a rainbow about its edge.
As a white tail deer stood still along the rock ledge.
An old locomotive passed along the tracks with a Click-a-de Clack.
And the whistle blowed as steam rose from her lofty stack.

In the far off distance on a tiny hill was a church with a steeple
high. And peaceful sounds of a bob bob white bids us sad goodbys.
This beauty is breath-taking as the warm summer breeze
rushes thru the Old Oak trees. So please my dearest love holdfast
our sweet memories.

—Jeanise "Bachelor" Karimi

TOGETHER WE CREATED LIFE

From the very first day I met you, I knew we were meant to love each other. I have so many memories of you, still fresh in my mind. There were times when our love was as rough as the seas, but the many happy moments we shared is what I'll always remember. In love, we gave life to our daughter. She is so beautiful! God decided to take you from us. You needed to be at peace. From above, you are watching. Each day she will grow and become a woman. You will help her to understand life. She has so much of you within her. Our families will help her to know you as though you were still with us. The hardest words to say to you were always Good-Bye. In my own words, I have tried, with many tears, to say I Love You One Last Time.

—Barbra E. Klee

PASSION

Today you rest, waiting for the approaching night,
But though asleep, you're ready to spring as a coil wound tight.

For you're here, just below the surface at a steady rhythmic hum,
Desire full force, a sentence to render all senses numb.

One soft touch, a breath so easy now struggles to free,
A passing glance, frantic eyes dart from there to here but do not see.

Thoughts adrift, never actually settling before moving to another,
Consuming all, like a baby greedily receives the breast of its mother.

Moments pass, warm passion cools as it has begun to ignite,
Rest it needs, preparing for the long approaching night.

—Rhonda Roberts

RAINY DAYS

Rainy days give peace to me, rainy days bring memory,
thunderstorms claim majesty, beauty reigns in all I see.

You've heard the old expression about judging books by covers,
we can't always distinguish our enemies from lovers.
Since fate would never have us know how long we'll be together
we should never judge a day by ever-changing weather.

We give no thought to climate as we meet each passing season
and yet from weather moods can change with neither rhyme nor reason.
A foggy day, a cloudy sky cannot determine whether
life may bring a smile to us to brighten up dull weather.

The sun, while bright, can still the air yet bring a warmth so stifling
we cannot always know for sure who with our hearts are trifling.
Our hopes must soar on clouds above as light as any feather.
Why can't we just learn to judge no day by its own weather.

—(Mrs.) C. Rusty Bowman

I WISH I WEREN'T ADOPTED

She's his little baby, he loves her but not me,
I know I'm not really his, but I can't change my history.
I wish I weren't adopted, I don't even know my dad,
And when I think about it, it makes me really sad.
I used to cry at night, in that old foster home,
But now I think it's loneliness, for I feel all alone.
Sometimes I see my mother, way back in my mind,
I know that she was special, she was one of a kind.
And I know she'll come back for me when the time is right,
And I will watch for her each and every day and night.
My new mom is real sweet, and she takes care of me,
But there's nothing like a real mom to soothe the pain inside of me.
My new sister is treated better, I know that for sure,
Just to know he loves her more, I cannot endure.
I want you to know my mother, wherever you are now,
Just to say that you are mine, I am very proud.
And when we're all in heaven, I'll be with you my mother,
Because I know, with our love strong, we will be together.

—Chantel Crocker, age 14

MY REWARD

Let me know you care
Just by being there!
Too many loving phrases
Send me running mazes!
My mind, a spinning whirl,
As my goodness you unfurl!
I want my verbal pay,
But, in my Father's way,
Not on this sphere,
Even from one so dear!
So be kind and smile;
Compliment, but wait awhile!

—Charlotte Baskett-Brown

SPRING

It won't be long till spring is
here
all fear and dreariness will
disappear
Birds will sing their song of
cheer
Flowers will bloom that
bloomed last year
The earth will be covered in
shades of green
No one need tell us, the time
is . . . Spring.

—Lottie Loree Huff

LOVE'S SHINING LIFE

Roses so pretty
Violets so blue
Like a white dove
we all fall in love
In the night
by the pale moonlight

Like a Knight in shining armor
from a long time ago
But the Knight does no harm
for she will fall in his arms

For as long as they shall live
Happy, sad, glad, or mad
together, they both shall give
themselves to each other

—Brenda Lundberg

S.O.S.

So lonely, all alone.
Till it rises like a moan.
From every thing I am
Comes a cry, to break the dam
That holds my feelings back
And from others hides the lack
Of love I have in me.
I hope they'll never see.

But if they never see
This emptiness in me
They can never help me find
The way to peace of mind
That I'll somehow achieve
If the lovers just don't leave.
And so, this is my plea.
Don't desert me, help me see.

—Sandra J. Craig

DORYPHOROS

Taunted daily
        by your presence—
Eyes so clear
        they absorb me,
An innocent smile
        that intrigues me,
A mind so full it spills
        from your lips,
Gently sprinkling
        those about you—
These move me
        in an unfamiliar way.

You, aloof, stand
Oblivious to my thoughts.
So real,
So close,
So always . . .

Untouchable.

—Amelia Caldwell

HUNTERS LAMENT

Fallen leaves
    Of lifeless brown,
Like defrocked angels
Down from pinnacles,
Drying on the ground.
Small specks of red
Upon those leaves
Drying to brown
In Novembers breeze,
Signal yet another passing.

A gleaming
Leaf shaped
Knife of flint
Ancient there
Among new browns
Cries aloud —
That given prudence,
The venue
Is not wrong.

—Tom Detwiler

ENJOY!

Rain falls gently
    bringing peace and a sigh.
So thankful we are
    for relief from high.
It seems to cool
    more than the ground.
It calms our nerves
    and refreshes, we've found.
Look, listen and
    feel the air.
This beauty we enjoy
    is much too rare.
The birds, the rain,
    and thunder too,
All part of nature,
    and beautiful, it's true.
The day begins well
    for a change.
Now, let's enjoy
    and not rearrange!

—Laurie R. Brooks

THE ANGRY SEA INSIDE MY HEAD

My mind is like the angry sea, it tosses and it twirls.
I feel the pain deep in its depths when upon the rocks it hurls.

I feel the darkness of the night, the solitude as well.
But then the anger starts to grow, the waves begin to swell.

The lightning flashes in my head and lights the darkened sky.
The thunder crashes also there and often makes me cry.

The sea grows very angry then, she throws herself around.
Any boat which tries to cross . . . a "mayday" they will sound.

In the morning, the sun comes up, she falls to sleep at last.
The fury of the night before is dead and in the past.

Then by day, she plays her role, she's soothing and she's kind.
She lays passive to the passing boats, and pretends she doesn't mind.

She knows down deep within her heart, the anger is still there.
The nights will come, the storms will crash . . .

But no one seems to care.

—Sharon Smith

A WRITER

A writer pours his soul out with his pad and pen,
He writes of dreams and properties far from the sight of men
He shouts louder than is heard, his voice the sword of life
He writes unrestricted thoughts of mind, keeping his soul
from strife.

People laugh; they cry, when they hear this man
Emotions trickle from fermented hearts, and he never lifts a hand
He holds them suspended for a time, frozen in their sightly state
He grins as he sees them, this is his toy with fate.

He loves to the gray the paper, as he turns the pages of time,
He writes of human fallacies, searching his body and mind
He writes about beautiful happenings, the time he's come to find
As he watches the world pass gently by, and edits the frames in line

To him the world's a movie, today is just a set,
The script are things he's remembered; the actors people
he's met
He loves to watch it over, each word a fresher screen,
Soon he awakes a new day, the poem was just a dream.

—Jamison

SALVATION ARMY

They want our pants!
    they want our shoes!
they're building a fortress in Newark and they need hangers.
An oven mitt whaps the Mayor of Bourne relentlessly
while big, pink beads tighten around his neck.
The Smothers Brothers are donating albums
Blender caps hastily knock Franki Valli unconscious
and take over his game of Chutes and Ladders.
bulky toasters launch CB radio belt buckles into orbit
pointy collars pierce the eyes of Helen Reddy
as a Whiffle bat clubs a nun, sending her reeling
into a vat of broken cameras
Americans from coast to coast pack the 70's into Hefty bags
and launch the decade into its meager existence
behind the Rayon Curtain
a Veteran screams himself awake
visions of a single pair of pressed white boy's briefs on a cliphanger
haunt his sleep
there is no hope . . .
Donna Summer has already hit top 10 in the record bin.

—M. Madri

As I sit here quietly and reflect upon my life,
I just can't help but think about the things that brought me strife.
I grew up under a mom who taught me love, respect, and fair play,
And a dad who taught me to believe in my dreams; they too could
 come true some day.
I fought the battle best I could with every part of me,
But somehow and for some reason, my success just wasn't meant to be.
I now am much older and wiser than some of my peers,
From hard knocks, knock-me-downs, and a body worn from years.
I look into the mirror and see a tiny tear forming in my eye,
For I realize that life now too has passed me by!

—**Sandy Spikes**

SWEET DEATH

Oh sweet death, come and rescue me before
I must bear one more heartache,
The pain inside my soul is too much for me to take.

Oh sweet death, take me before
my eyes must shed one more sorrowful tear,
Rescue me from the pain of life.

Oh sweet death, come for me before
my loneliness consumes me,
For I can't stand the agony of the nothingness that surrounds me.

Take me sweet death and put an end
to my tortured life.
Let me sleep the peaceful sleep, let me dream the endless dream.

—**Linda Kibler**

A PRAYER FOR MY TEAM

Dear Lord, help my team know what true sportsmanship really is,
And help them always to be good sports.

Help them to see their opponents for what they are,
Realize that they, themselves, are equal, and give their best.

Help them to see their goals clearly
And to work their hardest to win those goals.

Make them proud of their team, Lord, and what they represent,
Not only to themselves but also to others.

Give them strength and courage to go on after they have lost,
And give them enough faith and will power to try again.

Also, make them humble enough, both in winning and losing,
To be able to congratulate the other team.

But, most of all, keep them safe, dear Lord,
For they mean much to me.

—**Cherie Hankins Thornhill**

ENGLEHART'S FOUNTAIN IN WINTER

The deep snows lie on it like warm, white wool blankets,
 It's WHISTLER'S MOTHER WRAPPED IN WHITE, a beautiful sight!
A fountain is so precious God covers it in winter with layered coverlets,
As it gets colder He adds another layer. Winter here is November,
December, January, February, March, April—then spring freshettes
Send their dancing droplets dimpling still waters or gushing jets
Grasping for sunbeams, make roaming rainbows thank the sunlight bright.

Each snowflake is a promise new waters will wake, so remember,
Fountains need water, not words.

My neighbors, Ruby and Syd, stood at the great fountain in Rome
And couldn't help likening its beauty to the one in their town at home.
Years ago in New York the Prometheus fountain held me spell-bound,
Gail threw coins into a fountain in London, Canada to hear the sound,
Our fountain fascinates birds, even in winter bluejays, finches, snowbirds,
Chickadees, woodpeckers, grosbeaks gather and their sweet songs resound.

—**Ethel M. Tinney, B.A.**

THIS CHILD OF MINE

This child of mine
 so small I carry.
With hopes and dreams,
which I foresee.

Thru years of wonder
and strife we live,
we find this love of ours
grows more each year.
As years pass on
this child of mine,
can bring more joy and
peace we find.
You are my light
which shines so bright,
a light of life,
this child of mine . . . .

—**Janet Conti**

DECISIONS

Decisions, decisions,
Oh what revisions,
What torture we do endure.

When simply with practice,
We'd learn the act is
Neither a threat nor a lure.

It's simply selection,
General direction
To travel until we are sure.

So make them all lightly,
Inquiring nightly,
What's on the menu du jour?

—**Helen Regan**

DREAMS

My mind goes a-floating
 upon a carefree breeze,
up across the hilltops,
behind the leafy trees.

Like fireflies of the night
or lilies by a stream,
gentle breezes caressing
thoughts in a dream.

How vivid the images,
the reality so strong,
until my mind awakens
and my dream is gone.

—**Joyce E. Young**

TRUE LOVE

Love should be cherished
Whether friends or more
By loving each other
Without keeping score.

Someone that holds you
Through the darkest night
Love freely given
Not paid for at light.

If you share this love
You can only gain
'Cause anything less
Is just wasted pain.

—**Bunny Davidheiser**

ONCE THURSDAY'S ROSE
(or Lynn's Song)
The months have passed,
Winter has set in upon us.
The days grow long;
And was that I saw,
Yesterday—
A rose has died,
And parks closed.
Is it said to be—
This thing of happiness
Dies, for too many Thursdays
Have gone by—
For why does it happen,
How dreams cry—
How will it be,
Once the rose is
Dry.

—L. A. Bushman

LINCOLN
History acknowledges that great men champion great causes
And allows us to reflect as it pauses,
To honor his words, his name, the greatness that is his fame.
He shared center stage with others too.
Lest we not forget, Lee, Jackson, and Longstreet, to name just a few.
They fought well, and won their share of battles, the men of gray.
The Federal Cavalry met their match in Jeb Stuart who ruled the day.
This was a time of extreme sadness.
Americans dueled to death in mortal madness.
Many lives were lost as both sides suffered much pain.
The cost was high, but not in vain. We were a Nation again.
To keep the Union whole, was his singular goal.
A place in history is his forever, the Union they did not sever.
His life was our gift, his legacy, the Union not adrift.
A casualty of war, the Nation was suddenly robbed.
They mourned the loss of their President. He was gone.
Now he belongs to the ages.

—Dan Alden

DECEMBER FLOWER
In the snow shower
Stands a small tower
Blooms all year
My December Flower

Through rain, sleet and snow
Always she does grow
Lives her life in fear
Of what she doesn't know

If ever in bitter frost
My flower became lost
Winter will not part
Through all the world across

If spring doesn't come
What would be the fun
For I know in my heart
That she's the only one

—John G. Friedline

REQUIEM, J. F. K.
Lower gently the banners, our leader is lost.
He is on the great journey, the barrier crossed,
He strides into Valhalla through history's halls
Home now is the warrior from destiny's calls.

Home now is the warrior who sought to unite
Religions and races and nations despite
All the tensions and hatreds we must reconcile
To carry the torch in courageous profile.

To carry the torch that all men may be free;
This, then, is his message at Gethsemane.
From ramparts he won at so grievous a cost,
Fling high the brave banners, his cause is not lost.

Fling high the brave banners; proclaim the great dream.
His cause is unvanquished, though dimmed it may seem.
The drums are not muted; the trumpets still call
For peace upon earth and good will to all.

—Cecil Parr Martin

It was cold and clear that January day that dawned full of promises down at the Cape.
Seven eager souls ready to further the space program they all loved.
Lots of love and good wishes from the whole world were bestowed upon them.
They knew that all eyes were upon them; we knew them by name.

Minor delays, then all systems go; the beauty of liftoff, a sight to behold.
As Challenger left its pad, people everywhere stared in awe.
The spaceship climbed higher with Houston tracking and guiding the way.
The crowd below cheered them along as Houston gave the go ahead.

Full throttle, the order came, and seven brave souls were thrust into the waiting arms of Jesus.
Joy turned to horror as the scene unfolded. Children, grownups, friends, and relatives watched in terror as smoke filled the sky.
All that was left fluttered to the sea.

The world cried; things came to a standstill.
People were drawn to their T.V.'s seeking an answer to such a devastating tragedy, feeling such sorrow for seven who dared.
But despair no more, for Dick, Mike, Greg, El, Ron, Judy, and Christa now have all the answers.

They're seated in the master teacher's classroom.
They understand it all while those left behind may never know.
Yet ours is not to question, but to accept and go on.
Those brave seven accepted the challenge and rode the Challenger to the answer.

—Grace Parker

HERE'S . . . WINTER!

The beautiful flowers and
leaves fall
I stall
The wind becomes forceful
I am not as joyful
The white, pretty cold stuff
starts to appear
Why here?
I don't care
W-I-N-T-E-R
Shucks, it's not splendor
What can I say
I can ONLY surrender
There goes the day
The leaves fall
I must stall

—Bobbie

THE DAWN OF A NEW DAY

In the midst of the night
When the air is so cool.
There's a dew on the grass
And a mist on a pool.
You can hear but a cricket
And maybe an owl.
The moon is so full,
In the distance a howl.
The time goes by quickly,
The mist goes away.
The dew makes the grass wet
The birds start to play
The sky starts to lighten
The moon almost gone.
The world can get started,
For now it is dawn.

—Patricia E. Knelson

CLOUDS IN THE SKY

Standing so tall,
Is the mountain above.
Never bending,
Just sort of adjusting,
To the waves and crevices of the cloud.
Although at times,
It seems as though
The cloud forgets the mountain
By covering up its beauty,
The memory of the mountain
Will last forever.
For without the mountain,
The sky,
In which the cloud finds its
Future—
Would simply fall.

—Jill M. Thomas

THE MOONLIGHT BALLET

The weaver of my dreams, she brings
Feelings of delight, which cling
Tight to moments fleeting past
But memories of her, they last.
In shadowed moonlight, Lo! She goes
Dancing to the fate she knows—
Stepping to the beat she hears
Of all I love and all I fear.
Spinning fancies through the night
Which fade to vagueness, come the light;
Upon a stage of truth, she plays
With images unreal, that fray
So when I wake, they're quickly gone
But her! She's with me all day long—
She takes in my reality
Distorting it for nights to be.

—Chamile McChey

BLISS

Ahhh, to be a leaf
dancing upon the air,
turning over and over and around

                        lifted up,
tumbling, suspended   swooping down.

Floating, listlessly,
ahhh, carefree (truly free), relaxed.

A bird passes, eagerly searching for food,

                    soaring up,
jealous of my calmness,   dropping down.

Flying fast, then slow
with only warmth and clouds above,
forms and colors below.

                    climbing up,
Peaceful, level and steady then   floating down,

spiraling down

                        up
                    rising
                then
                        again.

—Roxann M. Stec

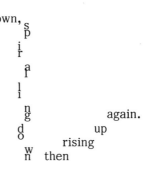

CAMERAS

Click! Click! Click!
Always snapping pictures
Mine are the best
Ever taken.
Really fantastic
Always great
Super shots.

—Lori Denise Mutch, age 14

CONTEST ANXIETY

Writing, writing,
What a dilemma!
Choose a topic —
But do I have 'ta?

Thinking, planning,
Outlining, editing;
Where this will end,
There's no telling.

Ideas, ideas
Are not always easy,
And often leave you
Feeling queasy.

—Terry M. Fontaine

THE MEADOW CAT

I dreamed one night
A pretty sight
Of wind and sun
And rain
The soft thick fur
Of a snow white
Cat
Prancing through the
Grassy plain
The chirp of a bird
The whistle of the
Wind
A song that may
Never end

—Mandi Tromm

I sat in a window,
A window that sees
The purple orange grove
With its blue and red trees.

I had a crocodile,
My friend and my steed,
Who told me to think
And listen with ease.

I thought and thought
Of marvelous keys,
And saw a planet
With no bees.

"How strange!" said it,
"And covered with fleas."
He mused and hummed
And made sense of this geas:

"The purple orange grove
of blue and red trees,
Gives a bath with
This dry lease."

—David M. Kelley

THE MAGIC PUPPET

Oh my little puppet, would you please
come off my shelf and play,

Why do you always need my hand to guide
you along the way?

You have mesmerized me so many a times,
like the quiet soft readings of nursery rhymes.

I believe in magic, and that dreams
and wishes come true,

Oh my little puppet, I believe in YOU!

—Jenni Dod Miller

MY OLD CAT

My old cat caught a rat,
And got fat!!fat!!fat!!
Then he said YUM-YUM to my tum-tum!!
And I said, Here kitty-kitty come,
Let's go have some fun!!
So we had some fun,
You could call it a TON of fun!!

After we had some fun,
My mom said, Go to the store!
So we went to the store,
Walked right in the door!!
Then we got a pack of gum,
And we went back home to have more fun!!!!

—Susan E. Hudman, age 9

WHEN THE HAWK'S AROUND

I can always tell when the hawk's around,
But I never know where to look.
There's often a rustle or cry from a bird,
And the myriad squirrels disappear.
Sometimes, there's a haze in the sky
Or a low-lying mist, as after a snow,
And I know how it must feel in battle
When it's too quiet and too dangerous to be out
And everyone waits for something to start.
Sometimes nothing happens at all.
The noise from the hedge sparrows signal
An all-clear, and I leave my window,
Knowing the hawk will eventually return.
He must live, too, and understands neither
Boundary nor armistice.

—Nancy Rutledge Pogue

FURRY FRIENDS

Strange bedfellows are these
Soft and cute and cuddly things
Under the blankets, toes will tease
But not to cease, the bedpost it clings.

Try not ever to strike its fancies
As everywhere they seek to climb.
Walking and digging in your favorite pansies
Sitting on your favorite book of rhyme.

Balls of yarn and catnip are their toys
Bouncing, leaping, running to claw
Anything that moves from girls or boys.
Then ignoring everyone with a wave of its paw!

A kitten is cute, you can bet on that;
But a cat is mischief, and always gets fat!

—Virginia Barber

GOD

I walked through a deep dark valley
Where man should never trod
and there I feared no evil
for I felt the hand of God

I stood upon a mountain top
and looked upon the scene
amazed at all the beauty
that nature always brings
my heart was filled with wonder
Such beauty grown from sod
and looking on this great big world
I see the hand of God

And someday I shall walk I know
Where mortals can not trod
by faith in Jesus Christ his Son
I'll see the face of God

—Sarah Pierson

UPSTAIRS

Jesus is my answer
He is a very good friend.
He will guide me through it,
Until the very end.
He knows all my troubles
He is with me every day.
He will stand beside me,
Every step of the way.
We are all God's children
He loves us everyone.
If we would study all the parables,
We would be disciples of his son.
Now this is very easy
And it comes from deep within.
If we only study and pray
Everything with him.
He knows all the answers
And he listens to my prayers
I know he stands beside me
Until I meet with him upstairs.

—Jean Kerans

A SINNER'S PRAYER

Lord, make me a shaking coward,
When it comes to doing wrong,
A constant thief of others' cares
Stealing many the whole day long.

Make me a winning gambler, God,
Of time dealt, to visit shut-ins,
A vagrant, gathering hand-outs
To feed the hungry, strength for wins.

Please show me how to get even,
With people, whose deeds do me good.
Teach me to love everybody,
But hate their sin acts, as one should.

I am a human sinner, Lord,
Trying hard to do what's right,
Would like other folks to know me
Cause my life reflects Jesus' light.

Lord God, You're the greatest master,
I love you and your caring ways,
Watch over, love, lead and guide me,
Through all given earth-living days.

—Grace Pierce

YOU ARE MY GOD

You called me back when I went astray
You gave me light in my darkest day
You loved me even when I did wrong
And in my heart You put this song

You are my strength You are my all
You are my bravery when on You I call
You hear my plea You fill my need
You are my God my all

You hold my hand each passing day
And shine Your light on my pathway
I thank You God for all You've done
I thank You for Your living Son

—Barbara G. Haggy

OUT-STRETCHED HAND

He holds us firm with out-stretched hand
No tighter grip has any man
That has always been God's plan
To hold us firm with out-stretched hands.

Reach out and hold that gentle touch
That's always there and means so much
And when life's fleeting like the sand
Just reach out for the Master's hand.

Strength that's ours if we just ask
And best of all it always lasts
If we'd just think about His plan
That God reaches out with out-stretched hand.

—Paula Leggett

THE HOLY ONE

In the magic of your beauty
I've seen a part of you that
is tragically hurt.
In the openness of the ocean
I have seen the perfect cure.
Its winds blow right through me.
Its eye allows no escape.
It's pure and it's righteous
and it does not hesitate.

In the darkness of the evening
star lights twilight all across the sky.
But you have seen of one so close
walk right from your sight and say goodbye.

—Mitchell Price

SPRING ETERNAL

Spring has come to adorn our land,
From the Mountain high to the Rio Grande.

South warm winds blowing, "Oh" so strong,
We often wonder what's gone wrong.

Geese flying North to seek their home,
Bring song and cheer that we're not alone.

New grass peeks high through morning dew,
While Robins serenade a year brand new.

Storm clouds roll over with thunder and rain,
Giving Farmers a trust for their golden grain.

Fruit trees all a bloom with color so bright,
Assures our Great Nation that timing is right.

God's promise perfected. Stated in his true book.
Known as "Resurrection." Let's all take a look!

—Edna Cleveland

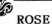

ROSE

My sis "Rose"
full of pose!
she calls our
clowns the Curio
for Heaven's hour
like a good country murio!

—Gloria Callaham

MUSIC MAN

If I close my eyes,
I can hear the
Tinkling of his
Piano keys . . .
The strum of his
Guitar strings . . .
And deeper in my mind,
I hear the songs
His voice sings . . .

Music man,
You are lost in time . . .
Sweet music man,
You are only in my mind . . .

—Crista M. Smith

MYRA BJORN

The big blonde Goddess of
The Sword cuts a wide path
In her world. The masses part
When she walks, a fathom tall
And hair a meter long,
Seems like a furlong!
Her sword is steel and
so's Her grip. Nice ice-blue
Blinkers that can chill or
Kill a man. It makes me glad
That Myra is on my side.
She laughs at me, her pupil,
But she doesn't mock or chide
Or scorn.
She takes me under Her wing
And her eyes dart around.
Myra Bjorn.

—Markie Hope

NANETTE

Nanette and I have traveled
Many, many miles
Nanette's always quiet
Never frowns, never smiles.

If I am feeling weary
Or just need to sit and cry
Nanette's the only one
Who doesn't ask me, "Why?"

Nanette's the perfect lady,
I need her as my friend.
Nanette always understands,
She accepts me as I am

Mother handed Nanette to me
Many years ago
From a box of Cracker Jacks
she came, my little Nanette doll.

—June Sohn

ODE TO A COAL MINE STRIKER

I'm sorry I cannot help you in your mines,
A new remedy must be sought.
Through my tears I have fought
In unknown lands in an unknown time
And in those battles, so grand and fine,
I have found what must be found,
In the land above the ground.

Inspired by the book The Red Badge of Courage.

—Carrie Nelson, age 12

THE HANGER

Mr. Hanger don't you ever get tired.
Don't you ever feel confused or wired.
You don't get any attention or one little mention.
But I think you're a neat little invention.
You're thrown on the bed and even the floor.
But usually picked up one time or more.
You hold up my pants, dresses, and skirts,
and sometimes you hold my fancy shirts.
But whether you come in satin or wire,
it doesn't matter because you hold my attire.

—Kimberly Reimels

THE CONFIRMED SMOKER

There was a man named Mr. Bloke,
Who continued and continued to smoke!
He puffed and puffed, coughed and coughed,
And nearly had a STROKE:

The Doctor said, "There is no hope,"
"For this poor unfortunate man,"
"He is VERY, VERY SICK,"
"But I'll sure do what I can!"

So the Doctor worked very, very hard,
Cleaning out this poor man's lungs,
But alas, there was nothing he could do!
The damage had been done!

So poor Mr. Bloke,
Went up in smoke,
To sing with the angels on high,
And rarely does a day go by,
You may still see him smoking in the sky!

—Myrtle M. Chartrand

TO A DEDICATED PSYCHIATRIST
(For Dr. Tahir M. Sheikh)

You're always there to lend an ear
Or to calm someone's raging fear.
Your dedication is beyond compare
And for your patients you truly care.
Leading people out of darkness is a part
Or helping the ache that's in their heart.
From a youth with a learning disability,
To someone in a nursing facility,
The depressed and forgetful there are many —
Some have family and some not any.
You help them through their bleakest days,
So they may feel the sun's rays.
Your days are long and sometimes frustrating
But a breakthrough can be exhilarating.
Time is short for family and friends
Yet their belief in you never ends.
They understand your work is God's call
To help His children one and all.

—Joan A. Iversen

LONELY ROSE

A moment when a lass
love is found —
Press close rose
your thorns —
My heart unhealed —
Only loneliness the
Rose hath found —

—Jennie Davis

STILL LIFE

Sitting pretty on a shelf
each in its little own place,
Smiles upon the face.
Arranged and rearranged
to suit the owner of this collection.
Still Life —
A recollection.
Tiny pieces trimmed in gold,
embossed in a metallic glaze.
I could sit and watch for days.
The majesty of the ornaments
makes impressions upon the mind,
And for some time,
leave this world behind.

—Sanora B. Hines

THE PURPLE TULIP

"Betty Jo" glows
she is on the go
to HEAVENS' Gate;
where she is within
her hair like gloss!
She blossoms like
A PURPLE TULIP
for she is;
Always cheerful
Like a couple
of Bluebirds:
Singing harmony
in the bright
morning
with Sunny!
Ha! Ha!

—Gloria Callaham

TEXAS TEXAS

Texas, Texas of the
Rolling plains

Many herds and much
Tall grain

Acres and acres of
Cotton white

Fields of bluebonnets to
Please our sight

Oil wells reaching to
The sky

Catching the eyes of the
Passer by

Oh, Texas, Texas of the
Rolling plains

—Gladys Bonnette

FOOTBALL POEM

Nebraska football helps the state
because the Cornhuskers are great.

Nebraska is a long, long state;
farmers grow food, factories make plates.
East and West sometimes fight and hate.

But, everyone gets together,
they crowd together at the gate.
They cheer, they get loud while they wait.
They all agree the team is great.

—Candice Marie Harkins

MY HOMETOWN

Rockwall, you are my hometown.
No finer place can there be found.
American Flags fly on town square.
Go lake sailing if you dare.
"Yellowjacket" banners through town stream.
A view of Dallas' skyline can be seen.
Go for a scenic country drive.
Makes you really glad to be alive.
Coming home I look forward to.
No other place has Rockwall's view.

—Martha Shipley

COUNTRY JAM

The dust hung heavy, white and thick;
While bullfrogs sang down by the crik,
We sat down on the concrete floor,
And listened to the music roar.

Charlie kept the beat real loud,
As Ricky's bass made a sensual sound.
Jimbo played at his usual par;
The best lead picker near or far.

We tapped our feet to the poundin' drum,
And swayed to the rhythm of the guitars strum
As Jimbo kept cookin' loud and quick,
And Ricky matched him lick for lick.
Jammin' in the country.

—Bonnie Sommerville

RURAL MAILBOX ARRAY

In clusters or lonesomely solitary,
some with faded names and rotting posts
or gilded tints and fancy stance, you wait,
all equally obsequious to the mailman.

Your "open door and open heart"
welcome the junk or precious art,
and faithfully, routinely each day
the carrier unloads surprise, shock, or woe.

You slouch there wantonly, mouth agape,
or wait in dejected despair,
ready to seize the moment
that converts neglect to glee.

You loiter there meekly demure and shy,
haunted by past great estate,
now surreptitiously servile
to tender welfare and pension checks.

You posture there satirically,
posing and smirking to express grand disdain
for the comic concern for charity pleas,
catalogues, circulars, and multiple bills.

—Wilbur Throssell

BETSY

Statuesque model of heaven warmed
   radiates from your style and grace.
Flowing without effort is not earned
   but can be dimmed by your face.

Your lengthy stride exudes best what has been
   for there is vision in your walk.
In your slim calves and thighs you have grinned
   and yet you will lie down to talk.

Stunned the first time I saw you in blue,
   you can still sweep me off my feet.
Your langorous nature leaves not a clue
   of when to rise or keep my seat.

Your breasts are lovely as they fly so high
   escorting me where ever I dream.
But you stretch out so sweetly when you sigh
   and are always more than you would seem.

—John R. Guillean

HI

Hi . . . I could not see you that day,
   You did not know who I was,
     Still . . . "Hi," you said,
     "Hi, Don."
The sound of your voice warmed my heart.
   Few people tell me hi,
   Fewer still even know I'm there.
   But there you were . . .
     "Hi," you said,
     "Hi, Don."
The words were simple,
The feeling . . . Awesome.
Was it the words . . . or that you spoke them?
     "Hi," you said,
     "Hi, Don."
Someday . . . When we meet,
I'll hug you . . . if I'm allowed.
Your kindness I'll return.
     "Hi," I'll say
     "Hi, Beth!"

—Donald J. Worthen

HEART STONES

Seven stones at the sea wall
   Have on them seven names
Of loves once tried and fallen for;
Evidence of lovers' games.

In youth I came to carve those names,
First to last in love's progression.
Thinking each would be the last;
Childishness is my confession.

The sea, like time, has washed away
The names from every stone
Except for one; all others though,
Without a trace are gone.

With my knife I gouge the name
On that one, deeper still;
To so protect it one more time
'Gainst the sea's tempestuous will.

Upon my heart, and daily deepens,
I, too, engrave the same;
And if it's said my heart is stone,
Yet on it is that name.

—Rod Randall

THE HEALING HEARTS

To open and blossom
   Perfectly as a flower.
Clean, pure as air
In the eucalyptus forest.
In your arms,
In my own arms.
Safety and warmth
Radiating through our hearts,
Radiating through my heart.
Independently whole buds
Blossoming.
Feeling the strength of new life
Pulsing in the soles of my feet.
The old coldness thawing away,
With golden flame.
The sun melting shadows,
Incinerating fears.
A new hope fills my soul.

—Rachel Unterseher

ESSENCE

Walk with me through fields
   of clover

   Lie within the blades
     of grass

   Breathe the faint scent
     of honeysuckle

   And watch the clouds form
     as they pass

Listen to the sound
   of nature

   Feel the warmth of earth
   bestows

   Taste the essence of
     this wonder

   Imagine life and how
     it grows

—Patty

SAILING

Come sail with me,
   let us enjoy the curves
of mother sea.
Riding her crests
and valleys of waves,
feeling the breeze
and salty spray.

Where else can we be
as water and sky? . . .
Lovers that kiss on the horizon.
Nestled among the waves
where time seems to stand still,
in a place of no comparison.

Yes, come sail with me
on our kin the sea . . .
for we, though of flesh
are of many waters.
Joyfully, let's share
in the sun, moon and air.
Our life sailing together as one.

—Faries Williams, Jr.

A FRIEND

A friend is someone who you can trust,
They won't fight or make a fuss;

They are always worthy and always kind,
They always tell you what's on their mind;

A friend is someone who'll never lie,
You can always trust them until you die;

A true friend is hard to find,
Now you have one no doubt in mind.

—Wanda J. Parker

YOU TOUCH MY HEART

You make the kindness just flow from
   my heart.
I want to describe the feelings, but don't
   know where to start
You warm my very soul, you
   touch my heart.
Why am I so nice to you?
I don't try to be.
It just flows from my heart
Like it knows . . .
You are my true friend.

—Christine Jewell

LEAVING

Why is it hard to leave a friend —
   Someone I've grown close to?
Why do I feel so empty inside —
The hurt that makes me blue.

It's time again for my life to change
And say good-bye to those dear.
Wondering if I'll ever see them again
Is something I'll always fear.

To think of the times I've wasted,
Not telling that person I care.
The next thing I know, my life has changed —
Suddenly, they're no longer there.

I say my good-byes; shed tears from my eyes.
As the day comes to an end,
I think of all the great times I've had
And wishing I had more time to spend!

Dedicated to Karlynne Fluharty 8/2/89

—Tehoni Addison

THE FRIEND I NEVER HAD

You liked me for a little while
   Who could not like me long
You gave me wings of gladness
And lent my spirits a song

You liked me for an hour
But only with your eyes
Your heart I could not capture
By storm or by surprise

Your mouth, that I remember
With rush of sudden pain
As one remembers starlight
Or roses after a rain

Out of this world of laughter
Suddenly I am sad
Day and night it haunts me
The friend I never had.

—K. Allen Wuori

ALONENESS

How beautiful to be alone,
   And yet to know
That just outside the circle
Of my aloneness
Friendship waits,
And needs but a beckoning
To warm my heart
With its presence.

—Grace Key

Where have all the flowers
   gone, winter seems frozen
   in time. The cold blue
   shadows of the barren trees
   and the ghosts of summer
   in the meadow, has taken
   on a thousand forms.
But — when I return from a
   winter's walk, I find a
   long ray of sunlight leading
   to Springtime
Tho' we are far away, our
   friendship is the bridge
   that closes the distance
   between us

—Virginia Hollingsworth Hickox

He sailed the seven seas
   And then once more
To hear the swaying trees
And guard the world from war.

The years quickly passed
And it would seem
That life moved so fast
He would never live his dream.

Twas a lady he sought
From Rome to China's Seas
And in Northern Places
And in Sunny Tropic Scenes.

Til a Birthday came round
That of his Corps
And that Lady he found
Right at a friend's door.

—C. W. Lynard

HOW I FEEL

I'll always be there for
   you, no matter what you say.
   Through the years, through
the weeks, and every single
day.
   You seem to say to your-
self, I've heard this all be-
fore,
   But the more that you
will say that, I'm there through
rich or poor.
   I know you don't under-
stand this, you think it's
all a deal.
   But the words on
this paper, are really how I
feel.

—Hollymarie Palma

THE PRIDE

The pride and determination
Shall forever lead the sad and heart broken
Into a world of smiles
And the poor
To the riches of heart and soul.
— **Sheron B. Hancock**

CHRISTMAS WITHOUT MY FATHER

The holidays are not the same.
They pass too fast.
They have lost their twinkle
That special sparkle that made them sweet.

The holidays now are a harbinger
Telling the year's ending.
The days grow dark, life slows down
Time grows shorter.

The holidays are not the same.
They have lost their innocence.
Truth has set in, childhood is gone,
The holidays are now my son's.

— **Rosemary Janes-Crabtree**

FATHERS DAY

Through the wear and tear of the years,
Even now, a smile lights up your face.
But through it all you have been there,
No one could ever take your place.

The love and support you gave us, Dad,
Your patience, no one could ever top.
You've sacrificed all for us, because
We're all chips off the old block.

Because it has been a labor of love,
We can never repay the debt we owe.
But Dad, we do love and appreciate you,
and we just wanted to let you know.

For the years you labored to see our needs met,
May God grant you health and happiness.
To replace the worries that we caused,
with peace and joy may you be blessed.

— **Rachel H. Warren**

WITCH DAY IS HALLOWEEN?

There is a witch, who makes a twitch, and
always gives a snort.

Just a touch of her hat, she can fly like
a bat, with her broomstick in her hand.

Children come out to see her fly all over
Zion City, but if you're late outside your
gate, why this is just a pity!

This ride she takes is once a year, on
every Halloween, No other time of any
nite is this green lady seen.

The black fat cat that paces round, is
one of many signs, That Halloween is
here again . . . A witch's special time.

So watch the hour on her special day,
when she decides to zoom, the flash
that shines before your eyes could be
her twinkling broom.

— **Christine Palomo**

PRESENCE

Christmas spirit
enveloped in song
day by day
coming closer
almost here
suddenly . . .
Peace.
then silence . . .
shifting snow in country wind
Christmas day has come.

— **Courtney Nicholas**

WHAT IS CHRISTMAS?
A CHILD'S QUESTION AT CHRISTMAS

Will there be some holly . . .
Will there be a tree?
Will there be a pudding,
Enough for you and me?
Will we sing the carols
They sang so long ago?
Will we have a turkey?
Will there be some snow?
Will there be some presents?
Will there be a sleigh?
Will we all be happy
When it's Christmas Day?

I think so . . .
Don't you?

— **Bonnie B. Goddess**

BIRTHDAYS

Birthdays are nice
They're like rolling
A lucky pair of dice.
You get cake and ice cream
With toppings with pleasure
That to seem,
Birthdays have joy and gleam.
You can scream with joy
With all your toys.
But that's not what birthdays
Are for . . .
They are
Love and care
For one another!

— **Theresa Schuerle**

CHRISTMAS TREE

We brought you in
and gave you a home,
But did you help us?
A definite no!
You started to lean up
against the wall —
Thankfully you did not
fall.
We gave you water every
day,
But when we touched you,
you started to sway.
The angel on top finally
dropped her head . . .
Then you, Christmas tree, fell
over dead.

— **Nora Graham**

TO LIVE, OR EVIL

Live to love, to compassion,
   to forgive.

Live to understand, to
   encourage, to comfort.

Live to give, to bless,
   to help.

Beware! Lest thou live
   to selfish mirror.

      To be evil, evil, evil.
                  —Axel R. Johnson

LONELINESS

Within every soul,
   lies a hidden place,
where love is a mask
and roses are weeds.
Ignorance is a solace and
insolence is a blessing.
I dwell there,
embraced by you.
Perhaps time is our defense,
or fear,
our master.

            —Emily Devaprasad

THOUGHTS ON LOVE

Listening to the wind,
   it is so inconsistent —
as are my thoughts.
Unable to predict,
the next movement.
Everytime is different . . .
Walking into it,
face down —
to be safe.
Will it feel refreshing,
as it passes by?
Will it unleash,
an unbearable pain?
By the time you decide,
"I am strong . . ."
The not so bad,
becomes so evil.

            —Lisa E. Pratt

CONFUSION

Darker shadows of clouds
      cover my dreams,
Encircle my world with fear,
      To only one escape
            there may be,
But only if you agree,
Placid thoughts envelop
      In my mind
Only to be confused by
      other ones already
            existing.
The choice is always
      difficult it seems,
Unbearable to even think.
Though might a miracle
      come to be,
   It would be much
      easier for me.

                  —Robin D. Walker

YOU'LL MISS ME WHEN I'M GONE

You'll hear my voice and see my face—
   And all the bad times you'll erase.
When I have gone my separate way—
   You'll miss me more and more each day.

You'll start to understand me then—
   And yearn to have me back again.
I know somethings I'd said were wrong—
But; times were rough and tension strong.

The problems we had weren't caused by me—
   And later on, you'll start to see.
                  —Kathy D. Gaither Smith Howey

WAIT FOR ME

I grieve for you everyday,
   But nothing takes the pain away.
I try to be strong,
   But I don't know for how long.
I'm afraid that it won't quit,
So I leave a light lit.
   I raise my head in silent prayer,
   So you know that I'm here.
So please promise me,
You'll wait and won't leave.
   I don't think I could take it,
   It's my heart, the pain will break it.
                  —Paula E. Goldsmith

TAKEN

Clear is not what is depicted
   Steamy windows — blown with moisture
Covering a view of terror
Yesterday — thank God is gone
Water trembling down her face
trickles bounce upon the glass
Lean against the wall in shock
Hurt so much in so short a time
Never has she known such danger
Clothing torn right off her flesh
thrown around as useless nothing
Unclean now she stands so bare
Drenched in water and in tears —
right behind a steamy window
Nothing of what has happened to her
can a shower ever do or change.

                  —Michelle Ortiz

WHY

Why does he hurt me so?
   He never did care,
He was never there.
He treats me bad one minute,
But loves me the next.
I don't believe he could ever really love.

Love was meant to be beautiful,
Not painful and hard.
He changes so fast,
You never know what to expect.
I wish he could understand,
How much he's hurt me.

He crushed my heart,
Spread it over the land,
The pieces forever lost,
Somewhere in the sand.
                  —"Nikki" Joanna L. Smitherman

GRATITUDE

Grateful am I for the right to live,
For a few short years, that I may give.
My heart and soul a chance to know
Of the wonderous beauty of flowers that grow.

The music of waters that rush swiftly by
The rapture of clouds up in the sky.
The glorious sun that rides in the blue
And last but not least my friendship with you.

—Robert I. Braatz

AS DAY BREAKS

As day breaks and shadows flee away,
you will only have memories of yesterday.

For today will come in fresh and clean
and those shadows of yesterday will not be seen.

As day breaks and darkness flees away,
a new sunrise will brighten the day.

From that moment on, you can choose your way,
a bright fresh start — or the shadows of yesterday.

—Conrad A. Reiber

I walk with you both nite and day;
Who I am, I will not say.
I'm in the deepest part of your mind;
you reach for me; yet cannot find.
Know who I am?
You want me; yet you fear me. Why?
I'm there for you, right by your side.
Know who I am?
I'll take you places you've never been;
Nor will you go there; ever again.
Know who I am?
I am your shadow; your lonely friend,
I'm with you when time ends.
Know who I am?
You look for me in several ways;
Soon you'll reach and you will find;
For there is no escaping me;
For I am the victor over all.
Know who I am??
I AM DEATH!!

—Thresa Baker

OBSERVE THE ETERNAL REIGN

Listen to the Darkness
It is here all around us
Acknowledge its presence
For no one will escape it

Befriended by her Sincerity
Trusted within her Entirety
Look upon it as Royalty
As its truthfulness is its Sovereignty

For all heavenly stars, She portrays a window
As She hides our guilt within her shadows
Seeking out the night to accommodate our lust
So we may feel secure — To penetrate our fears

Believe in Her Power,
For Her Reign has No End
Yet beware of Her Beauty
Since the Darkness of our lives shall also descend

—A. Thomas Grecco

It was at the break of dawn,
when I heard you had gone.

It was only when we developed
a great bond.

That you were taken away,
Just like that,
You were gone!

—Rebecca Avila

FORBIDDEN LOVE

Alas! I had stayed in the past
With my ageless ancient romance,
Out of touch with reality
And my abandoned womanhood,
Vowing never to love anew,
But keep fresh flashing memories
With sentimental souvenirs,
And reverent recollections
Of my fallen conquistador
Until the death of my own days.

—Marilyn W. Bowser

DARE TO CARE

Deep within I hear a voice
To care is more than to share.
Love others, as I love you
Carry their load, touch and care.
Under the skin, behind the veneer
Sense what they feel and conceal.
I love you, love them, from within.
They are the prize, let my Spirit rise
Spill out concern, wash over them
Want what is best, endure the test.
Hurt when they hurt, cry for the lost.
Stay in there, willing to share;
My love never divides, only provides
Holds them in arms that never harm
Soaks up their pain, helps them gain
A love that always comes through.
So, hear my voice, make that choice.
Forget what they say, it's O.K.
Just be there to care.

—Rose Harrison

A TALENT FOR LOVE

The world waits not.
Mates and friends
Have their lives to live.

So give of self
And heed not the
Dangers of love.

Parents don't train
The talent to love.
They can only corrupt.

And we live with the rot,
Until the talent erupts
In an orgasm of life.

Practice your capacity for love
With everyone, openly with grace,
And the talent grows and lives.

Giving blooms of joy and happiness
Until your life rejoices in the never
Filling cup of personal fulfillment.

—Arthur Winslow

MY DEAR ONE

As the rain thudded
Upon bluest rock,

My dear one awaited
Love caught in his thoughts.

The strangeness about him
The sadness within,

Caused radiant tear
Pure shame in the wind.

—Eu-wanda Jenkins

DREAM COME TRUE

In the cool refreshing air
of a moonlit night,
he awaits for her there
to come into sight.
A young couple in love
and full of romance,
the Father above
gave these two a chance.
When they are together
how the sparks do fly,
forever and forever
their love will survive.
So be patient my friend
for true love never ends!

—Lori McEwen

HAUNTED HEART

Of all those sacred moments
which have marked "maturity,"
None so forced my growth
as our final separation.

Then,
years of quiet hope
barely daring to be thought,
Melded with dusty daydreams
—All dashed (their secret glow.)

Now,
redirection of the mind
set with tight control—
Muffles the spark
you left behind.

—Irene Todd Baldwin

CHANGE

I can change
myself easier than I
can change
You.

I can change
my hair to a raven black
But I cannot
change yours.

I can disguise
my heart to seem
happy but I
cannot help yours.

I could change
my time on earth
which would be
inconvenient but final.

—Kimberly L. Henry

FIRST DESIRE

He dazzles me with depth, honesty,
and sincerity.

I feel his smooth words flowing
through me like a fresh breeze.

My teacher, my listener, my friend.

I'm enticed with crisp white textures,
sweet smelling inks, and vibrant dreams.

Trusting words from my soul, for the
world to see.

—Kris A. Gillespie

ALONE

There you were alone.
Lost in a world you've never even known.
The wish of life did not come true,
at least not for you.
Alone is a word most people cannot explain,
but that word is all you have, plus pain.
Lost in a world so dark and so gray,
it wasn't your fault;
it just happened that way!
Alone is at last, and last is forever.

—Stacy Lovelady

I TRIED

The night was young, and my heart was too
My feelings consisted only of you

I tried to fight them, but to no avail
My life was fading, everything dim and pale

I laid my heart out for you to see
And all I wanted, was for you; to love me

You're so far away, but oh so near
I cry out your name, but you never hear

I tried my hardest, that's all I can do
When you leave, my love does too

Your reply was kind, honest and true
And for that, I thank you

—Kris Seitz

THE RAVAGES OF SILENCE

Yes, I sense your languid stare
and your deceiving eyes,
fooling not I, you show your inner soul to me.
You hope to distract
the thoughts that I want to think.

No, you cannot turn my gazing stare
away from far-off laughter or sounds of joy,
you cannot keep dark thoughts deep within
and tempt me to bring them out,
only to be angered at again and again.

The parting curtains of positive, hopeful thoughts
far outshine your darkened veil of ugliness,
the gloom you sought to instill in me.

I cast my view, my lot, for happiness
and truth; the bright light of tomorrow
and all that awaits me —
to turn off the darkness
and start the light, shining once again.

—Ruth L. Macejak

OASIS

You are the bright sun of my dark despair,
You are the sunshine, you are the sweet air,
With you next beside me the world is our chair,
You're my oasis of living in a desert of no care.

—Enrico Minnucci

THE LONELINESS SONG

How does it feel not to dream
How does it feel when the fat lady sings
What do you do when the leaves don't fall
Where will you be when you're not at the ball

How does it feel not to hate
When there's no more time, no more dates
Only black you see with your sights
No whiskers on kittens or mosquito bites

The days are over, the nights are gone,
And when chaos rings and everything's wrong
Enchant the lines of the loneliness song . . . .

—Matthew Richard Blasdell

TRUTH

He said, "Go, speak the truth, in love."
But the truth was painful. I'd make you cry.
Please remember, I love you so much.
Because of that, I told you a lie.

I thought you wouldn't understand
If I would tell you all I knew.
I was afraid that you'd run away
And all that we had would be through.

I never sensed how you longed to know
What had happened, and when,
So I pushed the hurt down deeper.
I hoped we'd be free of it then.

But today I noticed, where I'd buried the hurt,
A tangled flower now lives.
In the very center, there's a broken heart.
No fragrant perfume it gives.

Oh, Little Flower, I'm so sorry.
How I wish you were happy and free.
I never meant to break your heart.
It was that lie. That lie . . . in me.

—Claudia J. Lent-Boutchyard

REMEMBERING WHEN

I remember when, we used to be friends,
I remember when, we used to love,
I remember when, we used to be one,
I remember when, we broke-up.

It has been a year, since we were one.
Now we are just friends, like we were before.
But there is still a spark,
        that shows when we are alone.
What-ever happened to our love?
Was it me, or was it you?
I know it's impossible to ask for another chance,
Since that's all this relationship ever was — pour — chance!

I guess now all we can do is, cherish the memories.
But don't forget what used to be.
Now all I can do is —
        REMEMBER WHEN!!!

—Precious C.L. Alls

FINDING LOVE

Alone by the ocean just gazing above
I wonder how people ever find love . . .
Do I wish upon a distant star
or is it deep within my heart?
I've found that love does not come fast
but I know love comes and I know it lasts.
If I see the world with loving eyes
I think it's then I'll realize,
If loving's the way I'm going to be,
then that's how love will come to me.

—Marisa L. Cilento

DESIRES OF LOVE

Thoughts of you racing through my mind.
  Feelings for you pounding in my heart.
Wanting you in my life is tearing me apart.
Hoping you'll want me too,
Keeps me holding on.
Being unsure of how you feel,
Confuses me.
Seeing you and hearing your voice,
Warms my soul.
Loving you, hurts
Because, I need you to love me too.

—Malinda Parks

A VERY SHORT FOREVER

Eyes
opening
coming aware
slowly realizing
exploring possibilities
appreciating the significance
discovering overwhelming desire
labeling the ensuing experiences
taking each other for granted
following the daily grind
some turbulent times
forgetting the call
losing the drive
and feelings
and then
closing
eyes.

—Mark S. P. Turvin

LOVE

His warmth, his courage,
his compassion through out,
Made me love him with-
out ever a doubt.

Love is beautiful like a
fragile red rose,
Yes true is the love you
and I know.

Love is a sweetness that is
so real,
Wanting yet afraid to tell
how you feel.

But together we can with-
stand the test of time,
With our hearts and our
souls forever intertwined.

—Darla Alese Richards

FOR MOTHER

Our Mother is Gone.
But it's only her body,
that we won't see anymore.
What we have left of her,
is her spirit, in, which,
will always remain.
We will cherish the memories,
and not forget the sad times.
For Death has to come, and
when it does, it brings much
pain to all.
We, should not fear death,
But the Lord above.
For He knows, best, when
our work is done.

—Sheler Sherlest White

WITH THIS RING

You live long trust
And the wearer whose gift this ring
Be ever but happy
Though you may feel strong.

So on and on the spell
That's been wove
Keeps us together
Though we may grow old.

But here's to the red
Of your birthstone ring
The wear'er of my dreams.
Has a new song to sing.

Wear it and flash it.
With your wedding band
And it leaves no doubt
As to where era you stand

You've been won
And we're one.
Happy Anniversary Dear.

—Dan (Chief) Moody

TO: MY SWEET LITTLE MAN MATTHEW JAMES

Oh my little Son
I love you so.
I wrote this poem
So you could know.

Just how much
Your Daddy and I care,
with so much love
in our hearts to share.

I pray the Lord will
watch out for you,
when you've grown
and I'm unable to.

I watch you sleeping
so sweet and small.
Someday you will be a man,
and will have forgotten this all.

But deep in my heart
Forever will be,
The memory of when
it was just you and me.

—Cathy Schmitt

WHERE APRIL WAKENS THE WILLOW TREE

In verdant spring and summer glow
we walked together through the years,
In autumn chill and winter snow,
through times of joy and times of tears.
You're gone, my love, but your heart must know
my heart will follow wherever you go.
I know some day you'll walk with me
where April wakens the willow tree.

—Alice C. Walker

FIRSTS

A Mother remembers—
Her first pains . . . His coming into this world.
His first cry . . . The joy that he lives.
His first word . . . "Mama!"
His first steps . . . To her waiting arms.
His first parting . . . Going reluctantly into school.
His first love . . . The pain of its ending.
His first prom . . . How handsome he was!
His first shave . . . The faint fuzz of manhood.
His first car . . . Old, but he loved it.
Her first telegram . . . "Killed in action."
Her first tears . . . For her first-born.

—Deen Underwood

DADDY

Daddy, sometimes I want to lay my burden
at your feet
And let you make life more pleasant and sweet
The trials and temptations and troubles each day
Make me want to cry and sing my sorrows away.
I want to reach to you, Daddy;
I want to hold your hand
I want you to direct me, give my life a plan.
I want to sing you my blues, loud and clear
'Cause Daddy, I know you have a listening ear.
I want to tell you my sorrows, my pain
and my grief
Because Daddy, you always gave me
a lasting relief.
I want to hold you, hug you, love you
and kiss you.

Daddy, I miss you.

—Maureen Medlen Newman

ROSE, "ROSA," MY MOTHER!

ROSA, my mother, is like a rose;
she spreads her petals of opening love
to her husband, to her children and it
all shows, with a beautiful pose.

ROSA, yes, she is a very good mother;
the soft spoken rose that is
kind, protective, and loving;
she is always concerned with others.

ROSA, oh she is a wonderful mother;
a rose that is so beautiful even in color;
I love her like no other.

ROSA, my mother, is just like a beautiful pink rose;
and when I think of that rose when it is a bud,
blossoming into a beautiful rose; yes I think of
Rosa, as she flourishes and prospers; that beautiful
rose, who is no other, than my **MOTHER!**

(Rosa Lee Frazier)

—Patricia Ann Frazier Rivers

LITTLE GIRLS
Tiffany and Amber Stephansen

As the sun comes up
Two little girls arise
You hear the patter of little feet
Coming down the hall.

Their faces are all bright smiles
As they say "Good Morning"
Ready to start a busy day
Out in the day's sunshine

One is brunette with rosy cheeks
The other is blonde with wide blue eyes.
Such happy faces
With not a care in the world.

How we love them "Lord"
Just as you do too
Look after them and keep them safe.
Through out their happy lives.

—"Grandmother"

YESTERDAY, TODAY AND TOMORROW

Yesterday you strolled into my life.
A tall, handsome stranger
with a look of wildness
in your baby blues.
The love and gentleness you
showered upon me quickly
melted the ice from
around the heart.

Today we live, love and
laugh together.
Our souls have intertwined.
One's pain or happiness is
felt as deeply by the other.

Tomorrow our love will be stronger.
There will never be another
love as pure.

Memories live forever.
I will always remember yesterday.
Live today for you, knowing
you will be there tomorrow.

—Susan Stangl

THE LOVE I'LL NEVER HAVE

The love I'll never have is
smart, nice and sweet,
Intelligent and charming
The kind no one can
beat. He would be
sweet as honey that
money couldn't
buy. And he'd
be smart as
Einstein and
nicer than a valentine. Intelligent
and charming as a prince in
a story book the kind no one
would over look.
For this is only a dream,
The kind that makes a
person wonder and
say: May-be some
day I'll have the
love I thought
I'd never have.

—Nikki Stigger and Jenny Harris

THE LADY IN RED

The lady in red.
Is still in my bed.
She came into my life.
She became my wife.
We've been married for years.
I love her up to my ears.
She's still my love.
We've been hanging on to each other.
We've been getting old together.
Her dress has faded into a light red.
But she's still my lady in red.
Honey, let's go to bed.

—Paige Marie Westover

FRIENDSHIPS

Friendships weave a tapestry
of beauty to behold,
The threads are strong and beautiful,
In a blend mutual and bold.
Our lives are a blend of happiness,
Often misery and agony untold,
Friends are there to sympathize,
If a story needs to unfold.
The tapestry will endure
for a lifetime,
With blessings more precious
than gold.

—Bennie Garlock

MOTHER, DEAR MOTHER

As I sat beside the bed, her
breathing so hard.
Knowing she was suffering but
ever so soft with our Lord.
Thinking of our days together, in
the past, so dear.
No tomorrows, death so near.
Into her face, I took one long look,
Those long hands, had held the Good Book.
Not knowing when our time will come.
You have had a long life, some
die so young.
That seems bad, for our time together
we are glad.

Goodby Mother, Dear Mother

—Mary Jo Stewart

AS WE GROW . . .

As we grow . . .
along the way
we stumble and fall,
bumps and bruises
colds and cuts;
you help us
through it all.
As we grow . . .
through the years,
you help ease our fears
although it may go unsaid,
how much we really care
you're not just a doctor,
You're our best friend!
"As we grow . . ."
Dedicated with love and kindness, a very special
doctor, W. Jud Fisher, D.O. Thanks to you!

—CIKH

THE SPEED OF LIGHT

The speed of light
    zooming through time
Throughout all of
    eternity.
Endlessly roaming
    to the ends of the earth
Never ceasing
    to ever stop going.
In and out
    weaving through and between
The shreads and shards
    of time.
Alone and cold
    endless and free
Chasing and looking
    for something unseen.

—Jennifer Colvin

Like the morning sunrise,
Like the fresh sweet dew,
Life is coming homeward
    from the sky to you.

Love's the cricket's new song
    in the knee high grass
Joy's the music sunward
    from the heart to shine.

Lately I have found the
    joy of inborn peace.
Love's new life awakening
    has its time for me.

By the joyous dawning,
By the hope-filled days,
Love's pure music sunward
from the heart to shine.

—Bernadette McClain

WITHOUT A SOUND

Autumn's multi-colored leaves
    wafting down,
Once green summer symbols
    falling to ground,
Without pomp, ceremony,
    without a sound.

Fragile filaments
    woven 'round and 'round,
Eight-legged art work,
    artifice to astound,
Coffin made by creature
    without a sound.

Marble's erected,
    weighs many a pound,
Cold rain is falling,
    memories abound.
I weep and say goodbye
    without a sound.

Brisk breezes blowing,
    billowing around,
Swirling my memories
    into a mound.
Leaves covering your grave
    without a sound.

—Bettie R. Dycus

LEAVES ARE FALLING

Leaves are falling everywhere,
    I try to gather them with
        great care;
The more I rake,
The more they fall.
I don't think this will ever
    end at all

—Erika Lee Harrington

THE HAWAIIAN IN ALASKA

The white world glistens,
    bathed in serenity.
The Snow Queen's realm
    stretches to infinity.
Her black lace dress of frozen trees
    is silhouetted against a frozen sky.
And my mind is still,
    lost in an alien beauty.

—Andrea Lewis

ON YOUR WINGS

If I had your wings
    I could learn to fly
I would leave the ground
And touch the lining of the sky.

Your wings are so strong
They lift me up on high
The wind is in my face
Water wells up in my eye.

Oh! How I envy you so,
You're not pinned, to the ground.
In one thought, you can go,
With only the slightest of sound.

Please, do not leave me
Now that I've; experienced
    this thing.
You hold the key,
On the tip of your wing.

—T. R. Jerome

MEDITATION

Upon this mossy bank I lie, —
    The summer sun is low;
The rippling lake before my eye
Reflects the radiance of the sky,
    And spreads a heavenly glow.

Enchanted, long I fondly gaze,
    Wrapped in sweet Lethe dreams,
Lost are the clouds of by-gone days,
Amid the golden beaming rays,
    Of what the present seems.

Those skies of dreamy violet,
    What amaranthine bloom?
What varied jewel deeply set
In lights of heaven's own covenant,
    lightens the nether gloom?

How blest we were to crown our days
    with radiance from above;
Along life's rude and rugged ways,
To scatter warm, effulgent rays,
    Here's peace and reverant love.

—Bruce D. Heald

FOG

All cold and very misty
I look right down the street at night
What do I see,
Fog I see
All cold and very misty.

—Steve Mason

FOR ME SHE PAINTED

For me
She painted, colors blending,
Open field with flower standing,
Fusing light and shadow with the dawn.
And free
Her spirit guides the brush,
Gentle strokes that never rush,
Musing on the form until it's done.

Her lines
Are graceful, simple, pure,
Young and fresh, but ever sure,
Knowing destination from the start.
And shines
The star and moon below
As signature for all to know,
Who find themselves enraptured by her art.

—Daniel L. Fleming

RAINY SPRINGTIME DAYS

When I first saw a picture of you
I was more impressed with what you knew.
But on one rainy, springtime day,
I finally saw your image from far away.
And using every wishing well and falling star,
I wished the distance to be less far.

When the day finally came to meet you,
I knew that all my opinions were true.
Your goodness had been greatly underestimated
And with your smile, my resistance was devastated.

I don't want your love as a meaningless fling.
When thinking of you, my heart sings.
Your happiness and safety is important to me
As I thought no man's could ever be.
All my deep love and caring for you is real.
And, someday, all this I'll need not conceal.

—Laura Kelley

NATURE HIGH

I found a place that is high above,
with endless waterfalls that flow with love,
a thousand trees reach for the sky,
a refuge for the birds that fly.

The streams that flow across the land,
flow together and make a stand,
a hundred pools in which to see,
the person you have come to be.

The sun's rays seemingly heaven sent,
reflect through the leaves in a wondrous tint,
and as the wind wanders through the trees,
there rides many scents upon her breeze.

For once you have happened upon this place,
and grasp its majestic grace,
the love which you experience there,
is the love you can always share.

—Dawn Desonée Webb

THE OLE HANGIN' TREE

For over a century,
proudly it stood;
A tall stately tree of
pine scented wood.
Legend says it once was
an "Ole Hangin' Tree,"
But that story hardly seems
likely to me;
For I thought I heard it say
through the breeze
As it whispered softly to the
far distant trees,
"I'm just an old tree that has
out-lived my time;
I'd rather be known as
The Old Lonesome Pine."

—Wilma M. Grissom

MOONWALK

Past the mighty oak,
standing tall beside
a place called home,
day courts the shadow's tide.
Twilight is fast fading
on painted hill,
darkness settling down
the mockingbird's trill.
Deer cross the meadow
at forest edge,
crickets play their banjos,
beyond a rocky ledge.
Night breaks forth
in starry song,
the moon walks round
its circled throne,
a reminder of the sun
to return in glory,
when the dawn awakens
the sparrow's story.

—Ronda D. Packard

NATURE'S MAGIC MOMENTS

There are moments in nature,
Almost magic it seems;
Events to be treasured,
And called up in dreams.

A walk in spring
On a balmy day,
Discovering green sprouts
Promising flowers on the way.

A lazy summer afternoon
Under a bright blue sky,
Imagining favorite places
In clouds drifting by.

The pungent smell
Of burning leaves,
Wafting by
On an autumn breeze.

The first snowfall of winter
As you look out and see
The world all around you
Covered in crisp, white purity.

—Diane Karp

THE WORTH OF A SMILE

Give an extra smile away;
  Go an added mile each day;
Sow the seed — for joy it brings
When it's sent on loving wings.

None resists so great a light —
Balm, magnetic, to the sight.
Smiles, accomplishing their goal,
Light up windows of the soul.

Wealth we own is so much gold —
Gives no comfort until sold.
Life is richer — more worth while,
When we give away a smile.

—Evelyn Garrett

THE EYE OF THE NEEDLE

No leafy boughs,
  No glowing lights,
No ho ho ho,
  No Christmas night,

No shining star,
  For kings to see,
No manger bed,
  No Calvary,

Had one young maid,
  Like a rich man said,
"I cannot, Lord,"
  And hung her head.

—Anne E. Bolles-Beaven

THE TOWER OF IGNORANCE

The chatter of a crowded room
  Echos through time.
Yet in my head, only the sound
of foolish children lets me
Know man still exists.

Let me know, Oh God of Man,
Where temptation lies.
Use time to show impatience.
Use a mirror to show conceit.

Let me see, Oh God of Man,
that love still survives.
In a world of lust and lies,
Let me know that our knowledge
    will thrive.

—Rebecca L. Martin

WAITING

I'm just sitting right here
  Right here in the lobby
Waiting for him
To be buried
I will miss him
So much
But I hope that he's happy
To be in heaven
With god
God will care for him,
Love him so much
And probably
Answer his prayers
So he's probably
In paradise
Thinking about us

—Cari Christenson

PEOPLE TO PEOPLE

Father to Son
  Mother to Daughter
    We all become one in the eyes of the Son
    We spent our lives living for tomorrow,
as yesterday slips away forever gone
        People to People
        Father to Son
        Mother to Daughter
We all are as one under the Sun

—Donald R. Adams

TIME

Time, time happens. You know it's
  going on, but still you wait.
  You see the clock spinning like dust
devils on the hill. Wait. Still you wait?
  You wait for right time, but no, it's
wrong time.
        Time! Time! Time!
  The time has come. The dust has cleared.
You go to see. Time didn't wait for me.
  All that's left is dust, no more
time for me.
  Time! Time! I need time!

—Chyrele A. Singletary

THE BEREAVEMENT

I saw angel, at the time a babe was he.
  He was soft and pink and downy like his mother hoped he'd be.
She longed to caress him and put him to her breast
But tearfully she knew we both need rest . . .

How long can three hours be?
It seemed like an eternity.
How much suffering Lord, can a broken body endure?
But might this pain be your plan for her cure?

There I stood at the mother's side
All the while wishing I could but hide
Hide from a world that allowed such pain
Hide from my God as though in shame.

The hours did pass and more till at last
These words burnt into me and caused me to curse
Our baby got tired
And he's gone on to rest . . .

—Jean Gonsoulin Toepfer

THREE GIFTS

I was looking out of the window just watching the rain
  As it beat and ran down against the window pane
Suddenly the rain stopped, then the snow and sleet began to fall
And I could hardly see out of the window at all

I thought what great gifts God sent down for us to see
Gifts of mythical beauty not made by you or me
Gifts that are uncreated by the hands of man
But created by God to fall upon the land

First God sent the rain, then the snow and sleet followed rapidly
Only God can do all this, send the rain, snow and sleet that's three
"Three Gifts" from God for all the world to behold
"Three Gifts" that are more precious than silver or gold

Thank you dear God for the rain pure precious water from the sky
Thank you for the snow, dear God, the earth it purifies
Thank you for the sleet, truly it gives moisture to the sod
"Three Gifts" sent to the world from heaven, we thank you dear God.

—Annie May Bruner

WHERE DOES THE SKY END?

There it ends — bright though
  Reflecting. Strange, dismal land
Still, heaven awaits.

—**Mark Weisenborn, age 9**

GOD'S GIFT

G God's gift is very special,
O Oh! Yes it really is,
D Does it have to do with people
  Or just a simple quiz?
S So why don't people worship Him,
  And why don't people care
  That sometimes God gets despaired?

G Go out there and try to help some people
  And maybe you can get them
  to go to the steeple.
I If you want to give it a try
  It's all right, you don't have to be shy.
F For you can help as much as I.
  So go out there and give it a try.
T This message is over I must say,
  But I hope it will help you each and every day.

—**Heather E. King**

DEAR LORD

While lying here all alone
  all I do is cry
I pray that God will talk to me
  again there's no reply
Dear Lord have I done something wrong
  have I not tried to be strong
Is it written for me to be alone
  to never love again
Do I deserve this broken heart
  a pain without no end
I've tried so hard to do what's right
  to never go astray
You know I'm dying deep within
  more and more each day
Take my hand, lead the way
  I will walk with you
Show me to the promised land
  where only skies are
  blue!

—**Barbara Cross**

MASTER

Lord, how masterful you are.
 You are creator, owner and lord over all that you survey —
From the highest peak to the lowest valley,
From ocean to mighty ocean,
All belongs to you.
You, alone, have the power to bless with many riches or to
    repossess those riches if they are abused.
Help me, Lord, to praise you in all things and to give the glory
    to you.
For without you, existence is meaningless.
You, alone, hold the key to everlasting life, hope, and peace.
Forgive my denials and failures.
Teach and strengthen me to change would be failures into
    successes;
That all efforts may be in accordance to your perfect will,
And that they may be pleasing in your sight.

I will praise the Lord with all my heart,
For no one is more worthy than He.

—**Stefanie Baker**

THE BEGINNING

The Adam in me
  wants Eve to see
  that i want to be
  the apple of Eve's eye.

—**Doug Presnell**

YOUR CHRISTIANITY IS SHOWING

Your Christianity is showing,
 the things you do,
the things you don't do.
People in need see you true.

Do you give your best
or just enough to pass the test
of everybody watching?
People in need see you true.

Is your time more important
doing the things you want to do?
Or is it spent for Jesus
shared with the multitude
of people in need — like me.

—**Aleta D. Nolan**

GOD EVER LOVES

God cares for me
 I am His child;
I trust in His
Abiding love.

When trials of life
Bog me down,
I just hang on
To God's strong hand.

He'll never leave me
We are told
So I am secure
Within His fold.

God ever loves me;
I am His child;
As I sing and praise Him,
He looks down and smiles.

—**Betty Ann Bilbrey**

THE CHRISTMAS ANGEL

The little girl sat
 upon the church steps
alone, and quiet, and cold —
while carolers sang,
joyously and rosy-cheeked,
those oh, glorious songs of old.

Shoppers hurried by,
paying no heed nor care
to the small, coatless child
huddled upon the church stair.

Darkness came, and thus the light,
Oh! And Christmas morning had come!
though —
there was a small child
asleep on the stair,
fragile skin as white as the snow.
Or was she asleep?
No, her little soul of love
had flown during the night
up to Heaven above.

—**Christal Brown, age 13**

PRESSURE

Pressure, pressure, burning hot
  See who's with it, see who's not
Building up and boiling over
See the rage from deep within
That's what happens
When you keep it in
Locked deep inside, no one can know
Now there's too much with no place to go
See it burst, see it fly
Now people start asking
What the Hell? And why?
Little pieces everywhere
Do you wonder? Do you care?

      —Kristin A. Ferguson

IS IT WORTH IT?

The wind was weeping;
  The clouds were crying;
All through the countryside
The tissues were flying.

"The trees are dead!"
The poor rabbit said.
"It's pollution that killed them,
And that's something to dread."

There'd been millions of trees
That were centuries old;
To the animals there
They were worth more than gold.

      —Emily Stitt, 14 years old

Once upon a time
  There were no wars
And no people to cause them

Life was pure, Life was simple
Creatures lived a lovely life
Until people came and tore it down

We need a door, or a hole, or a window
We could climb through it and rebuild
our world
There's a Light shining at the end of
the tunnel
We can climb through it and save
ourselves

      —Tracy Spielman

TIME TO CHANGE

The sky so gray,
  No children play,
No sound around,
Blood on the ground.

It's all the same,
That sad, sad, game,
The great big blast,
Now life has past.

They never learned,
That what they yearned,
Was up above,
The gift of love.

Before we see the final end,
Let's take the time to all be friends,
Let's all join up and take a stand,
So peace is spread throughout the land.

      —Krystina R. Shepherd

FLOWER CHILDREN

Children on a hill searching.
  Communes,
producing abstract snatches
of fragmented joy.
Fulfillment denied.

      —Phyllis E. Beaumonte

BOMBAY

Go gently into this good night;
  as travel to
    changes to through,
    gaze into sorrow soul.

Turn tragedy's corner, full face.
  See inside
    what's begging there,
  touch this open wound.

Breathe inside this poor man's musk.
  Let it tell
    Your heart its woe.
  This scent will leave its mark.

The street transformed, becomes lifeline
  that can not
    bear the weight
      of all a country's sins.

      —Margaret M. Paris

IN THE VALLEY OF OUR HEARTS' DELIGHT

The quiet buzzing of a bee,
  The flowers growing beneath a tree,
And rivers flowing to the sea
In the valley of our hearts' delight.

The scent of yellow daffodils,
The greenness of the rolling hills
Are jarred by harsh construction drills
In the valley of our hearts' delight.

The buildings tower toward the skies,
There's sadness as our valley dies
And sorrow filling empty sighs
In the valley of our hearts' delight.

The smog and smoke pollute the air,
The trees cut down without a care.
Our forests are now bleak and bare
In the valley of our hearts' delight.

      —Lisa Marie Calderon

BETTER THAN WAS GIVEN TO US

The sun goes its merry way from beginning
  to end of day.
Valley's golden and unplowed, sit like gold
  upon a crown.
Then darkness drapes its cloth of night,
  stars like diamonds is its sight.
The Earth green and blue as from space is
  seen, like a jewel on a raven's wing.
We are lucky if I may be so bold?
  To have this world, and all it holds!
But we make war and pollute the land, will
  our children think living here so grand?
No, I say! and stop we must and give to our
  children, better than was given to us!!

      —Lynn Pacione

You cannot see my smile
   In the darkness
As you sleep.

You may not even be able
   To see it in the sun
As we walk.

But when we're apart
   And horizons make the search infinite
Make yourself warm

And You'll be my smile.

—**William R. Euller**

THE WAY I FEEL

Ever since you gave me
   that glance,
I thought,

This heart needs a second chance.
Look me in the eyes and tell me no lies:

Should we really try?
Sometimes I want to laugh;
Sometimes I want to cry.

I don't know what to do
because I really do love you.

—**Beth Gibbs, age 14**

LOVE IS A DREAM

Love is a dream
   in a world of confusion
Love is a dream
   that comes true for some
Love is a dream
   that is easily shattered
Love is a dream
   that keeps us going
Love is a dream
   which can never die

—**Melanie L. Packer**

LOVE

This eternal light of love
   For you extends.
I see within your soul
Through the windows
Of your eyes.
My heart vibrates a rhythm
Of passion.
Endless harmony is ours,
Embracing the future
We share.

—**Gee**

LOVE

I've been waiting all
   my life, just for you.
   It's you I Love,
I thought you Loved me
   I need a Love,
that is mine,
   that is true,
one that will last a lifetime
   Maybe that
will consist of
   me and you.

—**Melissa K. Doden**

ONE

Two individual souls,
   Two backgrounds opposite
      our needs equal and same.

Two people, man and woman
      horizon of husband and wife.
Two acts of love; in hand in soul.
   two acts; one of the other
      our hand deserved of our soul.

Two lives of opposite, brought together.
Two lives, made as one.
Two souls joined,
   our hand the sign in act.

Our Two Is One.

End.

Written for Stephanie.

—**Mark Franks**

EYES OF STONE

We've had fights before but never
   like this.
      We've always made up,
      It always ended with a kiss.

   But here you stand before me
with a face so cold,
   With no emotions in your eyes
of stone.

   What's running through your
mind, don't you even care?
   What are you thinking of,
what's behind that icy glare?

   I'm about to leave you
and all that we have here,
   And I'll be like you and
not shed a tear.

   But just once before I
go and leave you alone,
   Just let me see behind
your eyes of stone.

—**Danyal Nelson**

ETERNITY

You're my special someone,
   The one I've always dreamed of,
The one I want to be with forever,
and the one I'll always love.

The love I feel for you,
can't be expressed in anyway.
I want to be with you,
each and every day.

You're there when I celebrate,
and when I feel blue.
It seems you're always at my side,
we're like one, not two.

Our love will never die,
I know that this is true,
Because everytime I see you,
I fall in love anew.

If I could have this one wish,
Do you know what it would be?
For us to be together,
for all Eternity . . . .

—**Becky Lidlow**

ALONE

Alone is an eagle with nowhere to fly,
Alone is a star with no sky.
Alone is at night when no one's awake,
Alone is being in an earthquake.
Alone is sitting and reading silently,
Alone is getting in a fight . . . violently.
Alone is when an eighth grader thumps you,
Alone is when your girlfriend dumps you.

Written in 1988 at age 9
—Nathan R. Woodruff

ALONE

The rain fell from the sky and kissed my face
each drop reminding me of days gone by.
I'll not forget for I don't want to try.
So many times we stood in this same place
and many times we shared a warm embrace.
We counted stars away up in the sky,
you're gone from me and only God knows why.
And now, for me, life is an endless pace.
The wedding vows we knew could not go wrong
for God did bless each day for you and me.
The fun we had, the love we found is gone.
Oh rain drops, give thy comfort now to me.
My time with you was not so very long.
I'll walk alone, for this was meant to be.

—Deloise B. Haugen

LINGERING LOVE

The heart is bruised, the pain austere,
When Death leaves one alone . . . .
To never hear that welcome step,
Nor that voice on the 'phone;
To never wash those clothes again,
Nor ever make that bed . . . .
To eat the breakfast all alone
Becomes a daily dread.
To never fill that coffee cup,
Nor share a glass of wine . . . .
Nor lay the clothing on that bed
Before you're off to dine;
To never see that Devilish Smile,
Nor hear that "laugh with ease" . . . .
My, aren't we glad for Super Times
To relive as we please?

—June DeFaye Adams

SOMETHING MORE

Every time I see you, I see it in your eyes.
Something that could have been everything,
    turned out to be a lie!

I don't know why I do things
    and often wonder why.
When I try to answer that question,
    all I do is cry.

Whenever I think of you
I can feel how much you cared,
It always made me feel better,
    knowing you were there.

I'm sorry that I hurt you
and you've heard this all before.
I tried to give you something,
    but I couldn't give you more!

—Valeree Jackson

EYES

Your eyes are like the twilight,
You are my light.
They are a shimmering pool,
An emerald jewel.
You are my Love,
You are a beautiful flying dove.
I Love You,
We are the perfect two.

—Courtney Baity

TRUE LOVE

You're the perfect person for me,
I'll describe and you'll agree.
You're loving, caring, gentle and kind,
You're the best woman I could ever find.
You're someone to whom I can talk,
Hold hands, kiss, argue, and walk.
But of course we'll make it through,
What I'm trying to say is
        I LOVE YOU!

—Jerry Strickland

TOMORROW

Day after day, night after night
My heart cries out for your love.
You've changed your mind with time
I wish that I knew why.
What did I do to push you away?
I've never more than loved you —
And mostly from afar.
I want to change your mind again
And, I hope, change your heart.
But if you can't love me
Say so now
And I'll say "good-bye";
But go on loving you
With hope that someday
You will love me,
And need me,
And call me.

I'll be waiting —
I believe in tomorrow.

—Susan M. Lewis

FOR CHRISTIE TOO

To sing together to the stars
Sharing our heartbeats
Listen to our strength

Loving for peace
Moist, water in the dust
Growing toward luxuriant calm.

Impulse, holding
touching . . . celebrating the softness
timeless.

Separate, yet together
Learning to give
affirm and understand

Dancing in a mutual
folkdance of cooperation
richness in poverty.

Achieving exquisite
communication lifted
by love endured.

—Michael S. Roth

THE FATE OF YOUR OWN

Though you have no reason to be
Something is expected you see
Life is not a pleasure
It is a test
A test to prove
Without a doubt
That you are worthy
Of first being in
And then being out
Your life is but a mystery
Constantly overwhelming
Totally annihilating
Every personal image
The one single feeling
The fate of your own
Ending in escape

—Ronald E Makinson

THE WANDERER

I am the Wanderer
Oh yes, the Wanderer.
I am he who walks the earth
    who follows life's own paths
I am he who climbs the mountains
    who descends into the valley's pass
I am he who sails the sea
    swaying on ship's tall mast
I am he who knows yet all
    he who has walked the past.
I am he who follows the trails
    the yet untrodden tracks
I am he who knows all ways
    from beginning to the last
I am he who has walked the sands
    who knows the desert traps
I am he who has seen the beginning
    who has seen the after-math.
Oh yes, my friend,
I am the Wanderer.

—Cassandra Buela

THE WAY THE ROAD TURNS

The eighteen wheeler churns through fog
    Tired clunking mass
Carries burdens of steel
The weary driver's cargo delivered

Deposits himself on the back stoop
Leaving boots on pasty linoleum
Stale coffee and overdue bills
Await the return

Demanding alimony and child support
Stuffed in envelopes and sent away
The raw wounds
Mount and throb

Time of youth, the tender wife
Hearth and palace on Ashton Lane
Blessed children
Gathered 'round his knee

Betrayed by time and dying dreams
Love extinguished, the moonlight pales
Wave and gather your eighteen wheels
And follow the turn of the road

—Kelly Hostetter

CHANGED

"Innocent, vulnerable, naive," of her was said.
Well, let it be known, that she is dead!

In her place, one not quite so pure.
This one thing, she knows for sure.

No one passes the wall inside,
It is now well fortified.

She learned that trust is for a fool,
and love, to some, only a tool.

Something said to get their desire,
And saying, "I love you," makes them a liar.

The new is not the old remade.
Though both are made of human clay.

What once was, can now never be.
The better of the two? I leave to thee.

—L. K. Seaton

A CROW WITH MANY FACES

Lonesome little child
    Torn from those she loves—
Taken as an infant
By a flock of lovely doves.
They appeared with all their splendor
And plucked her from my touch—
They raised her as they wanted
And . . . I love her oh so much.
So many miles between us
We're not allowed to write—
They've filled her mind with lies
And kept her from my sight.
Hope still fills my heart
My love for her still grows—
Little did she know . . .
Those doves were only crows.

—Virginia A. Carruthers

GET FUNKY NOT JUNKY DON'T USE DRUGS!

I'm balanced like a cat,
    I always land on my feet;
And when I hear those drums,
I get with the beat.

To rock and roll all day,
To rock and roll my way,
When I hear those drums play,
To this I say Okay!

So get funky,
Don't get junky,
And have fun when you get funky,
And not junky.

—Joanna Laws, age 10

Cold and clammy
    I rested my head against the cement pillow.
    The angels pranced by like dancing devils
For I was consumed by evil.

    The evil nipped at my lips and fingertips
Til I welcomed him in.
    It made me feel warm
As it burned at my soul.

    People like yourself look down at me.
You stare at the evil in me with disgust
    All because I have been taken.
My soul is captured inside a brown bag.

—Kenneth Darling

UNTITLED

In the late afternoon
As I lay on my bed
I watch the last rays of Sun
Slip past my window
I am bathed in golden light
I grieve for the past
I hunger for the future
And I revel in the present
For I am bathed in golden light

    —Charles A. Ross, Jr.

I AM WEARY

I am weary for no purpose
I go about my dreary
Little challenge, but sustenance

Security until my insecurity
    becomes secure.
Will it ever? Yes.
Perhaps not when I am
    there to see it.

Come early, release!

    —Paul M. McKenzie

REFLECTIONS

I sit by a mirror
And what do I see?
A face showing sadness
Is staring at me.

I think to myself
How can this be?
I'm not unhappy
I'm healthy and free.

My friends are the best
They're thoughtful and kind
And loaded with talent
Not easy to find.

So I look in the mirror
Now what do I see?
A face with a smile
That's the way it should be.

    —Dorothy Dorffi

BLONDS HAVE MORE FUN
I
I maybe a little bit older,
A little bit older than you.
But I like to be a blond
A blond just like you.
II
Some folks often tell me,
That blonds have more fun.
So I want to be a blond,
And have more fun like you.
III
So I'm going to bleach my hair
The same color as yours.
So I can be the belle,
Of the party next year.
IV
Now that I'm a blond
My brown hair won't do.
For I'm having more fun,
Like blonds often do.

    —Viola Hoyt

THE FLINCH

There is no illusion, it's a state of confusion.
Caught in between — something I've only seen,
Yet, right in the midst of an omnipresent bliss.
Came on like a cinch, got lost in the flinch.
The bliss can be found, it's still around —
hiding in overwhelm, since the flinch
holds the realm. Waiting and wondering
isn't very fun, maybe a flinch should be
allowed to shun. Suppose it isn't proper
to stop this itching, so hold a
smile and keep on flinching.

    —Michael Lafferty

WHAT DO YOU SEE?

What do you see when you look at me?
Do you see the wrinkles brought on by time,
Or the laughter behind the old laugh lines?
The crows feet put there by the smiles,
Or the gray in my hair brought on by the strife
Of fighting and working all of my life?
What do you see when you look at me,
Someone important in somebody's life,
A mother, grandmother, sister or wife?
All of these things I hope you can see,
For someday, you will look just like me!

    —Melba Winegeart Judah

MY DREAMS

My dreams may not mean much to others
But they seem to do alright for me
Sometimes Dreaming is all I ever do
A special moment to escape from reality

I can set my visions on a far away place
Or just around here, close to home
Sometimes when I'm Dreaming, I feel so good
When I dream, it seems I never feel alone

I can climb upon high mountains
Or fish in swift rapids on a creek
It seems I can do anything I want to
I can be whoever I want to be

Dreamland will always be my place of shelter
Whenever Reality becomes too hard to stand
I hope that I will be able to Dream On Forever
Keeping my sights on some far away Land

    —Damon Hofmeister

STRANGERS IN THE MIRROR

All our lives will increase two-fold
Before the dreams that we behold,
While all the books like open minds,
Will be left for us to read and define.

Then all the nightmares will grin and look
About the dreams that we mistook;
For all our lives we've taken tasks
To form our plays and wear our masks.

Then all the children come out to play
When thunderstorms begin the day;
To walk upon the endless fields
Grasp onto time and what it yields.

Then never take a moment's glance
For without our legs we shouldn't dance
And all the dreams would be something else,
If we weren't strangers to ourselves . . . .

    —Logan Douglas

FERNERY

O' Master
What is this
That can make me on
   a bright Spring day
Crave that Land of deeper silence . . .
In the night
Childhood fears·of ghosts return
When each shadow is an enemy
Coming to slay the soldiers
   by the bed
And after the soldiers are slain
What becomes of the general?
Salvation comes
When one human sound in the night
Dispels the sadness and childhood
   madness . . .
You say Father, there are no ghosts?
Then what is that strange creature
Smiling just behind you!!

—Rollie C Dowdle

TIME EXISTS

Among life's inconsistencies
   always reliable.
Constant, despite the varied
    perceptions of its passage
Not dwelling earthly as matter
    yet measured concretely
All entities relative to
    some point in its vastness.
Never in variance
   though seemingly so
As a minute quantity
    valued in terms of the beholder
May bear with it, into itself
Memories to color its future
    dull or bright
Definition dependent,
   as always, on the
Ever-changing perception
   of its never-changing
      passage.

—Myra Buller

DISTANT LIGHT

As I look out in the darkness,
  I see a distant light.
Through the trees it calls me,
in the dark of night.
I know not where it comes from,
but silently it calls.
Can happiness or sadness,
dwell within its halls?
It seems to beckon to me,
"Come follow my cold blue light."
As in a dream of long ago,
it penetrates the night.
What strange fascination.
Sinister thoughts begin to form.
Far, though imagination takes me,
it will all end with morn.
Not to return again till darkness,
this distant, haunting light.
Calling, calling to me,
in the dark of night.

—Don L. Fritz

TRANSPORT

The hunched, resonant stir
  of the vast ocean that is air,
hums softly beyond the reef of my wall.

I await my passage
to another island of humanities
making in the form of the earth-faathers,
remembered from long ago.

Leeward lies the way
and green and blue lights behind
lessen my fear while
no clocks are ticking.

There is a sun that cannot be seen
thus too the shades that rise
from off of Dracos tail,
and momentarily bite the night.

—Brian McMillan

SPIRIT'S PRESENCE

There's a ghost spirit in a presence,
  A deep, dark light.
Ghost, fly away and sway,
  Out of sight.

"Flying, Flying, I will go"
  He cries.
Sounding like winds,
  Out of the skies.

Going, leaving like heavy
  Rains.
As the spirit leaves; all I feel is
  Heavy pains.

He comes for another
  Presentation.
The spirit touches me; a burning
  Sensation.

He leaves again and never
  Returns.
Thank God he doesn't; for I never
  feel his burns.——Again!

—Melissa Fite

NIGHTLY VISITOR

Beneath the ground in twisted tunnels
Leading to graveyard tombs
Staying underground 'til dark
Hidden in decaying rooms

At night their loathsome, rubbery flesh
Is seen in the moonlight
Dirty, blood encrusted claws
Dig up the graves at night

Canine features watch around
For unwary midnight men
But as they watch, they see me not
For I'm beyond their ken

After feeding from open graves
As I stand—watching—scowling
They stare up at the silvery moon
And as one all start howling

Then as the sun begins to rise
They creep off one by one
These nightly visitors known as Ghouls
All gone when dinner's done

—Geoffrey Viney

INDECISION

I sit here without a clue,
Wondering what I should do.

I feel like I'm on a test,
Wondering what is coming next.

I sit here so perplexed.
An on going quest, to do my best.

I look for something new,
But I haven't got a clue.

I'm looking through my mind,
A poem I am to find.
I wish I could push the rewind.

Fast forward would be great,
But now it's getting late.

I know I must not pause,
For this would be the last clause.

   —Michelle Bradley, age 12

YELLOW FANTASY

When I dream—I dream of
Yellow stars and chocolate bars
I dream of yellow roses
And green garden hoses

When I dream—I dream of
Comic books and gourmet cooks
I dream of yellow yarn
And a big red wooden barn

When I dream—I dream of
Yellow hay and places far away
I dream of being alone
With just a dog and his bone

When I dream—I dream of
Green garden hoses watering my
Freshly planted yellow roses
And that my friend is my
YELLOW FANTASY

   —Elaine Pingel

WHAT MATTERS

I saw her once today
With her face turned to the sky,
Her thoughts were far away
I needed not wonder why;

You see for her and many more
The way they seem to feel,
No challenge left, nothing to explore
What in this world is real; . . .

The cheerful words that smother lies
Held deep within by many,
The secrets hidden in their eyes
You could buy for just a penny;

The deep warm feeling
Of a job well done,
The burdensome dealings
When you're on the run; . . .

It doesn't really matter
What took her thoughts away,
The only thing that matters
Is how she lives her day.

   —Del Robinson

LADY LOVE

Another day pass';
a restless soul weeps;
tearing for those who cannot cry.
She feels the pain;
of never having lived;
the fear of those who shall not die.

Birds nestle;
under green growing leaves;
a song is not to be found.
Her whispering voice;
in their listless breath;
her love cannot be bound.

So she weeps;
with the coming of the night;
escaping those who taint her sight.
Soon she flies on wings of gold;
flying free she broke the mold . . .

   —Mitchell Carter

FEELING COME — YET UNSEEN

Felt the slightest tingle
Went from toes to fingers
Like a fresh of rushing air
Thoughts from soul did bare
Winging their way to someone
A good feeling was said and done.
Nothing was about, even no one!
That went over and was gone
But thoughts sure linger on
Those that will be remembered
Started way back in September.
Until the way grew long —
Many a time without a song —
Because the road was weary,
And the days were dreary.
Thus was how the tale went on —
Because someone wasn't along! —
For somewhere down the way.
Not able to see — feel the rushing air
Meeting one another some other day!

   —Nellie Mae Crawford

FREE

I want to be free from this cage
 I don't belong here.
among the tears, disappointments and pain.
 I strike out at you, clawing.
wanting to tear you apart
 for hurting me,
waiting for you to open the lock
 on this cage around my heart,
so I can finally escape.
 I don't see you as my protector.
You are my enemy, now.
 I will not allow you to get
close enough to hurt me, again.
 I will lie here and pretend
I'm not aware,
 Then when you're not paying attention,
I will pounce on you and
 tear you limb from limb,
and then just walk away
    finally free!

   —Linda Sugalski

WHAT IF THERE WERE NO HOPE?

What if there were no hope, at all?
If all that we ever did and lived
Was as soon forgot — forever lost
The grandest light was but shadow dim.

To despair of our little children
They just happen, fickle fate
From nowhere to nothing, nohow
Hopelessness from start to futile end.

Thanks to the God of light and love
For He has ordained our rescue
In His Son, darkness did die
We embrace light, eternal love, hope!

Amen.

—Robert L. Larson

NONE SO BLIND . . . .

Dried up and shriveled are the autumn leaves;
Some blindly see but an annoying mess
And miss the beauty that they yield
While criticizing nature's dress;
They tread upon the fallen dead that lie there
on the ground, And deafened ears never hear.
Their lovely crunching sound! The lifeless forms
are gathered and cremated on a pile,
But the unique smell that they offer
goes unnoticed all the while! Only they who seek
for beauty with the spirit and the soul will
find it everywhere . . . . .
Among the Young . . . . .
Among the Old . . . . .

—Katheryn Clarke

Christmas is coming, let's
all gather round,
And sing praises to Jesus,
The Saviour we found.
Let's give Him the glory for
all He has done;
For forgiving our sins,
Yes, everyone.
God sent forth His Son, for
You and for me,
Then allowed Him to die, so
that we, could go free.
This wonderful gift, we can
all receive,
There is nothing to do, just
simply believe.

—J. Wilson Jones

DAILY PRAYER

Dear God above . . .
please help me through
the day . . .
help ease the pain
that may be brought
upon me . . .
forgive me for the sins
of yesterday . . .
let tomorrow be a new
start . . .
but for today Dear Lord . . .
. . . just let me have peace
within my mind . . .

Amen.

—Donna Marie Bowen

TEARS OF MUSIC

No dreams, nor hopes
with lavished thoughts;
night's long awakening beating heart
with no ends, nor start.

I walk a shadow of my mind
the web of ache;
and trembling muscles tighten,
soaring clouds darken,
winds blow
dust gathers for a wash over.

Forgotten soul, I love you words,
utterance of a formed speech.
Casual calls, remember not,
choking on uncertainties.

Unknowledged vision, I must trust?
cast thy eyes of devotion
never mourn!
Must I be of you? and you not of me?
heart of one not in thee;
tears of music, down beat pour;
in God I trust
forever more.

—Joellen Ryman

WILMINGTON GREEN

Is she Irish, or is she Scottish, or is she Welsh.
She sure is Rex, she sure is Daine.
Walking across the Wilmington green . . . .
Shekinah Glory in her hair.

Is she Irish, or is she Scottish, or is she Welsh.
She sure is Rex, she sure is Daine.
Walking across the Wilmington green . . . .
Jesus Christ on her mind.

Is she Irish, or is she Scottish, or is she Welsh.
She sure is Rex, she sure is Daine.
Walking across the Wilmington green . . . .
Shekiner Glory in her hair.

Envoy
Is she Irish, or is she Scottish, or is she Welsh.
She sure is Rex, she sure is Daine.
Chrisie Evert is her name . . . .
Walking across the Wilmington green.

—008 A New Beginning

FLAME?

Flame?
No.
In my spirit burns
A Pilot light,
It gives me a warm glow.

Flames flicker out
Pilot lights burn
Continuously
As long as the source feeds it.

This Pilot light
of mine
Is fed by
God's Love
Eternal.

Flame
Pilot Light
OH.

—Deborah Farrington

THE PAINTBRUSH

The quaking asp is a paint brush
    For the Master Painter's works—
The Earth and sky His palette—
Where hidden color lurks.
In the Fall He dips His paintbrush
In the gold of a harvest moon—
And gilds the acres of aspens
While the winds in the pine trees croon.
He dips His brush in the sunset
And with each mighty stroke
He paints with scarlet and crimson,
The thickets of maple and oak.
He dips His brush in the evening sky,
And with strokes precise and true—
He tints the lakes and the rivers
With cobalt and azure blue.
His colors spill over in Autumn,
They blend and mingle, and so
He dips His brush in the Milky Way,
And cleanses His picture with snow.

—Retha Gossett Jones

THOUGHT SEEDS

Seeds that are planted
        Should always be granted
        Their right to grow

Words that are spoken
        Should never be token
        But meant to show

Those thoughts you can feel
        Not onions to peel
        Which cause tears to flow

The ones that stay planted
        Are those that were granted
        The time to grow

No matter, no matter, no matter
        How strong winds shall blow

—Dave Burbee

IMPERFECTIONS

Trying to climb a huge old tree
    I endeavored to rise above infirmity
Avoiding each snarling limb
Unwittingly I tread upon him

Where did you come from, Majesty?
Utterly suprised by His Nobility
Certainly from royal blood, I know!
Noticing His luminous inner glow

The beauty of such graciousness
Far exceeded worldly success
But quickly I did glance seeing
His side had been lanced

Oh, who has done this ghastly feat?
Then I saw his bleeding feet!
Perceiving with an awful dread
I focused upon his blood stained head

Capturing his tear fulled eyes
Uncannily I realized—
These piercing wombs upon His Grace
Lay at my feet in great disgrace

—Theresa A. Herbert

It's a supernatural feeling to be
born again.
And to be among the chosen who can
call a King their Friend.
If you wonder how I know this, it's
plain for you to see.
The Bible is the Living Word and the
Author lives in me.

—Austin Ashby

ETERNAL LOVE

Love transcends death
    through the pathway,
of our spiritual lives;
grasping for the ties
that were formed,
in the physical existence
of our lives.

For love knows no death,
just a brief pause;
time when the entwining
souls link themselves eternally,
to begin the deeper dimension
of love's beauty,
in our spiritual lives.

—Linda Esparza

HEAVEN

Angels are heaven,
        So is God,
Pearly gates maybe,
        But never fog.

Rainbows are heaven,
        So are kites,
Unicorns maybe,
        But never fights.

Flowers are heaven,
        So are the trees,
Grass could be maybe,
        But never weeds.

Good is heaven,
        So is Aunt Sue,
I could be maybe,
        How about you?

—Alicia S. Weeber, age 11

I'd like to leave a lighted path
for some one else to trod.
It's not easy, yes it's hard
To walk the path for God.

I want to live a life
So when my time comes,
I can leave a lighted path
for some one else to run.

God knew the toils
That I would have;
He sent his only Son,
So I could leave a lighted path
for some one else to run

Today is almost over;
The sun is setting fast.
I pray I've left a lighted path
Today may be my last.

—Betty L. Buchanan

TEXTURES

Of blue and brown and gray combined,
Of past and future and ageless time,
Sharp angles, soft curves,
Points and circles,
Countless wonders, wondrous miracles,
Laughs and tears and love-filled years,
Needlepoint claws and velvet ears,
A gentle blend of all of these,
A picture of love,
My Siamese.

—Jacqueline Reid

NUBIAN

Across the barren desert we go.
It's so hot, but the black Arabian stallion
gallops on across the sand.

This gallant steed called Nubian
came one night, and his destination
was unknown.

He was traveling to some faraway land,
as he bravely crossed the desert sand.

An omen or symbol of death, he may be,
but riding so smooth and gently upon
Nubian's back that night was a dream to me.

—Charlene Corman May

MR. GOBLER

Oh, Mr. Gobler,
We've made the punch and peach cobbler,
But you're the treat,
Our bit of meat.
Come back here Mr. Gobler.
Where is Mr. Gobler?
He should be on the table,
There he is in the horse's stable.
Mr. Gobler got away—
We'll have no Thanksgiving Day,
Oh, yes we will!
Just be still—
We caught Mr. Gobler!

—Jada Lynn Brisentine, age 9

WALKING THE DOG

Young, frisky and proudly curling
his fluffy white tail over his back,
in a pretty neat plume: he
was tugging anxiously to go,
either the leash or my stride was
too short; I was supposed to be
walking him but he was pulling
me. Whoa! "Easy does it," no boring
stationary bike or grueling treadmill
ride, only a pleasant workout
for both of us; enriched and
refreshed by the picturesque beauty
of Mother Nature and our daily
brisk walks, on the road to fitness,
with my dog "Whimpy," the only male
Spitz in a litter of four, born February
9, 1989 to: "Princess Ladybug II" and
"Prince Sugar Bear."

Dedicated to: Ms. Norma G. Butler, R.N.
—Eliza Ruth Lamberson

CATERPILLAR

Caterpillar Caterpillar small
and furry, spin a cocoon
before the winter flurry.
When the summer comes, open
your cocoon, when you come out eat
your cocoon.

—Sarah Campbell, age 6

On her dainty little feet,
Going gracefully down the street,
Head held high as if to meet,
The one who knows she's so sweet.
Curves? right! as described in fiction,
Health and wind, in good condition.
Works so hard, others to fool,
Sorry, she used to be, my mule.

—Howard O. Wilkins

TEN LITTLE TURKEYS

Ten little turkeys came
to the door.
I took five and there's
still five more.
You make the stuffing
I'll make the bread.
"Let's hurry up and eat," I
said.

—Amanda Jo Buck, age 7

IMAGINATION

A pretty yellow butterfly
Flew over the elephant's back,
And as he flew he asked him why
The ducky went quack, quack, quack.

The elephant said, "I don't know
But why do you suppose
The turtle goes so very slow
While you can fly so fast?"

Little butterfly paused to think,
And a cat with mischief bent
Saw his chance and started to slink,
But butterfly up and went!

—Helen Iris

SAFARI
Shhh walk quietly
Lions and tigers I can see
Grass higher then my knees
Helps them not see me
Elephants in a herd
I'll not speak a word
Rhinoceros and caribou
Shouldn't frighten you
Dangling from a tree
A python I do believe
Jungle sounds pound loud and clear
So my mother I didn't hear
Go to your room and don't come out
I don't cry I don't pout
Shhh walk quietly
Come on Safari with me

—Deborah S. Nakagawa

THE DEER

So innocent, so scared,
they wander through the forest;
with dark, big eyes filled with fear
for they sense that danger is near

So beautiful, so gentle,
they are such feeble creatures,
with sensitive, soft features

Their coats are a velvety golden brown,
which glows in the shimmering sun.
Each step they take is precautious,
for their enemy, the wolf, is ferocious

How could man hurt or hunt
these lovely creatures?
They live and breed in fear,
yes, this is the deer!

—Ana Maria Ghetu

MAGGOT

Little Maggot
turn into a fly.
But quickly, but quickly it flys.

—Abram Morford

THE CLAM

Cool sand sifts
Through long fingers
Wrinkled by the water.

As the tide rolls on
And off of the beach
Foam's left dancing behind.

Each handful of sand
Brings the white treasure
More within reach.

While each gentle wave
Washes it farther
And farther from reality.

—Amy Pappas

FLIGHTS OF FANCY

Flying colors from New Guinean jungles,
you grace the skies and trees with
your lovely plumes; apodan wonders who
are known, yet unknown, to one and all.

Named for royalty that now exist
only in memories, you
have descriptions that do not do
your members justice.

From the Empress, King of Saxony, and
Count Raggi's to Queen Carola's
bird with six wires, ". . . and all guarded
by avian riflemen."

Wahnes' and the Arfak sixes produce a twelve,

all leading to a few with color.
Black-billed and White-billed sickle billeds
Grey-chested, Yellow-chested, Red,
and Blue.

From your many fairy tale names,
came legends of heavenly flights;
fairy-tale names, forever flying
till Death overtakes them.

—John F. Tashjian

AN ELEPHANT

There once was an elephant.
And he was so fat,
That he sat on a rock
And he made it flat.

—Jamie Rhea Brewer, age 9

WEE WET WINGS

There's a joy; there's a beauty,
An instinctive sense of duty
As a chrysalis emerges from its cage.
A tiny one begins to shiver.
Wee wet wings begin to quiver.
A caterpillar bows upon another stage.
From a slow, tiresome creeping
To a curled up winter sleeping
The butterfly so gracefully steps out.
It's a summer's secret story
Of a resurrected glory.
Reality views wonder inside out.

—Sister Mary Jude Litzinger, C.S.J.

IN A LIGHTER VEIN

A leech
bit deep
a lighter vein
and drank
a lethal dose
of humor.
And now
its body tickles
near hairy bristles;
a smooth skin
makes it grin.

—Thambi

THE LANDSHARK

The Landshark quieter than quick

His eyes engorging
Rare glance subdue

The Watery Cloud

Speechless encounter
Eyes upon her

So still in
the truth far from
the memory

Teeth embossed lifelessness
Landshark

Channel of pure expression

Doomed
I lie in a
Northern world
Another world

The Landshark
Eyes and jaws
of death
Love
For Gott*
The love

*Gott is German for God

—DES

NOW YOU'RE GONE

You trembled
in your sleep this morning
    as though
you were afraid
to let me go

There were .tears under your lashes
  I kissed them away
    and you
in innocent slumber
smiled

　　　　—Jacqueline McGuffey Young

THE BONDING

Deep within the firelight glow,
passion burns.

Gentle light reflecting upon
two champagne glasses.

Flames dance rhythmically,
to soft jazz music.

Sweet words are whispered,
pledges of devotion.

Loneliness extinguished,
souls joined eternally.

　　　　—L. Melyndia Wikander

ALL THE WONDERS YOU SEEK ARE WITHIN YOURSELF

My youth
  My family,
My children . . .
My Church
My God

My town
  And my Country

They're mine!
They belong to the future
They belong to the past

They are me

And I will live on —
  Forever

　　　　—Verda Seeklander

SOMETHING

Something awful,
    is always a faller,
        before it starts.

Something bad,
    is always awful.

Something O.K.
    is always going bad.

Something good,
    is always O.K.

Something nice,
    is always good.

Something special,
    is always getting nicer.

Something wonderful,
    is always special;
            forever.

　　　　—Thomas L. Kittle

MY HUSBAND AND I

As we sit at the table each morning,
  It sometimes can get very boring.

We enjoy our cup of coffee very much,
And as we talk it does keep us in touch.

As the day goes by, we like to kiss and share,
  My husband and I, we are a pair.
　　　　—Connie Biddy

POEMS TO READ IN THE DARK (3)

Your upturned face is a sunflower
    words spill from your lips like seeds
        fall upon my breasts
            take root
    become things that grow over the pavement
        below us.
I can read those words
    in the darkness
        cast by our bodies.
You turn slowly to follow me
    as if I were the sun
        reach down into the shadows
            for the poems at our feet
    stretch out your withered arms . . .
　　　　—Natalie Dunn

THE　　　　MAIDEN

As she brushed her silk-like hair
The moonlight caught her beauty
It held it solemnly for a touching moment

As the moment passed her by
The moonlight could not bear to leave
To leave the love it held for her
To leave and pass her by

It lingered in the room that night
Not able to bear leaving her on the morrow
So just before the daylight broke
It glided to her hair
And slipped into her lovely curls
Forever staying there.
　　　　—Rigel McKee, at age 12

ONE MORE CHANCE

Is Marriage a game of win or lose
Do you get to take turns and play by the rules
Can you quit if you're losing, are you forced to play
Who wins in marriage, who knows these days

All the rules are different, for each and every game
But how many rules for marriage, how many can you name
Love, Honor, and Cherish, so long as you both shall live
Is what you say on your day, it's the promise that you give

So when does one really win, when is it time to part
When all the cherished memories are invested in the heart
When all the love is spoken from special places in the heart
And honor is built up so much it can't be torn apart

And who is the judge in this game, who has the right to say
That built up love is all gone, and cherished memories floated away
Who counts the money, who rolls the dice
Who says who'll live, while memories die

While hearts are broken and honor fades
And love is drowning among the waves
And everyone losing just wants to give in
And have one more chance to win again
　　　　—Audrey Lynne Doolittle

MY HEART

My heart is hurt, but it
was worth the pain and suffering
I spent for you. My trust and
hoping has had my coping well
worth my days and nights with
you. You are my life, my soul,
and my hope. All worth my
time with you. I love you my
dearest, with my life and hope
we can spend our lives together.

—Patty Y. Woodall

LONELY NIGHTS

The silence of the night
Invades the darkest corners of my mind.
Afraid, that with each new day,
Or whichever road, what I will find.
The days drag by slowly,
Turning into those lonely nights.
Sleep doesn't come for hours,
Then the sun turns on its lights.
But I'll keep my candle burning,
Every minute, night or day.
I'll keep my love alive for you
Until you come home to stay.

—Marilyn E. Wright

EASTERN OREGON

The farmer's seed
of which I came
brought me up in a life
of honesty, purity and simplicity.

The farmer's seed
to which I will marry
will keep me
in touch with the fields and flowers.

The farmer's seed
will again be planted
my hips will cradle
the womb of our oneness.

The farmer's seed
planted in an endless
circle, bringing forth.

—Shannon K. Madison

MY CHOICE

I love to see the sunlight—
shine brightly through the trees.
I love to smell the flowers,
and to catch the falling leaves.

I love to watch the ocean,
and listen to the sounds.
I love to be with people,
yet—I love when no one's round.

There are many things I love to love,
and what I say is true,
there is nothing that I could love more,
than loving life with you.

I love the way you look at me—
I love to hear your voice,
I love to love you, can't you see?
A life with love's my choice.

—Judi Vick

OUR LOVE

When our love was new,
I truly did love you.

People said it wouldn't last.
But as the years have past

Our love has grown strong.
Our love was never wrong.

Our love has been sure.
And so it does endure.

Today I truly love you,
Like our love was brand new.

—Barbara Rishavy

SELFISH MY LOVE

Should it be selfish my love
To think of this end
My life on earth without yours
Spare my pain within

Should it be selfish my love
To think of this end
Your life on earth before mine
My life would end then

If you love the way I do
Darling you should know
Our love will live forever
When you go I go

—Ronnie Clark

ALONE

I'm just alone; not by choice
but by fault.
Many of my friendships
were illusions,
Falsely motivated by the
desire to be wanted.
An addictive pattern of
forgiveness.
Just afraid to be alone!
Now I know how to be a
friend — now
The only problem is,
I'm alone.

—Danyel M Long

FEELINGS

Waves splash without sound
Naivete abounds
Clarity surrounded by clouds
Knowledge becomes secondary
Feelings primary
Know not to feel
But to feel
So that all may become aware
Clearly surrounded now
But completely unseen
A feeling comes — then goes
Never to be seen
But felt with force
Only to be spun into wonderment
As the noiseless waves
Splash about the clouds

—Keith Frederic Dungan

FUTILITY

What sad abbreviation of life,
this boy who has bled his last.
No march in time, no drum, no fife —
No cadence as he hurries past.

Was your existence all for nought,
So painful you could not bear
To see what else thy God had wrought?
And only death ease your despair?

How many heard but did not listen
As you cried in an echoless void?
Who knew how soon your blood would glisten —
with what horrors your mind had toyed?

Come back, come back, let's try again!
It's such a futile, empty cry,
Regret for all that might have been.
Come back, young man — you need not die!

—Jeannette Gemelke

GUILT

Each step I take,
Each mile I walk,
I carry this horrid pain in my heart.
I let one thing go and all fell apart.
Each night I cried,
Realizing this pain,
This pain filled heart can beat no
more.
Trying to cope with the death of my
love.
I was willing to take all the blame.
I knew things wouldn't be the same.
Both eyes are filled with tears.
And the one heart was broken,
I gained back all my fears.
Just wanting to be happy,
Just wanting my love not to hate me.
Maybe he would be alive.

—Angela Martinez

LET NOT US MOURN

It is not for Bruce we mourn
        For his soul is now at rest
Our Lord Jesus took him Home
        For God knows for all what's best

His pain and suffering now are gone
        But Bruce really never died
He lives forever with our Lord
        And he walks right by his side

God gave to Bruce a special strength
        That no one on earth can measure
The "Love of Christ" is what it was
        And there is no greater treasure

Let not us mourn, because he's gone
        But fill our hearts with laughter
Because Bruce now is at his rest
        And has peace forever after

"Amen"

Written in the spirit of God as a memorial to
Bruce Lee Hiedeman in the hopes that the courage
and strength he showed in his life here on earth
will always be an example of faith for others to
follow.

—John A. Hiedeman

LIFE'S SURPRISES

Life is full of suprises
More than we can hold
So don't let it keep you in the cold
And in a constant hold

Life is too short and sometimes good
So don't stop it all because you could

—Louise M. Kozlowski

THE OLD WOMAN

The old woman sits behind the locked door
Afraid to leave her room anymore
There was a time she felt vital and strong
Now she feels useless and all alone

She peers at the people down below
Making up stories as she watches them go
Her family has long since gone away
Watching these strangers fills up her days

She watches the seasons pass her by
Sitting alone in her tiny room
She never thought it would end this way
She fears it will all be over soon

—Stephanie Bennett

I WISH YOU WOULD HAVE STAYED

You were there as a true friend to all
Soon distance but yet there
You were still there supposedly to come back
Always writing, still talking
But then suddenly nothing
You were gone

Don't try to send letters
They won't return
Don't try to call
No one will answer
Don't go to the door
For the bell won't ring.

Just send messages to heaven
The answers will always be there
You were the only one who knew why

—Jenny Lackey

SORROW

It can be caused by trouble,
It can be caused by pain,
It can be caused by hurt,
Sometimes by the rain.
It can happen when losing a loved one,
The weight of the pain feels a ton.

You want to tell somebody,
But instead you keep it inside.
At times you want to cry,
Your own pain is where you abide.
'Cause you feel like no one will care,
So with no one will you share.

You know you're not yourself,
But no one else could know.
Your heart grieves with the pain,
But your feelings, you won't show.
Sadness, sadness; is how you feel,
So the sadness, in your heart, you seal.

—George L. Hurta, Jr.

SUNDAY MORNING

So often at breakfast before we woke on Sunday. We thought of our busy father an country labour that's tough!

I remember last night the headlights of a lonely car. Pass me by so abrupt Mr.
Now it's raining again, I'd like to sail down river.
At night our kittens were playing.
Europe an I are wise of things you know. I think of growing up an who wonders what!
Before everything changes I would like to enjoy a good percentage.
The day I stood on the lawn, I thought of playing cards.
I have a dog for a pet I love him like a teddy bear.
Before I talk to Mom tomorrow I collect eggs in the barn.
I brought my friend home today we played together.
Two things I know math an a hero we know.
The lessons I take I experience.
Spring a nest of young birds, mountain yellow.
May I believe the horizon an sun set.
Bring the same to me apples in a basket.
We travel my parents an keep a light on.
My dad likes baseball an reaching his goal.
I save an like orange soda.
To get home I look an I better look well.
Check me I'm working now swing the weight.
My ice cream cone is dripping an she doesn't have a Kleenex.
I love white tape red cross an ice skating.
In town are my dominos, Let's go around.
To make the big time I got to make the hill top.
The less I like to see it was little miss.
This last of all was my baby shoe.
The sun left cold at dawn, shining was a star.
　　The End

　—Patrick J. Marenger

THE LEGEND OF PIPERVILLE

"J. C. Piper & Sons←—" read the bill, one at the highway; the other, bottom of the Hill.
They lead cattle buyers from across the country, Future Farmers of America, even a busload from Germany.

The Jersey farm was started by my grandfather, you see. Cyrus Piper was his name; he was just "Grandpa" to me.
Hard times they had, surviving the Depression. But the Jersey business prospered three generations.

Five brothers and one sister made up the family. Three brothers stayed with the dairy—Herb, Clair, and Louie.
'62 and '64 took away Louie and the Patriarch, leaving Herb and Clair to continue the trade they had embarked.

The breadth of the land spread from the bridge to the "slab." As dear as Dallas is to JR, so was the farm to my dad.
In winter when dusk was early, the barns with bright lights were filled. Ed Jenner, a regular Sunday guest, called it "Piperville."

There was a lane filled with blackberries, a huge garden with vegetables. Garden upkeep went to Cyrus (and many a grandson), the flowers to Mable.
The barn started with one building, then grew and grew; added were a bull barn, milk barn, parlor, and office to mention a few.

The old gray barn and tall white silo bring back memories—Of days taken for granted and times of ease.
Of summer days at the fairs, cattle sales, and awards—Of silver trophies, and purple banners with golden cords.

If only I could go back for just one day and relive those memories of yesterday—
To touch loved ones long since passed on, but we can not go back; we must go on.

Yes, this era is now gone and time marches on. The Pipers are scattered like seeds upon the ground.
My heritage I will not forget; it will always be a part of me. The past is past—the future is yet to be.

　—Deborah Piper Schultz

COUVER

Every heart courts a dream
not yet conceived
Impatient
aching of want
Beckoning
with relentless inner stirrings
and ceaseless murmurs
Waiting
upon the fullness of time
to entreat the heart to follow.

—Linda K. Portelance

The wind blew . . .

I watched as the leaf
drifted to the ground.

I picked it up and scotch-taped
it back on the tree.

It never came to life again.

I watched; I waited;

day faded into night.

The moon rose high

and was gone again.

I looked; I watched; I waited.

I never came to life again.

—Judith P. Thompson

IMPRESSIONS IN THE SAND

Collecting our thoughts
on the moist earth
like pieces of hardwood.

Looking to the sky
for inspiration,
seeing only a painted overcast.

Walking on, the cedar
scratching at our calves,
like memories overlooked.

Cedar, such a hard wood,
seasoned by time,
leaving impressions in the sand,
like certain events,
from the past.

—Bonnie S. Maldonado

PEACE IN GREEN

Quiet excitement
Heartbeats with no sound
Your voice is all I see
By grace you came to me
Love in blue

Humble royalty
Tears of salvation
Your pain I chose to be
By grace you came for me
Joy in purple

Wild contentment
Immortal love can sing
Your song is what I smell
Tho' from your grace I fell
Peace in green

—Peggy S. Jones

There comes a full, shining time
to defy the strong private mind
lilac days of rain cool my heart
to a swelling pastel fire
rich breath of jeweled skies
please keep the desert blaze
from my rivulet mountain.

violent storm and summer shower
now join hands in my home
hail beneath a horizon of rainbows
crystal streams in a whitened sky
thunder booms a happy panic in my heart
sunset at moon rise
billows into my silken eyes

—Susan L. Devasher

SILENT DOMAIN

A quiet dreary morning
Rain is in the offing
The sound of thunder in the distance
The birds and insects communicating

The sound of a plane high above
On its way to who knows where
A streak of lightning splits the sky
Then a roll of thunder there

A coolness comes from out of the woods
As the rain slowly approaches
Little dots upon the lake and now upon my arm
As the rain slowly encroaches
Upon my silent domain

—Doris I. Merkel

CHRONICLES

Thy past preserved within my pages,
I suppose a diary
Emotional thoughts
Of an emotion familiar to me,
If only to me
Chronicles of my tyme
Chronicles of my unusual rhyme
But my rhyme is not my reason,
Remembering a lost season, perhaps
And within my pages
Chronicles of people I have met
Perhaps only in thought, rather than words
An attempt in explaining
Perhaps that, my gaining . . . .
12/07/89

—D.R. Mote

THE WALNUT

A seemingly tough exterior
Creamy richness of color
Beauty in its shape.
Ridges making a definite pattern
Unique to feel, but not understood.
Unconscious of its wholeness.
It now lies in pieces
One man is responsible.
He wanted to get inside.
He drew out his tool.
His force splintered the silence.
Smashing, grabbing, tasting,
He devoured all of the meat.
Sate, he walked away,
And left the empty shell.

—Nicole Edington

SEEING YOU IN ME

I kissed my mirror
because I saw you there.

My prints stayed for days
waiting for an answer.

Our love was strong enough
to travel through reflections.

Now the mirror is clear,
as are my desires.

—**Sunny Peyton**

NEPTUNIANA

I fling open my mind
To hold the enormity of the universe
By looking up at the stars at night.

I look down in wonder
On the newborn babe in my arms,
An individual universe
Containing a million atoms.

At my feet
A blade of grass,
A drop of dew,
A grain of sand.

—**Anne Ahne**

SCARLET

Now come inside—my hope fail
to one song's sentinel
the scarlet quarter-moon
like a jack-o-latern grin
when it stares at you:
the Cantor
has fallen
we will have to wrest
the harp of seven score strings
to the last Kol Nidre
that will spare
the womb:
sweet, watery, honey-like womb

. . . . . let's talk about me
for just a minute

I'm the one who is losing.

—**Peter W. Acebal**

GEORGIA GAVE BIRTH

When Georgia gave birth
She opened up ebony eggs.
Black as the earth, that gave her life
Sweet, as the blood, passion in the day.

Georgia is the earth.
The timid and the brave suckled her.
Her breast is filled And
Strength lives in her hips.
Georgia is   liberated A
Root free;
She grows, around, through — In.

Beauty and Black.
Georgia is the isthmus,
The Appendix,
All conception is in her And
"She Shall be like a tree planted by
The river of waters."   Ps. 1,3

—**Lucien M. Shockness**

SOPRANO SAXOPHONE

The high note tries to go higher
On the horn that plays the song
that is music to my ears
The song that makes me think of you
Hold me, listen to the music
with me.
Let's fall in love all over again.

—**Perrian Locke**

SILENCE

Silence descends upon me
like a carpet of sand
covering my trembling body
no sounds from the land.

darkness is overpowering
light not to be seen
silencing my crying heart
loud the silent scream.

capturing my spirit free
in its heavy cover
grains of sand weigh me down
restrain me from my lover.

—**Sandy Higgins**

ILLUSIVE SHADOW

The sun is setting in the sky
I stand and watch it fall
I turn around and then I see
A shadow on the wall

I brush away the cobwebs
From a dream that couldn't be
It's faded, but it's there
Like the shadow I can see

The shadow hovers near me
Like a haunting melody
It drifts away and comes again
But I am never free

I'm looking forward to the day
When all my doubts have passed
My love will not a shadow be
And I'll know peace at last

—**Gertrude Robinett**

I WANT

Waking up quickly
shaking dusty sleep from my mind
i slap the buzz of the clock
And cry that i am alone

Waking up slowly
in a sweaty clogged waterbed
i kick the tangled sheets
And pray to be alone

Excitement and rejection
Never leave time to think
Except when you can't stand reflection

Security
Is not all it's cracked up to be
Except when it's not there

Why does it take two men to show me
That I have no idea what I want?

—**Jennifer Jean Bornsen**

SPRING

Spring is here,
When the rain drops to the ground.
When the sun rays blaze,
And the flowers bloom all around.

Spring is a special time of year.
Spring is fun.
Spring is a new beginning,
For everything and everyone.

—Toni Weller, age 10

MY WISH

Walk among the frozen fields
See the crystal flowers
Empty of spirit and purpose
Heads looking only upon the ground.
Where is the bright life that once
Filled these rapid creatures?
Oh — that I should be the sunlight
Feeding them with hope and assurance
Of the Spring to come.

—Suzanne J. Rivet, age 16

SPRING

Raindrops dance on the ground,
Newborn creatures are all around.
Everywhere there is green,
Sounds of rushing water come from the bubbling stream.
The air smells fresh and new,
The sky is a brilliant blue.
The birds come back from their little vacation,
To join in the lively celebration.
I wish it was always spring,
But I'll hold onto the memories it did bring.

—Kara Roggie

the SUN

the SUN,

the Shine,
the warm Summer breeze;

As I follow the steaming waters,
I catch a glimpse.

Then, before I can act,
the dart hits dead center.

Like flickering neon, I blink,

I must.

—Dave j. Forchette

FALLING LEAVES

The green of summer has faded away
Leaves are falling today.
As the leaves sparkle and glow
A red and gold show
A zephyr flees before you know
A color go round parades the air
Misty leaves are everywhere.
They fall to the earth as a feather
falls from the sky
Up so very high
You're held spellbound by their
awesome beauty
As they speak to you and me.

—Carolyn Holifield Otis

THE ALLEGRO OF FALL

The allegro of fall
Tiptoes on sunkissed-leaves
And rustles in pools
From her rain-drenched twilight
In spiraling-streams.

—Cherie Marie Hayes

SPRING

Summer is just around the corner. The beautiful flowers are blooming in the spring. The blossoms on the trees are bursting forth. The kites are flying around high in the sky. The birds dot the sky. I love spring and all its beauty.

—Lynda Krugger, age 16

WINTER SONG

The softly falling snow is a
symphony,
Each tiny flake lazily, lightly
falling,
Is a note in the music of the
winter song.

Be still, my Heart, and listen
with delight!
Awake to find the symphony
complete
In a world of white.

—Florence M. Taylor

SPRINGTIME SONG

This morning I woke and heard your trill
Bursting over my window sill.
You sang of your hopes for a space and a nest,
For a mate to share it . . . a spot to rest.
With a cheer-up you sang of eggs, a soft blue,
Of a shady tree to share with you.

Dear robin, I hope you'll find your mate
And nest in that tree by my back gate.
I'll watch again new life appear
As you start a family again this year.
When skies are blue and years are gone
They'll carry on your springtime song.

—Georgia McGriff Smith

WINTER BEGINS

A day without sun:
Veils of mist
white as the washed sky
spread over the pale grass

lift to the leafless trees
in ghost clouds
downy as baby birds
but cold

as I am
shivering
in the winter
of your absence.

—Aurora Alberti, M.D.

SO MANY THINGS TO DO

Today I must go everywhere,
Clean every corner,
Wash every chair.
There are so many
things to do,
I seem to have
No time for you!

(I'm sorry)

—Morgan Gaskin, age 9½

SWING OF LIFE

The child swings upon the sky
Just as far as she can eye,
She stops momentarily . . .
Just to be sure she can see

The path she has worn
Makes sure it's the life she's sworn,
To ride and glide in the blue . . .
Knowing to come down is the clue

For life's adventures and things to gain
Knowing the earth is where it's sane,
That above is a dream . . .
The swing's flight is the eye's gleam.

—Susan N. Bell

MY DAUGHTER'S EYES

Life would be so beautiful,
If I'd just take the time
To view it through my daughter's eyes
Than to see it just through mine.

There is wonder in most everything,
A beauty left unseen.
No color in the days that pass
Or so it often seems.

Those little eyes, they see so clear,
A miracle it's true.
They search for good in all of us,
No matter what we do.

My life would be its fullest
If I'd just take the time,
To view it through my daughter's eyes
Than to see it just through mine.

—Diana Dunlap

ADVICE TO A BELOVED DAUGHTER

Always keep a quiet spot
Tucked away within your heart.
A quiet place to harbor
Your soul's special, softer part.

The world will try to chain you
To its hustle and its haste.
Demand constant loyalty,
Lay your precious peace to waste.

Life will work to bend you down.
Unable to freely roam,
Always leave your secret soul
Packed away in your heart's home.

The quiet joys will save you
From the outside's pounding roars.
Silent rooms and poetry
Are the salves to heal life's sores.

—Susan Rustad Mills

CHILD

The masters' brushstroke,
The sculptors' hand,
The perfect canvas;
That, is a child.

—Nancy C. Bracy

GO TO BED LITTLE SLEEPY HEAD

Go to bed little sleepy head,
Little lids being so droopy,
Daddy's going to ready the bed.
Too late to make whoopie.

Go to bed, little sleepy head,
Dream clouds will be floating,
Up above your little bed.
Sand bags blue eyes coating.

Go to bed little sleepy head,
Our Heavenly Father protecting now,
Mother and Daddy in prayers led.
In His love will teach us how.

—Mildred Allen

SPORTS AND POETRY

Football is rough and tough
and baseball sure is hard stuff.

Hockey you really gotta be jockey.

Soccer is fun but you really gotta run.

Skiing is my passion,
but you really gotta buy the fashions.

Volleyball I say with a sigh,
you really gotta jump high.

Wrestling with Hulk Hogan
is really not my slogan.

So sports you can see
are for you and me.

If you want to be a star
just work very hard.

—Justin E. Brewer, age 9

WALLS

If walls could talk, I wonder what they
would say,
You know they hold the secrets of each
passing day.
A happy house has happy walls,
All shiny and bright, no worries at all.
A sad house may have gloomy walls,
Dark-colored woodwork, and paper to fall.
Each room has its own four walls,
To see you, to hear you, to echo your
call.
In winter it's cozy inside these walls.
The cold winds outside pose no worry
at all.
In summer these walls fill with
laughter and play,
Children hang posters to make them
look gay.
The nighttime comes and seems so
complete,
When you know your family's surrounded
by walls to sleep.

—Barbara Baty

THE DAY IN THE LIFE OF MUSICAL NOTES —

The notes of music arising early in the morning, floating never doting, always roaming, never moaning. Soaring even in the periods of greatest roaring.

The musical notes in soaring hear a sound, a sound that begins to resound, hello I am a cello, have you heard when I am mellow. Then the sound of all the instruments resounding in the hall, gives forth a call to the musical notes entering the hall. Come float with us as we arise to life's highest call.

—Lance Andersen

A DEDICATION BLESSING TO THE ONE I LOVE

Like the Dawn that greets the morning sun, May each day be bright, shiny,
and new, a delight to look forward to!
Like the calm of the rolling sea, May the waters
be calm and still for you, and bring you peace,
Like the rose in the Springtime, May our love
blossom and grow,
May the moisture of the gentle rain kiss you so
softly,
Like the swan, May you find the beauty and
splendor, as each day passes by,
Like the clown, May you discover something to
smile and laugh about,
no matter what fate brings in life, you will always
have me,
May God bless us and keep us in his care, May he
shelter us in his arms,
bestow his ever abiding love to us,
May we always put him first and trust him com-
pletely,
Have Faith in Jesus, letting him guide us now and
ever,
May we remain together, forever. Amen.

—Sherry K. Lewers-Caldwell

JOURNEY

I see a flower in the distance,
It looks so far away,
Do I dare tackle this long journey before me, to
reach it?
I must —
I would not forgive myself if I turned and walked
away.
Not knowing exactly what kind of a beautiful
flower, that which
caught my eye from all the rest.
I contemplate on which way would be the right
direction to start —
Go down and around,
Up and around,
or simply right through the middle.
I chose to go through the middle, take my chances,
The obstacles were minor, compared to my want.
When I reach the flower, I take a few moments to
admire the life which
it holds within itself.
The slight breeze and a ray of sunshine only add
to its magnificent
beauty.
I decided to leave it, full of life and spirit,
And just be thankful for the wonderful intimate
moments we shared together,
Just us two!

—Valerie Lawrence Morgret

GOOD-BYE, HALLOWEEN!

The doorbell now is silent;
No goblins can be seen.
The sidewalk's free of monsters —
Good-bye, Halloween!

The dog stares at the doorway;
The cat peeks 'round the chair.
Calm settles in the household —
No goblins anywhere.

Masks and costumes vanish;
The candy dish is clean.
No more trick-or-treaters —
Good-bye, Halloween!

—Michaele S. Russell

A NIGHT TO REMEMBER

It was a night to remember,
Mountains reflecting in a crystal clear pool.
The smell of mountain wildflowers wafting in the
breeze—
And the sound of a meadow lark singing its melody.
We sat next to the river—
And shared our hopes and dreams.

It was a night to remember,
Mountains reflecting in a crystal clear pool.
A doe and her fawn move silently through the tall
grass.
We are silently watching the golden sun set into
the mountains—
And the smell of rosemary and sweet clover fill
our nostrils.
As it became cooler, we snuggled closer together
and sat back to enjoy what was yet to come.

It was a night to remember,
Mountains reflecting in a crystal clear pool.
The large orange moon rose slowly into the night—
And the stars started their slow return to the
night sky.
As we turn to go back to our cabin—
We could hear a coyote let out its mournful cry.

—Judy Albjerg, age 15

I'LL HAVE TO SAY GOODBYE

There's no easy way to
say good-bye.
We always sit and
wonder why.
It's only for a while
that we will be apart.
So please remember me in your hearts.
Well I must leave
you now, only for a little while.
So please be brave
and wear a smile.
I gave to you my love
yes, I did my very best.
And the love you gave
to me it gave me happiness.
Well my friends, I thank
you for all the love you've shown.
But know I have to
travel this road alone.
No matter where I am,
No matter how far away.
I'll always carry the thought
with me, that we will be together again
someday.

—Yvonne King

LONELINESS

Loneliness — the experience of the mind
Whether you are alone or with others,
It creeps in and tries to destroy you.

There can be periods of loneliness
  Deeper than time itself
Trying to surrender you forever.

Mind lapses — lonely times
  You keep surpressed
And act as a mime.

Surrender your life or cope if
  You can, because
Loneliness is a fact of man.

—Carol A. Burney

LONELINESS

When there's no one to love,
When there's no one to care,
When all hope is gone,
When all will is gone,
When your heart is a black, black void,
When in your heart nothing exists,
When in everything there is no feeling,
It's a black hole.
It's a devil's hell.
It's where no sun can shine.
It's where no light can glow.
Loneliness sometimes is in one's
          heart and soul.

—Tina Marie Jellerson

PICEANCE

The monster screamed again last night
I don't know what makes him angry
Silent screams raced through my mind
His name, they say, is Lonely

I screamed back, Go away
And let me dream this one night only
About the one I met today
Go away you monster Lonely

Sweet dreams — I've had none tonight
Silent screams — I've heard many
Be gone for once, once and for all
Be gone you monster Lonely

—Martin Jon Miller

WHERE ARE MY TOMORROWS?

I see a lonesome shadow,
stretched across the afternoon,
The air is still and somber,
The day is almost through,

There's not a sound to echo,
that the silence shall not find;
though my heart it keeps your memory
forever and all time;

Somewhere in the distance,
a whippoorwill he sings;
My heart is melancholy
There's truth in the song he sings.

Yesterdays have gone before me,
They shall never come again,
But where are my tomorrows?
With you they'd never end!

—Eric S. Charlton

LONELINESS

Loneliness feels terrible,
One never knows when it will hit.
Sometimes we cry and weep
We know not why, we just cry.
Every day and every hour
Until the tears have disappeared,
And we start all over again.

—Judy Bolick

K.M.C.

I let you take from within my chest
  my heart.
It had never experienced such a
  wonderful warmth—
To it, you brought.
At first I thought that maybe
  I should not
But then my lonely heart
Would know not the warmth
  that you sought.
But now, that you are gone
I wish that I had not—
For my heart is broken
  from the sorrow—
To it, you brought!

—Darrin M. Peine

THE TEARS THAT WILL NOT DRY

The moments when it hurt to say
  The things which stained my mind.
The sometimes when I couldn't smile
Or good thoughts could not find.

The hours when I sat alone
And pondered on the past,
Or cried about the things I miss
The things that did not last.

When in despair and all alone
I cry, My God, to thee,
I know you'll heal my wounded heart
And set my spirit free.

I'll run to you in times of strife
Your love abideth nigh,
You wipe away the hurt, the pain,
The tears that will not dry.

—Eva W. Forde

LIFE WITHOUT YOU

Life seems very lonely
Now that you are gone.
I wish things were different,
But it's over; things are done.

I miss your boyish smile
And I miss your shining face.
I miss the way you used to,
With your fingers, my mouth trace.

Often I see you with other girls —
Like an Arab with his harem.
I hear your laugh and see your smile
And remember when we shared them.

We had something special —
That's very clear to see —
But, a bright-eyed girl
Still loves you; obviously me.

—Cyndi Spina

TEAM WORK

Me, myself and I are we
A truly wonderful team we three
When me can't do the job with I
We know myself will surely try

I like to walk and talk with me
Myself prefers her privacy
I and me like to play
Myself would rather think all day

But, when the times get really sticky
And life becomes a little tricky
We join together, our team of three
I, myself and me.

—Karen L. Bell

THE SPARK

First a spark glimmers and
glows, then into a flame grows.
Then a conflagration takes hold,
then a strong gentle hand reaches
out to an old man shivering in
the cold and snow.

—Patrick Bryan Witt

MY BABY HAS A COLD

My baby has a cold.
you really do deserve more!
I dialed your number
just to hear you "blow"
and say "Nello."

It's bad; I hate it!
But God knows the ladies of the world
need a break to build defense
against the perfect romeo!
So take a while —

Just tough the damn thing out
or go sniff your "Peace" roses
or just get drunk
and maybe you won't even
know when you're well.

—Eleanor Mabry

My boy friend — ART Thritis

He threw his arms around my neck
It was only just a little peck,
But he stuck his finger in my eye
It hurt so bad I couldn't cry.

He banged his fist upon my ear
It's no wonder that I cannot hear.
He bumped his elbow on my shoulder
I really guess I'm getting older.

He ran his knees up and down my back
I thought I was on a wailing rack.
He wrapped his arms around my knee
I didn't think that I'd ever get free.

He twisted my fingers and my toes
How I stood that—Goodness knows.
He gave my hip a great big kick
That is when I REALLY got sick.

To the hospital—I had to go
It was ARTHRITIS—wouldn't you know.
But—when I got home once more
Art was still knocking at my door.

—Catherine McClusky

THAT OLD FLU FEELING

First the shivers
Plunge me into an arctic lake
Then the shakes
Pan fry me in hell.

My bones ache all over
My feet are on pins and needles
But run I must—
I need the throne and basin quick.

Dust dry throat, red and raw
A rock is sitting on my chest
As my nose drips like a thawing icicle
Lord, do I feel miserable!

—Kathleen M. Ouellette

LYING SMILES

They say that eyes are
the window to the soul
Why then do we allow ourselves
to be so easily deceived by people
Are we so blinded by a smile
that we can't see its true meaning
Smiles in their own ways
are only lies. —
Lies used to hide our true
feelings and intentions
Just as a rotting carcass is
wrapped in white linen — so is pain
and hatred covered by a smile

—Brian Brock

WASTED

We shared a life together,
there were so many dreams and hopes.
Mine developed due to God's inspiration
and yours evolved from Dope.

We planned to live in a Co-op,
but you reasoned a homeless shelter fine.

We planned to start up a business
but our "bread" was spent on "dimes."

And now I survive without you
and endure this dismal toil.
For our life is what you wanted . . . nothing
like a beer can sowed in soil.

—Ronnie Clark

BRAIN SURGERY

Headache, had a whole new meaning
Headache, a new breed of pain
Headache, it throbbed with each heart beat
The headache of a trauma filled brain

Intense, sharp, pulsating,
knife edged, stabbing, tight,
how would you describe a headache
that drives sleep from you at night?

I found no relief on the pillow
concentrated, throbbing, dull.
Like my head was being clamped in a vise
a pressurized brain in an aching skull

Chewing was a big undertaking
Standing, a terrible strain
Light headed and dizzy I sat back down
The Headache of a swollen brain.

—Tim Koehn

SEASIDE

I watched the tide come in today
And wash the burned-out fires away
And clean the shore of human sloth
Then . . . spread a sandy tablecloth.

I watched the tide go out at morn
And saw my hasty footsteps borne
By careless wave to distant shore
And . . . dared to dream where seagulls soar.

—Willena Burton

NIGHT DREAMS

Looking up at the far away sky,
Emotions abound but none explain why.

Is there an answer, does anyone know,
Or is it a mystery that will continue
                    to grow?

Why does he like me, or does he at all,
Does my place in his heart have
        any substance at all?

Does he want what I want, can he
                know how I feel?
Like the stars up above, this dream
                doesn't seem real.

—Debra LaMantia

Some are not so risky
They fear a chance, to take
They'll never strive to reach their goals
If their feelings are at stake

You only have one life they say
To do with, what you can
And if another scoffs at you
You'll never take your stand

Yet courage helps and so does hope
These two you can't obtain
They're born with you and die with you
Their purpose, to sustain

Reach out now and find your dream
With me it may not lay
But if it does, I'll give you strength
To do what your dreams say

—Sean P. Smith

LIGHT VS. DARK

Preying upon the innocent
Like a thief in the night
slowly moving in for the kill
Darkness Prevails

A fawn sipping water from a clear brook
in an open meadow
all is serene and calm
Light Prevails

Darkness — not feeling
Light — not knowing

When Darkness clashes with Light
there is an explosion of crimson
that fills that once clear brook

Light has ceased to exist.
Darkness is the victor.

—Pamela Best

THE HUNT

Dawn —
Through the stillness comes
The sound of beating wings.
A shot rings out.
An Arctic Sea Duck falls.
A long way to go to die.

—Millie Sabasteanski

BLESSED

The day is dark and cold,
Clouds have formed,
And now it rains
I prayed to God for strength,
He sent His son to guide me
And Jesus is His name

I asked for strength
I asked for wisdom
The day goes by
And God has blessed me,
Once again
I see it clear,
As flowers in the field.

—Louis Hernandez

REFLECTIONS

Sweet dreams of remembrance
pale lights in the mist.
Soft muted thunder,
like heaven's dark kiss.
Your eyes bridge the distance
between dream time and now.
Sleek and sure as a cat
from the ground to the bough.
Lest you wake from your sleep
pure memories I hold;
like the love that I keep.
As a light in the window
can be seen from afar.
I have seen in my eyes;
a wish time cannot mar.

—Mary S. Hall

THE FLOWER OF FRIENDSHIP

Life is like a garden
and Friendship like a flower
That blooms and grows in beauty
with the sunshine and the shower
and lovely are the blossoms
That are tended with great care
By those who work unselfishly
To make the place more fair
and like the Garden Blossoms,
Friendship Flower grows more sweet
when watched and tendered carefully
By those we know and meet
and, like sunshine adds new fragrance
and raindrops play their part,
joy and sadness add new beauty
when there's Friendship in the heart
and, if the seed of Friendship
Is planted deep and true
and watched with understanding
Friendship's Flower will bloom for you.

—George E. Chenette

A GRECIAN DREAM

One day I fancied — in days of yore,
dwelling mid marbled columns on
a fair Grecian shore,
where blithe maidens cavort
playing on flutes and harps,
a music of mystic sort.
across the sea with ripples bright,
sun-beams today and moonlight tonight,
lie towering peaks with pastel hue,
how would a dream like this come true????

—**Earl W. Davis**

THE PILGRIM

I hear them coming . . .
this fetus-form that is myself
lying upon this wheeled and sheeted shelf . . .
"Good morning, Jennie, it's a beautiful day!"

Once upon a time,
I played in the sunshine
with clay dishes,
along a creek in Iowa . . .

They push the spoon between my lips,
but my mouth will not open . . .

I am on my way to the Source of my being.

—**Genevieve O. Miller**

Standing once in a candle, hollow —
There was no wick.
To look up many hundreds of feet
Lay flame in the center,
Above nothing.

Tiny gnome with me — we walked,
Stroked the walls — I said
"What is this?"
Gnome teased me, said
"Don't you know won't tell you Don't you know"
Said "This is you."
Stopped. I said
"Who are you then?"
Gnome said "I am no one,
I am you too."

Look down
My feet turn to wax.

—**Ayle Perry**

MY COLORS

My colors can save me.
All my colors lift me up.
Art is a lifesaver do you see.
All I need is paper, my colors and coffee in my cup.

At times I feel alone and lost.
Now I am poor for sure.
I know my art will one day really cost.
Sometimes I feel like I have a disease with no cure.

The power of art.
It is like a type of prayer or a beautiful song.
It can give you a fresh start.
Love, truth, beauty, with these words in your art
you can not go wrong.

My art saves my life it is a sacred act.
You may not think colorful art can save my life
but it can it is a real fact . . . .

—**Mr. Gerald S. Szewczyk**

I am Sharon.
I have an accent.
I dress funny.

I believed that my mother
could do/fix anything
religion is a primitive human invention.

—**Sharon E. Chitin**

MEN

They are sometimes nice.
Sometimes, men make us cry.
Some have a gentle touch.
Some have a rough touch.
Some are cute.
Some are homely.
Others are huggable and kissable.
Men are sometimes the untouchables.
Men are wonderful.
Men can be a pain in the heart.
Men think they are lovers.
Some think they are everything.
Some are lovers.
Some are everything.
Mine makes me feel wonderful.

—**Betty Jo Braim Stanley**

TIME AT A STAND STILL

When I laid eyes on you,
Love I knew this world belonged
to you and me. Darling with me
in your arms and I in yours
everything went to a stand still.

With us kissing so tenderly and
loving you wouldn't imagine.
With things twirling around in my mind,
All of a sudden, time just flew by
and we had to go but neither
One wanted to leave. All we wanted
was to stay wrapped up in our
own little world hoping that time
would stand still.

You can surely know my Darling
I will never forget the times
we are having together.

—**Mary Davis**

YELLOW

I took a dab of yellow
and brushed it through my mind,
It flowed into a pattern
while I stayed close behind —

"What picture shall I make of you?"
I asked the little blob,
"Something more than daffodils,"
It answered with a sob —

But springtime is your background,
"I saw that as we walked,"
and yellow said I'd stopped it there
because the road was blocked —

It told me I should clear a way
and make new paths to meet,
For first impressions cannot paint
a portrait that's complete —

—**Margie Knudsen**

I AM ME

I often walk this path alone
In thought and quiet prayer
These are my precious moments
Only mine and not to share

The breeze whispers its secrets
Nature singing for my ears alone
I enjoy this restful peacefulness
It is mine, my very own

I did not know, nor did I conceive
this strength I feel within me
renewed by unleashed freedom
Often denied my frailty

In time I must associate
with friends and family
But for now I am ONE UNTO MYSELF
I AM ME

> **—Isabel Fecteau Lowe**

NIGHT PATROL

Cement, pavement square and neat,
Lying silent by the street;

Tell me what is wrong or right,
Mute observer of the night?

Should I think, or should I Pray;
Or will I die along the way?

Although you have no eyes nor ears,
Soon when daylight slowly appears;

You will have witnessed much more than I,
From the many passers-by.

> **—Ed Williams**

THE MAN IN THE MOON

Have you ever seen the Man in the Moon?
It's dark, He'll be here soon.
To bravely stand watch—
As the stars play hopscotch.

The Man in the Moon comes to visit at night,
To make sure the stars shine bright.
He smiles and gives us a wink,
As the Sun begins to sink.

The Man in the Moon lights up the skies,
As he waits to award the prize.
And before the break of day,
He watches the twinkling stars play.

> **—Ethel Hiriart**

THE COLOR GREEN

It's the color, of the landscape.
And the leaves, on the tree.
It stands for life, not death.
It makes you alive, for life is precious.

I know the color green.
For, I seek the life, that is so dear.
And, express the love, that life brings.

In this age of self.
There are some, I hope.
Will redefine, the notes.
That all colors, will bring the hope.
To all, mankind.

> **—Stuart Lee Rosenberg**

THE NERD

The typical nerd,
He's not one of us.
Sitting all by himself,
At lunch or on the bus.
With broken rimmed glasses,
And checked bellbottom pants.
Hair is parted in the middle,
And always crawling with ants.
He thinks he is very cool,
But he has no friends.
He tries figuring it out,
And asks, "Does it end?"

> **—Julia Dickinson, age 14**

THE VISITOR

When the dripping is even,
Through the night,
Creeping and crawling,
Comes a bloody sight.
Its head is all tarnished,
With ashes and soot.
Into kids bedrooms,
It comes with a look.
So lock your door
You could be next,
You could be the victim,
Of this horrible guest.

> **—Jason Hill, age 8**

I AM NOT A MASOCHIST

It would be better
to be disemboweled—
Or eaten alive
by hungry mouths,
Than to stand before
a crowd and   speak.
Flesh ripping from my bones,
would be more tolerable, than

To feel the Whip
With every word
And be Mutilated
By attention.

> **—S. S. Garland**

BROTHERS

Way down deep in my heart
I find the love for you,
Even if you don't see things
In my point of view.

I love you dearly
Even if sometimes I don't show it,
And I'm sorry that
Sometimes, I do hit.

I'll love you always
Through good and bad,
Even if sometimes because of me
You are a little mad.

Thank you for being
There for me,
And my love, changing about you
Will never be!

> **—Heather Tuttle**

BALLOONS

As big as they are—
As bright as they are—
they're my balloons.
There's faces on them—
that look like 'toons.
Red and green and yellow,
they're plump like jello.

—Andy Hiriart, age 8

SITTING ON THE MOON

I see . . .
        dancing ballerinas
        reciting sonatinas.
Old folks walking, rumors talking.
Dreams wondering, thoughts pondering.
Music listening, swan lakes glistening.
Criminals lying, unborn babies dying.
Trees falling, loneliness calling.
The Devil working, world war lurking.
Water drowning, jealously frowning.
Clowns juggling, drug smuggling.
Aids killing, but no one feeling.
The cow just passed by,
and the dish with the spoon.
For I can see it all,
        Sitting on the moon!

—Jennifer Vallet, age 13

Why the blossoms come in May
and strew the carpet green
With colored flowers all around
and sunlight in between.

And why this spring-time joyfulness
while all about me gay
When I know the summer come
will burn it all away.

And why the lark so happy there
to sit upon the fence
And sing his song so loud and true
as if he's making sense.

And what this feeling deep inside
that turns my thoughts to you
Of wishing you could share this
while Iris is yet blue.

—Cheryl M. Green

EASTER DAWN

They rose early in the morning,
On the first day of the week.
Rushing to the grave of
The One they loved to seek.
The day was not quite dawning,
As they hurried on their way.
They could see as they approached,
The stone had been rolled away.
The grave cloth laid there empty.
The women cried and turned away.
They saw the radiant angel,
And they heard him say:
"He is not here but risen.
Come see the place where He lay."
This time with joy they turned away,
And rushed to tell the others,
What they had learned that day.

—Annell Markle

THE OUTSIDER

Ever walk up to a candy store
To find a locked door?
Or watch a family party begin
At the window, looking in?
Loving someone, but not able to fit,
No one must know, it's a secret!
Special occasions and holidays
Must they be shared, apart, always?

—Coretta M. Seguin

FOR ALWAYS, EVER

Mom is neat.
Mom is sweet.
I love her and she loves me.

Dad is rad.
Dad isn't mad (I hope).
I love him and he loves me.

We are together
For always, ever.
Because we have love for one another.

—Brandon Boice

THE OLD BOOKS

When to my old books
My soul takes a walk
Those books like fire
Come alive.
Always when I visit them
They rush right back to me.
Oh, what a feeling is there
In that strange encounter.
What an embrace takes place.
How can this meeting be described?
Here, only the feeling in the person
Can describe it.
Here, the feeling itself
Finds food for its Soul.
Oh, those old, old books,
What magnetic power they display.
And how much Love
They get from me.

—Paul Pascal

CREDIT CARDS

What do you think of a credit card
How do you really feel
Spending money, no holds barred
This is some big deal
Buy something now
Then you pay later
Yes you know how
Use your credit card if you prefer
You know what people say
When a card you do flaunt
It's the rent you pay
For things you want
That you can't afford
You always spend too much
And for this you'll never win an award
So be careful of what you do
Don't ever go too far
You never have a clue
Because you won't even win a cigar

—Country Girl

MEMORIES

Memories
Are they another man's dreams?
A reflection dancing on the clear lake.
An open book of pleasures.
The image of shadows on the wall.
The holding of yesterday's treasures.
A mirror reminding him of someone else.
The fear of the past.
A wonder of thoughts in the mind.
Ways of living in the future.
Or an image raising, overlooking the dead.
Vision.

—Grace M. Gelinas

HAUNTING MEMORIES

I know I fear the known . . .
   much more than the unknown.
For therein lies the despair
   that envelops my mind.
Robbing me of my quest.
   My desire is to let the fears
that make me afraid to be
   justifiably emersed in happiness
disseminate into oblivion.
   There is an urgency to get on with
my life in search for contentment.
   To let go of the fear
of being hurt — again.

—Betty Gray

SWEET DREAMS

Sweet dreams they say
but, is it true
why isn't it always that way?

Can't someday a dream awake
and hold out its hands for me to take

Carry me on and through all to see
open the doors and set me free

Happiness and Love for all to share
and bad and evil will disappear

Sweet dreams
Sweet dreams

Whatever that means

—Linda Nicole

Old photographs.
Was I prettier then? They are now.
Looking back, crying over lost mistakes.
The tattered memories,
like paper so worn it's Kleenex—
they don't help as much as I'd prefer,
to make my life the perfect melody
of peace and happiness.

The pain felt before,
is the same pain I'll feel later
and forever.
Learning from missed opportunities
was never a strong point.
The old photos just get older,
and more faded.

—Amy Winter

GENTLE SPIRIT

Lunar in space
Moths in orbit

Colors in good taste
Rainbows, ice cream, and Love.
Life is a weave.
Spin a yarn or two,
But keep the pattern simple.
Remember, I Love you.

—Audray Quill

FIRST LOVE

From the early years of life,
I have suffered much strife.
Remembering things I never did,
Still I wish I was a kid.
Teenage girls are a curse,
Long legged women are much worse.
Once they find how much you care,
Very quickly they will scare.
Even faster they will leave,
So you sit alone and grieve.
Until the day that they get dumped,
Coming knocking you'll be stumped.
Knowing not just what to do,
Simply saying "I hate you."

—Matt McBurnett

LINGERING

Cologne drifted in the air.
Was it a stranger's?
I didn't recognize the scent,
Yet it seemed so familiar.
My mind playing tricks on me?
   Just a possibility.
Maybe it's just an old lover's
   Long lost scent.
Haunting me from time to time,
Calling my mind to uncertainty.
   A stranger behind my back
   Wait . . . who could it be?
   It's only my boyfriend
With his cologne and roses for me.

—Elaine Pidlaoan

PARADISE ISLAND

I would like to go to Paradise Island,
And be there just with you.
We would be alone together,
Under the skies so blue.

We would sit there in the moonlight,
And count the stars above.
I would wrap my arms around you,
And tell you of my love.

I know I could make you happy,
If you would let me try.
While we played there on the island,
Sweetheart just you and I.

But I guess I am dreaming,
Of the island for us two.
For I haven't even told you,
I am in love with you.

—Wanda Hunter

LOVE'S BLINDNESS
What happened?
You were with me a whisper ago
In the pitch black of love's blindness
I did not see you go
I can hear you
Calling me
Reassuring me
I know you will not be back
You have gone where I cannot follow
I am lost
In the night
Please do not leave me here
Alone.

—Paula G. Brown

PREVAILING HOPE
Darkness surrounds,
heavily deafening.
The eyes hold the only sense,
and they too fail upon every second
when they succumb to the darkness,
and blink.
But lo in their waken time
they see lights.
Lights upon flickering lights above.
Each its own world,
each its own mystery.
The vast darkness enhancing
its life.

—Paula Kay Myers

WHY AM I?
Citronella candles burning bright.
Insects flying left and right.
The moon is high.
There are many stars in the sky.
I sit here all alone,
For, alas, no one else is home.
Looking at the lighted sky,
I sit here wondering,
Why am I?
Confusion burns in my soul.
As I'm sinking away from life,
I ask myself,
Why am I?

—Dana Desch, age 13

If I think positive, and I believe
that's right.
Soon I'll be happy every morning
and night.
Dark clouds surround me, but they're
drifting away
Blue skies, and laughter are coming
my way
Someday, I know my dreams will
come true.
For my Rainbow of Happiness is
long overdue.
Don't ever be afraid, don't ever
give in.
Have Faith in yourself and you're
bound to win.

—Patricia Penney

FOREVER IN MY HEART
Alas, the final day has arrived
The day I hear you say good-bye
I'll never forget you, my love still grows
Remembering your warmth the sunset glows

I'll hold in my heart our precious dreams
Refreshing love like a clear cool stream
Whenever I'm down and feeling blue
My tears will dry with every thought of you

And when you have gone and time has passed by
And age is upon me and I'm soon to die
I'll close my eyes remembering you that day
Then with a smiling heart I'll fade away.

—Elizabeth Anne Wrasman

POETIC WINE
Did Lily Pons divinely trill
When first she sang a happy tune?
Did Shakespeare nonchalantly pen
"MacBeth" between the dawn and noon?

Does one compose within a day
An immortal sonnet? One must dream;
Embellishing, enhancing it
Till it is poetry supreme!

Eternal poets think and dream
Until their lyrics flow like wine
And fill our goblets brimming full
With overwhelming song divine!

—Joyce Wiley Seefeld

BEYOND THE DESERT'S EDGE
The tempest has finally subsided.
I have endured the burning desert heat.
I've walked, in solitude, a long deserted mile.
As I look into a new horizon,
beyond the desert's edge.

Before me lies a fresh new start.
A strange new city, towers in the sky.
Radiant rays of life emerging from within,
beyond the desert's edge.

No sense looking back in retrospect.
Everything I ever had will forever be,
beyond the desert's edge.

—Pedro A. Reyes

STAY ON FIRE FOR GOD
Keep your heart on fire and all aglow
So your coals of faith will not burn low
Pray to God to kindle the fire on high
And help you reach his castle in the sky
Tell God you love him and really care
So in return his blessings he will share
Let God teach you how to live
So of your talents you will freely give
Receive love and peace in your heart
And forget your past and make a new start
When God talks to you be willing to listen
To hear in your life what is missing
Be ready when God knocks at your door
To receive his blessings and ask for more
Faith in God will kindle your burning desire
To let God's grace control your raging fire

—Thomas E. Harris

LOOKING BACK

Yesterday is full
of memories that are dear.

Tomorrow is full
of things that we don't want to hear.

Yesterday had
fondness and happiness and cares.

Tomorrow holds
loneliness and sorrow and despair.

Yesterday was what tomorrow will be.

—Felicia Lewis

A LANDLORD'S CRY

The American Dream, which is mine,
Became a nightmare . . . .
When those tenants didn't care,
And now there is no more time!

Something that is your very own,
Something they say you must share.
And now with a different tone,
It's really nothing you can spare.

I lose sleep, wondering why,
No one seems to even care.
There's no sense to even try,
Why is it, that I must share,

My piece of the American Pie!?

—Diane M. Gusciora

CYCLE

In love we are conceived
through God and in to God
with love we are received
for love and because of love
child to and into, Mother
Mother for and before, daughter
given birth by giving birth
meeting expectations, expectations met
conflicts emerging, conflicts merged
emotions imparted, parted emotions
letting go to learn, learning to let go
pupil to teacher, teacher to pupil
Parent into friend, friend unto parent
Life from love, loving for life

—Ana Underwood

C'EST LA VIE À VRAIMENT DE BOD FORMÉ

We live to love
life to respect
respect of inspiration
from within

We die of hate
death of no regard
regard of nothingness
from without

We give our lives
life to the young
young to learn our mistakes
from experience

We take to ourselves
selfishness of desire
desire of want
we live to love

—Jim Gallagher

WILD BANK

The titled print, hangs on a
    wall on 4 west,
    the playbill reads, "My
    Fair Lady."
The bouquet of purple iris
    tied with a green ribbon
curlycued.
You lie there, ravaged
    by the indignity of your
    mental illness,
Restrained . . . for self protection,
    the ironies of Wildbank.

—Patricia A. Nester

I must leave Norway now
Land of the roving Viking
As you found my land
A thousand years ago
So now have I found yours.
Your cool deep woods
Your lakes of beauty
The sky so blue that encompasses me
The mountains call and I would come,
But I must leave Norway now.

The hills stand here
Unchanged since Tecumseh roamed
At dawn deer drink at the river's edge
And jump, their tailes white flags waving.

—Alice R. Clupper

A NOTE OF THANKS

The morning breeze blows o'er my
    pillow,
    How sweet and fresh it seems;
It touches my cheek, and seems to
    lessen
    The turmoil of my dreams.
I close my eyes, in utmost ecstasy,
    Much pleasure doth abound;
The blowing of the little curtains,
    Scarcely make a whispered sound.
And once again, I thank My Father,
    For moments such as these;
For all the love and careful giving
    That came in on that breeze.

—Violet M. Penland

TAKE A LONG LOOK AT LIFE

Take a long look at life my friend,
    and tell me what you see.
Is it full of happiness and joy or
pain and agony

Is it full of happy things that only
we can share.
Or is it full of tales of heartache
and despair.

No matter what we do, of this you
can be sure.
Through all life's toils and trials
our friendship will endure.

So take a long look at life my friend
and tell me what you see.
    It won't always be like
this through all eternity!

—Nita Stokley

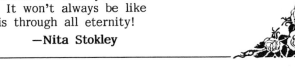

BELATED FATHER

When you first became a dad
You didn't know what you had,
You were so busy through the day
There wasn't time for you all to play.

You had no time to share in their fun
Or even to say —."I love you-hon,"
Hear their prayers, kiss them good night
To tuck them in, turn off the light.

You really did miss so much
First steps, first words and such,
Life is short, the years rush past
They all grew up so very fast.

Now with families of their own
I hope you would like it to be known
It really wouldn't have been so bad
To have had them call you "Dad."

—Charlotte Marschner

OH CANDLE

Oh candle in the window,
so shiny and bright.
Sometimes you give me hard times
when you go out.
When I come the next day.
And boy are you bright.
You live a while then you die,
I tried to resist you.
Oh candle in the window,
where do you live?
What is your name?
Oh dear little candle you
set my heart on fire.

—Rachael R. Kimbrough
written at age 8

WHY ME?

I'm sure there are many out there
Who's asked these same words too,
But are there many more like
me who always seem to be blue?
Why when there's trouble brewing
it always seeks out me.
When someone has to go without,
If someone has to lose their job
And if someone is to be in pain
It always seems to be me!
What have I done to suffer
so, I've forgotten how to smile.
My mother has told me to
take the first step, and
God will take the last mile!

—"Mae"

MY MOTHER

The sound of her voice
brings joy.

The smile on her face
brightens up my day.

She's the one that brushes
my sadness away.

Just when I thought happiness
would never stay.

—See Ka Xiong

BE KIND TO MOTHER

What a Blessing is one's mother!
But children don't seem to bother.
She can slave from morning till night;
Whether sick or not, that's alright.

Without her life is so empty.
Though your loved ones may be plenty,
There's no one that can fill her place,
No not one in this whole wide race.

Now be kind to your mother dear!
She loves you and has much to bear.
It matters not the trials she endures,
Tis your life's journey she treasures,

Little Deeds of loving kindness
And words of praise with tenderness,
To Mother the Dearest and best,
T'will be comforting when she's at rest.

—Evelyn Cromer Bowden

TO SOMEONE I MET TOO LATE

Awake and lonely at two a.m.
I think of you
I long to see you
Is this love?
Or only the heat of the August night?

My radio sings sad songs
Do I want you because of love?
Or love you because I'm lonely?
Does it matter?

I don't need promises
Love doesn't come with a guarantee
If you hold me
My night won't be so dark
Because you want me

—Rita Flener

THE LORD'S WAVES

Your waves rise up
so high and mighty
reaching for the sky,
strong by your power.

Then fall as if failing
while striving to touch shore
but cannot,
returning to try
once more . . . .

—Donitta Young

GOODBYE

Goodbye, my darling
And as you go away
Always remember I'll think of you
With each passing day

I cry as I watch
Your plane fly away
And I hope that I will see you
Again someday

Please don't forget me
But if you do
At least remember
How much I loved you.

—Stacy Timpson

DREAMS

I can recall when I was small
 I always loved to sing about
the characters in nursery rhymes
and other childish things
When I grew up into my teens
 to sing was my ambition
 and hoped someday someone
 would give me an audition
But now I'm old as time does fly
 my dreams have come and gone
 and still I love to sing
 But all the audience that I have
 is me myself and I.

—Teresa Antonelli

THE ONLY ONE

You're the only thing I ever knew,
 You're the only one I ever knew—
You're the only one in my past.

You're the only thing I think,
You're the only one I think—
You're the only one in my future.

You're the only thing I know,
You're the only one I know—
You're the only one in my dreams.

You're the only thing right now,
You're the only one right now—
You're the only one forever.

—Donna Moore

PARANOID

His mind is always paranoid,
 It spins off like an asteroid.
The pictures flowing through the eyes,
Distorting shapes and changing size.
Hallucinations then take place,
The pain is all over his face.
Distracting noises bother him.
His future looks dark, very grim.
He fights with all his will and might,
Hoping to see some guiding light.
When paranoia takes control,
The mind will start to rock and roll.
His sanity will be lost,
And all his life will be the cost.

—George S. Kim

BRINGING ME TRUTH

Do not come to me with false praise
 Do not shower me with half truths of
your worst days
Do not cover me with elusive advice
Do not darken my view, when you
have not yet seen the light
But do bring me the wisdom of your
pain
For from your grief, only we can gain
Bring me tales of what desires burn
For from your drowned passions, we
can learn
Do not color all that is bleak
See it for what it is, and we shall
find the truth we seek

—Wanda Griffith

PARASITE

Could a parasite ever be
 lonely, when he feeds upon
another?
Now who could love a para-
site, except the parasite's mother?
Greedy little monster, greedy
as greedy can be
Who do you remind me of,
why I guess it's me.
I hate to admit it, and yet
I know it's true.
In many, many ways, I'm
just like you.

—Grace M. Clark

HAPPY

Happy, I was Happy today.
 Being Happy is feeling BEAUTY!

Happy, I was Happy today.
Being Happy is feeling SWEET!

Happy, I was Happy today.
Being Happy is feeling EXCITEMENT!

Happy, I was Happy today.
Being Happy is feeling CHEERFUL!

Happy, I was Happy today.
Being Happy is feeling GREAT!

Happy, I was Happy today.

—Carmen Frenzel

DREAMS

The candle flickers in the draft
 As I wander in the past
The ashes of dreams
The ghost of hope
The feel of emptiness they evoke.

Behold, what is this I see?
A tiny sprig of destiny?
A glimmer of tomorrow
From seeds of the past
Rise up, rise up, hold on fast!

The future rises from the past.
As we turn to dreams to come.
Away from dreams, set with the sun.

—Mary Rose McKee

PATIENCE

It is quite an oddity of nature
 that occurs
 when one possesses
 the awareness
 required to withstand
 the subtle seduction
 of time.
 Such simplicity
 is captivating.
What makes this refined rebuttal
 most stirring
 are the gentle, easy
 mannerisms of its
 distinction.

—J.C. Aeed

The setting sun was sinking from the hill,
That wonderful day you came, our lives to fill.
Filling our hearts with your sunny smile and,
Filling our arms, with your many charms.

Your eyes so bright, your cheeks so tan,
We pictured you like your dad, one day a man.
Til then dear heart, live fully, have fun,
We are so very proud you are our Grandson.

—**Betty H. Partridge**

A CHRISTMAS CARD FOR HEATHER

To my granddaughter—
A happy time is Christmas,
But oh how sad 'twould be;
The sweet little face of Heather
On Christmas we did not see.
Just rush right over to Pa Pa's house—
Such pretty gifts there will be.
You'll have much joy and laughter,
'Cause they are from Ma Ma and me.
Dear Heather, Merry Christmas,
And many, many more.
I still will send you cards,
When I am eighty four.
          Love,
          Pa Pa

—**Doyle Elkin**

THE REDUCTION PRAYER
(To be said before each meal)

Dear LORD:

Before I put "this" on my lips
Soon to find it upon my hips,
Caution me of upcoming days . . .
Weddings—Showers—Balls—Soirees.

Remind me that I yearn for "thin"
That being "plump" just isn't in.
Give me strength to walk each day—
Help me melt these pounds away.

The weight comes off so very slow
Please keep me cheerful as I go.
Fill me with good, wholesome self-pride
For soon I'll be, "Mother-of-the-Bride."

—**Ceatta Mickey Beluscak**

WRINKLES

The signs of my age are showing.
New wrinkles appear everyday.
My skin has become less glowing.
The edges are beginning to fray.

I hear there's a new way to tighten
The skin near the eyes and chin.
A new way to change and heighten
The features that make us fit in.

I thought I'd get my face lifted,
To be accepted by all my peers,
But I thought how I have been gifted
By the wisdom of my many years.

I remembered what the Bible has said
About the world and it's loving its own.
So I grinned and climbed into bed
And just left my old face alone.

—**Cecil W. Pierce**

MY LOVE

My love I have with
golden hair
Streams upon my lap
Thy eyes are as the
sky above
Thy skin white as the
clouds themselves
Thou sings sweeter
than nightingales
That sing when the moon
is full
I love Thee and Thou
returns Thy love to me

—**Cathleen Sitton, age 9**

JOURNEYS

How far men had to travel
Their vigil then to keep . . .
To find, at last, the manger
And view the child, asleep.

How blessed are we this Christmas.
No journey need we fear,
When faith can whisper, "Jesus?"
And Love responds, "I'm here."

For them, the long dark journey
To seek their "promised Light . . ."

For us, Christ's shining Presence,
Illumining our night.

—**Mrs. Mary (Dexter) Hepner**

ANGELS FLIGHT
Prince of promise, angels delight,
Child of man, mornings light,
Dream of heavens flight.

Destination unknown,
Looking for a home.
Journey's end, my friend.

Infinite thread of time goes on.
Past, present and future
Are but one.

Night disintegrates,
Evil darkness overcome.
Light of day . . . the sun.

—**G. Diane Hayes**

CAMPING

          beautiful nature,
God's the creator
          beauty at its best,
cool enough for a vest
          campfires at night,
to my delight
          marshmallow roasting,
you can see them toasting
          hiking for fun,
let's all run!
          taking naps,
sleepingbags with snaps
          time to go home,
we have memories of our own.

—**Katherine M. Simone**

BEST FRIENDS

Our friendship is immeasurable
Unable to be put to words
You are there when the ocean is stable
Or when the tide turns
A friend of mine you'll always be
Forever 'til eternity
I am yours and you are mine
Best of friends throughout all times

—Diane Katherine Rinehart

FRIENDS FOREVER

My thoughts drifting, wandering away
From year to year, day to day
What I've done and what I'll do
My memories often float back to you

All the things I wish to know
Can't think of, can't let go
All my dreams and fears to be
The ones I might not ever see

Some friends are forever
Some will be
Friends forever
Like you and me

—Sarah Yarosevich

YOU ARE!

In the day I think
You are the sun,
Warming the air,
Making pedals beam in the light.

At night I think
You are the stars,
Singing to the heavens
With light twinkling in your eyes.

All the time I think
You are the sun, the moon, the stars,
Lighting the sky in the day
Brightening the sky at night.

—William Kenneth Brubaker, age 15

MY PEOPLE

The knowledge of my people
Is quite remarkable

They stand apart from the rest
Like shadows in the night

Gay and head strong they stand
In city streets or in crowds.

They are lustless people
Who give but expect nothing in return

Living apart from society
Gives them a new found courage

They speak with people in their minds
And love in their hearts

Oh, my people are not different
Because they encounter challenges

They are a special breed of people
And I wish you could see the way
They make me laugh.

—Coni B. Olivier

UPON A HILLTOP

I enjoy sitting upon a hilltop
in the bright sun.
I enjoy sitting upon a hilltop
having great fun.

I enjoy lying upon a hilltop
dreaming away.
I enjoy lying upon a hilltop
all covered in hay.

I enjoy standing upon a hilltop
standing under a tree.
I enjoy standing upon a hilltop
and heaving a sigh lazily.

—Samantha M. Wolfe

THE SETTING
A SUNSET OVER THE PLATTE RIVER

A bright yellow ribbon of light
Lay upon the river,
Long and winking.
Slowly turning to gold, then red.
The Sun a bright ball,
Tinged with pinks, and reds,
And purples.
Vagrant wispy clouds
Reflecting the colors
On a deep blue backdrop.
Slowly sinking beyond the horizon,
Peace, Serenity, all.

—Patricia Joyce Hill

TO A ROSE

I clip you from your tender stem
Very carefully, lest I spill some sup
Of crystal dew from your cup;
And lose your fascinating gem.
I shall but place you at my plate
To feed my soul, the while,
Grace be said — without guile,
To keep me 'till evening late,
Without a fear of what may come
For your philosophy will tell
Much in which to ponder on,
Deep delightful thoughts — O well,
How I wish I better knew the one
Who created a rose, a man, a hell!

—S. Elizabeth Gorley

WHAT IS A MEMORY?

A memory is the unplanned thought —
that flows from someone's past,
She brings to mind a special time —
that only did not last,
This memory is a hidden place —
that does not always show,
Yet in this place one finds the room —
to let their feelings go.

One should never fear a memory —
it's because of her they'll find,
The spark that brings in meaning —
from a time they left behind,
She teaches many lessons —
that gently point the way,
And after she is finished —
she softly slips away.

—William F. Hoffman, Jr.

THE LOST LOVE

There is no real love here
only heartache, that doesn't go away
No cure exist for this empty soul
At birth you have love, within you
until you live and it's taken away
The pain is too much for one to endure
If there is a love for this empty soul,
let it come before judgement day

—Catrina Anne Monts

DAWN

Greetings, provider.
You meet me on the horizon,
    and I once again sing my joy.
From dew-speckled grasses
    and snow-capped peaks,
I welcome your arrival with open arms
    and warmth in my heart.
Good morning.

—Heather J. Buchanan

CONFIDENCE

It is with me that goals can be accomplished
Just strive for whatever you have wished
Never give up and all will be achieved
For in the end it will be received
If you use me it can be done
The results will be seen in the long run
With me there isn't anything you can't do
But my only existence is through you
It is your force that makes me weak or strong
But in your possession I do belong

—C. L. Ferree

PHANTOM OF IGNOMINY

An illusion of reality
Invades our heads
A clarification of an illiterate world
Is much needed in this day and age
Prejudice
And stereotype
Two of the many we can do without
If we are so able-minded
As many of us are
We can subdue the hatred
As the Phantom of Ignominy
Invades our heads.

—Shawna Pauline Romolliwa, age 14

I am proud of what I am.
I have no money in my hand,
But I have wealth within my heart.
A richness of spirit that is a part
        of what I am.

I've love of family and of friends—
The kind of love that never ends.
Love that accepts me as I am—
A special someone in a Master Plan.

The better me
I try to be,
The more that love fills the span,
The more I'm proud
        of what I am.

—Pamela Watson

THE OCEAN AT NIGHT

The ocean is
A fierce, fiery creature,
Thrashing wildly in the darkness,
Humongous waves thundering at me on
the shore.
But from a faraway distance,
The ocean isn't scary anymore,
Just a beautiful, peaceful sight.

—Melissa A. Sparr, age 10

TAKE THE TIME

Take the time
to do something good.
Take the time
to help your neighborhood.
Take the time
to listen to the robins sing.
Take the time
it's worth more than a diamond ring.

—Tim Strong

FREEDOM

Freedom is something that means so much,
A smile, a laugh and a kind little touch.
Your touch is caring, and that's what I need,
    To Keep my heart from wanting to bleed.
    Some people say that Love is a Myth,
But you're the only one I dream of being with.
    I'm blinded with fear about being rejected,
    But with you I know I won't be neglected.
        If you're as true as you seem to be,
    Then It's with you that I want to be free.

—Lara Lee Holst

THE MAN UPON THE WALL

As I walk and search the halls
I see the man upon the wall
trapped on canvas by fading paint
his brilliant colors growing faint
He calls to me, he makes me cry
I cannot help, I tell him why
his eyes grow wide, a tear runs down
the smile that's become a frown
I turn away, I close my eyes
I run and run, and hear his cries
as I walk and search the halls
I avoid the man upon the wall

—Angela Kathleen Flannery

THE CONSEQUENCE OF CHOICE

Today's society if you're bored
will give you drugs to be stored
In your body to be kept
To help you manage life's attempt
But let me warn you, if you will
Of what happens as you pay the till
They'll digest you with their might
They will cause you to lose sight
Of things you thought precious and dear
They will tell you 'they were never there'
But as you ponder on your condition
A man will come with more sedition
And you will pay to be corrected
Of the belief you're not infected

—Jeffrey W. Schuller

398

STORMS

Storms
bring us to our homes.

The meeting
of concrete and wet.
I smell the announcement.

Thunder.
The sky speaks loudly to its creatures.

Lightning.
Flash the designs.
This is
your
time

Animals,
the Rain Maker speaks.
Dance in your dwellings.

Raindrops,
speak to us until dawn

as storms
bring us to our homes . . .

—Debra Ann Pappani

STAIRWAY

The brain is like a star
Shining from afar
Or like a galaxy
Expanding into reality

For when we see and hear and feel
It sometimes seems so unreal
When the thoughts begin to flow
Like a supernova's glow
It is then that we will know
What to do and where to go

For then the brain
Will become a mind
And the mind
We will surely find
Is unique and one of a kind

—Joseph Gregory Salvo

THE BLUES

The blues are not supposed to be
A way of life for you and me.
They are a way of venting steam
That pent up due to stress extreme!

They crop up at a time that's bad.
A time when mostly I feel bad.
I try and give myself a lift,
But feel like jumping off a cliff!

I wallow in despair and pain,
And drop down falling bad again.
I feel I don't deserve much joy.
I feel like someone's puppet toy.

Then when the Blues have gone away,
I hope to salvage what I may.
To run until the next mishap,
When all my happiness is sapped.

—Joe Coleman

CARING ABOUT YOU

I care about you very much, with all my heart,
right to the bottom of my heart.
The most important thing in the world,
which I needed so much or
I ever wanted a love in my heart
and you in my life.

—Cheryl Small

HOPE AND FREEDOM

We who have been born in this great land certainly have
been blessed,
For we have freedom and a chance for happiness;

To work towards a goal, and speak our mind,
To wake up in the morning without fear of any kind.

People from other lands come to us with hope;
To escape a life from which they could not cope,

With dreams and wishes, a new life to start,
And from this great country to never part.

To work freely, love, raise families and live,
And their skills and cause to this country give.

They learn from us, and we learn from them;
This makes our nation full of great men.

We'll fight to keep our freedom for others who come,
And welcome them as Miss Liberty has done.

United States Of America is the land I speak of,
Where the people stand together and reach out with love.

Don't ever take for granted the freedom you are given,
For we must work together to keep this land we live in.

—(Artist) Hope Marie Maki

NEVER BEEN TO THE MOUNTAINS

I've never been to the mountains, I've never been to the
great lakes,
But the visions I have in my mind are truly great.

I've been to the sea shore, walked down the beach;
Seen the moon over the water, it seemed close enough to
reach.

I've never seen the desert nor the long strips of plain,
But I know in my mind that they both need plenty of rain.

Everybody talks about the great islands, where the great
breakers roll;
But I've lived in my lonely spot, it seems to satisfy my soul.

I've never seen the big red wood trees that they say grows so
tall,
But there is none so stately that don't break when they fall.

I've seen the lowly dogwood on whose branches my Savior
hung,
I've seen the big pines that have grown in the southern sun.

I've seen the stately oak on whose limbs the acorns grow,
That feed the squirrels and the old black crow.

I've seen the magnolia and their flowers so sweet,
The beautiful holly tree with its berries so neat.

As I think and look at all the spacious things,
I think of the Great One that made them and sing.

How great thou art, oh Master Divine,
The world's Master and mine.

—Ollie H. Taylor

My mother just passed away,
We buried her yesterday,
God, we thank you for
  her love
That still guides us
  from above.

In memory of my mother, Wilma
Garner, Mrs. Sylvester Garner

—Steve Garner

SILENCE

The silence of the library is a wonderful thing
There is no one who laughs, raps, or sings
It is only broken by,
The sound of two girls talking

And in the distance I see books more and more
What are they all just sitting there for
I can from see a book about vases of Ming
Oh yes, silence is a wonderful thing.

—Sanjay Bhojraj

AN EARLY FROST

Standing tall full blossom
in view.
    A loved one lost why did
it have to be you.
    The colors were showing, you
were in your prime.
    No matter the reason, I guess
it was time.
    Memories of you are left, not
lost. Like of a rose in an
early frost.

—Mary (Page) Eckstein

My room I fill with bits of lace,
doilies, dresser scarves.
A ruffled edge adorns each space;
flowers bloom on the walls.

The bed is loaded, rounded,
with pillow-tops, appliqued;
the window sash surrounded
by curtain panels, filet'd.

An Irish rose, some hairpin work,
crocheted stuff abounds.
What inner drive does hereby lurk
to so decorate my surrounds?

—Jayne M. D'Agostin

CAUGHT

You caught me unawares
When you slipped back for the forgotten
    briefcase.
(I had been exulting in the joy
Of having the house to myself—
Of being free from your
Unwanted presence.) . . . . .
I tried to put on my mask
Of wifely concern,
But you caught the flash of dislike
And unwelcome that crossed my face.
. . . .
The hurt in your eyes tortures me still.

—Naidene Stroud Trexler

WHEN I WAS SLEEPING

When I was sleeping time sneaked by
When I was sleeping trees were dancing
When I was sleeping the wind was howling
When I was sleeping owls were eating
When I was sleeping people were dancing
When I was sleeping babies were crying
When I was sleeping my dreams came true

—Heather Mailand

A HOME WITHOUT LAUGHTER

A home without laughter,
Is as quiet as a tomb,
A home without laughter,
    Echoing from every room!

Now I live in a home,
    Where one hears laughter daily.
But it is so sad to find,
    That it is coming only from — ME!

—Bernice Couey Bishop

LOVELESS LIFE

I look into the mirror of past life
It reflects back feelings of sadness
Anger, and resentments in bitter sorrow
Empty love in the depths beyond
Love of life in the healing of the soul
Buried deep in my heart
Years of pain anchor it there
No release ever allows it to emerge
Uncertain emotions to hide it
Changing love beyond recognition
Loveless life of the past

—C.A. Harrington

bus from the south

That seaman—
he was all alone . . .
on a bus full of strangers.
He stood off   secluded,
    buried in his black trench coat,
                watching,
following with his dark eyes, hands
    inside his pockets,   silent.
Maybe he was 19,
    or 20.
But he never told me.
. . . he only watched.

—Tracy J. Cade

IDLE MINDS

Today I wrote a story book.
    For little folks to read.
tomorrow I'll write a love song,
just for you and me.

I'm always doing something,
I keep busy all the time.
like Pa, and Ma, before me.
I deplore Idle Minds.

Idle Minds, are worthless Minds.
Not worth a hill of beans.
in my opinion, Idle Minds.
Have never accomplished anything.

—James C. Price

SPARROW

Brownish-gray echos its cry
So lonely to thy ear
Small one chipping
   Away with song
So beautiful to hear.

—Persia L. (Polly) Gilbert

GUESS

You wake me in the morning
with your annoying monotone.

Some people would like to beat you,
though you are mechanically innocent.

Tomorrow I must get up at 8,
so I will set you for 11.

—D. Staiano

WONDERFUL CHILD OF MINE

Wonderful child of mine
I remember when you learned to climb
So many years we have left behind.

Will we still have time, to do all
the things we have left to do, and
say all the things we have left to say.

Wonderful child of mine.

—Celeste L. Kotter

FIRST KISS

      The first kiss scared me
that's why I went and told.

      The first kiss was daring
you certainly were bold.

      That first kiss was special

I hold it dearly in my heart

      That first kiss sealed a promise
that we would surely never part.

—J. Roach

POETRY

It's the eloquence of truth from deep thought,
exceedingly noble to me and has wrought
out of my own life's strenuous tribulations
victories in difficult and adverse situations.

To a different language and country born,
I tried meaningful poetry, without adorn,
banning melancholy with realistic style
in sensible rhyming words, all the while.

It simplified and softened the predicament,
writing and solitude bolstered armament
against destructive tension and stress,
changing my attitude, unlocking duress.

Rewards came in a challenging pleasure
and education, that's always a treasure.
To master this art makes one really think
that by coming to praises there's also a link.

Between endearment and joy to discover
the good and beauty for a poetry lover,
for the ones who understand and have feel
for great truths, and tell it — short and real.

—Gÿs J. van Beek

FALL

Fall is when winds blow,
leaves fall, and you play in
the leaves and climb
the fall trees.

—Leslie Anne Chouinard, age 8

NO COZY BAND TO TEA

For one, a magic flute,
Needless lessons to boot;
The other, a whistle of wood.
Inevitably, never could
This papa gain
On his son's fame.

—Jerry Pfeiffer

AWAITING WINTERS LOVE

Winds are howling through the trees,
coming up to winters freeze.

To look above a sun lit sky,
the winds do take thee up so high.

To sit and wonder, where my love,
will descend upon me, as a dove.

Wanting, waiting, for you here,
Wanting, waiting, for you to be near.

—RJI

DOVE

You may ask why,
A dove flies through the sky,
It means peace.

When two people are happily married,
There is a dove,
That stands for love.

The reason for this rhyme,
Is the dove sounds like you,
all the time.

—Hannah Wenzka, age 9

THIS THING WE CALLED OUR TIME

Why is it always me who is left behind?
You don't really have to say your goodbye.
I don't need to hear the words for all your whys.
I guess I've known for quite awhile.
Your heart and mind were closing me out
Leaving me behind. Treating me like a child
"In this thing we called our time."
Your eyes didn't know me anymore.
You walked away and I needed you.
My life fell on the line. Your lips said no more.
You would not hear; you didn't love
"In this thing we called our time."
Now, it's my turn. You hurt me inside
But I'll never say.
Leave me with a little pride
Through the tears that were cried.
Now, I don't want you to stay.
Torn apart, here in my heart, it's empty, cold and bare.
You became so unsure . . . when you left me behind.
"In this thing we called our time."

—Joan Carole Trier

About The Authors

Authors are listed in alphabetical order by name or pen name.

Maryann Abajian was born on Oct. 19, 1964, in Passaic, New Jersey. She is a housewife and mother. She married Antoine Abajian on Dec. 26, 1985. Her memberships are: Right to Life and Human Rights Organizations. **Her comments:** I have always been intrigued by nature and life in general. **Snow** was written a few years back. What inspired me to write it was, I was gazing out the window one night, looking at the snow, and the words just came into place!.. 127

Maryann Abajian

Howard O'Neale Adams has been reading poetry ever since he lived on a farm in El Paso, near Beebe, Arkansas. He was born on Jan. 21, 1919, the third son of Howard and Ethel Adams. He won an Athletic Scholarship to attend the University of Arkansas where he lettered in three sports; football, basketball, and track. He was co-captain of the basketball team and captain of the Razorback football team. He played six years Pro Football for the New York Giants, where he earned a spot on the regular team as end. The number on his jersey was number 30. He now is an NFL pensioner. He has received several honors. He married beautiful Theda Royster from Rogers, Arkansas. They have been married for forty-five years. Their marriage date was January 14, 1944. He coached and taught school in Sand Springs, Oklahoma for 32 years. He served in the U. S. Air Force during World War II. He has two children, Howard II, and Rebecca L. Adams. Howard is self employed and Rebecca is an attorney with her own Law Firm. She holds two degrees from Stevens College and a Juris Doctorate

Howard O'Neale Adams degree from Southern Methodist University, Dallas, Texas. We live in the country at Candlestick Beach, Sand Springs, Oklahoma. He plays guitar and writes music as a hobby. We live close to The Bald Eagles at Lake Keystone and he is an avid bird watcher. He watches the eagles every day as he walks a mile to the Dam and back from his home. We now have over 100 Eagles that nest here during winter months. There's plenty of fresh fish, rabbits, rodents, and squirrels here for them to eat. They migrate to Alaska in the summer months. We have five bird baths, seven bird houses, and three feeders in our yard. O'Neale now works half a day in daughter Rebecca's Law offices in Sand Springs, Oklahoma. Theda does lots of charitable work and is a house keeper...24

Shantay Marguerite Al-Kassir was born Aug. 15, 1961, in Los Angeles, CA. She previously attended West Los Angeles College. She is a Kindergarten Teachers Aide and a Finishing School Instructor. She married Ezzat Al-Kassir on Sept. 19, 1989. Her publications: **Semi-Automatic Weapons and Hunting** was published in **The Outlook Newspaper**, 1989. She received an award on **The Accident**, for best poem in 1978, which was published in the High School Poetry Book. **Her comments:** My poem, **The Young Widows Poem**, is dedicated to my late husband of only one month. He passed away at age 23 on Oct. 27, 1989. May God bless him and comfort me.......................161

Shantay Marguerite Al-Kassir

Martha L. Allums was born on July 24, 1937, in Tyler, Smith County, Texas. She attended Pan American University, Tyler Jr. College, San Jacinto Jr. College studying both Business and Banking Courses. She also had three years of creative writing classes. She is employed at the Lone Star Bank, N.A., Highlands in Houston, Texas. She married her husband, David, on May 22, 1981. Her memberships include: Fine Arts Club, San Jacinto College, Houston, Texas and Support for Theatre and Artist groups. Her publications include: **The Three of Us,** a narrative, published in **Prism** (1990); five poems published in **Prism** (1989); four poems published in **Prism** (1990); and a short story published in **Prism** (1990). Her awards include: 1990 First Place Narrative in the Fine Arts Contest at San Jacinto College and a 1990 Second Place Poetry in the Fine Arts Contest at San Jacinto College. **Her comments:**

Martha L. Allums After three years of creative writing classes, I was a copy writer for T.V. Commercials in my 20s. Writing is my <u>first</u> love. Themes relate to my observations of changing life in America, emotions of people and impressions I've known and meet....................104

Phyllis Altomare is the pen name for **Phyllis Arabik,** who was born on Sept. 15, 1946, in Springfield, Massachusetts. She attended Springfield Puttnum High School and Westfield State University. She is a hair stylist and owner of two Salons with twin sister. **Her comments:** A new phase of life for me has been poetry. Poems are another way of communicating. I thoroughly enjoy reading and writing them to the fullest. **Parade** is my favorite poem. These feelings are not only my own but many more like me, who would like to give special thanks to all our Viet Nam Veterans...........333

Phyllis Arabik

Linda Schaaf Aton was born on Dec. 9, 1942, in Louisville, Kentucky. She received a B.A. in Literature from Indiana University. She was an art student. She is a housewife, former teacher, photographer, and a sales clerk. She married her husband, Michael, in 1976. Her publications include: **Black Asphalt Roofs** published in Iron (Northumberland) 1976. **Her comments:** I wrote this poem on a napkin while taking off on a jet. And that is the way I write my poems. At the moment of inspiration, I take any piece of paper available. I don't wait until I get home to my desk..............................27

Linda Schaaf Aton

!AVIVA! Argonaut is the pen name for **Cary M. D. Haley** (also: **Cora P. Butt,** and **G. Howie Pharrtz).** Cary was born on May 3, 1950, at Wilmington, Delaware. After graduating from high school, Cary had three years of mixed college studies, which include: English Lit., Horticulture, and Computer Science. Cary's occupations include: Writer, Actor-Performer, and Poet. Cary's memberships include: San Francisco Arcaids Theatre, San Francisco; Actors' Theater for Children, Santa Rosa, California. Cary's publications include: **The Hawaiian Lover** published in Hawaii in 1960; **My Country Is Dying** published in **Bay Area Reporter** in 1974; and **Al(bert) Wagner** published in **Amer. Poetry Anthology** in 1990. **Cary's comments:** With 2,000+ pages of poetry completed and ready for publication, a broad variety of rhymed and unrhymed styles is evident. Subjects vary from children's simplistic idologies and thoughts to expressions of serious adult matters. Poems range in length from 2 words to several hundred lines. Styles vary from complete free form to imitating Keats, Browning, and Shakespeare. A favorite thing to do with the words has been to actually draw a picture with the words on the printed page and have that picture relate directly to the subject/theme of the poem..........142

Evelyn W. Bachtel was born April 21, 1913, at Elkins, WV. She graduated from Buckhannon High School, Buckhannon, WV in 1931. She is retired and a Contract Bridge Teacher. She married Roy E. Bachtel (now deceased) on Nov. 7, 1936. Her memberships include: Daughters of American Revolution; American Contract Bridge League; Wickenburg Country Club, Wickenburg, Arizona; and Las Senoras de Socorro. **Her comments:** The old swinging bridge crosses the Middle Fork River, in Ellamore, WV. It swings from Randolph to Upshur County. As a child I was fascinated by it, and spent many hours fishing and swimming beneath it..........71

Vivien Bellamy was born on March 28, 1935, in London, England. She received a British education. She is a housewife, "World Gospel Singer", and Scuba Diving Business, Maui. She married her husband, James, on August 18, 1956. Her memberships include: Asia/American Christian Truth Squad--(Accts) Korea, World Hope Foundation (Texas) (Canada), AARP (Maui), and Baptist Church. **Her comments:** An enormous thank you for my poem being accepted by Sparrowgrass Poetry, it was an exhilarated spurt for me the "first time" that I had dared to have my thoughts reviewed and was accepted for publication (after my husband's prompting). To open your letter of acceptance was to pursue my hearts desire a published book of poems, and ecstatic joy. My inspiration, where else, but the Almighty's Beauty is inexhaustible, on land, sea, or air, and themes just tumble out, so rich is life. Thank you again if no awards, your publication is my reward.............................300

Vivien Bellamy

Connie Biddy was born on Jan. 17, 1937, in Brooklyn, NY. She had 8 years of grammar school and 3 years of high school. She is a house wife and a mother with 5 children, who are all married. She married her husband, Olin, on Nov. 10, 1956. She used to belong to The Ladies Auxiliary of Copiague, NY, for a few years. **Her comments:** I always like to write poems. I was thrilled to be chosen to be in a contest, and to have it published in your **Poetic Voices of America.** I have 6 grandchildren and a wonderful husband..........................376

Connie Biddy

Bernice Couey Bishop was born on June 3, 1927, at Floyd County, Georgia. She attended high school at Dallas High, Dallas, GA; for three years, she went to the University of Georgia and for 62 years she has gone to the "school of hard knocks!" She received her Yeoman training at Iowa State College, Cedar Falls, Iowa. She is a retired Office Manager/Bookkeeper. She married Furman R. Bishop on July 7, 1946. She is a member of various Genealogical and Historical Societies; Writer's Digest Club, and other writer's organizations; Epilepsy Assn. of America; NCO Club; Floyd Medical Center Assn.; Rome/Floyd County Library Assn. and others. She is a former member of Rome Business Women's Club. Her publications include: **In The Solitude** published in **Great Poems of Western World,** 1990; listed **Who's Who in Poetry,** Vol. 5, 1989; **I Was There All the While** published in **Poetic Voices of America,** 1990; **Angel's Tears** published in **Selected Poets of the New Era,** 1990. She received the Golden Poet Award in 1988 & 1989 from World of Poetry, and Publisher's Choice Award from American Poetry in 1988 & 1989. **Her comments:** With paints of beautiful colors, an artist paints

Bernice Couey Bishop

a masterpiece; but with my pen, I too, paint beautiful pictures with the words of the poetry that I write. My inspiration comes from God, my family and my fellow man!..........400

Matthew Blasdell was born on April 25, 1974, at Iowa City, IA. He attends McDonough High School, Pomfret, MD. He is a ninth grade student. He wrote the poem **The Loneliness Song** when he was 13 years old. He has written several other poems and has completed a short story **Pack of Wolves.** He received the MIP award during this same year for achievements on his football team, the St. Charles Bears. Both of his godparents are University Professors at the University of Iowa. He currently attends McDonough High School in Pomfret, MD and is in the ninth grade..................357

Matthew Blasdell

Yalonda M. Bones was born on Nov. 1, 1971, at Ottawa, KS. She is currently a senior in high school. **Her comments:** Poetry unites all readers, no matter what age or race. Poetry enables the writer and reader to become one. I love to write in an intense and sometimes shocking way so that my audience will stop and think about what they have just read, and then apply it to themselves...12

Yalonda M. Bones

Joseph Anthony Booth was born on May 29, 1964, at Hartford, CT. He has completed grammar and high school, and took a two-year course in Forestry Conservation. But he is at his greatest peace when he can attempt to grab onto the muse of a nation, the world, and ultimately the universe and use the magic of words to share it with others. **His comments:** Poetry, as I see it, is a celebration of the senses, an explosion of color. The Nirvana of consistencies of who we are and what we want to be. It's an introspective exploration of the inner universe and our connection with infinity. My poem takes flight on the wings of the spirit and soars with the Freedom of an infinite majesty — The Imagination.

(Mrs.) Claranelle (Rusty) Bowman was born on Dec. 3, 1945, at West Palm Beach, FL. She had 1½ years of college. She works in Corrections at Volusia County Jail. She married Robert C. Bowman on Aug. 21, 1989. She is a member of the Nat'l Federation of Business & Professional Women's Clubs, Police Benevolence Assn. and First Baptist Church of Deland, FL. **Her comments:** My husband has inspired most of my work before our marriage and since. I also receive inspiration from various quotes, proverbs, etc. This poem was inspired by my love of rain (growing up in Hurricane Country) combined with the old adage, "You can't judge a book by its cover." When others complain about rain, I usually respond, "You can't judge a day by its weather."

(Mrs.) Claranelle (Rusty) Bowman

Marilyn W. Bowser was born on May 20, 1948, at Corapeake, NC. She has a B.A. Degree in History and Social Studies and graduate study. She is a teacher. She was married on August 8, 1970. Her memberships include: NEA, NCAE, Alpha Kappa Alpha Sorority, Gates County BELLES Inc., Autism Society of NC, Inc. **Her comments:** I have written more than 100 poems in my lifetime. I wrote poetry as a child, but stopped. I resumed writing about 1 year ago. Much of my spare time is spent writing poetry. I derive a great sense of pleasure and accomplishment from writing poetry. My inspiration comes from events in my life, people who touch me in a special way, and observing nature.

Marilyn W. Bowser

Reagan Elizabeth Boyce was born on Feb. 20, 1977, at Prince George Co., MD. She has completed pre-school thru seventh grade. Her publications include: a cartoon published in **Las Vegas Review Journal** 1989. She won the "Best Cartoon in the 6th grade category" in the **Youth Cartoon Contest** sponsored by the **Las Vegas Review Journal** in 1989. She received three original cartoon works as a prize. She attended Estes McDoniel Elementary School at the time. Her other awards include: Art Achievement Award 1989, and Presidential Academic Fitness Award 1989. **Her comments:** My inspirations for writing this poem were: my curiosity of the universe, my love for all animals and the want of an "A" in my English class.

Reagan Elizabeth Boyce

Justin Edward Brewer was born on Aug. 26, 1980, at Longview, WA. He is the son of Robert and Jeannie Brewer. He is currently in the 3rd grade at Catlin Elementary School, Longview, WA. His hobbies include: playing the piano, baseball, basketball, and soccer. **His comments:** This is my first poem I have ever written. My parents inspire me.

Justin Edward Brewer

Laurie R. Brooks was born on April 24, 1957, at Alton, IL. She has attended St. Matthews Grade School, Marquette High School, and Lewis & Clark Community College. She is a receptionist/secretary at McKinley Iron Inc. She is divorced. **Her comments:** I have written poetry since I was very young. It is my release from frustration and/or worry. My dream is to put all of my poems together and have a book of them published......................342

Laurie R. Brooks

Leon Harvey Burnes was born on April 3, 1930, in Tampa, Florida. He has attended Mont Verde School, St. Leo Academy, and Florida State Junior College. He is a retired Senior Chief in the Navy. He married his wife, Jeannie, on April 16, 1982. He is a member of the AARP, VFW, and is a Mason. His publications include: **The Journey,** a poem, published in July, 1988, and **Reflections of Life,** a book, published in December, 1989. **His comments:** I dedicate my poems to my family, friends, and foes. Just whom I might offend with this, the good Lord only knows. I do not wish to slander or reflect in any way. On the character of the people, whom these pages put at bay. So if the shoe fits, wear it, if not, then pass it by. But I hope you find a line or two, that suits both you and I..............................74

Leon Harvey Burnes

Kay C. is the pen name of **Kathleen (Kay) Alison Christie** born on Feb. 11, 1965, in Webster City, IA. She has graduated from South Hamilton High School in Jewell, IA, and has had 1 year as an Equestrian major at Northwest Community College in Powell, WY. She is a Laundry Supervisor (west) at Prairie View Nursing Center. She married Ian Christie on Sept. 21, 1985. She enjoys singing in the church choir and is a member of the Women's Bowling League. **Her comments:** My source of information comes from the feelings of life. Even a seemingly mundane day can cause a thought to form in my head, and when that happens, I just have to write it down. My poetry says a lot about what I'm feeling inside...111

Kathleen (Kay) Alison Christie

Patricia N. Calhoun was born on July 8, 1929, in Amarillo, TX. She is a high school graduate, and assisted teaching Speech. She is retired. Her publications are: **Great American Poetry Anthology** published in California, 1988. Her awards include: Golden Poet Award, 1987; Honorable Mention, 1987 and 1988. **Her comments:** Interested in nature, everyday happenings, all serve to inspire me and of course, the love of words..295

Millie "Naomi" Chandler, who goes by Naomi, was born on Oct. 10, 1927, in Salem, VA. She completed the 10th grade. Her father died when she was just 4 years old. Her mother died when she was 15 years old, and her "only" sister died just 2 months after her mother. She is a housewife and used to work for the American News Co., and the Gray Gasket Co. years ago. She married Henry Ernest Chandler on April 15, 1947. She has five grown children, three girls and one boy. She lost twin boys. Both she and her husband are life members of the D.A.V. (Disabled American Veterans). They are also members of the Calvary Baptist Church, Salem, Virginia. Her husband, Henry, is a disabled American veteran of World War II. He was a Tail Gunner on a B-17, and was in the last battle over Germany. He flew in eight combat missions. **Her comments:** I have never had a poem published before, but have always loved to write poetry! I was sitting on my front porch in a rocking

Naomi Chandler

chair, in August 1977, when the Spirit of God gave me this poem. I added the 7th through the 12th verses on Sunday, April 8, 1990. All the rest of the poem was written in August 1977. My source of information is the King James Version of the Bible and I do Truly feel that I was inspired by God to write this poem! All or any "praise" goes to God, The Father; God, The Son; and God, The Holy Spirit! Amen!.......................230

Versey Chapelle was born on June 30, 1950, in Guelph, Ontario. She is an Office Administrator working with Insurance Employee Benefit Packages. She married David Carr on June 30, 1990. She was a Communications Dir. for Barrie Balloon Busters for 2 years, and was a member of the Hot Air Ballooning Club, and was the Crew Captain for 4 years. **Her comments:** Resident of Barrie, Ont. Lived also in Bermuda and the Cayman Islands. One daughter, 13 years old. Greatly inspired by water -- have a family cottage on Georgian Bay for over 50 years. Enjoy hot air ballooning, own a 30 foot sailboat "Sae Bridd," hope to cruise Caribbean in future. Loves animals -- 1 Gordon Setter, 2 cats, turtles and fish..

Versey Chapelle

Evelyn Christiansen was born on Feb. 22, 1918, in Joplin, Missouri. After she graduated from high school, she self taught herself from books in the library, mainly philosophy, psychology and many of the classics including the Bible. She married Arvith Christiansen (now deceased) on Nov. 29, 1937. She is a member of the Senior Citizens of Belfair, WA. **Her comments:** The poetry submitted should be called **A Revelation**, since it came to me in this manner. The first line of it is a quote taken from Revelations Chapter 17, Verse 8 in the Bible...

Bonnie Colby was born on Dec. 19, 1949, in Spring Valley, IL. She has a B.S. in English, Speech, and Secondary Education. She is a teacher and runs a small junior high language arts program. She married her husband, Danny, on January 24, 1970. She is a member of the National Council of English Teachers, and Delta Kappa Gamma. **Her comments:** My main source of inspiration and an old friend, is my volume, **The Collected Works of Edna St. Vincent Millay,** that I have had since I was sixteen. Having read her poetry hundreds of times through the years has given me a sense of theme and an automatic feel for cadence and depth..

Bonnie Colby

Cookie is the pen name of **Florence Jean Watkins,** who was born on Sept. 20, 1933, at Fort Smith, AR. She completed the ninth grade. She is in Environmental Services-Sparks R.M.C. at Fort Smith, AR. She married Fred Watkins on May 6, 1988. She is a member of the Y.W.C.A. and United Pentecost Church. She makes posters for her Safety Program at Sparks Hospital, where she is employed. **Her comments:** My family and friends are very encouraging. My inspiration comes from God. I hope I can bless many people with my poetry. I write songs also and do pen and pencil drawings...

Florence Jean Watkins

Loren Craig-Young was born on Jan. 25, 1965, in Michigan City, IN. She is a fiction writing student at Columbia College. Her publications include: **Brown Brother** published in **Chicago Defender** 1980. **Her comments:** Poems to me are short vignettes of life, from a literary view. But living a piece of work is as important as expressing it. I sometimes believe there is no difference..........................

Bonnie K. Crockett was born on June 23, 1965, in Driggs, ID. She graduated from high school in 1983 from Tonasket, WA. She is a house wife and mother of two children, Blake and Fona. She married David W. Crockett on August 11, 1984. She is involved in their local rodeo club and church activities. **Her comments:** I get a lot of inspiration from people who are, and were close to me. Often different experiences give me ideas for topics of my poems...

Bonnie K. Crockett

Dr. Anne Bernice Smith Cunningham was born on Feb. 14, in Birmingham, Alabama. She attended Birmingham Public Schools, and received a B.S. Degree from Alabama A & M University, a M.A. Degree from Case Western Reserve University, and a PhD. from Walden University. She is a retired Elementary School Administrator. She is married to James Clinton Cunningham. Her memberships include: Doctorate Association of New York City; Board of Directors of the Kathryn Tyler Community Center; National Council of Negro Women; Women's City Club of Cleveland; Phi Delta Kappa Sorority; Alpha Kappa Alpha Sorority; Chairman of the Board of Christian Education-Bethany Baptist Church. Her awards include: Jennings Scholar for Excellence in Teaching, 1964; Principal of Bolton School, Recognition as a School to Visit-**Instructor Magazine,** Nov. 1969, because creativity and learning flourished in an atmosphere which encouraged students and teachers to think and experiment. **Her comments:** Poetry has always crept gently into our thoughts and dreams—always—again and again!

Dr. Anne Bernice Smith Cunningham

Gloria Jean Daily was born on Jan. 18, 1926, in La Crosse, WI. She graduated from Onalaska High School in June, 1943, and she received a Degree in 1975 as a Nursing Assistant from a Vocational School in La Crosse, WI. She is a homemaker, poet, singer, nursing assistant, waitress, dept. store clerk. She married Robert Kendal Daily (deceased 1985) on June 25, 1944. Her memberships include: Living Word Christian Church-"Handmaidens Of The Lord". Her awards include: Fourth Place-World of Poetry, 1988 and Golden Poet Award-World of Poetry, 1988 and 1989. Her publications include: **Dream -- A New Dream** in **Poetic Voices of America,** 1989; **He Painted My Soul** in **Treasured Poems of America,** Winter 1990; **Dreamers See God** in **Our Twentieth Century's**

Gloria Jean Daily

Greatest Poems, 1982 and **American Anthology of Midwestern Poetry,** 1988; **The First Snowfall** in **American Anthology of Midwestern Poetry,** 1989 and **New American Poetry Anthology,** 1988; **Ministering Angels** in **The Golden Treasury of Great Poems,** 1989; **I Miss You So — My Love** in **World Treasury of Great Poems, Vol. II,** 1989; **Love Diamonds** in **American Poetry Anthology,** 1989. **Her comments on her poetry:** God has been a constant source of inspiration to me since I was a young child; when I wrote my first poem at age seven. In high school, I wrote all of the poems for our High School Year Books. I began seriously writing again in 1980 and had my first poem published in 1982. I have been writing ever since and it has been a great source of Joy to me! My themes are basically Sacred; telling of God's great Love! I also write about nature and my family and friends. Occasionally, I also write about controversial things; such as "abortion"; I have also "tried my hand" at humor! Everything that I write is based on my faith and the unfathomable Love of God, our Father and our Savior, Jesus Christ.

Grace R. Dalzell was born on December 2, 1936, in Mexico City, D.F. She attended San Antonio College and St. Mary's University. She is a Medical Office Manager. She married Emmet O. Whitaker, Jr. on November 7, 1974. Her publications include: **The Little Girl** in the Summer of 1990, and **Jenny Is** in August of 1990. **Her comments are:** I am always amazed when I write poetry. The transformation of feelings to thoughts, thoughts to words, and words to poetry is an awesome and mysterious process. I view each piece of poetry that I write as a unique collection of my feelings and thoughts at a given time. I gain great pleasure from my ability to write, and consider it a beautiful gift.

Grace R. Dalzell

Mrs. Mary Lee Dauer was born on October 25, 1929, in Kendallville, IN. She has an A.B. Degree in Education. She is a retired school teacher. She married her husband, Ira E., on June 17, 1957. Her memberships include: N.E.A., Illinois Retired Teachers Assoc., Republican Presidential Task Force, Wood River Hospital Auxiliary, and International Graphoanalysis Soc. Her Publications include: **God's Wonderland** in **American Poetry Anthology,** 1988; **Winter Wonderland Sleep** in **American Poetry Anthology,** 1988; **Philosophizing** in **Best New Poets of 1988; True Value of Man** in **Best New Poets of 1988; Recipe for Happiness** in **American Poetry Anthology,** 1990; **Choices** in **American Poetry Anthology,** 1990; **On Being Successful** in **Poetic Voices of America,** 1989; and **Feelings** in **Poetic Voices of America,** 1990. **Her comments about her themes and sources of inspiration:** Nature, holidays, values, self-esteem, inspirational, and educational.

Florence Lillian Davis was born in Joaquin, Shelby County, Texas. She graduated from Joaquin High School. She was married to James Carroll Davis, (deceased). She is a homemaker. She has had a poem or two, now and then, published in her home town news papers for special occasions. She is a born again Christian and is a member of the Southern Baptist Church, and the AARP. **Her dedications to writing:** Feeling led to serve God, in a Special Service, through my pen. I have written **Devotionals In Rhyme** for many years. They have been inspired by people, places, things and activities. Last, but far from least, many are inspired from Bible study. My heart and pen desire to honor God to the best of our ability......................168

Florence Lillian Davis

Donna Evelyn-Marie Dennis was born on May 8, 1973, in Decatur, IL. She is a student attending Mt. Zion High School. She is a member of AFS, and the Spanish Club. **Her comments:** I really enjoy writing poetry. I have found that it is an effective way to express my feelings about events in my life and the world in general. Many different things have inspired me but I think the most important ones would be my loving family and my two favorite teachers, Mrs. Sheila Hogan and Mr. Royce Phillips, both people whom without I probably would not have made it through some of the hard times in my life..294

Donna Evelyn-Marie Dennis

Vladimir De Tonya was born on June 2, 1945, in Yugoslavia. He has a BA in Yugoslav Literature and History, from Zagreb University, Yugoslavia, and a MA in Yugoslav Literatures, from the University of Chicago. He is a Teacher, Translator, Social Worker, Ethnic TV Show Editor, and is presently associated with Lincoln Property Company, San Diego, CA. His publications include: **The Glass of the Joyous Table,** a book of poetry, published in Osijek, Yugoslavia, 1968; **The Moonlite Above the Watermill,** a book of poetry, published in Sarajevo, Yugoslavia, 1987; **Odysseus on the Atlantic,** a book of poetry, published in Privlaka/Vinkovci, Yugoslavia, 1987; and **Across the Two Boundaries,** a short novel, published in Privlaka/Vinkovci, Yugoslavia, 1989. He was awarded "The Best of Yugoslav Immigrant Poetry", Sarajevo, 1988. **He comments about his poetry:** Started writing poetry at the age of 12; always returning to the Nature for additional strength and inspiration. Everything is of my concern, especially universal love and friendship; just about any theme is welcome. Favorite authors poets: A. G. Matos, E. Dickinson, R. Frost, Rilke. If we all could stay just a little closer to the Earth, if we could..10

Vladimir De Tonya

Shirley A. Dittman was born on Nov. 8, 1936, in Clarion Co., PA, and is a high school graduate. She is a housewife and a singer in The Jimmy Dittman Round, Square, and Polka Dance Band. She is married to James J. Dittman, who she married on Aug. 16, 1957. Her publications include: **Resurrection Easter** published in **Progress News,** 1988; **Green & White Hats,** published in **Progress News,** 1987; and **I Trust Jesus,** a song, to be recorded on the **HALLELUJAH** album on The Rainbow label, 1990. **Her comments:** I am a collector of butterflies. I think they are very beautiful creatures. To me the butterfly is the symbol of the Christian Life. Their old life falls away and a brand new life appears. I have been writing songs and poetry since January 1988.........................95

Shirley A. Dittman

Richard Doiron was born on Jan. 22, 1947, in Moncton, N.B., Canada. He is a graduate in Journalism and is a free-lance writer. He is a member of the Canadian Boxing Hall of Fame--Builder, Community Theatre Director. His publications include: **Love?** published in a booklet, Ontario, 1978; **Exegesis** published in an U. S. Anthology, 1990; **A Boy At Heart** and **The Lobster Trap** published in a New Brunswick magazine, 1982. He was awarded the Certificate of Merit, Journalism in 1974. **His comments about his themes and sources of inspiration:** People, places, things. Unlimited themes. 2000 poems written to date. Especially moved by love. Enigmatic: Boxer-poet. Published 26 years..122

Richard Doiron

Denise M. Dudzik was born on Sept. 23, 1971, at St. Mary's Hospital, Green Bay, WI. She is a 1989 graduate of Pulaski High School, Pulaski, WI. **Her comments:** If we took the time to understand why the baby cries . . . then the child would not hide, the men would not fight and the people would not die..251

Denise M. Dudzik

Gloria M. Duke was born on Jan. 22, 1926, in Brainerd, MN. Her formal education is Virginia Jr. College, Virginia, MN; UK, Elizabethtown, KY; Wayne State, Detroit, MI; IBM and RCA Computer Schools. She is retired from the U.S. Treasury Dept., and the IRS--Supervisory Computer Systems Analyst. **Her comments:** I have always expressed my thoughts more easily and completely in written formats. Poetry is a natural outlet for any circumstance which holds special pleasure for me..15

Gloria M. Duke

Doris Harbaugh Eckart was born on Feb. 1, 1927, in Corydon, IN, which is in Harrison, Co. She graduated from Corydon High School in 1945 and attended Indiana University studying S. E. courses. She is a homemaker and a member of the Order of Eastern Star, and Trinity United Methodist Church. **Her comments:** My mother told me to put my thoughts on paper, and my themes come from the heart as life goes on in this beautiful world so many take for granted. I lived this poem. **A Smile and a Glance.** This is my first attempt at publication...106

Doris Harbaugh Eckart

Steven L. Eckols was born on July 20, 1952, in Gonzales, TX. He has a B.A. Degree in Government from Sam Houston State Univ. in Huntsville, TX, where he furthered his education after graduating from Gonzales High School, Gonzales, TX. He is employed by the United States Army. **He comments:** I am a poet and a songwriter, as well as a musical composer. I also draw and take photographs. There are many sources of inspiration for my works and a variety of themes...170

Steven L. Eckols

Pauline W. Elswick

Pauline W. Elswick is the daughter of Rosa and Bev Wells. She was born on Sept. 12, 1921, in Swords Creek, VA. She attended Honaker High School, Honaker, VA; Lincoln Memorial University, Harrogate, TN; and received her B. S. Degree in Elementary Education from Emory and Henry College, Emory, VA. She was an Elementary School Teacher for 33 years in Virginia and Tennessee; and is now a Bookkeeper for Starving Artist Cafe. She married Kermit Edward Elswick on Aug. 18, 1947. She is a life member of VA. PTA and has memberships to VEA, NEA, and Washington Co. Retired Teacher's Assoc. Her publications include: **Lavender Snow** published in **Treasured Poems of America,** Winter 1990, and **Country Sounds** published in **Treasured Poems of America,** Summer 1990. Her awards include: **Lavender Snow,** Fifth Place, Winter 1990, and World of Poetry Honorable Mention, Spring 1990. **She comments:** I wrote poetry in High School English, but never seemed to find the time or inclination until I retired from teaching in 1988. My inspiration is the World around me, my roots, and all the spontaneous, unexpected moments my head fills with all the words I need to write down as a legacy for my children and grandchildren.

Charles R. Eskew

Charles R. Eskew was born on Nov. 26, 1949, in Tucson, AZ. He has an Associate Degree in Engineering, and a Masters Degree in Theology. He is an engineer. He married his wife, Barbara, on March 17, 1984. He is a member of Knights of Columbus and is N.I.C.E.T. Certified. His publications include: **The Swan** published in **Golden Voices,** 1989 and **Christian Humor-An Absence** published in **Lyrical Fiesta,** 1987. He was awarded Golden Poet in 1988. **His comments:** Being quiet with ourselves lets the inner person surface. Our quiet times away from others nurture the soul struggling to safeguard our journey. In solitude we find our sanity when the world around us seems insane.

Eva M. Fanning

Eva M. Fanning was born on December 12, 1922, in Cedarville, AR. She went through the eleventh grade at Cedarville High School. She is a housewife. She married Donald D. Fanning on Feb. 25, 1947. She comments that she has always enjoyed poems.

James H. Farrell

James H. Farrell was born on Aug. 20, 1945, in Reno, NV. He attended local schools up to college level in Salinas, CA, at which time he entered the USN and had three tours in Viet Nam (decorated). He works for the Civil Service, Dept. of Defense. He is single. His memberships include: World of Poetry; Great Lakes Poetry; Chapel Recording; Sunrise Records; Majestic Records; Talent and Associated Companies, President, J.H. Farrell Productions. His publications include: **The Kid and The Poet** published in World of Poetry, 1988; **Growing Old** published in **World of Poetry,** 1989; **A Poet's Creed** published in **Great Lakes Poetry,** 1988 and **A Feather in the Wind** published in **Great Lakes Poetry,** 1989. He was awarded the Golden Poet Award in 1987, 1988, 1989. **His comments:** Anthologies of a simple poet, for which I have just completed, is based on fact or fiction, dreams or reality, in the readers own mind; and my life of dedication to poets, friends, and family to bring light where there is darkness, joy where there is sadness.

Eva Wynnetta Mone' Forde was born on March 5, 1975, in Huntsville, AL. She is a student in the ninth grade. She is an Assistant Childrens Choir Director, a Class Vice President, and a Choir member. **The Emptiest Time of My Life** is her only publication and she won an award on the same poem in 1987

Eva Wynnetta Mone' Forde

Roger D. Fox was born on May 11, 1954, in Albuquerque, NM. He has a B.A. Degree from the University of Albuquerque, in Albuquerque, NM, which he received as an English major. He is a custodian and an aspiring writer. His publications include: **Poetic Essence** published in **Great Poems of the Western World**, 1989 and **Search For Freedom** published in **Poetic Voices of America**, 1990. He was awarded the Golden Poet Award in 1989. **His comments:** Poetry, especially in Free-Verse style, is the calling I feel I have a talent for. I enjoy creative writing first and foremost in my life, and my writings deal basically with my personal life and interests. When an idea is striking enough and won't leave my mind, then it is inspiring enough to set on paper and work with. My Greatest source of inspiration has been my English teacher, Mentor, and ultimately close and dear friend, Professor Theodore Foss, whose help has guided me. I am thankful to God for this blessing

Roger D. Fox

Wistar Freeman was born on March 13, 1910, in Aberdeen, NC. He is a high school graduate and attended business college. He is retired and his wife is deceased. He is a member of the Musical Art Club and the Disabled American Veterans. **His comments:** I was inspired to write this poem after hearing many stories from combat soldiers about "The Ghost of the Seigfried Line." My hopes are that the great leaders of the world will sometime read this poem and realize how foolish war is. The ghost has spoke his message through me, a combat soldier

Wistar Freeman

Don L. Fritz was born on August 18, 1925, in Cleveland, OH. His formal education is: Independence High School, Cleveland Institute of Art, and Cleveland Trade School. He is a sculptor and owner of Metal -- Sculpt Creations. He married Eleanor M. Fritz on June 28, 1946. His memberships include: International Sculpture Center; The Artist; Blacksmith's Association of North America; and The American Legion. **His comments:** The natural environment that surrounds us, is my greatest inspiration

Don L. Fritz

Dolores Gaylord was born on May 14, 1936, in Detroit, MI. She is a high school graduate and had some college. She has been a secretary for over 25 years. Her publications include: **Friendship** in **Quill Books**, 1990; **Santa's List** in **Poetic Voices of America**, 1990; **Michelle** in **Literary Pathways, My Restless Heart**, 1990; and **Expressions** in **Laureates '89, Cader Publishing**, 1990. **Her comments:** My inspiration comes from many sources: my childhood, my life's paths, my children, and grandchildren. I see the beauty of nature all around me. My deep religious convictions have also been an inspiration to me. I find much gold in the true meaning of friendship. I enjoy writing and hope to accomplish a lot in this life time. Writing has given me the opportunity to express myself. It has opened many doors to me--as an outlet for my emotions. Sentiment means a lot to me. Without laughter, tears or joy, one cannot truly say they have lived a full life. My work is written from the heart--always

Dolores Gaylord

Tatiana Louise Gelardi was born on October 30, 1979, in Portland, ME. She is a 4th grade student at Consolidated School, Kennebunkport, Maine..87

Reené George, a widow, was born in Youngstown, Ohio. She is a high school graduate, and had 15 years of evening college. She is a church secretary. She was married to her husband, Raymond (deceased, 1987). Her memberships include: Toastmasters International, American Society for Quality Control, and Woods on the Fairway Craft Guild. Her publications include: **I Am the Sea** in **Toastmasters,** 1980; **Angel Without Wings** in **Toastmasters,** 1980; **Mountains of Life** in **World of Poetry,** 1989; **A String of Pearls** in **World of Poetry,** 1989. Her awards include: Golden Poet Award 1989; Honorable Mention (certificates for 2 poems) 1989; and Who's Who in Poetry, 1990. **Her comments:** When I was widowed in 1987, (in Ohio) my life has changed quite drastically. I reach up to God and the thoughts flow freely.........307

Reené George

Dawne Germann was born on July 27, 1947, in Kearny, NJ. She is a high school graduate. She is a Real Estate Associate. She married her husband, David, on July 14, 1984. She is a member of the Nat'l Assoc. Realtor, and NJ Assoc. Realtors. **Her comments about her source of inspiration with her poetry:** Temporarily paralyzed by a violent crime, I took to writing as therapy to understand my feelings...340

Dawne Germann

Kris A. Gillespie was born on May 31, 1964, in Hamilton, OH. She attended Fairfield High and received her diploma in 1983. She is now taking a creative writing course at British-American School of writing. She works at Lou's Machine Co., her father's company, as a secretary. She married A. Ray Gillespie on July 16, 1988. She is a member of the Brush & Easel Art Club of Hamilton, and is the Corresponding Secretary. Her awards include: 1984 Finalist for Miss Fairfield essay, **Living in Fairfield. Her comments:** I enjoy writing short stories, poems, and articles. I realize I'm just a beginner, and I am very interested in learning much more. But I have a long way to go. I'm thrilled to have gone this far in your contest.........356

Kris A. Gillespie

Leslie Thomas Hansen II was born on Oct. 13, 1942, in Hammond, IN. He attended Culver Military Academy in 1960; St. Joseph's College and received a B.A. Degree in 1969; and University of Dallas Graduate School in 1970. He works in investments and accounting. **His comments about the inspiration and themes for his poetry:** Viet Nam, the experience 1966-67, like so many others....255

Leslie Thomas Hansen II

Janet M. Harper was born on Sept. 8, 1960, in Owensboro, KY. She graduated from high school in 1978, and attended college in 1988 and 1989, majoring in Social Services. She is a writer and entrepreneur. She married Ron L. Harper on June 26, 1982. She was awarded Honorable Mention for poetry in 1990. **Her comments:** My source of inspiration lies within my deep faith and love for my family...187

Janet M. Harper

Minnie F. Harris was born on June 20, 1913, in Amherst County, VA. She graduated from Madison Heights High School, and John Tyler Community College, and attended Virginia Commonwealth University. She is a home maker. She married Robert Harris (now deceased) on April 23, 1938. She is a member of Christian Women's Club, Church activities, and works in the library. She has had no publications. **Her comments:** During my teen years I often tried to express my feelings about some event or experience in lines that rhymed. It was a way of expressing some deep thought. In my later years I have gone back to trying to write these inner feelings in verse form..231

Minnie F. Harris

Tracy L. Hauppa was born on March 18, 1973, in Chicago, IL. She is currently a junior at a parochial high school near Chicago with a college-preparatory curriculum. She is a member of the Queen of Peace Chapter of the National Honors Society; Editor of Graphics/Photography Department of School Newspaper..183

Tracy L. Hauppa

Cherie Marie Hayes was born on Nov. 5, 1928, in Los Angeles, CA. She is a graduate of the Los Angeles area UCLA. She is a house wife. She married Milton Cecil Hayes on Feb. 9, 1950. She is a member of Magnolia Park Senior Citizen's Club. Her publications include: **Rhythm of Spring** in **World Treasury of Great Poems,** 1989. She was awarded the Golden Poet Award in 1989. **Her comments about the inspirations and themes that influence her poetry:** They are mostly nature themes...382

Cherie Marie Hayes

Jennifer Herrewig was born on Nov. 27, in Hillsboro, WI. She is in the 7th grade. **Her comments:** I wrote my poem while I was in after-school detention in the 5th grade. My school principal found it and at first refused to give it back, because he loved my work...153

Jennifer Herrewig

Walter Mark Houseman was born on Sept. 14, 1945, in Wadena Saskatchewan Canada. He attended school for 14 years—Wenatchee Valley College 1977-1979 and was on the Dean's Honor Roll in 1977. He was in security for 9 years and is now disabled. He married Maureen Houseman on June 26, 1981. He is a member of the Fraternal Order of Police. His publications include: **Born A Rebel** published in the U.S. in 1989; **Bring Down the Strong Holds of the Cults; Thoughts and Prayers, Inspirational; Soul Warriors.** His awards include: For Weaponry, 1984; Patrolman's Academy, 1979; and Dean's Honor Roll, 1977, in which he was the only one. **His comments:** Since I am disabled, I have a lot of time and God is my inspiration..............................135

Walter Mark Houseman

Judy C. Howell was born on May 18, 1949, in White County, Sparta, TN. She attended Bon-De-Croft Elementary for 8 years and White County High School for 4 years. She is an inspector for Wagner division of Cooper Ind. Inc. She is divorced. **Her comments:** My inspiration for **TaLonna Love,** came from my lovely 13 year old daughter, TaLonna. I felt this poem could serve as a message to other parents, showing them how divorce divides their families and breaks so many hearts...61

Judy C. Howell

Tensía LaToya Hyde was born on Jan. 23, 1980, in Chicago, IL. At the present time, she is an honor student in the fourth grade at St. Marks the Evangelist. She is a member of the Junior Girl Scouts. She won first place Catholic league 220 in track. **Her comments:** I would like to thank my aunt, Kimberly Williams, for inspiring me to share my thoughts in writing with others...336

Tensía LaToya Hyde

Jeán Pierre is the pen name of **John Brutsche,** who was born on June 4, 1963, in Manhattan. His formal education includes: Laguardia Community College, Francis Lewis High School. He is a bus operator. **His comments about the inspiration of his poem:** Inspired by Estela, to whom I dedicate this poem...257

Edelia Jenson was born on July 14, in Newell, Iowa. After graduating from Newell High School, she attended the University of Iowa for one year and McPhail School of Music and Dramatic Art in Minneapolis, MN for one year plus private lessons. She was a former coach of declamatory contest work and occasional judge. She was also a former play director and did occasional acting. She married Walter DeWitt Jenson (deceased) on Feb. 24, 1923. She is a member of the Lac D' Esprit Federated Club, and Past Matrons Club of the Order of Eastern Star. She had **Portrait of Texas Love** published in **Poetic Voices of America** in 1990. She was awarded Best dramatic reading in high school contest (winner), 1918. **Her comments:** I have enjoyed poetry for many years and frequently recite poetry during the day. I enjoy sharing poetry with others...228

Edelia Jenson

Josephine Lamitina Johnson was born on March 2, 1923, in Rock Glen, New York, which is a small rural community in western New York. She is a house wife. She has been married to Robert P. Johnson for 25 years. Her publications include: **Just For Me** in **Poetic Voices of America**, 1988; **My Wonderful Friend** in **Poetic Voices of America**, 1989; **My Brother** in **Treasured Poems of America**, 1989; **Abused Child** in **Poetic Voices of America**, 1990; **My Very Special Friends** in **Poetic Voices of America**, 1990; **The Lamitina Family** in **Treasured Poems of America**, 1990. She was awarded Honorable Mention, 1988, and the Golden Poet Award and Trophy, in 1989, by World of Poetry, for the poem **My Brother.** She was also listed in Who's Who in Poetry, 1990. **Her comments about her poetry:** I have been very lucky to have such beautiful people in my life and wanted them to all know how very much they have made my life so beautiful. I thank my wonderful husband, my beautiful family, and all my dear, dear friends. I love you all. **Dedication of her poem: My Nephew Buddy** In memory of my dear

Josephine Lamitina Johnson

nephew "Angelo" who was taken away from us so quickly by a drunken driver. He was a wonderful nephew, son, brother, friend, who loved everyone who knew him. He had so much to live for and so much love in his heart for everyone, he made our lives so much brighter just by being around us. He has left so many beautiful memories behind and a loving family who will love him forever. Until we meet again "My Dear Nephew" you will live on in our hearts forever. We love you "Angelo" and miss you so much. Love and Kisses XXXXOOOOXXOXOX From "Aunt Jo Jo"..................130

Lynn H. Johnson was born on February 9, 1946, in Gary, Indiana. She is a high school graduate with an A.A. Degree and is working on her B.A. Degree in Elementary Ed. at William Penn College, Oskaloosa, IA. She will receive the B.A. Degree in 1992. She is a college student. She married her husband, Gerald, on February 9, 1974. She is a member of the SISEA and is the Executive Accountant for the College Yearbook. **Her comments:** I have been writing poetry and short stories since I was thirteen years old. My inspiration was and still is, my dear grandmother who passed away two years ago. She taught me how to speak from my heart through poetry. She wrote several poems that I have and cherish and I plan to pass mine down..150

Lynn H. Johnson

Alexander W. Jones Jr. was born on Jan. 15, 1943, in Roxboro, NC. He attended A & T State College, NC and has a Bachelor of Science Degree and has attended Kean College, NJ. He is a teacher at Piscataway Public School District. He is the son of Alexander W. Jones Sr. and Hilma S. Jones. His memberships include: NJEA, PTEA, MCEA, United Way, and St. Martin de Porres Society. He has had **Wing'd Heart** published in **SEED News Letter** in 1989. **His comments:** My writing comes out of an urgent need to articulate my experiences and to give voice to the haunting spirits of my ancestry. It is also a way for me to record my observations about the awesome genius of mother nature. This poetic patchwork helps me preserve feelings and knowledge from experiences which have informed my identity and cultural consciousness..311

Alexander W. Jones Jr.

Henry Michael Jones was born on Sept. 19, 1947, in Dayton, OH. He has an Associate Degree in Business. He is a telephone repairman. He is a member of the Audubon Society and Telephone Pioneers. **His comments:** I usually write introspectively and am somewhat surprised, but always pleased, when others enjoy my writing..235

Henry Michael Jones with ace #1 grandson

Jeanise "Bachelor" Karimi was born on Nov. 12, in Caruthers, CA. She has attended Caruther High School, Fresno State University, Fresno, CA. She is a home maker and a writer. She married Jamal Karimi on July 30, 1981. **Her comments:** My themes are inspired by my friends, my husband, my two children — Jason and Jachelle — and my ability to write. I give total credit to God..............340

Jeanise "Bachelor" Karimi

James Karr was born on March 16, 1956, in Cleveland, Ohio. He has a B.S. in Communications and graduated from Ohio University in 1978. His publications include: **The Dragon** in **Days of Future Past I**, 1989, and **Transient Respite** in **On the Threshold of A Dream II**, 1990. He was awarded the Editors Choice Award in 1989 for the poem **The Dragon. His comments:** Poetry is my effort to audibilize the "still small voice" within me, within everyone. To peer behind the veil of the common and ordinary and to touch, if but for a moment, the transcendent quality of living that is life itself..............209

Randy Lynn Keatts was born on Aug. 26, 1965, in Dover, TN, which is in Stewart County. His formal education includes the 12th grade at Stewart County High School. He is a repair handler at Osh' Kosh B' Gosh. He is a member of the Tennessee Sheriffs' Association. His awards include: 6 years Perfect Attendance at Dover Elementary, 1972 to 1978; 4 years Perfect Attendance at Stewart County High School, 1979 to 1983; 1 year Perfect Attendance at Osh' Kosh B' Gosh, 1988 to 1989. **His comments:** I wrote this poem hoping it would bring a whole new meaning to life. This poem tells that you can't hide your problems, emotions, your pain. There is a place on earth just waiting for me. Everyday life is poetry. You bring your inner thoughts out on paper. I love to dance, put puzzles together and I enjoy nature itself..............265

Randy Lynn Keatts

Heather Elizabeth King was born on Aug. 29, 1980, in Cumberland, MD. She is attending Horace Mann Lab School (North West Missouri State University) at the Fourth Level (9 years of age). **Her comments on the factors that influence her inspirations and themes:** My family, church and concern or love of people. I enjoy writing poetry. It's fun..............363

Heather Elizabeth King

Yvonne DeLane King was born on May 17, 1948, in Hamilton, OH. She is a graduate and is employed in nursing. She married Thomas King on Dec. 14, 1985. **Her comments:** I generally write according to how I feel that day. The poem I submitted was written for the girls of my ex-sister-in-law at her death..............384

Yvonne DeLane King

**Albert S. Knowles
BA, ALP, RA**

Bert Knowles, BA, ALP, RA is the pen name of **Albert S. Knowles, BA, ALP, RA,** who was born on Jan. 6, 1915, in Orange, NJ. He has a BA Degree from Rutgers University College, New Brunswick, NJ, in Literature and History, and a diploma in American Law & Procedure from LaSalle, Chicago. He has served in the NJ National Guard, is a Major in the U.S. Marine Corps Reserve, NJ National Guard Federalized, and served in WWII and the Korean war. He has been retired since 1975 and he married Catherine Knowles on Nov. 30, 1974. He is a life member of both the National Wildlife Federation and the Men's Garden Club of America. He became a member of The National Authors Registry in Aug., 1989. **His comments:** I've been writing poetry, about 630 poems. I am working on two novels of historical myth, a series of children's poems, Sea Saga series of poetry, and picture story poems. I am permanently disabled and retired since 1975. I'm interested in collecting fine books in Literature, History, Art, Horticulture and Religion. Special Note: All my poems are taken from a lifetime of beautiful experiences, fanciful, fictional and reality. I specialize in general interest: Poetic stories; Picture poems; Poetic rhyme; Poetic rhythm; Sea Saga poetry; Children's adventure story poems; Nature poetry--all seasons; Rhymed narrative; and Religious theme. No free style. No Haiku. No Freeform. Just poetry. The verse from the Romantic Period--none finer...247

Narcisa P. Kuske

Narcisa P. Kuske was born on March 18, 1934, in the Philippines. She has a Bachelor of Science in Education, major in Science and minor in English. She writes poems to compose to songs. She married Herbert Kuske (deceased) on April 1, 1974. She is a NSA member, which is all about the study and practice of Buddhism. She is also a Charter member of the Presidential Task Force for President Bush. Her publications include: **United States of America March** in July, 1988 and **All Things Bright and Beautiful** in July, 1988. She received her first royalty check in 1988. **Her comments:** As of now, I am enjoying writing, most specially when I received the letters that my works were accepted. Now, I am just waiting when to be making good money in the future. At present not very much yet. But it is okay............239

Robert Allen Lebo

Robert Allen Lebo was born on July 4, 1964, in Bristol, PA. He has a high school diploma, and attended Philadelphia Police Academy, Sheriff's Academy-Dickinson Law School, and various police related college courses. He is a police officer. His memberships include: Fraternal Order of Police, Deputy Sheriff's Association of PA, Bristol Twp. Police Benevolent Assoc. **His comments:** This is my first publication, but my inspiration comes from my personal living experiences and feelings...280

Mary Antil Lederman

Mary Antil Lederman was born on April 3, 1925, in Los Angeles, CA. She graduated from St. Mary's High School, Cortland, NY, in 1943 and has received an A.B., Magna Cum Laude, in 1946 from Syracuse University (Lib. Arts, English maj., French/Spanish minor) and a M.Ed. in 1968 from University of Virginia (French). She is a retired language teacher, taught 23 years at Albemarle H.S., Charlottesville, VA, Dept. Chairman of For. Langs. She married Donald George Lederman on Dec. 26, 1946. Her memberships include: Phi Beta Kappa, Phi Sigma Iota, Delta Sigma Rho, Tabard, AATF, VRTA, FLAVA, Poetry Society of Virginia, Alliance Francaise, and AARP. Her publications include: Prose articles published in **Albemarle Magazine,** 1989 and **The Observer,** 1990; **Tomorrow . . .** in **Per Annos,** 1943; **School Daze Doesn't Faze** in **Venture,** 1988; **The Larch in Winter** in **The Piedmont Writer,** 1989, and **Poetic Voices of America,** Summer 1990; and **Musings of a Beached Whale** in **Orphic Lute,** 1990. Her awards include: 1st Place for **Musings of a Beached Whale,** 1990 (Humor Contest); 2nd Place for **The Larch in Winter,** 1990 from Sparrowgrass Poetry Forum; **Politic Limerick** won Honorable Mention, from Poetry Society of VA, 1989 (Limerick Contest); **Just Too-Too,** 2nd Place from Poetry Society of VA, 1990 (Limerick Contest); **Supernovas Gone Too Soon,** 3rd Place from Poetry Society of VA, 1990 (John Lennon Contest-song lyric). **Her comments:** I love lyricism

Continued on next page

in poetry, painting and music. I feel that good poems are thoughts expressed musically; just as good music is poetry expressed in sound. Lyricism is the magic ingredient woefully lacking in much "modern" art, music and poetry, where our esthetic senses are assaulted instead of caressed, un-fortunately

Nellie Lohr was born Sept. 15, 1940, in Girard, PA. She is a graduate of Rice Ave. Union High School, Girard, PA; Tech. School Machine Shop; and Tech. School Data Processing. She is a machine oper. at General Electric, Erie, PA, Local 506 and is also a Lic. Private Dect. She married Charles Dale Lohr Sr in 1970. **Her comments on her inspirations and themes:** My love for our creator. I drive more than 30 miles one way for work every day. This is my quiet time for me to be alone with God. Also my love for my husband, children, and grandchildren, and our wonderful lovely America

Nellie Lohr

Paola Luz was born on Feb. 11, 1964, in Manila, Philippines. She is a professional photographer (since 1982), and a professional singer and song writer (since 1986). Her memberships include: Organization of Filipino Singers, Recording Artist Under Contract with Dyna Records Philippines, Member of the PEPSI New Generation Artists. Her publications include: "Dear Paola" (regular column) in **The Philippine Star,** 1986; Art Review (column) in **Pinaglabanan Art Magazine,** 1984; poems--**Prism, The Whitest Wall, My Sad Pen Wilbur,** etc. in an article about her in **The Chronicle,** 1988; **Stand Alone, When You Love, Break Free,** etc., songs she composed and recorded for her album, 1988. Her awards include: Gold Record for Outstanding Sales of Record, 1989; Second Place Cultural Center of the Philippines Best Photograph & Best Photographic Series, 1982; Certificate of Poetic Accomplishment for the poem **Prism,** 1990. **Her comments:** I was a professional photographer for almost five years, then I became a professional singer and song writer about 4 years ago. I just completed my first album in '89, I have already received one gold record off of the album, another song has been the most requested song on the radio for nearly six months.

Paola Luz

The album is called **Stand Alone.** I have toured all over the Philippines and am very popular here. I had my own radio program on Sundays and have front acted for MENUDO and MIAMI SOUND MACHINE. I have been writing poems since I was 10 years old. I am now writing a book.

Alan Larry Lykins was born on July 24, 1964, in Boone, IA. He attended Des Moines Area Community College for 1 year, and in 1986 graduated from Iowa Central Community College with a degree in Broadcasting. He is a radio announcer and he married his wife, Barbra, on Aug. 26, 1989. He had **For Now** published in **Whispers in the Wind,** 1990. **His comments:** I'm fascinated by the poetry of Robert Frost. I've been writing poetry since 1980 and my main source of inspiration comes from daydreaming. I also get inspiration by watching people in everyday life.

Alan Larry Lykins

Eleanor Mabry was born March 10, 1940, in Stanly County, Norwood, NC (Piedmont, NC, many say it's the most beautiful place in the world). She completed high school, and has had courses in antiques and real estate brokerage and appraisal. She works part-time as an Antique's dealer. She is divorced. **Her comments:** I live in a very small town; the town where I was born. You adjust to small town living and learn it is a beautiful way of life. I was named from a poet and friend of my mother's, Eleanor (Mrs. Peter) Taylor, Charlottesville, VA. Poetry is an outlet for many of my emotions. It's like having a friend by my side whenever I need to talk. Needless to say my poetry ranges from tranquil to explosive.............................386

Eleanor Mabry

Merritt Mage was born on Nov. 2, 1949, in Seattle, WA. Merritt's education includes 2 yrs. of university level, at U. of WA, Seattle; plus much travel, Tao, and Life: "Scholar of the Road"- the Way; the Tao. Merritt is an Assoc. Member of the Old South Church, Copley Place, Boston, MA, and is employed as a laborer. **Comments on inspirations/themes:** A handful of Stardust from the land of Oz; sandals full of Holy soil from Eretz Israel; and a quiver full of ideas aimed at you: **Hen, Hesed, Emet,** all rolled into **One: Yeshua Meshiah**..6

Patrick J. Marenger was born on June 10, 1953, in Escanaba, MI. He is a 12th grade graduate and is a flat tar roofer (unemployed). **His comments on his inspirations and themes:** Original feeling of a walk in the woods and leaves rushing...379

Patrick J. Marenger

Helena Marsh (Srokowska) was born on Aug. 20, 1949, in Saint Andrews, Scotland. She attended Fulton Montgomery Community College, and Suny College of Technology at Oswego. She is a teacher in Occupational education--cosmetology. She married Trevor Marsh on Aug. 9, 1986. Her memberships include: National Cosmetologist Assoc., Saratoga Chamber of Commerce, and Vocational Industrial Clubs of America. **Her comments on her inspirations and themes:** Viet Nam War--My brother's return and the difficulties of his adjustment to normal life. Our family's disappointment with his attitude towards life...151

Helena Marsh

Ralph E. Martin was born on Dec. 27, 1924, in Medford, MA. He attended George Washington University and received his BA in 1950. He is a retired manager of Railroad Retirement Board Field Office, Richmond, VA. His publications include: **Wondering** published by Sparrowgrass Poetry Forum, Inc., 1990; **Fishing** published by Riverrun, 1990; **Ducks** published by Old Hickory Review, 1990; **Surf Surges** published by American Poetry Assoc., 1990. His awards for poetry include: **Wondering,** Hon. Mention, The Poetry Center, 1990; **Footsteps in Snow,** 3rd Prize, Major Poets Contest, 1973; **Duck Hunting,** Hon. Mention, Major Poets Contest, 1972. **His comments:** I try to compare "what is" to what "may be" and this may exist in a state of abstraction that envelops the open willing mind in such a way that the pen takes charge and the writer is not entirely responsible for the results...284

Ralph E. Martin

James J. McKay was born on Feb. 14, 1950, in Fall River, MA. He has a B.A. in Economics from Ohio State University, and a M.A. in Economics from Ohio University. He is a manufacturing manager and a poet. He married Madeleine McKay on April 15, 1978
....

James J. McKay

Verna Ollis McKinney was born on Oct. 14, 1969, in Crossnore, NC. She attended Avery County High School and has a high school diploma. She is a secretary. She married Michael McKinney on July 25, 1987. **Her comments:** At the tender age of 9, my Daddy, age 44, died suddenly of a heart attack. With 3 of her 5 children at home, my Mother raised me to the best of her ability. Giving more than I could ever return to her. She did without necessities so she could supply my wants. Not only material things did she give, but she gave 110 per cent of herself. Teaching me values in life and being a wonderful example, her virtues as a Christian woman are only one of the many abilities I try to pattern my life by, so for giving so much of herself, I dedicate my poem to My Mother, Willie Taylor Ollis

Verna Ollis McKinney

Maureen McNeil was born on March 7, 1952, in Cleveland, OH. She attended Erieview Catholic High and was in the Class of '72. She has been an alternator assembler for 10 years. **Her comments:** My inspiration for writing poems all come from deep within-my inner self. Any occasion from a happy to a sad feeling, a sunny day to a rainy day, can inspire me to write. People, places and things can cause a poem from me to be written. I find my best poems are written when I'm depressed. That's where my true feelings exist -- inside myself. Then they are put on paper -- as a poem

Maureen McNeil

Linda Meche was born on April 11, 1954, in Franklin, LA. She is a high school graduate and is a house wife. She married Adam Meche Sr. on May 18, 1985. She is a member of First Assembly of God in Franklin, LA. **Her comments:** I pray that my writings be used to attract readers to Jesus Christ. Five years ago, He became the Light to my darkened world. May His light shine through me

Linda Meche

Lucrecia Mervine was born on Oct. 18, 1976, in Johnstown, PA. She is currently attending All Saints Catholic School in Cresson, PA. She is a member of the youth choir at St. Francis Xavier parish in Cresson. **Her comments:** I have had to maintain a great deal of understanding in my life. My father died when I was 5 years old. I know now that I have to continue my life and move along. Together, my mother and I take care of each other. My loving mother, Betty Mervine, my family, and all our close friends are my source of inspiration. They are always there to guide and support me. When the going gets rough, I always remember how much I'm loved and cared for, by all of my friends and family.....................................107

Lucrecia Mervine

Mlgo is the pen name for **Mary L. Ohler,** who was born on May 4, 1930, in Garrett, PA. She is a 1948 graduate of Meyersdale High School, and is a factory worker at Flushing Shirt Co., Grantsville, MD. She married Roy I. Ohler on Nov. 11, 1951. She is the Financial Secretary of ACTWU Local 673, and is a member of Meyersdale Elks Lodge No. 1951, and Zion Evangelical Lutheran Church. **Her comments:** I write from the heart. Truth inspires me. My themes are mostly personal as well as general. I like people, nature, and seasonal themes. I've written special poems about my family and friends. I have a husband, 5 daughters, 4 sisters, a brother, a mother (father deceased), and many, many friends. I love and enjoy them all. My pen name (initial) is "Mlgo"..198

Mary L. Ohler

Anita Gale Moore was born on Sept. 3, 1944, in Elvins, MO. She graduated from Elvins High School in 1962. She operates a day care in her home for "Special Children". She married Carol Gene Moore on Sept. 19, 1962. She is a member of the Calvary Assembly of God Church in Festus, MO, and sings in the choir, and plays the organ. Her publications include: **Inspirations From the Heart,** a book, published in New York in 1987; **He's Never Too Busy** and **Mother,** published in West Virginia in 1989; and **I Have Jesus,** published in California 1989. Her awards include a plaque (for poem **Mother**) in 1989 and 2 recording contracts on lyrics and music she wrote in 1989. **Her comments:** All my inspiration comes from God. He gives me all my poems, songs, music, and everything I write................................89

Anita Gale Moore

Lori Denise Mutch was born on Sept. 4, 1975, in Joplin, MO. She has completed the 8th grade and is entering Girard High School in Girard, KS. This is her 1st work to be published. **Her comments:** I live in the country on a farm, and love wildlife, nature, and photography. Also, I enjoy the outdoors and these things are what inspires me to write...................................346

Lori Denise Mutch

Jan Neville was born Oct. 3, 1934, in Chicago, IL. Her education includes: B.A. (Theatre), University of Denver; M.A. (Librarianship), University of Denver; Ph.D. (Speech Communication), University of Denver. She is a Public School Librarian/Media Specialist, and married George Russell Neville (now deceased) on June 13, 1959. She is a member of League of Historic American Theatres, Speech Communication Association, and Toastmasters International. Her play, **Elizabeth Palmer Peabody,** was performed in 1975. **Power, Interpersonal Needs,** and **Communication Behavior** was her Doctoral Dissertation in 1989. Her awards include: nominated, Best Actress Fanny Award, 1974; winner, Elwood Murray Best Speaker Award, 1979; winner, Area Toastmasters Tall Tale Contest, 1988. **Her comments:** My inspiration comes from life around me which triggers in my memory quotes from playwrights, authors, poets, and song writers who become echoes in my writing. My mother, Margaret A. Chapman introduced me to the bluebird of happiness....322

Jan Neville

Brenda Newton was born on Dec. 21, 1950, in Hancock County, KY. She is majoring in English at Owensboro Community College in Owensboro, KY. She is a wife and mother. She married her husband, Sherman, on Dec. 23, 1966. **Her comments:** Poetry's vivid perception of endless subjects uplifts the mind, opens the senses and rescues our emotions from anonymity. In my work **The Writer,** it is my desire to reveal the "blood and sweat" that goes into the author's work and the anguish and joy at its completion. My heartfelt thanks to my family for supporting and understanding my dream to be a writer...288

Brenda Newton

Rhonda L. Nunes was born on Sept. 12, 1961, in Stockton, CA. She has a B.A., cum laude, from UCLA (1984) and a M.M. from University of the Pacific (1986). She is a free-lance composer/performer-musician/artist. Her memberships include: UCLA Alumni, American Woman Composers, and American Musicological Society. Her publications include: **String Sextet, opus 6** (Master's Thesis) published in Stockton by the University of the Pacific, 1986 and **Memories** (poem) published in **Westwind** (UCLA), 1984. Her awards include: Stephen's Scholarship (UCLA), 1983-1984; Honorable Mention in The National Federation of Music Clubs Composition Contest, 1985 and Frank Thornton Smith Memorial Scholarship, 1982. **Her comments on her inspiration and themes:** Life—

Rhonda L. Nunes

and the love of it . . . there is nothing else that is important in comparison—love, art, our relation to the world around us are parts only of its composition . . . At times, I am so happy to be alive that I dance—I try to do this as often as possible—to be in touch with one's own physical reality is to rejoice in the body as the supreme expression of life...162

Reuben Oglesby was born on Oct. 16, 1935, in Garfield, GA. He attended Rutgers University, Dale Carnegie School of Human Relations and Effective Speaking, Armstrong A.E.C. and home bible studies. He is an optimist, farmer, researcher, poet, free-lance writer and local biblical radio personality. His memberships include: A.M.E. Church, NAACP Assoc., Disabled American Veterans, Optimist International and Habitat for Humanity International. His publications include: **A Plea From Death Row** in **Focus,** 1987; **Most Wonderful Time of Year** published by Sparrowgrass Poetry Forum, Inc., 1990; and **Words of Wisdom, Weekly Quotations** published in **Metro County Courier** 1989 and 1990. He has been awarded several awards including the highest achievement in human relations, effective speaking and how to stop worrying and start living, etc., 1968. **His comments:** I don't like to boast but in my opinion I believe that this poem to you and only you is probably one of the best love poems that has ever been written, and that includes King Solomon's love poems too because it has universal love appeal that can be used everyday of the year and by persons of all ages......308

Reuben Oglesby

Kenneth Earl Oldham

Kenneth Earl Oldham was born on Aug. 2, 1959, in Clayton, NM. He is a high school graduate from Clayton High School. He is a stocker at Clayton Ranch Market (local supermarket). He married Martina Oldham on Aug. 2, 1980. He is a Lion's Club member. He was awarded a diploma for song lyrics by Music Success Association in Nashville, TN in 1977. **His comments:** God is always first in everything. His great care for me, his blessing me with my wonderful family; wife, Martina, daughters, Tanisha Lomai, and Rheeannon Kolis, ages 7 & 4. I realize my total need for, and dependence on God. I feel like I can understand the feelings others have about life, and I feel like I can write about it..................57

Donald Lester "Duke" Palmer Jr. was born on February 11, 1965, in Martins Ferry, OH. He is a high school graduate and is self-employed. He married Cammy S. Palmer on Feb. 18, 1983. He is a member of the First Christian Church. He had the **Sad Man** published in **The Intelligencer**, 1989. **His comments:** The works of society and common beliefs are handed down to us through the generations. We find ourselves torn between society and our own feelings -- I believe in me, my heart and my soul......................216

Donald Lester "Duke" Palmer Jr.

Debra Ann Pappani was born on Nov. 17, 1953, in San Jose, CA. She attended Presentation High School, San Jose, CA. She pursued medical school before writing career and has a degree (Cert. Med. Asst.). She is a writer. She is a member of Humane Society of United States of America. Her publications include: **Just Look Into My Eyes** published in October 1981 and a 2nd ed. in March 1983; **Closer To My Soul** planned to be published in 1990. **Her comments on her inspirations and themes:** Favorite poet--Emily Dickinson--also any type of haiku. My first book of poetry sold 800 copies within 3 months. In my own published books, I have been applauded on my alliteration and my style that has overtones of ambiguity; I enjoy leaving many works up to the reader. I have had 3 autograph days in my area, 2 TV appearances, and copies of my 1st book have sold in Hawaii. I have also taught two creative writing classes.........................399

Debra Ann Pappani

Merri Lu Park was born on Feb. 15, 1944, in Austin, TX. Her education is the planet Earth. She is a poet, writer, and photographer. She is a member of Texas Photographic Society and Kauai Writing Hands. Her publications include: **Rainbows Before Breakfast,** her book, published in Hawaii, 1989 and **The Rooster** published in **Poetic Voices of America,** 1990. **Her comments:** My poetry, like my photography, is intended to create both an intellectual and an emotional response within the ear/eye of the reader/observer. Blossom   seed-poems   blossom...........................76

Merri Lu Park

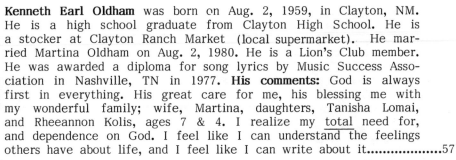

Kenneth G. Place was born on July 19, 1922, in Milwaukee, WI. He has a B.S. from Milwaukee State Teachers College, and a M.A. from Wisconsin State College (Milwaukee). He is a retired Elementary School Principal. He married his wife, Annette, on Sept. 20, 1986. He is a member of Administrators and Supervisors Council. **His comments:** I had just met (a month before) my wife-to-be and in a reflective mood, on a stormy winter night, I went for a walk. When I returned, I penned this poem!......................253

Kenneth G. Place

Emma Pletcher was born on July 11, 1928, in Somerset, PA. She is a high school graduate and is retired from General Motors Co. She married her husband (now deceased) on August 23, 1947. She is a member of Ladies Auxiliary of Meyersdale Fire Co. **Her comments:** Most of my poems were written in times of sadness or despair. It served as a release for my emotions..271

Emma Pletcher

Caroline Price is the pen name of **Penny Caroline Price,** who was born on Aug. 1, 1966, in Fort Worth, Texas. Her formal education is High School at W. E. Boswell, Saginaw, TX, and she graduated at Sierra Nevada Job Corp Center, Reno, NV. She is a typesetter/typographer. She married Dewayne Price on March 4, 1989. **Her comments on her inspirations and themes for her poetry:** Source of inspiration--my husband and Elizabeth Barrett Browning--of **Addicted To Your Love,** May 16, 1989. Not nearly as good, hope to be as good one day!..308

Caroline Price

Dan E. Ragsdale was born on Aug. 16, 1972 in Huntingdon, TN. He graduated from Gorman Christian School in 1990. He is a student. **His comments:** I like nature, irony, philosophy as themes. My inspirations are my 3 foot boa constrictor, my family, the great state of Tennessee, but most of all I thank the Lord for all things..298

Dan E. Ragsdale

Teresa E. Ralston was born on June 6, 1960, in Tampa, FL. She received her GED in Feb. of '85 and became a certified machinist on June 6, 1986. She is a poet. She married Robert E. Ralston on April 1, 1985. Her publications include: **Struggling Parents? or Struggling Children?** published by New American Poetry of Anthology, 1988; **I Had a Dream Last Night?** published by American Poetry Ass. in April 1990. Her awards include: Award of Merit for **Struggling Parent? or Struggling Children?,** Nov. 21, 1987; Golden Poet of the Year, Aug. 27, 1988; Silver Poet of the Year, 1989. **Her comments:** I sometimes think we all need to be reminded of small, but important details in life that we all take for granted from time to time. Trying to understand life on its own terms is sometimes frustrating...........................167

Teresa E. Ralston

Charisma Reddy is the pen name for **Marepally S. Reddy.** She was born on Feb. 15, 1954, in Asia. She has a Master of Arts, M.A., (English Literature) and a GED. She is a Co-ordinator for General Development of Education (C.B.O.) B.F.F.Y. She is married to Kuchokulla Reddy. She is a member of A.S.R.C. and a recent N.R.A. Her publications include: A poem published in **Dr. Ambedkar News Letter,** 1981; an editorial/poem published in **Pratibha News Letter,** 1981-82; two short stories published in **National Newspaper,** 1982-83; an editorial/poem published in **St. John's News Letter,** 1989-90; and published/complete lay-out **B.F.F.Y. News Letter The Bugle,** 1989-90. **Her comments:** Poetry flows in me spontaneously on Dreamy days—those Enlightening moments—when I truly experience Astral planes. I perceive everything at an immensity of depth. What my eyes 'see' others 'don't'. It is for my eyes only. My poems spring from my Apocalyptic visions. When I wrote **Fire In Passion,** I felt it emerged--because--not my Mortality but Immortal SOUL was put on FIRE—when I reached the Apex of Glory of Love. True Love is beyond Immortality. Nothing could Emulate it.........................30

Marepally S. Reddy

Lydell Reed was born on Sept. 11, 1966, in Jackson, MS. He is an anti-submarine warfare technician in the U.S. Navy. He had **Hilter's Friend** published in **Wings, 1990. His comments:** Poetry is when a dew-covered lawn becomes a "green velvet carpet layered in diamonds." Other forms of writing exist while poetry breathes

Lydell Reed

Margie Ann Reeves was born on Aug. 27, 1952, in Wichita, KS. She has a Legal Assistant Degree and studies in Communications. She is a Legal Assistant. Her memberships include: Epsilon Sigma Alpha International since 1983; Central Oklahoma Association of Legal Assistants since 1985; Associate Member American Bar Association; Associate Member Oklahoma Trial Lawyers Association; National Association of Legal Assistants; Associate Member Oklahoma City Oil & Gas Title Analyst Association; Board Member for Life Program--Oklahoma County, OK; Junior Achievement Consultant; Midwest City Regional Hospital Volunteer; and Hugh O'Brien Youth Foundation Counselor. **Her comments about her inspirations and themes:** Love of nature and life. Helping others

Constance K. Richardson was born on Oct. 3, 1914, in Waltham, MA. She has a B.A. from Tufts University, 1936, "In Humanities," and a B.S. from Bemidji State University, 1971, "Education, pre-school -- K." She is a retired teacher. She married Charles A. Richardson (deceased 1990) on Oct. 7, 1939. She is a member of National Association for Education Young Children, Mn. Branch, and Women of Evangelical Lutheran Church. Her publications include: **A Quiet Place** published in the Spring of 1990, and **A Prayful Hope for All Who Work With Children** published in the Fall of 1977. Her awards include: Evelyn House Award--Oct. 1977, for outstanding service to children, and Commemorative plaque--Sept. 1986, given to her husband and her for establishing Wee Folks Garten Child Care facility for the children of working parents in the area. **Her comments on her inspirations and themes:** My own 4 girls when in 4-H, they had me finish their demonstrations with a poem. This poem is one of learning to cope alone, after 50 wonderful years

Constance K. Richardson

Patricia Ann Frazier Rivers was born on Feb. 7, 1954, in Savannah, GA. She attended Gilbert Haven Elementary School, Alfred Ely Beach High School, and Savannah State College. She has a BBA Degree in Office Administration & Management. She is a Tutor at the YMCA in Savannah, GA. She sings in the church choir and is a member of Collegiate Secretaries International (C.S.I.), Savannah State College. She writes creative poetry for church engagements and enjoyment. She is a speaker of church functions. **Her comments:** What inspired me to write the poem about my mother, was I watched her raise 8 children; myself, the eldest. She always worked hard to raise all eight of us, so one Mother's Day I wrote a poem about her

Patricia Ann Frazier Rivers

Lavada Robbins was born on June 4, 1930, in Skelton, WV. She attended school through the eighth grade and has her GED. She is the mother of five children and grandmother of ten. She is a receptionist at the Ritzz Hair Design. She is divorced. **Her comments:** I get my inspiration from life. **Hungry Lust** came from a newscast A man on drugs killed a lot of people. One in particular was a police officer and an elderly woman

Sally Rock was born on July 24, 1949, in Plattsburgh, NY. She had **Memories** published in **The News** (Southbridge, MA), 1987. Her awards include: United Press International (2nd Place Feature), 1987; New England Press Assoc. (1st Place Special Category), 1987. **Her comments:** The inspiration for the themes of my poetry comes from everyday people and everyday situations. The actual writing of my poetry is my way of giving back what life has given to me.....................106

Sally Rock

Roxanne is the pen name for **Roxanne Jones-Steidle.** She was born on Nov. 25, 1948, in Vermont. Her education is LIFE! She is a legal assistant, writer, and psychic consultant. She married Dennis Steidle on Valentine's Day. Her publications include: **Dreams** published in The New York Poetry Society Anthology, 1985 and **Me & Trees** published in some anthology in Texas, 1985. She was awarded $50 cash for **Dreams**, 1985. **Her comments on her inspirations and themes:** Love and life, on all levels and planes of existence, are the sources of inspiration for everything I do but especially for exhibiting and expressing the gifts and talents I was so fortunate to be born into this life with.......198

Roxanne Jones-Steidle

Jennifer A. Russell was born on Sept. 21, 1971, in Oklahoma City. She has a high school education. Her occupation is homeland. She is a member of D.E.C.A. **Her comments:** I let my feelings do the writing. I try to express my feelings in a poem...31

Jennifer A. Russell

Ralph J. Ryan, III was born on April 16, 1942, in Cleveland, OH. He has a high school education. He is a scheduler for United Airlines, and is divorced. He had **Remembrance** published in **Golden Treasury of Great Poetry,** World of Poetry, 1989. His awards include: Who's Who in Poetry, World of Poetry, 1990; Golden Poet Award 1988 and 1989. **His comments:** I write free verse, I write of my experience in a way a therapy to wrench out of myself, my feelings that others may know they're not alone.........................324

Ralph J. Ryan, III

Lori J. Ryder was born on July 16, 1974, in Orlando, FL. She is in the 9th grade. She had **No Lullaby** published in **Poetic Voices of America, 1990**.......238

Lori J. Ryder

Juanita Ruth Sanders was born on May 10, 1926, in Frost, TX. She graduated from high school in 1944, and received a B.S. Degree in 1961. She is a teacher. She is a member of Texas State Teachers Association. Publications: At present time I have written about 35 children's educational poems that fit with Science, English, Math, Social Studies, and Fire Prevention. Then I put music to them and we sing the songs in class. Awards: Children songs, 1989, on television 2 times, and in two newspapers--no awards--. **Her comments:** I get my inspirations and ideas for my poems, sometimes, by past experiences. I pray the Lord gives me the words to write down.

Juanita Ruth Sanders

I am only the instrument. When I begin a poem, usually, my pen or pencil does not stop until the end of the poem. I have used nature, love, and lot about life. I take no credit but give the Lord the glory...185

Mary Faye Brumby Sherwood was born on May 11, 1912, in Marietta, GA. She has an Association Arts and B.S. and three years of special work on Shakespeare and English. She has worked for 25 years as a manufacturer and 2 years teaching. She married John B. Sherwood on May 11, 1986. Her memberships/social organizations include: Presbyterial office, member of AAUW, Treasurer of Business & Professional Club, Member of N.C. Historical Comm., served in N.C. House of Representatives and N.C. Senate. Her publications include: **Things I Love** published in **Christmas Lyrics**, 1939; **Farmer Will** published in **Bay Leaves**, 1977; **Loneliness** published in **Sixty N.C. Poets**, 1974; and **On Genealogy** published in **Tar River Poets**, 1976. Her awards include: Distinguished Service Award of N.C., 1984; **Farmer Will**--Honorable Mention, book, 1977; Who's Who of American Women, 1970-71. **Her comments:** I have been married 4 times so my name may be under Brumby, Shires, Hull or Sherwood. My inspiration comes mostly from nature and love of people, sometimes sadness for the poor and lonely..........................208

Mary Faye Brumby Sherwood

Pat Clark Simpson was born on Oct. 20, 1959, in Sparta, TN. She attended 1st thru 6th grades at Doyle Elementary School, 7th thru 12th grades at White County Middle and High School. She is a Classified "A" Operator at Mallory Controls. She married Arthur Simpson on Nov. 20, 1975. **Her comments:** This poem **Save the Stars & Stripes** was written to be used as the theme of a Baby Show Float for my daughter, Jerrica Joni, when I entered her in the White County Fair as Betsy Ross in September of 1989. We took fourth place out of 28 contestants...24

Pat Clark Simpson

Linda Green Slone

Linda Green Slone was born on Jan. 4, 1952, in Willard, OH. She attended Garrett Elementary School--Primer--8th grade, Garrett High School--4 yrs., Alice Lloyd Junior College--graduated 1973. She is a secretary for J. & S. Battery Service Inc., Hippo, Ky. She married James Edgle Slone on Aug. 25, 1973. Her memberships/social organizations include: Caldwell County Geneological Society, NC, "I love geneology. I've been tracing family roots." 1968-1971 Member of National Beta Club. Her awards include: In 1971 she graduated from High School, second in her class and she received the salutatorian award, English award, library award and the Governor's merit award, and she was on the Dean's list in college 1971-1973. **Her comments:** This will be my first poem to get published. I started writing poetry in college. I love reading poetry. My husband, the love of my life, inspired me to begin writing poetry. We were dating when I first started writing and he has been encouraging me to write more. My high school English teacher got me interested in poetry, also.................................102

Reta J. Robinson Smartt was born on Sept. 20, 1966, in McMinnville, TN. She attended Warren County Senior High School, McMinnville State Area-Vocational Technical School, Motlow State Community College. She is a loan processor/secretary for First National Bank, Manchester, TN. She married Michael Smartt on Aug. 11, 1990. Her poem **Daddy** was published in **Poetic Voices of America**, Spring 1990. **Her comments:** My poems are a way for me to sort out my feelings, fears, and dreams. A way to deal with the worries of every day problems and a way to show those I love, how much they have touched my life...165

Reta J. Robinson Smartt

Judy McLamb Smith was born on July 29, 1945, in Four Oaks, NC. She has a BA in Sociology, Georgia State University, and a Masters in Behavioral Disorders, Armstrong State College. She is self-employed. She married Bobby Smith on Oct. 15, 1980. **Her comments:** I enjoy observing life and writing about it; usually my poems are philosophical in nature as a result. I, like most people, question man's existence in the universe and my poems tend to be religious to some extent...............................234

Judy McLamb Smith

Melva Gail Smith was born on Nov. 4, 1960, in Louisville, KY. She is a graduate of Ballard High School, 1979. She studied communications for 4 years at the University of Louisville and has a certificate of Museum study from the Canadian Museums Association. She is a director of services, Museum United Services Enterprise. Her memberships include: Order of the Eastern Star, Fraternal Order of Police, Women of the Moose, American Association of Museums. She has had over 20 news articles published in **The Louisville Cardinal**, 1982. **Her comments:** I was inspired to write **We Were There**, after looking at a scrapbook containing photographs of my life long friend, Tonya. Although the miles separate us, our friendship continues to grow. Lasting friendship is rare, and should never be taken for granted. As for myself, I enjoy Ballroom dancing, writing, travel, museums,

Melva Gail Smith

and the arts. I have been employed by 2 museums for a total of 7 years, and have founded a museum service, with emphasis upon the role museums play in education 164

Millie Sparks was born on July 25, 1939, in Douglas, WY. She completed elementary and high school, Douglas, WY, (father a rancher), and is a graduate of Business College, Denver, CO. She works in marketing and is a freelance writer. Her memberships include: Orange County Guild for Infant Survival, Southeast Escrow Assoc., Plate Collector Clubs, National Notary Assn., and Coordinator/Commentator of Philanthropic Fashion shows—15 yrs. Her publications include: **Security Alert,** mo. column, published in **Plate Collector Magazine,** 1983-86; **Teddy Bears** in **Plate Collector Magazine,** 1985; **Ramblin' Round the Halls** (editor's column) in **The Converser,** 1956-57; **A Girl Named Steve** in **Retailer Publication for Employees,** 1975. Her awards include: Pen & Quill award, 1956-57; Americanism essay—Hon. Mention, 1955; S.E.E.A. Millie Sparks Scholarship, 1989. **Her comments:** My motivation for writing comes from the heart. Any subject I write about or anyone I write about must genuinely inspire me before I begin. I have

Millie Sparks

two books started. One is entitled **Earth Angels with Heavenly Purposes;** the other is called **Please Save a Place for Me.** Both are about real people in real situations. This poem, **Gentle Love,** has inspired many to realize that the gentler love is, the more effective and real it is...133

Melissa A. Sparr was born on March 31, 1979, in Tinley Park, IL. She is in the 6th grade at Bannes School. She helps with the publication of the School Newspaper every month, 1989-90. She received the superior achievement award in band, 1989, and 1st place award in cheerleading, 1988. **Her comments:** I think my poetry expresses my feelings in a way I can not describe. It lets me pour all my thoughts out. My sources of inspiration are very simple. My yearning to go to the beach, and I was mad at winter for being so long and cold. So I wrote a poem about the ocean.......................398

Melissa A. Sparr

Scott Stinespring was born on Sept. 26, 1953, in Waynesboro, VA. He works for Vector Industries. He is a member of both Association For Retarded Citizens of Augusta, and Bethlehem Lutheran Church. He had the poem **Nick & Rick** published in Poetic Voices of America, 1990. He was awarded Employee of the Month—Vector Industries, 1988. **His comments:** I have written short stories, presently working on a children's story; but this is my first attempt at poetry..299

Scott Stinespring

Gloria Stagi Stopford was born on Aug. 19, 1925, in Monessen, PA. She graduated from Monessen High School, ranked 20th out of class of 310. She is a secretary in three companies: H. J. Heinz Co., Mellon Institute of Industrial Research, and Corning Glass Works. She married her husband, Jess, Jr. (deceased), on April 23, 1949. Her memberships include: Order of Eastern Star Copporas Cove 1070, Amateur Organists' Assoc., International, Killeen-Copporas Cove Organ Club, Roller Skating Rink Owners' Assoc. for semi-professional roller dancers. Her publications include: **God's Country At Dawn,** in **World Treasury of Great Poems,** 1989; **That's Life** in **American Poetry Anthology,** 1989; **Love** in **American Poetry Anthology,** 1989; and **Ode to a Slumbering Child** in **Diamonds & Rust,** 1989. Her awards include: Golden Poet Award (World of Poetry), 1989; Poet of Merit Award (American Poetry Assn.), 1989; and Editor's Choice Award (National Library of Poetry), 1989. **Her comments:** My poetry addresses itself, almost exclusively to the problems which confront us as individuals and cause those unfortunate breaches to occur, which could be prevented if we only took time to reflect and meditate more often. My most frequent source of inspiration is the catalog contained in my memory of all those myriad Bible chapters we had to memorize back in those little Sunday school rooms in that Monessen, PA Methodist Church. I have a humorous side, however, which emerges when I'm

Gloria Stagi Stopford

not trying to solve world problems. I believe it's called satire—I commented to someone recently, "When you're rich and famous, they call it "satire"—When you're poor and struggling, they put you away!!!"..313

Lee Stratton was born on June 23, 1953, in Waterloo, NY. He is a high school graduate. He is a radioman first class in the U.S. Navy. **His comments:** The inspiration for the poetry that I share comes from my Lord God in heaven. It is a gift that he has blessed me with. I am led to use this gift to spread love and joy to all who would read it

Lee Stratton

Tanno was born on Oct. 21, 1954, in Phoenix, AZ. Her education includes: M.A., Cal State University, Fullerton, 1989; B.F.A., Cal State University, Fullerton, 1988; San Jose City College, 1974-77; West Valley College, Saratoga, CA, 1973-74; and she successfully passed the C-BEST EXAM, 1988. Tanno has a graduate degree, with an emphasis in drawing and painting; a solid background through both field research and studying under successful artists and scholars. Tanno has a broad artistic perspective resulting from extensive travel abroad: --Europe: self-education through exploration of every museum and gallery humanly possible; Lisbon, Rome, Madrid, Milan, Venice, and Nice; 4 weeks in 1981; --Japan: lived on the island of Okinawa for 9 months in 1984; --Mexico: Puerta Vallarta, Mazatlan, Mexico City, Acapulco. Visited 7 times between 1975-79; --Hawaii: painted extensively on the islands of Maui, Hawaii, and Oahu. Visited 10+ times between 1971-81. She is an active artist, personally attuned to the world of art and environment. She has a talent for creating a stimulating, challenging, learning environment. She has demonstrated success in establishing art classes and programs. Tanno married Joseph Threat on Nov. 28, 1981. Tanno is a painter and sculptress. She is presently tutoring 8 children in Cypress, CA, ages 4-8, in media exploration, Sept. 1989 to present. She founded the support group of artists entitled DAB. Currently consists of 25 southern California artists. Local group shows arranged every two months. Organizes exhibitions, meets curators, writes monthly news letters and press releases. She assisted in computer logo design for a major California corporation. She is the owner of Fine Art by Tanno, San Clemente, CA; consists of art sales and consultations, since January 1989. She participated and donated work to Laguna Canyon Paint in. She will have **Karen** published in **Women Under Discussion,** a book by and about Women Artists, in approx. 1991. Her exhibitions include: Oct. 1987--Exit Gallery, CSUF; Nov. 1988--Gorman Fine Art Gallery "Erotica 88" juried competition Santa Monica, CA; Dec. 1988--West Gallery, CSUF juried competition; April 1989--Pacific Art Co., exhibit of 7 local artists San Clemente, CA; May 1989--Weisman Foundation Graduate Purchase Show for purchase selection; July 1989 to present--Americana Gallery on display Laguna Niguel; Oct. 1989--Master of Art Exhibition CSUF; Oct. 1989--Ivey Gallery DAB group show Los Angeles, CA; Nov. 1989--Motzie Gallery Laguna Beach, CA; Feb. 1990--Ariel Gallery 3 person show Soho, NY; May 1990-Art Store "Response to Environment" DAB group show, Irvine, CA; approx. May 1990 (1991?)--**Women Under Discussion** a book about female artists. Poem entitled **Karen** to be published; May 1990--Tohoboho Gallery; San Diego, CA, 2 woman show entitled **Two Wild Women. Her comments:** I often write poems which I include with my paintings or sculpture. The poem **Summer** accompanies a painting of the same title. I often write and create about my female experiences

Bobbie E. Teague was born on Dec. 10, 1943, in Paris, TN. He has a high school education. He is the owner of a Janitorial Service, which has been in operation for 12 years. He married Venita Teague on February 3, 1967. **His comments:** I love writing poetry and also composing songs. I hope one day to join the ranks of famous writers who have contributed so much to help mankind

Bobbie E. Teague

William R. Thies was born on Oct. 26, 1942, in Cincinnati, OH. He received his Bachelor of Arts in 1972 from the University of Cincinnati. He is a Gradeschool Teacher and Athletic Director. He had **Stars Over Cincinnati** published in **Student Book of Poetry,** U.C. (Raymond Walters Branch), 1970. **His comments:** My poetry reflects thoughts and experiences I have had in the past...201

William R. Thies

Amy Elizabeth Thom was born on Jan. 5, 1980, in Aurora, IL. She is in the 5th grade, Quest program (gifted children) with an A average. **Her comments:** I love writing poetry--sometimes it seems that all I have to do is sit down and poems just jump out of my pen. Other times, all I can do is scribble on my paper. I also love reading, writing stories, going shopping, visiting different places, and riding horses. One day I hope to become either a famous writer, a world peace activist, or a happily married housewife...98

Amy Elizabeth Thom

Elizabeth "Bettye" Thompson was born in Atlanta, GA. Her publications include: **Snow** in **Coatesville Record,** 1959; **Valentine** in **Coatesville Record,** 1961; and **Ode To My Children** in **Village News,** 1989. **Her comments:** I am a great lover of poetry and have written most of my adult life. To read my work is like reviewing my entire life, which is centered around my deceased husband, five children and one adopted son; plus several household pets. My grandchildren also play a major part in my poems. **Destiny** is an example. I am now in my 70s and live in Coatesville, PA, where I quietly pass my time, frequently writing poetry...215

Ethel M. Tinney, B.A.

Ethel M. Tinney, B.A. was born in Armstrong Township near Earlton, Northern Ont., Canada. When she was ten years old she passed the High School Entrance Examination and was studying Zoology, Botany, Latin, Geometry. After high school she went to North Bay Teacher's College, U. of Toronto for Geology. In 1982, she received a Bachelor of Arts Degree from Laurentian University. A school teacher who loved teaching, her publications include: In local weekly newspapers about 100 poems;, **The Indian's Sled** published in **Anthology of American Poetry; God's Glow** published in **Glad Tidings Magazine,** 1973; **I Heard Your Violin** published in **Lincoln B. Young's Anthology** in 1970s and **World of Poetry Books** in 1980s. Her awards include: Won International Contest Prize in Adult Contest when still a teen at high school; won watch with 40 diamonds on it for 1 poem; Golden Poet awards in 1988 and 1989; Won trips for 2 to USSR, (Moscow, Leningrad & Kiev) and Finland, 1979 and 1980; Won trips for 2 to Holland (also visited Germany). She is a member of her local museum. **Her comments:** Much of my inspiration comes from living in region known as the James Bay Frontier Area--only one generation settled. Also have had pet cub bears, very tame ravens and enjoy wild life...343

S. Kay Tomblin was born on June 6, 1947, in Orlando, WV. She is an administrative assistant/automobile dealership. **Her comments:** I wrote my first poem 4 years ago for my sister's birthday . . . most of my poems are written personalized for family and friends. This is my first attempt at having one judged professionally and I am thrilled to have my first entry chosen for publication...54

S. Kay Tomblin

Linda Diane Trathen graduated from high school in 1976, and is a hostess at Willows Inn Restaurant, Wickenburg, AZ. Linda Diane Trathen is a fun loving young lady who enjoys hiking, fishing and exploring old history in the west. She loves the Arizona desert and vacationing in central Nevada. Since 1987, Linda has learned how to shoot and now owns a twelve gauge shotgun. Linda's life began on October 17, 1958, in Eloy, Arizona. Her family is from Oklahoma and Linda is part Creek Indian. Linda spent much of her life in Blythe, California until she moved to Wickenburg, Arizona in 1986. She has three beautiful daughters--Michelle, Lori, and Kari--that are the pride of her life. If Linda is not exploring the desert, she might be found at Phoenix Airport with her hand held scanner listening to the tower and pilots communicate. Linda admires airplanes and has become quite a collector of old airliner models displayed joyfully throughout her living room. Linda has been writing poetry since junior high school. She became inspired to write **Hillbilly Okie,** on a stormy summer night in Wickenburg in 1988. Linda's special friend, Pixie Garrett was born in Arkansas. Linda put Arkansas and Oklahoma together then put it on paper, titling it **Hillbilly Okie**..209

Linda Diane Trathen

Mark Wayne Triboulet was born on May 19, 1969, in Upland, CA. He is attending Point Loma Nazarene College in San Diego, majoring in Psychology and minoring in Religion and Literature. He is a timekeeper for Walden Books DC. His publications include: **Run Away** in **American Poetry Anthology,** 1990; **I Love You** in **American Poetry Anthology,** 1990; **Feeling Blue** in **American Poetry Anthology,** 1990. **His comments:** I write from the heart, my feelings and my thoughts and, of course, my dreams are in each of my poems. My inspiration is my love for poetry and others. I thank God for this gift he has given to me; and I thank my parents for their love for me..44

Martha Deen Underwood was born on Jan. 18, 1945, in Louisville, KY. She has a B.S. in Education from the University of Texas at El Paso, and a Masters in Education from Lesley College, Cambridge, MA. She is a Computer Literacy Teacher for 7th and 8th grade at Eastwood Middle School. She married Hamilton Underwood on April 17, 1976. Her memberships include: El Paso Writer's League, El Paso Manuscript Club, Delta Kappa Gamma, Am. Asso. University Women (AAUW). Her publications include: **I Am A Poet** published in **Best New Poets,** 1989; **I Am a Teacher** published in **Delta Kappa Gamma News,** 1989; **Aspen Interlude** published in **Am. Assoc. University Women News,** 1989; **Pony Express Race** published in **El Paso Prospectors News,** 1989--all were poems. Her awards include: 1st place Humorous Poetry--Writers League, 1989; 4th Place Religious Poetry, 1989; 4th place Children's poetry, 1989. **Her comments:** Poetry explores the landscapes of the mind, moving writer and reader into wider fields of vision, expressing then, new ways of observing the world. The writer reaches out to people he may never meet, except through his poem. A poem develops new life every time a reader brings his own experience to it. Shared, it takes on new meaning with every reader..358

Deen Underwood

Rebecca Valdivia-Godoy was born on Sept. 28, 1958, in Watsonville, CA. She attended Notre Dame Grammar School in Watsonville; Notre Dame High School in Salinas, CA, (graduated 1976); Cabrillo College in Aptos, CA; and Calif. State Univ., Fresno, CA. She is employed at Migrant Education, a supplemental program within the Pajaro Valley Unified School District in Watsonville, CA. She is married to Alfonso Godoy and has three sons--Frank, Richard, and Philip. Her awards include: 1st place-Santa Cruz County Fair, 1988 and 1st place-Santa Cruz County Fair, 1989--in Spanish Poetry. **Her comment:** My inspiration comes from my life & life itself, my culture and my family..282

Rebecca Valdivia-Godoy

Callie Elizabeth Walker was born on April 5, 1976, in Texarkana, TX. She has completed Kindergarten through Jr. High School. She has had some poetry published. **Her comments:** As a 13 year old, I was inspired to write poems as a way to express my inner feelings. Violence in the school and on t.v. played an important part in my selection of writing. Poetry is a hobby and a way to release pressure in our society

Callie Elizabeth Walker

Lora Waller was born in Dec. 1958, in San Diego, CA. She has attended Hilo High School, Hilo, HI, and Carson High School, Carson City, NV. She has also attended two trade schools--one in business, and the other in photography; and a college: correspondence and in residence. She is a housewife and is married to her husband, Bill. Her publications include: **Daily Tennis Practice After School** published in Hilo High Yearbook, **Blue and Gold,** 1975 and **Invasion** published in **Nevada Appeal Newspaper,** 1985. She was awarded Best First Hour Mult-Media Presentation in 1976. **Her comments:** My thoughts and poems and literary themes, come from life's experience and human dreams. My Lord my God influences my mind, and I end up loving all mankind

Lora Waller

Dana-Marie Walter was born on August 1, 1971, in Washington, DC. She has had 12 years of high school and attends college part-time. She is a clerk typist/student (occupation: CT for Chemical Dynamics and Diagnostics). **Her comments:** This poem is dedicated to my dear friend Eugenia Louise Mays whose friendship I adore because she gave me a flower for a smile

Dana-Marie Walter

Robin Elaine Wening was born on April 30, 1946, in New York City, NY. She has a B.A. in Spanish/Education and a M.A. in Curriculum & Instruction (Foreign Lang. Education). She is an information specialist (with specialty Advertising company). She married Tyler Wening on Oct. 7, 1972. She is a member of Miniature Book Society. **Her comments:** The majority of my work is for special occasions and oral (<u>custom</u> poems) reading to groups- (i.e., birthday greetings, weddings, births, anniversaries, recognition) and most always is either humorous or very specific personally. So, when I create and submit a serious piece for consideration, I am dipping into a different area of my "creative volcano!" I am proud, flattered and honored to have been selected for inclusion in this anthology

Robin Elaine Wening

Craig Alan Whitney was born on Jan. 3, 1973, in Elk Grove Village, IL. He has completed kindergarten through the sophomore year of high school. He is a circulation page at a local public library. **His comments:** I know I'm a good writer! All my friends see my work and I only hear good things about my work when they read it. I've been writing for 2½ years and I love every minute of it........................292

Craig Alan Whitney

Barbara Barnes Wright was born on May 3, 1943, in Fayetteville, TN. She has a high school education. She works as a Human Resources Coord., at Jack Daniel Distillery. **Her comments:** There is no cure for life or death except to enjoy the brief interlude. The poem, which I wrote following my mother's death, reflects feelings that I dealt with, and the message of self-expression helped me better handle my grief. The subject matter excludes no living being and could serve as sound advice to all........................254

Barbara Barnes Wright

Jacqueline Ruth McGuffey Young was born on June 26, 1946, in Stanford, KY. She is a medical records secretary. **Her comments:** The body of **Now You're Gone** emerged into life through love. Its title imprisoned by death. Sharing this part of me, was inspired by the realization death is not the finality, in retrospect, tis love........................376

Jacqueline Ruth McGuffey Young

Carl L. Youngblood was born on Jan. 1, 1940, in Williamsport, IN. He graduated from high school in West Lebanon, IN. He was a dairy farmer until 1976 and is presently employed at Quaker Oats in Danville, IL. He married his wife, Susan, in 1980. He had **Heaven on Earth** published in **American Poetry Anthology** in 1989. **His comments:** I began writing poetry in 1974, after the death of my dad, which brought me to the realization of the importance of having a personal relationship with God in Heaven to give us added strength that we can rely on, at any given time, if we but ask through prayer daily........................41

Carl L. Youngblood

Kenneth Devaughn Younger was born on April 16, 1956, in Indianapolis, IN. He plans to get a B.S. in nursing. He is a U.S. Army Nurse Recruiter. He was awarded Top New Recruiter in 1989. **His comments:** A poem to B for all to C, 1 message 2 show family, friends @ foe. Be all that you can be!........................303

Kenneth Devaughn Younger

Muriel Zieman was born on March 19, 1919, in St. Paul, MN. She has a college education at a Business college. She is a secretary and is divorced. She has been active in the Lutheran church for most of her life. This is her only publication. **Her comments:** I have always enjoyed writing all my life and interested in reading real often. My daughter is studying to be a writer and she talked me into entering this contest and thought my poem would be accepted. The poem is inspired by my daughter and son-in-law's new home! 300

Muriel Zieman

008 A New Beginning is the pen name of **Charlie Earl Porter.** He was born on Nov. 13, 1948, in Magee, MS. He graduated from Spartan School of Aeronautics and attended TN State, Christian Bro. Col. and Memphis State. He is a private investigator. His memberships include: St. Phillip's Order of the Golden Fleece, and Full Gospel Business Men's Fellowship In. He has publications in **Great Poets of the Western World,** Sacramento, CA, 1989 and **Who's Who In Poetry,** Sacramento, CA, 1990. He was awarded the Golden Poet Award in 1989 and is listed in **Who's Who In Poetry,** 1990. **His comments:** Shame is the medium by which the universe is measured. To be in harmony in thoughts one has to know what you think so poetry gets a criticizing gaze..372

Charlie Earl Porter

Index of Authors

Authors are indexed under the name or pen name that appears with their poem.